Que's Big Mac® Book,

4th Edition

Mark Bilbo
Neil Salkind

Que's Big Mac Book, 4th Edition

Copyright© 1993 by Que® Corporation

All rights reserved. Printed in the United States of America. No part of this book may be used or reproduced in any form or by any means, or stored in a database or retrieval system, without prior written permission of the publisher except in the case of brief quotations embodied in critical articles and reviews. Making copies of any part of this book for any purpose other than your own personal use is a violation of United States copyright laws. For information, address Que Corporation, 11711 N. College Ave., Carmel, IN 46032.

Library of Congress Catalog No.: 93-84123

ISBN: 1-56529-075-5

95 94 93   4 3 2 1

Interpretation of the printing code: the rightmost double-digit number is the year of the book's printing; the rightmost single-digit number, the number of the book's printing. For example, a printing code of 93-1 shows that the first printing of the book occurred in 1993.

Screen reproductions in this book were created using ImageGrabber from Sebastian Software, Bellevue, WA.

Publisher: David P. Ewing

Associate Publisher: Rick Ranucci

Publishing Plan Manager: Thomas H. Bennett

Operations Manager: Sheila Cunningham

Book Designer: Amy Peppler-Adams

Indexers: Joy Dean Lee

Production Team: Claudia Bell, Danielle Bird, Julie Brown, Laurie Casey, Brook Farling, Michelle Greenwalt, Carla Hall-Batton, Michael Hughes, Heather Kaufman, Bob LaRoche, Jay Lesandrini, Caroline Roop, Linda Seifert, Sandra Shay, Amy Steed, Michelle Worthington

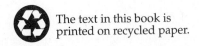

The text in this book is printed on recycled paper.

Title Manager

Shelley O'Hara

Acquisitions Editors

Chris Katsaropoulos
Sherri Morningstar

Product Development Specialist

Kathie Jo Arnoff

Production Editor

Cindy Morrow

Editors

Elsa M. Bell
Lori Cates
Barb Colter
Bryan Gambrel
Barbara K. Koenig
J. Christopher Nelson
Virginia Noble
Brad Sullivan

Technical Editors

Burt Goldstein
William Hartman
Bob Jorritsma
Lisa Riddle Lynch

Additional Technical Support

Patricia R. Brooks

Editorial Assistants

Julia Blount
Sandra Naito

Composed in **ITC Garamond** and **MCPdigital** by Que Corporation

About the Authors

Mark Bilbo still remembers being introduced to a little, beige "toaster" sometime in 1984. His remark about how cute it was is not really worth recording for posterity. He immediately returned to his belief that the S-1000 bus would rule the world. Yet, about a year later, he found himself halfway across the continent at Monogram Software with one of those toasters sitting on his desk. Things haven't been quite the same for him since.

His obsession with the Macintosh way is probably second only to Guy Kawasaki himself. He has, in turn, been a technical support representative, a programmer, a consultant/support person, and nearly everything else for a television show, as well as a full-time writer.

Chased by smog, gridlock, and traffic jams, he fled Los Angeles to return to his area in East Texas and even now plans for the day that he and his Mac will live deep in the woods where only the birds can find them.

Neil J. Salkind lives in eastern Kansas and has taught child development at the University of Kansas for 20 years. He has written more than 30 computer books on various topics, including spreadsheets, word processing, and graphics. He also has published several college-level textbooks and written more than 100 papers dealing with children and families.

Trademark Acknowledgments

A ll terms mentioned in this book that are known to be trademarks or service marks have been appropriately capitalized. Que cannot attest to the accuracy of this information. Use of a term in this book should not be regarded as affecting the validity of any trademark or service mark.

1-2-3 and Lotus are registered trademarks of Lotus Development Corporation.

Apple, AppleTalk, Centris, HyperCard, ImageWriter, Lisa, Mac, Macintosh, Macintosh Plus, Macintosh SE, Macintosh SE/30, MacPain, MacWrite, and Quadra are registered trademarks and MultiFinder is a trademark of Apple Computer, Inc.

IBM and IBM PC are registered trademarks of International Business Machines Corporation.

Microsoft, Microsoft Excel, Microsoft Word, PowerPoint, and MS-DOS are registered trademarks of Microsoft Corporation.

WordPerfect is a registered trademark of WordPerfect Corporation.

Contents at a Glance

Introduction 1

Part I   Macintosh Basics

      Quick Start: Learning the Essentials 15
1   Getting Started 31
2   Understanding the System 103
3   Managing Disks 143
4   Managing Files 179
5   Configuring the Macintosh 209
6   Customizing the Macintosh 233
7   Printing 267
8   Using Fonts 297

Part II   Macintosh Software

9   Buying Software 325
10   Working with Word Processors 337
11   Using Spreadsheets 381
12   Using Databases 415
13   Using Integrated Software 437
14   Using Finance and Business Applications 459
15   Desktop Publishing 501
16   Using Graphics Software 537
17   Using Communication Software 575
18   Using Multimedia 611
19   Using Utility Software 629
20   Learning and Having Fun 651

Part III   Macintosh Hardware

21   Buying Hardware 687
22   Reviewing Macintosh Models 693
23   Choosing Input Devices 715
24   Choosing a Display 723
25   Choosing a Printer 737
26   Expanding the Macintosh 755
27   Adding Accessories 769

Part IV   Advanced Topics

28   Networking 779
29   Using Connectivity Software 805
30   Using HyperCard 815
31   Programming the Macintosh 845
32   Maintenance and Troubleshooting 879
 A   Using System 6 899
 B   System Specifications 913
 C   System Error Codes 919
 D   Directory of Products 927
 E   Vendor Guide 981
       Glossary 1009
       Index 1039

Contents

Introduction 1

Who Should Use This Book? 2
A Road Map to This Book 3
How to Use This Book 4
A Brief History of the Macintosh (In the Beginning...) 5
The Birth of the Macintosh 6
The Future of the Macintosh 9

Part I Macintosh Basics

Quick Start: Learning the Essentials 15

Starting Your Macintosh 16
Using the Mouse 17
Using the Macintosh Menus 19
Working with Windows 20
   Closing a Window 22
   Moving a Window 22
   Resizing a Window 22
   Scrolling a Window 24
   Opening Additional Windows 25
Cutting, Copying, and Pasting 26
Printing a Document 27
Ending a Work Session 28
Quick Start Summary 29

1 Getting Started **31**

Setting Up the Macintosh 32
  Preparing to Set Up the Macintosh 32
    Adjusting Monitor Height and Distance 32
    Preventing Screen Glare 33
    Considering Keyboard Positions 33
    Judging Office Furniture 34
  Looking at Macintosh Models 35
    Compact Macintoshes 36
    Modular Macintoshes 39
    Tower Macintoshes 42
    Laptop Macintoshes 42
  Connecting the Macintosh 47
  Setting Up a Printer 48
    Connecting a Serial Printer 49
    Connecting a SCSI Printer 50
    Connecting an AppleTalk Printer 51
Understanding the Desktop 52
  Viewing the Desktop 52
  Understanding the Finder 54
  Understanding the Desktop File 55
Using the Mouse 55
  Pointing 56
  Clicking 56
  Double-Clicking 57
  Dragging 58
  Using Modified Clicks and Drags 61
Understanding the Menus 61
  Choosing Commands 61
  Using Option Menus 64
  Using Hierarchical Menus 66
  Using Scrolling Menus 67
  Using Pop-Up Menus 68
  Using Keyboard Equivalents 69
  Considering the Finder Menus 70

Understanding Windows 72
   Moving a Window 73
   Sizing a Window 73
   Zooming a Window 75
   Scrolling a Window 75
   Closing a Window 76
   Using Multiple Windows 76
   Considering Window Types 79
Understanding Dialogs and Alerts 81
   Using Dialog Controls 81
      Command Buttons 82
      Radio Buttons 83
      Check Boxes 83
      Text Boxes 83
      List Boxes 84
      Keyboard Control 84
   Understanding Alerts 85
Understanding Macintosh Keyboards 86
   Modifier Keys 87
   Function Keys 89
   Special Keys 89
   Desktop Commands 91
Understanding Macintosh Text and Graphics 92
   Typing Text 92
   Moving the Insertion Point 93
   Deleting Text and Graphics 95
   Replacing Text 96
   Understanding the Clipboard 96
   Copying Text and Graphics 97
   Moving Text and Graphics 97
   Undoing Mistakes 98
   Typing Special Characters 99
   Considering Other Text-Editing Features 101
Chapter Summary 102

2 Understanding the System 103

Understanding System Software 104
   Understanding System Software Versions 104
   Installing System Software 105
Viewing the System Folder 107
Understanding Icons 110
   Selecting Icons 110
   Editing Icon Names 111
   Moving an Icon 112
   Copying an Icon 113
   Deleting an Icon 114
   Opening an Icon 116
   Getting Information about an Icon 117
   Locking and Unlocking Icons 119
   Creating and Using Aliases 120
Understanding Multitasking 122
   Starting Applications 122
   Switching Applications 124
   Copying between Applications 126
   Hiding Application Windows 126
   Quitting Applications 127
   Adjusting Memory Use 128
   Using Background Copying 130
Using the Apple Menu 131
   Working with Supplied Applications 131
   Choosing Apple Menu Items 131
   Considering the Supplied Applications 132
      Alarm Clock 132
      Calculator 134
      Chooser 134
      Key Caps 135
      Note Pad 136
      Puzzle 137
      Scrapbook 137
   Acquiring System Information 139

Acquiring Help 140
    Using Balloon Help 140
    Displaying Finder Shortcuts 141
    Obtaining Application Program Help 142
Chapter Summary 142

3   Managing Disks 143

Reviewing Storage Devices 144
Using Floppy Disks 145
    Understanding Floppy Disk Structure 146
    Understanding Floppy Disk Types 146
    Inserting and Ejecting Floppy Disks 148
    Ejecting Jammed Disks 149
    Initializing Floppy Disks 150
    Copying Disks 154
        Copying a Floppy Disk to Another Floppy Disk 154
        Copying a Floppy Disk to a Hard Disk 155
    Locking and Unlocking Disks 156
    Caring for Floppy Disks 157
Using Hard Disks 158
    What Are Hard Disk Drives? 159
        A Brief History of Hard Disks 159
        Understanding SCSI 160
        Understanding How Hard Disks Work 161
        Hard Disk Types 162
    Connecting Hard Drives 164
    Initializing Hard Disks 165
    Partitioning Hard Disks 166
        Hard Partitions 167
        Soft Partitions 168
    Optimizing Hard Disks 168
    Compressing Hard Disk Data 170
    Securing Your Files and Applications 170
    Caring for Hard Disks 171
Using Other Disks 171
    CD-ROMs 172

Magneto-Optical Disks 176
Floptical Disks 177
The Big Mac Recommendation 177

4   Managing Files **179**

Understanding Files 180
How Files Are Stored on Disk 180
How the Macintosh Recognizes Files 180
How Icons Represent Files 181
How the Hierarchical File System Works 182
Working with Files 183
Opening Files 183
Opening by Double-Clicking 183
Opening by Dragging and Dropping 185
Opening within a Program 185
Organizing Files 186
Creating, Naming, and Deleting Folders 189
Nesting Folders 189
Labeling Files 190
Labeling a File 190
Removing a Label 191
Sorting by Label 191
Aliasing Files 191
Creating an Alias 192
Locating Original Files 192
Considering Some Uses of Aliases 193
Searching for Files 195
Using the Find Command 195
Narrowing a Search 196
Working with Stationery Pads 200
Working with Folders 201
Viewing Files 201
Viewing by Small Icon 201
Viewing by Name 201
Viewing by Other Orders 202

Using Outline Views 202

Navigating Folders 203

Making File Backups 205

Backing Up Floppies 205

Backing Up Hard Disks 206

Using Other Backup Methods 207

The Big Mac Recommendation 208

5 Configuring the Macintosh 209

Setting General Options 210

Setting the Desktop Pattern 210

Setting the Insertion Point Blinking Rate 211

Setting Menu Blinking 212

Setting the Time 212

Setting the Date 212

Setting International Options 213

Setting the Date and Time Formats 213

Setting Date Format Options 214

Setting Time Format Options 216

Setting the Number Format 217

Setting Keyboard Options 219

Setting Key Repeat 219

Setting Keyboard Layout 219

Setting Memory Options 220

Setting the Disk Cache 221

Setting Virtual Memory Options 221

Setting the 32-Bit Address Mode 223

Setting the Monitor Options 223

Setting Color Options 224

Identifying and Arranging Monitors 225

Setting Mouse Options 226

Setting Mouse Tracking Speed 226

Setting Double-Click Speed 227

Setting Screen Brightness 227

Setting Sound Options 228

Setting the Alert Sound 228
Setting the Sound Volume 229
Setting the Startup Disk 230
Setting Trash Options 231
Chapter Summary 232

6   Customizing the Macintosh **233**

Setting Color 234
   Setting the Text Highlight Color 234
   Setting Window Frame Color 235
   Using the Macintosh Color Wheel 236
Setting the View 237
   Setting the View Font 238
   Setting the Icon Grid 239
   Setting List View Icon Size 240
   Showing Folder Size 240
   Showing Disk Information 241
   Changing List View Columns 241
Setting Physically Challenged Help Options 242
   Using Close View 242
   Using Easy Access 243
      Using Mouse Keys 244
      Using Slow Keys 246
      Using Sticky Keys 246
      Setting On/Off Audio Feedback 247
Changing Sounds 248
   Adding Sounds 248
   Removing Sounds 250
Customizing the Apple Menu 250
   Adding and Removing Apple Menu Items 251
   Sorting Apple Menu Items 251
Setting Automatic Startups 255
Customizing Icon Appearance 256
Labeling Icons 258
   Applying Labels 258
   Customizing Labels 258

Adding Control Panels 260
   Installing a Control Panel 260
   Removing a Control Panel 261
Adding System Extensions 261
   Installing System Extensions................................262
   Removing System Extensions 262
   Preventing System Extension Startup 262
Adding Keyboard Layouts 263
   Installing a Keyboard Layout 263
   Removing a Keyboard Layout 263
   Choosing a Keyboard Layout 264
Chapter Summary 265

7   Printing 267

Understanding Types of Printers 268
   Dot-Matrix Printers...269
   Inkjet Printers 270
   Laser Printers 271
   Color Printers 273
      Color Inkjet Printers 273
      Thermal-Wax-Transfer Printers 273
      Phase-Change Printers 274
      Continuous-Tone Printers 275
   Plotters 275
   Typesetters 276
Understanding Printer Drivers 277
   Installing Printer Drivers...................................278
   Choosing a Printer Driver 279
Printing a Document 281
   Setting Page Setup Options 282
   Setting Print Options 283
   Using Background Printing 284
Using Laser Printer Languages 286
   Understanding PostScript 287
   Using PostScript Tools 288

Printing with a PostScript Printer 289
Programming with PostScript 290
Using PostScript Utilities 290
Using PostScript Programs 293
Sharing PostScript Files 294
Chapter Summary 296

8   Using Fonts **297**

Defining Fonts 298
Understanding Font Types 302
Understanding Font Rasterizing and Search Order 302
Using Fonts on QuickDraw Printers 303
Using Fonts on PostScript Printers 304
Understanding Fonts On-Screen 307
Installing Fonts 308
Working with Fonts 310
Creating Fonts 311
Downloading Fonts 311
Previewing Fonts 312
Using Font Utilities 312
Type Enhancement Utilities 313
Font Conversion Utilities 315
Font Managers 315
Adobe Systems Font Utilities 315
Some Tips for Font Use 321
The Big Mac Recommendation 322

Part II Macintosh Software

9   Buying Software **325**

Types of Software 326
Word Processors 326
Spreadsheets 326
Databases 326

Integrated Packages 327
Financial and Business Programs 327
Desktop Publishing 327
Graphics 327
Communications 328
Multimedia 328
Utilities 328
Learning and Fun 328
Sources of Software 328
Evaluating Software 329
Memory Considerations 330
Macintosh Type Considerations 330
System Software Version Considerations 331
Understanding Version Numbers and Compatibility ... 331
Understanding Warranties and Return Policies 333
Understanding Technical Support 334
The Big Mac Recommendation 335

10 Working with Word Processors 337

Creating Documents 339
For Example... 339
Opening Documents 343
Saving Documents 344
Editing a Document 346
Deleting Text 346
Inserting Text 346
Moving Text 347
Searching for and Replacing Text 350
Formatting Documents 352
Setting Margins 352
Setting Tabs 353
Creating Tables 354
Justifying Text 354
Using Fonts, Sizes, and Styles 356
Adjusting Line Spacing 358
Working with Pages 358

Understanding Special Functions 359
    Using the Spelling Checkers and Thesauri 360
    Using Merge 360
    Using Sort 362
    Using Glossaries 363
    Using Macros 364
    Using Tables of Contents and Indexes 365
    Using Graphics 366
    Using Document Translation 368
Using Specialized Word Processors and Add-Ons 369
    Spelling Checkers 369
    Thesauri and Dictionaries 370
    Grammar Checkers 371
    Writing Assistants 373
    Using Equation Generators 374
    Predesigned Documents 375
    Text Editors 375
    Desk Accessories 376
    Specialized Word Processors 376
Choosing a Word Processor 377
The Big Mac Recommendation 378

11   Using Spreadsheets 381

Understanding Spreadsheet Programs 382
    Understanding Spreadsheet Components 382
    Considering Uses of Spreadsheet Programs 383
    Considering Benefits of Spreadsheet Programs 384
Using Worksheets 385
    Understanding the Worksheet Screen 386
    Creating a Worksheet 389
    Entering Data in a Worksheet 389
Formatting a Worksheet 390
    Aligning Cell Entries 390
    Formatting Numbers 391
    Working with Fonts 393

Using Formulas 394
    Entering Formulas 394
    Using Operators 397
    Using Functions 398
Creating Charts 400
    Creating a Chart 402
    Adding Text 402
    Formatting Charts 402
Using the Spreadsheet as a Database 403
    Creating a Database 404
    Sorting a Database 405
    Finding and Extracting Information 407
Creating Macros and Using Macro Languages 410
Assessing Compatibility among Spreadsheet Programs ... 411
Considering Smaller Spreadsheet Programs 413
The Big Mac Recommendation 414

12 Using Databases **415**

Understanding Databases 416
    Understanding Fields, Records, and Files 416
    Comparing Flat-File and Relational-File Databases 418
        Flat-File Databases 418
        Relational-File Databases 419
Choosing a Database Program 421
Creating a Database 422
    Designing a Database 422
    Creating a Database File 424
    Entering Data 425
    Searching for Records 425
    Creating a Layout 427
    Importing and Exporting Records 427
Using Small Databases 428
Using Specialized Databases 430
    Graphical Databases 430
    Bibliographical Databases 430
    Contact Managers 431

Appointment Managers 431
Grade Managers 433
Client and Employee Managers 434
The Big Mac Recommendation 435

13   Using Integrated Software 437

The Idea behind Integrated Packages 438
ClarisWorks 439
Transferring Information 440
Considering Module Integration 443
Surveying the Modules 447
Sharing Information with Other Programs 449
Moving to Stand-Alone Packages 450
Microsoft Works 451
Surveying the Modules 452
Works Add-Ons 455
Other Integrated Packages 456
The Big Mac Recommendation 457

14   Using Finance and Business Applications 459

Using Personal Finance Programs 460
Understanding Accounts 460
Creating Accounts 461
Entering Transactions 462
Creating Reports 464
Choosing a Personal Finance Program 465
Quicken 465
Managing Your Money 466
Dollars & Sense 468
Using Tax Preparation Programs 469
Using Other Financial Programs 471
Using Accounting Software 471
Understanding Accounting Programs 472
Considering Other Accounting Packages 475
Considering Forecasting and Planning Programs 481

Considering Creative Problem-Solving Programs 483
Using Spreadsheets as Financial Tools 486
Considering Statistical Analysis Programs 487
Considering Features of Statistical Programs 488
Descriptive Statistics 489
Group Differences 490
Measures of Association and Prediction 492
Regression 492
Nonparametrics 492
Considering Graphical Presentation 493
Considering Some Specific Statistic Packages 494
Considering Project-Management Packages 495
MacProject 496
Other Project Managers 499
The Big Mac Recommendation 500

15 Desktop Publishing 501

Understanding Desktop Publishing 502
Using a Service Bureau 504
Comparing Traditional Publishing with
Desktop Publishing 505
Learning Design Basics 507
Considering Design Techniques 509
Adding Special Effects 515
Manipulating Text 519
Using Style Sheets and Templates 522
Using Default Pages 523
Using Predesigned Style Sheets and Templates 523
Surveying Desktop Publishing Applications 525
PageMaker 525
Ready, Set, Go! 526
QuarkXPress 527
Interleaf Publisher 527
Other Packages 528
Buying a Desktop Publishing Package 530
Using Desktop Publishing Utilities 532

Capturing Screens 532
Learning Desktop Publishing 534
The Big Mac Recommendation 534

16 Using Graphics Software 537

Understanding Graphics Software 538
Using Paint Programs 539
MacPaint 2.0 540
Other Paint Programs 540
Paint Desk Accessories 542
Using Draw Programs 542
MacDraw Pro 543
Illustrator and FreeHand 546
Using Programs with Paint and Draw Capabilities 548
Canvas 548
SuperPaint 3.0 548
Storing Graphics Images 550
Working with Color 551
Selecting Color Applications 552
Producing Color Documents 553
Using Color Utilities 554
Using Clip Art 554
Creating Your Own Clip Art 555
Tracking Clip Art 556
Creating Three-Dimensional Graphics 558
Using Computer-Aided Design (CAD) Programs 561
ClarisCAD 562
AutoCAD 563
Other Programs 563
Creating Graphs and Charts 565
Picking the Appropriate Chart Type 566
Picking a Graphing Package 566
Using Scanners 569
Using ThunderScan 570
Using Optical Character Recognition
(OCR) Software 571

    Buying OCR Software 572

    Using Gray-Scale Scanning 573

    Fine-Tuning Scanned Images 573

    Using Color Scanners 574

  The Big Mac Recommendation 574

17 Using Communication Software 575

  Reviewing Telecommunication Requirements 576

    The Modem 576

    Communications Software 576

    The Phone Line 577

    The Connection 578

  Defining Terms 578

  Using a Modem 580

    Modem Protocol 580

    Modem Speed 582

    Error Checking 583

    MacBinary 585

    Facts about Fax 586

  Choosing a Modem and Modem Software 586

    Considering Some Guidelines 587

    Considering Available Modems 588

  Assessing Telecommunication Costs 589

  Buying Communications Software 590

    MicroPhone II and Pro 591

    White Knight 595

    Smartcom II 596

    Specialized Software 596

  Using Electronic Mail 597

    Public E-Mail Services 597

    Public E-Mail Software 598

    Private E-Mail 598

  Exploring the World of Bulletin Boards 599

  Using Information Services 600

    CompuServe 601

    GEnie 602

America Online 602

Dialog 603

BRS 603

Orbit 603

Dow Jones News/Retrieval 604

NewsNet 604

Prodigy 604

CONNECT 605

The Well 605

How to Choose an Information Provider 605

On-Line Addiction and Billing Problems 606

Using Fax Modems 608

The Big Mac Recommendation 609

18   Using Multimedia

18   **Using Multimedia** **611**

Understanding Multimedia 612

Using Sound 613

Using Video 615

Using QuickTime 616

Using Multimedia Software 618

Using Multimedia Utilities 623

Using Photo CD 624

Choosing Multimedia Hardware 626

The Big Mac Recommendation 627

19   **Using Utility Software** **629**

Essential Utilities 630

Backup Programs 630

Data Recovery and Hard Disk Maintenance
     Programs 632

Virus Programs 635

Diagnostics 637

Useful Utilities 638

Data Compression 639

Startup Managers 641

Resource Managers 642

Finder Enhancers 643

Security Utilities 645

Macro Utilities 646

Utility Packages 647

The Big Mac Recommendation 649

20   Learning and Having Fun **651**

Considering Educational Software 652

Elementary Skills 652

Secondary Skills 658

Software Instruction 662

Language Instruction 663

Typing Programs 663

Considering Games 664

Athletic Games 665

Flying and Driving Games 668

War Games 670

Detective and Adventure Games 671

Brain Teasers 671

Arcade and Board Games 672

Card Games 675

Other Games 676

Best Game Ever 677

Considering Music Programs 678

Considering Posters and Calendars 680

The Big Mac Recommendation 683

Part III Macintosh Hardware

21   Buying Hardware **687**

Sources of Hardware 688

Evaluating Hardware 690

Understanding Warranties and Return Policies 690

22 Reviewing Macintosh Models 693

Compact Macintoshes 695
  Macintosh Classic II/Performa 200 695
  Color Classic 695
Modular Macintoshes 696
  Macintosh LC III 696
  Performa 400 697
  Performa 600 697
  Macintosh IIvx 698
  Centris 610/650 698
Laptop Macintoshes 699
  PowerBook 145 700
  PowerBook 160 700
  PowerBook 165c 700
  PowerBook 180 701
  PowerBook Duo 210/230 701
Tower Macintoshes 702
  Quadra 800 702
  Quadra 950 703
Older Macintoshes 703
  Macintosh Classic 704
  Macintosh IIsi 704
  Macintosh SE/30 705
  Macintosh IIcx 705
  Macintosh IIci 705
  Macintosh IIfx 706
  Macintosh LC/LC II 706
  Quadra 700 707
  Quadra 900 707
  PowerBook 100 708
  PowerBook 140 708
  PowerBook 170 708
Obsolete Macintoshes 708
  The Original Macintosh 709
  Macintosh 512K/512Ke 709

Macintosh Plus 709

Macintosh II 710

Macintosh IIx 710

Choosing a Macintosh 710

On the Horizon 712

23   Choosing Input Devices 715

Choosing a Keyboard 716

Choosing a Mouse or Trackball 718

Choosing a Tablet 719

Choosing a Scanner 719

Choosing a Video Camera 720

The Big Mac Recommendation 721

24   Choosing a Display 723

Understanding How Monitors Work 724

Understanding Displays 725

Choosing a Display 727

Considering Apple Monitors 728

Considering Non-Apple Displays 729

Choosing a Video Card 731

Adding Video to PowerBooks and Compact
Macintoshes 732

Choosing an Overhead Display 733

Protecting Your Screen 734

The Big Mac Recommendation 735

25   Choosing a Printer 737

Understanding Printers 738

Considering Apple Printers 739

Considering Apple's Dot-Matrix and Inkjet Printers 739

StyleWriter II 740

ImageWriter II 741

Apple Color Printer 742

Considering Apple's Laser Printers 742
    LaserWriter Select 300/310 742
    Personal LaserWriter NTR 743
    LaserWriter Pro 600/630 744
Considering Non-Apple Alternatives 745
  Connecting Parallel Printers 745
  Considering Non-Apple Laser Printers 746
  Considering Non-Apple Color Printers 747
Caring for Printers 748
  General Printer Care 748
  Servicing Your Printer 749
  Caring for Dot-Matrix Printers 750
  Considering Laser Printer Maintenance 752
The Big Mac Recommendation 753

26   **Expanding the Macintosh** **755**

Choosing Storage Devices 756
  Understanding Storage Devices 756
  Understanding SCSI Connections 756
  Choosing a Hard Drive 757
    Capacity 757
    SCSI Termination and ID Selection 758
    Seek Time 758
    Other Considerations 759
  Choosing an Optical Drive 759
  Choosing a CD-ROM Drive 759
  Choosing a WORM Drive 760
  Choosing a Magneto-Optical Drive 761
  Choosing a Tape Drive 762
Choosing Expansion Cards 762
  Understanding Expansion Cards 763
    Understanding Memory Cards 763
    Understanding NuBus 764
    Understanding PDS 764
  Choosing an Accelerator Card 765

Choosing a Math Coprocessor 766
Adding an Apple II Card to an LC Series Macintosh 767
The Big Mac Recommendation 767

27 Adding Accessories **769**

Power Line Protectors 770
Carrying Cases 771
Dust Covers 772
Security Devices 772
Anti-Glare Filters 772
Diskettes and Disk Files 773
Stands and Bases 774
Furniture 775
The Big Mac Recommendation 776

Part IV Advanced Topics

28 Networking **779**

Understanding Network Basics 780
Defining AppleTalk and LocalTalk 780
Defining Servers 782
Defining Types of Networks 783
Daisy Chain 783
Backbone 784
Star 785
Token Ring 786
Defining AppleTalk Zones 786
Defining Bridges 786
Setting Up a Network 787
Planning Considerations 787
Constructing a Small Network 788
Using PhoneNET 790
Using EtherNet 791
Using Shared Peripherals 792
Communicating by Remote Control 792

Using File Sharing 793
   Configuring File Sharing 793
      Setting Sharing Options 794
      Creating a New User 795
      Creating a New Group 797
   Sharing Folders and Disks 798
   Setting Options 800
   Controlling Sharing 800
   Accessing Shared Items 802
  The Big Mac Recommendation 803

29   Using Connectivity Software **805**
Communicating with IBM PCs and Clones 806
   Transferring and Translating Files 806
   Working with Disks 809
   Running IBM Software 810
      Using a Hardware Solution 811
      Using Software Solutions 811
Using Your Mac with Mainframes 812
The Big Mac Recommendation 814

30   Using HyperCard **815**
Defining HyperCard 816
Learning HyperCard Basics 817
   Starting HyperCard 817
   Setting the User Level 818
   Understanding the Building Blocks 819
   Using Commands 821
Working with an Existing Stack 822
   Opening a Stack 822
   Adding and Deleting Cards 823
   Cutting, Copying, and Pasting Data 823
   Moving through a Stack 824
   Converting a Stack 825
Creating a New Stack 825

Copying from an Existing Stack 825
Linking Cards and Stacks 828
Printing Stacks and Cards 830
Using HyperTalk 831
Examining a Script 832
Viewing Some Examples 833
Creating Music and Sound 834
Adding Visual Effects 835
Using Interactive Scripts 837
Using Loops 838
Working with the Date and Time 838
Considering Alternatives to HyperCard 840
Selecting HyperCard Applications 841
Indexing Stacks 842
Travel Stacks 842
Generating Reports 842
Using XCMDs and XFCNs 842
Finding Stacks Sources 844
The Big Mac Recommendation 844

31   Programming the Macintosh **845**

Getting Started 846
Understanding the Programming Process 847
Defining a Good Program 848
Debugging Your Program 849
Understanding Computers 850
Understanding Microprocessors 850
Understanding Machine Language 851
Understanding Assembly Language 852
Using Compilers and Interpreters 853
Understanding Object-Oriented Programming 854
Understanding Interfaces 855
Programming with the Toolbox 856
Understanding the Event-Driven Environment 858
Understanding Memory Management 858
Understanding Apple's Human Interface Guidelines 859

Choosing a Language 860
  Understanding High-Level Languages 861
    BASIC 861
    Pascal 862
    C and C++ 862
    LISP 863
    LOGO 863
    Forth 864
    Miscellaneous Languages 864
  Using Object-Oriented Programming 865
  Defining Artificial Intelligence 868
Using ResEdit 869
  Understanding How a Resource Editor Works 869
  Changing Icons 872
  Changing Menu Commands 874
  Changing Alert Boxes 874
  Changing Fonts 874
Finding Resources for Macintosh Programmers 876
  Apple-Related Resources 876
  Macintosh Associations 876
  Publications 876
  On-line Forums and Roundtables 877
  User Groups 877
The Big Mac Recommendation 877

32 Maintenance and Troubleshooting 879

Practicing Preventive Maintenance 880
  Avoiding Electrical Spikes 880
  Avoiding Heat 880
  Avoiding Dirt 881
  Avoiding Dust 881
  Cleaning the Mouse 882
  Avoiding Static 882
  Avoiding Computer Viruses 883
  Traveling Safely 884
  Protecting against Theft 885
  Considering Computer Insurance 886

Considering Ergonomics 886
  Reducing Glare and Easing Eye Strain 886
  Protecting against Radiation 886
  Avoiding Muscle Strain and Carpal Tunnel
    Syndrome 887
Troubleshooting 888
  Determining the Problem 888
  Fixing Startup Problems 889
  Locating Software Conflicts 890
  Recovering Lost Files 892
  Locating Hardware Problems 893
  Fixing SCSI Problems 894
  Fixing Printer Problems 896
Deciding Whether to Upgrade 897
The Big Mac Recommendation 898

A   Using System 6 899

Considering a Switch to System 7 900
Considering Differences between Systems 6 and 7 901
  Icons 902
  Menus 902
  Windows 903
  Documents 903
  Folders 904
  Control Panels 904
  Extensions 904
  Printers and Fonts 905
Using MultiFinder 905
  Starting MultiFinder 905
  Adjusting Memory Use 908
  Disabling MultiFinder 909
Using Desk Accessories 909
  Installing and Removing Desk Accessories 910
  Accessing Desk Accessories 911
Installing and Removing Fonts 911

B System Specifications 913

C System Error Codes 919

Apple System Error Codes 920
  General System 920
  I/O System 920
  File System 921
  Disk 922
  Memory Manager 923
  Resource Manager 923
Sad Mac Codes 924
  128KB ROMs 924
  Sad Mac Codes for Macs with 256KB and
    Larger ROMs 925

D Directory of Products 927

Product Listing by Category 928
  Accounting 928
  Animation 929
  Artificial Intelligence 929
  Backup 930
  CAD/CAM 930
  CD-ROM (Drives and Software) 930
  Clip Art 931
  Creativity Tools 932
  Data Analysis Programs 932
  Databases 932
  Desktop Publishing 933
  Disk Compression Programs 934
  Draw/Paint Programs 934
  Educational Programs 935
  Fax Modem/Machines 936
  File Management 936
  Fonts 937

Furniture 937
Games 938
Graphics/Screen Capture Programs 939
Home Finance 939
HyperCard Programs 940
Information/Time Management 940
Integrated Software 941
Keyboards 941
Languages 941
Macros 942
Math/Statistics Programs 942
Memory Upgrades/Accelerators 942
Mice/Pointing Devices 943
Modems 944
Monitors 944
Multimedia Tools 945
Music Programs 946
Networking 946
OCR Programs 947
Outliner 947
Portable Macs 948
Presentation Programs 948
Printers 948
Programming 949
Resources 950
Scanners/OCR Software 950
Screen Savers 951
Security Software 951
Spelling Checkers 952
Spreadsheets 952
Supplies 953
Telecommunications 953
Utilities 953
Word Processing Programs 955
Word Processing Add-Ons 955
Product Listing (Alphabetically Arranged) 956

E Vendor Guide 981

Glossary 1009

Index 1039

Introduction

hy such a big book about a computer that has a reputation of being easy to use? Because the Macintosh environment has grown by leaps and bounds over the near decade since the computer's introduction, and this growth shows no signs of slowing. Apple Computer, Inc. is hard at work designing better Macintoshes and Macintosh peripherals, such as disk drives, scanners, and printers. Thousands of third-party developers also are designing and producing new software, hardware, and other goodies to match the demands of Apple's new products.

All this growth calls for a single reference book that explores the growing Macintosh universe. This book attempts to survey most aspects of the Macintosh world—from taking the machine out of the box to purchasing software and hardware. It even discusses the possibilities of the Macintosh future.

In this book, you find information about almost every aspect of the Macintosh, including the following:

- The basics you need to get your Macintosh up and running— including instructions for setting up your Macintosh system

- Information about Macintosh applications; reviews of word processors, spreadsheets, databases, personal finance managers, utilities, and more

- Information on games—both educational and just for fun

- Information about desktop publishing and its potential application to your needs

- Guidelines for selecting software and hardware

- Information about upgrading your Mac

- An introduction to programming your Macintosh

- An introduction to HyperCard

- Guidelines for keeping your Macintosh (and your data) safe

- Information about networking and telecommunications

Whatever you do with the Mac, you can find helpful information in *Que's Big Mac Book,* 4th Edition. In addition, appendixes provide information ranging from how to select the Macintosh that is right for you to an extensive directory of products and where they are available.

Who Should Use This Book?

Whether you are a beginner who doesn't know the difference between an icon and an ImageWriter or an advanced Macintosh user who is interested in the latest desktop publishing applications, *Que's Big Mac Book,* 4th Edition, is for you.

No matter what types of experiences or what level of expertise you have with the Macintosh or general computing, you can pick up this book, open to any page, and begin learning about the Macintosh world. The book is organized and written so that the information contained in any one of the chapters can stand alone, yet references other chapters when appropriate.

If you are a beginning Macintosh user, certain features of this book are especially helpful, such as the following:

■ The quick start at the beginning of the book, which gets you up and running without delay

■ The basic step-by-step approach that leads you through complex procedures with numerous screen illustrations

■ Advice on buying software and hardware, including information about warranties, return policies, and smart ways to protect yourself from purchase disasters

For example, just a brief look at word processors for the Mac reveals that Microsoft Word, WordPerfect, WriteNow, and MacWrite Pro are only a *few* of the myriad programs that can help you accomplish the same basic tasks. If you want to know what separates these word processors from one another, and if you are looking for a special feature, the word processing chapter can help you choose between these leading word processing programs.

For Macintosh experts, this book contains plenty of information, such as the following:

■ The basics of keeping your Macintosh healthy by preventive maintenance

■ The fundamentals of programming with the Macintosh and a guide to programming resources

■ Ideas for networking and communicating with the Macintosh

■ An introduction to the worlds of multimedia and the data sharing and communication between IBM PCs and Macs

A Road Map to This Book

Que's Big Mac Book, 4th Edition, consists of 32 chapters organized into four major parts: "Macintosh Basics," "Macintosh Software," "Macintosh Hardware," and "Advanced Topics." At the end of the book are several appendixes.

Part I, "Macintosh Basics," gives you quick and clear instructions on everything from plugging in your Macintosh to printing your first document. This section contains timesaving tricks that can even help the most proficient Mac users. Next, you find answers to the "everything you wanted to know about the Mac" questions. In this section, you learn about working with the basics of the system, manipulating and storing information as files on disks, and printing. This section is a must-read for all new Macintosh owners.

Part II, "Macintosh Software," gets to the heart of software—the do-it part of the software/hardware pair. Numerous applications are discussed and compared, including word processing, spreadsheet, database, desktop publishing, and graphics packages. You learn about the Mac's unique graphical user interface (GUI), which remains fairly consistent between applications. Because of this consistency—for example, many menu structures and hot key combinations are the same in different packages—you can quickly learn additional Mac programs once you learn the basics of one program.

This part covers all the major software categories and what you can use them for. Do you need to write a business report or a term paper that includes references to the population of Tibet? No problem. You can get the information you need by going on line with a variety of information services. You can even talk to a friend across the street or fax a document across the world by using your Macintosh's communications capabilities.

Part III, "Macintosh Hardware," gives you an overview of and guidelines to expanding and adding to your Macintosh. You read about memory upgrades, adding hard disks, accelerating your Macintosh to greater speed and performance, purchasing surge protectors, and more.

Do you know how to shop through the mail? What kinds of questions should you ask when you mail order? What about your needs next week? Next year? What about those discount, guaranteed-forever floppies? This part discusses the currently available Macs. It even covers the future of the Mac—what Apple intends to introduce over the next few years.

In Part IV, "Advanced Topics," you tackle topics such as networking and see how one office can have many Macintoshes sharing printers, modems, large disks, and more. You learn about Macintosh tools like HyperCard and the basics of doing your own programming. You learn how easy it is to share information between Macintoshes and IBM PCs, provided you have the right tools. Preventive maintenance and basic troubleshooting are also covered. You can use the information in this part to do more than type a letter—you learn how to make your Mac shine.

How to Use This Book

Don't try to read too much too soon. The fast readers are not always the best ones. If you are new to the Macintosh, one of the great pleasures in learning is taking your time and allowing yourself the luxury of discovering new things (and possibly making mistakes). Rushing can lead to more and bigger mistakes, which lead to frustration.

Don't be afraid to try new things. You may be a beginner and have no experience with desktop publishing, scanners, or other advanced Macintosh tools and features. Don't worry. Everyone starts at the beginning, and even the experts didn't know much when they first picked up a mouse. This book and your enthusiasm make a perfect combination for exploring everything the Macintosh offers. Although you may not be able to purchase enough software to try everything you want, user groups and other clubs often have available on-site programs open to members.

Work through the examples. Nothing works better than learning by doing. Even though people often think that watching (or reading) is enough, they need to exercise their knowledge so that it becomes a part of a larger base of understanding.

The Macintosh was born out of a strong desire to create a fun and useful "appliance" computer. To a great extent, the goal was reached. Yet, although learning to use a Mac is easier than learning to use a PC, it still takes time.

Don't rush yourself or have unreasonable expectations and demand too much from yourself in too short a time. Explore at your leisure and you will find yourself learning much quickly.

A Brief History of the Macintosh (In the Beginning...)

Since Apple Computer's beginning in 1977 (and especially since the introduction of the Macintosh in 1984), the company has set the standard for a new way of working with computers and continues to be a major influence on the design of hardware and software.

Apple Computer, Inc., was born out of the dreams of two people: Steve Jobs and Steve "Woz" Wozniak. Woz was the "whiz kid" with an appetite to learn all he could about computers, and Jobs was the person who was going to (and did) put it all together and market the resulting machines. The rest, as they say, is history. Both college dropouts (Jobs from Reed College in Oregon and Wozniak from the University of Colorado), the two men spent some time exploring career and lifestyle alternatives. In fact, their experiences outside the more traditional world of college probably had a significant impact on Apple's becoming an incubator of ideas, where people were free to think broadly about the future of computing.

Wozniak and Jobs eventually ended up in what is now known as Silicon Valley and founded Apple Computer, Inc. The Silicon Valley area, located in northern California not far from San Francisco, already had a stockpile of electronics manufacturers with factories filled with technicians. The raw material for the revolution that would occur was in place.

Jobs' and Wozniak's introduction during the early 1970s led to a collaboration and, under Wozniak's direction, the building of the Apple I, the result of Wozniak's lifelong ambition to build his own computer. In his desire, Woz had contacted companies such as Hewlett-Packard (for whom he worked at that time), but they weren't interested in the idea and saw no potential in what they viewed as a limited market.

Before the two entrepreneurs knew it, they were in the computer business. For a little under $700, anyone could (and many did) own this "garage computer creation." The Apple I led to the Apple II, and things began to take off. The infrastructure that was established in the Silicon Valley employed thousands of people, many wanting to be part of an upstart company that seemed to offer the freedom to explore new ideas and financial goals.

But success also presented difficulties, mostly on the side of management and growth. Clearly, what the fledgling Apple Computer, Inc., needed was a skilled manager who also understood the emerging field of personal computers. The person who filled this role was Armas Clifford "Mike" Markkula, a 33-year-old retired multimillionaire, who was so intrigued by the two Steves' plans that he agreed to come on board as the chief executive in 1977.

With Markkula's money invested in the firm, Apple incorporated and went public in 1977, for about $25 a share. In 1983, Apple sales passed the $1 billion mark (early in 1993, Apple announced in Tokyo the shipping of the 10 millionth Macintosh). Markkula really got things going when he encouraged Wozniak to quit his job at Hewlett-Packard and go full time with Apple so that his creative energies could be devoted fully to the new products that future needs would demand.

Wozniak left Hewlett-Packard. Then Jobs hired John Sculley away from Pepsi-Cola. Jobs eventually left Apple after a failed power struggle with Sculley for control of the company, and went on to produce the NeXT computer, a powerful, highly acclaimed computer that has not yet become a major player in the personal computer market.

Apple Computer, Inc., became a haven for the counterculture computer wizard. With the success of the Apple II and the peripherals and software that helped create an even more successful market came plans for, and the realization of, an entirely new type of computer: the Macintosh.

The Birth of the Macintosh

If you could have looked in on the group of 15 or so people who were in charge of creating the first Macintosh, you would have seen a mixture of young, committed, and passionate people who dreamed of creating a computer unlike any the world had seen.

The first attempt at a graphic interface computer was the Lisa—which became the prototype for the Macintosh and the beginning of that dream. The Macintosh was a vision for Jobs, and he saw it as the people's computer, not unlike the Volkswagen of the 50s and 60s, which was seen as transportation for the masses. The Lisa was Apple's hope to capture a large portion of the business world's computer needs by delivering a powerful but easy-to-use office computer. The Lisa was a powerful $10,000 computer, reviewed positively in the computer press. The first computers were shipped in April, 1983—with great expectations. The Lisa was much like the Macintosh—using graphics and that now-familiar, easy-to-use mouse.

Although the Lisa was in a major part due to the hard and creative work of many people at Apple, ideas for the Lisa stemmed from earlier research done at the Xerox Corporation's Palo Alto Research Center during the 1970s. There, computer engineers developed the concepts of a computer with a graphical interface, which Jobs saw on a visit. The only problem was that Xerox did not have the vision that Jobs had. Though Xerox developed the first true personal computer before any other company and essentially created the graphical user interface (which Xerox called Star and now renamed Global View), the company failed to market the computer—not believing that the personal computer's time had come. The idea of a graphical computer floundered.

Some people left Xerox to work for Apple and to head up the Lisa project, and the concepts developed at Xerox worked their way into the new Apple products.

The Lisa was slow, but what hurt sales most was the price tag. Ten thousand dollars for the then-unexplored world of personal computing applications caused many businesses to pull back. The result? Anticipated sales of 10,000 turned into actual sales of about 6,500, and the 1983 introduction of the IBM PC (and the later introduction of Lotus's best-selling 1-2-3 spreadsheet) started to take the business world by storm. The crest that Apple had been on for the preceding five years was beginning to fall. Apple had never been well established in the business community, and the battle looked like it would be even harder than anticipated—indeed, it was. Sales fell considerably; without the continued sales of the Apple II, there would not have been an Apple Computer, Inc.

The Lisa project, which Jobs originally wanted to direct, didn't go very well because of personal conflicts and vague management goals. The Macintosh project, however, which Jobs *did* direct, became an inspiration to produce a computer that could do much of what the Lisa was acclaimed for but with less power and at a much lower cost. Jobs' intent, which probably led to the "Computer for the rest of us" slogan, was to create something that everyone could afford and easily learn to use—a computer with software that was user-friendly. This machine was to be the computer you could set up within 10 minutes after you took it out of the box and begin using in another 5 minutes. For most Macintosh users, these goals have been met, although increasingly sophisticated and demanding software can at times require more than the user's intuition.

To increase the new machine's attractiveness to consumers and to third-party software (and eventually hardware) developers, the designers intended the Macintosh to be the people's machine—one design and one configuration of the peripherals. In this way, add-ons could be shared freely, and one standard for software design and implementation could evolve. In fact, the standard Macintosh was so standard that the original Macintosh could not be opened without the use of a special tool kit; developers believed that the owner would have no need to go inside the machine and add anything. The Macintosh could not—in fact—be expanded at that time.

In 1984, the $2,495 Macintosh computer was ready to be sold to the public, and along with the tremendous accomplishments of the team who developed the Macintosh came an advertising campaign to match. To this day, people still talk about the commercial that cost more than $500,000 dollars to make and more than $1,500,000 to show on Super Bowl Sunday in 1984. This commercial tried to communicate the message that the Macintosh was unlike anything you had ever seen before. Although there was some doubt and trepidation about the content and presentation of the commercial, which showed a high-tech world of office drudges in a rather dungeon-like setting with a *1984* Orwellian talking head challenged by a young woman wielding a sledge hammer, it turned out to be a rousing success commercially and artistically.

The Macintosh has gone on to become the most popular personal computer of all time, creating a cult of users unmatched by any other corporate product. While the company still experienced growing pains and had to deal with an almost fatal financial mess with too much inventory in the early 1980s, Apple and its Macintosh continue to lead the way in easily accessible products.

Ironically, the currently leading business machine—the IBM PC and clones—has now fallen to the ideas first presented by Apple. After years of mocking the Macintosh as a "toy" computer, several millions of IBM PC and PC clone users have bought (and still are buying) the graphical Microsoft Windows user interface, which helps to make the PC more Mac-like.

For the Macintosh true believer who survived the dark years when no one knew whether the Macintosh and Apple would survive at all, the situation has a surreal, *Alice in Wonderland* feel to it. Software manufactures on the DOS side of the world now compete to be "Mac-like" in order to sell to IBM PC and PC clone users. IBM broke ranks with Microsoft and has now turned to join forces with Apple in developing the next generation of computers.

Although the Macintosh is still considered by many to be a "niche" computer (one that fills certain specific needs and occupies only a certain fraction of the total market), a window of opportunity has opened. DOS has begun to crack—showing its age—as the old IBM PC standard technology strains with maintaining out-of-date standards. Meanwhile, the graphical user interface is now positioned to become the dominant standard of the future personal computer.

The Future of the Macintosh

Predicting the future of computers is a risky business. When I was in college (I'm dating myself here: the Macintosh was still a gleam in Steve Job's eye when the event I'm about to detail occurred), a panel of major computer industry employers was convened by my university to discuss with the students of the department the "next ten years of computers." The most honest comment came (if memory serves me correctly, the irony is just too much to stand) from the—I believe—Xerox representative who confessed that no one really knew what the next decade would bring.

Considering that I had been a teenage hobbyist when the first microprocessor chip was introduced by Intel and still own my first single board computer (with a whole 256 bytes—not kilobytes, *bytes*) of memory, I concur with the statement. The first, full microprocessor chip was introduced around 1974. Ten years later, the Macintosh was introduced. The industry went from hand-built-and-soldered hobbyist computers to the Apple II (IIe and IIc), the IBM PC, and the Macintosh. Now, another decade is passing and the end of this ten years will bring tiny computers that are far more powerful than the two-car-garage-sized computers of several years ago. Even now, the Macintosh I have written this book on is more powerful than the room-filling minicomputer at the business where I had my first programming job 13 years ago.

My current career of writing books for nonprogrammers using computers simply did not exist when I graduated from college. Nonprogrammers didn't use computers. Who knows what the next decade will bring?

But we do have an idea of what is on the drawing boards today. And the future is rather amazing. Apple announcements include the following:

- *The PowerPC.* A totally new computer that will deliver speeds of 10 to possibly hundreds of times the current models.

- *Casper.* A voice recognition system that will enable you to talk to your computer, giving voice commands rather than using a mouse or keyboard. (Some such systems are already offered, though rather limited in power and fairly expensive in price.)

- *Handwriting recognition. Star Trek*-like clipboard-sized computers you can scribble notes on and choose commands with a pen-like pointer. "Pen-based" computers already exist, but are still a bit on the rough side.

- *Wireless networking.* Macintoshes will link to networks when you walk into a building. In the not-so-distant future, your Macintosh may never be out of touch with your company's computers—even if you are on the road, in a plane, or in the jungle. (In fact, if the Global Positioning System performs as expected, your Macintosh may be able to *guide* you out of the jungle or through a new city.)

- *Newton.* The "personal digital assistant" (or PDA) that—in initial introductions—will enable you to jot down notes, keep your schedule, and communicate with other computers, as well as other features. Later versions may talk to you and understand spoken commands.

- *Project Taligent.* A new operating system that will be object-oriented and licensed to other computer manufacturers and developers. The operating system is code named *Pink*. This is really the key to the IBM-Apple joint venture's success because it will be capable of running on a variety of systems that currently have difficulty "talking to each other." Your next word processor will work the same way whether you are using an IBM, Macintosh, or some system not yet introduced.

- *Project Kaleida.* A joint IBM-Apple venture to develop a multimedia platform with standard formats, making it easier for developers to create applications that work with different operating systems.

- *Project Enterprise.* Aimed at making it easier for Macintoshes and IBMs to connect and communicate with one another.

- *PowerOpen.* A new operating system that will provide a common platform for the Mac, IBM, UNIX, and others.

When will all of these sci-fi features be at your dealer? Look for the first PowerPC to arrive around the middle of the decade. Then watch for increasingly powerful machines to be rolled out as the turn of the century approaches. Just before the PowerPC, you should see Casper appear on a new generation of Macintosh computers currently dubbed the "Mac III."

Newton is coming fast. Expect to see the introduction before mid-decade. Early units may not perform to the full "dream specifications," but will be a major step toward the science-fiction idea of a companion computer.

Pen-based systems will become more prevalent in mid-decade, but will probably not be extensively useful until later. Few users will give up the speed of typing for the slowness of handwriting, but I expect pen-based systems to eventually obliterate the spiral notebook and the clipboard. Already, UPS uses a rudimentary pen system for customer signatures when packages are delivered. The day is not far away when you will be approached by poll takers and opinion surveyors with relatively flat computers rather than reams of paper. College students may soon carry about pen-based computers that can be docked with their Macintoshes (unless professors do not mind voice recognition computers taking notes—images of a professor lecturing to desks with nothing but Newton PDAs dance through my head).

Beyond these announcements and potentials, no one is quite sure about future of the Mac. A revolution is brewing that may break around the turn of the century. Many experts believe that we are reaching the end of the usefulness of silicon—the material all computer chips are made of. Even now, computer engineers find that the speed of electrons (close to the 186,000 miles per *second* of light) is too slow (!) and that electrons—so small that billions could dance on the head of a pin—are too large and cumbersome to work with.

The promise of optical computers—those that use laser light rather than electricity to perform calculations—is astounding. Parallel processing, which uses more than one microprocessor simultaneously, promises incredible speeds. (One prototype uses 64,000 microprocessors to attack problems all at once; the Macintosh has only one microprocessor.)

Once it was postulated that a computer that had the same number of connections as the human brain would fill the Empire State building. That conjecture is now severely out of date. By the early decades of the next century, the same number of connections in the brain may be in your desktop Macintosh.

But for now, we have the Macintosh, putting power undreamed of only a couple of decades ago on our desktops. For now we have an easy-to-use, friendly, and useful companion to aid us in our work, help us deal with finances and taxes, and entertain us at the end of a long day.

This book is your companion guide to our current science fiction future that snuck up on us all rather unexpectedly and will help you put all that high-tech wizardry to work.

Part I

Macintosh Basics

Includes:

Quick Start: Learning the Essentials
1 Getting Started
2 Understanding the System
3 Managing Disks
4 Managing Files
5 Configuring the Macintosh
6 Customizing the Macintosh
7 Printing
8 Using Fonts

Learning the Essentials

Everyone has to start somewhere. This Quick Start is
written especially for people
who aren't familiar with the
Macintosh's basic functions
and features. You can learn
more about any of the topics
covered by reading the rest
of Part I, "Macintosh Basics." Work
through the steps in this Quick
Start, and you will accomplish tasks
with your Macintosh that you
didn't think possible in such a
short amount of time.

Starting Your Macintosh

The location of the power switch on the Macintosh depends on the model. The four basic models are described here:

- *Compact Macintoshes*. The self-contained, all-in-one-case Macintosh, such as the Classic II and the Performa 200, has a power switch on the back of the computer, on the left side near the power cord. The switch is a "rocker" type. You press the upper half of the switch to turn on the computer. The LC, LC II, and Performa 400 have a similar switch, although these units are modular.

- *Modular and tower Macintoshes*. These models have separate monitors (with the exception of the LC, LC II, and Performa 400), and you turn on these computers by pressing a key marked with a left-pointing triangle, the Power On key. This key is located at the top of Apple keyboards but may be in other locations on non-Apple keyboards.

  Note that if pressing this key does not turn on your Macintosh, the "master" power switch may not be turned on. This power switch is a round button located on the back of the Macintosh. Press the button; it should click and remain pressed. From then on, you can turn on the computer by pressing the key that displays the left-pointing triangle. (If you are unable to locate the power switch, see Chapter 1, which includes diagrams of the backs of the current Macintosh models.)

- *Laptop Macintoshes*. Laptops have a "sleep" feature that enables them to be in a low-power state without actually being turned off completely. You "wake" the laptop by pressing any key. If pressing a key does not wake the laptop, you need to press the power button located on the back of the computer (hidden by a "flip down" lid on many laptops). It is a round button located on the left side when the laptop is facing you.

The following actions occur when the Macintosh powers up:

- A beep tells you that your Macintosh is on.

- Your screen comes to life, and you see a small Macintosh welcoming you with a smile. If you don't see this Macintosh, your hard disk probably doesn't contain the System Software needed to start the Macintosh. If your computer does not start, you may have to install the System. Turn to Chapter 2, "Understanding the System," for instructions on how to do this. Other possible problems are covered in Chapter 32, "Maintenance and Troubleshooting."

- A `Welcome to Macintosh` message appears. This message indicates that the System Software has been located and your Macintosh is starting up.

- The "Desktop" appears. The Desktop looks similar to that shown in figure QS.1. (If your Desktop looks different, don't worry about this now.) In the top right corner is an *icon*—a small picture—that represents the disk containing your System Folder.

Fig. QS.1
The Macintosh Desktop.

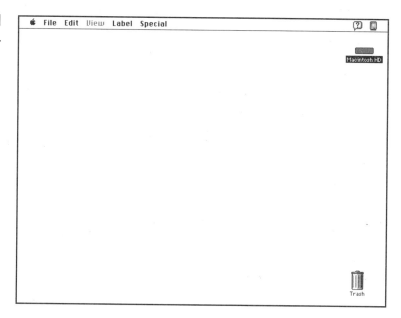

The appearance of the Desktop indicates that all is well and your Macintosh is ready for use.

Using the Mouse

The *mouse* is one of the vital connections between you and your Macintosh, and one of many different types of input devices. You use the mouse to make selections on the Desktop and to perform a variety of operations. To use the mouse efficiently, you need to learn and practice certain mouse techniques.

Practice moving the mouse around on a solid surface or mouse pad. (*Mouse pads* are available through a variety of sources; for more information, see Chapter 27, "Adding Accessories.") As you move the mouse, the mouse pointer on-screen moves in the same direction and a proportional distance.

You use the mouse to point to an icon (or text or a graphic) and to select it before you can perform any operation that affects the icon. For example, you must highlight the icon that represents a file before you can move or copy the file to another location.

In figure QS.2, the mouse pointer is placed on top of the Macintosh HD icon. You now are using the mouse to point to this icon.

Fig. QS.2

Pointing to the start-up disk's icon.

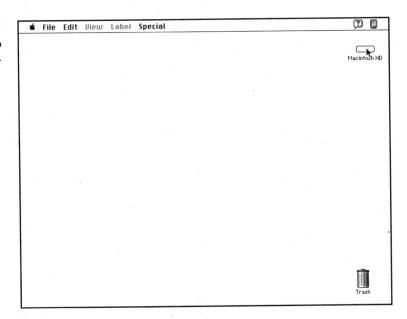

Three important mouse operations are clicking, dragging, and double-clicking. To *click*, you place the mouse pointer on an icon or another item, and then press and release the mouse button once. *Double-clicking* is the same as clicking but uses two quick clicks rather than one.

To *drag*, you place the mouse pointer on the item, and then press the mouse button and hold it down while you move the item to a new location. When you release the mouse button, you have finished dragging. Chapter 2 explains mouse concepts in greater detail, and Chapters 5 and 6 show you how to customize and adjust the mouse's response.

Place the mouse pointer on the Macintosh HD icon and click the mouse button once. The icon darkens to indicate that it has been selected.

Selecting the icon means that the next action you take is applied to the disk that this icon represents.

To deselect an icon, move the pointer off the icon and click elsewhere on the Desktop (the screen).

You move icons by dragging them. One reason for moving an icon is to rearrange the order of the file icons on your Desktop. Follow these steps to drag the Trash icon to another location:

1. Place the mouse pointer on the Trash icon in the lower right corner of the screen.

2. Press the mouse button and, while holding it down, drag the Trash icon to another location on the Desktop.

   Note that an "outline" of the icon follows the mouse pointer as you move the mouse (see fig. QS.3).

Fig. QS.3
Dragging the Trash icon from one location to another.

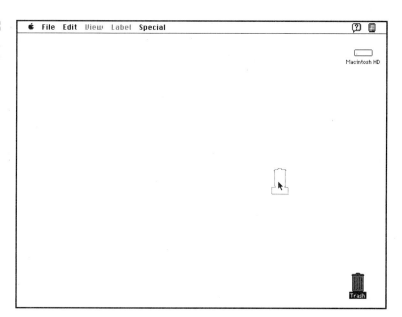

3. Release the mouse button.

Using the Macintosh Menus

At the top of the screen is the *menu bar*, which contains a series of menus. Each menu offers various commands, as shown in figure QS.4. These commands provide you with tools to do many things.

Fig. QS.4
The System 7 Finder
menus.

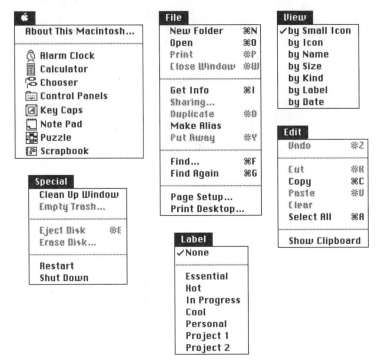

When you are working with menus, the menu items or commands that are *dimmed* are not active and have no effect if you choose them. To select a command from a menu, follow these steps:

1. Move the mouse pointer to the File menu; then press and hold down the mouse button to display the commands on the menu (see fig. QS.5). As you drag the mouse pointer over each command, the command is highlighted; you make the selection when you release the mouse button.

2. Press and hold down the mouse button while you move the mouse pointer to the command you want to choose. Then release the mouse button.

Working with Windows

When you double-click an icon that represents a file, a window opens to display the contents of the icon. You "look through" a window to work with a file's contents.

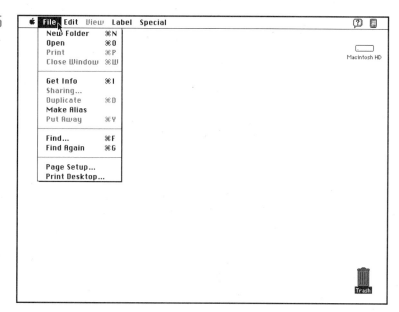

To open any window, double-click the icon that represents the file, folder, or disk whose contents you want to display. Figure QS.6 shows the results of double-clicking the Macintosh HD icon. The Macintosh displays names and information about some of the different files and folders on that hard disk. In figure QS.6, you also see the various parts of the window labeled.

Here are descriptions of the main elements of the window:

Title bar	Indicates the name of the file, folder, or disk that the window represents. Also used to move a menu on-screen.
Close box	Used to close the window.
Zoom box	Used to change the window quickly between two sizes.
Scroll bars	Used to view the contents of the window up, down, left, or right, enabling you to view items that do not fit inside the window's current size.
Scroll arrows	Used to view the contents of the window by small amounts.
Scroll box	Used to view the contents of the window by large amounts.
Size box	Used to change the window's size.

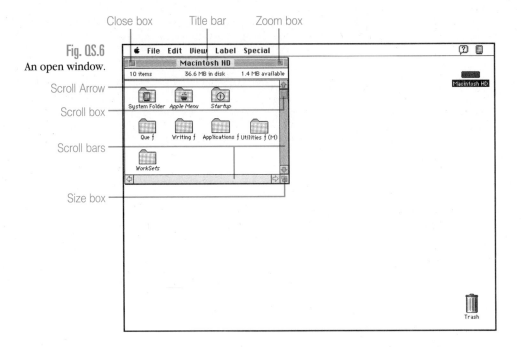

Fig. QS.6
An open window.

Close box   Title bar   Zoom box

Scroll Arrow

Scroll box

Scroll bars

Size box

Closing a Window

To close a window, click the close box, located in the upper left corner of the screen. The window closes and "shrinks" back to an icon.

Moving a Window

To move a window, place the mouse pointer on the title bar, press and hold down the mouse button, and drag the window to its new location. An outline of the window follows the mouse pointer (see fig. QS.7). When you release the mouse button, the window is moved. One great Macintosh feature is that you can have more than one window open at the same time. Only one window, however, can be active. You can tell which window is active because the active window has horizontal lines in the title bar.

Resizing a Window

To change the size of a window, drag the size box, located in the lower right corner of the window (refer to QS.6). When you drag the size box to resize a window, the upper left corner of the window remains stationary. An outline of the window follows the mouse pointer (see fig. QS.8). You can drag the size box in any direction to change the size of the window. When you release the mouse button, the window assumes the new size.

Fig. QS.7
Moving a window.

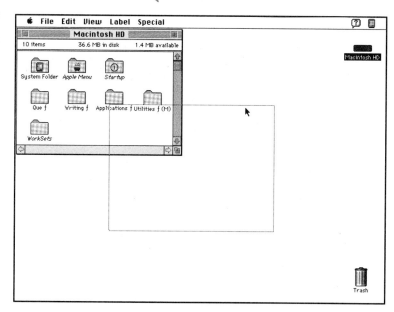

Fig. QS.8
Resizing a window.

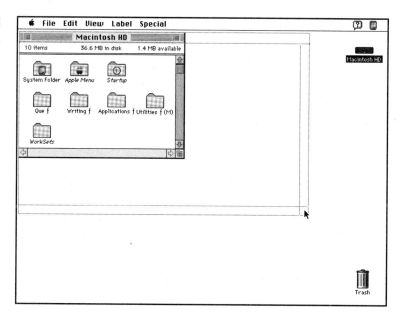

You also can change the size of a window by clicking the zoom box, located in the upper right corner of the window. Using the zoom box rather than the size box toggles the window between the last size you set with the size box and a size that displays as much of the contents of the window as is possible.

Scrolling a Window

Often all the information contained in a document or in another file, folder, or disk cannot fit on one screen (especially if you reduce the size of the window with the size box). In such cases, you may need to scroll through a window's contents. *Scrolling* enables you to view one screenful of information at a time. As you scroll, you see different parts of the window's contents. Scroll bars run horizontally along the bottom of the window and vertically along the right side of the window.

To scroll through the contents of a window, use one of these methods:

■ Place the mouse pointer on one of the scroll arrows at the ends of the horizontal or vertical scroll bars and click (see fig. QS.9). Each time you click the scroll arrow, the contents of the window move up or down one line.

Fig. QS.9

Clicking a scroll arrow.

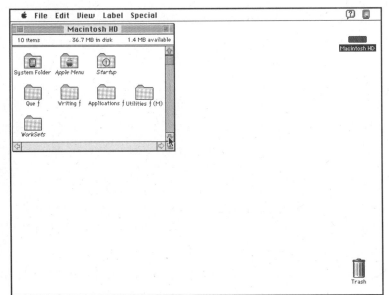

- Click the scroll bar above or below the scroll box. Each time you click, a new screenful of information appears.

- Place the mouse pointer on the scroll box. Drag the box up or down the vertical scroll bar, or to the right or left in the horizontal scroll bar. The information in the window shifts in the same direction, in an amount relative to the distance you dragged the scroll box. If you drag the scroll box about halfway down the vertical scroll bar, for example, you move to a point about halfway through the window's contents. Release the mouse button at the place you want to stop.

I f you have only one window of information, the scroll bars remain white (refer to the horizontal scroll bar in fig. QS.9). Otherwise, the scroll bars are gray (see the vertical scroll bar in that figure).

Opening Additional Windows

You can have several windows open at the same time. If you click a folder icon with one window already open, a second window opens. Figure QS.10 shows two open windows. Both windows can be resized and moved. Even though two windows are open, only one is active—the window with lines in the title bar. (In figure QS.10, the MacLinkPlus folder is the active window.) The second window always opens on top of the first. Windows open in the same position as when they were last closed.

When more than one window is open, click the one you want to make active. If you cannot see the window you want, resize the active window (using the size box) and move the other windows.

Y ou also can move an inactive window by holding down the Command key and dragging the window by its title bar. In figure QS.10, for example, you hold down the Command key, move the mouse pointer to Macintosh HD (the title of the inactive window), and press and hold down the mouse button. You then can move the window without making it active.

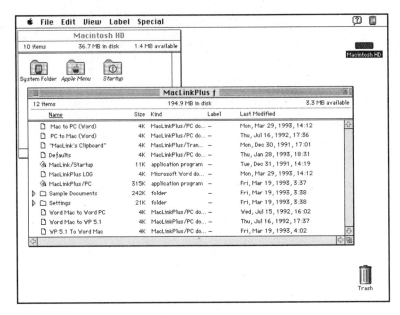

Fig. QS.10

Two open windows.

Cutting, Copying, and Pasting

You often need to remove material from one document window and place the material into another document window (in the same application or in a different application, such as from an accounting package to a word processor). Or you may need to copy the same information to more than one location. To accomplish either task, use the Cut, Copy, and Paste commands, located on the Edit menu. Follow these steps to make the changes:

1. Select the text or graphic you want to cut or copy by clicking the name or icon, or by dragging the mouse pointer over the name or icon.

2. From the Edit menu, choose Cut or Copy.

   Any cut or copied information is placed in the *Clipboard*, a temporary storage area. The Clipboard can hold only one selection at a time. When you execute another cut or copy operation, the contents of the Clipboard are replaced.

3. Activate the window of the document where you want to place the cut or copied information.

4. Move the mouse pointer to the position in the new document window (or in the same window) where you want the information to appear.

5. From the Edit menu, choose Paste. The copied (or cut) text or graphic appears.

Printing a Document

To print a document, choose Print from the File menu. In the Print dialog that appears, make your choices, or accept the default values by clicking the Print (or OK) button. In Chapter 7, "Printing," you learn about the available printing options.

When you print, you see a Print dialog similar to the one in figure QS.11. Notice that the dialog in this figure is for printing with an ImageWriter LQ. Dialogs appear whenever you need to provide additional information so that the Macintosh can continue its work.

Fig. QS.11

The ImageWriter LQ Print dialog.

You may be able to print a document without being inside the application program that created the document. You do this by printing "from the Desktop." Be careful, however, because some applications do not enable you to print files from the Desktop.

To print a file from the Desktop, follow these steps:

1. Highlight the icon that represents the document you want to print.

    To print more than one file from the same application, Shift-click each file name. To Shift-click, hold down the Shift key while you click the mouse button.

2. From the File menu, choose Print.

The Macintosh displays the appropriate dialog, and you can print from there. For this method to work, however, the program that created the document must be on your disk. If you do not have the application, your Macintosh tells you that it cannot find the required program. This printing technique actually opens the program that created your document and tells that program to print the selected document. That program's Print dialog is displayed, and the document is printed after you make your selections and click the Print (or OK) button. After printing, that program quits.

Ending a Work Session

To turn off your Macintosh safely, *always* choose the Shut Down command from the Special menu unless you are using a laptop Macintosh.

If you are using a laptop Macintosh, you probably will want to use the Sleep command in the Special menu. This command puts the laptop in a low-power state but keeps all your documents open. The documents will be immediately available to you when you wake the Macintosh by pressing a key. Use the Shut Down command when you need to power down the laptop completely—if, for instance, you are not going to use your computer for a day or so.

No matter how tempted you may be, *never* simply switch off the power. Your Macintosh needs to update files and do a little "housekeeping" so that the next time you start up, things are in order and ready to go.

Macintoshes that turn on from the keyboard automatically power off after the shut-down sequence is completed. They can then be powered up by the Power On key (the one with the left-pointing triangle) on the keyboard.

Macintoshes that use manual power switches display a message at the end of the shut-down sequence, informing you that it is now safe to turn off your Macintosh. At this point, you may switch off the power.

Quick Start Summary

Even if you have never previously touched a Macintosh, you should have mastered some of the fundamental skills by now. Clicking, double-clicking, dragging, choosing menu options, cutting, copying, pasting, and printing are techniques you use in almost every Macintosh activity. The rest of the chapters in Part I cover these techniques and others in greater detail to give you the tools to master your Macintosh more fully.

Getting Started

This chapter guides you through some of the basics of the Macintosh. You see how the various Macintosh models are set up; that is, how the different components are connected and made ready to use. This chapter does more than tell you how to connect your Mac. It first helps you to thoroughly consider your workspace and how to best set up the area in which you will be using the Macintosh.

The chapter then introduces you to the main parts of the Macintosh interface. The *interface* is the system that enables you and your Macintosh to communicate. You are probably already familiar with the Macintosh interface, which uses a mouse, menus, and graphics. In this chapter, you begin to learn the basics of how to use the interface to control your Macintosh.

Setting Up the Macintosh

One of the best features of the Macintosh computer is that it can be set up easily. Few other computers can be unpacked and prepared for use in so short a time as the Macintosh. This chapter explores some safety and comfort issues that you need to consider when setting up your Mac. It then explains the parts of the Macintosh and leads you through the setup procedure.

Preparing to Set Up the Macintosh

Ergonomics—which refers to the health and comfort of computer users—has become a buzzword in the computer industry. Buzzword or not, the positioning of your computer and yourself can affect your health. Carefully consider the arrangement of your work area and the placement of the various components of the Macintosh.

Adjusting Monitor Height and Distance

The ideal height for a monitor places the viewing area of the screen at eye level. You can determine a good height for your monitor by sitting at your desk or table and looking straight ahead. Your eyes will naturally seek the best location for the center of the monitor.

You can raise the monitor or the Macintosh (if the monitor is built-in) by purchasing a stand through your dealer or through mail order (see Chapter 27, "Adding Accessories"). Alternatively, you may want to consider a computer desk with a hutch that allows you to place the computer or the monitor at a more ideal height.

The distance a monitor is located from your eyes is also important. The ideal distance can vary from person to person but is generally about a foot—approximately the distance you find naturally comfortable for reading a book.

At the same time, however, many people are concerned about the potential risks of radiation from monitors. Unfortunately, in order to cut down on the possibility of radiation, you need to stay approximately 28 inches from the monitor—over twice as far as the ideal focus distance of your eyes.

The studies on so-called video display terminal (VDT) radiation are inconclusive. You have to decide how far from the monitor you want to work. Many users believe that the stresses of an improperly set up work area and bad work habits (whether voluntary or not) are more problematic than the small amount of radiation monitors emit. Others disagree. On the bright side, responsible manufacturers such as Apple take pains to reduce the emissions of their monitors.

Preventing Screen Glare

When light from a window or light fixture reflects off the Macintosh screen, the on-screen image appears "washed out." Additionally, you may see an image of the light source reflected in the screen. This reflection—called *screen glare*—forces your eyes to work extra hard to see the display, and can therefore cause eye strain.

You can avoid screen glare by positioning your monitor so that it does not reflect the room's source of light. Don't place your Macintosh close to a window (this also helps prevent direct sunlight from falling on the Macintosh). And don't position the monitor where a light source is reflected on-screen.

If you can't avoid the room's light from falling on the screen (perhaps the room's light fixture is in the center of the ceiling and the light reflects no matter *where* you move the monitor), consider purchasing a lamp that you can position as needed. Make certain that the lamp provides adequate and comfortable lighting throughout the room. Indirect, diffuse lighting is best. My favorites are the newer halogen floor lamps that aim the lighting at the ceiling, casting a diffuse but bright light throughout the room. These lamps can also be adjusted to comfortable lighting levels.

Considering Keyboard Positions

Repetitive strain injuries (RSI), including carpal tunnel syndrome, have become a major concern for computer users in recent years. The repetitive motions of typing and using the mouse can potentially cause painful and debilitating injuries that lead to costly medical treatment.

Because each computer user is different, no specific set of rules will definitely prevent the condition. However, the following general guidelines can lessen your chances of ever experiencing such an injury:

- Position your keyboard so that your hands and arms are as relaxed as possible. The keyboard should be at a height so that your elbows are bent at right angles, and you do not have to bend your wrists when you type.

- Consider purchasing a wrist rest, which fits in front of your keyboard and lets you rest your wrists as you type.

- Consider purchasing a desk with an adjustable keyboard shelf so that you can lower the keyboard to a comfortable height. If you don't want to purchase an entire new desk, you might want to buy a shelf to attach to your current desk (see Chapter 27, "Adding Accessories").

- Take frequent breaks during long typing sessions. Make phone calls, do some filing, go get a cup of coffee—do anything that gets you away from the keyboard for 5 or 10 minutes every hour or two.

- Don't disregard any pain or numbness that you feel. If you notice pain or strain, see a doctor.

Judging Office Furniture

Your choice of desk, chair, and other office items can contribute to your health and comfort or affect them adversely. Carefully consider your body's most comfortable position and select furniture accordingly.

Your chair should have good back support to help keep your back straight. While a high-quality chair can be expensive, medical costs for back problems are considerably higher.

Some users find the so-called "back chair" to their liking. These odd-looking chairs actually place you in a kneeling position that causes your back to be straight. You might want to consider purchasing one of these chairs, but keep in mind that quality means higher cost. The less expensive versions of these chairs cannot be adjusted and hence may cause more problems than they solve. Some users also complain that these chairs cause their knees to become uncomfortable and even to hurt over long periods of time.

Overall, your body should be relaxed when you are sitting at your desk. The height of the desk should allow your arms to be relaxed as your wrists rest on the surface; your elbows should be approximately at a right angle. A desk that is too low can cause you to "hunch over" as you work. One that is too high can cause you to strain slightly (keeping your arms up) as you work.

Pay attention to small amounts of strain. As you test desk and chair combinations, you might tend to disregard minor amounts of strain. But over time, the strain can build up. Be very careful when choosing office furniture.

Looking at Macintosh Models

A pple releases new Mac models at what seems to be a furious rate. During the few months that it took to write this book, for example, Apple released no fewer than 10 new models. For up-to-the-minute information about new models, see your Apple dealer.

There are some 30 different Macintoshes in existence today. Though not all of these models are currently in production, a great number are still in use and are available in the used Macintosh market. Fortunately, the different models fall into four categories that allow them to be considered together. These categories are compact, modular, tower, and laptop.

R egardless of which Macintosh model you are using, you can run System 7, the most recent Macintosh operating system. This book is based on System 7.

Compact Macintoshes combine all parts except the keyboard and mouse in one casing. The current compact models are the Classic II, the Performa 200, and the Color Classic.

Modular Macintoshes have separate monitors. These are the members of the Macintosh II family, such as the Macintosh IIvx, the Performa series, the Centris series, and the LC series.

Tower Macintoshes are the more powerful Quadra computers. The Quadras are primarily workstations—meant for computer-aided design, high-powered graphics work, and the like. The monitors are separate on these units, as well, but the computer itself is intended to stand on the floor near a desk rather than on it as a modular Macintosh is designed to do.

Finally, *laptop* Macintoshes are—as the name implies—meant to sit in the lap or on a small table. This category includes the PowerBook and

Duo series. These smaller Macintoshes contain a flat display that folds up from the computer itself. (The older portables also fall into this category though they are much too large and heavy to place in one's lap.)

Each of these categories is considered so that, whichever Mac you have, you can familiarize yourself with the important parts of your Macintosh, set up the computer quickly, and then begin using it.

As you view the back of your Macintosh, take careful note of the major connections. You can see a symbol—or icon—located near each connection. This symbol helps you identify the connection. For example, the serial port generally used for connecting a serial printer has an icon of a printer near it. Macintoshes that have monitor ports have a small monitor symbol near the port. In general, cables have matching symbols to help you locate the outlet into which you insert each of them.

Compact Macintoshes

The compact Macintosh continues the orginal Macintosh design. At its inception, the Macintosh was intended to be small, self-contained, and easily connected. The hallmark of these units is that the monitor is contained within the computer casing. Three compact units are current: the Classic II, the Color Classic, and the Performa 200. However, four other versions are still in use and available in the used computer market. These older units are the Plus, the Classic, the SE, and the SE/30. Three compact Macintoshes are now obsolete and not considered in this book: the original Macintosh (called the 128K), the 512K, and the 512Ke.

Figures 1.1 through 1.4 show the backs of compact Macintoshes. Note that the Classic does not have a sound input port.

When connecting your Macintosh, you are most concerned with the locations of the power receptacle, the power switch, the Apple Desktop Bus (ADB) ports, and—if you have a printer—the serial ports or the SCSI port.

Note that the Plus does not have the ADB ports. Rather, the mouse has a port of its own, and the keyboard plugs into the front of the computer through an outlet that looks like a telephone jack. This outlet is near the bottom of the Plus's front, off to the right.

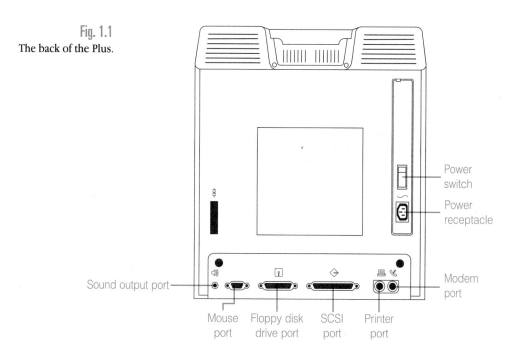

Fig. 1.1
The back of the Plus.

Power switch

Power receptacle

Sound output port

Modem port

Mouse port

Floppy disk drive port

SCSI port

Printer port

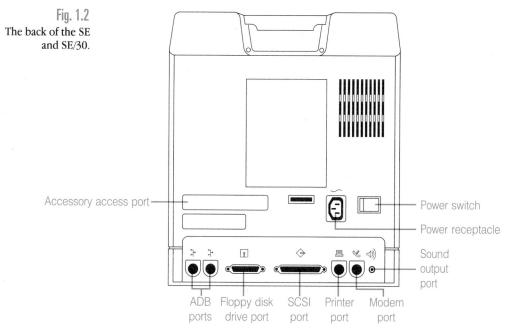

Fig. 1.2
The back of the SE
and SE/30.

Accessory access port

Power switch

Power receptacle

Sound output port

ADB ports

Floppy disk drive port

SCSI port

Printer port

Modem port

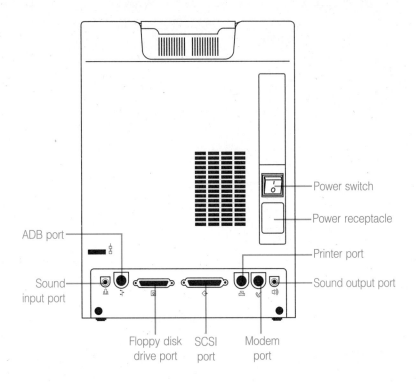

Fig. 1.3
The back of the Classic,
Classic II, and
Performa 200.

ADB port

Sound
input port

Power switch

Power receptacle

Printer port

Sound output port

Floppy disk
drive port

SCSI
port

Modem
port

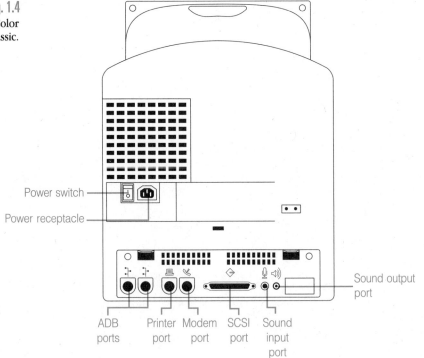

Fig. 1.4
The back of the Color
Classic.

Power switch

Power receptacle

ADB
ports

Printer
port

Modem
port

SCSI
port

Sound
input
port

Sound output
port

Modular Macintoshes

Modular Macintoshes have separate monitors and generally offer more expansion options than the compact units. The cases of these Macintoshes are intended to sit flat on a desk with the monitor resting on top. Figures 1.5 through 1.10 show the backs of the modular Macintoshes.

Fig. 1.5
The back of the Macintosh LC series and Performa 400 series computers.

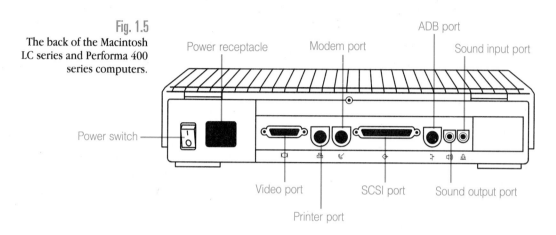

The LC III has the same ports, arranged in the same way, as the other LC models, but the back of that model does differ slightly from the others.

Fig. 1.6
The back of the Macintosh II, IIx, and IIfx.

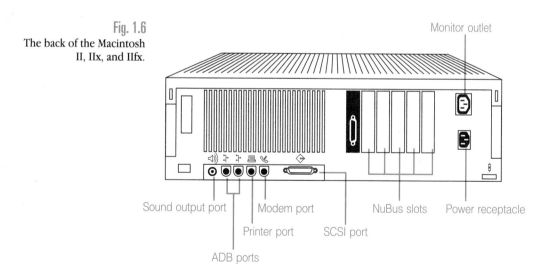

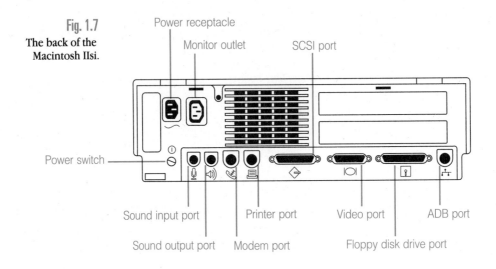

Fig. 1.7
The back of the
Macintosh IIsi.

Power receptacle

Monitor outlet

SCSI port

Power switch

Sound input port

Sound output port

Modem port

Printer port

Video port

Floppy disk drive port

ADB port

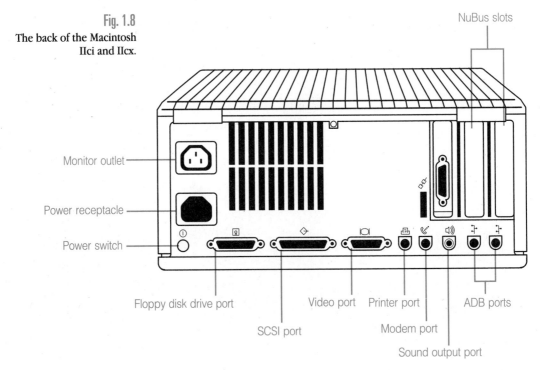

Fig. 1.8
The back of the Macintosh
IIci and IIcx.

NuBus slots

Monitor outlet

Power receptacle

Power switch

Floppy disk drive port

SCSI port

Video port

Printer port

Modem port

Sound output port

ADB ports

Note that the IIcx does not have the video port shown in figure 1.8.

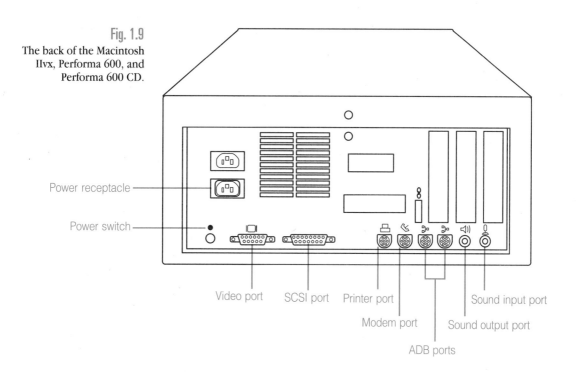

Fig. 1.9
The back of the Macintosh
IIvx, Performa 600, and
Performa 600 CD.

Power receptacle

Power switch

Video port   SCSI port   Printer port

Modem port

ADB ports

Sound input port

Sound output port

Although the Centris 610 is a slim-line model, smaller than the 650, its back is similar to that of the 650. It has all the same ports (except the EtherNet port in the most basic version of the 610) in the same order. The primary difference is that the 610 does not have the NuBus slots.

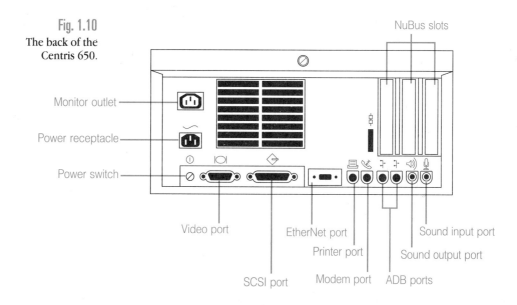

Fig. 1.10
The back of the
Centris 650.

NuBus slots

Monitor outlet

Power receptacle

Power switch

Video port

EtherNet port

Printer port

Sound input port

Sound output port

SCSI port   Modem port   ADB ports

When connecting your modular Macintosh, you are most concerned with the locations of the power receptacle, the power switch, the Apple Desktop Bus (ADB) ports, the video port (machines with NuBus slots usually have this port in one of the slot locations), the monitor power outlet (if one exists; the LC, LC II, LCIII, Performa 400, Performa 405, and Performa 450, for example, do not have monitor outlets), and—if you have a printer—the serial ports or the SCSI port depending on your printer's type.

Tower Macintoshes

The Quadra series of Macintoshes are the most powerful Macintoshes to date. They are intended for intense, power-hungry applications such as computer-aided design, heavy graphics work, networking, and the like. These machines stand up like a tower rather than sit flat on a desk. Quadras are designed to stand next to a desk, and the monitor and keyboard reside on the desk.

Figures 1.11 and 1.12 show the backs of these units.

The newer Quadra 800 actually has three NuBus slots, one more than is shown in figure 1.11.

When connecting your tower Macintosh, you are most concerned with the locations of the power receptacle, the power switch, the Apple Desktop Bus (ADB) ports, the video port, the monitor power outlet, and—if you have a printer—the serial ports or the SCSI port depending on your printer's type. If you are connecting your tower Macintosh to a network, you may also be concerned with the location of the EtherNet port.

Laptop Macintoshes

Laptop Macintoshes do not have to be connected before they are used. Because they are meant to be portable, they are self-contained and ready to use. However, you do want to know the connectors' locations on these units, however, in case you want to attach external disk drives, printers, and other options to them. And, of course, you want to know where the power switch is located.

Figures 1.13 through 1.18 show the backs of the laptop (and the Portable) Macintoshes.

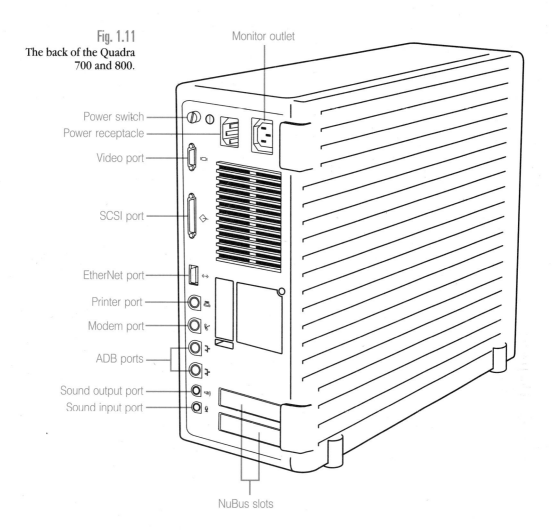

Fig. 1.11
The back of the Quadra
700 and 800.

Monitor outlet

Power switch

Power receptacle

Video port

SCSI port

EtherNet port

Printer port

Modem port

ADB ports

Sound output port

Sound input port

NuBus slots

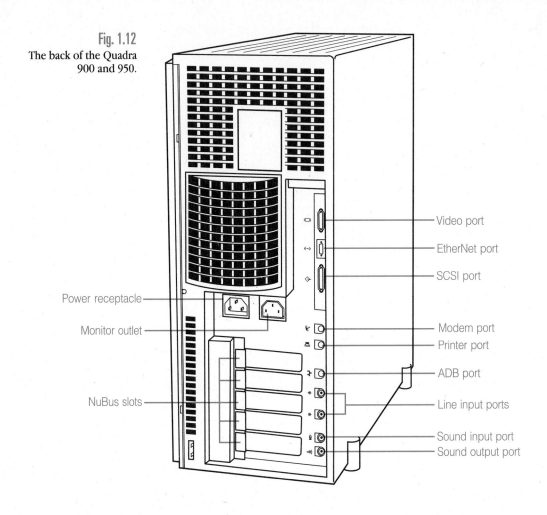

Fig. 1.12
The back of the Quadra
900 and 950.

Video port

EtherNet port

SCSI port

Power receptacle

Monitor outlet

Modem port

Printer port

ADB port

NuBus slots

Line input ports

Sound input port

Sound output port

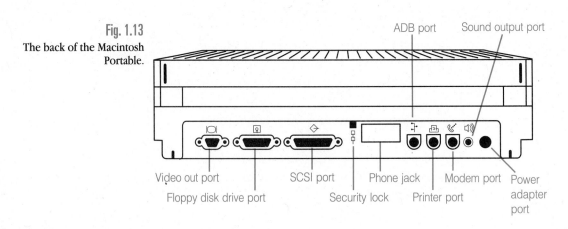

Fig. 1.13
The back of the Macintosh
Portable.

ADB port

Sound output port

Video out port

Floppy disk drive port

SCSI port

Security lock

Phone jack

Printer port

Modem port

Power
adapter
port

Fig. 1.14

The back of the
PowerBook 100.

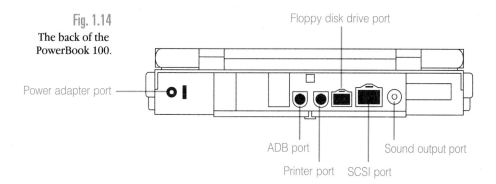

Floppy disk drive port

Power adapter port

ADB port

Printer port   SCSI port

Sound output port

Fig. 1.15

The back of the PowerBook
140, 145, 160, 165c, 170,
and 180.

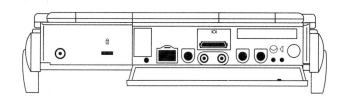

Note that the PowerBook 140, 145, and 170 do not have the video port shown in fig. 1.15. This port was added to newer models. All the other ports are the same.

Fig. 1.16

The back of the PowerBook
Duo 210 and 230.

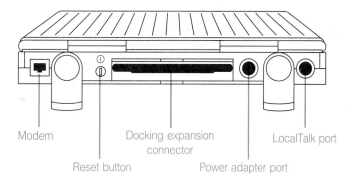

Modem   Docking expansion
connector

Reset button   Power adapter port

LocalTalk port

The Duo series of Macintosh laptops introduces a new version of a concept called docking. *Docking* is a method of attaching a laptop computer to full-sized peripherals such as monitors and printers. The idea is that the travelling computer has a "home port" of sorts.

You can dock Duo Macintoshes in more than one way. Two methods involve plugging a docking unit to the back of the laptop. Cords run from the docking unit to an external floppy disk drive, full-sized monitor, printer, or other full-sized hardware peripheral.

The Duo series also has a docking unit that resembles a desktop computer. This unit can contain such options as additional memory and larger hard drives and also has connections for a full-sized monitor, printer, or other full-sized hardware peripherals. You slide the Duo laptop itself into the docking unit, rather like a video cassette, and the laptop is automatically connected to the hardware options installed in the docking unit or connected to the unit.

Fig. 1.17
The back of the Duo MiniDock.

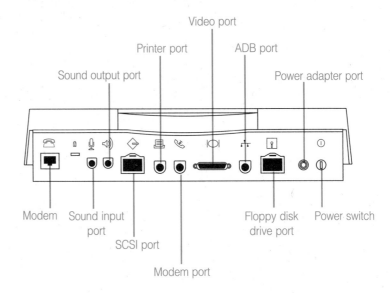

Fig. 1.18
The back of the Duo Dock.

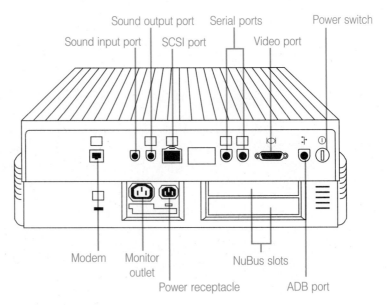

In the case of the laptop units, you will be most concerned with the location of the power switch and the power adapter outlet.

Connecting the Macintosh

One of the Macintosh's great strengths is the ease with which you can set it up. Only a few steps are required to connect the machine and begin doing work.

To connect a Macintosh, you only have to attach the power cord, the keyboard, the mouse, and the monitor—in the cases of modular or tower Macintoshes—to the computer. Use these steps:

1. Plug the power cord into the power receptacle on the back of the Macintosh.

2. Plug the other end of the power cord into your surge protector.

3. Plug the keyboard cable into one of the ADB ports on the back of the Macintosh (some compact units such as the Classic and Classic II have only onc ADB port on the back).

   The keyboard cable has ADB plugs on both ends. The icons on these plugs will match those on the back of your Macintosh.

4. Plug the other end of the keyboard cable into one of the ADB ports on your keyboard.

   Most Mac keyboards have two ADB ports. This allows you to place the mouse on the left- or right-hand side of the keyboard depending on whether you are left- or right-handed. Connect the keyboard cable to the opposite port on the keyboard.

5. Plug the mouse's ADB plug into the keyboard.

The Plus is connected differently. Rather than perform steps 3 through 5, you connect the keyboard by plugging it into the phone-jack-style plug at the base of the Plus's front. You then connect the mouse to the mouse port on the back of the Plus.

If you have a Macintosh with a separate monitor, connect the monitor's video-input cable to the video port on the back of the Macintosh. This cable ends in a flat connector that is very different from the monitor's power cord.

Then connect the monitor's power cord. If you have any of the LC Macintoshes or a Performa numbered in the 400s, the monitor's power cord has a standard three-pronged plug that you plug into your surge protector.

If you have one of the Macintosh II series, Centris series, Quadra series, or Performa 600 computers, often the monitor's power cord ends in a three-pronged plug with a hood that prevents you from inserting the plug into a wall receptacle or a power strip. This plug only fits into the monitor power outlet on the back of the Macintosh.

Your Macintosh is now connected and ready for use.

Setting Up a Printer

Setting up a printer can actually get a bit more complicated than setting up the Macintosh itself. However, the task is not overly difficult.

The first step is to identify the connection method that your printer uses to communicate with the Macintosh. There are three basic types: serial, SCSI, and AppleTalk.

Table 1.1 lists the Apple printer family and the types of connections used by the printers.

Table 1.1
Apple Printer Connections

Printer	Connection Type
ImageWriter I	Serial
ImageWriter II*	Serial
ImageWriter LQ	Serial
StyleWriter	Serial
StyleWriter II*	Serial
Personal LaserWriter SC	SCSI
Personal LaserWriter NT	AppleTalk
Personal LaserWriter LS*	Serial
Personal LaserWriter NTR*	AppleTalk
LaserWriter/LaserWriter Plus	AppleTalk
LaserWriter IISC	SCSI
LaserWriter IINT	AppleTalk
LaserWriter IINTX	AppleTalk
LaserWriter IIf*	AppleTalk

Printer	Connection Type
LaserWriter IIg*	AppleTalk
LaserWriter Select 300*	Serial
LaserWriter Select 310*	AppleTalk
LaserWriter Pro 600*	AppleTalk, Serial, Parallel
LaserWriter Pro 610*	AppleTalk, EtherTalk, Serial, Parallel

* Currently in production

If you have a printer from a company other than Apple, you need to check the manual to determine the connection type. But any printer that works with the Macintosh uses one of these three connection types.

The following three sections outline how each of the three types of connections is set up. The instructions are brief, rather than detailed, due to the broad variety of printers. Apple printers are the easiest to connect because of Apple's use of icons near the ports. You should be able to match icons on the cable, the printer, and the Macintosh to connect your printer. You can also refer back to figures 1.1 through 1.18 to view the back of the various Macintosh models and locate the ports named in the following sections.

If you need more detailed help, check your printer's manual for instructions specific to your printer.

Connecting a Serial Printer

Connecting a serial printer only requires that you connect the cable (which should accompany the printer) between the printer and the Macintosh. The printer should have a single round port that matches the size of the plugs on the cable. Which end of the cable you use is irrelevant; the two ends are identical. Note that the plug fits only one way in the port. On most cables, one side of the plug is flat and should be facing upwards. If the plug does not go in easily, do not force it. Instead, try rotating the plug before attempting to insert it into the port.

The other end of the cable plugs into one of the two serial ports on the back of your Macintosh. Unless you have a modem, you can use either serial port, but the most logical one to use is the printer port, which is marked with a small icon of a printer. The flat side of the cable plug should be facing up and, again, the plug should be easy to insert if it is oriented correctly.

Connecting a SCSI Printer

This type of connection is the most complicated. The SCSI interface can be difficult to set up properly. However, if you have only one device (your printer) to attach, the connection is not overly difficult. The following discussion assumes you have only your printer to connect to the SCSI port.

The SCSI cable should have come with your printer or been sold to you by your dealer at the time you purchased the printer. This cable is rather bulky, with flat connectors on each end. These connectors may or may not be the same size. The plugs may have screws that secure the plug in the port (the more convenient ones have knobs that allow you to hand-tighten the screws).

Locate the SCSI port on the back of your Macintosh (refer back to figures 1.1 through 1.18 if necessary). Note that the SCSI port is trapezoidal in shape. This is good because the port matches the plug and allows you to insert the plug only in the correct way (that is, you cannot insert the plug upside down).

Match the shape of the plug to the port and push the plug onto the port. The plug should insert easily. Press firmly to make certain the plug is fully inserted. Tighten the screws to secure the plug, but do not over-tighten them. A turn or so should suffice.

Many 50-pin SCSI ports have clips rather than screws.

The other end of the cable should attach to a SCSI port on the printer in the same manner as to the Macintosh. Again, you cannot insert the plug upside down due to the trapezoidal shape. Hence, if the plug does not insert easily, you may have it turned upside down—or be attempting to connect to the wrong port (some printers have more than one port type available).

After physically connecting the printer, you need to set the SCSI ID number. The method for setting SCSI IDs varies from printer to printer. Generally, you find a physical switch located on the printer (many times on the back near the ports) that allows you to choose a number between 0 and 7, inclusive. These switches can take various forms. Some are knobs, others are thumbwheels, and yet others are push buttons (usually recessed). You need to check your printer's manual for the exact method of setting the SCSI ID number.

The important point is to set the number so that the printer has a unique ID number. That is, no two devices can have the same number.

You should not use the number 7 because this is the SCSI ID number of your Macintosh computer. If you have an internal hard drive installed by Apple, you do not want to use the number 0 because this is the SCSI ID number of your hard drive.

If your internal hard drive was supplied by a company other than Apple (perhaps you had it installed later or purchased your Macintosh from a dealer who uses hard drives from other companies), you can determine the SCSI ID number of the hard drive by using the Get Info command in the File menu (see the "Getting Information about an Icon" section in Chapter 2).

If you have no SCSI devices attached to your Macintosh other than your printer, you are usually safe using a number between 1 and 6, inclusive. If your printer does not print at all, however, you may want to check the SCSI number of your internal hard disk to determine whether the printer is set to the same number. Again, it should not be.

Finally, you should check the termination of the SCSI chain. The general rule is that the first and last devices in the SCSI chain must be terminated. That is, the first device attached to your Macintosh should be terminated, the intervening SCSI devices should not be terminated, and the last SCSI device must be terminated.

Note that the Quadra 900 and 950 are exceptions to the preceding rule, in that the Quadra itself is counted as the first device in the chain and is terminated. Hence, you only terminate the last SCSI device attached to the chain.

Termination is accomplished in various ways with SCSI devices. Some have an external plug that looks like the plug at the end of the SCSI cable. Others have switches (many times hidden behind access panels). Some have "jumpers"—small metal connectors that you move physically.

Check your printer's manual to determine the termination of your printer and the method of changing the termination. To save yourself trouble when purchasing a SCSI device, make sure that the SCSI ID number is easy to set (push buttons are best), and that the device is externally terminated.

Connecting an AppleTalk Printer

Laser printers are the most common printers using the AppleTalk method of connection. AppleTalk is the Macintosh's built-in networking system. Essentially, when you connect an AppleTalk printer to your Macintosh, you create a small network of your own. LocalTalk is the Apple networking system consisting of cables and corrector boxes (called LocalTalk boxes).

You should have two LocalTalk boxes or the equivalent (the most common competing version is Fallaron's PhoneNet boxes). The boxes are not included with the printer. You must purchase them (and the cable) separately. These boxes are small (about 2 inches by 1 inch by 1 inch) and have short cables protruding from one end. The other end has two round outlets or phone jacks. The short cord of one box plugs into the printer port on your Macintosh. The short cord of the other box plugs into the printer. A cable or length of phone cord runs between the two boxes.

When connecting the box to the Macintosh, make certain you use the printer port (the port with the printer icon by it). The modem port (with a phone handset icon) does not work as an AppleTalk printer connector.

Connect the two boxes by plugging one end of the cord in one box and the other end in the other box. You use only one of the two connections in each box. Nothing else connects to the other outlet unless you later add another networked device.

Understanding the Desktop

Once your Macintosh is connected, you are ready to turn on your computer and start learning about it. This section starts the "basic skills" part of this chapter. Here, you learn about the Desktop—the workspace of your Macintosh.

The designers of the Macintosh had several goals in mind when they designed the computer. One goal was to make the computer as easy to use as possible. They did this by creating an environment that allowed the user to interact directly with the Macintosh's operating system software. They used the metaphor of the top of a desk—an area on which can reside documents, tools, and other items needed to do work.

Viewing the Desktop

If you worked through the Quick Start, you have already seen the Desktop. The Desktop is one of the first things to appear on your Macintosh screen. Before the Desktop appears, however, some other things happen that you may be curious about.

When the Mac's power comes on, several important procedures begin. A program that is "hard-wired" and part of your Macintosh's read-only memory (ROM) sends a signal to the central processing unit (the brains of the Macintosh). This signal tells the computer to start a software routine that "boots," or starts up, the computer. One of the things that the boot routine does is locate a file called System in the System Folder. The System file contains the basic operating instructions that present the displays you see on the opening Desktop and provide the tools you need to perform tasks such as cutting, copying, pasting, and printing. These instructions are in the System Folder and are loaded into the Macintosh's memory every time you start the computer.

Your Macintosh also runs a check at this time to determine whether all its internal parts (such as the memory) are working properly.

All this activity takes place quickly, and soon you see the Desktop itself (see fig. 1.19).

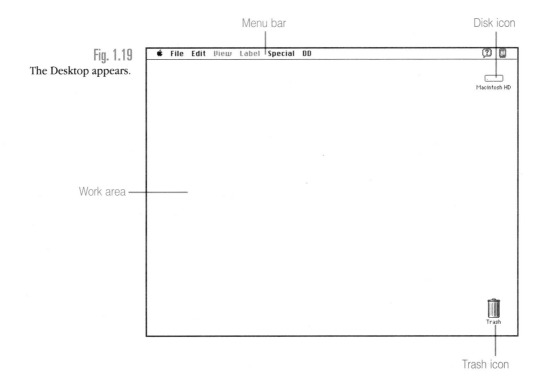

Fig. 1.19
The Desktop appears.

The figure shows my Desktop (which is by far much neater than the top of my real-world desk). You may see a difference or two between the figure and your own Desktop. The basics, however, remain the same.

Note that if you are using one of the Performas or a Macintosh running the Apple At Ease program, your Desktop will appear significantly different from the figure. You still want to read on in this section, however, (especially if you have a Performa series Macintosh) because the information will help you understand your Macintosh more fully.

The large gray portion of the Desktop is the work area. In the work area reside the icons representing disks, documents, folders, application software (Microsoft Word, for example), and other items with which you work.

The Desktop is not totally blank initially. Some items are already present. In figure 1.19, you see the menu bar, two disk icons, and the Trash icon.

The disk that contains the System files is the startup disk. The icon that represents this disk is always located in the upper right corner of the Desktop, like Macintosh HD is in the figure. The icons representing other disks (other hard drives, floppy disks, and so forth), appear below the startup disk icon. Chapter 3, "Managing Disks," covers disks more fully.

The Trash can is displayed in the lower right corner. This special purpose icon is used—as the icon's appearance suggests—to delete items from your disks.

Above the Desktop's work area is the menu bar. The menu bar contains the menus that, in turn, contain the commands you use to work on the Desktop. Several menus appear on the menu bar in figure 1.19: Apple (represented by a small apple symbol), File, Edit, View, Label, Special, Help (represented by a balloon with a question mark), and Application (the computer-looking icon at the far right of the menu bar). Using the menus is covered in a following section, "Understanding the Menus."

For the time being, simply note the location of the menus and understand that they contain the commands you use when working on the Desktop.

Understanding the Finder

If you look at the far right end of your Macintosh's menu bar, you see a small icon of a Macintosh (refer back to 1.19). You saw in the previous section that this icon represents the Application menu. This icon changes to reflect the currently running software—called the "foreground" or "active" application.

When the Desktop first appears, you are already running an application program although you have done nothing more than turn on your Macintosh. This program is called the Finder and is always the first program to start running because it is the manager of the Desktop.

The Finder keeps track of the images that appear on your Desktop. When you start working with disks, files, folders, and other items on the Desktop, you are using the Finder and its commands.

The active application always places its menu bar at the top of your Macintosh screen, just above the Desktop work area. Hence, the menus you see in figure 1.19 are the Finder's menus. The menus' commands are Finder commands.

The Finder performs such work as copying disks, files, and folders, deleting items in the Trash, cleaning up and organizing the Desktop, and shutting down your Macintosh.

Because of the relationship between the Finder and the Desktop, you may hear the Desktop referred to as the Finder Desktop. This is merely another way of referring to the Macintosh Desktop.

Understanding the Desktop File

Although you do not see it, the Desktop file (or set of files in System 7) exists on every Macintosh disk. This file (or set of files) contains information that informs the Finder about the size of the disk, the files and folders contained on the disk, the icons used on the disk, and other information. Without this file, the Finder cannot find anything.

You should be aware that Desktop files are accessed so frequently by the Finder that they can become corrupted over time. At least, they can become rather large (especially on large hard disks) and take up valuable disk space. To limit the occurrence of these problems, you should rebuild your Desktop file at least once a month (heavy users should consider rebuilding once a week, as I do).

Instructions for rebuilding the Desktop file are found in Chapter 32, "Maintenance and Troubleshooting."

Using the Mouse

One of the most notable features of the Macintosh was the early application of a rather old concept. The concept of the mouse is almost half a century old now, but has only recently been used in a widespread fashion.

The Macintosh mouse was designed to be simple. This small device rolls along a surface, moving an on-screen pointer. The single button is used to control and manipulate the various parts of the Macintosh interface. The mouse is very heavily involved in your use of the Desktop.

There are four basic mouse concepts that you must know to use the Macintosh. These concepts are *pointing*, *clicking*, *double-clicking*, and *dragging*.

Pointing

As you move the mouse, you see that a small arrow moves on-screen in the same direction. This arrow is the mouse pointer. You point at something by moving the mouse pointer until its tip is on the desired object. Figure 1.20 shows the mouse pointer pointing at the Macintosh hard disk icon.

Fig. 1.20
Pointing at the Macintosh HD icon.

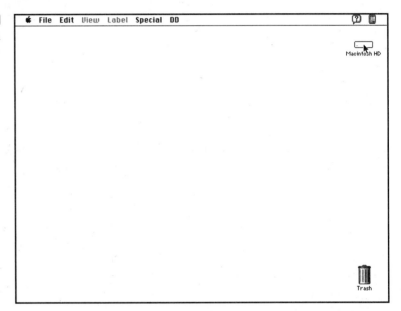

Clicking

Clicking involves the use of the mouse button. The word "click" is used as a verb in the Macintosh world, as in the sentence "Click the hard drive's icon."

You click an item by pointing at it and then pressing the mouse button one time quickly. Do not hold the mouse button down; rather, press and release in a smooth, quick motion.

Items that have been clicked darken to indicate that they have been selected (see fig. 1.21).

Fig. 1.21
Macintosh HD has been
clicked.

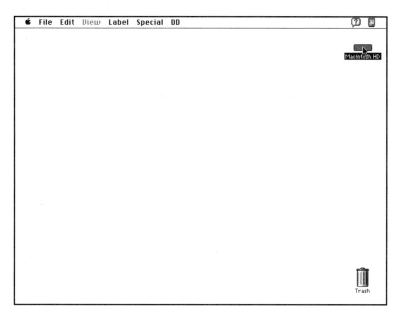

You use clicking to select a single item for a menu command to operate on. You also use clicking to "push" buttons and mark choices in Macintosh on-screen controls. (The "Understanding Dialogs and Alerts" section in this chapter discusses various controls in the Macintosh interface.)

Double-Clicking

As you might guess from the name, double-clicking consists of two clicks. To double-click an item, you point at it with the mouse pointer and then press the mouse button twice in rapid succession. Double-clicking functions in several different ways, depending on the type of object you double-click.

Double-clicking is the standard way to open an icon to display the contents of a disk, folder, or file. If you want to see the contents of the Macintosh hard disk, for example, you double-click its icon (see fig. 1.22).

The double-clicked object turns gray, indicating that it is open.

Note that double-clicking has many uses; for example, double-clicking the icon of an application program (such as Microsoft Word) starts that program. The "opening" metaphor works better when you double-click a document (such as one created by Microsoft Word) and the application starts up to display the contents of the document.

Fig. 1.22
Macintosh HD's contents
displayed.

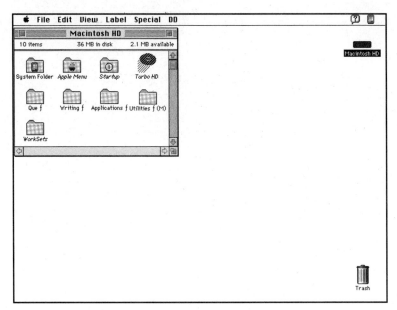

When you are working with text, double-clicking changes meaning
again. Double-clicking is used by text-handling programs to select a
single word or number (see the "Understanding Macintosh Text and
Graphics" section later in this chapter).

Two interesting clicks are the triple-click and the quadruple-click. A
triple-click, as the name implies, is the same as the double-click, but you
press the mouse button three times in rapid succession. The quadruple-
click uses four presses of the mouse button.

Some word processors introduced the triple- and quadruple-clicks to
select larger amounts of text. Microsoft Word and WriteNow, for
example, use triple-clicking to select a paragrah. However, neither triple-
nor quadruple-clicking ever caught on as widely as double-clicking. In
fact, apparently no one is using the quadruple-click at present.

Dragging

Dragging is a very essential concept. You use dragging a great deal in
your use of the Macintosh. Dragging's uses include moving icons or
other objects, moving through menu commands, and selecting groups
of items or blocks of text.

The basics of dragging are very simple. You point at something, press and hold the mouse button, and then move the mouse. You release the mouse button at the end of the drag.

For example, to move the Macintosh HD icon by dragging it, follow these steps:

1. Point at the icon.

2. Press and hold the mouse button.

3. Move the mouse.

    You see an outline of the icon being dragged as you move the mouse (see fig. 1.23).

4. When the outline is positioned where you want the icon, release the mouse button.

    The icon moves to the new location.

Fig. 1.23
Dragging Macintosh HD.

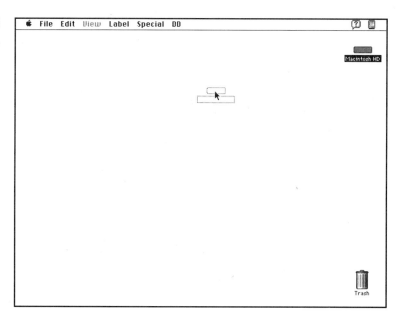

You can select groups of icons by enclosing them in a marquee. You point to a corner of the area you want to select (not to any particular icon) and drag diagonally to the opposing corner. A box shows the selection area (see fig. 1.24). Release the mouse button to select the group.

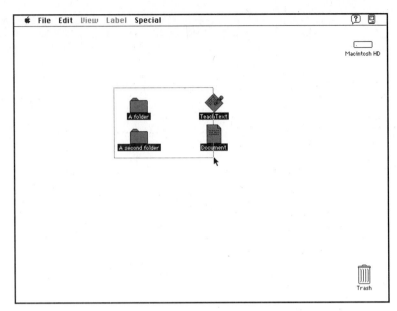

Fig. 1.24
Dragging to select
a group of icons.

As you can see in the figure, icons selected in this manner darken, just as when you select a single icon. You can combine these two types of dragging to move more than one item at a time. Drag to select a group of icons and then drag any one of the icons. All selected icons move together. You can use this method to delete several icons by dragging them to the Trash.

Other sections and chapters cover the various uses of dragging. The following section, "Understanding the Menus," for example, discusses making menu selections by dragging. Selecting text is covered in the "Understanding Macintosh Text and Graphics" section later in this chapter. And you learn more about working with icons in Chapter 2.

The important point for new Macintosh users to remember is the sequence of actions in dragging. New users have a tendency to press the mouse button too late at the start of the drag, or to release the mouse button before reaching the end of the drag. The mouse movement is bracketed by the button actions. The mouse should not be moving while the button is being pressed or released.

Using Modified Clicks and Drags

As Macintosh software became more complex, the single mouse button did not offer enough flexibility. Hence, Apple introduced new kinds of clicks and drags which involve an action at the keyboard. The keys used are the Command, Shift, Option, and Control keys. These keys are called modifier keys because they modify the meaning of a key press or mouse action. When you see a notation such as "Shift-click," the meaning is that the Shift key is held down while you click. A "Shift-drag" is a drag performed while you hold down the Shift key.

The general rule is to press and hold the key. Then perform the click or drag. After clicking or dragging, release the keyboard key.

The most common of these are the Shift-click, the Command-click, the Option-click, and the Shift-drag. You encounter these often.

Understanding the Menus

Every Mac program has its own menu bar. This menu bar contains menus with commands specific to the particular program. Although menus and commands are specific to their programs, the basic menu concepts and the techniques for using the menus remain the same. Macintosh programs also have menus other than those that appear on the menu bar. This section discusses the different types of Mac menus and their uses.

For example, when the Macintosh first starts, you see eight menus on the menu bar: the Apple (⌘), File, Edit, View, Label, Special, Help, and Application menus (see fig. 1.25). As discussed in the "Understanding the Finder" section, these are the menus of the Finder application which runs at startup.

Choosing Commands

As mentioned in the "Using the Mouse" section, you choose menu commands by dragging. Specifically, in the case of menus on the menu bar, you do the following:

1. Place the mouse pointer on the name of the menu—the File menu in this example.

2. Press and hold the mouse button. The menu "drops down" allowing you to see and access the commands in the menu (see fig. 1.26).

You can preview the contents of a menu in this way without choosing a command. When you release the mouse button, the menu disappears and you can proceed on to another menu. To choose a command from the menu you have caused to drop down, you continue with these steps.

3. Drag down through the commands.

   You see that each available command is highlighted by a black band as you drag through the menu, like the Make Alias command is in figure 1.27.

4. When the desired command is highlighted, you release the mouse button.

   The highlighting blinks to confirm your choice and then the command is performed.

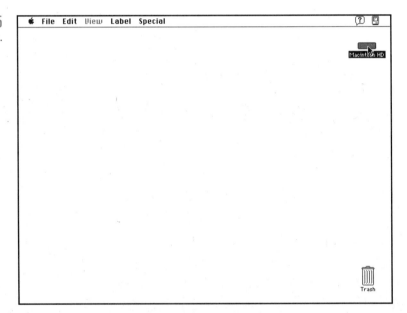

Fig. 1.25
The Finder menus.

Another important point about menus concerns commands that are *grayed out*, or dimmed. Consider the Print, Close Window, and Duplicate commands on the File menu of figure 1.27. You cannot choose these commands at this time, so they are dimmed and have a grayish appearance.

Fig. 1.26
The File menu drops
down.

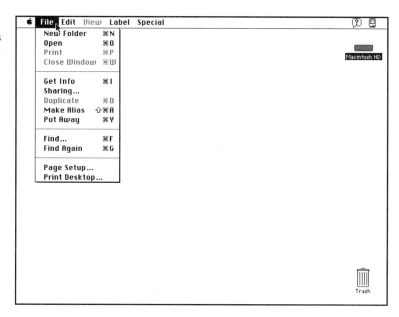

Fig. 1.27
Highlighting the
Make Alias command.

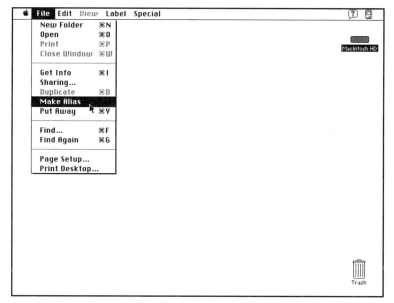

When a command is dimmed, you must perform some action before choosing the command. Commands are rather like verbs in English. They perform action. Hence, they often require an object to act upon. The Duplicate command, for example, requires that you select an item (such as a document) to be duplicated before the command is available to you. The Close Window command is dimmed because no windows are present on-screen. With no windows open, you cannot perform the action of closing a window.

Note at this point the ellipses (...) to the right of some of the menu commands indicate that further action is required. That is, commands, such as New Folder, perform their function as soon as you choose them. Others, such as Find, require further action (in this case, you need to indicate what you want to find). Generally, a dialog appears with the appropriate options (see "Understanding Dialogs and Alerts" later in this chapter).

You definitely need to understand this relationship between objects and menus. Keep in mind that commands act on some object, whether it is a disk drive icon, a document, a piece of text, or something else.

Note the available commands in the File menu of figure 1.27. Also note that the hard disk icon, Macintosh HD, is selected. The active commands in the File menu will, if chosen, act on the disk Macintosh HD. In the figure, for example, the Make Alias command is being chosen while Macintosh HD is selected. Hence, when the mouse button is released, an alias will be made of that disk drive's icon. (Aliases are covered in Chapter 2, "Understanding the System.")

This is the most common type of menu and the most common use of menus you will encounter in your use of the Macintosh. However, there are other types of menus that you use differently. The following sections explore these menus.

Using Option Menus

Some menus contain options instead of commands. That is, the available selections in the menus perform no direct action, but rather configure an application or document in some way.

Menus containing options indicate that an option is active by placing a check mark to the left of the option in the menu (see fig. 1.28).

Fig. 1.28
A typical Font menu with
the Geneva option chosen.

Font menus are one type of option menu, and you see them often in your use of the Macintosh. Note that in figure 1.28, the menu is indicating that the Geneva font is currently chosen. You can change this by dragging down through the menu options and choosing another font. The check mark will then appear next to the new choice. In this kind of option menu, you can only make one choice. Choosing the Courier font, for example, disables the Geneva font choice. Only one kind of font can be used at any one time (that is, although documents can contain more than one font, you can only type in one font at a time).

Some option menus contain options that *toggle*. That is, choosing the option turns it on, and choosing it again turns it off. In these kinds of option menus, you can choose more than one option. A typical example is the Style menu (called Format menu in some applications), which is found most often in word processing programs. Figure 1.29 shows the Style menu of the WriteNow word processing program.

Fig. 1.29
The Style menu with
several options chosen.

You can see by the check marks that the Bold and Italic style options are chosen. The mouse pointer has highlighted the Superscript option, and when the mouse button is released, this option becomes active and a check mark appears to the left of it on the menu. The effect is that the next thing typed (or any text currently selected) is raised above the baseline (as footnote numbers are) and appears in bold italic type. If you want the type to be bold superscript only, choose the Italic option again to deactivate it.

In other words, selecting the same menu turns these options on and off. They are toggled. You should again note at this point that not all options in a menu can be chosen separately. Some are mutually exclusive. For example, choosing the Plain Text option from the Style menu of figure 1.29 turns off all other styling options. Plain text has no styling of any kind. Another example is that the Condensed option cannot work with the Extend option because they are opposites. Choosing one turns off the other.

The exact results of choosing options often depends on the particular application. The important thing to understand at this point is that options in menus are turned on and off by choosing them as you would a command. The check mark is your indicator as to which option or options are currently active.

Using Hierarchical Menus

You may have noted in figure 1.29 that the Underline and Color options have right-pointing arrows next to them on the Style menu. These arrows indicate the presence of a kind of menu called a *hierarchical menu*.

As Macintosh software became more complex, more menu space was needed. Apple developed the hierarchical menu to allow menu choices to contain further menus.

If you are dragging through menu choices and the highlight band encounters a hierarchical menu, another menu appears (see fig. 1.30).

Fig. 1.30
The hierarchical Underline menu in WriteNow.

As long as the highlight band is on the Underline menu and the mouse button is pressed, the menu stays on-screen. If you release the button at this point, no action is taken because Underline has a submenu and is not an option or command.

To choose one of the options in the Underline menu, you must take some further steps:

1. Continue to hold down the mouse button.

2. Move the mouse pointer to the right, into the secondary menu.

   The highlight band appears in the menu.

3. Drag through the menu choices until the highlight band is on the desired option or command.

4. Release the mouse button.

Your choice is accepted (commands blink to confirm and options are checkmarked), and the menus disappear.

New users may find hierarchical menus a bit difficult to use at first. Even experienced users of the Macintosh sometimes have a hierarchical menu disappear when they attempt to make a choice from it. The point to remember is to move the mouse straight to the right and into the menu before dragging up or down. If you deviate up or down, the menu may vanish before you can make your choice.

Using Scrolling Menus

As stated before, Macintosh software has continued to increase in power and complexity. This has meant that the user has a greater number of options available. At the same time, however, the menu system of the Macintosh was strained by the sheer volume of choices.

Apple created the scrolling menu to further address the problem of an increasing number of menu choices. Menus can hold far more choices than merely the number that can be contained on-screen at any one time. Menus that you are able to customize can grow to enormous sizes. Font menus are a good example, as users have added more and more fonts to their Systems. The System 7 Apple menu also can be customized and grow quite large.

You know you have encountered a scrolling menu when you see a downward-pointing triangle at the bottom of a menu.

Microsoft Word, for example, permits you a great deal of flexibility in customizing menus. You can add or remove commands and options at will. Hence, it is possible to create long, customized menus that are longer than the screen displaying them.

The downward-pointing triangle indicates that more options are available than can currently be displayed. You reach these options by dragging down through the menu choices and passing the end of the menu. The options below the bottom of the menu display scroll (move) upwards onto the menu, and you can then drag to one of them and choose it.

When a menu is scrolled in this fashion, the options at the top of the menu scroll up and off the screen. An upward-pointing triangle appears, indicating that options are available above the top option displayed. You reach these options by dragging upwards and passing the top edge of the menu display. The menu then scrolls downward, and the options reappear and become available for choosing.

Note that through all of this, the mouse button must remain pressed, or the menu disappears entirely.

Using Pop-Up Menus

One of the more interesting menus that Apple has created is the pop-up menu most often seen in dialogs (see "Understanding Dialogs and Alerts").

You can usually tell that you have encountered a pop-up menu by the appearance of the menu. The current choice of a pop-up menu is displayed in a rectangle, like the name option in figure 1.31. Note that the rectangle is *shadowed* and appears to be three dimensional. This appearance alerts you to the presence of a pop-up menu.

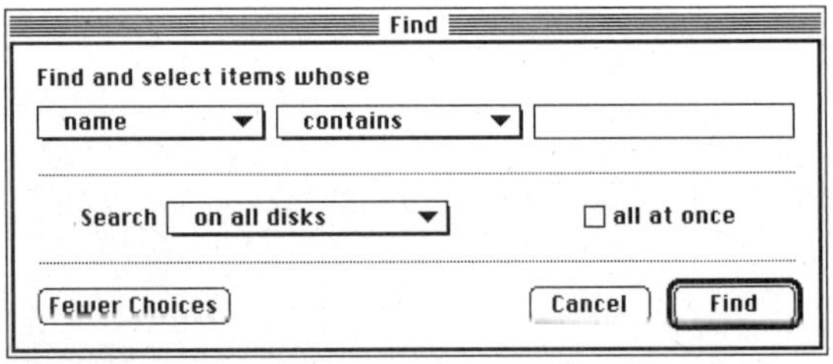

Fig. 1.31

A pop-up menu displaying the name option.

To access the pop-up menu, place the mouse pointer inside the rectangle, and then press and hold the mouse button. The menu appears (see fig. 1.32).

Fig. 1.32

The menu pops up.

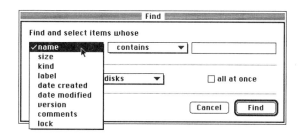

When the menu pops up, you can drag through its options to make a choice as you would with any other menu. After making your choice, you see that it is then displayed in the rectangle containing the pop-up menu.

Using Keyboard Equivalents

As you become more proficient in your use of the Macintosh, you will surely begin to look for ways to perform work more quickly and efficiently. One of the drawbacks of a computer that uses a mouse is that you must frequently remove your hand from the keyboard to make menu choices and perform other actions.

There are shortcuts, however, that enable you to make menu choices without removing your hand from the keyboard. That is, you bypass the mouse by using the keyboard to make a menu selection.

Figure 1.27 showed you the Finder's File menu. You may have noted that some of the commands had a four-leaf clover symbol (⌘) followed by a letter to their right on the menu.

The four-leaf clover symbol is the Command key symbol. You should see a similiar symbol on one or two of the keys on your keyboard to the left or right of the space bar. Alternatively, the Command key may actually have the word "command" printed on the key top. You also may see an apple (⌘) on the key. Regardless of its exact appearance, this is the Command key.

Refer back to figure 1.27 and consider the New Folder command. To the right of the command is the Command key symbol followed by the letter N. This indicates that you can choose the New Folder command from the keyboard by doing the following:

1. Press and hold the ⌘ key.

2. Press the letter N.

3. Release both keys.

This action has the same effect as choosing the New Folder command from the menu using the mouse.

As menus grew, so did keyboard equivalents. Originally, only the Command key was used in making keyboard choices of menu items. Now many applications use the Shift, Control, and Option keys. Sometimes a combination of keys is used.

The standard symbols for the keys that you encounter in menus are shown in table 1.2.

Symbol	Key
⌘	Command
⇧	Shift
⌥	Option
⌃	Control

Table 1.2
Key Symbols Used
in Menus

Considering the Finder Menus

Being an application, the Finder has menus. These menus contain the commands that allow you to operate on files, folders, disks, windows, and other items that make up the Macintosh system.

A few of the menus are rather special and are available to all applications. The Apple menu, for example, can be customized (see Chapter 6, "Customizing the Macintosh"). Rather than containing commands, this menu can contain a great variety of items such as documents, applications, folders, and so on. Figure 1.33 shows a typical Apple menu.

Fig. 1.33
The Apple menu in
System 7.

The other Finder menus are the following:

File. This menu enables you to get file information, locate files, and perform common tasks such as opening, saving, and printing files. This menu also contains commands related to the Apple networking system called File Sharing.

Edit. This menu provides you with the commands to select, cut, or copy information within a file, or to move text and graphics from one location to another within a document or from one file to another.

View. This menu enables you to decide how you want to view the contents of a Macintosh window or a disk. You can view files by name, date, or small or large icon, for example.

Label. This menu enables you to label files, folders, and disks to better organize them.

Special. This menu enables you to rearrange the contents of a window, turn off your Macintosh (Shut Down) safely at the end of a work session, restart the Macintosh, eject and erase disks, and empty the Trash can.

Help. This menu allows you to access the Apple Help system, which provides information about items on-screen when you point at them with the mouse pointer.

Application. This menu lists all currently running applications, permits you to switch between them, and enables you to hide or show the windows of applications.

System 6 users will notice some differences. The Apple menu in System 6 has a different appearance and is more limited in function than it is in System 7. A Color menu is available in System 6 to those who have color Macintoshes. The Color menu enables you to apply a color to any icon. In System 7, color is applied by using the Label menu.

For now, it is only important to understand the basic contents of each of the Finder menus. The specific uses of the commands are covered in more detail in later chapters (primarily in Chapters 2, 4, 5, and 6).

Understanding Windows

The concept of overlapping windows was developed by Xerox in the early 1970s. The concept was quite revolutionary in the days when computers displayed only single pages of text (really partial pages, given that displays were usually around 24 lines long) at a time.

Windows were not widely used on computers until the Macintosh became popular a decade or so after the concept was invented. The concept has subsequently gained such popularity that even IBM and IBM clone users are scrambling to buy a package named after the concept, and software manufacturers are now found bragging about how "Mac-like" they can cause an IBM PC to be (which is not very; Windows is still a very primitive version of a graphic user interface and can probably still be beaten hands down by an old Mac Plus in the ease-of-use category).

Windows on the Macintosh are aptly named. They allow you to "see into" your disks and files. Most of your work on the Macintosh is done in a window of some kind.

The most common kind of the window is the one you see when you double-click a disk icon. A window appears to display the disk's contents (see fig. 1.34).

Fig. 1.34
A window displaying the contents of External HD.

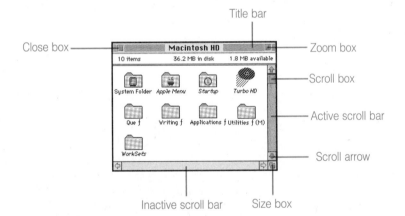

Although there are many different kinds of windows, the kind in figure 1.34 is by far the most common. (The dialogs and alerts in the "Understanding Dialogs and Alerts" section of this chapter are windows of a special kind.)

Because of the overlapping nature of windows, you are able to work with more than one at a time. Several can be on-screen at once, each displaying the contents of a folder, file, or disk.

The window shown in figure 1.34 is the kind that enables you to view the contents of disks and folders. Hence, it contains information specific to files, folders, and disks. The first is the *title bar*, which contains the name of the disk or folder whose contents are displayed. In this case, the contents of the disk External HD are displayed.

The name in the title bar helps you keep track of which file, folder, or disk you are viewing. Each window that is open on-screen has a name in its title bar.

Below the title bar, you find some information specific to disks that you do not see in other windows, such as those opened by word processors. The first piece of information is to the left. You see that the window displays the number of items contained on Macintosh HD: 10. In the center, you see that the disk has 36.2 megabytes (MB) of information stored. Finally, to the far right, you see that 1.8 megabytes of space are still available for use on Macintosh HD.

Windows have several features that enable you to manipulate them in order to work with them or for convenience. These are explained in the following sections.

Moving a Window

Having overlapping windows is an advantage only if you can move them. And you can. You can move a window by dragging its title bar. As you drag the window, you see a gray outline following the mouse pointer (see fig. 1.35).

When you release the mouse button, the window fills the gray outline and appears in the new location.

Sizing a Window

You can also change the size of a window. You do this by dragging the size box in the window's lower right corner. Again, a gray outline follows the mouse pointer as you drag (see fig. 1.36).

When you release the mouse button, the window fills the area of the gray outline. Note that windows do have size limits. Obviously, you cannot size a window larger than the size of your screen. But you are also limited as to how small you can make a window. You can tell you have reached the limit of a window's size when the gray outline refuses to move further.

Fig. 1.35
Moving a window.

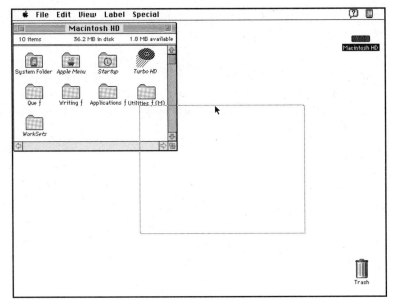

Fig. 1.36
Resizing a window.

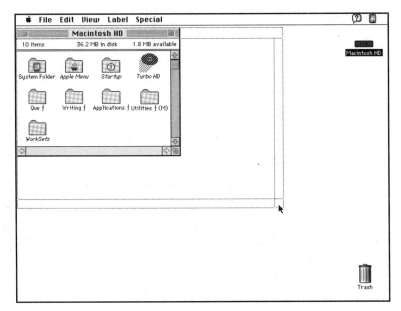

Zooming a Window

Related to sizing a window is the zoom feature. After you have resized a window, you can toggle between full size and its new size by clicking the zoom box in the window's upper right corner. The next click on the box again returns the window to the size you that you set.

In the Finder, the zoom is "intelligent." That is, clicking the zoom box resizes the window in such a way as to display as many of the items in the window as possible. Many times, this means that all the contents of the window can display (unless there is a very large number of items in the window).

Scrolling a Window

If a window has more items to display than can be shown in its present size, one or both of the scroll bars becomes active. An active scroll bar is gray and contains a scroll box (refer back to figure 1.34).

To see more of the items in the window, you scroll the window. You can scroll a window in one of three ways: clicking the scroll arrows, clicking the scroll bar, or dragging the scroll box.

Clicking one of the scroll arrows moves the window a short distance (windows containing text scroll one line for each click on the arrow). You click the arrow that points in the direction of the items you want to see. In figure 1.34 for example, the side scroll bar is active. You can view the objects that are below the window frame by clicking the downward-pointing arrow. Because the arrow moves the contents of the window only a small amount, you may need to click the arrow more than once. You can cause the window to scroll repeatedly by pointing to the arrow and then pressing and holding the mouse button, rather than just clicking.

If you click in the gray part of the scroll bar, the window scrolls in larger increments. Rather like paging through a book, or a legal or steno pad, clicking the scroll bar "flips" to another page of items.

The scroll box serves a dual purpose: it is at the same time an indicator and a control. Note the location of the box in figure 1.34. Because the scroll box is at the top of the scroll bar, you know that you are viewing the "top windowful" of items. If you click the downward-pointing scroll arrow or click in the scroll bar, you see the scroll box move to indicate the direction and the amount of scrolling done. That is, for example, if the scroll box is halfway down the scroll bar, you know you are looking at the middle windowful of items. If the scroll box is at the bottom of the scroll bar, you are viewing the last windowful of items.

You can drag the scroll box to any position in the scroll bar. You can, for example, return quickly to the top windowful of items by dragging the scroll box to the top of the scroll bar. Conversely, to see the last windowful, drag the scroll box to the bottom of the scroll bar.

Closing a Window

When you have finished using a window, you need to close it. Otherwise, you end up with what has come to be known as *screen clutter*. Dozens of windows scattered across the screen, making the display confusing and difficult to work with.

Also, closing a window in most applications prompts the application to save the contents to disk.

To close a window, you click the Close box in the window's upper left corner. Alternatively, you can use the Close Window menu command. The Finder has a Close Window command, as you saw in the "Understanding the Menus" section. This command closes the "frontmost," or active window.

Another reason you want to close an open window is that each open window requires memory. If you have a large number of windows open, you may encounter error messages to the effect that you are running out of memory. If you receive such a message and have many open windows that you are not using, close those windows. This may free enough memory to enable you to continue working.

Using Multiple Windows

With the Macintosh, you can have as many windows open on your Desktop as the application you are using and the memory in your Macintosh can support.

In figure 1.37, five windows are open, but none has been resized or moved. Figure 1.38 shows three windows that have been resized and moved; you can work with any of these windows while the others are still in view.

You should understand that regardless of how many windows you have open, only one is active.

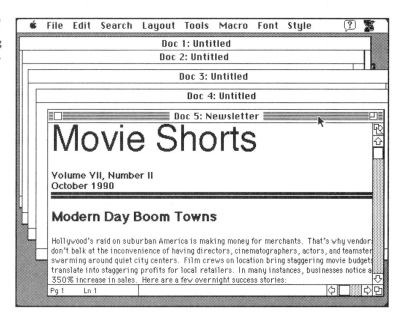

Fig. 1.37
Several overlapping windows.

Fig. 1.38
Windows that have been resized and moved for simultaneous viewing.

The active window is the one with the horizontal lines in the title bar. Any action you take by choosing a command or option from a menu, or typing on the keyboard, occurs in the active window.

You can activate one window at a time by clicking any part of the window that you want to make the active window. Unfortunately, windows that are completely covered by other windows cannot be accessed this way. When this occurs, you have to resize or move windows so that you can see the hidden one that you want to work on. Many applications also have a Window menu, which enables you to activate any one of many different open windows by choosing the name of the window from the menu.

Many Macintosh programs come with a tiling feature, which enables you to view all the open windows simultaneously. One program that provides tools to work with windows is Microsoft Excel. Figure 1.39 shows four Microsoft Excel windows that were tiled by using the Arrange Windows command on Excel's Window menu.

Fig. 1.39
Four tiled windows.

	File	Edit	Formula	Format	Data	Options	Macro	Window	

| Normal | | | | | Σ | B | I | | | | | | | | | |

| | 120 | | | =AVERAGE(B11:B19) | | |

Moving Average

	H	I	J	K
19	-0.18	13.87	-0.37	
20	-0.10	13.89	-0.29	
21	-0.12	13.94	-0.24	
22	-0.38	14.03	-0.23	
23	-0.40	14.02	-0.12	
24	-0.48	14.08	-0.08	
25	-0.47	14.26	-0.16	
26	-0.33	14.33	-0.13	

Analysis of Prod-Sales

	A	
11	13	32
12	04	35
13	06	38
14	09	39
15	11	41
16	14	41
17	06	42
18	03	44
19	05	46

Consolidated Income

	A	B
12	Operating Income	
13	Operating Expenses	
14		
15	Income Before Profit Sharing	
16	Employee Profit Sharing	
17		
18	Income Before Taxes	
19	Current Taxes	
20	Deferred Taxes	

Personal/Family Budget

	A	B
1	Personal/Family Budget	
2		
3	Year: 1907	
4		
5		
6		
7	INCOME	
8	Salary #1	
9	Salary #2	

Ready

At times, you will want to close all the windows on the Desktop. You can click the close box for each open window or select the Close command from the File menu. An easier alternative, however, is to hold down the Option key and click the active window's close box. All the windows close, and you are left with a clean, empty Desktop. This option always works in the Finder. Many, though not all, application programs use this option also.

You can save time the next time you start up by using this option when ending a work session because all windows are automatically closed and you then start next time with a clean slate. Your Macintosh does not have to reopen the windows and draw their contents the next time you start up, so it does not take as long to get started.

To move a window on the Desktop when the window is not active, place the mouse pointer on the window's title bar, press the Command key, and then drag the window by its title bar. This moves the window but does not activate it. Normally, whenever you click on any part of a window, it becomes the active window. Using this Command-drag allows you to view the contents of a window that you do not want to work with or make active at present.

Considering Window Types

You encounter many kinds of windows in your use of the Macintosh. But they are all variations on a theme. The window type used as an example in this section is the most common, but you should be aware of other window types.

Consider the window shown in figure 1.40.

Fig. 1.40

The Norton Utilities main
window.

This window has a title bar but no close box, zoom box, size box, or scroll bars. You cannot resize this window, and to close it, you must quit the program. You can drag the window if you need to, because the window has a title bar. Because the window's entire content is always displayed, no scroll bars are provided.

The Calculator desk accessory provided in your Apple menu displays a window that looks very different, but is a window nonetheless (see fig. 1.41). You can drag this window by its title bar and close it with the close box. No scrolling or resizing is possible, however.

Fig. 1.41

The Calculator window.

Not all window types reduce the number of functions available. Many application programs add features and functions to windows. Microsoft Word, for example, adds the capability to split a window so that you can view more than one part of a document inside the window at one time.

Among the many varieties of windows, you see some with functions specific to an application program. You need to consult the application program's manual for specific instructions on using the additional features. Because of the uniformity of the Macintosh interface, however, you should be able to spot familiar parts in almost any window type and know how to use them.

One special case of the window is the dialog, which you see often. Dialogs (and alerts) are the topic of the next section.

Understanding Dialogs and Alerts

The Macintosh computer is built on the concept of being "user driven." Rather than having an application dictate your choices to you, restricting you to only certain actions at certain times, the Macintosh provides a great deal of flexibility, allowing you to issue almost any command at whatever time you see fit.

However, at some points, the Macintosh requires information before it can proceed and carry out a command. At this point, the Macintosh presents you with a dialog in which you may choose various options or type information (such as a name for a new document) to inform the Macintosh how you want to proceed.

In a similar vein, sometimes the Macintosh has an important message or warning that you must know about. Perhaps your memory is running low and the Macintosh needs to make certain you know of this condition. At this time, you see an alert informing you of the problem.

Dialogs and alerts can contain controls that enable you to respond and inform the Macintosh as to how you want to proceed or simply to acknowledge the condition about which the Macintosh is informing you.

Using Dialog Controls

A dialog is the Macintosh's way of asking you for additional information. In figure 1.42, for example, you see a dialog for printing. When you choose the Print command from the File menu, the application you are currently using needs additional information before it can execute the command.

Fig. 1.42
A typical Macintosh dialog.

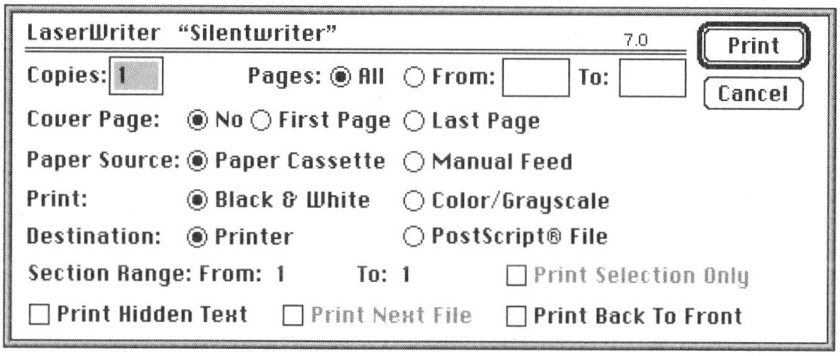

Dialogs come in different shapes and sizes, but each one requires that you make some kind of a response. Dialogs also almost always contain an OK button or a button (such as Print) indicating what operation you want to perform, and a button marked Cancel to cancel your choices.

Look a little more closely at the dialog shown in figure 1.42, which prepares a Microsoft Word document for printing. The dialog contains two kinds of buttons—round radio buttons and rectangular command buttons. This dialog also contains square check boxes and text boxes.

These items are controls; they enable you to inform the Macintosh concerning your wishes. There are several different kinds of controls that can appear in a dialog.

Command Buttons

You use command buttons to issue or confirm many kinds of commands and actions. The most common command buttons are the OK and Cancel buttons. In figure 1.42, you see that instead of an OK button, the dialog contains a Print button. When you click the Print button, the application prints according to the settings you made in the dialog's options.

A ny button with a bold double line around it, like the OK button, can be activated by pressing the Return key. You usually can cancel a choice by pressing the Command-period (⌘-.) key combination or the Esc (Escape) key.

Some command buttons are followed by an ellipsis (for example, the Find File... button in Microsoft Word's Open dialog). The ellipsis indicates that clicking the button leads you to another dialog. Command buttons usually put in effect the choices you make with radio buttons and check boxes. Some dialogs offer an Options button, usually located near the OK and the Cancel buttons. This button provides you with additional options for the tasks handled by the dialog in which it appears. The Options button in the Page Setup dialog, for example, provides the printing options shown in figure 1.43. Additional command buttons—such as Help (for getting help), Eject (for ejecting the current disk), and Disk (for changing disk drives)—appear in some dialogs.

Fig. 1.43
Other options available for
the LaserWriter printer.

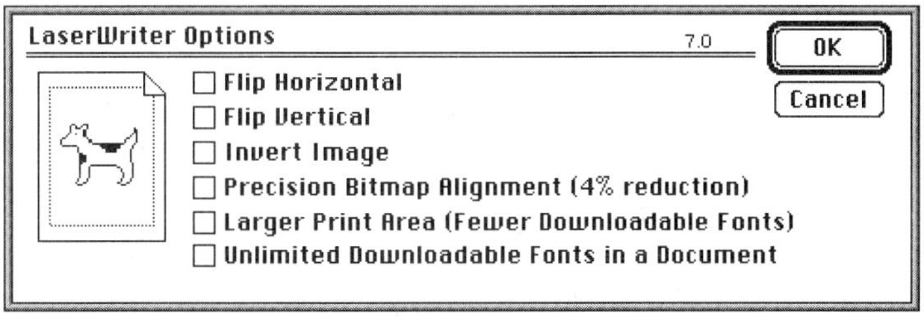

Radio Buttons

Radio buttons earned their name because you can choose only one at a time, rather like a station selector on a radio. You cannot press more than one at a time and tune in several stations. You press only one and tune in only one station.

You can click only one radio button at a time because options controlled by radio buttons are mutually exclusive. For example, in figure 1.42, you cannot have both Paper Cassette and Manual Feed as the Paper Source.

Radio buttons indicate the chosen option by displaying a round dot in the button next to the active option. You can see that the active Paper Source option in figure 1.42 is the Paper Cassette option. The Manual Feed option has no dot in its radio button and is not active.

Check Boxes

You can choose check boxes in any combination. You can click as many as you want. Check boxes indicate that the option they control is active by displaying an X in the box. An empty check box indicates an inactive option.

You activate an option controlled by a check box by clicking in the check box. An X appears in the box, and the option becomes active. To deactivate an option, you click in the check box again, clearing the X from it.

Text Boxes

Sometimes dialogs require that you type information into them. You see a text box in the dialog when this is necessary (see fig. 1.44).

Fig. 1.44
Microsoft Word's
Save File dialog.

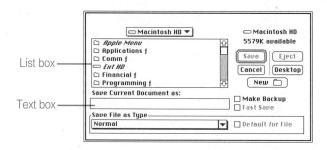

List box

Text box

You can see the text box below the line Save Current Document as: in the dialog shown in figure 1.44. In this text box, you type the name under which you want to save the document.

List Boxes

In figure 1.44, you also see a box containing a listing of the files and folders on the disk Macintosh HD. Dialogs frequently display disks, files, folders, and other items in list boxes from which you choose the item you want to work with. In this example, you can choose the folder in which you want to store the word processing document by opening the desired folder.

Note that an active scroll bar is to the right of the list box. This indicates that the list contains more items than the list box can display at any one time. You can scroll the contents of the list box in the same manner as you scroll a window (see the "Understanding Windows" section of this chapter).

Keyboard Control

Many dialogs permit you to control them from the keyboard. The most common buttons have standard keyboard control. Table 1.3 shows you the keyboard controls available in Standard File dialogs.

Table 1.3
Keyboard Controls
for Dialogs

Button or Action	Key Combination
OK (or default button)	Return or Enter
Cancel	⌘-. (period) or Esc
Eject	⌘-E
Desktop	⌘-D
Select next item in list box up	↑

Button or Action	Key Combination
Select next item in list box down	↓
Open next folder up	⌘-↑
Open folder selected in list box	⌘-↓
Select next disk	⌘-→ or ⌘-←
Select list box or text box	Tab

Some applications offer even more control over dialogs. Microsoft Word follows the general rule that you can choose any button in a dialog by pressing the Command key and the first letter of the button. Other application programs have similar shortcuts. You need to consult your application program manual for application-specific shortcuts.

Understanding Alerts

An alert is rather simple, usually containing an alert icon, a text message, and one or two buttons (see fig. 1.45).

Fig. 1.45
The Trash warning alert.

The alert in figure 1.45 is typical of alerts. The exclamation icon indicates to you that this is an important message. In this case, you are about to delete the contents of the Trash and remove the items from your disk.

You have two options represented by the two buttons: OK and Cancel. Clicking the OK button confirms to the Macintosh that you wish the action to proceed. Clicking the Cancel button causes the action to cease. Clicking either button dismisses the alert.

Some alerts permit no choices. They inform you of an existing condition that has prevented a command from being completed (see fig. 1.46).

Fig. 1.46
An alert showing that the Open command cannot be performed.

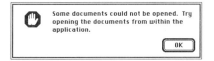

You can see that the message is more urgent by the "stop" symbol in the alert. Your only choice in the case of alerts such as that in figure 1.46 is to press Return or click the OK button.

Understanding Macintosh Keyboards

The Macintosh keyboard, like any computer keyboard, is based on the standard typewriter keyboard with which you are probably already familiar. There are some differences that are important to note, however. You will also want to know how to use the keyboard to perform functions specific to the Macintosh computer.

Figures 1.47 and 1.48 show the two primary Apple-supplied keyboards.

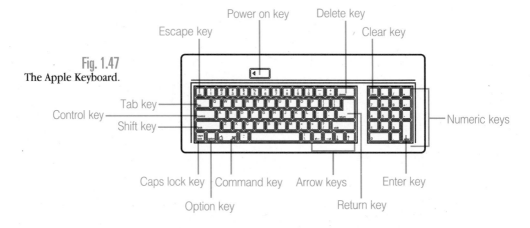

Fig. 1.47
The Apple Keyboard.

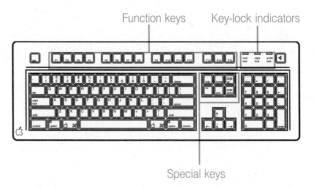

Fig. 1.48
The Apple Extended Keyboard II.

If your keyboard is from a third party (that is, not from Apple), the exact arrangement of your keys may differ from those in the figures. However, the variation should not be great. Keyboards have achieved a certain uniformity in recent times and do not vary as widely as they once did.

Modifier Keys

As the name implies, modifier keys modify the meaning of a keypress. If you have used a typewriter, you are already familiar with one modifier key: the Shift key. The Shift key on typewriters or computers modifies the meaning of a keypress. When you hold the Shift key down, you type an uppercase letter rather than a lowercase letter. The keypress's action has been modified—changed from one action to another.

Although typewriters have only one modifier key, computers have several. The Macintosh uses a total of five modifier keys (although two of these keys' functions overlap). The modifier keys are: Shift, Caps Lock, Control, Option, and Command (⌘).

The Shift key and the Caps Lock key perform similar functions, in that both modify keypresses to result in uppercase letters rather than the lowercase versions. There are, however, two important differences to note.

First, the Shift key must be held down to be active, whereas the Caps Lock key becomes active when pressed and must be pressed again to become inactive. The latter is important to note if you are used to the Shift Lock of a typewriter. A typewriter's Shift Lock is disengaged when the Shift key is pressed. Caps Lock is deactivated only when the Caps Lock key is pressed a second time.

Secondly, when the Shift key is pressed, the symbols above the top row of numbers are typed (for example an exclamation mark instead of the number 1). The Caps Lock key has no effect on the number keys or other nonletter keys (such as the colon/semicolon key). Even with Caps Lock active, you must press Shift to obtain the symbols above the numbers.

You can use the Shift key on the Macintosh to modify more than just the letter, number, and other character keys. In most cases, for example, you can use the Shift key to modify the action of the Tab key. Normally, the Tab key tabs to the right. Holding down the Shift key while pressing the Tab key in most Macintosh applications causes a tab to the left. This key combination is called a Shift-Tab.

The Shift key also can modify the function keys so that you can invoke more than one action with one function key. Pressing F1 can cause one action, but holding down the Shift key and pressing F1 (called Shift-F1) can invoke an entirely different function.

This is also true of the Control, Option, and Command keys. Some application programs permit many functions to be assigned to a single function key. Pressing F1 invokes a function, pressing Shift-F1 invokes another, pressing Control-F1 invokes a third, and so on.

Further, you can go on to combine modifier keys to produce such combinations as Shift-Command-Option-F1, where you hold down the Shift, Command, and Option keys while you press the F1 key. This allows up to sixteen different functions to be assigned to one function key, for a possible 240 different functions for the fifteen function keys.

Of course, carrying things this far can lead to confusion. Who can remember so many functions? But the potential is there.

The important thing to note here is that it is not uncommon to modify keys by using the four primary modifier keys. (Caps Lock is usually used for shifting the letter keys to uppercase, and only in very rare and unusual cases to invoke functions.)

The Shift, Control, Option, and Command modifier keys also can modify the function of the mouse, as discussed in this chapter's "Using the Mouse" section.

You use the Command key primarily in conjunction with the letter and number keys to invoke menu commands from the keyboard, as discussed in this chapter's "Understanding the Menus" section. The Command key is not limited to this use, however. You can use this key to modify keys such as the space bar, the arrow keys, the Delete key, and so on. Whether this is done in your application program depends on the designer, so you need to consult your manual for details.

The primary function of the Option key is to invoke a second set of symbols for the letter and number keys. This enables you to type unusual characters such as the symbol for the British pound, Spanish ñ's, and other foreign characters. This use of the key is covered in this section under "Typing Special Characters."

One special use of the Option key is in compatibility with the IBM PC. The IBM PC has an Alt key that is used to invoke options in a way that is similar to the way the Macintosh Option key functions. Hence, in application programs that are meant to be compatible with the IBM PC version of the application, it is common to use the Option key in the same way as would use the Alt key in the PC version. The Option key is frequently used in this manner when you run IBM PC application software on your Macintosh, as discussed in Chapter 29, "Using Connectivity Software."

The Control key was added by Apple mainly to increase compatibility with the IBM PC standard computer and other computer systems which make use of the Control key to generate special characters. Hence, you encounter the use of the Control key largely in communications programs (see Chapter 17, "Using Communication Software"), which enable you to connect by phone line to other computer systems. You can encounter use of the Control key in application programs that are designed to be compatible with the IBM PC version of the application.

Function Keys

The Apple Extended Keyboard II and many third-party keyboards have a top row of function keys, usually 15 of them labeled from F1 to F15. The latter three have additional labeling: *Print Screen*, *Scroll Lock*, and *Pause*. These labels are for compatibility with IBM PC software and are not used in Macintosh application programs.

The purpose of a function key is to invoke a command or set of operations when the key is pressed, thus saving time by allowing quick access to frequently used commands or actions. Function keys have long been present on IBM PC standard keyboards, but have only come to the Macintosh in more recent years. They have been present long enough, however; a wide variety of application software now uses the keys.

Apple has assigned functions to the first four keys, F1 through F4. They correspond to commands in the Edit menu. From left to right, the commands are Undo, Cut, Copy, and Paste. The remaining keys F5 through F15 are available for use by application programs.

The exact use of these keys is up to the application program, so you need to check your manual for specific details.

Special Keys

Several special keys are present on Macintosh keyboards. These keys have various functions you need to know about.

The following keys are found on the standard Apple and extended Apple keyboards, as well as on third-party keyboards.

> **Esc (escape).** This key is a holdover from the distant past of computers. The key's orginal function was to send a character that alerted a computer that a special control character was about to be sent. These days, the key is rarely used for this purpose although you may still encounter a need for it if you regularly connect to a larger computer system by phone or network. Usually, the

Macintosh uses this key as an equivalent of the Command-period (⌘-.) key sequence, which cancels an operation (see the "Understanding Dialogs and Alerts" section of this chapter for more on the Command-period key combination).

Power on. The Macintosh II series, the Performa 600, the Color Classic, the Centris series, and the Quadra series computers use this key to turn on the Macintosh. Instead of flipping a power switch, you press this key and the power is switched on by an internal switch. On other Macintoshes (the Classic II, LC II, and so forth), this key performs no function.

Arrow keys. The four arrow keys are used to move the insertion point in the indicated direction in word processing applications and other application programs that use text. In System 7, these keys also enable you to move around on the Desktop without using the mouse (see "Desktop Commands" in this section). You also can use these keys in dialogs to select files, folders, and disks (see "Understanding Dialogs and Alerts" in this chapter).

Numeric keys. The numeric keypad has the ten digits (0-9), a decimal point (.), symbols for the four common mathematical operations—addition (+), subtraction (–), multiplication (*), and division (/)—an equals key (=), a Clear key, and an Enter key. These keys are used to enter numbers in "ten-key" fashion like a calculator. You use the Clear key to clear a selection and the Enter key primarily to confirm an entry without moving the insertion point (you see this mainly in spreadsheet programs; see Chapter 11, "Using Spreadsheets," for more on these applications).

The following keys are found on the extended Apple keyboard and many third-party keyboards:

Help. Many programs use the Help key to invoke their Help function. This is not universal, but is up to the application program's designer to decide whether to use this key for that purpose. Ironically, Apple does not use the Help key to invoke System 7's Balloon Help feature.

Home, Page Up, Page Down, and End. These four keys are used by many word processing and other programs to move the insertion point. You generally use Home and End to move to the top and bottom of the window, respectively. Page Up and Page Down generally enable you to scroll the window up a page or down a page. You need to check your manual to determine the exact meaning of these keys in your application software.

Del. This key is usually employed by word processing and other text-handling programs to delete a single character to the right of the insertion point, rather than to its left as the Delete (Backspace) key does.

Desktop Commands

System 7 introduced the ability to select items and move about the Desktop with the keyboard rather than the mouse. This can be a time saver since you can now do many operations that usually required the mouse without taking your hands off the keyboard.

Table 1.4 shows the keyboard Desktop commands and their mouse equivalents.

Table 1.4
Keyboard Desktop
Commands

Action	Key(s)	Mouse Equivalent
Open a selected icon	⌘-↓	Double-click icon
Select an icon	Type first letters of name	Click icon
Select next icon by name in alphabetical order	Tab	Click icon
Select previous icon by name in alphabetical order	Shift-Tab	Click icon
Select next icon to left*	←	Click icon
Select next icon to right*	→	Click icon
Select next icon up	↑	Click icon
Select next down down	↓	Click icon
Make Desktop active	⌘-Shift-↑	Click Desktop
Open window enclosing active window (move up one folder level)	⌘-↑	None
Expand outline of selected folder**	⌘-→	Click outline triangle
Collapse outline of selected folder**	⌘-←	Click outline triangle
Expand entire outline	⌘-Option-→	Click each outline triangle
Collapse entire outline	⌘-Option-←	Click each outline triangle

Works only in icon views.

**Works only in list views.*

(See Chapter 4 "Managing Files" for more on outlines, icon views, and list views.)

If you are a new Macintosh user, you will most likely begin by using the mouse to perform almost every action on your Macintosh. As time goes on, however, you may want to find shortcuts to help you speed up your work. The shortcuts in table 1.4 can help you navigate on the Desktop and select files, folders, and disks. You may find these more convenient.

Understanding Macintosh Text and Graphics

One of the features that gives the Macintosh the reputation of being easy to learn and use is that basic text and graphics operations are performed in the same manner in all Macintosh applications.

You may have already heard of "cut and paste" and thought the phrase rather reminiscent of elementary school days. Far from being derogatory, however, this description is actually a compliment to the simplicity of text operations.

Regardless of the additional features a word processor, spreadsheet, database, or other application program may add, the basic text-handling operations remain the same. You only have to learn the operations once no matter how many different applications you use. These basic operations also apply to the Finder and can be used in naming, renaming, and editing the names of files, folders, and disks. (Chapter 2 explores how the text operations are applied to the icons of these items.)

The application TeachText, which is included with your Macintosh and probably already installed on your hard drive, is used as an example in this section. You can use this application to practice the text and graphics operations.

Typing Text

The most basic and necessary text operation is typing text. You already know, of course, that typing text requires the skill of pressing the correct keys. But you should also know a few important points about text typing in the Macintosh environment.

Consider figure 1.49.

The vertical, blinking bar indicated in the figure is the *insertion point*. This bar indicates the location at which text (or graphics) will next be inserted, whether typed or pasted.

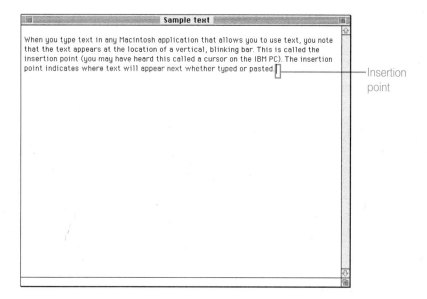

Fig. 1.49
A paragraph of text in
TeachText.

Sample text

When you type text in any Macintosh application that allows you to use text, you note that the text appears at the location of a vertical, blinking bar. This is called the insertion point (you may have heard this called a cursor on the IBM PC). The insertion point indicates where text will appear next whether typed or pasted.

Insertion point

As you type, you see that the insertion point moves to the right as text appears. The bar continues to the right until it reaches the right margin. The bar then moves down one line and appears at the far left of the new line. Text that does not fit on the line automatically "wraps" to the next line without your having to press the Return key. This automatic action is called *word wrap*. On the Macintosh, unlike on a typewriter, you press the Return key at the end of paragraphs only. The computer handles line breaks for you.

You can move the insertion point to any position in the text-editing window. This flexibility is important when you are editing text because you have access to virtually all the text in a given file.

Moving the Insertion Point

The last line of the paragraph in figure 1.49 contains a typo. The sentence is missing the word "indicates." You can press the Delete key to back up to the location where the word is missing and then type the word; that is a wasteful approach, however, especially because you can easily move the insertion point to and place text at any location in your document.

To move the insertion point, you can use the mouse or the keyboard. To use the mouse, place the mouse pointer where you want to insert text. Note that the mouse pointer changes from the familiar arrow to a vertical bar with curled ends (see fig. 1.50). This is called the I-beam pointer.

Fig. 1.50
Moving the insertion point.

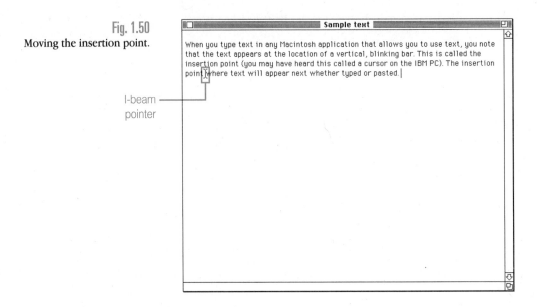

I-beam pointer

When the I-beam pointer is in place, click the mouse button. The insertion point appears at the location of the I-beam pointer. You can then type the text you want to insert—in this case, "indicates." Note that existing text is shifted to the right, rather than overwritten, to make room for the new text.

You also can use the arrow keys to move the insertion point. Each press of an arrow key moves the insertion point one character or one line in the direction of the key's arrow. Holding an arrow key down invokes the key repeat, which causes the key's action repeat for as long as the key is pressed.

Note that many applications give you the ability to move more quickly than the single character or line at a time that you can move by using the arrow keys. Usually this requires using a modifier key (such as the Command key) with an arrow key. Whether this feature is provided depends on the application program. You need to check your program's manual.

Deleting Text and Graphics

You can quickly delete any amount of text and graphics from a document by first selecting the text or graphics and then pressing the Delete key.

The primary way to select text or graphics in a document is to drag the mouse pointer through the desired selection. For example, if you want to delete the phrase *that allows you to use text* from the paragraph in figure 1.50, you do the following:

1. Place the insertion pointer (the mouse pointer) at the immediate left of the word *that*.

2. Press and hold the mouse button.

3. Drag the insertion pointer across the phrase.

   You see a highlight band encompassing the selection (see fig. 1.51).

4. When you reach the end of the selection, release the mouse button.

5. Choose the Clear command from the Edit menu, or press the Delete key.

Fig. 1.51
Selecting text.

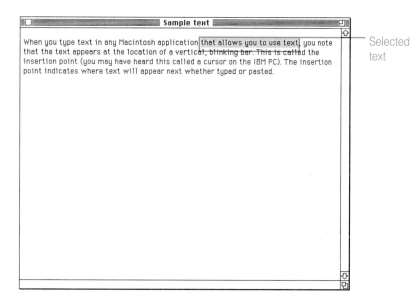

Sample text

When you type text in any Macintosh application that allows you to use text, you note that the text appears at the location of a vertical, blinking bar. This is called the insertion point (you may have heard this called a cursor on the IBM PC). The insertion point indicates where text will appear next whether typed or pasted.

Selected text

This process works equally well for text and graphics in a document. And your selection can contain both. The selection indicates the beginning and end of the deletion. The highlight band gives you a visual cue concerning the scope of the deletion.

Note that a shortcut exists for selecting single words. Rather than drag across the word, place the mouse pointer on the word and double-click. This action selects the word.

Replacing Text

If you need to retype a short section of text, you can use a procedure similar to that of deleting text to do so quickly and easily. Use the dragging method (or double-clicking if you only need to retype a word) to select the text to be replaced. Then instead of deleting the selected text, type the new text. The selected text is deleted and replaced with the newly typed text. The replacement text does not have to be the same size as the selected text. You can replace a word with a sentence, a paragraph with a word, or any other replacement you like. The surrounding text automatically moves to fit the new replacement text.

Understanding the Clipboard

The text-editing procedures discussed up to this point are helpful but limited. Up to this point, no method of moving text around your document or duplicating text has been discussed. You need to understand one component of the Macintosh System software, however, before you use the commands to perform these procedures.

The commands in the Edit menu of the Finder and all text-handling applications make use of a part of the System software called the Clipboard. The Clipboard is a temporary storage area that holds text and graphics for later use. (The Clipboard is not actually limited to these two kinds of objects, but they are the focus of this section.)

The Clipboard is not part of any particular application. Rather, it is part of the System software itself. Because of this, the Clipboard operates the same in every application.

The important point to remember about the Clipboard is that it always contains the contents of the last selection that was cut or copied. Each time a selection is copied or cut, that selection replaces the previous contents of the Clipboard.

One interesting feature of the Clipboard is that, because of its independence from application software, the contents of the Clipboard are not lost when you quit or switch from an application. You can copy or cut a selection in a document, for example, quit that application, and start another one (or switch from one active application to another). The Clipboard's contents are still intact, and you can then paste them into a document of the newly active application.

Chapter 2 covers this use of the Clipboard in the discussion on multi-tasking. For now, it is important to understand that the Clipboard retains the last copied or cut selection right up to the moment you shut down your Macintosh.

Copying Text and Graphics

Duplicating text or graphics is simple when you use the Clipboard. You can use the following steps to duplicate a selection of text or graphics anywhere in a document:

1. Select the text or graphics.

2. Choose the Copy command from the Edit menu; you also can press ⌘-C, or F3.

   A copy of the selection is stored in the Clipboard.

3. Place the insertion point where you want the text or graphics to appear.

4. Choose the Paste command from the Edit menu; or press ⌘-V, or F4.

   This action copies the contents of the Clipboard at the location of the insertion point.

You can repeat steps 3 and 4 as many times as you wish. Remember, the Clipboard retains the last selection copied or cut.

Moving Text and Graphics

There are times you want to move text or graphics from one location in your document to another. You do this with the Clipboard in a manner similar to the copying procedure discussed previously. Use these steps:

1. Select the text or graphics.

2. Choose the Cut command from the Edit menu; or press ⌘-X, or F2.

   The selection disappears from your document and is stored in the Clipboard.

3. Place the insertion point where you want the text or graphics to appear.

4. Choose the Paste command from the Edit menu; alternatively, press ⌘-V, or F4.

   The Clipboard's contents copy at the location of the insertion point.

You can repeat steps 3 and 4 as many times as you want to duplicate the selection throughout your document or in another file. Again, remember that the Clipboard retains the last selection copied or cut.

Undoing Mistakes

The Macintosh recognizes that sometimes people make mistakes. You might type over the wrong word, delete the wrong sentence, or paste the wrong paragraph. The Undo command on the Edit menu is intended to come to your aid at such times.

The Undo command reverses the effect of the last action you performed. If you have just deleted a word, Undo restores the word. If you have just cut a paragraph, Undo pastes the paragraph back into your document.

To undo your last action, choose the Undo command from the Edit menu. Alternatively, press ⌘-Z or F1.

You must use the Undo command immediately after an action because the command only reverses the effect of the last action. If you make a mistake but do not realize the error until you have performed several more edits, you cannot use Undo to correct the error. Rather, you need to edit to correct the mistake.

Keep two points in mind here. First, your application software may provide a means for undoing more than just the last action. This is a feature provided by some word processors and other application programs.

Second, you may not always be able to undo your last action. The choice of which actions can be undone are up to the designer of the application program. You know that an action cannot be undone if the Undo command is dimmed on the Edit menu (the command may also read "Can't Undo" in its dimmed state). Generally, however, the Undo command can undo the last text edit action.

Typing Special Characters

Although not apparent from the appearance of the keyboard, the Macintosh permits you to type a great many special characters, such as foreign letters, the symbols for major foreign currencies, common mathematical symbols, and more.

You access these special characters by using of the Option key, which, in this case, acts in a manner similar to the Shift key. When the Option key is held down, the letter and number keys of the keyboard are modified to produce special symbols rather than the usual characters. You can access additional symbols by holding down both the Option and Shift keys while pressing character keys.

You can view the available characters by using the Key Caps application which is installed on your Apple menu. Choose Key Caps from the menu and the Key Caps window appears (see fig. 1.52).

Fig. 1.52

The Key Caps window.

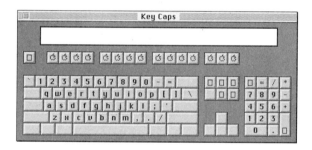

Key Caps displays a keyboard that closely matches the appearance of the keyboard attached to your Macintosh. You see the letters and numbers produced by the keys displayed in the squares representing the keys.

You can see the usefulness of Key Caps when you hold down the Option key while the Key Caps window is on-screen. The Option key or keys displayed in the Key Caps window darken to indicate that they are being pressed, and the characters assigned to the keys in the window change (see fig. 1.53).

Fig. 1.53

The Key Caps window with the Option key pressed.

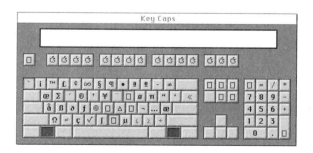

If you look closely at figure 1.53, you see that the British pound symbol has taken the place of the number 3. What this indicates to you is that the British pound symbol is produced by holding down the Option key while pressing the 3 key.

I f you have trouble remembering the location of a symbol, try pressing and releasing the Option key several times while you watch the desired symbol. You see the letter or number of the key alternate with the symbol. This can help you locate the key to press.

The accents pointed out in figure 1.53 require a bit of explanation. Many foreign words require accents of various kinds (Spanish words, for example, make use of the tilde over the letter n to create a separate letter). The accent keys allow you to add accents to letters by following these steps:

1. Press and hold the Option key.

2. Press the key corresponding to the desired accent.

3. Release the Option key.

4. Type the letter to be accented.

Note that nothing is typed when you do step 2. The Macintosh waits until you indicate the letter that is to be accented before displaying a character on-screen.

Try this a few times while in Key Caps. When you release the Option key in step 3, you see that Key Caps displays the letters that you can accent in this manner. The keys containing these letters have a bold outline on the key tops displayed in the Key Caps window.

Remember that you can also generate special characters by pressing character keys while holding down the Option and Shift keys. Holding down these keys in Key Caps displays the characters that can be obtained with this key combination. If you have an extended keyboard, you can also obtain some additional special characters by holding down the Control key. (It is interesting to note that in the Chicago font, you can type the four-leaf clover Command symbol by pressing Control-Q.)

Key Caps initially displays in the Chicago System font. This is the font in which the menus, menu commands, window names, and other System-related items are displayed. You can see the symbols of other fonts by choosing the desired font from the Key Caps menu that appears on the menu bar when Key Caps is on-screen (see Chapter 8, "Using Fonts," for more on fonts).

You can close Key Caps by clicking the Close box in the upper left corner of the window, or by choosing Quit from the File menu.

Note that Key Caps uses your current keyboard layout. For most users, this is the standard QWERTY layout found on typewriters. However, it is possible to use other layouts such as the Dvorak keyboard. Chapter 6, "Customizing the Macintosh," covers the use of other keyboard layouts.

Considering Other Text-Editing Features

Various application software packages offer editing features beyond the basic System-supplied features discussed in this section. Some offer enhanced selection features. Many word processing applications, for example, allow you to select a paragraph by triple-clicking within the paragraph. Many applications enable you to select text by use of the arrow keys and a modifier (usually you use the Shift key in conjunction with an arrow key).

Two notable features in word processors (and other applications) that I think should be standard are the unlimited undo offered by Nisus and the drag-and-drop offered by Microsoft Word, Microsoft Excel, and Nisus (the feature's name in Nisus is called Intelligent Cut and Paste). Unlimited undos enable you to undo not just your last action, but also the several actions before. (With sufficient memory and disk space, you should be able to restore a document all the way back to pre-edit condition!)

But I have to confess that the drag-and-drop feature has become my favorite new editing feature. Drag-and-drop is an alternative to Cut and Paste and is a logical extension of the Macintosh interface. With drag-and-drop, you can select text or graphics then drag it to the location you wish the selection to occupy, reducing the number of steps moving a selection usually requires. Drag-and-drop is an idea that goes in the "why didn't somebody think of that sooner?" category.

I expect unlimited undos and the drag-and-drop to become standard over time.

In any case, word processors and other applications offer a great variety of enhancements to the basic text-editing capabilities of the Macintosh. However, you can rest assured that the basics will be supported in any text or graphics program. This means that once you have learned basic editing skills, you can apply them immediately and then go on to learn the additional features later.

Chapter Summary

This chapter has been concerned with the basics of the Macintosh. You have seen how to set up the Macintosh and connect its various parts, and you have explored some of the fundamental parts of the Macintosh interface.

Some important points to remember:

- The Desktop is the workspace of the Macintosh interface and is intended to reflect its real-world equivalent: the top of a desk.

- The Finder is an application program that manages the Desktop, copying files, opening applications, emptying the Trash, and performing other household duties.

- The menu bar at the top of the screen contains menus that contain the commands that enable you to "drive" the Macintosh.

- Menus can contain commands, options, other menus, or all three.

- Some menus are scrollable, containing more commands or options than can be displayed at one time. Others are nested and called *hierarchical*.

- Pop-up menus can be located almost anywhere, but usually appear in dialogs. You can detect a pop-up menu by the shadowing seen around the rectangle of the menu.

- Windows enable you to "see into" files, folders, and disks.

- Dialogs are special cases of windows and enable you to set options, choose items to be operated on, or respond to various conditions.

- Alerts are limited dialogs meant to inform you of important conditions such as limited memory or errors.

- Modifier keys—Shift, Control, Command, Option, and Caps Lock—modify the meaning of keypresses, and at times mouse actions, to provide a wider variety of options in issuing commands to your Macintosh.

- The use of a modifier key is indicated by placing the name of the key used before the action (e.g., ⌘-Q, Shift-click, Shift-Control-F1).

- The Copy and Cut commands copy a selection to the Clipboard, and the Paste command copies the contents of the Clipboard to the location of the insertion point.

- The Clipboard retains the contents of the last copied or cut selection.

The next chapter delves more deeply into the Macintosh System Software to give you a better understanding of how your Macintosh computer works and how you can best put your Macintosh to work.

Understanding the System

Computers are not the mystical boxes of genius that many people once believed them to be. They are simply machines that follow instructions extremely quickly. These instructions are largely responsible for the power and utility of your computer. The more sophisticated your computer, the more you are able to do with it. The System Software that you install on your hard disk provides a great deal of power; its graphical interface, in fact, distinguishes the Mac from other popular personal computers and character-based operating systems.

This chapter explains the contents of the System Folder, provides instructions for installing the System Software (if it is not already installed), and outlines some of the basics of System Software operation.

This chapter introduces you to *icons*—the graphic representations of files, folders, and disks—and how they are used. You will also discover *multitasking*—the Mac's capability to run more than one application at a time. You learn the basic uses of the Apple menu and its supplied mini-applications (often called *desk accessories*). Finally, you are introduced to the Balloon Help system so that you can get assistance when you need it.

The information in this chapter is based on Versions 7 and 7.1 of the System Software and covers the P enhancements of the software that are shipped with the Performa Macintoshes.

Understanding System Software

A computer cannot operate without instructions. Many of the basic instructions for the Mac are included in *read-only memory* (ROM). In other words, basic instruction sets that direct such operations as reading files from the disk drive, drawing windows, and creating menus are built into the machine. These sets of instructions make up what is called the *Toolbox*.

Like a real box of tools, the Toolbox cannot do things by itself. Instead, the tools in the Toolbox wait for someone to come along and use them. The user in this case is the System Software, which executes your commands and acts as the overall operator of the Mac. Whenever you click a mouse or press a key, the System Software uses the tools of the Toolbox to respond.

The System Software makes the Macintosh come alive. Without it, the Mac is merely an expensive paperweight.

Understanding System Software Versions

During the production life of the Macintosh, Apple has released several versions of the System Software. New System Software versions result from progress; Apple has periodically made improvements in the efficiency with which the System operates and the options it provides. Each improved version is given a new version number. Major revisions in System Software are distinguished by changes in the digit preceding the decimal (4.0, 5.0, 6.0, 7.0, and so on). Feature changes that result in less than a full revision are indicated by changes in the tens position following the decimal (6.1, 6.2, and so on). Minor changes and *bug fixes*— corrections to errors found after release—are indicated by changes in the hundreds position (7.0.1, 7.0.2, and so on).

Before System 6, Apple updated the parts of the System Software set individually or in groups and made no attempt to standardize the revision numbering of those parts. Finder 4.1, for example, might be intended to work with System 3.1 and MultiFinder 1.1. Individual numbering was fine as long as there were only a few component parts of the System Software, but that was no longer the case by the time System 5 was released. At this point, the number of System Software parts had grown so great that it was difficult to keep the correct versions of the parts together. As a result, Apple decided to unify the numbering scheme to indicate which versions of which parts worked together.

System 6 was the first revision to use this unified numbering scheme. All of the component parts of System 6 had a version number of 6.0 or higher. In the same way, all of System 7's parts have a version number of 7.0 or higher.

Version 7.1 of the System Software is now available; although it has additional features, it is still a version of System 7.

Installing System Software

You should have at least six floppy disks in your System 7 software set, including the following:

- Install 1
- Install 2
- Tidbits
- Printing
- Fonts
- Disk Tools

Here's how you install System 7:

1. If your Mac is already turned on, choose the Restart command from the Special menu. When the screen goes blank, insert the Install 1 disk into the internal disk drive. Otherwise, insert the disk immediately after turning on the Macintosh.

   The Welcome to the Apple Installer message shown in figure 2.1 appears.

Fig. 2.1

The Welcome to the
Apple Installer
message.

2. Click OK. The Easy Install screen appears (see fig. 2.2). The Easy Install option automatically determines the software you need to install for the model you are using. The Customize option enables you to select the exact combination of System files and other available resources to install.

Fig. 2.2

The Easy Install screen.

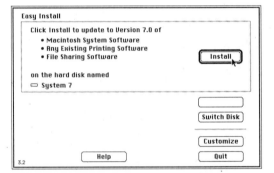

Use the Customize button only if you are familiar with the parts of the System Software that you need. The Easy Install option determines which parts of the System you need and is much easier to use. The only advantage to using the Customize option is that you can reduce the amount of disk space used by System Software by installing only those parts you actually need. (Easy Install engages in a bit of overkill in order to make certain you have everything you need.)

Until you understand the parts of the System Software, it is best to let the Installer decide what you need.

The Easy Install window lists the System 7 components that will be installed.

You also have the chance at this time to specify a disk drive for System storage. Your Macintosh should recognize your hard disk and indicate it on-screen; if it does not, click the Switch Disk button until you see the name of your hard disk.

3. Click Install to start the installation process.

4. Follow the instructions, inserting each disk into the floppy drive as your Macintosh tells you to do so. A hand cursor tracks the progress of the installation, ticking off fingers to indicate that activity is occurring.

When installation is finished, your Macintosh gives you the option of shutting down or restarting.

5. Click the Restart button. Your Macintosh ejects the Installer disk and restarts using your hard disk and the System Software installed on it.

Viewing the System Folder

Your Macintosh operates according to a complex set of instructions contained in files in the System Folder. Several different types of System files are stored in this folder. This chapter examines the System files and their assigned jobs.

Basically, the System Folder contains the information that tells the Macintosh how to do the following:

- Construct the Desktop and control its appearance and operation
- Allocate memory as needed
- Keep track of icon locations
- Load and run programs (called *launching*)
- Print text in one of the available fonts, styles, and sizes
- Save and open files

Without the files in the System Folder, your Macintosh is useless. The System Folder is contained on the startup disk because it contains instructions necessary for starting and running the Mac.

The System Folder is called the *Blessed Folder* by programmers; its special status is shown by its icon—a miniature Macintosh (see fig. 2.3).

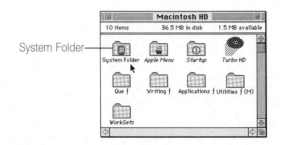

Fig. 2.3
The System Folder's
Macintosh icon indicates
its important status.

Within the System Folder, different icons represent the different types of System files and folders (see fig. 2.4). The icon for the Apple Menu Items folder contains a small Apple, for example, and the Control Panels folder icon contains an adjustment slide like the ones you use to adjust settings on the actual control panels.

Fig. 2.4
The contents of the
System Folder.

Table 2.1 describes the different files located in the System and Utilities folders for System 7 (including version 7.1 revisions and P enhancements for the Performa Macintoshes).

Table 2.1
The Contents of the
System Folder for System 7

Icon	Folder/File	Description
	Apple Menu Items	This folder contains applications, files, folders, aliases, and other items you choose to place on the Apple menu.
	Clipboard	This is where cut and copied text and graphics are stored temporarily until they are retrieved for use at a later time.
	Extensions	This folder contains files that enhance the operation of the System Software. These files used to be called INITs (for INITialization); they start automatically when you turn on your Macintosh and do things such as adding search capabilities to your Open dialogs.

Icon	Folder/File	Description
	Finder	The Finder is the manager of the Desktop. (See Chapter 1 for a full discussion of its functions.)
	Scrapbook File	The Scrapbook File permanently stores and enables retrieval of text and graphics that you select using the Scrapbook application, discussed later in this chapter.
	Control Panels	This folder contains control panels for customizing monitors, sound, memory, and the appearance of your Desktop, among other things. (The control panels that come with your Mac are discussed in Chapters 5 and 6.)
	Note Pad File	This file contains any notes or memos that you enter using the Note Pad application.
	System	The central, controlling portion of the System Software resides in this file; other items, called *resources*, are also included. The System file uses a suitcase icon because of the Mac standard of storing resources in suitcase files. The System file is also one of the few that you can open in order to view and change the contents (see Chapter 6, "Customizing the Macintosh," and Chapter 8, "Using Fonts").
	Preferences	This folder contains preference and option setting files created by programs according to the choices you make while running those programs.
	PrintMonitor Documents	This folder contains files that are being printed in the background while you are working on other projects with your Macintosh.

For your Mac to work correctly, you must have the files and folders shown in the top two rows of figure 2.4. You might have additional items; if you don't, you will probably add them as you add features to your Macintosh.

To avoid System crashes, make sure that only one System file appears on your startup disk. Make sure that you copy only the files you want to your hard disk because many applications come with a System Folder and System files. Do not copy any of the System files present on a floppy disk to your hard disk.

Understanding Icons

In order to understand the Macintosh interface, you need to understand the use of *icons* to represent software and hardware options. Each icon is a small picture that represents an item such as a file, a folder, or a disk.

In the Macintosh interface, you manipulate icons to tell the computer what actions you want to take place. As an example, you can drag an icon of a file from one disk to another to instruct the computer to copy the file from the source disk to the target disk.

One of the advantages of using icons to represent items is the uniformity that such an approach affords. Because the rules for using icons remain essentially the same regardless of the item the icon represents, you have fewer commands to remember. For example, the action required to copy a file to a disk is the same as the one required to copy an entire disk to another disk. In each case, an icon is dragged to the target disk; only the icons themselves differ.

This section covers the rules that govern icon use. These rules can be applied to any icon whether the icon represents a file, a folder, or an entire disk. There are a few variations, but these are far less numerous than the variations found in DOS. (Disk commands are very different from directory commands in DOS, for example, while in the Macintosh interface they are quite similar.)

Selecting Icons

You use the mouse to select and manipulate icons, and the rules for selecting icons are few and simple:

- To select a single icon, click the icon.

- To select several icons located close to one another in a window or on the Desktop, drag from a point at the upper left of the icon group to a point at the lower right of the group. (You can actually drag in any direction—the important thing is to surround the icons with the selection box that appears when you drag the mouse pointer.)

- To select several icons that are not located close to one another, click the first icon, and then Shift-click each remaining icon of the group.

If you need more information, read the section "Using the Mouse" in Chapter 1.

Editing Icon Names

At times, you might need to rename or edit the names of existing icons. You might need to change the name of an icon to make it more expressive of the icon's contents, for example, or to bring it into line with the naming conventions used with other icons.

This is how you rename an icon:

1. Click the name of the icon you want to rename.

    Or

    Click the icon and press Return.

    A border appears around the name of the icon.

2. Type the new name.

    When you begin typing, the old name disappears and the new one appears in its place. The insertion point moves to the right as you enter characters.

3. Press the Return key or click the Desktop to confirm the new icon name.

Figure 2.5 shows how these three steps look on-screen.

Fig. 2.5

Renaming an icon.

Editing an icon name is just as easy. When you edit, you modify what is there instead of changing the entire name.

To edit an icon name, follow these steps:

1. Click the name of the icon you want to edit.

    Or

    Click the icon and press Return.

A border appears around the name of the icon and the mouse pointer becomes an I-beam cursor.

2. Place the I-beam cursor to the right of the character you want to edit.

3. Click the mouse once, and the insertion point appears inside the icon name.

4. Use the Delete or Backspace key to delete characters.

5. Type any new characters.

6. Press the Return key or click the Desktop to confirm your changes.

Moving an Icon

To move an icon, simply drag it to the new location. If you are moving the icon from one location to another on the same disk, the icon is *transferred* to the new location.

If you drag an icon from one disk to another, the icon is *copied* to the destination disk but does not disappear from the source disk. To remove the copied icon from the source disk, drag that icon to the Trash.

Note that the Desktop is considered part of your startup disk, which can lead to some interesting situations. If you move an icon from your startup disk onto the Desktop and later move the icon back onto your startup disk, you are moving the icon rather than copying the file or folder that the icon represents. However, if you move an icon from another disk onto the Desktop and then move that icon onto the startup disk, the file or folder that the icon represents is copied to the startup disk.

These complications arise from the fact that icons *represent* the files or folders being moved. The item represented by an icon remains on disk even though the icon appears on the Desktop.

To return an icon to the disk that contains the file or folder the icon represents, select the icon. Then choose the Put Away command from the File menu.

T I P

If you move an icon while pressing the Option key, a copy of the icon with the same name as the original is created. This *Option-drag* method forces a copy to occur even at times when a move would normally occur—for example, when dragging an icon from one folder to another on the same disk.

If you attempt to move an icon to a location where an icon with the same name already resides, you receive the warning message shown in figure 2.6.

Fig. 2.6
An icon with the same name is already present.

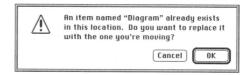

An item named "Diagram" already exists in this location. Do you want to replace it with the one you're moving?

Cancel   OK

Clicking the OK button replaces the existing icon with the one being dragged in. Clicking Cancel cancels the operation, leaving the existing icon untouched.

Copying an Icon

Occasionally you might find it useful to duplicate existing icons. Perhaps you have created an icon that contains information you want to use again, in slightly modified format, to serve the purposes of another project. Or perhaps you simply want to store an icon in another location on the Desktop. Duplicating a selected icon can help you accomplish these and other tasks.

In any case, it is not difficult to copy an icon. Follow these steps:

1. Select the icon you want to copy.

2. From the File menu, choose Duplicate.

A new icon appears with a name identical to the original except for the addition of the word *copy* at the end. If you make a copy of that copy, then you get *copy 1*, *copy 2*, and so on. This copying process creates an exact duplicate of the items represented by the original icon. If the icon represents a folder, for example, both the folder and the contents of that folder are duplicated.

Holding down the Option key while dragging an icon is the same as selecting the icon and choosing the Duplicate command. The Option-drag method is simply a shortcut for the Duplicate command.

Deleting an Icon

Deleting an icon requires the use of the Trash icon. As you drag the icon to the Trash, an outline of the icon follows the mouse. When the icon to be deleted is in the proper position, the Trash icon darkens (see fig. 2.7).

Fig. 2.7

Deleting the Schedule icon.

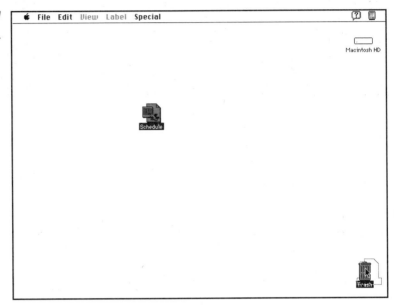

Releasing the mouse button drops the icon into the Trash, but does *not* delete the icon. Instead, the icon remains in the Trash just as a wadded piece of paper sits in a trash can. To permanently delete the icon, you must empty the Trash using these steps:

1. From the Special menu, choose Empty Trash.

   A warning alert appears informing you of the number and size of the icons to be deleted and requesting confirmation of the command (see fig. 2.8).

2. Click the OK button or press Return.

This process empties the Trash and deletes all the icons inside. Note that you can abandon the Empty Trash command before any deletions take place by clicking the Cancel button rather than the OK button.

Fig. 2.8
Confirming the Empty
Trash command.

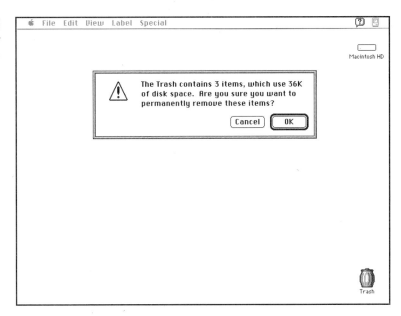

In System 7, the Trash is emptied only when the Empty Trash command is chosen. When the sides of the Trash icon begin to *bulge*, the Trash has items inside.

Unfortunately, items in the Trash continue to take up space on disk. If you do not empty the Trash regularly, you might run out of disk space because of the buildup of icons you thought you had deleted.

This arrangement also has a distinct advantage, however, in that you can recover icons from the Trash any time before you choose the Empty Trash command. Here's how:

1. Double-click the Trash icon to open it.

   The Trash window appears and displays the contents of the Trash (see fig. 2.9).

2. Drag the icon (or icons) out of the Trash window.

   Or

   Select the icon (or icons), and then choose Put Away from the File menu.

3. Click the close box of the Trash window.

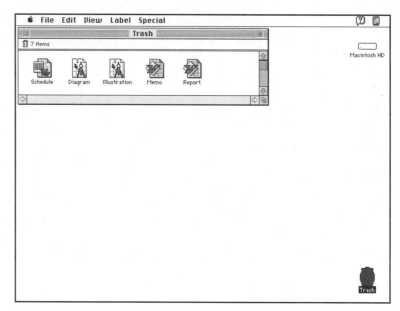

Fig. 2.9
Icons in the Trash.

Opening an Icon

Icons can be *opened* in three different ways. Two of these methods can be used with all icons; one applies only to icons that can be opened by application programs (an icon representing a word processing document, for example).

The first, and most common, method is to double-click the icon. This method works with any icon that can be opened. (Some icons—primarily those associated with System files—cannot be opened at all; you will receive an alert to this effect if you try to open such an icon.)

The second method is to select the icon, and then choose the Open command from the File menu. This method is rarely used because double-clicking is much easier.

The third method, which is new in System 7, applies only to icons that can be opened by applications. To use this *drag and drop* method, follow these steps:

1. Drag the icon onto the application program's icon.

    If the application program is capable of opening the icon, the application program icon darkens (see fig. 2.10).

2. Release the mouse button and the icon opens.

Note that opening an icon can have slightly different meanings depending on what the icon represents. When an icon representing a disk, folder, or the Trash is opened, a window opens to display its contents.

A window also opens when you open an icon that represents a document of some kind (a spreadsheet, word processing document, and so on). But in this second case, the application program that created the document must also be started (or launched) in order to open the icon and display its contents in the window.

The only case in which the contents of an icon are not displayed when the icon is opened is when you open the icon of an application (word processor, spreadsheet program, database program, and so on). This step launches the application rather than displaying its contents. In other words, opening an application program's icon is how you start an application program.

Fig. 2.10
Opening the icon Report
with WriteNow 3.0.

Getting Information about an Icon

You can obtain information about an icon (and thus the item that it represents) by using the Get Info command on the File menu of the Finder. Simply select the icon (or icons) about which you want to obtain information; then choose the command. An *Info window* appears for each selected icon.

Info windows for folders and disks are slightly different from those for files (see fig. 2.11).

Fig. 2.11
Info windows about the
Applications folder and the
Macintosh HD disk.

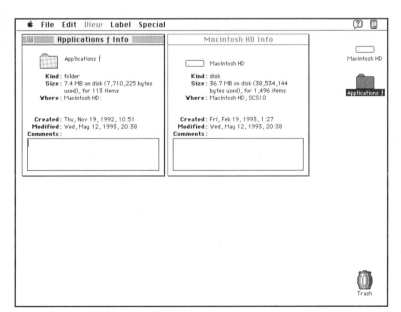

The Info window for an icon includes the following information:

Name
: The name of the icon appears to the right of the icon in the window.

Kind
: The icon's kind (folder, disk, application program, document).

Size
: The size of the file, folder, or disk the icon represents appears in MB (megabytes) for large items and K (kilobytes) for smaller items. The exact number of bytes is also displayed. The Info windows for folders and disks also display the number of items stored.

Where
: The location of the item. The name of the disk on which the icon resides is displayed followed by any folders that contain the icon.

Created
: The date the icon was created. For a file or folder icon, this is the date the file or folder was created. For an application program icon, this is the date the manufacturer prepared the application for distribution. For a disk icon, this is the date the disk was formatted and prepared for use.

Modified
: The date of the last change to the item the icon represents.

Version
: For application program and file icons, this is the manufacturer's version number. This information can be helpful if you need assistance from the manufacturer's technical support line. Document icons display this line of information with an *n/a* entered, because these documents don't have a version number.

Comments
: This window enables you to type comments about the icon and store them for later reference. Note that this field isn't terribly useful because any comments you enter are lost when you rebuild the Desktop, a maintenance procedure you should do often (see Chapter 32, "Maintenance and Troubleshooting," for more on rebuilding the Desktop).

You can prevent changes to application files (or other files) by using the Locked check box associated with their icons (see "Locking and Unlocking Icons" in this chapter). Document icons have a Stationery Pad check box that enables you to create templates of documents (see Chapter 4, "Managing Files," for more on stationery pads). Alias icons display a button enabling you to locate the original icon to which they point (see "Creating and Using Aliases" in this chapter).

To close an Info window, click its close box.

Locking and Unlocking Icons

Locking an icon prevents changes to (or deletion of) the file(s) that the icon represents. If you have worked hard to create a large, important spreadsheet, for example, you can lock its associated icon to prevent your valuable file from being accidentally deleted.

To lock an icon, follow these steps:

1. Select the icon by clicking it.

2. From the Finder's File menu, choose Get Info.

3. Click the check box to the left of the Locked option in the Info window that appears.

4. Click the close box of the Info window.

Now your icon is locked. If you place a locked icon in the Trash and then attempt to empty it, you receive a warning alert like the one shown in figure 2.12.

Fig. 2.12
A locked icon is in the Trash.

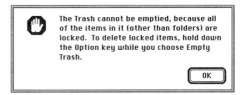

> The Trash cannot be emptied, because all of the items in it (other than folders) are locked. To delete locked items, hold down the Option key while you choose Empty Trash.
>
> OK

Note that a locked icon in the Trash *can* be deleted if you hold down the Option key when you choose the Empty Trash command. In either case, think twice before deleting a locked file.

After locking the icon for a document, that document cannot be changed by an application program. You can open it, view its contents, and even change its contents on-screen, but you cannot replace the original document with the altered document on disk. When you attempt to save such changes, you must create and name a second document. The document with the locked icon remains unchanged.

By locking the icon of an application program, you may reduce the chances of virus infection. However, many application programs change themselves in order to store user preferences and other important information in their own files. If programs that work this way are locked, they may not operate properly.

To unlock an icon, use the same steps you used to lock it. When you click the check box a second time, the X is removed and the lock option is deactivated.

Creating and Using Aliases

An *alias* is an icon that represents and provides access to another icon. Aliases act as *pointers*, serving solely to inform the Mac of the location of the original icon. Like the primary icons that already have been discussed, an alias can be used to access the contents of a particular file, folder, or disk. You can place an alias in any location on any disk; when you want to open the item, just double-click the alias.

With aliases, you can keep multiple copies of important files without wasting disk space. Because each alias only uses about 1KB of disk space, you can create virtually as many aliases as you wish and place them in strategic locations to give you handy access to important items.

If you are working on a project that involves large numbers of word processing documents stored in different folders, for example, you could place an alias of your word processor application in each folder containing project documents. This technique provides quick access to the word processor by making it unnecessary for you to open the folder in which the application resides. Chapter 4, "Managing Files," explores some of the ways in which aliases can help you organize documents and other files.

Aliases are easy to create. As figure 2.13 shows, an alias looks exactly like the original icon except for its italicized name. To create an alias, follow these steps:

1. Select the icon for which you want to create an alias.

2. From the File menu, choose Make Alias. The alias appears.

Fig. 2.13
Examples of alias icons.

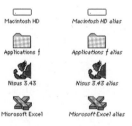

You can make an alias of an alias, but why bother? This method creates a *chain* of aliases in which each alias depends on the previous alias. If you delete an alias from which another alias was created, the later alias will be unable to locate the original icon. To keep things tidy, only create aliases from original icons.

Note that a *duplicate* of an alias (created with the Duplicate command) points to the original icon. Hence, making a duplicate of an alias is the same as using the Make Alias command on the original icon.

Although alias creation is a useful feature of System 7, you still need to know where the original icon of the file, folder, or disk is stored. To find out, select the alias; then choose Get Info from the File menu. When you click the Find Original button in the Get Info box, your Mac takes you to the location of the original icon (see the section "Getting Information about an Icon" in this chapter for more on the Get Info command).

You should also note that the Info window of the alias has an Original information line that tells you the name of the disk and folders in which the original icon resides.

Aliases behave exactly as the original except for these key differences:

■ An alias can be deleted without affecting the original icon.

■ An alias can be renamed without affecting the original icon.

■ An alias can be moved and copied without affecting the original icon.

You can, for example, make an alias of your hard disk and place it in any location you find convenient. Double-clicking the alias opens the hard disk window. Dragging an icon to the alias of the hard disk copies that icon to the hard disk. But throwing the alias in the Trash and deleting it *does not* affect your hard disk in any way.

After making an alias of an icon, don't move or delete the *original* icon from the disk on which it was located when you created the alias. Otherwise, the alias will not be able to locate the original icon and an error message will appear when you click the alias (see fig. 2.14).

Fig. 2.14
The original icon
cannot be found.

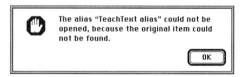

The alias "TeachText alias" could not be opened, because the original item could not be found.

OK

You may move the original to a different location on the same disk where it resided when its aliases were made. You may also change the name of the original to your heart's content. But if you remove the original icon from the disk—even if you store the icon on another disk in your Macintosh—you must create new aliases for the icon.

Understanding Multitasking

One of the most useful and powerful features of the Mac is its capability to run more than one program at a time. This capability is called *multitasking*.

Macintosh multitasking arrived with the MultiFinder, which became a standard part of the System Software with the release of System 6 (though it was introduced prior to that release). MultiFinder enhanced the Finder and provided a means for starting as many application programs as available memory could support.

MultiFinder also made it possible to access the Desktop at any time without quitting a running application. With it, you can switch freely between running applications (and desk accessories) and even use the Cut, Copy, and Paste commands to move information from one application to another.

Instead of using two Finders like System 6, System 7 incorporates multitasking fully. It also adds a number of multitasking features that were not available in the days of MultiFinder.

The only problem you might encounter when using these features is the amount of memory you need. Obviously, if you attempt to run more than one application at a time, you use more memory.

You need about 4MB of memory to take advantage of the power of multitasking. But my suggestion is to upgrade your Mac to around 8MB or even 12MB of memory (assuming it can be upgraded). Memory upgrades are relatively inexpensive and you can never have too much memory.

Refer to Chapter 26, "Expanding the Macintosh," for more on memory upgrades. Also see Chapter 5, "Configuring the Macintosh," for information concerning 32-bit addressing; this option affects your Macintosh's ability to utilize memory.

Starting Applications

To start an application, you must open that application's icon. The section "Opening an Icon," earlier in this chapter, introduced you to the three methods of opening icons. With the Mac's multitasking capability, you can use any of these methods to start an application at any time so long as you have enough available memory. It doesn't matter how many applications are currently running.

Usually you need to switch to the Finder application in order to start an application program (see the next section "Switching Applications," for details), but a shortcut is available. You can put your most-used applications, documents, and aliases in the Apple menu; by doing so you make them available regardless of which application you are currently using. Chapter 6, "Customizing the Macintosh," covers the techniques for using application programs and documents in the Apple menu.

If you get enough applications running at once, you might run low on memory. If this condition occurs when you attempt to start an application, you receive a warning alert (see fig. 2.15).

Fig. 2.15
Not enough memory to
run an application.

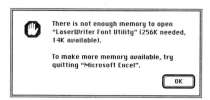

The alert helpfully tells you the amount of memory needed to launch the desired application program and the amount available. As the figure shows, a suggestion of an application program that can be quit to free up memory might also be offered. Your only recourse when you receive this alert is to click the OK button, and then close open windows or quit application programs to free up memory.

In some cases, the Mac offers to free up memory for you by quitting an application that is apparently not in use (as indicated by its lack of open windows). If this occurs, an alert like the one in figure 2.16 appears.

In the example given in the figure, the Mac has determined that the application program Microsoft Excel is not being used currently (it has no open windows). Quitting this application would free up enough memory to enable the chosen application program to start.

When presented with such an option, you can click the Quit Application button (or press Return) to permit the suggested action to occur. Alternatively, click Cancel to dismiss the alert and choose another application program you want to quit.

Refer to the section "Adjusting Memory Use," later in this chapter, for information about monitoring memory usage.

Fig. 2.16
The Macintosh offers to
quit an application to free
up memory.

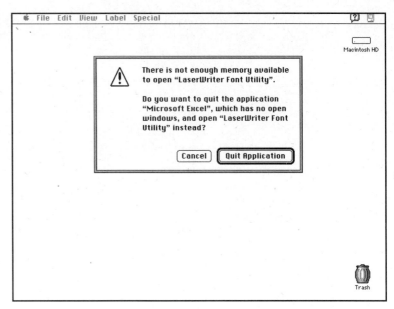

Switching Applications

After starting the desired applications, you can switch freely from one to another. The application program (including the Finder itself) that is active is considered to be in the *foreground*. Other applications are in the *background*. Only one application program may be in the foreground at any time.

The background applications, however, can still perform work. Depending on the way they were designed, some applications can work in the background while you work with another application in the foreground. Check the manual of the application program to determine whether this feature is available to you.

To *switch* to another application and thus make it the foreground application, choose its name from the Application menu at the right side of the menu bar. This menu is represented on-screen by the icon of the current foreground application. It appears initially as a small Macintosh (indicating that the Finder is the foreground application), and then changes appropriately whenever you switch applications.

The Application menu lists the applications you are running. The foreground application has a check mark to the left of its name. To switch to another application simply choose the name of the application program from the menu (see fig. 2.17).

Fig. 2.17
The Application menu lets
you switch to another
application.

When you switch applications, the menu bar displays the new application's commands and any windows belonging to the selected application are brought forward on-screen.

If the windows representing different applications overlap (see fig. 2.18), try an alternative method for switching from one application to another. Simply click a window behind the current window and the application to which it belongs becomes the foreground application. You can also bring the Finder to the foreground by clicking the Desktop or any icon on the Desktop.

You can also use the following methods to bring an application to the foreground:

- Double-click the application program's icon.

- Drag a document to the application program's icon (the *drag and drop* method of opening a document).

- Choose the application from the Apple menu (if it is installed in that menu).

Fig. 2.18
The windows of running
applications can overlap.

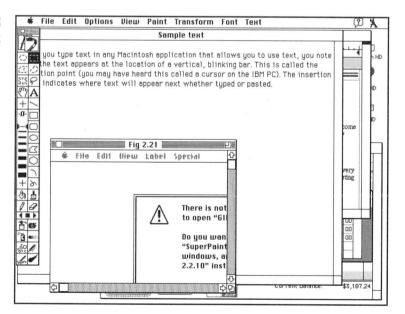

Copying between Applications

Thanks to Macintosh multitasking, you can copy information from one running application to another easily. You might want to transfer the information in a spreadsheet, for example, to a letter you are writing in your word processor.

To copy information between running application programs, use the Clipboard. (See the section "Understanding the Clipboard" in Chapter 1 for more details concerning the Clipboard.) Here's how:

1. Open the document to which you want to copy information (the *destination document*).

2. Select the information you want to copy.

3. From the Edit menu, choose Copy. Alternatively, press ⌘-C or the F3 key.

4. Open the document from which you want to copy information (the *source document*).

5. From the Application menu, choose the name of the destination document's application program. The document appears as the application program becomes active.

6. Place the insertion point in the location at which you want the information to appear.

7. From the Edit menu, choose Paste. Alternatively, press ⌘-V or the F4 key.

When you have completed these steps, the information appears in the destination document. If you want to move information from one document to another instead of copying it, simply replace the Copy command with the Cut command in step 4.

Note that System 7 offers an alternative way for documents to share information. See Chapter 28, "Networking," for information on the Publish and Subscribe feature of System 7.

Hiding Application Windows

When a number of applications are running, the screen can become filled with windows. This condition has come to be known as *screen clutter*. Fortunately the Application menu provides commands that help alleviate such clutter (see fig. 2.19).

Fig. 2.19
The Application menu
offers ways to avoid
screen clutter.

The menu contains the following commands:

Hide [*foreground application*]. This command always includes the name of the foreground application program. Choosing it hides the windows of the foreground application and switches to the next visible application.

Hide Others. This command (the one highlighted in figure 2.19) hides the windows of all applications other than the foreground application. When you use this command, the first Hide command becomes unavailable because no other applications are visible.

Show All. This command makes the windows of all running applications visible again.

If you choose another application from the Application menu after using the Hide Others command, the windows of the previous foreground application remain on-screen. To avoid this screen clutter, hold down the Option key when switching applications. This step hides the windows of the previous foreground application when you switch to another application.

Quitting Applications

You can always quit the foreground application by choosing Quit from the File menu (or using the shortcut ⌘-Q, which is available in most cases). But you can also quit all applications at once when you are finished working with your Macintosh without having to choose the Quit command in each one.

Use the following steps to quit all applications at once:

1. From the Application menu, choose the Finder. Alternatively, click the Desktop.

2. Choose the Shut Down command.

These steps cause the Mac to quit all applications and then shut down. If you have not saved your work to disk, the applications prompt you to do so. If you like, you can substitute the Restart command in step 2. This action quits all applications and then restarts the Mac.

Adjusting Memory Use

You might need to check your memory usage from time to time. For example, you might want to determine whether you have enough available memory to run an application. To determine your current memory usage, choose the Finder from the Application menu, and then choose the About This Macintosh command from the Apple menu. The About This Macintosh window appears (see fig. 2.20).

Fig. 2.20
The About This Macintosh
window.

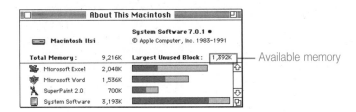

The About This Macintosh window shows a listing of each running application and the amount of memory used by each application. The window also shows the System Software's memory use. The amount of available memory appears as the Largest Unused Block. This number determines the size of the application that you can launch.

The amount of memory allocated to each application appears by a bar to the right of that application's name. The shaded portion of the bar represents the amount of memory being used by the application. Application programs work best when they use no more than about three quarters of their allocated memory to run. This provides them with extra memory that can be used when opening documents and performing various necessary functions in executing commands. If a very large percentage of the memory use bar is shaded, you might want to increase the amount of memory allocated to the application.

To determine and/or alter the amount of memory an application uses when running, use these steps:

1. Quit the application if it is running.

2. Select the application program by clicking the application's icon.

3. From the File menu, choose Get Info.

The Info window opens (see fig. 2.21).

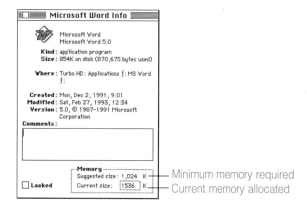

Fig. 2.21
The memory requirements
for Microsoft Word.

The Current size field in the Memory section of the Info window
indicates the amount of memory that the chosen application uses when
running. In the figure, for example, this field indicates current memory
usage by Microsoft Word.

To increase an application program's memory partition, double-click the
Current size field in the Info window, type a larger memory amount, and
then close the Info window by clicking its close box. Try adding memory
in 32KB increments, running the application after each increment until
the memory usage looks good.

To free up memory in order to make space for new applications, you can
take one or more of the following actions:

- Close open windows.

- Quit one or more application programs.

- Reduce the memory use of one or more applications.

- Reduce the size of the disk cache.

- Use virtual memory. (Not all Macintosh models provide this
  option.)

- Install more physical memory.

If you decide to quit applications to free up memory, choosing the
About This Macintosh command from the Apple menu provides helpful
information about the amount of memory application programs are
using. This information enables you to determine which applications
would free up enough memory for you to start the new program.

Generally, don't reduce application memory unless you have previously increased memory for that application. To change the application's memory partition size, double-click the Current size field in the Info window, type a smaller memory amount, and then close the Info window by clicking its close box. Do not reduce the partition size of the application program below the value shown in the Suggested size field.

Setting the Disk cache is covered in Chapter 5, "Configuring the Macintosh"; installing more memory is covered in Chapter 26, "Expanding the Macintosh." Note that the 32-bit addressing setting can also affect the amount of memory you have available. See Chapter 5 for more information concerning this option.

Using Background Copying

System 7 adds the useful feature of *background copying* to its multitasking capabilities. With this feature, you can work in open applications while copying icons in the background.

To use background icon copying, follow these steps:

1. Launch the applications in which you want to work.

2. Switch to the Finder.

3. Drag the icons to copy to the target destination.

4. From the Application menu, choose the name of the desired application.

Note that you cannot use the double-click or drag-and-drop methods to start applications while icons are copying. Copying icons keeps the Finder busy and unavailable for launching applications.

You can work with any application other than the Finder while copying icons. You might notice a slight slowing in the speed at which an application program runs because the Macintosh is occupied with the copy process.

Note that you can also work in an application during a long emptying of the Trash (perhaps you are cleaning off a large number of icons from a disk and it is taking too much time). Whether you are copying icons or emptying the Trash, you can choose another application from the Application menu and keep working.

Using the Apple Menu

In the System Software versions prior to System 7, the Apple menu could only contain *desk accessories*—mini-applications meant to complement running application programs. System 7 permits you to install any icon you like in the Apple menu and then access that icon by choosing it from the menu.

Apple still ships the desk accessories that have been part of the Apple menu for many years now. This chapter provides more information about these useful mini-applications.

Chapter 6, "Customizing the Macintosh," covers the process of installing other items in the Apple menu.

Working with Supplied Applications

Before multitasking, Macintosh users were confronted with some significant problems. For example, if you were working with a word processor and discovered that you needed to use a calculator application, you would have to quit the word processor before you started the calculator. What a pain.

Apple solved some of this difficulty by creating the *desk accessory*. Desk accessories are small, dedicated applications that can be invoked even if another application was running. They appear on the Apple menu and are always available.

Now that multitasking has come to the Macintosh, however, there is less need for desk accessories. With the advent of System 7, the desk accessory *per se* has been abolished. All application software is treated the same, none has to be installed in special ways (as desk accessories once did), and the Apple menu can host any number of items.

Small, dedicated applications still exist, however, because many of them are just too useful to give up. And how much space can a calculator program really require, anyway?

The term *desk accessory* is still used, but for System 7 users, a desk accessory is simply a mini-application.

Choosing Apple Menu Items

Any item listed on the Apple menu can be accessed by dragging down with the mouse until the desired item is highlighted (just as you choose commands from other menus). When you release the mouse button, the chosen item (application, folder, document, or what have you) opens and appears on-screen.

Considering the Supplied Applications

Apple supplies the following desk accessories: Alarm Clock, Calculator, Chooser, Key Caps, Note Pad, Puzzle, and Scrapbook. This set of accessories is essentially unchanged since the introduction of the Macintosh in 1984 except for the removal of the Control Panel (which is now a folder rather than a desk accessory).

In fact, with the exception of the Puzzle, the desk accessories provided by Apple have remained essentially unchanged since the Macintosh was released. This fact has puzzled some Macintosh users.

Of course, these days you are not limited to the applications supplied by Apple. Many other small, dedicated applications exist that perform a number of useful functions. The supplied applications from Apple are merely a good starting point from which you can proceed.

The following sections offer brief descriptions of the supplied applications and what they do.

Alarm Clock

When you choose Alarm Clock from the Apple menu, a clock appears on-screen. Click the small lever to the right in the Alarm Clock window to display the Alarm Clock's settings (see fig. 2.22).

Fig. 2.22
The Alarm Clock.

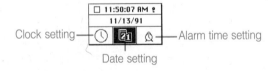

As figure 2.22 shows, the Alarm Clock displays the time (as set by your Macintosh System clock; see Chapter 5, "Configuring the Macintosh," for details) in the top panel and the date in the middle panel.

The three icons in the bottom panel represent buttons that let you set the time, date, and alarm time.

To reset any of the Alarm Clock information, follow these steps:

1. Click the appropriate button. To reset the time, for example, click the clock button at the left of the lower panel.

2. In the middle or upper panel, click the part of the time, date, or alarm setting that you want to change. When you do this, a small set of arrows appears to the right of the current setting.

3. Click the up-arrow key to advance the part of the time, date, or alarm setting you want to change. Click the down-arrow key to move the setting back. Or click the value you want to change (such as the *11* in *11:50:07 AM*), and then type the new number (such as **12**) to reset the time.

   Note that if you set the alarm time, you also need to click the small switch to the left of the alarm time to turn on the alarm. The switch is up when the alarm is on and down when it is off.

4. Click the close box to save the new settings.

You can also move the Alarm Clock to a new location by dragging the top panel of the Alarm Clock window.

When the Alarm Clock is active, you can copy and paste the time or date to another application. Just select the appropriate information in the lower panel, and then choose the Copy command from the Edit menu.

When the alarm time arrives, your Mac beeps and the Apple of the Apple menu flashes. If your Macintosh is not turned on when the alarm time arrives, you get the beep and flashing Apple when you turn on the computer.

Many new users are confused when their Apple flashes when they first start the Macintosh. Over the nine years of the Mac's life, this must have been the most commonly asked question: "Why is my Apple flashing?"

The answer is that the alarm was set—for whatever reason—before the Mac was shipped. Because the Macintosh's internal clock is battery-powered, the alarm clock has patiently been trying to tell someone that the alarm has gone off since the Mac was placed in a box at the factory.

To stop the flashing, simply choose the Alarm Clock from the Apple menu, and then click the close box. You might also want to turn off the alarm altogether before closing the Alarm Clock; otherwise it will inevitably go off again.

Calculator

Suppose you are in the middle of an application, and you need to make a quick calculation. You could get the result you need with a formula in a spreadsheet program, but it would be much faster and simpler to use the Calculator (see fig. 2.23).

Fig. 2.23

The Calculator.

The Calculator works much like a hand-held calculator. You select the appropriate numeric keys by clicking them with the mouse or entering the values from the keyboard (using the numeric keypad is easiest). If you use the keyboard, you must press the equal sign (=) or Enter, not the Return key, to get the final answer.

To multiply 56 by 43, for example, use the following steps:

1. Enter the value **56**.

2. Enter the operator *.

3. Enter the value **43**.

4. Click the equal sign (**=**), press the equal sign on the keyboard, or press the Enter key.

Calculator performs the calculation and displays the answer.

One of the best things about Calculator is that you can cut and paste the result of the calculation into your current document. To do so, choose the Cut or Copy command from the File menu to place the values in the Calculator window in the Clipboard. You can then select any document, click to place the insertion point, and choose the Paste command to insert the calculated value at the location of the insertion point.

Chooser

The Chooser is extremely important because it enables you to choose the type of printer you are going to use (see figure 2.24).

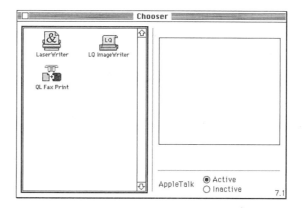

Fig. 2.24
The Chooser window.

After you select Chooser from the Apple menu, you need to indicate which type of printer you are using. You see the icons of available printers displayed in the left list box of the Chooser window.

The Chooser also enables you to activate the AppleTalk networking system, to select file servers, and to choose AppleTalk zones in a network (see Chapter 28, "Using Networking").

You need to use the Chooser at these times:

- When you use a printer for the first time.

- When you change from one printer to another (from a dot-matrix printer to a laser printer, for example).

- When you change the port to which the printer is connected.

- When you want to select a device (such as a modem) in a different AppleTalk zone.

The Chooser is covered in greater depth in Chapter 7, "Printing," and Chapter 28, "Networking."

Key Caps

One reason the Macintosh has become so popular is the ease with which you can change fonts. (A *font* is a set of characters of a particular design; see Chapter 8, "Using Fonts," for more information.) Key Caps provides a preview of the fonts that are part of the System file. The Key Caps on-screen keyboard then shows you how each character in the font appears. If you select the *Chicago* font, for example, the characters on the keyboard represent the way the Chicago font appears in a Macintosh document.

Key Caps enables you to view the font's special characters. To see the special characters, choose Key Caps from the Apple menu. Press the Option key; press the Option-Shift key combination to see another set of special characters. The keyboard of special characters shown in figure 2.25 is the result of pressing the Option key when displaying the Palatino font.

Fig. 2.25

Special characters shown in the Key Caps window.

As you enter characters (using the mouse or the keyboard), they appear at the top of the Key Caps window so that you can view combinations. You can copy text from Key Caps to the Clipboard and then paste it into documents. Chapter 1, "Getting Started," discusses how Key Caps can help you generate special characters.

Note Pad

The Note Pad is intended to enable you to jot down notes for later reference (see fig. 2.26). To use the Note Pad, follow these steps:

Fig. 2.26

The Note Pad.

1. From the Apple menu, choose Note Pad.

2. Type any text you want.

3. When you're finished, close the Note Pad.

The contents are saved automatically; the next time you select the Note Pad, the contents you entered appear again. The Note Pad holds up to eight pages of text. You can page through the pad by clicking the turned-up corner of the page in the lower left corner of the window. One click turns one page.

Puzzle

The Puzzle is an imitation of the small, plastic tile puzzles you have probably already seen. You simply rearrange the tiles to make a picture. In this case, the picture is (what else?) the Apple logo from Apple Computer.

Actually, you can use any graphic in the puzzle. Here's how to insert a new graphic:

1. Open the application that you used to create the graphic.

2. Select the graphic.

3. Copy the graphic using the Copy command on the File menu.

4. Open the Puzzle.

5. From the Edit menu, choose Paste.

The graphic is pasted onto the puzzle. If you prefer a more traditional puzzle, choose the Clear command from the Edit menu and you see numbers on the tiles. To restore the graphic, choose the Clear command again.

One thing I'm *not* going to tell you about is the sound that you hear when you solve the puzzle. That's something you must find out for yourself.

Scrapbook

Let's say you're working on a job that uses the same text or graphic, such as a company logo, in more than one document. You might be working in one application (perhaps in Microsoft Word or WriteNow) or in several different applications (such as the Excel spreadsheet and the PageMaker page-layout program). The simplest way to use the same information multiple times is to store it in the *Scrapbook*, which works like a permanent Clipboard.

The Scrapbook, a file maintained in the System Folder and accessed from the Apple menu, enables you to collect graphic images, text, or sounds to be used at a later time. Unlike the Clipboard, the Scrapbook stores items permanently. When your Macintosh is turned off, the information in the Clipboard disappears, but information in the Scrapbook is retained.

Figure 2.27, for example, shows one of the seven graphics screens in the Scrapbook shipped with the Macintosh at the time of this writing (the contents of your Scrapbook may vary). You can scroll through the Scrapbook as you scroll through any other window. Drag the horizontal scroll box to the left or the right to browse through the Scrapbook entries, or click one of the scroll arrows to move quickly to the preceding or following entry.

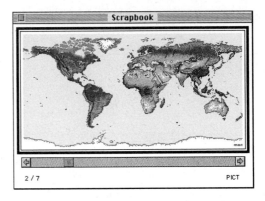

Fig. 2.27

The Scrapbook window.

The graphics, text, or sounds that you copy or cut and paste into the Scrapbook are stored prior to the entry displayed in the Scrapbook window when you use the Paste command.

To add an entry to the Scrapbook, follow these steps:

1. Open the application containing the picture, text, or sound that you want to store in the Scrapbook.

2. Select the item you want.

3. From the Edit menu, choose Copy. Alternatively, choose Cut.

4. From the Apple menu, choose Scrapbook. The Scrapbook window appears.

5. Scroll to the location desired if you don't want it first in the Scrapbook.

6. From the Edit menu, choose Paste.

To use an item from the Scrapbook, follow these steps:

1. From the Apple menu, choose Scrapbook.

2. Click the scroll arrows or the gray scroll area to scroll to the item you want.

3. From the Edit menu, choose Copy.

4. Open the application or document into which you want to insert the item from the Scrapbook; position the insertion point where you want to insert the item.

5. From the Edit menu, choose Paste. The object appears in your document.

To remove text or graphics from the Scrapbook, follow these steps:

1. From the Apple menu, choose Scrapbook.

2. Click the scroll arrows to scroll to the item to be removed.

3. From the Edit menu, choose Clear.

Acquiring System Information

You have seen how the About this Macintosh command in the Apple menu can help you determine memory usage. The command also provides other System-related information that can come in handy when you are talking to a technical support representative.

Figure 2.28 highlights some of this useful information.

Fig. 2.28
The About This Macintosh Window.

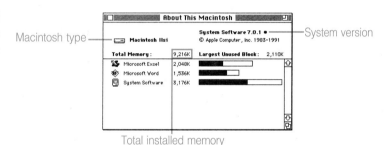

As you can see, the window displays the type of Macintosh you are using, the System Software version your machine is currently running, and the total amount of installed memory.

One interesting bit of information you can obtain in this window is the exact amount of memory being used by an application (of the memory allocated to the application in the Info window—see "Adjusting Memory Use" in this chapter for details). To get this information, follow these steps:

1. From the Apple menu, choose About this Macintosh.

2. From the Help menu, choose Show Balloons.
   (The next section covers Balloon Help.)

3. Point at the memory use bar to the right of the application program's name in the About This Macintosh window.

A balloon appears that lists the amount of allocated memory being used by the application (see fig. 2.29).

Fig. 2.29
The amount of allocated memory used by Microsoft Word.

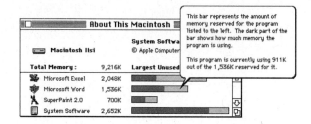

4. Point at the memory use bar of other application programs, as desired.

5. From the Help menu, choose Hide Balloons to stop displaying the balloons.

Acquiring Help

Sometimes you might need assistance as you work with your Macintosh. Fortunately, Apple added a built-in help feature to System 7 that can help you learn about the various parts of the Macintosh interface. This feature, called *Balloon Help*, is available at all times.

Using Balloon Help

To use Balloon Help, follow these steps:

1. Place the mouse pointer on the question mark balloon in the upper right corner of the Desktop.

2. From the Help menu, choose Show Balloons (see fig. 2.30).

Fig. 2.30
The Show Balloons command.

When Balloon Help is turned on, relevant help messages appear wherever you place the cursor. (You don't even have to click the mouse!) You can point at any item on the Desktop and a brief explanation of that item appears on-screen. Or you can drag through a menu (slowly, to give the balloons time to appear) and see explanations of the menu choices (see fig. 2.31).

Fig. 2.31

Help for the Make Alias command.

Most applications designed for use with System 7 take advantage of Balloon Help.

To stop the balloons from appearing all over your Desktop, choose Hide Balloons from the Help menu.

Displaying Finder Shortcuts

Initially, you might have trouble remembering the many shortcuts offered by the Finder. Fortunately, you have a ready reference to them at all times. Simply choose Finder Shortcuts from the Help menu to view five pages of shortcuts (see fig. 2.32).

Fig. 2.32

Finder shortcuts displayed on-screen.

You can flip through the pages by clicking the Next button. A Previous button appears when you are displaying pages 2 through 5. The Next button disappears when you reach the end of the pages.

Click the close box of the window to dismiss the shortcut display.

Obtaining Application Program Help

As application programs have been upgraded to work with System 7, software designers have taken advantage of the Help menu and Balloon Help features. In applications that are compatible with System 7, you can obtain help by choosing the *Application name* Help command from the Help menu (see fig. 2.33).

Fig. 2.33
The Microsoft Word Help command.

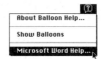

Chapter Summary

This chapter covers many of the basics of the Macintosh interface. You should now be comfortable with operating your Mac and be well on your way to making full use of the machine.

Here are some points to remember:

- System Software handles the most basic and necessary functions of a computer. Without System Software, the Macintosh could not perform useful work.

- The current System Software version, Version 7.1, indicates that this is the first feature enhancement of the seventh major revision of the System Software.

- The components of System Software reside in the System Folder. Only one System Folder should be present on any one disk.

- Icons represent other items such as files, folders, and disks.

- Multitasking enables you to run more than one application program at one time, provided you have sufficient memory.

- The Apple menu can contain any icon.

- Apple supplies several useful mini-applications, formerly called *desk accessories*, that appear on the Apple menu.

- The Help menu enables you to activate the Balloon Help feature of System 7 and to obtain help by pointing at any Desktop or menu item.

CHAPTER THREE

Managing Disks

W elcome to the world of
information management
and media: SCSI, floppy
disks, densities, hard drives,
access times, formatting,
tape backups, sectors,
tracks, and more. Probably
the most significant breakthrough computers have created in
information management is the
ability to save and share information without using paper.

This chapter discusses different types of storage media and focuses on floppy disks, hard disks, and optical storage devices such as *CD-ROM* (Compact Disc Read-Only Memory) and *WORM* (Write-Once, Read-Many). Discussions on managing the files on your disks and making backups are also included.

Reviewing Storage Devices

The simple floppy disk used to be all that was available for storing information. During the past ten years, however, some phenomenal developments in storage technology have occurred. Most of these developments are now available to the average user.

Table 3.1 lists the various storage media available to Macintosh users, the approximate capacity of each media, and the intended uses of each.

Table 3.1
Storage Devices, Capacity, and Uses

Device	Capacity	Use
Floppy disk	720KB-1.44MB	General purpose, backups, file transfer. Most application software comes on floppy disk.
Hard disk	20MB-1,000MB	Storage media of choice for most Macintosh users. Used to store System software, applications, documents, other files. Hard disks also come in a removable cartridge format that enables you to switch hard disks almost as easily as floppy disks.
Tape	100MB-5,000MB	Backup of hard disk drives, especially on networked systems.
WORM drives	128MB-600MB	Backup and archiving. WORM drives can be written to and read from, but not erased.
Magneto-optical	128MB-1,00MB	Rapidly replacing WORM drives, these drives can be erased and written to again. Good for network backups and archiving large amounts of data.

Device	Capacity	Use
CD-ROM drives	600MB	Access to large amounts of information; especially useful in multimedia work. CD-ROM drives can be read from but not written to or erased.
Floptical	21MB	Laser-guided floppy disk drives that enable you to store larger amounts of data on special 3.5-inch disks. Good for transporting large amounts of information or backing up larger hard disks.

Using Floppy Disks

The letters, reports, and computerized drawings you produce have to be stored somewhere. One of the most frequently used medium for Macintosh file storage is the floppy disk, a small circular cutout of plastic material (often Mylar) coated with a magnetic material such as iron oxide. With both floppy and hard disks, the electrical impulses (the information) generated by the read/write heads in your disk drives are stored as magnetic domains that can be recorded (written) or played back (read) by applying another magnetic field to generate current. In the fundamental language that computers use, your Macintosh sends these impulses as ones or zeros (high-current or low-current levels, respectively), using a binary (off/on) system of communications.

Although some floppy disks come in soft or flexible covers, the disk you use with your Macintosh is contained in a rigid case. The combination of convenient size (small enough to fit into a shirt pocket) and protective covering makes transporting your disks safe and easy. The capacity and the size of floppy disks the Macintosh uses also have changed. Initially, the 3.5-inch disk could be formatted for 400KB worth of information, then 800KB, and now 1.44MB (1,440KB) with the new SuperDrive (also called FDHD). The SuperDrive first appeared with the Macintosh SEs and is now the standard disk drive. By using the SuperDrive's capacity to read MS-DOS-formatted 360KB, 720KB, and 1.44MB disks, you immediately see the Mac's versatility.

Understanding Floppy Disk Structure

From the outside, you can see that a Macintosh floppy disk comes in a plastic case that has a protective metal door. A user shouldn't open this door or touch the material inside. When you insert the disk into the drive, the door opens, providing the read/write heads access to the disk. In the corner of the disk is a small cutout with a tab that enables you to *write protect* a disk.

When the write-protect tab is pushed back, leaving the hole open, the disk is locked, or protected. You can read the files on the disk, but you cannot write to the disk, save information, or alter the disk's contents. If you try to change its name, the cursor remains an arrow over the name and a lock appears in the disk window.

G et into the habit of locking your original application disks (the ones that came right out of the box) to avoid accidentally erasing or changing an important file. When the hole is closed, the disk can be modified.

Figure 3.1 shows an 800KB floppy disk. (The construction of the 1.44MB high-density disk is the same, but it has a square hole in the upper left—when you view the top of the disk—that indicates to the drive that the disk is a high-density disk.) On the inside, you find a circular disk made of essentially the same material as an audio cassette tape. A lining on the inside helps keep the disk free of contaminants that can destroy your data. As the disk turns (at about 300 revolutions per minute), the disk lining picks up small particles of dust and debris. If the disk is used excessively, these particles can build up and affect performance. Therefore, making more than one backup of files stored on your floppy disks is a good idea.

Understanding Floppy Disk Types

Many different sizes of floppy disks are available, but the disks you use with your Macintosh are 3.5 inches square and can hold either 800KB or 1.44MB of information. *KB* (for kilobyte) represents 1,024 bytes, or individual characters of information. *MB* (for megabyte) represents 1,024 kilobytes (1,048,576 bytes).

A double-spaced page containing 33 lines of text with 65 characters per line is about 2,145 bytes, or approximately 2KB. At this rate, a standard 800KB floppy disk can hold 400 pages of text. A 1.44MB (or 1,440KB) disk can hold about 800 pages of text.

Fig. 3.1
Diagram of a 3 1/2-inch
floppy disk.

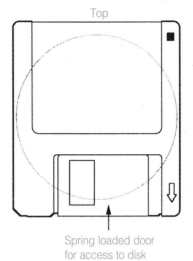

Top

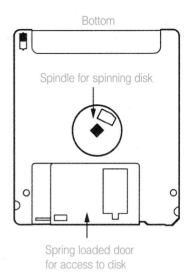

Bottom

Spindle for spinning disk

Spring loaded door
for access to disk

Spring loaded door
for access to disk

Because other information also must be recorded on a disk, an 800KB floppy disk actually holds only about 785KB. A 1.44MB disk ends up with just over 1.3MB of available storage space. The "lost" space is tied up in invisible files and formatting information necessary for the disk to store information.

The original Macintosh used single-sided disks and disk drives that were capable of storing only about 400KB per disk. Only one side of these disks was used, hence the term "single sided" (an odd name, really, since the disk media obviously had two sides; one simply went unused because of drive technology at the time).

With the introduction of the well-known and long-lived Macintosh Plus, Apple began using double-sided disks and drives capable of using both sides of the disk media. Therefore, the floppy disks stored twice as much information (800KB). Early models of the Macintosh II and Macintosh SE series used the newer drives and disks.

Since the later models of the Macintosh SE, Apple has been using the SuperDrive, which uses high-density floppy disks capable of storing more than a megabyte of information on each floppy disk.

All the Macintoshes from the Classic on up come equipped with these Floppy Drive High Density SuperDrives (FDHD). SuperDrives also can read from, write to, and format 400KB and 800KB disks.

You should be aware of two distinctive characteristics of high-density disks and drives. First, the disks are not manufactured in the same way as double-sided disks and, therefore, cannot be initialized in double-sided drives. (A later section discusses initializing.) Second, double-sided drives are packed with a plastic stabilizer that pops out when you turn on your Macintosh for the first time. This plastic stabilizer keeps the ceramic heads in the drive from being damaged while the computer is being transported. High-density drives don't come with this stabilizer and, to avoid damage, you shouldn't place a stabilizer in them.

Inserting and Ejecting Floppy Disks

Floppy disks can only be inserted in *one* way. Refer to figure 3.1. The top of the disk should be visible as you prepare to insert the disk into the drive. The edge of the disk with the metal shutter enters the drive first. You see the arrow on the disk indicating the direction of insertion. This arrow should be in the upper-left corner.

Note that floppy disks *do not* have two "sides," despite the name "double-sided." That is, you *cannot* turn a disk over and "play" the "other side." Inserting a disk with the spindle visible (that is, upside down) can damage your floppy disk drive (and potentially cost you a couple hundred dollars in repairs!). A disk that is inserted correctly will "glide" in. Never try to force a floppy disk into the drive.

When you insert a disk, a disk icon should appear on your Desktop. This occurs for disks that have been initialized; disks that have not been initialized cause a message to that effect to appear on the Macintosh screen. Responding to that message is covered later in the section "Initializing Floppy Disks."

A disk that is in your floppy disk drive can be ejected in one of three ways:

- *Drag the disk icon to the Trash icon.* This *does not* erase your disk. Instead, the disk is ejected from the disk drive. This is a case when the graphic "metaphors" of the Macintosh fail. Dragging something to the Trash normally means you are disposing of it. With a disk, you are simply ejecting (or more technically, *dismounting*) the disk.

- *Select the disk by clicking on its icon, then choose Put Away from the File menu* (or press ⌘-Y). This achieves the same effect as dragging the disk icon to the Trash icon.

■ *Press ⌘-Shift-1.* This ejects the disk in the internal disk drive. ⌘-Shift-2 ejects the disk in the first external drive (if you have one). ⌘-Shift-0 ejects the disk in the second external disk drive (if you have one). This method of ejecting disks has one drawback: A dimmed image of the disk icon remains on the Desktop and the Macintosh may later demand that the disk be returned to the disk drive. This method is best used for temporary removal of a disk. (Suppose, for example, that you insert a disk you want to store information on, and then find that the disk is write-protected; press ⌘-Shift-1, adjust the write-protect slider, then reinsert the disk.)

A fourth (and actually fifth and sixth) method exists, but is only to be used in cases of dire emergency. This method is covered in the next section.

Ejecting Jammed Disks

Once in a while, a floppy disk may become jammed in your disk drive and refuse to eject. This can occur because of a label peeling off and sticking slightly, a problem with the disk drive itself, or (as I experienced recently) a corrupted System file not recognizing that a disk is in the drive. (Few things, incidentally, are more frustrating than to *know* a disk is in the drive, but have your Macintosh refuse to acknowledge this fact.)

Try the following steps, in this order, when such a problem occurs:

1. Try the previously mentioned three methods at least once each.

2. From the Special menu, choose Restart. (The Restart command ejects *all* ejectable disks.)

3. If step 2 does not eject the disk, restart the Mac and press the mouse button as the Macintosh starts up. Holding down the mouse button as the Macintosh starts causes any disk in the internal drive to be ejected.

I f you cannot choose Restart, you may have a software problem. You can (and should try to) force the Macintosh to restart. Press ⌘-Option-Power On key to restart Macintosh IIs and Quadras; compact units and the LC Macintoshes have a Restart button on the left side (the front-most of the two buttons); PowerBooks have Restart buttons on the back of the computer.

Finally, if and *only* if all else fails, try step 4.

4. Turn off the Macintosh. Straighten a paper clip and insert the straight part *gently* into the small hole immediately to the right of the disk drive. Press *gently*, though firmly, with a steady motion. Do *not* force the disk if it refuses to move.

If all of these methods fail, check your warranty and call your dealer.

A n interesting side note to the paper clip trick is that in the earlier days of the Macintosh, when drives were less robust (to be fair, drives on all personal computers of the time were less than perfect), you rarely saw Macintosh users without a straightened paper clip on their desks. (At the time, these mutilated paper clips were termed *MacTool*.) I've used a Macintosh IIsi for the last year, and I've only had to resort to the "paper clip trick" once—because of a peeling disk label.

On the more serious side, you are inserting a piece of metal into a piece of electrical equipment—something we usually spend time insisting loudly that children not do. Proceed carefully. The paper clip should only go in about a quarter of an inch. If you find that your paper clip is going deeper than this, you are not hitting the right spot. And be sure that you insert the paper clip straight, not off to one side.

Initializing Floppy Disks

When you buy a floppy disk, it is blank and unreadable by the Macintosh (unless you purchase preformatted disks, which are more expensive). To help you understand what initializing a disk does, imagine that your blank disk is a parking lot with no painted stripes to mark parking spaces—this is how the disk appears to your Macintosh before you initialize (or format) the disk.

Suppose that cars are pieces of information; with no marked parking spaces, they may be able to park, but the result will be chaotic. After you complete the initialization process (paint parking spaces), the information (like the cars) has a place to park in an orderly, easily managed fashion. If the disk is new, the initialization process adds parking slots so that information can be recorded and stored. If the disk already has been used, initialization tows away the cars (erases any old information), erases the lines, and repaints the lot to ready it for more information.

Initialization is the first step you take to prepare a disk for storing information. If you insert an uninitialized disk into the Mac, you are prompted to initialize the disk.

CAUTION

Never initialize an application disk! If you do, you erase all information from the disk—including the program. In fact, the first thing you should do is write protect the original disks, make copies of the disks, and store the originals in a safe place.

Only initialize a disk under two conditions. First, you have to initialize a new disk so that it can accept data. When you place a new disk in one of your drives, you see a message asking whether you want to initialize the disk (see fig. 3.2). Note that the message of the figure may also read This disk is unreadable rather than This is not a Macintosh disk. Both messages mean the same thing: the Macintosh realizes that it cannot use the disk in its present state.

Fig. 3.2
Initializing a disk.

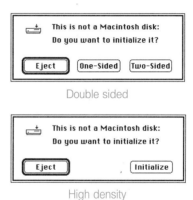

CAUTION

Should you see one of these messages when you insert a disk that you have used previously and that you know contains information, click the Eject button. Do *not* permit the Macintosh to initialize the disk. The disk is damaged in some way, but the information (or at least some of the information) may be recoverable, provided you do *not* initialize the disk.

Instead, turn to Chapter 32, "Maintenance and Troubleshooting," for tips on recovering failed disks.

When you initialize a double-sided disk, you are offered the option of initializing it as a one-sided or two-sided disk. The latter option is the one you will normally click. The former is included for compatibility with older Macs that use 400KB single-sided disks. (These disks are no longer common, so this option is rarely used.)

When you insert a high-density disk, the Mac recognizes that the disk is high density. Consequently, you are offered only one initialization option—the 1.44MB format.

Click the appropriate initialization option. The Mac warns you that the process of initialization erases all information on the disk. This isn't a problem if the disk is blank; click OK. Then you are prompted to name the disk; type a name that is up to 27 characters long; then click OK. (If you do not provide a name for the disk, the disk is named Untitled.) The disk is initialized and prepared for use.

The second condition under which you should initialize occurs when you have a used disk and no longer need the information on the disk, or when you want to destroy the data on the disk. In either case, you want to clean off the disk to make it "new" again. To initialize a previously used disk, follow these steps:

1. Insert the disk into the floppy disk drive.

2. On the Desktop, click the disk's icon to select it.

3. From the Special menu, choose Erase Disk.

   A dialog appears that asks whether you want to erase the disk.

4. If the disk is double sided, click One-sided or Two-sided. If the disk is high density, click Initialize.

   If you change your mind and want to abort the initialization process and retain the disk's information, click Cancel.

CAUTION

For reasons I cannot fathom, the Mac requires you to confirm the initialization of a blank disk, warning you that the information is erased in the process. On the other hand, it does *not* require confirmation when you initialize—and thus erase—a disk the Macintosh *knows* contains information.

In other words, once you click one of the initialization options of step 4, the Macintosh merrily erases the disk without further confirmation. In other words, use the Erase Disk command with caution.

Fortunately, a helpful icon appears in the dialogs. Refer to figure 3.2. You see an icon that shows a Macintosh with an arrow pointing to the floppy disk drive. This icon—which might look slightly different on your Mac—shows which drive the initialization will occur on. If you see an icon of your hard disk instead of the floppy drive, click Cancel!

When you initialize a disk, those "parking stripes" don't get put down just anywhere. A formatted disk is organized into *sectors* and *tracks*, as shown in figure 3.3. (The figure shows a simplified version of a double-sided disk.) Each sector is like a slice of pie, and the tracks divide the disk into concentric circles. Each sector contains the same amount of information, but some tracks contain more sectors than others. An initialized high-density disk contains twice as many tracks as a double-density disk and can hold twice as much information.

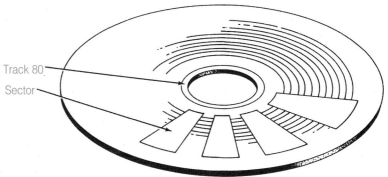

Fig. 3.3
A disk divided into sectors and tracks.

Track 80

Sector

When your Macintosh saves information on a floppy disk, it records the physical location at which the file is stored. The Mac System takes these addresses and constructs a directory of the file names (the Desktop file). This directory is an invisible file or collection of files that is created on each disk. The Desktop file stores on the disk the file addresses and associated icons. The Desktop file normally shows no icon and uses several tracks for storage. Each time you add information to a disk by saving a file, your Macintosh adds the name the file is saved under and its icon to the Desktop file.

When you select a file to work with, the Macintosh finds the file name in the Desktop file, notes the address, goes to that location on the disk, and reads the necessary information. When you erase the file, you don't actually erase anything more than the address or location of that file on the disk. The data in the file can be restored, as you learn in Chapter 32 "Maintenance and Troubleshooting."

Copying Disks

The process of copying disks is quite simple and it is one that you will need to do frequently as you install software, transfer documents, make backup copies, and do other work.

Copying a Floppy Disk to Another Floppy Disk

To copy all the information (files folder, and so on) from one disk to another is a relatively simple procedure, but it can get a bit tricky if you have only one floppy drive. Use these steps if you have only a single floppy drive:

1. Insert the *target disk*—the disk you want to copy the information *to*.

2. After the disk's icon appears, choose Eject from the Special menu or press ⌘-Shift-1 to eject the disk.

   This step removes the disk from the drive but leaves the icon—which is dimmed—on the Desktop.

3. Lock the *source disk*—the disk you want to copy information *from*.

   To lock the disk, turn the disk over and push the write-protect slider up so that you can see through the small, square hole. High-density disks have two square holes, but only one has a slider.

4. Insert the source disk into the disk drive.

5. Drag the icon of the source disk onto the dimmed icon of the target disk. When the icon of the target disk darkens, release the mouse button.

   You see a dialog asking you to confirm the copy process (see fig. 3.4).

Fig. 3.4

A prompt asking you to
confirm the disk copy.

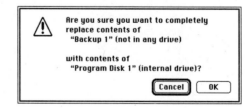

6. Click the OK button.

Now put on your dancing shoes and get ready to do what has come to be known as the *floppy disk shuttle*. The Macintosh immediately ejects the disk in the drive and demands the other disk. Then, as the copy proceeds, the Mac continues to periodically eject a disk and demand the other. This process continues until all the information from the source disk is copied to the target disk.

You can avoid some of the trouble of copying from disk to disk by using a *disk copy utility*. These are usually included in utility software bundles. For example, Norton Utilities for the Macintosh has a disk copy utility called Floppier that makes life a bit easier. (I use it myself being that I passionately hate the floppy disk shuffle.)

If you have two floppy drives, you can skip the rigmarole that single floppy drive users have to endure. Simply insert one disk into one drive and the other into the other drive. (Remember to lock the source disk so you do not inadvertently erase it.) Then drag the source disk's icon onto the target disk's icon. You see the confirmation dialog (refer to fig. 3.4). Click OK.

One important note: this process works if the two disks are of the same size (for example, two double-sided disks). If they are differing sizes, things are a touch different. First, the target disk *cannot* be smaller than the source disk. The Macintosh will simply inform you that you cannot perform the copy. Second, if the target disk is larger (say 1.44MB high density) and the source disk is smaller (an 800KB double density), use the procedure in the next section ("Copying a Floppy Disk to a Hard Disk").

Copying a Floppy Disk to a Hard Disk

Although many (if not most) application programs now come with installation programs (many using the Apple Installer), some still require you to copy the disks to your hard drive. Additionally, you might want to copy the entire contents of a data floppy disk to your hard disk in order that you can work with the data.

Copying a floppy disk to a hard disk is very simple. Drag the icon of the floppy disk onto the icon of the hard disk. When the hard disk icon darkens, release the mouse button. The floppy disk is copied to the hard disk and its data stored in a folder that has the same name as the floppy disk.

Alternatively, drag the floppy disk icon to an open window or a folder icon on the hard disk. This procedure creates a folder at the area you dragged to, and the folder contains all the information on the floppy disk. The folder has the same name as the floppy disk.

Locking and Unlocking Disks

One procedure I recommend you perform as soon as you get the shrink wrap off a new application program even before making a backup copy of the disks—is to turn the disks over and lock them.

You lock disks by pushing the write-protect slider upward so that you can see through the square hole. (Refer to figure 3.1 if you need to locate the write-protect slider; remember that high-density disks have two square holes, but only one of these holes has a slider.)

This procedure locks your disk, preventing it from being erased or changed. When you insert a locked disk into the floppy drive and double-click the disk icon, you see a Lock icon (see fig. 3.5).

Fig. 3.5

A locked disk displays a
Lock icon.

This Lock icon indicates that the disk cannot be erased, icons from it cannot be deleted, and other disks cannot be copied onto the disk. If you attempt to change the disk's contents, the Macintosh refuses and displays a message reminding you that you cannot alter a locked disk (see fig. 3.6).

Fig. 3.6

A message reminding you
that a locked disk cannot
be changed.

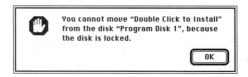

When you select a locked disk's icon, the Erase Disk command is dimmed and the Macintosh refuses to copy information onto the disk.

B esides locking program disks, be sure to lock important data disks. This guarantees that you won't accidentally overwrite the information on the disk.

But suppose that you need to change the contents of a locked disk? Simply push the write-protect slider back down so that the write-protect hole is closed. Then insert the disk into the floppy disk drive. Alternatively, if you discover that the disk you've just inserted is locked, press ⌘-Shift-1 to eject the disk, move the write-protect slider, and reinsert the disk. The disk is now unlocked, and you can change, delete, or copy over its contents.

Caring for Floppy Disks

Caring for your floppy disks properly is extremely important. Always follow these six commandments:

I. *Keep your disks away from all heat sources.* The plastic disk melts at a relatively low temperature—160° Fahrenheit. If your disk melts, no one can recover the data for you. Extreme cold also can damage your disks.

II. *Keep your disks away from magnetic fields such as refrigerator magnets or magnetic paper clip holders.* The x-rays emitted from screening machines at airports and other security checkpoints are not harmful, but metal detectors are deadly to your data because they have electromagnetic properties that erase your computer disks. Don't carry your disks through the metal detector.

Other sources of potential problems (believe it or not) are your TV, your telephone (but not your modem, because it doesn't ring), your printer, and even your Macintosh itself in certain cases. Each have magnetic elements strong enough to render your disk damaged (at best) or useless (at worst). Disks should not be placed on or too close to your printer or other computer equipment. The Macintosh contains a powerful power supply. Your internal hard drive and internal floppy drive(s) are protected from this source of magnetism, but if you place disks too close to the Macintosh's power supply (located close to where the power cord enters the machine), you can erase the disks over time. A distance of about a foot or two is usually sufficient.

III. *Store your back-up disks in a safe place.* Many users, especially those who use computers in their business activities, keep one backup disk on site and another at a different location. The likelihood that both will be destroyed is very low.

IV. *Keep the outside of the floppy disk case clean.* If removing a label leaves a glue residue, use lighter fluid or nail polish remover to clean the disk. But use these fluids carefully—liquids can seep into the inside of the disk and damage the media. Apply the liquid sparingly to a cloth, never on the casing of the disk.

V. *Keep your disks (and your other computer equipment, for that matter) away from food, coffee, and cigarette smoke.* The plastic material inside a floppy disk is very thin, and the read/write head must make contact with the disk to transfer or read data. Even a smoke particle 0.00025 of an inch thick can damage the disk or the read/write head. (It's actually very hypocritical of me to give out this advice, especially since I'm eating lunch as I write this. *But* be aware that you are taking risks by violating this rule and that one good spill could cost you hundreds of dollars in repairs.)

VI. *Keep your disks protected from dust by storing them in a closed container.* Disk containers are available from your dealer or favorite mail order company.

If you damage a disk or its rigid plastic holder—or spill liquids on the disk—it is *possible*, though not advisable, to transfer the media from one disk casing to another. To do so, pry open the disk case, remove the media, dry the media with a soft towel (keep you fingers off the media!), and then place the disk in a new disk casing. (Yes, an innocent disk must die for this trick to work.) Carefully seal the new casing with ever so tiny amounts of glue.

However, you do this at your own (and your floppy drive's) risk. In seven or so years of using the Macintosh professionally and personally, I've never encountered any data worth the risk of a several-hundred-dollar out-of-warranty repair to a floppy drive. (Your dealer's most likely response when you drag the damaged computer into the store will be, "You *%&# did *WHAT?*")

A far superior alternative for important data is to contact your dealer for data recovery services. Or check for such services in the ads in the back of major publications such as *MacUser* and *MacWorld*. These services do exist and specialize in recovering data from both floppy and hard disks that have died.

Using Hard Disks

If you don't have a hard disk already, you aren't being very kind to yourself. A hard disk allows you to store large amounts of information and access it at far greater speeds than possible with floppies. And hard disks are a relatively cheap addition to your Macintosh—an upgrade well worth the money.

When hard disks were first introduced, a 10MB (megabyte) drive was considered large. Today, 20MB drives are the low end, "cheap" hard disk drives and may soon fall out of production. Most users will want to consider starting at the bare minimum of 40MB and more likely around 80MB to 100MB. The larger the initial purchase, the lower the cost in the long run. A single 100MB drive will cost less than purchasing, say, four 20MB drives over the course of a couple of years.

What Are Hard Disk Drives?

Hard disks store and access data much faster than floppy disks, and they provide much more storage space. If you use applications that require large amounts of storage, such as graphics or spreadsheets, you may find that a hard disk is a necessity. Making the decision to buy a hard disk is even easier now that competition has dramatically reduced the prices of hard disks.

Furthermore, an increasing number of hard disks now match the capacity of the technologically more advanced optical storage devices. Gigabyte drives that store around 1,000 megabytes have become available and, in some cases, are priced at less than $1,500.

A Brief History of Hard Disks

The need for better data-handling capacity quickly became apparent as personal computers grew in popularity. Floppy disks are not adequate to handle and store the large amounts of data processed by personal computer users. Mainframe computer facilities first used hard disk technology when they switched from tape to *disk packs* (large plastic cases of coated aluminum platters). These disk packs greatly increased the speed with which mainframes could access and use information stored on the platters.

IBM developed the technology for the hard disk drive, named Winchester. In the early 1980s, the manufacturing cost of hard drives dropped as demand for hard drives in personal computers increased. Manufacturers began offering hard disk drives as options on personal computers. The hard disk drive now is standard on all new Macintosh models.

Because of high development costs, lack of supply, and lack of competition, early Macintosh hard disk drives often sold for more than $2,000, despite their relatively small capacity of about 10MB. Today, Mac hard disks have storage capabilities of as much as 1,000MB—a hundred times that of the original drives.

For a hard disk to function, the computer originally required a *controller card* that enabled the drive to communicate with the computer's operating system. You do not have to install such a card in order to use a hard disk drive on a Macintosh. The controller is incorporated into the drive and is configured to communicate in a standard way called *SCSI* (Small Computer System Interface, pronounced "scuzzy"). SCSI is explained in the following section.

Understanding SCSI

Rather than require the user to select the proper controller card, install the card, and configure the hard disk—procedures necessary for IBM PC users—Apple adopted a special type of interface to Macintosh computers. This interface, known as SCSI (Small Computer Systems Interface) and pronounced "scuzzy," enables data to be transferred from the hard disk to the computer and back again at a high rate of speed (1.5MB to 3MB per second on current Macintoshes, with a maximum potential of 5MB per second). SCSI has become an industry standard for connections between disk drives and other peripherals; Macs now are equipped with a SCSI port, where the external hard disk drives are connected.

While a full explanation of SCSI is beyond the scope of this book, you should know a few points about SCSI as it relates to the Macintosh:

- SCSI enables you to connect up to eight SCSI devices together in what is known as a *SCSI chain*. That is, each device has a cable that connects to the next device, rather than having each device connect to a central device. (In this case, the Mac would be the central device.)

- Each device on a SCSI chain has a *unique* ID number. These numbers run from 0 to 7. The Macintosh, which is on the SCSI chain, always has the SCSI ID number 7.

- If you have an internal hard disk drive in a Macintosh with a SCSI port, the internal drive also has a SCSI ID number. Apple always sets its internal drives to 0. Other vendors may use different numbers. In any case, you can find the SCSI ID number of any drive attached to the Macintosh's SCSI chain by clicking the drive's icon and choosing Get Info from the File menu. (See Chapter 2, "Understanding the System," for more on the Get Info command.)

- Because of the numbering scheme, if your Macintosh has an internal hard disk drive, you already have two ID numbers in use. Hence, you have only six available for external hard disk drives and other peripherals. Remember that no two devices can have the same SCSI ID number. Your Macintosh will not be able to function properly if two or more devices share the same number.

- A SCSI chain must be *terminated*. This ominous-sounding term simply means that there must be devices attached to the chain that reduce noise in the chain and assist the interface in reliably transmitting data. The general rule is that the first and last device *outside* of the Macintosh must be terminated.

- The exception to the preceding rule is the Quadra computer, which has a terminated SCSI drive inside the computer. This drive counts as the first device in the SCSI chain, so only the last external SCSI device attached to a Quadra SCSI chain should be terminated. To be on the safe side and make sure that you're getting all the necessary information, however, check your Quadra manual before you hook up SCSI devices.

- Things can get a bit complicated when you hook up a SCSI chain with several devices. Proceed carefully and keep your manuals handy. And don't be afraid to admit defeat and call your dealer for assistance. SCSI chains have been known to defeat even power users.

Understanding How Hard Disks Work

A floppy disk is made of a flexible, coated plastic material. In contrast, a hard disk is a thin platter (or platters) made of metal or glass. Whereas floppy disks spin in hundreds of revolutions per minute (rpm), a hard disk can spin at around 3,600 rpm. A floppy disk only spins when it is accessed; a hard disk, on the other hand, spins continuously. (Power-Book hard disks, however, turn off when the computer is not in use in order to save power; this means that sometimes you have to wait momentarily for the drive to spin back up to full speed before you can access the drive.)

The speed of the hard drive means that much data can be transferred quickly, and that you can access information immediately—you don't have to wait for the disk to begin moving. Hard disks are also very speedy because they generate a cushion of air upon which the platter floats; this air cushion prevents the head from actually touching the disk surface.

Hard disk speeds are measured in the following ways:

- The speed at which the computer can find the information it is looking for, which is called the *access time* or *seek time*.

- The speed at which the hard disk can transfer data from the disk to the computer's memory, which is called *rate*.

- The *interleave ratio*, which is a measure of the numbers of times a disk must spin for all the desired data to be read.

Average access and *seek time* are measured in milliseconds (thousandths of a second). One great advantage of hard disks over earlier methods of storing information (notably tapes) is that the hard drive does not search sequentially (as tapes must) through each file from the beginning of the directory to find a specific file. Instead, a hard disk drive uses a random-access method that enables it to go directly to the information requested.

The *transfer rate* is largely dependent on the SCSI bus. Hard disk drives have become so fast that many regularly exceed the speed at which the Macintosh SCSI can transfer information to the Macintosh. In time, the newer and faster "SCSI-2" interface will replace the current SCSI system, resulting in faster transfer rates. You can, if you want, upgrade many Macintoshes to SCSI-2 by purchasing a separate card. Usually such upgrades are limited to Macintosh IIs with NuBus or PDS slots. (See Chapter 26, "Expanding the Macintosh," for more information on this upgrade.)

M ost Macintosh users will be content with the 1.5MB to 3MB transfer rate of the current SCSI. But SCSI-2 holds great promise with potential speeds of up to 10MB per second. Users with large amounts of data who regularly work with huge files might consider moving up to SCSI-2 immediately.

The speed at which a hard disk can transfer information to or from the computer's central processor (CPU)—which holds all instructions on what to do with the data—is related to how efficiently the information is read, or the *interleave factor*. This ratio is a measure of how much data is read per revolution of the disk. A ratio of 1:1 indicates that each sector on the hard disk is read as it passes the read/write head. If the ratio is 2:1, every other sector is read, and so on. The higher the ratio, the more times the disk has to spin for all the data to be read. The more times the disk spins, the longer it takes to read the data. Interleave is not a major concern on the Macintosh, although you may see references to the term. Most current hard drives have an interleave of 1:1.

Hard Disk Types

Three types of hard disk drives are available: internal, external, and removable drives.

The *internal* hard disk drive is a drive placed inside your Macintosh housing. The obvious advantage here is that the drive takes up no desk space. Few users are confident enough to brave opening a new Macintosh and installing a drive—voiding the warranty in the process. Fortunately, you can have a technician install a hard disk for you. (Note that the technician *must* be Apple certified or your warrantee will still be voided.) Another advantage is that internal drives are less expensive than external drives.

External hard drives are free-standing units placed under, next to, or even on the back of your Macintosh computer. You usually just need to plug in these external drives—following the rules for SCSI chains—and they are ready to use. These drives are generally more expensive than their internal cousins, but they do not require a technician (Apple certified or otherwise) to hook up to the Macintosh. You can connect them easily yourself.

Removable hard disks allow you to remove the drive media much like you remove a floppy disk—enabling you to take the data storage unit with you. Although these disks technically are not "hard" because they are made of materials similar to floppy disks, they can store a great deal of information and access it quickly. SyQuest drives, for example, use 44MB and 88MB floppy-type disks; these drives are fast and reliable.

The primary advantages of removable disk technology are security and increased convenience. No one can read your data if the data isn't in the computer. Also, you can have separate disks for different purposes: one disk for office records, another for the year's budget reports, and so on. And your work is easily transportable!

The disadvantages of removable disks are expense and incompatibility. These data cartridges can cost up to $120 each. And although removables are easily transported, they come in three different standards: Bernoulli, SyQuest, and Ricoh, none of which are compatible with each other. Bernoulli offers compatibility to IBM PC users of Bernoulli drives, but—oddly—it does not offer compatibility between its own different-sized disks. SyQuest is generally the most used disk in the Macintosh world and with service bureaus. Ricoh is a relative newcomer.

If you need a removable in order to share data with other users or with a service bureau (such as a printer), find out which type of removable the other user requires. In order to be compatible, you need to purchase a drive with the same mechanism. If you only want to use disk media for archiving or security purposes, don't worry about this consideration.

Connecting Hard Drives

Because hard disk drives for the Macintosh have been designed so carefully, connecting your external drive is usually fairly easy. If you have no other SCSI devices to connect, make sure that the drive is terminated. (Check your hard drive manual for the exact procedure; procedures vary widely from drive to drive.) Set the SCSI number to any number other than 0 or 7. Make sure that your Macintosh is turned off, and then plug in the cable that came with the hard disk or the one that you purchased from your dealer. You plug the cable into the SCSI port in the back of your Mac (see Chapter 1, "Getting Started," for more information). Now restart your Mac.

If you have more than one SCSI device, you need to add the hard disk to your SCSI chain. Review the earlier section "Understanding SCSI." Then proceed with these steps:

1. Check your cabling.

   One of the most annoying aspects of working with SCSI chains is that there are two *different* connectors to be concerned with. The SCSI standard calls for a rather large, 50-pin connector to connect to SCSI devices. Apple decided to use the 25-pin connector you see on the back of the Macintosh. In a rather perverse fit of imitation, some SCSI device manufactures imitated Apple and use the 25-pin connector, while others use the 50-pin standard connector.

   Hard drive manufacturers that include cables with their drives (and not all do) often assume that their device will be the first connected to the Macintosh. The company provides the appropriate cable for this connection. Suppose, however, that you intend to connect the drive elsewhere. This dilemma is annoying—especially if you have another SCSI device with a 50-pin connector. Adding a single device to a SCSI chain can often mean reorganizing the entire chain or having to buy a new cable.

2. With the Macintosh and all other devices, hook the SCSI chain together.

   Figuring out the cable situation comes first. Termination and SCSI IDs can be set more easily.

3. Set your hard disk drive's SCSI number to any number between 1 and 6 not already in use. (Suppose, for example, that you have a CD-ROM drive with an ID of 3; you then would not use the number 3.)

4. Determine the termination of each device and reset as needed.

   Remember, the first and last device on the chain *must* be terminated unless you own a Quadra. In which case, your internal drive is counted as the first device and is already terminated.

   No other device should be terminated.

5. Turn on all SCSI devices, and then start your Macintosh.

In most cases, all your SCSI devices appear and all are fine. If not, shut down your Macintosh and start back with the first step, rechecking each device's cabling, termination, and ID number. If this does not work, take a long walk, have a hot bath, rent a Mel Brooks video, and *then* calmly call your dealer.

Initializing Hard Disks

Because hard disks are generally shipped already initialized (and many now have software already installed), you shouldn't have to initialize a new drive. However, you may need to initialize a drive if you purchase a used Macintosh or have a software problem that corrupts your hard disk's file structure beyond repair. (See Chapter 32, "Maintenance and Troubleshooting," for more on disk repair and recovery utilities.)

Hard disks come with utilities that enable you to initialize and prepare them for use. Apple ships a Disk Tools disk with the System software disk set. You can use this disk to start up your Macintosh from the internal floppy drive; then you can use the Apple HD SC Setup utility program to initialize, test, and update an Apple hard disk drive.

To initialize a drive, do the following:

1. Start up from the Disk Tools disk.

   When the Desktop appears and the disk icon becomes available, double-click the Disk Tools disk icon. The Disk Tools window appears, which contains the Apple HD SC Setup utility program (see fig. 3.7).

Fig. 3.7
The Disk Tools window.

2. Double-click the Apple HD SC Setup icon.

   The Apple HD SC Setup dialog appears with six buttons: Initialize, Update, Partition, Test, Quit, and Drive.

3. Click the Drive button until the desired hard disk is selected and displayed in the dialog. (The SCSI ID number of the disk will be displayed.)

   You will not be able to select non-Apple drives.

4. Click the Initialize button.

   You are asked for confirmation of this command (see fig. 3.8).

   Remember, the next step will *erase* your hard disk.

Fig. 3.8
Confirming the Initialize
command.

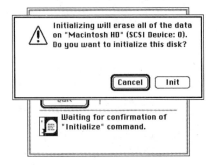

5. Click the Init button.

6. After the drive has been initialized, click the Update button to update the necessary driver software.

7. Click the Test button to check the drive's readiness.

   If the drive passes the testing, you are finished and have a working drive.

8. Click the Quit button.

If the drive fails the test, check with your dealer; you may have a mechanical problem in your hard disk drive.

Partitioning Hard Disks

The Apple HD SC Setup utility and other utilities enable you to partition—that is, subdivide—a hard disk into sections that act as separate hard disks. This is primarily useful to owners of very large hard disks (100MB to 200MB and up) because partitioning enables them to break large disks into smaller units of more manageable size.

This book doesn't cover explain *how* to partition your hard disk; check your Macintosh manuals for the specific procedure. Rather, this section *defines* partitioning so that you can decide whether or not you want to use it.

The Apple HD SC Setup utility is not the only available partitioning utility. In fact, it performs only one of two different methods for creating disk partitions.

There are two kinds of disk partitions: *hard* and *soft*. The following sections define these two partition types.

Hard Partitions

Hard partitions are completely independent of each other, although they reside on the same disk. The advantage of using hard partitions is that you can store data of different formats on the different partitions. Apple uses hard partitioning mainly so that Macintosh users can set up a separate partition for a second operating system, such as the Apple A/UX Unix system.

Hard partitions have the additional advantage that one partition can "crash" without affecting the other partitions. This is not true of soft partitions, as you read in the following section.

One disadvantage of hard partitions is that you must set up the partitions when you initialize the disk. If you decide that you want to adjust the size of hard partitions, you have to back up the data on the hard disk and then reinitialize the disk.

Consider using hard partitioning if you need to split a disk into sections that will be used for different operating systems, by different users on a network, or by those who want to isolate data in order to reduce the risk of total disk failure.

Several manufacturers offer hard disk partitioning software. Symantec's Norton Utilities 2.0 includes Norton Partition, ALSoft Power Utilities includes MultiDisk, and Drive 7 by Casa Blanca Works includes partitioning. Chapter 19 "Using Utility Software," discusses these utility packages and others.

Soft Partitions

Soft partitioning sets aside a part of a disk and treats this part as if it were another disk. The partitions are "subunits" of the larger disk partition rather than fully realized separate sections. Soft partitioning enables you to set aside areas of your larger disks for special uses. You cannot, however, store data of a non-Macintosh format in these partitions.

Soft partitions have an advantage that hard partitions do not: they can be resized pretty much as you need when you need. You do not have to back up and reinitialize the hard disk.

One disadvantage of soft partitions, however, is that the various partitions do not "crash" independently, as do hard partitions. While a soft partition can become corrupted without affecting the entire disk, if the main partition of your disk fails, any soft partitions on the disk go with it.

Consider using soft partitioning if you need to store sensitive information. Many partitioning utilities that perform soft partitioning allow you to encrypt the partition so that the data in the partition cannot be accessed by anyone but you (or those who have the encryption key).

Optimizing Hard Disks

Your hard disk stores data in sectors in much the same way a floppy disk does. If one sector is not large enough to contain all the information in one file, the computer stores the data where the drive can find the space—often in a sector completely removed from the sector containing the rest of the file.

When you use your hard disk frequently—adding new files, reading and resaving old files, deleting files, and so on—the files tend to be split and stored at different places on the disk. When you choose to open a file, the system has to locate all these pieces and rebuild the entire file. This process can take a considerable amount of time, depending on how large and how *fragmented* the file is.

To keep your disk from becoming too cluttered, you can rebuild the Desktop at least once a month. (I do it about once a week.) Simply hold down the Option and Command key when you start your Mac (after any System extensions load but before the Desktop appears.) The Finder reorganizes the Desktop and clears out unnecessary files; however, you lose all the information you have entered into the Get Info boxes. This procedure helps clean up your disk and may slightly improve the performance of the hard disk drive.

NOTE

FileSaver, a control panel that is included with Symantec's Norton Utilities 2.0, enables you to keep the comments in your Get Info boxes. This control panel saves all your Finder comments when you rebuild the Desktop. You then can use Norton Utilities to restore the comments.

You also can optimize your disk by using disk optimizer software such as Optimizer (part of MacTools from Central Point Software), DiskExpress II (from ALSoft), or Speed Disk (in Symantec's Norton Utilities 2.0). Figure 3.9 shows Speed Disk's main screen displaying information about the disk to be optimized. Optimizer utility programs reunite fragmented files, taking all the pieces of a file and placing them in contiguous (or adjacent) blocks so that each file is in only one area of the disk. DiskExpress II works in the background, keeping your disk optimized while you work.

Fig. 3.9

Speed Disk preparing to optimize Macintosh HD.

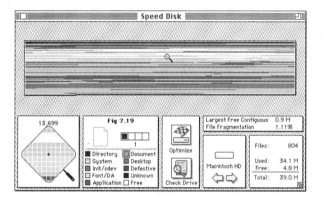

You also can defragment the disk manually (if you have the time). Here's how:

1. Back up all the application and data files on your hard disk to floppy disks.

2. Reformat your hard disk by using the Apple HD SC Setup hard disk utility that comes with your System disks.

   Don't just erase or throw away all the files on the disk; reformat the hard disk.

3. Reinstall the files from your backup to your clean hard disk.

4. Copy all the application and data files to your disk.

Compressing Hard Disk Data

Because data seems to magically increase to fill all available hard disk space, you might find yourself in the same situation as me: shuffling files on and off of floppies, archiving old materials as fast as possible, and generally trying to squeeze every bit of space available on your hard disk.

You can save a great deal of disk space by using one of the data compression utilities discussed in Chapter 19, "Using Utility Software."

Two approaches are available for data compression. The first involves *archiving* files. Programs such as Stuffit Deluxe by Alladin Systems and Disk Doubler by Salient enable you to create archive files that can be as small as one half the normal size of a file.

Stuffit SpaceSaver by Alladin Systems, AutoDoubler by Salient, and More Disk Space by Alysis automatically compress files that you are not using and decompress the files as you use them. DiskDoubler does automatic decompression as well as automatic recompression, but it requires that you specify the files and folders to be compressed.

A compression utility of some kind is a must for all Macintosh users. Even if your disk currently is not full to the point of bulging, it will be. Trust me; you can never have too much disk space.

Securing Your Files and Applications

Although you don't work at your Macintosh wearing a trench coat and sunglasses (you don't, do you?), security is a legitimate concern that needs to be taken seriously. Several Macintosh applications (such as Word and Excel) enable you to use a password to protect your files, and several new products are devoted solely to controlling access to your files.

Some available options enable you to password protect individual folders and set access options for them—for example, read-only access. Some keep track of any attempts to access your files. Believe it or not, an electronic "shredder" is even available that totally erases files. (In normal circumstances, using the Trash deletes the Desktop entry for a file, but the data remains until it is overwritten by another file.)

Chapter 19 "Using Utility Software" discusses several options you can purchase for securing your hard disk data.

Caring for Hard Disks

The rules for caring for a hard disk are about the same as the rules for caring for floppy disks. They include the following:

- *Keep a hard disk away from strong magnetic sources.* Placing your hard disk right up against your printer's power supply is probably not a good idea, but hard disk drives *are* better shielded than floppy disks, so you don't have to be quite so cautious.

- *Remember that liquids, food crumbs, and smoke can damage a hard disk drive.* Food crumbs aren't likely to fall into a well-designed hard disk drive case, but stranger things have happened.

- *Protect your hard disk from physical shocks, especially when it's running.* One good jolt and the read/write heads might touch the surface of the rapidly spinning media platter, wiping out a megabyte of data. (This is called a *head crash*, and just saying the phrase can give computer people weak knees.) Moving a hard disk drive when it is on and spinning is also not a good idea.

- *Don't turn the disk drive.* Because the disk platter spins at such a high rate of speed, it's something like a gyroscope. Turning the disk drive can set up some conflicting stresses in the media platter.

Keep in mind at all times that a hard disk drive's read/write heads float just *barely* above the media platter—the gap is so small it is dwarfed in size by a single dust particle. While an occasional bump may not hurt your drive, always handle your drive with care and take as few chances as possible.

Using Other Disks

Floppy and hard disks have dominated the personal computer scene for several years. But, like all technologies, they are showing their age. Newer technologies are appearing and maturing that promise to offer greater storage capacity than the standard floppy and hard disk are capable of.

This is not to say that floppy and hard disks will vanish tomorrow or next week. But, your choices for data storage have widened and will continue to do so. Eventually, one of the newer technologies will mature to the point that it will threaten to replace the floppy and hard disk. Most likely, you'll see the magneto-optical erasable drives becoming the dominant storage system in the not-too-distant future as magnetic media approaches its limits and optical increases in speed.

Before optical completely replaces magnetic media, "flopticals" will probably become a major player in storage media. The floptical merges floppy technology with optical to squeeze 20MB or so out of a 3.5-inch floppy disk.

But even before any major change happens, you already have access to different storage options. Most notable is the CD-ROM, which is rapidly catching on in the Macintosh world. The CD-ROM is *read only*—you cannot write to the disks—but provides such massive storage amounts (500MB to 600MB) that whole, shelf-bending encyclopedia sets can be stored on only a disk or two.

The following sections explain these other options in greater detail.

CD-ROMs

Remember when you used to go to the library to find out the number of hairs on the average person's head, how many red blood cells are produced in one day, or the exact square mileage of Asia? You would use the encyclopedia. Now, with your Macintosh, you can have the same amount of information available on a couple of compact discs. Like their audio counterparts, CD-ROM drives use a laser beam to read information from the CD-ROMs. (In fact, the technology is so similar that you can actually play audio CDs on a CD-ROM drive!) Because the light beam is so minute, lots of information can fit in a small space.

A single CD-ROM (*Compact Disk-Read-Only Memory*) can hold around 500MB of data—equivalent to about 625 double-sided floppy disks and 350 high-density disks. But remember that these disks have a read-only memory (ROM); therefore, you can read from these disks, but you cannot write to them. In other words, you cannot alter the contents of a file.

You may wonder how a compact disc (the same kind that your Chris Isaak, The Who, or Brandenburg Concerti recordings are on) can hold so much information. Tiny lasers record the data as infinitesimal pits on the surface of the disk; the size of the pit determines the value (1 or 0) of the information. Sound, text, visual images, and other data are turned into streams of ones and zeros that are burned into the media encased in the plastic of a compact disc. (This process explains why you get the rainbow "mother of pearl" effect when you move a CD about in the light; the tiny holes refract the light, breaking it into its component colors.)

Better yet, compact discs and other optical storage media are not so easily damaged by crashes, coffee spills, magnetism, or dirt. Granted, they are not indestructible and should not be handled carelessly, but they are much tougher than floppy and hard disks.

CD-ROM drives are SCSI devices, so all Macs can use them except the 128 and 512. When you purchase a CD-ROM drive, you receive the software needed to have the disks mount and appear on your Desktop. With this software installed, you treat the CD-ROM as you would a locked disk—remembering that you cannot change information on the disk nor save anything to the disc. You do, however, have access to immense amounts of information (see fig. 3.10).

Fig. 3.10
The Nautilus Intro 6 CD contains almost 440MB of software, graphics, and sounds.

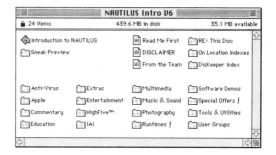

> The Nautilus disk shown is offered by Nautilus, a monthly CD-ROM "magazine" company. You subscribe to the CD-ROM magazine and receive a CD every month. At 400+ megabytes per month, a year's subscription is 5 *billion* bytes of software, graphics, sounds, and other items each year.

The AppleCD 300 CD-ROM drive comes with nine sample discs, including the one shown from Nautilus. Also included are

- Two discs of demo software—one games and one applications—showing you the wide array of software available for the Macintosh.

- A Kids Read disc with the story of Cinderella done in stunning color and read by the computer.

- An educational disc about Mozart that not only teaches about Mozart's music, but also plays the music.

- A stunning presentation called "From Alice to Ocean" about a woman's solitary voyage across the Australian desert. (I was hooked when I looked at this one and sat glued in front of the monitor, watching the desert scenery go by on my monitor.)

■ Two Apple sampler discs.

■ A sample Kodak PhotoCD disc that introduces you to the newest aspect of the CD-ROM world: developing photographs from negatives to CD-ROM. This capability enables you to view, edit, print, or otherwise work with your own photographs. Figure 3.11 shows a sample of this stunning feature (which you really *must* see in full 256 color mode).

Fig. 3.11
A sample photo from the Kodak PhotoCD disc.

The possibilities for the PhotoCD technology are amazing for small businesses. Pictures can be taken, developed to CD, and then used with Macintosh desktop publishing software such as Aldus PageMaker or Aldus Personal Press to create brochures, flyers, advertisements, and the like with a relatively small investment. Home users can take advantage of PhotoCD as well, making their own slide shows and Christmas cards.

CD-ROM offerings are growing by leaps and bounds; many established manufacturers—such as Apple, CD Technology, Denon America, NEC, and Toshiba—offer CD drives. (The AppleCD 300 was used in the production of this book, and the experience has me adding my pennies to figure out how soon I can own one myself.)

The collection of CDs available is almost exploding. Companies such as EduCorp now have full catalogs filled with almost nothing other than the vast collections of graphics, software, music, and sounds on CD-ROM.

Mail order catalogs now have whole sections devoted to disk collections, with such offerings as the *Sports Illustrated CD-ROM Sports Almanac*, which has statistics from 1931 to 1991; *Front Page News* by Wayzata, with over 340,000 (!) articles from 14 U.S. and international news services; *800 College Boards* by Queue, which is a collection of programs to aid students in taking college level tests; and many, many others.

Despite the tremendous amount of data that CD-ROMs can store, they have some limitations that slowed their initial acceptance. The drives are still somewhat expensive, averaging about $600-$700. (Apple goes right around this problem by simply including the CD-ROM player with the newer Macintosh IIvx and the Performa 600.) The edge has been taken off this price as CD-ROM prices have fallen dramatically. Early CD-ROMs cost from $100 to as much as $500. Lately, prices have come down to much more reasonable and affordable levels and range from $40 to $300. The *Sports Almanac* CD-ROM, for example, costs only $39. The *Front Page News* CD comes in at $89—rather reasonable for several hundred thousand newspaper clippings.

Another limitation has been that CD-ROM drives are rather slow. Their seek times are far higher than the average hard drive, and they transfer information much more slowly. (One factor contributing to this lack of speed is that the standard adopted for CD-ROMs was intentionally kept extremely close to the audio CD format, which slowed data access somewhat.) However, the speed issue is being addressed; the AppleCD 300, for example, operates at twice the old CD-ROM speed, and the sheer volume of information available on CD-ROM makes up for a bit of sluggishness in access speed.

One cool feature of CD-ROM drives is that they let you play audio CDs. Apple includes the CD Remote application with its CD-ROM players, which play audio CDs through the headphone jack of the CD-ROM player (see fig. 3.12).

Fig. 3.12
Listening to a CD while writing *Que's Big Mac Book*.

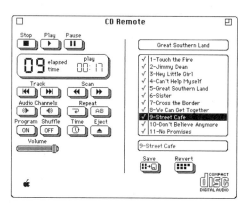

CD Remote enables you to label the tracks of the CD, order them in a play list, shuffle play tracks, repeat the CD, and perform other CD player functions. The CD Remote application runs in the background and does not interfere with running applications.

Other CD-ROM manufacturers offer similar capabilities so you may want to shop around. I'm quite impressed with the AppleCD 300, however, and wouldn't hesitate to recommend that you visit your dealer and see it for yourself.

Magneto-Optical Disks

Another type of optical drive, the rewriteable *magneto-optical drive*, differs from a CD-ROM disk in one important way: you can write to the disk as well as read from it. Magneto-optical disks are ideal for recording information that you want to archive or save for a long time.

3.5-inch magneto-optical disks store about 120MB per disk but are just slightly larger (in thickness mainly) than the standard Macintosh floppy disk. The drives cost around $1,500 to $2,000 dollars, which is rather steep, but for large amounts of data that must be stored over long periods of time, no other media comes close to this one. The disks are impervious to magnetic fields and are rated to last 30 or more years without significant data degradation. At present, the drives with Sony mechanisms are receiving the best reviews. (Drives such as the Optima Technology DisKovery 128MO and the PLI Infinity Optical 3.5-inch have received good reviews for their reliability.)

For even greater storage capabilities, there are the 5.25-inch magneto-opticals that have a capacity ranging from 650MB to 1,000MB. The drives run in the $2,000 to $4,000 range and media costs are high, but the cost per megabyte makes the drives *very* attractive for massive archiving. This last assertion is especially true when you consider the durability of the media and longevity of the stored data.

Magneto-optical does have its drawbacks—the foremost being a steep initial cost. The drives cost as much as many Macintosh computers, and the media cost from about $50 to as much as $200 per disk. Still, the massive amounts of storage bring the cost per megabyte down to a reasonable level for businesses that have long-term archiving needs.

Magneto-optical is still rather slow, which is primarily what keeps it in the "backup and archiving" category. I expect this to change, and in some cases it has already changed significantly. Pinnacle Micro is advertising the "optical hard drive" with a hard disk speed access time of 19 milliseconds. DGR technologies advertises a drive with a "short seek" time of 9 milliseconds. The PMO-650 drive and the DGR 128REM are probably representative of the near future when magneto-optical will begin to give magnetic hard disks a run for their money.

The biggest drawback that I see involves compatibility. Disks used in one drive do not necessarily work in other drives. But this lack of compatibility is reminiscent of the early days when floppy disks had a dozen different standards and could not easily be transported between drives. It did not take long for the market to shake out the industry and for only a couple major standards to remain. At present, businesses and individuals considering magneto-optical should check carefully to assure that their disks will be compatible with other drives they plan to use.

Floptical Disks

Finally, you may soon see more *flopticals*, a special kind of floppy disk that uses laser guidance to squeeze 20MB or more on 3.5-inch magnetic media. There are still questions about the drive and media reliability, and compatibility problems exist between drives. There's no question this technology could mature quickly since it is based on the known quantities of magnetic storage technology. Many of the drives also read standard Macintosh disks, doing double duty.

Perhaps the biggest question about the longevity and widespread acceptance of floptical is whether magneto-optical will simply leapfrog the technology—which it appears to be doing—and leave floptical only in the history books.

The Big Mac Recommendation

This chapter familiarized you with options for storing data and the related hardware. You should now understand your options in the areas of floppy disks, hard drives, and the newer optical disks. Also covered were the basics of floppy and hard disk use and care.

Your best bet today in the area of data storage is still the magnetic hard disk. The average Macintosh user would do well to consider a hard disk in the 80MB-200MB range, whether purchasing a new Macintosh or upgrading an existing one. (See Chapter 26, "Expanding the Macintosh," for additional help in choosing hard drives.)

A CD-ROM drive is a good addition to your Macintosh as soon as you can afford it. At the very least, take a trip to your dealer to experience the AppleCD 300 and what CD-ROMs have to offer.

Magneto-optical is a technology to watch, but the average Macintosh user will not have much call for it. On the other hand, businesses that deal with large amounts of data and need long-term archiving will want to seriously consider these drives.

CHAPTER FOUR

Managing Files

F iles are a major part of the use of a computer of any kind. Because you will use files a great deal in your work on the Macintosh, you need to understand how files are stored and represented on the Macintosh.

Understanding Files

A *file* is defined as information stored on disk and is also called a *document*.

Files on the Macintosh are a bit different than on other computers such as the IBM PC and clones, although they have a great many similarities. The way files are stored on disk is very much like the way any other computer stores its files, but the way the Macintosh uses files is different.

How Files Are Stored on Disk

In Chapter 3, "Managing Disks," you learned that a disk is formatted into rings called *tracks* (or cylinders). Each track is further broken up into sectors of the same size, but you know that not all files are the same size.

The Macintosh (like any computer) stores files by breaking them into pieces that will fit the sectors. For each file, the Macintosh maintains a table that informs it where each piece of the file is located and in what order the pieces go. The pieces of a file may not be located next to each other on a disk (although this is the ideal organization); the pieces may be scattered across the disk.

When pieces of file are scattered across a disk to a great extent—as inevitably occurs on any computer—your disk is said to be "fragmented," and the operation of your computer may slow as it takes progressively more time to reassemble a file.

You can remedy this problem by using an item of software called a *disk optimizer* (see Chapter 19, "Using Utility Software"). An optimizer reassembles files on your disk into contiguous locations for quicker access. You do not have to worry about this problem on floppy disks, only on hard disks.

How the Macintosh Recognizes Files

The Macintosh places two items of information in every file to identify the creator code and the type code. The *creator code* is a four letter (or letter and digit) code that each software application that creates files has as its unique identifier. Apple ensures the uniqueness of the creator code by enabling software manufacturers to register their creator codes with Apple so that duplication does not occur (otherwise, you might never know which application software might attempt to open a file). Microsoft Word uses MSWD as its creator code, for example.

Each application then has a set of *type codes,* which are also four characters in length, that identifies different types of files the application creates, uses, and maintains. Some type codes are standard. TEXT is used commonly for text files, and PICT is used for the PICT graphics standard files, for example. Other type codes may mean something only to the application that assigns them.

When you double-click any icon, the Macintosh reads these two codes to determine how to respond to your double-click. If you double-click an icon that represents a file with the creator code of MSWD, for example, the Macintosh knows to start Microsoft Word to open the file for you.

How Icons Represent Files

The small pictures called *icons* represent files, folders, and disks. By acting on these icons, you inform the Macintosh what you want done to the files stored on your disk.

Icons are not the files themselves but represent the files. The Macintosh has an invisible file (in System 7, a collection of invisible files) called the Desktop file that maintains a listing of which files are represented by which icons. When your Macintosh starts or you open a disk or folder containing files, the Desktop file is read and the icons that represent your files appear on-screen. Figure 4.1 shows some different application icons and associated document file icons.

Fig. 4.1
Application and
document icons.

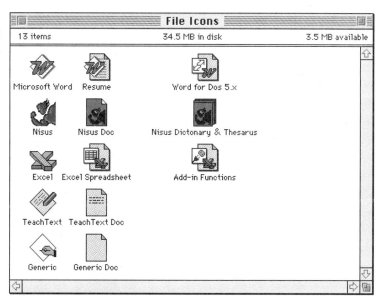

The first column shows five application icons; the second column shows a document created by each application. The third column shows a sample of a file icon that is unique to the application (if any). If the creator of the application does not provide an icon, Macintosh uses the icon labeled Generic to represent the application. The document icon to the right of the generic icon is a generic document icon used for files the Macintosh cannot identify (usually because the creator application software is not present on your disk).

How the Hierarchical File System Works

Apple added what is known as the Hierarchical File System (or HFS) with the introduction of the Macintosh Plus in 1986. HFS enables you to *nest* folders to different levels—that is, a folder can contain another folder. The benefit of this nesting is that you can divide a disk using folders and then further subdivide a folder with other folders. Although most users find anything beyond about five levels to be confusing and cumbersome, you can repeat the subdivision as much as you like (see fig. 4.2).

Fig. 4.2
The levels of folders
in HFS.

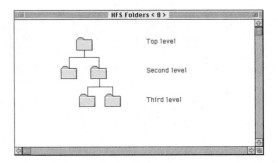

The top level of folders is the one that you see on the Desktop or in the windows of disks that you open. The second level in figure 4.2 consists of two folders contained within the folder on the top level. The third level shows two folders that are contained within the right folder of the second level.

Think of a filing cabinet drawer. In the drawer are folders—these are the top level of folders. Within each folder you may find documents, folders, or both. These are the second level. Within the second-level folders, you again can find documents, folders, or both. These are the third level.

This way of organizing folders enables you to subdivide your files. You can label the top-level folder "Meeting Minutes." You can label the second-level folders by month ("January," "February," and so on). You can subdivide the third level into folders for each week ("Week of May 2nd" for example).

Another advantage of HFS is that you can have duplicate file names so long as they do not reside in the same folder. You can have a report broken into sections, for example, and then have each stage of its revision (with the same names) in separate folders with dates that indicate which version of the documents the folders hold.

Working with Files

You need to know how to access files on the Macintosh because you will be working with them so much of the time. This section discusses how you can open files, organize files, search for files by using the Find command, create and work with the special kinds of files called *stationery*, and view files in folders.

Opening Files

The Macintosh provides three ways to open a document. Two of them are used to open documents while you are at the desktop in the Finder—the double-click and drag-and-drop methods. Both open the document by starting (launching) or switching to the appropriate application program to allow you to work with the document. The third method, using the Open command in an application program, enables you to open a document while within an application program. This method uses the Open dialog, which is common to all Macintosh application programs and may be a bit confusing at first glance.

Opening by Double-Clicking

When you double-click an icon, the Macintosh understands that you want to open the disk, application, or file. When you double-click a file icon, the Macintosh reads the creator code and then searches your disks for the appropriate application program. After the computer finds the program, the application program starts and the file is opened.

You may encounter a situation where you have a file whose creator is not on the disk. This situation results in the error message shown in figure 4.3.

Fig. 4.3
The file cannot be opened.

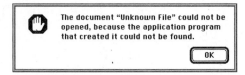

If you encounter this message, click the OK button; the message dialog disappears from the screen. Then, if you own a copy of the application program that created the file, install this program.

From the appearance of the file's icon, you may be able to determine the application program that created the document. You also can use the Get Info command to determine the name of the creator application program: select the document by clicking once on its icon, and then choose Get Info from the File menu.

Also the Kind field uses the name of the creator application program. This approach may not always work. Sometimes you may see the word *document* in the Kind field.

Not having the creator application program does not mean you cannot open and use a document. Many application programs can translate the files of application programs. Nisus, MacWrite Pro, Microsoft Word, and others have the capability of translating and opening the files of several different application programs.

Another possibility is that the TeachText program supplied by Apple and installed on your hard drive along with the System Software files may be able to open the file. If this is possible, you will see the dialog shown in figure 4.4.

Fig. 4.4
The file can be opened by
TeachText.

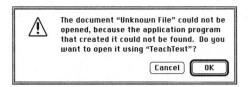

Click the OK button or press Return to open the file using TeachText. The TeachText program is a very simple program and will most likely not offer you much in the way of tools to work with the file. You will be able to view the file, however, which may give you a clue as to the program that created it.

Opening by Dragging and Dropping

To use this method to open a file, you drag the file you want to open onto the application program's icon (see fig. 4.5).

Fig. 4.5
Opening a file by dragging and dropping.

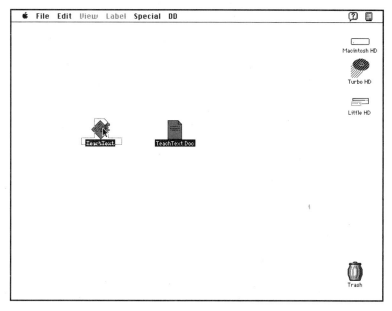

If the application program's icon darkens, you release the mouse button. The application starts and the file opens, ready for work.

The application program's icon will not darken if the application program cannot open the file in this manner. The application program still may open the file, but you must use the Open command. Check the manual that accompanies the application program for further information.

Opening within a Program

Within an application program, you open a file by using the Open command in the File menu.

After an application program is started, you can open files by performing the following steps:

1. From the File menu, choose Open. The Open File (or Open Document) dialog appears. Figure 4.6 shows an example of the Open dialog from within the Nisus word processing application.

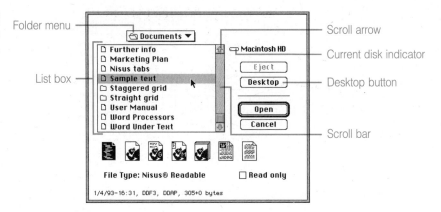

Fig. 4.6
Opening a file
within Nisus.

Folder menu

Scroll arrow

Current disk indicator

List box

Desktop button

Scroll bar

2. Double-click the name of the desired file.

   Alternatively, you can click the file's name and then click the Open button.

Open dialogs have several operations you can use to locate and open files. These options include the following:

■ *Folder menu.* Enables you to select a folder on the current disk. Displays the name of the currently selected folder or the name of the current disk if no folder is selected.

■ *List box.* Shows the files that you may open.

■ *Scroll bar and scroll arrows.* Allow you to scroll up or down the list of files.

■ *Current disk indicator.* Shows which disk's contents you are viewing.

■ *Desktop button.* Displays the files on the desktop and the icons for all mounted disks. Enables you to double-click on an element to indicate which disk's contents you wish to view.

Organizing Files

You probably will change the organization of your hard disk as your needs change and as you add applications and files to your Macintosh. This section discusses some ways of organizing files on disks. To illustrate the process, assume that you own the following software:

Microsoft Word

MacWrite Pro

Excel

Quicken

Assorted utilities, such as MacTools, and the tools that come with the System disks

Basically, you want to set up the hard disk with folders for the general categories of word processing, utilities, spreadsheets, finance, and of course, the System. Remember that if you don't have a System folder or the System file on the Desktop, your Mac doesn't know where to look to get started. The top level of folders (also called the *root* or *root directory*) in this hierarchy looks like the directory shown in figure 4.7.

Fig. 4.7

The root level for the hard disk named R&D Department.

To create a folder at the top level, you use the New Folder command in the File menu of the Finder and then name the new folder (see the next section "Creating, Naming, and Deleting Folders"). When you open a new folder by double-clicking the folder's icon, you see that the folder contains no files or folders because you haven't added anything. Use the New Folder command to create folders named Word and MacWrite. (These folders will contain all the files for these programs.) You then can add the appropriate files by dragging them into the folder.

T I P

M any users like to use the character created by pressing Option-F at the end of a folder name to indicate that it is a folder. This avoids the confusion that can arrive from having an application (such as Nisus) in a folder of the same name. Instead, the name of the folder is something like "Nisus ƒ." You also can use the word *Folder* as the System Folder does.

Your organization is as follows:

- All Word application files, folders, and document files in the folder called Word

- All MacWrite Pro application files, folders, and document files in the folder called MacWrite

- All system files in the folder named System Folder (this should have already been done for you)

- Any other utilities in the folder named Utilities

Some users choose not to place the actual document files they create using a particular application in the same folder as the application itself. Where you place your document files is a matter of personal preference and work habits, but you may want to follow these suggestions:

- A folder for each application (Word, PageMaker, Excel, for example) or a folder for each category (Word Processors, Utilities, and so on)

- A folder for each project

This system keeps all related data in one location and greatly simplifies the process of making backups. Each folder or file in the HFS system has a path, or a description of the location of the file in the HFS tree. A file named Sara stored in the Letters folder on a hard disk named R&D Department, for example, has the path R&D Department:Word Processing:Letters:Sara. You normally do not have to deal with paths, but you will see them in Info windows.

The following guidelines should help you organize your hard disk:

- Try to limit the number of files in a folder so that you can see them all at a glance when you view by name, date, or kind.

- Keep the organization as simple as possible. If you have 200 folders in one folder, you will have difficulty locating a needed file. The less clutter you have, the more efficiently you can work with your disk and the Desktop.

- If you have a special application that you use frequently, such as a word processing program, create an alias and place the alias near the files you work with frequently.

Another way to help organize the files on your hard disk is through the use of a utility that partitions the hard disk into several sections. You can take a 100MB hard disk, for example, and partition it into one 50MB and five 10MB hard drives. Partitioning becomes especially important as the size of the hard drive increases. You then can use each partition for a different project. See Chapter 19, "Using Utility Software," for more on hard disk management tools that enable you to partition a disk.

Creating, Naming, and Deleting Folders

When you decide that you want a folder to contain a group of items, you must first create the folder. Follow these steps:

1. From the File menu, choose New Folder. A folder appears named "untitled folder."

2. Type the name of the folder and press Return.

Folder names have the same restrictions as those for other icons. You may use up to 31 characters but cannot use a colon (:). Use names that help you remember the contents of the folder—names like Memos, Memo Folder, Company Memos, Personnel Memos, and so on.

You can rename folders the same way you rename any icon. Click on the folder's name to select it and then type a new name.

You can delete a folder just as you delete any other icon—by dragging it to the Trash.

Nesting Folders

As stated in a previous section, folders can contain more than just document files and applications; folders can contain other folders. If you have a large number of icons in one folder, you may want to nest some folders within a main folder to further organize the documents and applications.

In figure 4.8, you can see that the contents of the System Folder are divided into groups such as Apple Menu Items, Startup Items, Extensions, Control Panels, and Preferences. This organization is easier to deal with than the previous versions' System Folder that did not divide System Software items.

Fig. 4.8
The System Folder's organization.

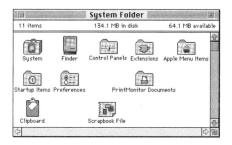

The folders in the System Folder are special, and you can see that they carry symbols to note that these folders differ from the average folder. You can use the same idea of nesting folders to organize your icons, however.

You can nest folders, for example, by opening a Memo Folder and then creating as many folders as you need by using the New Folder command. You then drag your memos to the new folders according to the categories you created.

You can then further subdivide any of the new folders by opening them and using the same process to create folders within the new folders. You can carry on this process, nesting folders within folders, to any depth you need. Of course, if you create too many folders, you reach a point where the nesting becomes more confusing than helpful.

When using nested folders, you may reach a point where you see far too many windows on-screen. Rather than closing each window by clicking the close box, hold down the Option key and click the close box of any folder window. All open windows close.

Labeling Files

The Label menu enables you to add text and—if your Macintosh works with color—colors to your icons. You may use this capability to further organize your icons, search for icons, and sort icons. Apple provides seven labels initially: Essential, Hot, In Progress, Cook, Personal, Project 1, and Project 2. You can use the Labels control panel to change the labels so that they better suit your needs (see Chapter 6, "Customizing the Macintosh").

If your Macintosh uses color, you also see a rectangle to the left of each label. Apple presets the colors as it does the labels, but the colors also can be changed.

Labeling a File

To label a file, follow these steps:

1. Click on the file's icon (or disk's icon or folder's icon) to select the file.

2. Choose one of the seven labels from the Label menu.

The labeled icon shows no apparent change in the icon views on a black-and-white-only Macintosh (such as the Mac Classic II). On a color Macintosh (such as the Color Classic or LC III), the icon changes to the color in the Label menu to the left of the chosen label.

Removing a Label

In any of the list views, the label appears in the Label column if you have set the Macintosh to display this column in these views (see Chapter 6, "Customizing the Macintosh").

To remove a label, follow these steps:

1. Select the file's icon by clicking on it.

2. From the Label menu, choose None.

Sorting by Label

In any list view (by Name, by Kind, and so on), you can sort icons in order of the labels you have assigned them by choosing the by Label option in the View menu. You also can click the Label column heading in the list view to change the sort order. Your icons then are grouped according to the labels assigned to them and sorted alphabetically within label groups.

Although the labels do not appear in the two icon views (by Small Icon and by Icon), you may use them to sort your icons by following these steps:

1. From the View menu, choose by Label.

2. From the View menu, choose by Icon (or by Small Icon).

3. Press and hold the Option key.

4. From the Special menu, choose Clean Up by Label.

5. Release the Option key.

The icons are ordered by label, sorted alphabetically within label groups left to right and top to bottom.

Aliasing Files

The System 7 introduction of aliasing addressed an irritating problem with the Macintosh. After you have accumulated the applications you find useful and have stored them neatly in folders, you may discover that you are repeatedly opening and closing folders to gain access to them. With aliasing, this nuisance can be solved, and some new, useful possibilities open up.

An *alias* is like a copy of an icon. The entire contents of the icon are not copied; only the picture and some information about the icon's location are copied. This copy results in a sort of image of the original that is small (only about 1KB) and that still operates similarly to the original.

You can double-click an alias of an application program, document, folder, or disk just as you can double-click the original. This method enables you to make unlimited copies of an icon and place them where you want without having to move or fully copy the original.

Think of aliases as icons with maps. When you double-click an icon, the Macintosh reads the map, locates the original, and orders the original to open.

An alias and the original icon function differently in some ways. When you copy an alias, you do not copy the original; you make another alias with the same map pointing the way to the original. If you delete an alias, the original is untouched. If you change the name of an alias, the name of the original is not affected.

If you move an original icon to another disk, the alias cannot find the original. You may move the original icon anywhere on the same disk, however.

Although you can make an alias of an alias, this procedure is not generally recommended. The map of the second alias leads to the first alias, which leads to the original icon. If the middle alias is ever deleted, the second alias cannot find the original icon, even though the original has not been touched.

Creating an Alias

You can create an alias by following these steps:

1. Select the file's icon by clicking it.

2. From the File menu, choose Make Alias.

The alias appears and bears the same name as the original icon but with the word *alias* appended (see fig. 4.9).

The name of an alias always appears in italics except when an alias is placed in the Apple Menu Items folder. The name appears in regular font in the Apple menu. Alias names appear in italics even in the Open document dialog.

Locating Original Files

A full or very large hard disk makes it easy to misplace files. You may know the location of an alias but may have forgotten the location of the original file. The Get Info command can help you.

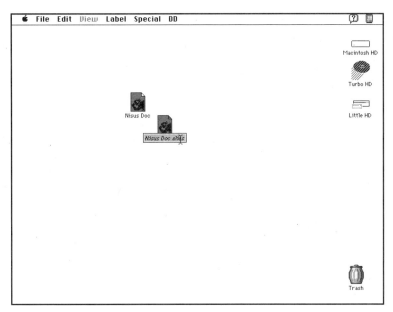

Fig. 4.9
Creating an alias.

To locate the original icon of an alias, follow these steps:

1. Click the alias to select it.

2. From the File menu, choose Get Info. A new button, Find Original, appears in the window.

3. Click the Find Original button. The folder or disk containing the original icon opens.

You also can determine the location of the original by reading the Original information line in the window below the Created and Modified lines. Disks and folders are separated by a colon (:) in this path information. Read the line from left to right. The first name is the disk on which the file is stored. The next name is the folder (if any) you must open to reach the file. The next names are folders nested within the first folder. The last name is the name of the original file.

Considering Some Uses of Aliases

The most basic use of aliases is to place application program aliases and other icon aliases in the Apple Menu Items folder, as discussed in Chapter 6, "Customizing the Macintosh." This method enables you to leave the originals in their folders and yet gain access to them from the Apple menu.

Similarly, you can use aliases of files and applications when you place icons in the Startup Items folder (see Chapter 6). This saves you disk space by placing the small alias that points to the file or application in that folder rather than the original file or application.

You can place an alias of your most used files and application programs right on the desktop to keep the application available.

One of the most interesting uses of aliases involves the capability of making aliases of files on one disk and placing the aliases on another disk. This applies to floppy disks, hard disks, and disks that reside on a file server to which you are connected by a network. When you double-click the alias, the System Software then searches for and requests the disk (if it is not present) on which the original resides. This use of aliases can help you to save disk space. If you have a hard disk, you eventually will run low on space.

You may decide to store files or applications you use infrequently on floppy disks. After you move the icons of the files and applications to the floppy, you can then make aliases of the icons and store them in a folder on your hard disk. This uses far less room than the originals. When you double-click one of the icons, the Macintosh prompts you to insert the appropriate disk.

If you do use floppy disks for storing originals, be certain to write on the disk label the correct name of the disk. The Macintosh will ask for the disk by name, and you will want that name clearly written on the disk label.

You can make aliases of other disks and store them on your hard disk. This is more useful to those connected to a file server (a remote hard disk) that requires mounting the file server volume through some log-in procedure. You can make an alias of the remote volume and then access it by double-clicking the alias.

If you habitually group project icons into folders, you can place aliases of the applications you use in that project in the folder with the documents. Similarly, document files that apply to more than one project are good candidates for aliasing.

With aliases, you can easily access the same file, folder, application, or disk from more than one location. If you need to place a name and address file in the folder that contains your word processor as well as the one that contains your database, for example, just create an alias and place the original in one location and the alias in the other.

K eeping an alias of the Apple Menu Items folder and the
Control Panels folder on the Desktop or at the root level of
your disk enables you to easily place new things in the Apple
menu or to access control panels without going through several
different windows to reach the System folder.

Searching for Files

If you own a hard disk, you may one day discover you have so many files
on the disk that you misplace one. Finding one file is often as trying as
the proverbial search for a needle in a haystack. Fortunately, Apple
provides a method of locating icons on any disk drive—hard disk users
need this feature more than floppy disk users. This method is the Find
command in the File menu.

Using the Find Command

To use the Find command, you first choose Find from the File menu (or
press ⌘-F). The Find dialog appears (see fig. 4.10).

Fig. 4.10
The Find dialog.

Find
Find: [   ]
(More Choices)   (Cancel)   [[Find]]

In its simplest form, you use the Find dialog by typing the name of the
file you want to locate and pressing the Return key or clicking the Find
button. The Cancel button dismisses the dialog without performing a
search.

While a search is in progress, you may see a progress dialog indicating
that the disk is being searched. The dialog also has a Stop button. Stop
the search by clicking on this button. This dialog appears only if the disk
you are searching is large and therefore takes some time to search.

If a match is not found, a message is displayed. Click the OK button to
dismiss the dialog.

After a file is located that matches the search request, the Find command opens the folder or disk on which the file is located and highlights the file.

If the located file is not the one you wanted to find, use the Find Again command in the File menu (you may press ⌘-G). The Macintosh searches for and displays the next file with the name that contains the string of letters you typed in the Find dialog.

Repeat the Find Again command as many times as you want until the Macintosh beeps, indicating that the last file with the name containing the string you typed has been found.

The Find command searches all disks connected to the Macintosh. That means that if you have a floppy disk inserted in the disk drive, it is searched as well as all hard drives in, or attached to, the Macintosh.

The Find command pays no attention to upper- and lowercase letters. Searching for *MAC, Mac,* or *mac* locates the same icons.

Narrowing a Search

The Find dialog has an option that enables you to narrow the searches. This is the More Choices button you saw in figure 4.10. Clicking this button expands the Find dialog (see fig. 4.11).

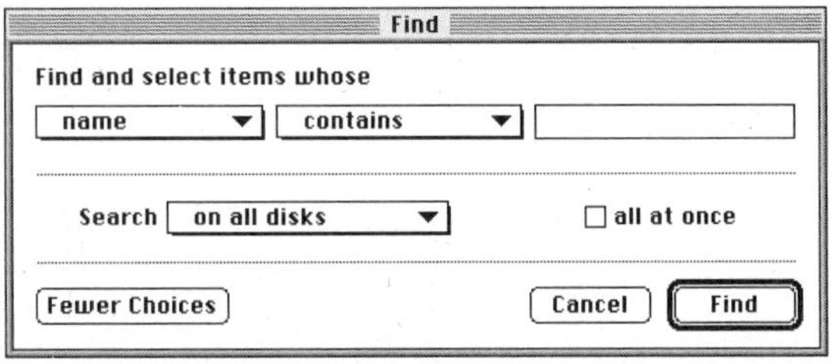

Fig. 4.11
The expanded Find dialog
has more options.

The many options offered in this expanded dialog are controlled by pop-up menus. Each of the three shaded boxes in the dialog is a pop-up menu.

The first pop-up menu, the Search By menu, gives you a choice of what type of search is to take place. After you make a selection in the first menu, the upper part of the Find dialog changes, displaying pop-up menus from which you can choose search restraint criteria.

Table 4.1 lists all the search criteria available in the expanded Find dialog.

Table 4.1
Search criteria of the
Find command

Search By	Constraints	Range or search text
Name	Contains Starts with Ends with Is Is not Doesn't contain	All text
Size	Is less than Is greater than	Some number of K
Kind	Contains Doesn't contain	Alias Application Document Folder Stationery (any kind)
Label	Is Is not	Any of the labels you have defined
Date created	Is Is before Is after Is not	Any date
Date modified	Is Is before Is after Is not	Any date
Version	Is Is before Is after Is not	Any version (number or text)
Comments	Contain Do not contain	Any text
Lock	Is	Locked Unlocked

Having so many different search options can confuse you. A few examples may help clear the confusion. The simplest is a search by name. Suppose that you are looking for a document that begins with *Mac*, but you do not want to find documents such as *Emac* or *Promac*. Set the Find options as shown in figure 4.12.

Fig. 4.12
Settings to search for files
that begin with *Mac*.

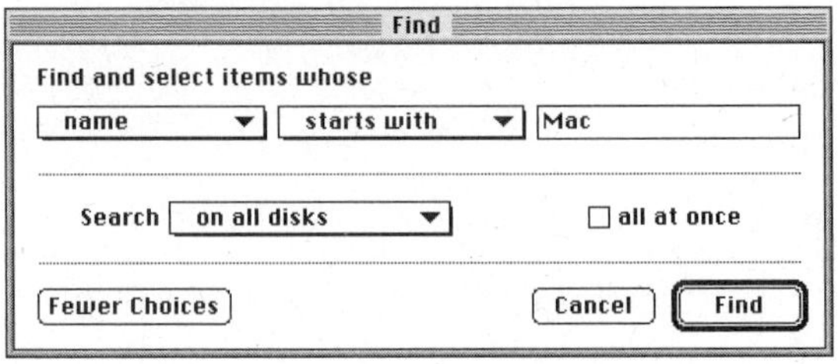

Another example may be to locate every file that you changed on a specific day. Set the options as shown in figure 4.13.

Fig. 4.13
Settings to search for files
modified March 12, 1994.

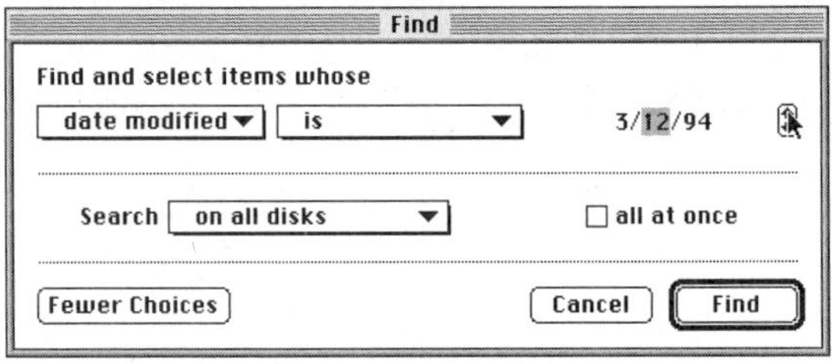

You can change the date part of the search by clicking the month, day, or year. A small control appears with two arrows. You can increase the selected part of the date by clicking the small up arrow. You also can decrease the selected part of the date by clicking the small down arrow. Finally, you can click any other part of the line—month, day, or year—to change the date in the same manner.

In the previous sections, you learned that searches take place on all mounted disks. With the Search menu, however, you also may narrow the choice.

The Search menu varies according to the Macintosh's hardware. The first option, On All Disks, is always present. Then each mounted disk is displayed, enabling you to choose the disk you want to search. Your hard disk or disks are listed. If a disk is inserted in the floppy drive, this disk also appears in the menu.

The On The Desktop option enables you to search for icons on the Desktop. The last option, The Selected Items, enables you to search through a group of files or a folder you previously selected or files you found and selected by a previous search.

You also can combine the various types of searches. You can search for all document files created this year with the Microsoft Word program, for example.

This search requires using the All At Once option and the Search menu. You must perform this search in stages, however, with one search for each criterion you want to use. To find the previously mentioned Microsoft Word document files, set the Find dialog as shown in figure 4.14.

Fig. 4.14

Settings to search for document files created in Microsoft Word.

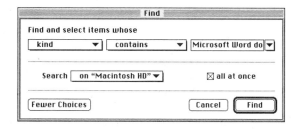

This search displays a text listing with the located file selected, rather than displaying the located files one at a time. You then would choose the Find command again, but not the Find Again command—that would repeat the same search. Set the Find dialog as shown in figure 4.15.

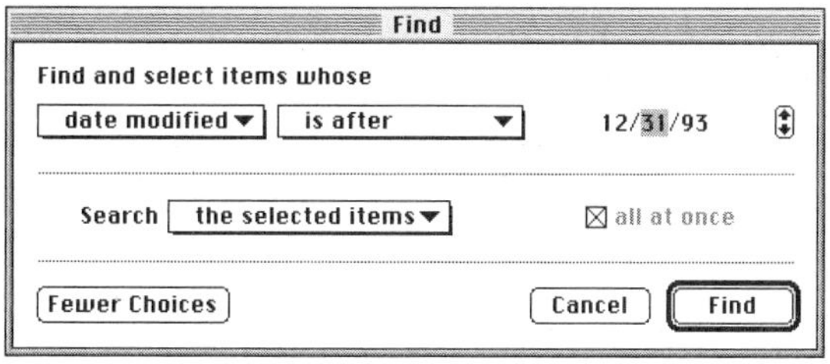

Fig. 4.15

Settings to search the already located files by date.

Again, any located files are displayed in a list view and are selected.

Because all the files are selected, when you drag one of the file icons to a disk or to another location, you drag the file icons as a group. In this view, be careful to place the mouse pointer directly on the small icon of one of the selected files before you press and hold down the mouse button. Otherwise, all the located files are deselected, and you must repeat the search.

You can choose the Find command again and proceed with more searches to narrow the selection of icons. Be sure that you leave the Search menu set to The Selected Items option.

The Find command has too many possibilities to explore in the scope of this book. Be adventurous and experiment. You cannot hurt data by searching with the Find or Find Again command, so try some search combinations to get a feel for the true power of this option.

Working with Stationery Pads

One feature unique to document files is *stationery*. This feature enables you to create template documents that contain data, such as letterheads, predefined financial spreadsheets, graphics, and so on. You can store frequently used information in a *stationery pad,* from which copies can be "torn off" and used to create new document files.

After you design a document that you want to use over and over, such as letterhead, you may want to turn the document into a stationery pad. This way, the Mac automatically opens a copy of the document when you double-click its icon and at the same time protects the contents from accidental changes.

To change a document into a stationery pad, select the document file by clicking its icon, and then choose Get Info from the File menu.

In the lower right corner of the Info window, you see a Stationery pad option. Click the check box. This step places an X in the box. The icon of the document file changes to appear as a stack of documents—a stationery pad—rather than just one document.

The icon of the document file on the disk now also appears as a stationery pad.

To change a stationery pad back into a regular document, follow the same steps. This time, the X is removed from the Stationery pad check box, and the icon returns to the previous state.

When you double-click a stationery pad, a copy of the stationery pad file is made containing the formatting and information you placed in the document file before you changed the file to a stationery pad. If the creating application program understands stationery pads, you will see an untitled copy of the document file open that contains the predesigned formatting and information. If the application does not understand stationery pads, the System takes over first, asking you in a dialog to name the new document file that will be created by copying the stationery pad. Then the application program will start, and the copy you named will be opened.

Stationery pad files are perfect for holding your company letterhead, a preformatted letter, a complex but often used spreadsheet format, or other document files that you use often.

Working with Folders

Folders on the Macintosh work much like folders in the real world. They hold document files and other folders and can be labeled to aid you in organizing your disks. One difference between the Macintosh version of folders and the real world of folders is that Macintosh folders also can contain application programs (whereas in the real world you would never have filed your typewriter in a manila folder).

Viewing Files

By now, you have learned how the contents of disks and folders can be viewed as icons with the by Icon view. This view usually is sufficient for small numbers of icons but can become difficult to use when a folder or disk contains large numbers of icons.

Viewing by Small Icon

The first option you may consider is the by Small Icon option in the View menu. Figure 4.16 shows a folder viewed by Small Icon.

Fig. 4.16
Viewing a folder's
contents by Small Icon.

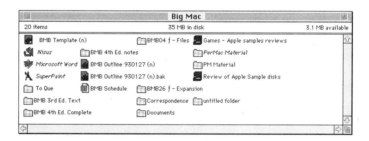

This view is good for a large number of icons because they are displayed in a small space. You may find that picking out an icon in this view is difficult.

Viewing by Name

Choosing the view by Name option from the View menu results in a display similar to that shown in figure 4.17.

Fig. 4.17
Viewing the System Folder
by name.

Big Mac				
19 items		35 MB in disk		3 MB available
Name	**Size**	**Kind**	**Label**	**Last Modified**
BMB Template (n)	5K	Nisus 3.43 station...	—	Thu, Jan 28, 1993, 19:01
Nisus	1K	alias	—	Wed, Jan 27, 1993, 17:51
Microsoft Word	1K	alias	—	Sat, Feb 27, 1993, 18:16
SuperPaint	1K	alias	—	Thu, Jan 28, 1993, 19:20
▷ To Que	421K	folder	—	Tue, Mar 9, 1993, 12:29
▷ BMB 3rd Ed. Text	876K	folder	—	Fri, Mar 12, 1993, 13:07
▷ BMB 4th Ed. Complete	2,274K	folder	—	Wed, Mar 10, 1993, 19:09
▷ BMB 4th Ed. notes	117K	folder	—	Fri, Mar 12, 1993, 12:54
BMB Outline 930127 (n)	27K	Nisus 3.43 document	—	Mon, Mar 8, 1993, 10:55
BMB Outline 930127 (n)...	27K	Nisus 3.43 document	—	Sun, Mar 7, 1993, 16:39
BMB Schedule	21K	Microsoft Excel do...	—	Thu, Mar 11, 1993, 18:09
▷ BMB04 ƒ - Files	497K	folder	—	Fri, Mar 12, 1993, 20:12
▷ BMB26 ƒ - Expansion	18K	folder	—	Wed, Mar 10, 1993, 19:09
▷ Correspondence	4K	folder	—	Wed, Feb 24, 1993, 7:11
▷ Documents	108K	folder	—	Fri, Mar 12, 1993, 14:40
Games - Apple samples r...	2K	DiskDoubler™ App ...	—	Fri, Jan 22, 1993, 13:14
PerMac Material	1K	alias	—	Tue, Feb 23, 1993, 13:06
▷ PM Material	56K	folder	—	Wed, Feb 24, 1993, 7:13
Review of Apple Sample ...	2K	DiskDoubler™ App ...	—	Fri, Feb 5, 1993, 23:24

This view gives you an orderly, alphabetical listing of the icons. You also are told the size of the icon, the kind of document, and when the document was last changed.

Viewing by Other Orders

The by Date, by Size, by Label, by Kind, by Version, and by Comment options result in the same basic display as by Name, but the icons are sorted in order of the date the documents were last changed, their size, or their kind, respectively.

The latter two, by Version and by Comment, may not be immediately available to you. You will need to add them to your View menu if you wish to use them (see Chapter 6, "Customizing the Macintosh").

A quick way to switch between the text views—Name, Size, Date, and so on—is to click the heading in the folder's window. That is, to sort icons by Name, click the Name heading in the window. To sort by Size, click the Size heading and so on.

Using Outline Views

The list views—by Name, by Size, by Date, by Label, by Kind, by Version, and by Comment—are often referred to as "outline" views. This description is given because these views can display more than just the files and folders of the top-level folder, but all the nested folders as well (see figure 4.18).

Fig. 4.18
Viewing a folder in
outline view.

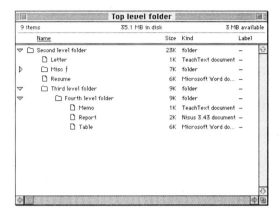

The small triangles to the left of the folder icons enable you to open the folder in outline view. Click the triangle, and the contents of the folder are displayed. The triangle points downward to indicate that the folder is open. Note that each level is indented to the right to show that the contents are at a lower level. Items aligned vertically (such as Letter, Misc ƒ, Resume, and Third level folder) are at the same level.

The outline feature of list views is handy when you have many nested folders. You can view the contents of the folders you need at the same time and select items from folders at different levels (you may Shift-click any visible file or folder to select them, regardless of level).

You also can easily control list views from the keyboard. The up-and down-arrow keys select folder or file icons up or down. Pressing ⌘-right arrow when a folder is selected opens the folder. ⌘-left arrow closes the selected folder. ⌘-Option-right arrow opens the selected folder and all folders nested within the folder to display its entire contents. ⌘-Option-left arrow closes the folder and all folders within it.

Navigating Folders

The nesting of folders can result in the need to open and close folders quite a bit while searching for a particular file, application program, or other item. Fortunately, the Macintosh has some commands that aid you in navigating through nested folders.

Folder windows have a folder menu that enables you to jump "up" in the levels of nesting quickly. To access the menu, hold down the Command key and click the name of the folder in the title bar of the window (see fig. 4.19).

Fig. 4.19
Opening the second level
folder, bypassing the third.

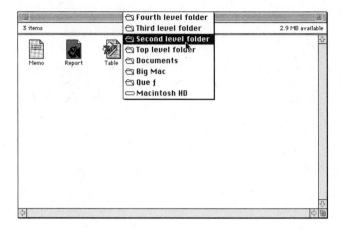

Folders are listed in the menu in reverse order. You see the name of the current folder at the top of the menu. The next folder down is the folder that contains the current folder (the Third level folder in figure 4.19). The next folder down is the folder which contains the folder that precedes it (the Second level folder contains the Third level folder). Each folder in the path is listed until you see the hard disk itself (Macintosh HD).

Move the mouse to highlight the folder or disk you want to open, and then release the mouse button and the Command key. The selected item then opens.

You also can hold down both the Command and Option keys before clicking the folder menu and choosing a new folder. This action causes the new folder to open and the current open folder to close.

You also may use the keyboard to navigate through folders. Use the up-, down-, left-, or right-arrow keys to select a folder (or other icon) in the current disk or folder window. The selected folder, file, or other item can then be opened by holding down the Command key and pressing the down-arrow key—the same as double-clicking the item's icon.

The ⌘-up arrow combination opens the folder that contains the current folder window, as if you had used the folder menu to select the next folder in the menu. To open Third level folder in figure 4.19, for example, you could press ⌘-up arrow rather than choose the folder's name from the folder menu.

Adding the Option key opens the new folder while closing the previous folder (in the example, the Third level folder opens as the Fourth level folder closes).

After you select a folder, you may press the Return key to select the folder's name. You then may type a new name. Press the Return key again to confirm the new name.

Making File Backups

Unfortunately, many users never realize the importance of backing up files and disks after they have lost a file they have spent hours, days, or even months creating. Get into the habit of backing up your files at the end of each work session so that you are not the one with the missing 342-page dissertation.

Backing Up Floppies

You can copy any file from one disk to another by dragging the icon representing the file from the source disk to the destination disk.

To back up an entire floppy disk, drag the icon representing the disk you want to copy to the destination floppy disk. When you do this, your Macintosh asks you whether you want to replace the entire contents of the destination disk with the contents of the source disk, naming the disks. When you see this message, take a moment to make sure that you no longer need the contents of the destination disk. Remember that copying the contents of an entire disk to another disk erases all of the destination disk's contents before the copying takes place.

When you are ready, click OK (or press Return); your Macintosh copies all the files and folders on the source disk to the destination disk. If any files or folders on the destination disk have the same name as any on the source disk, your Macintosh asks whether you want to replace them. Click Yes to confirm.

You can back up a day's work quickly by using the Find command to locate all files modified on today's date (see the section "Using the Find Command" in this chapter). Then drag the located and selected files to a floppy disk.

When you receive new software, always make backups of the original disks and work with the backup copies. Save the originals and store them in a safe place.

Backing Up Hard Disks

Although you may go through your Macintosh routines carefully and think that you never would inadvertently lose or erase a file, you can never be sure that an accident will not happen to you. Almost all users lose important information at one time or another because they have failed to back up their files. Like insurance, backup copies enable you to continue working when disasters strike—disasters caused by power failures, system crashes, or human error.

You can choose from a number of different methods for creating your backups. The simplest, fastest method is to back up individual files. At the end of each work session, make a backup copy of the files that you have worked on during that session. One way to remember the files you have worked on is to view them on-screen by date or to use the Find command. Copy these files to a floppy disk and label the disk as a backup with the names of the files.

Y ou would do well to remember the "grandfather, father, son" rule of backups. Keep three sets of backups. Assuming that I work on this book every day (which, by the way, is true), I would back up the changed files each day. Then, if today is Thursday, I would keep the disks for Tuesday and Wednesday as well, reusing the disk from Monday's backup.

Thursday is the "son" backup; Wednesday, the "father" backup; and Tuesday, the "grandfather" backup. Even in the unlikely event of a disastrous failure such as losing the hard disk *and* the backup disk as I was attempting to restore backed-up files, for example, two more backups exist. I would lose only about a day's work.

If your work is more critical than that, you can back up more frequently or keep more days of backups. But keep at least three backup sets. Preferably, keep one set in another location if your work is important.

After 12 years of working with computers, I have found that you can *never* have too many backups or be too paranoid. I always use the "Las Vegas" approach. I always ask myself how much I can afford to lose. You never know when a disk will fail and you will be stuck re-creating your work.

You also can do a global backup of your entire hard disk, backing up the full set of folders and files. Good backup software (discussed in Chapter 19, "Using Utility Software") stores the entire contents of the hard disk on several different floppy disks and maintains the original disk organization. You can do a complete backup without using backup software, of course; just select all the files in each folder and copy them to floppy disks. A commercial program can compress the files, however, so that they fit on fewer floppy disks and break up large files across more than one floppy disk. Global backup is a good weekly habit to get into; with this method, you catch any files you may have missed when backing up individual files.

Finally, you can back up in an incremental fashion, backing up files that have been modified or added since a certain date. Most users prefer this method because it backs up only those files that have been changed. Why back up 60MB of files when they are backed up already and have not been changed?

The method you choose for backing up depends on how often you work with your files, how much time you are willing to spend backing up, and how much data you are willing to lose in the event of a crash.

Using Other Backup Methods

Tape backups are an alternative to using floppy disks as your primary backup medium. A tape backup device is, in effect, a tape drive that can back up large amounts of data quickly.

Tape backups have two advantages over floppy disk backups. First, tape backups are very fast, backing up megabytes in minutes. Second, you need only one tape cassette as opposed to approximately tens of floppy disks to back up a full 160MB (or more) drive. With backup software, you even can schedule timed backups while you sleep, because you don't have to sit at the computer swapping disks as you must with floppy disks. Another type of tape is digital audiotape (DAT); one tape can hold a gigabyte (1,000 megabytes) of data.

The primary disadvantage of tape backups is price. Tape drives are expensive (see Chapter 26, "Expanding the Macintosh," for more information). Normally, only professionals and businesses purchase them. Average users can usually get by with floppy backups.

Another alternative for backing up large amounts of data is the newer magneto-optical drives. These optical disk drives can store about 120MB on a single 3.5-inch disk or as much as 650MB on a 5.25-inch disk. They have a media life far greater than tape or floppies; your data can last for decades. Again, both the drives and the optical disks are expensive, but for long term storage of large amounts of important data, nothing can beat them.

For businesses (or even professionals) that have extremely critical data, new systems are available that simultaneously write to two hard drives. This "mirroring" of your hard disk means that either drive can fail at any moment, but you will lose almost no data at all. Such systems are very expensive but may be what you need if you just cannot afford to lose data.

The Big Mac Recommendation

Now that you have seen how the Macintosh handles files, how icons represent them, and how you can organize them, only one recommendation needs to be made.

That recommendation is to back up and often. Whether you use your Macintosh for home or business, you need backups. Nothing is worse than a hard disk failure when you have no backups to safeguard your data. Like fire insurance, you don't buy it expecting your house to burn down. Your house may never even smoulder, but that one time the fire roars through makes the insurance worth it.

For the average user, backing up the floppies of application programs onto other floppies, storing the originals in a safe place (a safe-deposit box is a good choice), and then doing periodic backups of data as it changes is probably good enough. To add safety, a full disk backup with a good backup program is suggested. For business users and those on a network, a backup regime with a good quality backup utility program is a necessity. A loss of an entire day's work can be disastrous. See Chapter 19, "Using Utility Software," and Chapter 26, "Expanding the Macintosh," for more information.

CHAPTER FIVE

Configuring the Macintosh

Y ou can customize the Macintosh to fit your individual work habits and taste—more so than any other personal computer. This chapter and the next cover the configurations and customization features available and how you can use them to meet your needs.

This chapter introduces the control panels, also called control panel devices or CDEVs (pronounced *see-dev*). This small software item acts— as the name implies—as a control for various configuration and customization options.

Control panels reside in the Control Panels folder in the System Folder. You can access this folder in one of two ways. You can double-click the System Folder to open it, and then double-click the Control Panels folder. Alternatively, you can choose Control Panels from the Apple menu. In either case, the Control Panels folder opens, displaying the Control Panels currently installed on your Macintosh (see fig. 5.1).

Fig. 5.1
The contents of a typical
Control Panels folder.

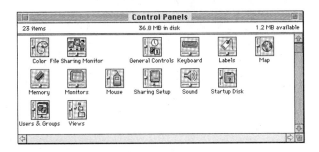

The content of your Control Panels folder may vary from that in figure 5.1, depending on which Macintosh you own and the exact configuration of your System software.

Setting General Options

The General Controls window determines the settings of the Desktop. The settings include such things as the pattern of the Desktop, the rate at which menus blink when selected, the time and date setting, and the insertion point blink speed.

Open the General Controls window by double-clicking its icon. A window opens and displays the controls (see fig. 5.2).

After you have set the general options, you confirm the changes and dismiss the window by clicking the close box in the upper left corner of the General Controls window.

Setting the Desktop Pattern

You can set the pattern on the Desktop with the Desktop Pattern control in the General Controls panel (refer to fig. 5.2). The pattern is a 32X32 grid that repeats itself until it covers the Desktop background.

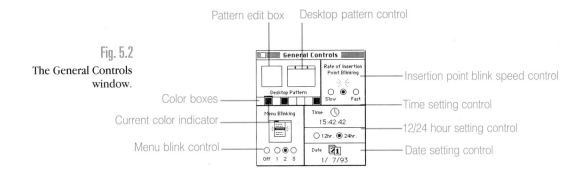

Fig. 5.2
The General Controls
window.

You can choose from two ways to change the Desktop pattern. Click the pattern edit box on the left to add or remove dots. The box to the right then shows a tiny version of the Desktop and displays the resulting pattern. When you achieve the desired pattern, click in the box on the right to set the pattern.

Alternatively, you can click the left or right arrows at the top of the Desktop pattern control to change the pattern. Approximately 38 patterns are available for your use. When you see the one you want to use, click the box to set it. The background of the Desktop is then redrawn in the selected pattern.

Color Macintosh users have the additional option of using color on the Desktop. Click in one of the color boxes to choose the desired color. When you click one of the boxes, the current color indicator moves to outline that color. To place the color in the pattern edit box, click in the box. Each individual dot you click changes to the currently selected color.

You can change the color of the color boxes. Double-click the color box you want to change. The standard Macintosh Color Wheel appears, and you can choose a color by clicking the wheel and clicking the OK button (see Chapter 6, "Customizing the Macintosh," for more about the Color Wheel).

Setting the Insertion Point Blinking Rate

When you work with text on the Macintosh, a vertical bar indicates the location at which text will be inserted. This is the *insertion point*. You can change the speed at which the insertion point blinks.

The Rate of Insertion Point Blinking control (refer back to fig. 5.2) consists of three buttons: Slow, Medium, and Fast. Click any of the three buttons to choose a speed. A sample insertion point blinks at the speed you have chosen.

Setting Menu Blinking

When you choose a menu item (command or option), the item blinks three times to confirm your choice. You can change this to one or two blinks, or you can stop it from blinking.

Choose a menu blink amount by clicking one of the three buttons numbered 1, 2, and 3; the menu above the buttons blinks that number of times to confirm your choice. You also can turn off menu blinking by clicking the Off button.

Setting the Time

The Macintosh has a built-in clock maintained by a battery. After the clock is set, the clock should maintain good time and rarely need adjustment, except when daylight saving time begins and ends. You change the time with the Time control (refer back to fig. 5.2).

Use these steps to set the time:

1. Click the hour, minute, or second to select it. Small control arrows appear to the right of the time.

2. Click the up arrow to increase the time by one or the down arrow to decrease it by one. Alternatively, you can type the numbers to set the hour, minute, or second.

3. Change the a.m. or p.m. settings by clicking the up or down arrow. Note that you must type only the letter **A** for a.m. or **P** for p.m. if you use the keyboard method.

4. Click the clock icon to confirm your setting.

5. To change to 12- or 24-hour time, click the button next to the setting you want to use.

In 24-hour mode, 1 to 11 p.m. is represented by the numbers 13 through 23. Midnight is considered to be hour zero (0), because it is the beginning of the day. If you choose 24-hour time, you do not use a.m. and p.m.

Setting the Date

You set the date similarly to setting the time. Use the following steps:

1. Click the day, month, or year to select it. Small control arrows appear to the right of the time.

2. Click the up arrow to increase the date by one or the down arrow to decrease it by one. Alternatively, you can type the numbers to set the day, month, or year.

3. Click the calendar icon to confirm the setting.

Setting International Options

With System 7.1, Apple has moved to "unify" the releases of System software worldwide. System 7.1 is the first release of System software that does not require specific versions for different countries. To achieve this, Apple has added the ability to conform System 7.1 easily to local customs in such things as the display of dates, times, and numbers.

Your Macintosh comes with these settings configured to conform to the country in which it is sold, and you should not have to change these settings. However, it is good to know how you can do it if you travel or move to another country, or if you find the dates, times, and numbers displayed in a manner other than is customary for your area.

Setting the Date and Time Formats

The Date & Time control panel enables you to set the format of dates and times in the Macintosh System. This feature enables you to accommodate international variations in date and time formats. For example, many European countries separate the parts of time—hours, minutes, and seconds—with periods instead of colons. To access the control panel, open the Control Panels folder in the System Folder by choosing it from the Apple menu. Then double-click the Date & Time control panel. You see the control panel's window (see fig. 5.3).

Fig. 5.3

The Date & Time control panel.

This window displays the current date and time in the current format. Note that you can change the date and time in this window with the following steps:

1. Click on the part of the date or time you want to change (the day, month, year, hour, minute, or second). A control appears to the right of the date or time.

2. Click the up arrow to increase the selected item by one, or click the down arrow to decrease the selected item by one.

3. Click outside the date or time field to confirm your setting.

Alternatively, you can type the date or time item, then press Tab to move to the next item to the right. You can then confirm your setting by pressing Return.

Setting Date Format Options

To set the date format, click the Date Formats button. The Date Formats dialog appears (see fig. 5.4).

Fig. 5.4
Setting the date format.

Long date parts menus

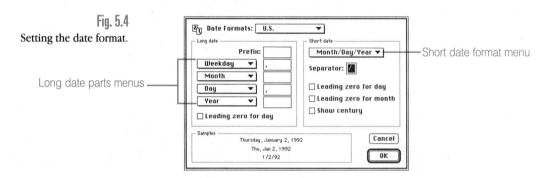

Short date format menu

At the top of the dialog is a pop-up menu that contains predefined date formats. The current setting in figure 5.4 is *U.S.*, for United States.

Your Macintosh may already come with other predefined formats. If so, you choose the desired date format from the Date Formats pop-up menu. If the Date Formats menu does not contain the date format you want to use, you can contact your dealer to obtain the format, or you can set a custom format.

If you decide to create a custom format, note that the Date Formats dialog is divided into two sections of settings that affect the display of dates: Long date and Short date. The Long date section sets how the full date is displayed. (The full date contains the names of the weekday, the month, the date, and the year, as in *Monday, January 25, 1993*. A short date uses only numbers, as in *1/25/93*.)

To set the Long date format, use these steps:

1. If you want a prefix to precede the date, double-click in the Prefix field, then type the prefix. You can type up to four characters that will display before the date. You can skip this initial step if you don't want to set a prefix.

2. From the first pop-up menu under the Long date heading, choose the part of the date you want displayed first. You can choose the Day (which is a number, such as 25), the Weekday (Monday), the Month (January), or the Year (1993). You can select None to display nothing in this position.

3. Double-click in the field to the right of the menu.

4. Type the character that will follow the part of the date you have chosen from the pop-up menu.

You can type up to four characters. For example, in figure 5.4 the weekday (Monday) will be followed by a comma and a space (the space is present, but it's not visible in the field).

Repeat steps 2 through 5 for each of the three following date part menus. Note that the Samples section displays how your date will appear. You can adjust your settings until you achieve the desired date format.

Finally, you can cause the day number to be two digits long at all times by clicking the Leading zero for day check box. This means that the date will display as January 02, as opposed to January 2.

To set the Short date format, follow these steps:

1. Choose the Short date format from the Short date format menu. This menu offers four options: Month/Day/Year, Day/Month/Year, Year/Month/Day, and Year/Day/Month.

2. Click in the Separator field, then type the character you want to separate the parts of the date. You can type one character. Usually, you type characters such as the slash, the dash, the period, and so on.

3. If you want the day number to always be two characters, click the Leading zero for day check box. This causes the day to display as 02 rather than simply 2. This setting does not affect days higher than 9.

4. If you want the month number to always be two characters, click the Leading zero for month check box.

5. If you want the century to be displayed, click the Show century check box.

This option adds the first two digits to the year display. 1993 is displayed, as opposed to 93.

As with the Long date settings, your settings are reflected in the Samples section.

When you have finished making changes, confirm your settings and close the dialog by clicking OK or pressing Return. If you want to dismiss the dialog without making changes, click Cancel or press Command-period (⌘-.).

Setting Time Format Options

You also can set the time format in the Date & Time control panel. To do this, first click the Time Formats button. The Time Format dialog appears (see fig. 5.5).

Fig. 5.5

Setting time formats.

As with the date formats, you can choose predefined formats from the Time Format menu. Choose the country whose format you want to use. Again, if the country does not appear, check with your dealer or set a custom format with the following steps:

1. Click the 24 hour or 12 hour button.

   24-hour time counts the hours after noon as 13 through 0 (zero being midnight). This format is often referred to as "military time."

   If you choose the 12-hour option, you have an additional step. (You can skip this next step if you chose 24-hour time.)

2. Click the 0:00 option button if you want noon and midnight to display as 0:00. Click the 12:00 option button if you want noon and midnight to display as 12:00 (as is common in the United States).

   If you want to have the time followed by characters such as AM and PM, continue with these steps:

3. Double-click in the Before noon field.

4. Type up to four characters that will follow the time displayed if the time is before noon (for example, type **AM**. Remember that you must type a space before AM if you want the characters to be separated from the time).

5. Press Tab.

6. Type the characters you want to follow the time if the time is after noon (again, you have four characters). For example, use **PM.**

   It is interesting to note that the characters you enter will be appended to the time even if you choose the 24-hour time display.

   You can change the character that separates the parts of the time. Continue with this step:

7. Double-click in the Separator field.

8. Type the single character you want to separate the parts of the time (the colon, period, and comma are examples).

   Finally, you can cause the hour to be displayed as two characters at all times (a zero precedes times from 0 to 9) with this step:

9. Click the Use leading zero for hour check box.

Your changes are reflected in the Samples section at the bottom of the dialog. An example of a time before noon is displayed to the left, and an example of a time after noon is displayed to the right.

When you have finished making changes, confirm your settings and close the dialog by clicking OK or pressing Return. If you want to dismiss the dialog without making changes, click Cancel or press Command-period (⌘-.).

Setting the Number Format

Formats for numbers can vary from country to country. For example, some countries use periods to indicate decimal parts of numbers, whereas others use commas. You can conform your Macintosh to the local custom by using the Numbers control panel. Open the control panel by choosing the Control Panels folder from the Apple menu and double-clicking the Numbers control panel. You see the control panel's window (see fig. 5.6).

Fig. 5.6
Setting the number format.

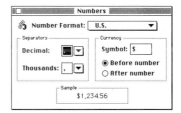

As with the Date & Time control panel, this control panel gives you access to predefined formats. You can choose the format you want to use from the Number Format menu. If the country whose format you want to use is not present in the menu, you can contact your dealer or set a custom format.

You can change two major components of number display in this control panel: Separators and Currency. Separators are the symbols used to separate the decimal part of a number from the whole number part, as well as to divide the thousand parts of a number. Currency concerns setting the symbol displayed for currency (the U.S. dollar symbol and the British pound symbol are examples).

Set a custom format with the following steps:

1. Double-click in the Decimal field and type the character you want to have separate the whole part of a number from the decimal part. Then press Tab.

   Or

   Choose a separator from the pop-up menu to the right of the field (indicated by the downward-pointing triangle.) The menu offers three choices: a period, a comma, or a space.

2. Type a character to separate the thousand part of a number. (For example, in the U.S., we use a comma to separate every three digits in a number. Many other countries use a period for this purpose.)

   Or

   Choose a separator from the pop-up menu to the right of the field. The menu offers four choices: a period, a comma, an apostrophe, or none (no separation at all).

Set a currency symbol by using the following steps:

1. Double-click in the Symbol field.

2. Enter up to three characters.

3. If you want the currency symbol to precede the currency number, click the Before number option button. If you want it to follow the currency number, click the After number button.

The Samples section shows the effect your settings will have on the number display.

When you have finished making changes, confirm your settings and close the dialog by clicking OK or pressing Return. If you want to dismiss the dialog without making changes, click Cancel or press Command-period (⌘-.).

Setting Keyboard Options

A few options enable you to conform the keyboard to your preferred work habits. You can set the speed at which held-down keys will repeat and the delay before repeating begins. You can also choose alternative keyboard layouts if you have installed more than one.

You set keyboard options by first opening the Control Panels folder, then double-clicking the Keyboard control panel. The Keyboard window opens (see fig. 5.7).

Fig. 5.7
The Keyboard control
panel window.

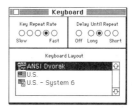

When you have set the keyboard options, you can confirm them and dismiss the window by clicking the window's close box.

Setting Key Repeat

The top two controls in the window affect the repeat rate of the keys. Key repeat is a feature that types a character repeatedly when you hold down a key. You can use this feature to create a dividing line of dashes or a string of periods.

You can set the key repeat rate from Slow to Fast by clicking the desired button. This is the speed at which the characters will be repeatedly typed.

The delay that occurs before the key is repeated can be set from Long to Short. Clicking the Off button prevents the keys from being repeated, regardless of how long they are held down. To determine the best settings for your use, you must experiment.

Setting Keyboard Layout

Keyboard layout controls which character is typed when you press a key. You usually use an American QWERTY layout—the standard typewriter arrangement of keys. Other arrangements are available through various sources. One such arrangement is the Dvorak key layout, which places your most-often-used keys within easier reach of your strongest fingers, reducing the amount of movement you make in typing.

In the lower part of the window is a list box that displays installed keyboard layouts. If you have only one keyboard layout—you have not installed another—this window does not appear, because there is nothing to choose. The highlighting band around ANSI Dvorak indicates that the keyboard is currently using the Dvorak keyboard arrangement. •

Change this selection by clicking any layout you have installed. You can obtain the Dvorak or other keyboard layouts through your dealer or from on-line services such as CompuServe.

Setting Memory Options

The Memory control panel enables you to set the options that control memory-related items such as the disk cache, virtual memory, and the 32-bit address mode. The disk cache uses memory to help speed accesses to your hard disk. Virtual memory enables you to set aside part of the hard disk to be treated as memory in order to run large programs. The 32-bit address mode setting enables you to control the way the Macintosh accesses memory and allows for accessing much greater amounts of memory.

To access memory controls, you open the Control Panels folder, then double-click the Memory control panel. You see the Memory window (see fig. 5.8).

Fig. 5.8

The Memory control panel window.

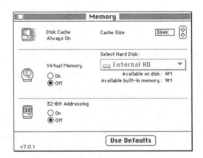

When you are finished setting memory options, you can confirm them and dismiss the window by clicking its close box.

Setting the Disk Cache

The disk cache is a part of memory set aside for use in accessing your disk drive. Disk accessing is considerably slower than for memory chips. Hence, a disk cache stores frequently used information in memory to reduce the number of times a drive must be accessed, speeding up the operation of the computer.

The cache size control has two small arrows that are used to set the amount of memory the disk cache uses. Clicking the up arrow increases the cache size by 32KB until a size of 256KB is reached. At that point, the cache increases by amounts of 128KB with each click. Clicking the down arrow decreases the disk cache by the same amounts. The size of the cache is displayed to the left of the controls.

The cache should be set at least to 32KB of memory for each physical megabyte you have installed in your machine. For a 5MB Macintosh, for example, the cache should be set to 160KB.

The easiest method of setting the cache size properly is to click the Use Defaults button. The cache size is set automatically.

You can increase the cache size for greater disk accessing speed; however, remember that each increase in cache size reduces the amount of available memory for your application programs to run in. If you want to try a larger cache, do so, but pay careful attention to the speed increase. If you do not notice an increase in speed, spending the extra memory is probably not worth it.

Setting Virtual Memory Options

Virtual memory is available on all Macintoshes that have a 68030 or greater CPU or all Macs with a 68020 CPU and a Paged Memory Management Unit (PMMU). Beginning with the introduction of the Classic II and LC II, all current Macintoshes have this chip. You can easily tell whether you can use virtual memory by opening the Memory control panel. If you cannot use virtual memory, no virtual memory control is in the window.

Virtual memory enables you to set aside part of your hard disk to act as memory. This makes much more memory available than is physically installed in your Macintosh. Application programs are "paged" in and out of the actual physical memory as they run.

There are two drawbacks to virtual memory. You lose the hard disk space, and the "memory" on the hard disk is significantly slower than physical memory. But if you only infrequently need more memory, virtual memory can be of great help.

You must set aside an amount of disk space equal to the amount of memory you currently have installed plus the amount of memory you want to add. For example, if you have 8 megabytes installed in your machine and want to add four more megabytes, you must set aside 12 megabytes of disk space. There are also limits to the amount of memory your Macintosh can access. The Macintosh IIsi, for example, can use only a total of 8 megabytes of memory (unless it is operating in 32-bit address mode; see the next section). Setting aside a 50MB hard drive as virtual memory does not affect this limitation; you still only have 8 megabytes with which to work.

To use virtual memory, do the following:

1. Click the On button in the Virtual memory control.

    The Select Hard Disk menu becomes active (see fig. 5.9).

Fig. 5.9

Setting virtual memory options.

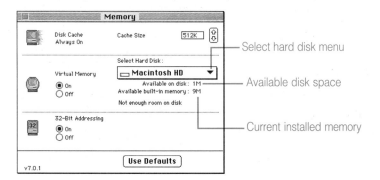

2. Choose the hard disk you want to set space aside on from the Select Hard Disk menu.

    If you do not have enough space on the hard disk for virtual memory, you will see a message below the Select Hard Disk menu, as in figure 5.9.

3. Optionally, click the increase or decrease button to adjust the size of the virtual memory.

    The Macintosh automatically sets an amount of virtual memory, and you do not normally need to adjust this amount. Additionally, the Macintosh may not permit you to make any adjustment to the amount of virtual memory. Note that if you increase the amount of virtual memory over the automatic settings, you may slow the operation of your Macintosh.

4. Click the close box of the Memory control panel.

5. Restart your Macintosh.

After restarting the Macintosh, choose the About this Macintosh command from the Apple menu. The memory amount should reflect the added virtual memory amount.

Turn off virtual memory by clicking the Off button in the Memory control panel, then restarting your Macintosh.

Setting the 32-Bit Address Mode

The 32-bit address mode enables the Macintosh to access, in theory, memory sizes of up to some four billion bytes. There are practical limitations, not the least of which is that no memory modules of such size yet exist.

Note that not all Macintosh models can use 32-bit addressing. Those that cannot will not display a 32-Bit Addressing control section in the Memory control panel.

You activate 32-bit addressing by opening the Memory control panel, clicking the button to the left of the On option, closing the control panel, then restarting your Macintosh. To turn 32-bit address mode off, use the same procedure but click the Off option.

It is not advisable to use 24-bit address mode unless most of your software is not compatible with 32-bit addressing mode. Check with the manual or manufacturer of each software package to verify that this is the case. Software application programs that are not compatible with this addressing mode will crash if you attempt to run them with this addressing mode turned on. All current applications run in 32-bit mode.

If you need to run an application program that requires 24-bit addressing when not all of your applications are compatible with that mode, you can turn on the option before using the application program. Then you can turn it back off when you are finished.

Setting the Monitor Options

This section applies only to Macintoshes that can have more than one monitor or have color capabilities. The Monitor control panel enables you to set various options for color monitors or for multiple monitors. You can set the number of colors the monitor uses for display, as well as change the orientation of multiple monitors.

Access the monitor options by opening the Control Panels folder and double-clicking the Monitor control panel. The Monitors window opens (see fig. 5.10).

Fig. 5.10
Setting monitor options.

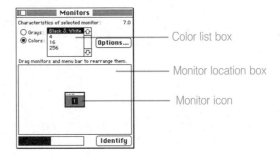

Color list box

Monitor location box

Monitor icon

The appearance of this control panel varies depending on your Macintosh and configuration. Figure 5.10 shows the panel for a Macintosh IIsi with a single monitor.

When you have finished setting the monitor options, confirm your settings and dismiss the window by clicking the close box.

Setting Color Options

Color-capable Macintoshes use various numbers of colors—black and white, four colors, 16 colors, 256 colors, and up into the millions of colors. You can change the number of colors your monitor uses to display information on the screen.

In the Monitors control panel, the Color list box displays the numbers of colors you can use. From top to bottom, you see the least number of colors (starting with black and white) to the greatest number (256 colors in fig. 5.10). To set the number of colors you want to use, click the option in the list box.

The greater the number of colors you use, the better the display will appear; however, the greater number of colors you use, the more memory is used and the slower the Macintosh runs. Black and white may be less appealing than color, but your Macintosh will run at its fastest speed.

If you use a particular color setting on a regular basis, you will want to set the color options to allocate memory for the color setting. Use the following steps in the Monitor control panel:

1. Click the Options button.

    If your Mac has built-in video, the Memory Allocation dialog opens (see fig. 5.11).

Fig. 5.11
Setting the color memory
options.

2. Click the maximum number of colors you will use.

   Set the memory allocation to the maximum number of colors you will use. This sets aside memory to dedicate to video display. If, for example, you plan to use the 256-color setting most, click the Up to 256 Colors/Grays option. You set this option only once. You do not have to reset it when you change the number of colors you use (unless you make a major change such as installing a new monitor or a color card for increased color capacity).

3. Click the OK button.

   You can now choose the color setting you want.

   Color-capable Macintoshes can also display in shades of gray rather than color. Instead of colors, this display option uses varying shades of gray. Using a large number of shades of gray gives the display a feeling of "depth" that is absent in the stark black and white setting. Clicking the Grays button then enables you to choose the number of shades of gray you want to use, up to the maximum number of colors your Macintosh is capable of.

Identifying and Arranging Monitors

If you have more than one monitor connected to your Macintosh, you will be concerned with the exact locations of the monitors. If the second monitor is to the left of the first, for example, the Macintosh should be aware of this fact so that it will display items to the left of the main monitor on the second monitor (otherwise, you might move the mouse to the right and find it appearing on the monitor to the left).

To inform the Macintosh about the locations of the monitors, do the following in the Monitors control panel:

1. Click the Identify button.

   A number appears on each monitor. This number corresponds to the small monitor icons in the Monitor location box of the Monitors control panel.

2. Drag the monitor icons to reflect the physical locations of the monitors.

For example, if monitor two is to the left of monitor one, drag monitor icon two to the left of monitor icon one.

Some experimentation is called for to align the monitors properly. Move the mouse around to make sure that you have the monitors positioned properly (when the mouse pointer goes off of one monitor, it appears immediately on the other in line with the direction of motion).

Setting Mouse Options

When you move the mouse, the mouse pointer responds by moving across the screen of the Macintosh. You can adjust the speed of the pointer and the response of the mouse button.

Access the mouse controls by opening the Control Panels folder, then double-clicking the Mouse control panel; the Mouse window opens (see fig. 5.12).

Fig. 5.12

Setting mouse options.

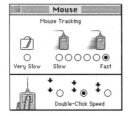

After setting the mouse options, confirm your choices by clicking the window's close box.

Setting Mouse Tracking Speed

Mouse Tracking determines the speed at which the mouse pointer moves in response to the movement of the mouse. The settings range from very slow—used for graphics tablets or for making very fine adjustments in a graphic—to Fast. The faster you set the mouse pointer's response, the less distance you must move the mouse to cross the Macintosh's screen. Choose a speed by clicking one of the seven buttons.

You will have to experiment to determine the setting that is best for you. If you have a small monitor, try using a setting between Slow and Fast, then adjust up or down. For larger monitors or multiple monitors, start with the Fast speed, then reduce the speed if you find yourself over-shooting your intended mark.

Setting Double-Click Speed

The Double-Click Speed controls determine how quickly you must press the mouse button for the Macintosh to interpret it as a double-click. The extreme left setting enables you to click more slowly, and the extreme right setting requires the double-click to be a rapid succession of button presses.

To determine the best settings, you must experiment. Try setting the control to the middle double-click speed at first. If you find that the Macintosh often interprets your double-clicks as two single clicks (a double-clicked icon is selected but does not open, for example), you may need to decrease the double-click speed. Conversely, if you find that icons are opening when you mean merely to select them, increase your double-click speed setting.

Setting Screen Brightness

A few Macintoshes adjust screen brightness with a control panel rather than with a mechanical knob or slider. Among these are the Classic and Classic II.

To set the brightness of the screen, open the Control Panels folder and double-click the Brightness control panel. The Brightness window opens (see fig. 5.13).

Fig. 5.13
Adjusting screen brightness.

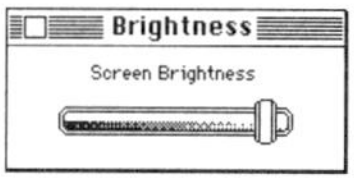

To use the Screen Brightness control, place the mouse pointer on the slider and drag it along the control. Move to the left to decrease screen brightness, and to the right to increase it.

Setting Sound Options

By now you probably have heard your Macintosh issue a warning or alert by beeping. You may want to be able to set the volume level of this beep. You will also want to know that you can change this sound to one you find more pleasing. On Macintoshes with built-in recording capability (these Macintoshes come with a microphone), you can record new sounds of your own. To set sound options, you use the Sound control panel.

Access the sound controls by opening the Control Panels folder, then double-clicking the Sound control panel. You see the sound controls (see fig. 5.14).

Fig. 5.14
Setting sound options.

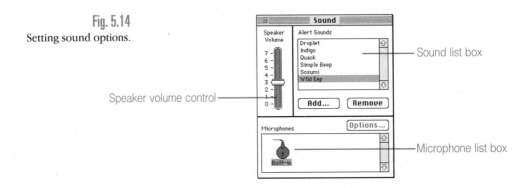

Speaker volume control —

Sound list box

Microphone list box

When you are finished setting the sound options, confirm your settings and dismiss the window by clicking the close box.

Setting the Alert Sound

To set the alert sound you want to use, click the sound in the sound list box. You may need to scroll the sound list to see all of the available sounds.

When you click on a sound, you will hear that sound through the Macintosh's speaker (unless the speaker volume control is set to 0). You can listen to each of the available sounds by clicking once on each in turn. Then, when you have settled on a sound you want to use, click on it before closing the Sound control panel.

If your Macintosh is capable of recording new sounds, you will also see the Microphone list box as well as the Add, Remove, and Options buttons. You can use the microphone provided with your Macintosh to add sounds to the sound list box, using the following steps:

1. Click the Add button.

   You see the dialog shown in figure 5.15.

Fig. 5.15

The dialog to record new sounds.

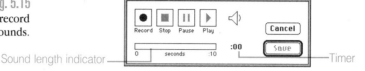

Sound length indicator ——— Timer

2. Place the microphone close to the source of the sound.

3. Click the Record button.

   You will see the timer begin to fill like a thermometer as the sound length indicator counts upward. This indicates that sound is being recorded. At the bottom of the timer, you see a number of seconds indicating the amount of time you have for the sound. In figure 5.15, 10 seconds is displayed as the amount of time you have for a sound.

4. Click the Stop button.

   Click the Play button to hear the recording. If the sound is not to your liking, record another by repeating steps 3 and 4.

5. Click the Save button.

   You are prompted to name the sound.

6. Type a name, then click the Save button.

The sound is added to the sound list box.

Setting the Sound Volume

You change the volume of the sounds your Macintosh makes by dragging the Sound Volume control slider to a new setting. The maximum setting is 7, and the lowest is 0. A setting of 0 turns off the sound. The menu bar flashes when you would normally hear the alert sound.

For unexplained reasons, the Macintosh IIsi has a habit of losing its voice. The sound capability ceases to function. At the time of this writing, Apple has found no cure for the problem, but it is easy to get around. Use the following steps:

1. Open the Sound control panel.

2. Drag the Sound Volume control slider to 7.

   You should hear sound. If you do not, try sliding to 0, releasing the mouse button then repeating step 2. When you hear sound, continue.

3. Drag the slider to the desired setting and close the Sound control panel.

Setting the Startup Disk

Although you should never keep more than one System Folder on any one disk, you can have separate System Folders for separate hard disks. The Macintosh has a normal search order when it starts. First, the floppy drive is checked to see whether a startup disk (one with a System Folder) is present. Then the Macintosh checks the SCSI bus in order of the SCSI identification numbers for a disk drive that contains a System Folder. The first folder it locates is the one it uses.

The result is that if you have more than one startup device on a second hard disk or a networked disk, the Macintosh always uses the first it finds and never proceeds to any others.

To change the order, you must use the Startup Disk control panel. You access this control by opening the Control Panels folder, then double-clicking the Startup Disk control panel. You see the Startup Disk window (see fig. 5.16).

Fig. 5.16
The available startup disks are displayed.

The two icons in the window in figure 5.16 indicate that two disks exist that can be used as startup devices. You may see only one, or you may see several, depending on the number of disk drives attached to your Macintosh.

You can choose one of the drives to be the startup disk by clicking the desired icon and closing the control panel.

The next time you start the Macintosh, it uses the chosen startup disk. Note that the floppy drive takes precedence over the setting of the Startup Device control panel. This way, you can always start the Macintosh from a floppy, even if the selected hard disk fails.

Setting Trash Options

The Trash has one option that you will want to know about. When you choose the Empty Trash command, you normally see a warning message noting the number of items in the Trash and the amount of space they take up on disk. You have the chance to change your mind about deleting these items.

If you don't want to be asked each time you empty the Trash, you can eliminate the alert with the following steps:

1. Click the Trash icon to select it.

2. Choose Get Info from the File menu (or press ⌘-I).

   You see the Trash Info window (see fig. 5.17).

Fig. 5.17
Setting the Trash option.

3. Click the Warn before emptying option check box.

4. Click the Info window's close box.

The Trash no longer warns you before emptying. You should set this option only if you are very certain about what you place in the Trash, because you will not be warned when you choose the Empty Trash command before the items are deleted.

You can reverse the setting of this option with the same steps.

Chapter Summary

This chapter covered some of the ways you can configure the Macintosh to suit your needs and work habits. You have seen how you can use control panels to set various options to tailor the working of the Macintosh.

You are not limited to the control panels included with your Macintosh. Many are available that can enhance the functioning of the System Software and help you work with your Macintosh. The next chapter covers ways you can use supplied control panels to customize your Macintosh further and how you can install third-party control panels, System extensions, and other options.

CHAPTER SIX

Customizing the Macintosh

T his chapter covers options that you can customize on the Macintosh. You're less likely to need these settings as much as you use those in Chapter 5, "Configuring the Macintosh," but these settings can help streamline your work habits, making the Macintosh more enjoyable to use.

Chapter 5 introduced control panels, and explained how they are accessed and used. This chapter goes further, explaining how you can install and remove control panels. This chapter also introduces the *System extension*—software items that add to the functioning ability of the System Software—and discusses the installation of alternate keyboard layouts. In these installation procedures, you see how you add and remove "resources" from the System file.

You also see how to alter the display of windows to suit your needs, how to add and remove sounds, and how to configure the Apple menu.

This chapter also covers the customizing of icons; you see how icons can be set to open at startup time, altered in appearance, and labeled to help you organize them.

Setting Color

If your Macintosh is color-capable, you can set the color used in the window frames and the color used as the highlight when you select text. You control both options from the Color control panel, which you access by opening the Control Panels folder and double-clicking the Color control panel. The Color window appears (see fig. 6.1).

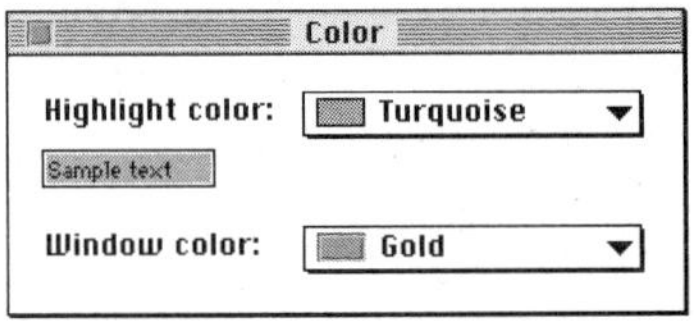

Fig. 6.1
The Color window.

Fig. 6.1
The Color window.

When you finish setting the color options, click in the window's close box to confirm your settings and close the window.

Setting the Text Highlight Color

The colored band you see indicates the color used to highlight selected text. To change the color setting, follow these steps:

1. Place the mouse pointer on the Highlight color pop-up menu.

2. Press and hold the mouse button. The menu pops up (see fig. 6.2).

Fig. 6.2

The Highlight color pop-up
menu.

| Purple |
| Yellow |
| Green |
| Turquoise |
| Red |
| Pink |
| Blue |
| Gray |
| Black & White |
| Other... |

Highlight color:

Window color:

NOTE

Note that the menu choices normally have a color box that displays the color. Because figure 6.2 is in black and white, however, you can't see these colors.

3. Drag to the desired color and release the mouse button.

    Choose one of the nine colors (Purple to Blue, Gray, or Black & White, the initial setting), or choose the Other option. This option invokes the Macintosh color wheel, which you can use to choose a color. (The color wheel is covered in the next section.)

    To the left of the menu, a text sample displays how the highlight color appears when in use.

NOTE

If your monitor is set to black and white, your text will be displayed with the black-and-white setting.

Setting Window Frame Color

You set the color of the frames of the windows displayed on-screen the same way that you set the highlight color. Choose from the Window color menu. You have six color options (Gold through Blue), Gray, Black & White, and Standard. The initial setting, Standard, is a purplish color.

You cannot create a custom color for window frames by using the color wheel, as you can with text highlighting. Also, the window frame colors do not display well (or at all) in a display configuration of less than 256 colors. (See Chapter 5, "Configuring the Macintosh," for setting the number of colors displayed by a monitor.) Unless you use 256 or more colors in your display, you will probably want to leave the setting to Standard.

Using the Macintosh Color Wheel

When the color wheel appears on color-capable Macs, it enables you to choose a color to use. As you have seen, the color wheel enables you to choose a highlight color from all the possible colors your Macintosh can display (see the previous section, "Setting the Text Highlight Color").

When the color wheel appears, you see the dialog shown in figure 6.3.

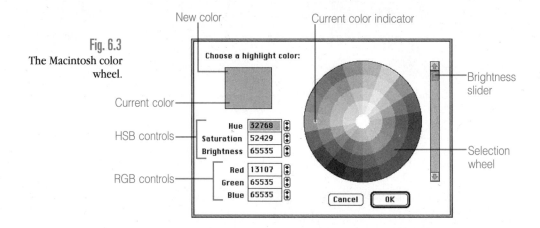

Fig. 6.3
The Macintosh color wheel.

You can choose a color in one of three ways. You can use the HSB system of selecting a color. The HSB system describes colors in terms of the hue (color), saturation (the amount of color), and value represented in the dialog as brightness. To use the HSB system, follow these steps:

1. Double-click in the Hue field.

2. Type a number between 0 and 65,535.

   Note that the hue value for red is 0, for green is 21,845, and for blue is 43,690.

3. Press Tab.

To set the Saturation amount and the Brightness amount, repeat these steps using the respective fields.

Alternatively, you can click the up or down arrows to the right of the field. The up arrow increases and the down arrow decreases the amount of Hue, Saturation, or Brightness.

As you enter the numbers or click the arrow controls, the current color indicator in the selection wheel moves to the color you selected. The new color field also displays the color next to the current color field so that you can compare the colors.

The RGB controls enable you to specify a color as a mix of Red, Green, and Blue—the primary colors of light (in contrast to the primary colors of paint, which are red, yellow, and blue). You use the RGB controls in the same way that you use the HSB controls. That is, you can double-click in the Red field, and then type a number between 0 and 65,535. This indicates how much of the color red you want to use (0 being none and 65,535 being the most possible).

To obtain white, enter an equal mix of all three colors.

To easily choose a color in the dialog, use the color wheel. To choose a color in the color wheel, simply click the mouse pointer on the color you want to use. You can then drag the brightness slider up to increase the brightness of the color, or down to darken the color.

Regardless of the method you use to choose the color, the new color displays above the current color, enabling you to compare your color choice with the current color.

After you choose a color, click OK or press Return to confirm your choice and dismiss the dialog. To leave the dialog without saving changes, click the Cancel button or press Command-period (⌘-.).

Setting the View

You can display the icons in disk and folder windows in various views. The View menu controls these views, which consist of two main types: icon and list. You can customize these views. You can change the font and font size used in the display of icon names, and set the grid used to organize icons in a checkerboard style or a staggered formation. You can also configure window views so that icons snap into their proper place whenever you move them—aligning to an invisible grid.

In the list views, such as View by Name and by Kind, the small icons you see can be made larger. You also can control the information displayed in these views.

To perform all these functions, use the Views control panel, which is in the Control Panels folder. To access the control panel, double-click the Views control panel icon. You then see the window shown in figure 6.4.

The control panel is divided into three sections. The top section controls the font and font size used in list views, the middle section controls the arrangement of icons in icon views, and the bottom section controls the display of list views.

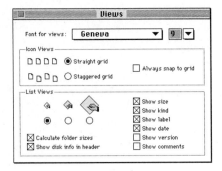

Fig. 6.4

The Views control panel.

Setting the View Font

Any font installed in your System can be used in icon displays. (Chapter 8, "Using Fonts," covers the process of installing fonts.) The standard font used in icon displays is Geneva. This font displays the best because Apple specifically designed it for use on-screen. You can and may want to experiment with other fonts.

To change the font, choose the new font from the Font menu (see fig. 6.5).

Fig. 6.5

Choosing the Garamond font.

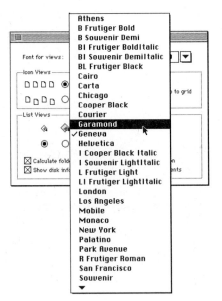

The font updates immediately; you don't have to close the Views control panel window to see how your choices look. With that in mind, open a window or two, and then open the Views control panel. Test a few choices to see which font you like best before you close the window.

You also can change the font size. To change the size of the font, type a size number between 6 and 36, and then press Return. Alternatively, you can choose from the font size pop-up menu to the right of the font size field.

In the font size menu, some sizes appear in outlined characters, but others appear in normal black characters. The normal characters indicate that those font sizes are not installed in your System and do not look as good on-screen.

Setting the Icon Grid

If you used the Special menu's Clean Up command or one of its variations, the icons align on an invisible grid. If you hold down the Command key as you drag an icon, you also see this grid in action; the icon "snaps" to the grid when you release the mouse button.

When aligned on a straight grid, some icon names overlap. You can address this problem by using a staggered grid. Figure 6.6 shows a straight grid in the top window and a staggered grid in the bottom window.

Fig. 6.6
Straight versus staggered grids.

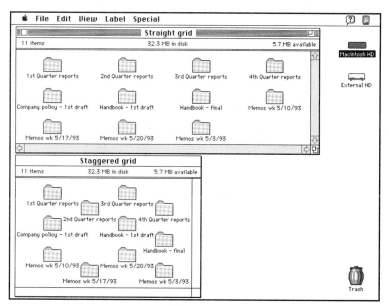

To change to either grid, click the Staggered grid option button or the Straight grid option button in the Views control panel window.

Unlike the font setting, the grid setting does not take immediate effect on folders created earlier. You must choose the Clean Up command for each window to which you want the setting to apply. The new setting applies only to changes made after you choose the grid setting. For example, if you create a new folder, the icons align according to the new grid setting.

The Always snap to grid option means the grid setting you selected is in effect when you move an icon. Usually, an icon aligns on the grid when you perform one of the following tasks:

- Create a new folder and copy icons to that folder by dragging them to the closed folder icon.

- Choose the Clean Up command from the Special menu.

- Hold down the Command key as you drag an icon.

With the Always snap to grid option turned on, an icon aligns with the grid as soon as you release the mouse button. To turn this option on or off, click in its check box. An X in the box shows the option is on. To temporarily reverse the setting of this option, hold down the Command key when you drag an icon; that is, Command-drag the icon. For example, if the Always snap to grid option is off, Command-dragging an icon causes the icon to align to the grid when you release the mouse button.

Setting List View Icon Size

Beneath the three icons in the List Views section of the control panel, the three round buttons determine the size of the icons to the left of the icon names in the list views. This option takes effect immediately. To choose a size, click the button beneath the sample icon in the Views control panel.

The smaller two sizes are usually best. The third size can be rather unwieldy, although full-size icons are easier to see and identify.

Showing Folder Size

The Calculate folder sizes option is one of the most welcome View control panel options introduced with System 7. Before this option, users used the Get Info command in the File menu to determine the size of a folder. With the new option, you can display the folder size in the list views.

When you copy folders to a floppy disk, the folder size information can be very helpful because you can determine whether those folders fit in the available space. Also, when you try to make room on a full hard disk, you can locate the largest space-consuming folders.

To activate the Calculate folder sizes option, click in the check box to the left of the option. The option takes effect immediately, and the sizes of the folders in kilobytes are displayed in the Size column of the list view.

The Macintosh may slow a bit, because the computer calculates folder sizes each time you open a folder or disk that contains folders. This option is slow enough that you actually can see the folder sizes appear as they calculate. Users of older machines, such as the original Classic and LC, may find this option too time-consuming. If so, deactivate the option by clicking in the check box a second time.

Showing Disk Information

In a regular icon view, the top of the window displays how many items appear in the window, the amount of total information (in MB—megabytes, or KB—kilobytes) on the disk, and the amount of remaining available space. You can add this information to the header of a list view with the Show disk info in header option. To activate or turn off the option, click the check box to the left of the option.

Changing List View Columns

The default columns used in the list views are Name, Size, Kind, Label, and Date (the date the file or folder was last modified). Two more columns also are available: Version and Comments.

The Version option adds a column with the application program's version number. The Comments option displays the comments entered in the Info window (see Chapter 2, "Understanding the System," for more on the Get Info command).

If you click one of these six options on the right side of the Views control panel, you toggle the option—switch the option on or off. An option is on when an X appears in the check box.

The Name column, which you cannot turn off, does not appear on the Views control panel. You also cannot change the order in which columns appear. The order is Name, Size, Kind, Label, Date, Version, and Comments.

The View menu (see Chapter 4, which explores viewing files) is altered according to the columns you select. The columns you include are added to the View menu as sort options. Those you remove from the view also are removed from the menu. You then can choose the Sort option from the View menu to sort a folder or disk window by any of the six columns that you include.

Setting Physically Challenged Help Options

Apple's philosophy is that the computer is a tool for everyone, and the company made provisions for those who have difficulty seeing, as well as for those who have trouble manipulating the keyboard or mouse. Those who have difficulty seeing the images on the Macintosh screen can use the Close View control panel. Users who have trouble with the mouse or keyboard can utilize the Easy Access control panel.

Using Close View

Close View is a control panel that enables you to magnify the images on the Macintosh screen. This effect can help those who have difficulty seeing the images on-screen, or those who need to do precise work.

Close View is not installed automatically with the System Software, and may not be on your Macintosh. However, you find the control panel on the Tidbits disk in your System Software disk set. This chapter covers installing control panels later.

To access Close View, first open the Control Panels folder and then double-click the CloseView icon. You see the CloseView control panel (see fig. 6.7).

Fig. 6.7
The CloseView control panel.

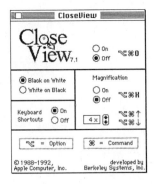

Magnify the images on-screen by using the following steps:

1. Click the On button in the top section of the control panel, or press Option-⌘-O.

   A rectangle appears around the mouse pointer, indicating the area of the screen that will be magnified.

2. Click the On button in the Magnification section of the control panel, or press Option-⌘-X.

   The screen is magnified. Move the mouse pointer to the area(s) you want to view.

The Magnification area of the control panel enables you to adjust the magnification of the screen from twice the normal size (2x) to as much as sixteen times normal size (16x). You see the magnification amount displayed in the control panel (in the figure, the control panel is set to magnify the image four times normal size—4x).

To increase the magnification, click the upward pointing arrow of the magnification control, or press Option-⌘-up arrow. To decrease magnification, click the down arrow of the control or press Option-⌘-down arrow.

You have two other options available. You can reverse the screen's image from black on white to white on black by clicking the White on Black button.

Because many programs now use keyboard shortcuts, you may find that the Option-⌘ shortcuts of the CloseView control panel interfere with another program. To avoid this conflict, click the Off button in the Keyboard shortcuts section. The Option-⌘ shortcuts are disabled; you must use the mouse to change the options in the CloseView control panel.

When Close View is active, you may notice some slowing of the Macintosh's operation.

To close the CloseView control panel, click in its close box. Note that if the keyboard shortcuts are on, they work even if the control panel is closed.

Using Easy Access

If you have difficulty manipulating the mouse or using the keyboard, you will welcome Easy Access. Easy Access is a control panel that enables you to substitute the numeric keypad for the mouse and slow the acceptance of key presses to prevent the Macintosh from accepting accidental key presses. Easy Access also enables you to use "sticky keys," which allow you to press keys in sequence instead of holding the keys down together for key combinations.

Note that those who work with graphics also often find the Mouse Keys feature useful in precision work.

Easy Access, unlike Close View, installs automatically on the Macintosh when the System Software is installed. If you find that the control panel is not present, however, you find it on the Tidbits disk of your System Software disk set. This chapter covers installing control panels later.

To access Easy Access, open the Control Panels folder, and then double-click the control panel's icon. The control panel opens (see fig. 6.8).

Fig. 6.8

The Easy Access control panel.

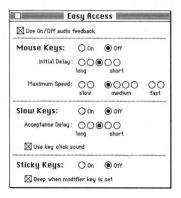

To close the control panel, click the close box of its window.

Using Mouse Keys

Mouse Keys enables you to use the numeric key pad to move the mouse pointer and to click and double-click items. To activate Mouse Keys, click the On button in the Easy Access control panel.

You can now perform mouse functions with the keypad (see table 6.1).

Table 6.1

Mouse Keys

Keypad Key	Mouse Action
0	Press and hold mouse button
1	Move mouse pointer down and left
2	Move mouse pointer down
3	Move mouse pointer down and right

Keypad Key	Mouse Action
4	Move mouse pointer left
5	Click mouse button
6	Move mouse pointer right
7	Move mouse pointer up and left
8	Move mouse pointer up
9	Move mouse pointer up and right

The Initial Delay option in Mouse Keys enables you to set the amount of time the keypad key must be held down before the mouse action performs. Click one of the five option buttons. The buttons toward the left increase the delay; the buttons toward the right decrease the delay.

When you press one of the direction keys (1 through 4 and 6 through 9), the mouse pointer moves only slightly, which enables you to make minute adjustments to the mouse pointer's position. If you continue to hold one of the direction keys down, the mouse pointer begins to move, increasing in speed as the button is held down. To adjust the maximum speed to which the mouse pointer accelerates, click one of the Maximum Speed option buttons. The buttons to the left reduce the mouse pointer's speed; the buttons toward the right increase the maximum speed.

Users of large screens may find that one of the two fast options is best.

The direction keys should be easy enough to understand. Press the key that moves the mouse pointer in the direction you want (for example, the 9 key in the upper right of the keypad moves the mouse pointer to the upper right).

The two keys used for the mouse button, 0 and 5, may need further explanation. Consider the 5 key your "click" key and the 0 key your "press and hold" key. When you need to click the mouse button, press the 5 key. To double-click, press the key twice.

When you need to press and hold the mouse button, as you do when you make menu choices or drag icons, for example, press the 0 key to press and hold the mouse button. You can then use the direction keys to drag the mouse pointer. Note that you "release" the mouse button by pressing the 5 key, *not* the 0 key. The 0 key only presses and holds the mouse button; it does not release it.

Using Slow Keys

Slow Keys helps prevent the acceptance of accidental key presses by delaying the acceptance of a key press. To activate Slow Keys, click the On button. You then set the delay (amount of time a key must be held down) before a key press is accepted by clicking one of the Acceptance Delay buttons. The buttons to the left increase the delay; those to the right decrease the delay.

Slow Keys automatically assumes that you want a key click sound to inform you when a key is accepted. Control the click sound with the Use key click sound option check box. An X in the box means that the click sound is on. To turn the click sound on or off, click in the check box.

When the click sound is on, you hear a click from the Macintosh speaker whenever a key is pressed. Then, as the key is held down, you hear a *second* click, which indicates that the key press has been accepted. Releasing a key before the second click is the same as not pressing that key. With a bit of practice, you can become accustomed to the "click-click" sound of accepted keys.

Using Sticky Keys

Sticky Keys enables you to press modifier keys—Shift, Command, Option, and Control—in sequence instead of together. For example, to eject a disk from the internal floppy drive, you press the Command, Shift, and 1 keys at the same time. With Sticky Keys, you can press Command, and then Shift, and then the 1 key.

To activate Sticky Keys, click the On button in the Sticky Keys section of the Easy Access control panel. You see a small icon appear in the upper right corner of your screen that indicates the status of Sticky Keys (see table 6.2).

Table 6.2
Sticky Key Symbols

Symbol	Meaning
⊔	Easy Access on
⬆	Modifier key held
⬇	Modifier key locked

To use Sticky Keys, press the modifier key you want to use. You hear a beep and see the symbol shown in table 6.2. The middle symbol indicates that a modifier key is being held.

You then can press another key to complete a key combination sequence. For example, to execute a ⌘-N key combination (which most programs use to create a new document), you first press the Command key. You see the second symbol from the table in the upper right corner of your screen.

You then press the N key. Because the Command key is being held by Sticky Keys, the result is ⌘-N. Alternatively, you can press other modifier keys. To execute ⌘-Shift-Option-S, you press the Command key, and then the Shift key, and then the Option key, and finally the S key. A beep acknowledges each modifier key, which is held until the sequence is complete.

If you need a key held for a period of time, you may want to type a word in all caps (thus needing the Shift key held) or want to perform more than one menu command, you press the modifier key twice. You see the bottom symbol of table 6.2. The modifier key is then held until you press it again.

For example, you may want to save a document, close the document, and then create a new one. This procedure involves using the keyboard commands ⌘-S, ⌘-W, and then ⌘-N in most Macintosh programs. To do this procedure with Sticky Keys, follow these steps:

1. Press the Command key twice to hold it.

2. Press the S key.

3. Press the W key.

4. Press the N key.

5. Press the Command key again to release the key.

Note that you can turn on Sticky Keys from the keyboard even with the control panel closed. Press the Shift key five times in a row. Conversely, Sticky Keys automatically shuts off if more than one modifier key is pressed at the same time or if a modifier key and another key are pressed at the same time.

Finally, to eliminate the beep that confirms a modifier key press, click the check box named Beep when modifier key is set option. To turn the beep back on, click in the option check box again.

Setting On/Off Audio Feedback

Easy Access is automatically set to notify you audibly when any of its three features is turned on or off. A rising tone indicates that a feature is turned on, and a falling tone indicates that any feature is turned off. If you do not want this audible feedback, click the Use On/Off audio feedback option check box. To turn the audio feedback on, click the check box again.

Changing Sounds

The sound capability of the Macintosh is both famous and infamous. The fame and infamy occur for the same reason—the Macintosh can produce a large number of sounds, from simple beeps to full music scores.

Users delight in adding sound to the Macintosh, and have done so with a gusto that at times has probably annoyed families and co-workers.

Since the introduction of the LC, Macintoshes have shipped with microphones, which enable you to add sounds. Unless you add software and possibly hardware, you are limited to adding alert sounds. For more on more advanced sound uses, see Chapters 18 and 20.

Adding Sounds

When the Macintosh informs you of a potential problem, you hear the alert sound. You probably already heard this sound in your use of the Macintosh. You can change the alert sound, as discussed in Chapter 5, but you can also add new sounds if your Macintosh is a model that can record sounds. You know your Macintosh can record sound without additional hardware or software if the computer includes a microphone.

To access the sound recording capability, first open the Control Panels folder, and then double-click the Sound control panel. You see the Sound control panel open (see fig. 6.9).

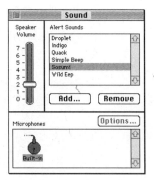

Fig. 6.9
The Sound control panel.

If your Macintosh can record new sounds, you see the Microphones list box, as well as the Add, Remove, and Options buttons. The Microphones list box in the figure shows only the built-in microphone. If your Macintosh is equipped with other recording equipment, you see other microphones or sound sources displayed in this list box. Choose one by clicking its icon.

Note that the Options button is not active for the built-in microphone, as there are no options for this sound source. Other sound recording equipment can provide options that you can set (see the manual for the equipment).

To add sounds to the Alert Sounds list box, follow these steps:

1. Click the Add button.

   You see the dialog shown in figure 6.10.

Fig. 6.10
The dialog for recording new alert sounds.

2. Place the microphone close to the source of the sound.

> **NOTE**
>
> If you are using a sound source other than the built-in microphone, step 2 may not apply.

3. Click the Record button.

   You see the seconds timer "thermometer" begin to fill, in imitation of a thermometer, as the sound length indicator counts upward. This indicates that sound is being recorded. At the bottom of the timer, a number of seconds indicates the amount of time you have for the sound.

4. Click the Stop button.

   To hear the sound and decide whether it was recorded correctly, click the Play button. If the sound is not to your liking, you can record another by repeating steps 3 and 4.

5. Click the Save button.

   You are prompted to name the sound.

6. Type a name, and then click the Save button.

The sound is added to the sound list box. You can select it by clicking it.

As you may have noticed, the buttons of the dialog act like a typical tape recorder. You may already understand that clicking the Pause button stops the recording temporarily. Click the Record or Pause button, and then proceed with the recording.

Click the Stop button to stop the recording. Unlike the Pause button, however, when you next click the Record button, the sound is lost and a new one recorded.

Note that you are not necessarily limited to the built-in microphone, even if you do not have additional sound equipment for your Macintosh. Apple includes an adaptor that plugs into the microphone jack of your Macintosh. The adaptor enables you to attach a standard line level sound source (such as a CD player), and record from that sound source using the same steps above.

The adaptor accepts RCA plugs, the kind used in regular stereo hookups.

Removing Sounds

Removing a sound from the Alert Sounds list box is quite simple. Follow these steps:

1. Open the Sound control panel.
2. Click the sound to delete.
3. Click the Remove button.

    A dialog appears, asking you to confirm the deletion.

4. Click the OK button or press Return.

Customizing the Apple Menu

Before System 7, the Apple menu was primarily the home of desk accessories. Now, in System 7, the Apple menu can hold any item you can open, including disk icons, folder icons, and applications.

To open anything in the Apple menu, choose it from that menu. You can start applications and open documents and folders with a quick menu choice instead of searching through folders for the icon you must double-click.

The new Apple menu also enables you to sort the items in a menu alphabetically. You can change the order of the items by changing the names of the icons.

To access the Apple Menu Items folder, double-click the System Folder to open it, and then double-click the Apple Menu Items folder to open it.

Note that the customizing discussed in this section requires no software in addition to System 7. But customization options that you may be interested in purchasing are available for the Apple menu.

Adding and Removing Apple Menu Items

To add any item to the Apple menu, place it in the Apple Menu Items folder, which you find in the System Folder. Avoid dragging every item you want available in the Apple menu into this folder, because installing items in the Apple menu folder takes up space and moves your icons into the folder, disorganizing your hard disk. Using aliases is the best approach.

You can place small items in the folder. For something as small as the Apple-provided Alarm Clock application, for example, you need not take the trouble to make an alias. Simply drag the Alarm Clock into the folder.

For large items, or items that you want to leave in their original locations, make an alias of them and place the alias in the folder.

To use the alias method of adding items to the Apple menu, follow these steps:

1. Select the icon of the item you want to add to the Apple menu.

2. From the File menu, choose Make Alias.

    The alias is created.

3. Drag the alias into the Apple Menu Items folder.

Repeat these steps for each item you want to add to the Apple menu. You can add items at any time, and those items immediately appear in the menu.

To remove any item from the menu, perform the following steps:

1. Open the Apple Menu Items folder.

2. Drag the icon to another part of your disk, or drag the icon to the Trash.

3. Close the Apple Menu Items folder.

The item immediately disappears from the Apple menu.

Sorting Apple Menu Items

If you drag icons or their aliases into the Apple Menu Items folder, the System sorts them in the Apple menu in alphabetical order. You may, however, want them to appear in another order. For example, you may want often-used applications to appear at the top of the Apple menu. Or you may want to group applications according to your work habits.

You can use a utility such as Now Menus from Now Software to group applications (see Chapter 19, "Using Utility Software"), or you can precede the names of the items in the Apple Menu Items folder with characters that cause them to sort in the order you want.

The order in which items are sorted is as follows:

1. Items with names preceded by a character from table 6.3.

Table 6.3
Characters Sorted before Letters

Character	Key(s) to Create the Character
space	space bar
!	
"	
«	Option-\
»	Shift-Option-\
"	Option-[
"	Shift-Option-[
#	
$	
%	
&	Shift-7
'	
'	Option-]
'	Shift-Option-]
(	
)	
*	
+	
,	
-	
.	
/	
0	
1	

Character	Key(s) to Create the Character
2	
3	
4	
5	
6	
7	
8	
9	
;	
<	
=	
>	
?	
@	

2. Items with names that start with letters. These names then are sorted in alphabetical order. Letters with diacriticals (accents, umlauts, etc.) sort with their regular counterparts (the umlauted "a" appears after "a," but before "b," for example).

3. Items with names preceded by a character from table 6.4.

Table 6.4
Characters Sorted after Letters

Character	Key(s) to Create the Character
[	
\	
]	
^	Shift-6
_	
{	
|	
}	
~	

continues

Table 6.4
Continued

Character	Key(s) to Create the Character
[	
†	Option-T
°	Shift-Option-8
¢	Option-4
£	Option-3
§	Option-6
•	Option-8
¶	Option-7
ß	Option-O
®	Option-R
ç	Option-C
™	Option-2
′	Shift-Option-E
¨	Option-U
≠	Option-=
∞	Option-5
÷	Option-/
±	Shift-Option-=
<	Option-,
>	Option-.
¥	Option-Y
µ	Option-M
∂	Option-D
Σ	Option-W
∏	Shift-Option-P
π	Option-P
∫	Option-B
ª	Option-9
º	Option-0
Ω	Option-Z
¿	Shift-Option-/
¡	Option-1

Character	Key(s) to Create the Character
¬	Option-L
√	Option-V
ƒ	Option-F
≈	Option-X
Δ	Option-J
«	Option-\
»	Shift-Option-\
…	Option-;
–	Option--
—	Shift-Option--
◊	Shift-Option-V

For example, an icon or alias with a name starting with a space will be at the top of the Apple menu. Items with names that start with a number (or any character in table 6.4) precede items with names that start with letters.

An item with a name that begins with an open bracket follows items with names that begin with letters. Items with names that start with a diamond (the last character in table 6.4) are at the end of the Apple menu.

In the table, the key combinations with difficult-to-locate characters appear in the column Key(s). An "option" indicates that you hold down the Option key. A "shift" indicates that you hold down the Shift key.

Avoid naming items with consecutive characters at first. Skip a few (for example, use space, and then the pound sign, and then the apostrophe). This enables you to insert items later.

Remember also that items that begin with one of the characters are further sorted alphabetically. You can use the characters to precede groups of items, which are then sorted by name.

Setting Automatic Startups

When you work on a particular project, you may find yourself starting up the same application programs, and opening the same folders and documents each time you start your Macintosh. To automate this process, you can use the Startup Items folder that you find in the System Folder.

When the Macintosh starts, items in the Startup Items folder open as if double-clicked. Use this folder to store anything that can be opened with a double-click and that you want opened automatically at startup.

To access the Startup Items folder, first double-click the System Folder. You then see the Startup Items folder (you may have to scroll before you see the folder).

Avoid dragging every folder, application, document, and other item you might need into the Startup Items folder. The items then are out of place. By dragging some icons into the folder, you might copy them and unnecessarily use space on your disk.

The best procedure is to create an alias of each item you want to open at startup and place the alias into the Startup Items folder (see Chapter 2, "Understanding the System," and Chapter 4, "Managing Files," for more on aliases).

To add items to your Startup Items folder, use these steps:

1. Select the icon of the application program, disk icon, folder, or document that you want to open at startup.

2. From the File menu, choose Make Alias.

3. Drag the alias into the Startup Items folder.

Repeat these steps until you add all the items that you want open at startup.

To cancel the opening of any item at startup, perform the following steps:

1. Open the Startup Items folder.

2. Drag the alias to the Trash.

3. Close the Startup Items folder.

To temporarily override the opening of the items in your Startup Items folder during startup, press and hold the Shift key immediately before the Desktop appears (right after the Welcome to Macintosh message disappears). You may need to practice to get the timing just right. When your hard disk icon appears on the Desktop, you can release the Shift key.

Customizing Icon Appearance

In System 7, you can change the appearance of icons. This procedure requires a graphics program, but is relatively easy to do. Follow these steps:

1. In any graphics program, select the image you want to use for the icon.

2. From the Edit menu, choose Copy.

3. Switch to the Finder (choose Finder from the Application menu, for example).

4. To select the icon to be changed, click it.

5. From the File menu, choose Get Info.

6. Click the icon's image in the Info window.

   A box appears around the icon (see fig. 6.11).

Fig. 6.11
The Misc. Info dialog indicates that the image is selected and ready to be replaced.

7. From the Edit menu, choose Paste.

   The contents of the Clipboard replace the icon's image.

8. To save your changes, click the close box of the Info window.

You can copy an icon's image to the Clipboard by using steps 4 through 6, and then choosing Copy from the Edit menu to copy the image to the Clipboard. Then you can paste the image into other documents that can accept graphics.

You can, for example, copy an icon's image to a graphics program in the manner described in the above paragraph. You can also alter the icon's appearance, and then use steps 1 through 8 to paste the altered image back to the icon.

If you want to restore a custom icon to its original icon, select the icon in the Get Info box. Then choose Clear from the Edit menu.

Labeling Icons

The Label menu enables you to label your icons with text. On color-capable Macintoshes, you can also label the icons with color. You can use this capability to organize your icons and to search for and sort icons (see Chapter 4, "Working with Files," for more on organizing files with labels).

In the Label menu, Apple provides seven labels: Essential, Hot, In Progress, Cool, Personal, Project 1, and Project 2. These labels may be changed to suit your needs.

If your Macintosh uses color, you see to the left of each label a rectangle that displays the label's color; these also can be changed.

Applying Labels

You can apply a label to an icon in the Label menu with the following steps:

1. Click the icon to select it.

2. Choose the desired label from the Label menu.

The labeled icon shows no apparent change in the icon views on a black-and-white Macintosh. On a color Macintosh, the icon changes to the color in the Label menu that appears to the left of the chosen label.

In any of the list views (such as view by name), the label appears in the Label column if you set the Macintosh to display this column in these views (see the section "Setting the View" in this chapter).

Remove a label with the following steps:

1. Click the icon to select it.

2. From the Label menu, choose None.

Customizing Labels

Initially, the Label menu reads from top to bottom: None, Essential, Hot, In Progress, Cool, Personal, Project 1, and Project 2. You can change these labels to better reflect the work you do. Because you can sort and search based on labels, think of labels that help you group your work.

You can change any label except None, which you use to remove a label as described in the previous section. You can change the other seven labels to suit your needs.

To change a label, use the following steps:

1. Open the Control Panels folder (choose Control Panels from the Apple menu).

2. Open the Labels control panel by double-clicking the Labels icon.

3. Double-click in the text field of the label you want to change.

4. Type the new label.

The labels must be 31 characters or less and cannot contain a colon (:). If you attempt to type a colon, a slash (/) results.

You can then click in the close box to close the control panel, or repeat steps 4 and 5 for each label you want to change.

If you have previously labeled icons, the icon label changes to reflect the new label.

To change the color of the label, follow these steps:

1. Click the color box to the left of the label text (a double-click is not necessary in this case).

   The color wheel opens.

2. Choose the color you want to use (see "Using the Macintosh Color Wheel" in this chapter).

3. Click the OK button in the color wheel.

   The label's color is then changed.

You may want to keep open a window that displays some icons labeled with the labels whose colors you are changing. This way, you can see how the icons will appear as you make changes in the Label control panel. On-screen, colors do not always display exactly as they appear in the color wheel, and you may want to see the overall effect of your changes before you close the Label control panel.

When you finish changing your labels, click the close box of the Label control panel to save your changes.

Adding Control Panels

You have seen how control panels work to configure your Macintosh (see Chapter 5, "Configuring the Macintosh"). You now should know that the control panels supplied with your Macintosh are not the only ones available. A great variety of control panels are available to enhance your computer.

Control panels can be as diverse as a screen saver, an alarm clock, a hard disk format protector, a virus-protection system, and other functions. Many come with software packages. For example, the Now Up-To-Date package comes with a Reminder control panel that enables you to set the reminder function of your calendar, determining when and how you are notified of upcoming events.

O ccasionally, you might encounter the term *CDEV*, which is the System 6 and previous systems' term for control panels. (CDEV stands for Control panel DEVice.) CDEVs and control panels are the same thing.

Installing a Control Panel

If you purchase a software package that includes a control panel, and you want to install that feature, do the following:

1. Drag the control panel to the System Folder.

   You see a notice like the one in figure 6.12.

Fig. 6.12
The control panel installation notice.

> ⚠ Control panels need to be stored in the Control Panels folder or they may not work properly. Put "Madness™" into the Control Panels folder?
>
> [Cancel] [OK]

2. Click the OK button.

   The control panel is copied into the Control Panels folder, which is located in the System Folder.

3. Restart your Macintosh to cause the control panel to become active.

Removing a Control Panel

For a control panel to be inactive, it only has to be removed from the System Folder (and, hence, the Control Panels folder). You do not have to delete the control panel from your disk. Follow these steps to remove the control panel from the System Folder:

1. Open the Control Panels folder.

2. Drag the control panel out of the folder.

   You can drag the control panel to the icon of the disk on which the System Folder resides. This action moves the control panel to the disk window, but outside the System Folder.

3. Close the Control Panels folder.

4. Restart your Macintosh.

Because a control panel outside the System Folder does nothing, you can store the program anywhere on your disk, or you can drag the control panel to the Trash.

I nstead of managing your control panels by dragging them in and out of the System Folder, you may want to consider a startup manager utility that enables you to turn control panels on and off. See Chapter 19, "Using Utility Software."

Adding System Extensions

At startup time, your Macintosh loads and runs System extensions, which are small utility programs that enhance the functioning of the System Software. The System extensions enhance the functioning ability of your Macintosh by adding features such as menus in your Open and Save dialogs, saving files automatically, and protecting from viruses.

P eriodically, you may encounter the term *INIT*, which is the System 6 and previous systems' term for System extension. INITs and System extensions are the same; only the name changed.

Installing System Extensions

Install System extensions in the same way that you install control panels: drag them to your System Folder. Follow these steps:

1. Drag the System extension to the System Folder.

   Like control panels, the System Software issues a notice here, which informs you that the System extension needs to be copied to the Extensions folder.

2. Click the OK button.

3. From the Special menu, choose Restart.

An icon should appear below the Welcome to Macintosh message that appears as the Macintosh starts. Most System extensions place an icon on-screen to indicate that the System extension is loaded and functioning.

Removing System Extensions

Removing a System extension is like removing control panels. Follow these steps:

1. Open the Extensions folder in the System Folder.

2. Drag the System extension out of the folder to another location on the disk.

   You can place the System extension anywhere except in the System Folder or Extensions folder.

3. From the Special menu, choose Restart.

S tartup managers can help you control System extensions as well as control panels, enabling you to turn them on and off without moving them in and out of the System Folder. See Chapter 19, "Using Utility Software."

Preventing System Extension Startup

In System 7, Apple provides a feature that enables you to override System extension startup, which you may need to do if one or more of your extensions cause compatibility problems (see Chapter 32, "Maintenance and Troubleshooting," for more information).

To prevent all System extensions from loading, hold down the Shift key as your Macintosh starts. Press the Shift key when the Macintosh icon appears on-screen and hold until the Welcome to Macintosh message appears. You should see a note in the Welcome dialog that indicates that the System extensions have been disabled.

If you run into trouble that appears to begin with a System extension, restart the machine and hold down the Shift key as the Macintosh starts. You then can remove the suspect System extension and try again.

Adding Keyboard Layouts

The Macintosh enables you to use different keyboard layouts. For example, you can switch to a Dvorak keyboard or a foreign keyboard with little trouble.

Keyboard layouts are available through your dealer and on many on-line systems. See Chapter 17, "Using Communication Software," for more about on-line information systems.

Installing a Keyboard Layout

Installing a keyboard layout is essentially the same as installing control panels and System extensions. There is one important difference. Before you attempt to install a keyboard layout, you must quit all running applications. Only the Finder can be running when the System file itself is changed; keyboard layouts are copied into the System file.

When you drag a keyboard layout to the System Folder, a dialog informs you that the layout must be copied to the System file. Click OK and the copy proceeds.

Removing a Keyboard Layout

Because keyboard layouts reside in the System file, removing those layouts requires a different procedure from that of control panels and System extensions. Follow these steps:

1. Quit all running applications other than the Finder.

2. Open the System Folder by double-clicking it.

3. Open the System file by double-clicking it.

You see the System file open (see fig. 6.13).

Fig. 6.13
The System file opens.

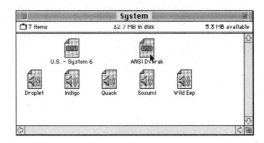

4. Drag the keyboard layout out of the System file.

You can drag the layout icon to any location, but outside the System Folder is best.

5. Close the System file and the System Folder.

Choosing a Keyboard Layout

After a keyboard layout is installed in the System file, that layout becomes available for you to use. You can switch between keyboard layouts by using the Keyboard control panel. Open the Control Panels folder, and then double-click the Keyboard control panel. The bottom half of the control panel lists the installed keyboard layouts (see fig. 6.14).

Fig. 6.14
The Keyboard control panel with the Dvorak keyboard layout selected.

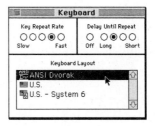

Click the layout you want to use, and then click the close box of the control panel.

Chapter Summary

You can customize the Macintosh in a great many ways to suit your personal work habits and tastes. In this chapter, you saw how you can adjust the highlight color, change how icons are viewed, change the appearance of icons, add and remove sounds, organize the Apple menu, and set other options. This chapter also discussed ways that you can further customize your Macintosh by adding third-party software items such as control panels, System extensions, and keyboard layouts.

One customization capability not covered in this chapter is that concerning fonts. The use of fonts is covered in Chapter 8, following the related topic of printing.

CHAPTER SEVEN

Printing

lmost everyone who uses a personal computer has to print hard copy at one time or another. If you use your Macintosh primarily for desktop publishing, design, or preparing business documents, a printer is an essential part of your system. Although you can view the contents of a file on the monitor, a well-designed, tangible document is indispensable for communicating your ideas to others.

Whereas once, only the ImageWriter printer was available for the Macintosh, you now can choose among a large assortment of printers. Software options, interface cards, and tools are available that enable you to use non-Apple printers with your Macintosh. This chapter can help you decide which printer best fits your needs.

This chapter also discusses the different types of printing technology and printer options. The final section of the chapter introduces programming languages, which give you the power to design and use special effects on your laser printer.

Understanding Types of Printers

One important decision is the type of printer to buy. Of the various printers available, each type uses a different technology to produce printed copy. Sometimes, the differences are negligible; at other times, they can turn a document that could have ended up at the bottom of a stack of papers into an effective, persuasive tool that communicates your ideas clearly.

Printers can be divided into several basic categories: dot-matrix, inkjet, laser, color (thermal-wax-transfer, phase-change, continuous-tone), plotters, and typesetters. The basic technologies of these printer types differ, and many models of each type are available.

Perhaps the most important criterion for choosing a printer is the quality of the output, which usually is related to price. Designing and constructing equipment that produces high-quality output simply costs more.

Although price and quality are related, price is not the sole criterion for determining the quality of a printer. For judging the quality of a print-out, a standardized measure of print quality is better than an arbitrary dollar figure. A printer's quality is best measured by the number of dots per inch (*dpi*) that the printer produces or the resolution at which the printer prints.

The ImageWriter, for example, produces approximately 72 dpi horizontally and 80 dpi vertically in its Draft mode. The next level up, Faster, provides an easier-to-read, denser image. The Best option produces an even more distinct image.

Laser-printer output ranges from 300 dpi to 1,200 dpi (300 to 600 is the range for Apple printers) and produces attractive copy. Finally, commercially produced output exceeds 1,000 dpi. Linotronics printers operate at around 1,270 dpi to 2,500 dpi, which is as good as actual typesetting.

Color printers have become more affordable in recent years and are catching on quickly. Inkjet color printers are the most affordable; many print at a resolution equal to that of the average laser printer. Thermal-wax-transfer, phase-change, and continuous-tone printers offer greater print quality but are priced so high that only businesses generally purchase them.

Dot-Matrix Printers

If you examine a dot-matrix printout closely, you see that each letter or graphic consists of a series of organized dots. Dot-matrix printers work exactly the way that their name implies. Print wires strike a ribbon, producing the dots that make up the characters you see on the paper.

The impression is made by a set of small print pins, or print wires, that are part of the print head. These print wires remain inside the print head until your Macintosh sends a graphic or text code to the print head, indicating which combination of wires should be "fired." When the wires are fired, they protrude from the print head, hit the ribbon, and make an impression on the paper. All the wires are the same size and shape, and they produce clean, uniform marks on the paper. The more wires in the print head, the higher the quality of the printout.

Figure 7.1 shows how a dot-matrix printer produces text as the print head moves across the paper. The print head does not create a character all at once; instead, the print head creates only the upper part of the character and then moves on to the next character, moving back and forth across the entire line. You can see the individual dots that make up the collective image of a character. In a conventional dot-matrix printer, each pin creates one part of the character and then moves to the next position, one character at a time.

A particular type of dot-matrix printer—the letter-quality printer—uses the same technology to create an image, but with one difference. Rather than advance the paper to leave spaces between the dots, the letter-quality printer advances the paper only fractions of spaces so that the dots touch one another. As a result of these incremental passes, the character appears to be an almost continuous stream of ink. Some printers, including the ImageWriter II in Best mode, double-strike the character with a slight offset to accomplish the same result.

The speed of dot-matrix printers is measured in characters per second (*cps*). This speed can vary, depending on the quality of output you want. The higher the output quality, the more "hits" the print head has to make; hence, the longer the printing process and the fewer characters produced in a given amount of time.

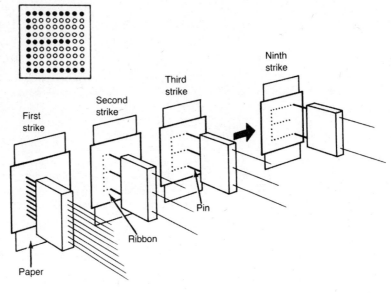

Fig. 7.1
How a dot-matrix print head creates an image.

First strike

Second strike

Third strike

Ninth strike

Paper

Ribbon

Pin

Inkjet Printers

Inkjet printers paint the image of a character or graphic on paper by spraying ink through a small nozzle, spraying droplets of ink on the page where they are needed, and the droplets dry quickly. Inkjet printers can be inexpensive substitutes for laser printers because they print quickly (as much as 10 times faster than dot-matrix printers) and can produce attractive graphics.

Apple's StyleWriter is an inkjet printer that retails for less than $400. The printer is rather slow but produces high-quality print, approaching the quality of laser-printer output. Apple has introduced a new version of the StyleWriter, the StyleWriter II, that offers enhanced performance.

Color inkjet printers are the least expensive color printers available, ranging in price from about $700 to $2,000. Print resolution ranges from about 180 dpi to 300 dpi. Color inkjet printers can be expensive to use, however, because they require more-expensive paper (clay-coated is best; regular paper can wrinkle because it soaks up the ink) and several colors of ink.

Laser Printers

Laser printers often are the preferred printer for several reasons: The quality of their output is outstanding; they are fast (some produce as many as 15 pages per minute); and in contrast to the noisy dot-matrix printers, they are quiet. Having a laser printer is like having your own printing press. Laser technology has helped create a revolution in computer printouts.

Laser printers, once only for high rollers, now are within the reach of almost everyone. You can buy a basic laser printer for about $1,000 to $2,000. Laser-printer technology also is becoming more sophisticated, enabling users to take advantage of increasingly sophisticated software. (A comparison of Apple and other popular laser printers appears in Chapter 25, "Choosing a Printer.")

Laser printers use technology similar to that of copy machines but use laser light to produce extremely high-resolution images (300 dpi resolution is common; resolution up to 1,200 is available). Printers with 300-dpi resolution place about 6 million dots on a page, producing a denser image than is possible with a dot-matrix printer. As a result, you avoid the jagged characters produced by a dot-matrix printer.

Figure 7.2 illustrates the sharp image a laser printer can produce.

Laser printers produce beautiful images

The laser-printing process begins when the computer transmits a signal (a "blueprint" for the page to be printed) to the printer. The printer then translates the signal and prints the page. The following step-by-step description shows the relatively simple process by which a laser printer produces a page of characters or graphics.

1. The smooth metal drum rotating inside the laser printer is electronically cleaned (neutralized from the last printing) and then charged, positively or negatively, by a charging corona wire.

2. The charged drum is exposed to a laser beam. Through the use of a mirror, the beam hits the drum at a precise angle, creating the image on the drum.

3. The parts of the drum exposed to the laser become demagnetized, leaving a charged image of the signal that is part of your document.

4. As the drum turns, the magnetized surface picks up a thin coating of toner wherever the light strikes the drum. This toner is a mixture of carbon, metal shavings, and plastic dust. The material sticks to the magnetized parts of the drum.

5. The drum continues to revolve into position for transferring the image to paper.

6. As the paper moves through the feeder, it is charged by another corona wire. The opposing charges of the drum and the paper cause the magnetized toner to transfer from the drum to the paper.

7. The paper passes through a fuser that uses pressure and heat to melt the plastic dust, fusing the image onto the paper. You now have a laser-produced printout.

One of the most important considerations in choosing a laser printer is the language that the Macintosh uses to describe the page to the printer. Macintoshes use two main languages to communicate with printers: QuickDraw, a built-in imaging system used to draw images on the screen; and PostScript, a language created by Adobe that has become the standard in laser printing. (For more information on PostScript, see "Using Laser Printer Languages" later in this chapter.)

Laser printers that use QuickDraw (such as Apple's Personal LaserWriter LS) are more affordable than PostScript printers, although the print quality may be lower. QuickDraw printers, however, are quite suitable for home use and even for small-business use.

PostScript laser printers use the Adobe standard language to describe the printed page. PostScript laser printers come in three varieties: level 1, level 2, and clone.

- Level 1 PostScript is the original PostScript language. Printers based on this language still are the most common, although level 2 printers have been available for a while now.

- Level 2 PostScript is an enhanced version of the PostScript language that—in time—should replace level 1.

- PostScript clone printers attempt to interpret the PostScript language but do not actually use the PostScript interpreter provided by Adobe. These clone printers generally are less expensive but have received less-than-satisfactory reviews, and even have shown compatibility problems.

If you primarily print text and do not need to take your documents to a professional printer, you can do well with a QuickDraw laser printer. A small-business user, however, should consider a PostScript printer, especially if graphics frequently are included in printed documents.

For a further discussion of how QuickDraw and PostScript work, see "Understanding Printer Drivers" later in this chapter. For more information on QuickDraw and PostScript printers, see Chapter 25, "Choosing a Printer."

Color Printers

As stated previously, color printers are becoming more affordable and popular. Four main technologies for color printing exist: inkjet, thermal-wax-transfer, phase-change, and continuous-tone. This list is in order both in quality and price.

Regardless of the exact technology, the main method used to create colors on a printed page is called *CMYK*, referring to the use of the colors cyan, magenta, yellow, and black in combination to create colors. If you recall your elementary-school days of mixing blue, red, and yellow to create different colors, you have a basis for understanding the CMYK method.

The difference between mixing colors and the CMYK method of printing is that the dots of color are not actually mixed but are placed close enough together that your eyes perceive them as mixed (the exception is the continuous-tone printing process, covered at the end of this section). This process, which is called *dithering*, is achieved in several ways. The different dithering methods are not discussed here. Suffice it to say that the best way to judge a color printer's dithering method is to view a printed page. The better the colors look, the more successful the dithering method is.

Color Inkjet Printers

Inkjet printers are the most affordable color printers, ranging in price from $800 to $2,000. Print resolution varies from 180 dpi to 300 dpi (or higher). Color inkjet printers work much like their black-and-white counterparts, spraying onto the page in the form of dots to build up the desired image. The main difference is that color inkjet printers use more than one color of ink.

Thermal-Wax-Transfer Printers

Thermal wax transfer currently is the dominant color-printing method. Printers that use this technology use sheets or ribbons of colored wax, which is transferred in dots to the page by heat in a process rather similar to dot-matrix printing.

These printers produce high-quality images with laser-printer resolution (around 300 dpi). Although 300-dpi resolution is not photograph-quality, these printers are suitable for use by businesses that need color presentations and illustrations with graphs, charts, and graphic images.

The price and operating cost of thermal-wax-transfer printers generally put them out of reach of the average home user but within that of the small-business and professional user. Prices currently range from about $5,000 to $10,000; lower prices are expected as the technology advances.

Because of the special paper needed and the cost of the wax, the per-page cost of operating these printers can be fairly steep. Several manufacturers (such as Seiko) are adapting their printers to use the same paper as laser printers, but the print quality is better on thermal-wax-transfer paper, which is more expensive. Expect to see this change, however, as new printers are introduced.

One distinctive feature of many thermal-wax-transfer printers (usually, the higher-priced printers) is their capability to print on a wide variety of media, such as transparencies for use in overhead projections. At least one printer (the high-end Seiko ColorPoint PSX Model 14) even can print on iron-on transfer media, which suggests some interesting small-business possibilities.

Phase-Change Printers

Phase-change color printers are cousins to thermal-wax-transfer printers in that they use colored wax, but they use a different method of transferring the wax. A phase-change printer melts the wax before transferring it to the page, where the wax hardens back into a solid.

The great advantage of using phase-change printers is that you can use ordinary laser-printer-quality paper. Phase-change printers thus are cheaper to operate than thermal-wax-transfer printers, although they generally are more expensive to purchase, with prices ranging from $7,000 to $10,000.

Because phase-change printers are better suited to printing on plain paper than on transparencies, they are suitable for business and professional users who create more paper documents than overhead presentations.

The technology is relatively new, but many people expect phase-change printers to replace thermal-wax-transfer printers as the technology advances.

Continuous-Tone Printers

The highest-quality (and highest-priced) color printer is the continuous-tone printer. These printers, which range in cost from $10,000 to $20,000, use a process that resembles the color-mixing example. Rather than dither colored dots, continuous-tone printers vaporize colored dyes and then transfer the dyes to special paper in such a way that the dyes actually blend to form colors. The result of this dye-sublimation procedure is stunning color images that approach professional Linotronic print quality.

The cost of purchasing and operating continuous-tone printers, however, makes them practical only for businesses that are interested in creating or adding to an in-house print shop.

Plotters

The Macintosh can create images on paper in many ways, and a device other than a printer may be just what you need if you use computer-aided design applications (see Chapter 16 for a discussion of these graphics software packages). In many cases, a plotter is a good alternative to color printers.

A plotter uses a pen or a set of pens to produce line drawings. Plotters often are used for special jobs that require large paper sizes (for example, 2 by 3 feet), such as drawings used in construction and in computer-aided design/computer-aided manufacturing (CAD/CAM). Because the lines produced by plotters are not interrupted, the lines are smoother and more precise than those produced by a dot-matrix or color-dithering printer. A plotter can use multiple pens; you tell the plotter which pen to use to draw which lines, symbols, designs, or charts. The color of the printout varies according to the colors of the pens you use.

Two advantages that plotters have over printers are the size of the documents they can produce and the number of colors in which they can print (limited only by the number of pens and the colors of the ink in the cartridges). In computer-aided manufacturing, for example, you can create a drawing the size of the actual product to be made and then use the paper as a pattern. This practice is used with great success in the aircraft industry.

Plotters are expensive but serve a specific purpose. Macintosh users can choose among several models, such as those manufactured by Hewlett-Packard and Toshiba.

Typesetters

You get resolution of more than 1.5 million dpi when you print your Macintosh files on a high-performance typesetter. Typesetters (produced by companies such as Linotronic, Varityper, and CompuGraphic) produce visually striking graphics.

Figure 7.3 compares a printout at 72 and 144 dpi from an ImageWriter, at 300 dpi from a LaserWriter, and at 1,270 dpi from a Linotronic. As you can see, the text and graphics produced on the Linotronic typesetter are crisper and better suited for serious desktop-publishing work.

Fig. 7.3
A comparison of several grades of printing.

WHAT'S NEW?	Draft ImageWriter printer at 72x80 dpi
WHAT'S NEW?	ImageWriter printer at 144x160 dpi (2 passes)
WHAT'S NEXT?	Laser printer at 300 dpi
WHAT'S NEXT?	Linotronic at 1,270 dpi

Because typesetters are very expensive, costing $10,000 or more, they are impractical for all but professional printers. If you need to have files printed at this high level of resolution, you can go to a commercial shop that specializes in printing on high-quality typesetters. The initial charge can be quite high—the print shop must produce a plate that is used to reproduce your document—but quantity costs can be low. You probably will not use this service for a term paper, but you may want to use it for a wedding invitation.

You also can mail your disks or send your files by modem to firms that charge less because of lower overhead costs.

T I P

Many universities have art and design programs that use typesetters and may charge much less than commercial printers for the same quality. You may have to register as a student to take advantage of this service, however.

A major difference between a typesetter and any laser printer (even one that prints at very high resolution) is that laser printers use toner, whereas typesetters use photographic material (film) to create actual pictures of an image. Typesetters, therefore, can produce much more precise and well-defined images.

If you need lots of high-quality printing, you may find a high-resolution laser printer to be cost-effective. These printers, which print at more than 1,000 dpi, now are available for less than $10,000.

Understanding Printer Drivers

When Apple defined the way the Macintosh communicates with printers, the company decided to create an industry standard to simplify printer usage. Although *simplify* is a relative term, the Macintosh world generally has averted the problem of printer incompatibility that exists in the IBM PC world.

Each printer has a unique piece of software called a *printer driver*, which tells the computer how to communicate with the printer. The driver translates the print commands issued by the Macintosh into instructions that control or drive the printer.

In simplified form, the Macintosh printing process can be explained this way: the Macintosh uses its built-in QuickDraw routines (also used to draw on your screen) to "draw" the printed page in memory, and then sends the page to the printer driver for translation into a form that the printer can understand. This process is why QuickDraw printers (such as the Apple StyleWriter and the Personal LaserWriter LS) are usually less expensive than PostScript printers. QuickDraw printers "speak" the same language that the Macintosh uses to draw images, so little translation is required. The disadvantage is that the Macintosh itself is required to do the drawing work. Thus, the higher the printing resolution, the more work the Macintosh must do to instruct the printer. QuickDraw printers can tie up your Macintosh for printing when you would rather be doing other work.

PostScript printers translate the mathematical QuickDraw language into the mathematical descriptions of the PostScript language. The Macintosh does less work because the computer can describe a square, for example, by two corner points rather than draw the entire image. PostScript printers cost more because they include microprocessors that translate the mathematical PostScript descriptions into images, but these printers also are faster. Your Macintosh can send the mathematical description of the page to the printer quickly and then turn to other tasks while the printer is interpreting the image and printing the page.

In any case, all printers require a driver of some sort to translate the Macintosh's QuickDraw commands into whatever language the printer "speaks." You must have the correct printer driver to use any printer.

If you have an Apple printer, the Apple Installer puts the proper driver on your startup disk when the System Software is installed. If you have a printer made by another company, however, you must install the printer driver before you proceed with printing. See your printer manual and the next section in this chapter for information.

Installing Printer Drivers

If your printer is not an Apple Computer printer or if you purchase a new Apple printer to replace your current one, the driver for your Apple printer may not be installed in your System Folder.

First, you must locate the disk that contains your printer driver (in the case of Apple printers, the Printing disk in the System Software disk set). If you have a non-Apple printer, consult the manual to determine the exact disk.

The following example is for Apple printers, but you follow the same basic steps for other printers (your printer manual contains more information). To install a printer driver, follow these steps:

1. Insert the disk containing the printer driver.

2. Double-click the disk icon to open the disk. You should see the printer-driver icon or a folder related to printing (see fig. 7.4).

Fig. 7.4

The Printing disk window.

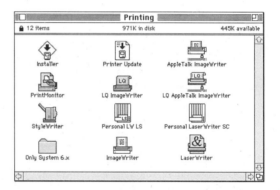

Figure 7.4 shows the icons of the printer drivers supplied by Apple; yours may be different. Usually, the printer-driver icon is named after your printer and looks something like the printer.

3. Drag the printer-driver icon to the System Folder. You see a message like the one shown in figure 7.5.

Fig. 7.5

Dialog instructing users to place printer drivers in the Extensions folder.

4. Click the OK button to continue. You then can eject the disk containing the printer driver and choose the printer driver with the Chooser, as discussed in the next section.

Some printer-driver suppliers use installer programs to place the printer drivers in the appropriate places on your disk. If your driver comes with such a program, use the installer program. The Apple Installer program (for more information on this program, see Chapter 2, "Understanding the System") installs drivers for any Apple printer.

In most cases, dragging the printer-driver icon to the System Folder works fine.

Choosing a Printer Driver

After installing the printer driver for your printer, you must tell the Macintosh which printer you are using so that the computer can call on the correct printer driver. You need to perform this procedure only once unless you use more than one printer.

Even if you do not have a printer, you may want to choose a printer driver, especially if you are working on a document that later will be printed on a Macintosh that is connected to a printer. Choosing the driver for the printer on which the document is to be printed ensures that the document's formatting conforms to that printer.

Before you use a printer for the first time, or if you must switch printers, you must choose that printer and its driver through the Chooser.

Open the Chooser by choosing it from the Apple menu. The Chooser window opens (see fig. 7.6). In the Chooser, you see icons of the printer drivers installed in your System Folder (along with other communications drivers, such as AppleTalk).

Fig. 7.6
The Chooser window displaying printer drivers.

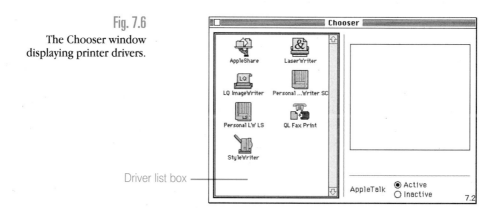

Driver list box

If you do not see the icon for your printer, you may have more printer drivers than the Chooser window can display. Scroll down through the list. If the icon for your printer still does not appear, the driver may not be installed (see "Installing Printer Drivers").

After you find the icon for your printer's driver, click the icon. If you are using a serial printer (such as a StyleWriter or Personal LaserWriter LS), you then see the serial-port selection icons in the Chooser: a printer icon and a telephone icon (see fig. 7.7).

Fig. 7.7

The serial-port selection icons.

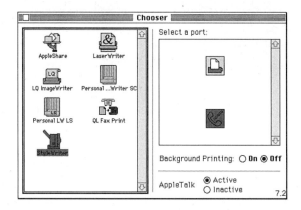

Click the icon that represents the port on the back of the Macintosh to which you connected your printer (usually, the printer port, represented by the printer icon). Then click the close box to close the Chooser. A message box appears, advising you to choose the Page Setup command in all open programs (see fig. 7.8).

Fig. 7.8

A Page Setup message.

Click the OK button. Thereafter, in each program that is open or running, choose the Page Setup command from the File menu and click the OK button in the Page Setup dialog to conform the program to the new printer setup. Your printer now is ready to be used.

If you choose an SCSI printer, such as a Personal LaserWriter SC, you do not see the serial-port selection icons in the Chooser because the printer is connected to your SCSI port, and the driver is aware of this fact. You do, however, see the message shown in figure 7.8. Click the OK button, and you are finished.

If you select an AppleTalk LaserWriter or other AppleTalk printer when AppleTalk is off, you see a message about activating AppleTalk (see fig. 7.9).

If AppleTalk already is active, you do not see the message shown in figure 7.9; instead, you see a list of available AppleTalk printers on the right side of the Chooser window. Click the one you want to use.

Click the Chooser's close box. You then see the Page Setup message shown in figure 7.8. If AppleTalk was not active when you chose the AppleTalk printer, you need to restart your Macintosh (choose Restart from the Special menu) to activate AppleTalk. You then need to open the Chooser again to select the AppleTalk printer you want to use.

Printing a Document

The basic steps for printing are essentially the same for all printers, although print options vary greatly from printer to printer. Essentially, you follow these steps:

1. Set the Page Setup options for the document. (You do this only once for a document unless you switch to another printer, in which case you need to reset the options.)

2. From the File menu, choose Print. You see the Print dialog for your printer.

3. Set the Print dialog options.

4. Click the Print (or OK) button to print your document.

The next two sections discuss printing options. You will, however, need to refer to the manual that came with your printer for more detailed information.

Setting Page Setup Options

Page Setup options include paper size and print orientation. To access these options, choose Page Setup from the File menu of the program you are using. You see a Page Setup dialog (see fig. 7.10).

Fig. 7.10
The Page Setup dialog for an ImageWriter LQ.

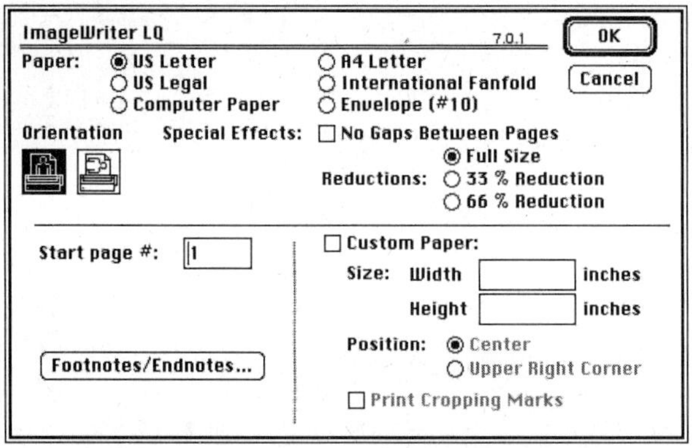

The dialog shown in figure 7.10 is for the ImageWriter LQ. The upper half of the dialog is typical of the dialog for dot-matrix printers; the lower half has been added by the word processing program Nisus. The Macintosh permits programs to add to the Page Setup dialog to enable you to set program-specific print options.

Figure 7.11 shows the Page Setup dialog, in the same program, for a LaserWriter.

All Page Setup dialogs contain options that enable you to choose paper size, page orientation (either landscape or portrait), the degree of reduction and enlargement, and various special effects. For a detailed description of the options available for your printer, check your printer's manual.

After you set the Page Setup options for a document, you do not have to set them again unless you need to make changes. Page Setup options are stored on disk with the document. Simply click the OK button to confirm your choices.

Fig. 7.11

The Page Setup dialog for a
LaserWriter.

```
┌──────────────────────────────────────────────────────────────┐
│ LaserWriter Page Setup                          7.1.2    ┌─OK──┐│
│ Paper: ⦿ US Letter  ○ A4 Letter                          └─────┘│
│        ○ US Legal   ○ B5 Letter   ○ │ Tabloid    ▼│  ┌Cancel┐  │
│        Reduce or │100│%           Printer Effects:  └──────┘   │
│        Enlarge:                   ☒ Font Substitution?┌Options┐│
│        Orientation                ☒ Text Smoothing?   └───────┘│
│        ┌┐┌┐                       ☒ Graphics Smoothing?        │
│        └┘└┘                       ☒ Faster Bitmap Printing?    │
│        Start page #:  │1 │        ☐ Custom Paper:              │
│                                      Size:  Width  │      │ inches│
│                                             Height │      │ inches│
│                                    Position: ⦿ Center          │
│       ┌Footnotes/Endnotes...┐                ○ Upper Right Corner│
│       └─────────────────────┘      ☐ Print Cropping Marks       │
└──────────────────────────────────────────────────────────────┘
```

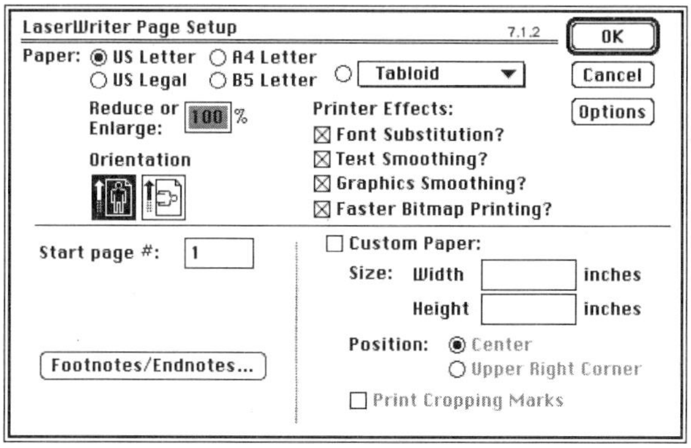

Setting Print Options

After you confirm the Page Setup options, you can print your document
by choosing the Print command from the File menu. When you choose
this command, you see the Print dialog (see fig. 7.12).

Fig. 7.12

Preparing to print a
document in Nisus.

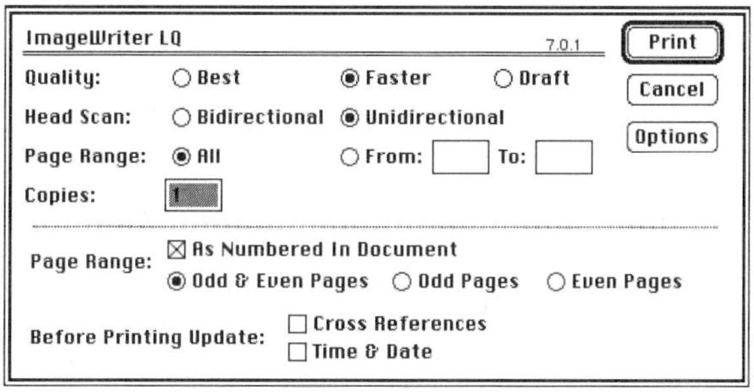

```
┌──────────────────────────────────────────────────────────────┐
│ ImageWriter LQ                              7.0.1    ┌Print─┐  │
│ Quality:    ○ Best      ⦿ Faster   ○ Draft          └──────┘  │
│ Head Scan:  ○ Bidirectional ⦿ Unidirectional ┌Cancel┐         │
│ Page Range: ⦿ All       ○ From: │  │ To: │  │ └──────┘        │
│ Copies:     │1│                              ┌Options┐        │
│                                              └───────┘        │
│ Page Range: ☒ As Numbered In Document                        │
│             ⦿ Odd & Even Pages ○ Odd Pages ○ Even Pages       │
│ Before Printing Update:  ☐ Cross References                  │
│                          ☐ Time & Date                       │
└──────────────────────────────────────────────────────────────┘
```

Figure 7.12 shows the Print dialog for the ImageWriter LQ, to which the
Nisus program has added information. Figure 7.13 shows the Print
dialog for a LaserWriter in the same program.

All Print dialogs contain options that enable you to choose the number
of copies to be printed, the range of pages to be printed, and the paper
source (paper tray, manual feed, and so on). You access these options by
clicking the Options button in the Print dialog.

You can accept the default options—which print one copy of all of the
pages of the document—by clicking the Print (or OK) button in the
dialog or by pressing Return.

Fig. 7.13
The Print dialog for a
LaserWriter.

```
LaserWriter "LaserWriter"                    7.1.2    [ Print ]
Copies: [1]       Pages: ⦿ All  ○ From: [    ] To: [    ]  [ Cancel ]
Cover Page:    ⦿ No ○ First Page  ○ Last Page
Paper Source: ⦿ Paper Cassette   ○ Manual Feed
Print:         ⦿ Black & White    ○ Color/Grayscale
Destination:   ⦿ Printer          ○ PostScript® File
─────────────────────────────────────────────────────────
                 ☒ As Numbered In Document
Page Range:      ⦿ Odd & Even Pages  ○ Odd Pages   ○ Even Pages

                          ☐ Cross References
Before Printing Update:   ☐ Time & Date
```

To confirm your choices and initiate printing, click the Print (or OK) button in the Print dialog.

Using Background Printing

Background printing refers to the capability of a printer driver to store a document in a disk file. The driver sends the file to the printer as quickly as it can process the information. The advantage of this approach is that you can continue to work on your Macintosh while a document is being printed.

You can use background printing only with certain printer drivers. To determine whether your printer driver offers background printing, follow these steps:

1. From the Apple menu, select Chooser. The Chooser window appears.

2. Click your printer's driver. If background printing is available, the Background Printing option appears in the Chooser window (see fig. 7.14).

Fig. 7.14
The Background Printing
option.

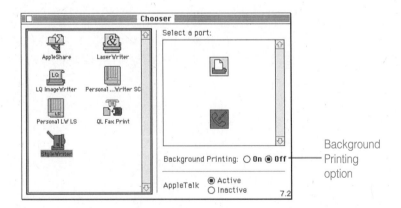

Background
Printing
option

3. Usually, the option appears already activated. If you need to turn it on, click the On radio button.

4. Close the Chooser window by clicking its close box.

When the Background Printing option is on, the dialog box that informs you that printing is in progress disappears quickly, even before printing is complete, because the document has been stored on the disk. You can continue to work while printing proceeds.

When a document is printing, a new program starts: PrintMonitor. To see the PrintMonitor window, choose PrintMonitor from the Application menu (see fig. 7.15).

Fig. 7.15
The PrintMonitor window.

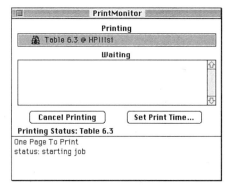

The PrintMonitor window has the following sections:

■ *Printing.* Lists the name of the document that currently is being printed and the name of the printer.

■ *Waiting.* Lists the documents waiting to be printed.

■ *Printing Status.* Displays the print status of the current document.

The window has the following control buttons:

■ *Cancel Printing.* Stops the printing of the current document.

■ *Set Print Time.* Enables you to set a time at which the document is to be printed.

When you click the Set Print Time button, a dialog appears. Click the date or time that you want to change, and two arrows (up and down) appear, enabling you to adjust the print time.

You can delay a print job indefinitely by clicking the Postpone Indefinitely button. The job is held until you set a print time with the Set Print Time option.

PrintMonitor has options that affect the way the program works. Access these options by choosing the Preferences command from the File menu when PrintMonitor is on-screen. You see the PrintMonitor Preferences dialog (see fig. 7.16).

Preferences...

Show the PrintMonitor window when printing:
⦿ No   ○ Yes

When a printing error needs to be reported:
◆ ○ Only display ◆ in Application menu
◆ ○ Also display icon in menu bar
◆ ⦿ Also display alert

When a manual feed job starts:
○ Give no notification
◆ ○ Display icon in menu bar
◆ ⦿ Also display alert

[Cancel]   [OK]

These options include the following:

Show the PrintMonitor window when printing. If this option is on, the PrintMonitor window appears whenever printing occurs. If the option is off, PrintMonitor appears only as a command in the Application menu; to display the PrintMonitor window, you must choose the command from that menu.

When a printing error needs to be reported. When a printing error occurs, PrintMonitor can notify you by displaying the printer icon in the menu bar, and by displaying an alert dialog. Click the options you want to use.

When a manual feed job starts. Some jobs require you to feed paper into the printer by hand. You can have PrintMonitor notify you before a manual-feed job (by displaying the printer icon in the menu bar, or by displaying the printer icon and an alert dialog), or you can opt not to be notified. Make your choice by clicking the radio button next to the option.

When the options are set, click the OK button. Click Cancel if you want to close the dialog without saving any changes that you made.

Using Laser Printer Languages

Laser printers have become very popular because they produce clear images that approach typeset quality. At the same time, laser printers offer a variety of fonts, styles, and sizes, usually limited only by the printer's internal memory. A basic understanding of laser-printer languages is necessary to understand the capabilities of Apple's various laser printers as well as those offered by third-party printers.

Understanding PostScript

As opposed to QuickDraw printers, which require the Macintosh itself to do all the work in printing a document, PostScript laser printers have microprocessors that do the work. These printers actually are computers, some with the processing power of full Macintosh systems. In fact, if you have an older Macintosh attached to a newer printer, the printer may have *more* processing power than the Macintosh.

Like all computers, PostScript printers have a language that they understand and in which they can be programmed. That language is PostScript, which is a set of commands that describes the contents of a page in compact mathematical terms. In PostScript, the drawing of a square, for example, can be initiated by a single command line that provides the basic parameters of the square. Printers that use QuickDraw must be fed the square one dot at a time.

You might say, in greatly simplified terms, that a printer with a PostScript interpreter "knows" what a square is. The Macintosh need only tell the printer where to place the square, how big to make it, and how thick to make the lines that compose it.

A PostScript printer generally has a set of fonts built into its read-only memory (ROM). The Personal LaserWriter NTR, for example, has 35 resident fonts and prints these fonts beautifully. If you use the resident fonts, the result is superb. Downloadable PostScript fonts and fonts designed specifically for laser printers also give you excellent copy. If you use a bit-mapped font, however, you may be disappointed by the results. You may end up with severe jaggies and fonts that look terrible.

PostScript printers do not store the actual fonts or the shapes of the characters themselves; instead, they store the directions that enable the laser printer to construct typefaces of the size and style you specify.

Languages such as PostScript are called page-description languages (*PDL*) because they describe the contents of a page. PostScript is the most popular PDL. The PostScript language describes the shape of each character or graphic to be printed as a mathematical formula. PostScript printers then create the characters and graphics in the requested sizes and styles, using the mathematical description of the font or graphic.

As discussed earlier in this chapter (in "Understanding Printer Drivers"), the Macintosh issues print commands in the form of QuickDraw commands. The printer driver translates these commands into PostScript commands and then sends the commands to the printer, which understands the commands and creates the desired images.

The primary advantage of PostScript is that it enables you to program your printer for many special effects. PostScript's capabilities are discussed in more detail in the following sections.

PostScript is not the only PDL in existence, although it has become the dominant one. Even Apple at one point attempted to compete with PostScript by introducing TrueType, an alternative font technology intended to be part of a PDL called TrueImage. System 7 and the newer Apple printers support TrueType fonts, but whether TrueImage ever will compete successfully with PostScript is questionable. (TrueImage may not continue to exist, so the point may be moot.)

In any case, although other PDLs may be interesting, the continuing dominance of PostScript—especially with the introduction of the more advanced Level 2 version—makes PostScript the focus of the remaining sections of this chapter. The next chapter further discusses TrueType fonts, which are included with System 7. Newer Apple printers support these fonts, which are offered by several manufacturers.

Using PostScript Tools

When you work directly with PostScript, as with any other programming language, you enter a set of commands. In programming languages such as BASIC, you use commands to create a program that performs a certain task (for example, totalling a column of numbers). In PostScript, however, your commands result in an image to be printed on your LaserWriter or a typesetting machine.

PostScript and other PDLs (such as UltraScript and Impress) were developed to take advantage of laser printers' extensive capabilities. Adobe, the leading developer and manufacturer of fonts and of PostScript, licenses the fonts and PostScript to printer manufacturers, who embed them in their printers' ROM. Some manufacturers sell PDLs as separate software products, but these products have been less successful than PostScript. Other manufacturers include non-PostScript PDLs in their printers' ROM, giving Adobe some competition. Early indications are that you may save some money by purchasing such printers, but clones are not always 100-percent compatible. If you create only simple graphics and use few fonts, a clone probably will be all right, but the safest bet is to avoid clones, especially if you do graphics-intensive work or extensive desktop publishing.

Printing with a PostScript Printer

Because PostScript does not affect the on-screen appearance of a document, you cannot see PostScript changes on-screen. To view the changes, you must print your document unless you have a utility such as LaserTalk (discussed later in this chapter in "Using PostScript Utilities").

If your PostScript printer does not contain the equations for a particular font on your Macintosh, your printer cannot draw the font from scratch. Instead, your printer may substitute a built-in font. For example, New York may print as Times, Geneva as Helvetica, and Monaco as Courier if you choose the Font Substitution option in the Page Setup dialog for an Apple laser printer. If you did not choose this option, the printer attempts to generate a bit-mapped version of the font—something to be avoided, because bit-mapped versions of fonts generally are not as appealing as the built-in or downloaded versions. (For more information on font downloading, see Chapter 8, "Using Fonts.")

Figure 7.17 illustrates the difference in quality between printing with and without the Font Substitution option.

Fig. 7.17
Printing with and without
the Font Substitution
option selected.

This is New York with font substitution.

This is Geneva with font substitution.

This is Monaco with font substitution...

This is New York without font substitution.

This is Geneva without font substitution.

This is Monaco without font substitution...

Your LaserWriter helps you improve the quality of printed output by providing the Font Substitution and Smoothing options shown in figure 7.18.

To achieve the best printing of fonts, make certain that you have the font you want to use in a form that your printer can best reproduce. Chapter 8, "Using Fonts," discusses in greater detail the process by which printers reproduce fonts. For now, you need understand only that PostScript uses commands and mathematical formulas to generate high-quality fonts and that you can work directly with these commands, if you want, by programming in PostScript.

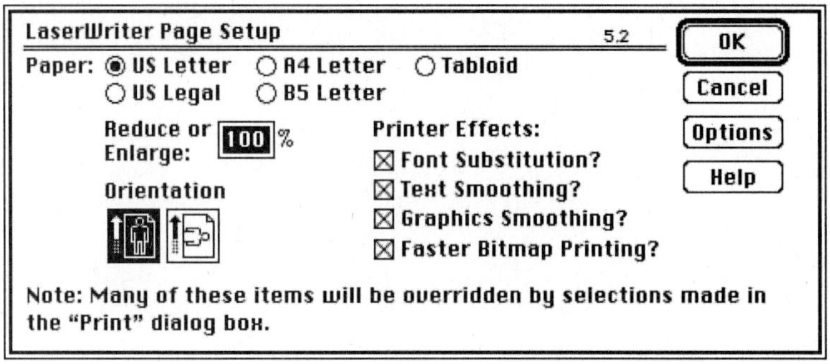

Fig. 7.18

Font substitution and
smoothing options in the
Page Setup dialog for
Aldus FreeHand.

```
┌─────────────────────────────────────────────────────────────┐
│ LaserWriter Page Setup                        5.2    ┌──────┐ │
│                                                      │  OK  │ │
│ Paper: ◉ US Letter   ○ A4 Letter   ○ Tabloid        └──────┘ │
│        ○ US Legal    ○ B5 Letter                   ┌────────┐ │
│        Reduce or ┌───┐                             │ Cancel │ │
│        Enlarge:  │100│%   Printer Effects:         └────────┘ │
│                  └───┘     ⊠ Font Substitution?   ┌─────────┐ │
│        Orientation        ⊠ Text Smoothing?       │ Options │ │
│                           ⊠ Graphics Smoothing?   └─────────┘ │
│        ┌──┐ ┌──┐          ⊠ Faster Bitmap Printing?┌──────┐   │
│        │↑⚇│ │↑⚇│                                    │ Help │   │
│        └──┘ └──┘                                    └──────┘   │
│                                                              │
│ Note: Many of these items will be overridden by selections made in │
│ the "Print" dialog box.                                      │
└─────────────────────────────────────────────────────────────┘
```

Programming with PostScript

Renowned computer buffs tremble, ace programmers shake,
technowizards fall, and the author shudders at the very thought of
programming in PostScript. But you can avoid much of the pain of
programming in PostScript by using a host of utilities.

Some programs show you what your PostScript code will look like. As
QuickDraw's color 32-bit fonts and Apple's TrueType fonts become
more common, you will see more programs that display what your
printer will print. (Chapter 8 describes System 7's capability to preview
fonts.)

Using PostScript Utilities

Several PostScript utilities help you use PostScript to your advantage and
even give PostScript capabilities to non-PostScript printers. If you are not
familiar with PostScript and don't want to take the time to learn it, these
utilities and stand-alone programs may be just what you need. Most
PostScript utilities translate into PostScript code the effect that you want
to achieve, just as compilers take a BASIC command and translate the
command into the 1s and 0s of the computer's assembly language.

The first (and perhaps the best) of these PostScript utilities is LaserTalk
from Emerald City Software. LaserTalk is a programming tool that
enables you to interact with the PostScript commands in your laser
printer's memory. After you open the window that lists the PostScript
procedures, you enter the PostScript code that you want your printer to
follow.

LaserTalk is especially good for beginners because it provides feedback every step of the way. If the printer does not understand the command you enter, a message appears. If you don't see a message, you can continue with the next command. While you are working, you can consult the status box, which displays the amount of memory still available, the current file name, and other information.

In programs such as Aldus FreeHand, you cannot see the images that you create on-screen. LaserTalk and similar utilities, however, display a reasonably faithful reproduction of what will print (see fig. 7.19). You also can browse through dictionaries of PostScript files and use the built-in debugger to determine why your listing does not work.

Fig. 7.19

A LaserTalk screen displaying a graphic altered by PostScript commands.

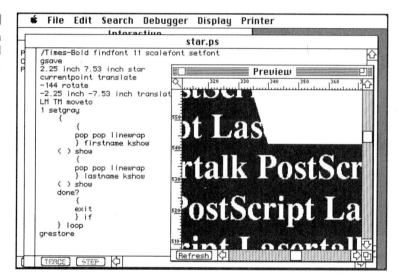

Similar PostScript utilities are PostHaste (from MicroDynamics) and Postility (from PostCraft International). Postility, for example, offers many of the same features as LaserTalk and some special menu items that cut down the tedium of PostScript programming. The Insert Font command in the Special menu, for example, enables you to insert a specific font with a particular style (such as Times Roman Bold) through menu selections rather than through complicated PostScript commands such as /**(fontname) findfont**.... If you change fonts several times during a procedure, you will appreciate this convenience.

Some word processing programs enable you to work with PostScript. Microsoft Word, for example, provides a predefined style that enables you to insert PostScript commands into a document. The PostScript commands are inserted as hidden text and are sent directly to the printer for interpretation when the document is printed (see fig. 7.20).

Fig. 7.20
Adding a watermark in
Microsoft Word.

```
% Word Under Text
/Times-BoldItalic findfont
/FontSize 72 def
/TextToPrint (CONFIDENTIAL) def
FontSize scalefont setfont
/printDraft
{0 0 moveto TextToPrint show} def
wp$x 2 div wp$y 2 div translate
45 rotate
TextToPrint stringwidth pop 2 div neg
FontSize 2 mul 3 div 2 div neg
translate
.95 -.05 .6
{setgray printDraft -1 .5 translate} for
.9 setgray printDraft
```

Marketing Plan

Introduction

The MovieView Division represents Donovan's best opportunity to dominate market
research for the film industry. This new Donovan division will be one of the first research
organizations devoted exclusively to quantitative research and analysis for motion picture
producers. We see two main target markets:

- Producers who want to test the appeal of actors, actresses, locations, and so forth
  prior to filming

This PostScript code prints the word *CONFIDENTIAL* in gray (a watermark) at a 45-degree angle across the page. Word's page-layout glossary contains several common PostScript examples, including the watermark example shown in the preceding figure.

The Macintosh version of WordPerfect also enables you to enter PostScript commands in your documents by creating a PostScript object in your text. This object is a box into which you enter the desired PostScript commands.

In System 7, you can work with PostScript commands by printing a document to disk rather than to the printer. This procedure creates a file containing the PostScript commands that you then can send to the printer. To create a file of this type, choose the PostScript File option in the Print dialog for the Apple LaserWriter (see fig. 7.21).

Fig. 7.21
Creating a PostScript file.

```
LaserWriter "LaserWriter"                    7.1.2    [ Save ]
Copies: 1        Pages: ● All ○ From:     To:         [ Cancel ]
Cover Page:    ● No ○ First Page ○ Last Page
Paper Source: ● Paper Cassette ○ Manual Feed
Print:         ● Black & White   ○ Color/Grayscale
Destination:   ○ Printer         ● PostScript® File
Section Range: From: 1    To: 1            ☐ Print Selection Only
☐ Print Hidden Text   ☐ Print Next File   ☐ Print Back To Front
```

A word processing program can open this file as a text file, enabling you to view and work with the PostScript commands. Using this procedure, you could create a graphic, print the graphic to disk, and then open the PostScript file as text. By copying the commands into a document and adding a few of your own, you could, for example, use a logo as a watermark rather than simple text.

B e advised that printing files to disk results in very large files. A one-page, text-only, 5KB Word document printed to disk by the author resulted in a 529KB PostScript file! You should limit your printed-to-disk documents to a fairly small size to keep them manageable. Printing a complex, multiple-page text-and-graphics document to disk probably is not a good idea; you may run out of disk space. Focus instead on smaller text or graphics to be used in a special way (for example, as a one-word watermark or a simple logo).

Word processing programs such as Microsoft Word and WordPerfect are discussed in Chapter 10, "Working with Word Processors."

Using PostScript Programs

One PostScript program that produces outstanding graphics is Cricket Draw (from Computer Associates). This drawing program has two features that are of interest to PostScript users. First, Cricket Draw enables you to view the results of your work on your monitor without having to print the graphic. Second, because you can see the graphic on-screen, you also can print the graphic on an ImageWriter, although the resolution is not nearly as crisp as on a laser printer.

Aldus FreeHand and Adobe Illustrator also offer a large selection of predesigned techniques, often called *procedures*, for creating different patterns. Figure 7.22 shows 10 patterns you can create with procedures.

The patterns you can create include the following:

- Triangles
- Balls
- Swirls
- Romans

- Crepes
- Hearts
- Solid lines
- Snowflakes
- Waves
- Checkers

You can apply procedures easily, in any combination, to any shape.

Fig. 7.22
Ten FreeHand patterns.

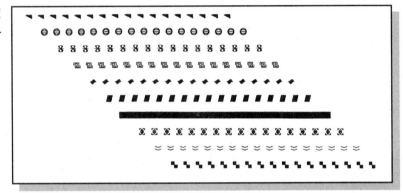

Sharing PostScript Files

You can create a PostScript file through programs such as FreeHand under one condition: the program in which the PostScript file was created must be saved as an Encapsulated PostScript file. A variety of programs accept this file format. Keep in mind, however, that Encapsulated PostScript files occupy a great deal of space because each file includes a great deal of information about (and instructions for) printing. When you save a file in FreeHand, for example, FreeHand attaches the extension EPS to the file name and saves the file as an Encapsulated PostScript file.

Figure 7.23 shows a QuarkXPress document that has imported an EPS file.

Fig. 7.23
Transferring a PostScript
file to another program.

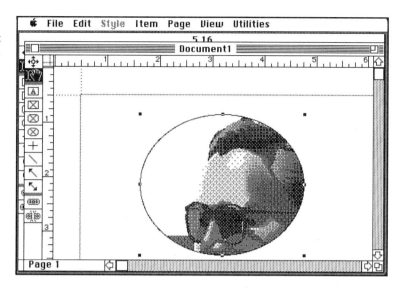

All these tools are great if you have a PostScript printer. But what if you cannot afford a PostScript printer? Or what if you have a non-PostScript printer but want to take advantage of some PostScript-like features? Welcome to Freedom of Press sold by Custom Applications.

Freedom of Press is an award-winning printing utility that transforms Mac-generated PostScript codes into information that non-PostScript printers can understand and use. Following are a few examples of what Freedom of Press can do:

■ Provide 35 high-quality outline fonts, such as those available in the LaserWriter Plus.

■ Scale typefaces to any point size and rotate them to any angle.

■ Work with more than 50 output devices, including the most popular non-PostScript laser printers, and with inkjet, dot-matrix, and color thermal printers.

■ Print in batches to help you save time.

To run Freedom of Press, you need at least a Macintosh SE/30 with a hard disk, 1.5MB of RAM, and 2.5MB of disk space. Freedom of Press sells for about $250 to $300, but when you consider that you can use any printer and get PostScript capability, the investment in Freedom of Press may well be worthwhile.

System 7 users can purchase Freedom of Press Light, which sells for less than half the price of Freedom of Press, and use PostScript with the Hewlett-Packard DeskWriter C, Canon BJC-820, or any QuickDraw printer (including those from the popular GCC line). Included are 17 outline fonts.

Chapter Summary

No matter how many hours you spend slaving over a keyboard, your work does not boil down to much unless you can communicate it to others. The way you most often communicate ideas and information is through a printed document.

You currently have several choices in the world of Macintosh printing, and even more choices will be available soon. You can begin with a relatively inexpensive dot-matrix printer and move up to a powerful PostScript printer with many resident fonts. Even if you write beautifully, no one will notice your message if you print with a frayed ribbon or a damaged drum on your laser printer. Marshall McLuhan probably did not have in mind a Macintosh and printer when he said that the medium is the message, but these words seem to ring true as printing technology becomes more sophisticated, more accessible, and less expensive.

CHAPTER EIGHT

Using Fonts

Your choice of fonts—their size, style, and weight—and the appearance of the words on a page is similar to a painter's choice of shapes, brush strokes, and textures. Your finished document is more than words, and you can make your document more effective if you know something about the world of type.

The word *font* traditionally has meant a set of characters of a particular design; a *typeface*, therefore, has represented a specific font such as Helvetica, Garamond, or Palatino. This definition is not exactly adhered to in the Macintosh world. Originally, every different modification of a typeface was a font; Helvetica Bold was a separate font from Helvetica Italic. Recently, especially since the introduction of System 7, fonts on the Macintosh have come closer to the traditional meaning in that variations in font styles are merged together in a single font file.

Defining Fonts

Type talks to the reader, and the shape of the type conveys a message. Figure 8.1 illustrates how type can convey a formal message or one that is contemporary and upbeat. You need to be able to distinguish clearly among the fonts you use and to determine the best font for the job at hand. The following information gives you the basic tools to make distinctions between font styles and appropriate uses.

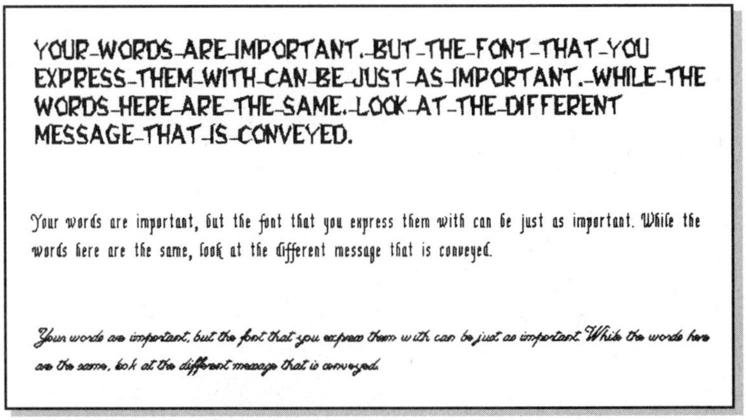

Fig. 8.1

How the typeface affects the message.

A *type character* consists of different components, as shown in figure 8.2. Characters are positioned on an imaginary line called the *baseline*. The height of an uppercase character is called the *cap height*. Lowercase characters have an *x-height*. The part of the character that extends below the baseline is called a *descender*, and the part that extends above the x-height is called an *ascender*.

Fig. 8.2

The components of type
characters.

Fonts can be divided into categories based on different sets of characteristics, including size, weight, width, angle, family, and style. One of the most obvious differences among fonts is whether they are serif or sans serif (see fig. 8.3). *Serifs* are the little crossbars added to the ends of letters, as in Times or Palatino. Serif type often is the first choice for the body of text because the serifs help break up the monotony, and the text is easier to read. *Sans serif* text, such as Helvetica or Avant Garde, adds a quality of boldness that is terrific for headlines, especially when a heavy weight is used. You can hardly go wrong with this combination of copy and headline fonts.

Fig. 8.3

A comparison of serif and
sans serif Macintosh fonts.

This is Times, a serif font.

This is Helvetica, a sans-serif font.

Type size usually is expressed in the standard printer's measures of *picas* and *points*; 6 picas equal an inch, and 12 points equal a pica. An 18-point character is 1.5 picas or 0.25 inch high, for example. Most applications enable you to set type size in inches, picas, or points, but the most frequently used measuring unit is points, such as 10/12 (10 on 12), meaning 10-point characters with the baselines spaced 12 points apart. The distance between baselines (from baseline to baseline) is known as *leading*. You can get some idea of how many lines of type will fit into how much space by using table 8.1. The logic is pretty straightforward: if an inch is 72 points, a 12-point letter takes up 6 lines. This handy chart can help you in your planning. If you have one inch of column space, for example, you can fit 6 lines of 12-point type in that space.

Table 8.1
Lines per Column Inch

Column Depth (in inches)	Leading (in points)										
	6	7	8	9	10	11	12	15	18	20	30
0.25	3	3	2	2	2	2	2	1	1	1	1
0.50	6	5	5	4	4	3	3	2	2	2	1
0.75	9	8	7	6	5	5	5	4	3	2	1
1	12	10	9	8	7	7	6	5	4	3	2
2	24	21	18	16	14	13	12	10	8	6	5
3	36	31	27	24	22	20	18	14	12	9	7
4	48	41	36	32	29	26	24	19	16	12	10
5	60	51	45	40	36	33	30	24	20	15	12
6	72	62	54	48	43	39	36	29	24	18	14
7	84	72	63	56	50	46	42	34	28	21	17
8	96	82	72	64	58	52	48	38	32	24	19
9	108	93	81	72	65	59	54	43	36	27	22
10	120	103	90	80	72	65	60	48	40	30	24
11	132	113	99	88	79	72	66	53	44	33	26
12	144	123	108	96	86	79	72	58	48	36	29
13	156	134	117	104	94	85	78	62	52	39	31
14	168	144	126	112	101	92	84	67	56	42	34
15	180	154	135	120	108	98	90	72	60	45	36
16	192	165	144	128	115	105	96	77	64	48	38
17	204	175	153	136	122	111	102	82	68	51	41
18	216	185	162	144	130	118	108	86	72	54	43
19	228	195	171	152	137	124	114	91	76	57	46
20	240	206	180	160	144	131	120	96	80	60	48
21	252	216	189	168	151	137	126	101	84	63	50
22	264	226	198	176	158	144	132	106	88	66	53
23	276	237	207	184	166	151	138	110	92	69	55
24	288	247	216	192	173	157	144	115	96	72	58
25	300	257	225	200	180	164	150	120	100	75	60
26	312	267	234	208	187	170	156	125	104	78	62
27	324	278	243	216	194	177	162	130	108	81	65
28	336	288	252	224	202	183	168	134	112	84	67

Remember that the amount of space used between baselines is somewhat arbitrary. Commercial printers generally use about 120 percent of the font's size, but you should use what looks right to you and what works well with the font you have chosen.

Type weight refers to the heaviness of the letters. Figure 8.4 shows the contrast between Helvetica Condensed and Helvetica Condensed Bold. The lighter the type, the more delicate and less obtrusive the type appears. Heavy types, such as Cooper, really make the point but often have to stand alone because anything else around them gets dwarfed.

Helvetica Condensed

Helvetica Condensed Bold

Type style refers to the boldface, outline, italic, and other style options that you see on many Macintosh applications. Also, some different styles have been added to more recent applications so that you can choose superscript, condensed, shadow, and others. Most of these styles are available on the Style menu or as part of the Font or Format menu of an application program. As a result, you do not have to go outside the application for special effects. Figure 8.5 shows a sample of different type styles.

This is Bold

This is Outline

This is Underlined

This is Italics

Understanding Font Types

You must understand the three basic kinds of fonts that exist in the Macintosh world. These are screen fonts, PostScript fonts, and TrueType fonts.

The *screen font*—also called a *bit-mapped font*—is used on your Macintosh screen. When you type, the Macintosh consults the currently selected font and uses that font's character set to draw each letter, number, or symbol. These fonts also are used to print to non-PostScript printers (and even PostScript printers in certain cases—cases to be avoided; see the section "Using Fonts on PostScript Printers" for details).

The PostScript font is used for the characters on a printer, usually a laser printer. Non-PostScript printers such as the dot-matrix ImageWriter II and the inkjet StyleWriter II use screen fonts—unless you have a utility such as the Adobe Type Manager or you are using TrueType fonts. The PostScript font category has become the standard for personal computers even beyond the Macintosh.

Apple and Microsoft jointly developed the TrueType font to address one problem discussed here. The difference between the screen font and printer font can lead to problems in document design; what you see on-screen is not necessarily what you see when you print. TrueType eliminates the use of separate screen and printer fonts. This font rasterizing system was intended to be part of the TrueImage page description language (see Chapter 7, "Printing," for more information), but of late it appears that both TrueType and TrueImage are faltering against the strength of PostScript.

Understanding Font Rasterizing and Search Order

You know from Chapter 7, "Printing," that you print a document by choosing the Print command from the File menu. You may be wondering what exactly happens, however, after you choose the Print command and click the Print (or OK) button in the Print dialog. Even if you are *not* overconcerned with just how a printer prints, you do need to understand the basics of this process in order to effectively use fonts.

When you initiate printing, the Macintosh begins to describe the page to be printed by using the commands of QuickDraw, the built-in imaging system used to draw everything that appears on your Macintosh screen. In simplified terms, the Macintosh "draws" the page to be printed in memory in a manner quite similar to the way it "draws" the page in memory that corresponds to your screen. The page to be printed is passed to the printer driver, which then begins to interpret the page into a language that the printer can understand.

In order for an image in memory to be printed, the image must be *rasterized*. The Macintosh or some other processor must perform what is called "raster image processing" (RIP or RIPing), which essentially means turning the page into a series of dots that are then placed on the paper page by the printer.

If your printer does not use PostScript, the Macintosh itself performs the RIPing, converting the memory image into a series of dots which are then fed to the printer. (This is why printers such as the StyleWriter and the QuickDraw laser printer Personal LaserWriter LS can be connected to the serial port; the Macintosh sends them one dot at a time).

Using Fonts on QuickDraw Printers

The fact that the Macintosh must do the raster image process for the printer is the reason non-PostScript printers are slow and why they tie up the Macintosh during printing. The Macintosh does all the work and feeds the bit maps to the printer along with a few printer commands.

Now you are ready to understand why there are three different basic categories of fonts. Screen fonts are used by QuickDraw to display your text on-screen. Screen fonts are bit maps, which means that they are already made up of individual dots. QuickDraw only has to select the correct bit map and transfer it into memory to display a character on-screen.

If you have only screen fonts and a printer, these same bit maps are sent to the printer and placed on the page. This results in an average- to low-quality printing because the resolution of screen fonts is not very high (only 72 dpi).

TrueType is built into System 7, and System 7 includes several TrueType fonts. System 6 can use TrueType fonts, too, but must have an Apple-supplied System extension in order to do so.

To obtain a higher quality print, you can use PostScript or TrueType fonts. These fonts are described mathematically rather than by maps of dots and therefore result in a much higher quality of print. If your printer is a non-PostScript printer, however, the printer cannot under-stand the mathematical language used to describe the PostScript fonts, and the screen version of the font is still sent to the Macintosh.

You can get around this in one of three ways. One is to use Adobe Type Manager (ATM) by Adobe Systems. This System extension unifies Adobe's screen and printer fonts, enhancing the display of fonts on-screen as well as the printing of fonts on non-PostScript printers. You also can use a software PostScript interpreter such as Freedom of Press by Custom Applications. If you have System 7, you can use Freedom of Press Light.

While all three of these options enhance printing quality, they have drawbacks. Using ATM with PostScript fonts or TrueType fonts definitely enhances the printing of text, but neither solution improves the printing of PostScript graphics. If you do more work with text than graphics, or you don't use PostScript graphics, these solutions will probably work well for you.

Freedom of Press and Freedom of Press Light give you PostScript font *and* graphics capabilities, essentially turning your printer into a PostScript printer. The Macintosh does all the work still, however, and this type of software PostScript interpreter increases the work load and slows your Macintosh even more during printing.

Heavy users of text and graphics will want to consider purchasing a PostScript printer or upgrading their non-PostScript printer to PostScript. Many printer manufacturers offer such upgrades.

Users considering purchasing a printer will want to look at PostScript printers. PostScript laser printers have come down sharply in price and are quite affordable.

Using Fonts on PostScript Printers

If you have a PostScript printer, the printer driver converts the page into a series of PostScript commands and then transmits these to the printer. The printer—using its own microprocessor—RIPs the page, translating the PostScript commands into dots to be placed on the page.

This type of printer reduces the workload of the Macintosh, and the printing will not tie up the Macintosh for long, especially if a printer spooler is in use. See Chapter 25, "Choosing a Printer," for more on print spoolers.

The communication process that goes on between the Macintosh and a PostScript printer is rather involved, especially if you use a mix of Post-Script and TrueType fonts. When you initiate printing to a PostScript printer, the Macintosh considers the fonts in your document and queries the printer to see whether the same fonts exist in its read-only memory (ROM) or on an attached disk. (Many high-level printers allow fonts in addition to those in the ROMs to be stored on a hard disk attached to the printer. See Chapter 25, "Choosing a Printer.") Current laser printers contain around 35 fonts, so the chances that the Macintosh will find the font are reasonably good unless you use a great many fonts.

If the printer responds that the font exists, the Macintosh sends the page and the printer takes over, RIPing the page and printing it. If the printer responds that the font is not resident, the next action of the Macintosh depends on whether the document font in question is a TrueType font.

If the font is not a TrueType font, the Macintosh searches the Font folder in the System Folder for a PostScript printer font equivalent to the font in the document. On finding a PostScript printer font, the computer sends the font to the printer (a process called *downloading*). The printer stores the font in memory, and the Macintosh sends the page to be printed.

If the Macintosh fails to find a printer version of the PostScript font, the Macintosh creates a bit map for the font and sends that to the printer. The resulting print quality is usually less than satisfactory in such cases.

Apple LaserWriter printer drivers offer an option called Font Substitution in the Page Setup dialog. This option is initially turned on. The option causes the Macintosh to substitute the Times font for New York, Helvetica for Geneva, and Courier for Monaco when printing. The reason for this option is that the New York, Geneva, and Monaco fonts look better on-screen, but the Times, Helvetica, and Courier look better on the printed page. Apple printers all contain the latter fonts resident in ROM.

The spacing between the substituted font and the screen font might differ and produce unsatisfactory results. If possible, use the same screen font as you will use to print the document.

Alternatively, if the font in the document is a TrueType font, the Macintosh queries the printer to determine whether it has the TrueType font in memory (as many of the newer Apple LaserWriters do). If so, the page is sent and the printer prints.

If the printer replies that it does not have the TrueType font, the Macintosh responds by downloading not only the font, but also the TrueType rasterizer, to enable the printer to print TrueType fonts.

Now, as if all of this process is not complicated enough, a good question is this: what happens if a PostScript printer font and a TrueType font of the same name are resident in the Font folder? Simple answer: you cannot have two fonts of the same name in the Fonts folder.

The upshot of all of this is

- ROM-resident fonts are the best to use. They are in your printer's permanent memory and do not require the Macintosh to do anything but send the page.

- If you are using any PostScript fonts, get ATM for better screen display and non-PostScript printing.

- PostScript fonts should be installed in pairs; both the screen font *and* printer font should be installed. Then when you are ready to print, the Macintosh can find the printer font and send it to the printer.

- If you want to use a PostScript version of a font, remove any True-Type version from your Font folder. Otherwise, the TrueType font may preempt the PostScript font.

I f you have one or two PostScript printer fonts that you want to use a great deal during a work session, you can speed the printing process by downloading the font to the printer's RAM so that the font will be resident and the Macintosh will not have to download the font itself. You can use the Apple LaserWriter Font Utility to do this with Apple printers. Third-party printers often come with a download utility that works with them.

RAM does not retain its contents when the power is switched off; the downloaded font will not be resident in memory the next time you turn on the printer. You will need to download it again. Also, bear in mind that your printer needs memory to print your document. If you download every font you *might* need, you can overload your printer's memory. The printer may not have enough memory to print, or it may have flushed out some of the fonts to make room for new fonts being downloaded, thereby negating the benefit of downloading the font. The next call for the font will require the Macintosh to download the font.

If you find yourself using more and more fonts, you may want to upgrade your printer's memory, add a hard drive, or buy a more powerful printer (see Chapter 25, "Choosing a Printer").

Understanding Fonts On-Screen

To confuse matters further, note that you need to be careful when you install fonts and use them on-screen. Some interesting things happen in System 7 that you will want to be aware of.

Each point size of screen fonts is treated as a separate font. When you have a bit-mapped screen font of a particular point size installed and a TrueType font of the same name (as you will if you use the Apple Installer to install the System Software), the bit-mapped screen font is the one that displays on-screen. In most cases, it is the one you *want* displayed, because the bit-mapped screen fonts are optimized for the best on-screen viewing.

I use the Courier font in 12-point size for writing, for example. This font is ideal for text submitted to publishers because it is a *monospaced* font—one that places the same number of characters per inch on a line. Courier font is rather typewriter-like; its consistent font helps publishers estimate page size and word count.

The bit-mapped screen font Courier 12 is installed in my Font folder, as is the TrueType Courier font. Hence, the Courier 12 screen font is used for displaying 12-point text on-screen while the TrueType font is used for printing (and because my printer is not a PostScript printer, using TrueType fonts is ideal). At the same time, if I choose to display Courier font in 48-point size, this screen font size is not installed in my System Folder, and TrueType takes over. The TrueType font in the larger sizes looks good on-screen, and the printing is very attractive, of course.

Were I to remove the Courier 12 screen font, however, the TrueType font would be called upon to display the 12-point size on-screen. In fact, I tried disposing of the screen fonts—leaving only TrueType fonts—in order to reduce the size of my rather enormous System Folder (which is over 10MB these days).

What I discovered was that the TrueType font is not readable on-screen at the smaller point sizes. This isn't actually supposed to happen, I thought. I was under the impression that TrueType eliminated the need for separate screen and printer fonts. Apparently, it does not always do so.

In any case, my printer is a very old dot-matrix but produces excellent quality text with TrueType fonts. I found, however, that I still needed the bit-mapped font for screen display of the smaller point sizes of the fonts I use. You may have the same experience.

You must experiment to determine the best font mix, which leads to the next section's topic: how to install and remove fonts of all kinds on the Macintosh.

Installing Fonts

Installing fonts has become much easier with System 7 and 7.1. No special utility is needed as was true with System 6. (System 6 uses the Font/DA Mover utility to install fonts; this utility is provided on the System Software disk set.)

Remember that you must install both the screen and printer font if you use PostScript. To use a TrueType font or a regular screen font, install the desired font. You can identify different kinds of fonts by their icons (see fig. 8.6).

Fig. 8.6

Different font icons.

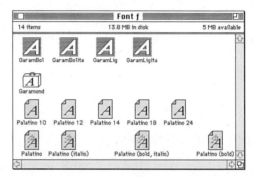

The top row shows the PostScript printer font Garamond in four styles: bold, bold italic, light, and light italic. These icons are Adobe's icons and may not apply to fonts supplied by other font manufacturers. The icon used will be distinctive, however.

The next row shows a single font suitcase. *Suitcases* have their history in earlier versions of the System Software; these special files were intended to hold fonts and the mini-applications called *desk accessories* that were installed in the Apple menu.

Suitcase files have lived on even though desk accessories are no longer separate from regular applications (desk accessories in System 7 can be double-clicked just like any other applications). Fonts do not have to be in special files but can be manipulated directly. Font suitcases remain a convenient way, however, to group related sets of fonts.

You can view the fonts in a suitcase file by double-clicking the suitcase. When the suitcase window opens, you see icons like those shown in the third and fourth rows of figure 8.6. You can move fonts in and out of a suitcase file by simply dragging the font icon. Hold down the Option key and drag to copy the font.

The third row of icons represent bit-mapped screen fonts. You can tell this because of the single letter *A* on the icon of the font file. This single *A* differentiates the bit-mapped fonts from the TrueType fonts of the fourth row, which display the triple *A* in different sizes, suggesting the ability of a single font file to display a font in different sizes.

The following installation procedure applies to all of these font icons. You may install fonts at any time, but your running applications may not recognize the new font until you have quit the application and restarted it. You also should keep in mind that you cannot replace a font when applications other than the Finder are running. Follow these steps to install a font:

1. Drag the font to the System Folder. The System Software recognizes the font files and displays a message indicating that the files must be stored in the Fonts folder (see fig. 8.7).

Fonts need to be stored in the Fonts folder in order to be available to the Macintosh. Put these fonts into the Fonts folder?

Cancel   OK

2. Click the OK button in the dialog box.

The Fonts folder exists only in System 7.1. In System 7.0, the fonts are copied to the Extensions folder. In System 6, the printer fonts are simply copied into the System Folder itself and no dialog appears at all.

System 6 users should note that they must use Font/DA Mover to install screen fonts in the System file rather than drag them to the System Folder. See Appendix A, "Using System 6."

To remove a font, System 7.1 users must follow these steps:

1. Quit all application programs.

2. Open the System Folder.

3. Open the Fonts folder.

4. Drag the font icon out of the Fonts folder and out of the System Folder.

5. Drag the font icon to another part of your disk or to the Trash.

Y ou cannot remove fonts from the Fonts folder or replace
them if any application other than the Finder is running. If
you attempt to do so, you receive an error message (see fig. 8.8). If
you see this message, click the OK button and start the procedure
for removing fonts again.

Fig. 8.8
Changes cannot be
made at this time.

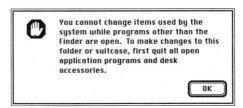

You cannot change items used by the
system while programs other than the
Finder are open. To make changes to this
folder or suitcase, first quit all open
application programs and desk
accessories.

OK

System 7.0 users must follow these steps to remove a font:

1. Quit all application programs.

2. Double-click the System Folder to open it.

3. Double-click the System suitcase file to open it. The screen and
TrueType fonts appear in the System window.

T he printer fonts are located in the Extensions folder rather
than the Fonts folder. To remove this type of fonts, double-
click the Extension folder to open it.

4. Drag the font icon out of the System Folder and drop it into
another part of your disk or into the Trash.

Working with Fonts

Several applications and utilities that deal with fonts are worth noting.
These products help you create new fonts, substitute fonts, and work
with fonts in other ways. This section discusses several you will want
to consider if you need more font capability than is built into the
Macintosh.

Creating Fonts

In the area of creating new, professional fonts, the dominant application is Fontographer by Altsys. Fontographer enables you to edit PostScript and TrueType fonts as well as draw new fonts. Guidelines help you to see the ascent, descent, baseline, origin, and width of new characters. The application offers an autotrace feature that automatically traces images from the Scrapbook or high-resolution scans. Several special effects such as scaling, skewing, and rotating also are included.

Bit-mapped screen fonts can be generated automatically from your created font. Then the font can be adjusted as needed and "hinted" (a process that improves screen appearance).

Fontographer can generate fonts that can be installed on the Macintosh, IBM PC, and the NeXT computer. You can preview a created or edited font, adjust character spacing (kerning), and print a key map showing how the characters correspond to the keyboard keys.

This is only a sample of the application's extensive features. Fontographer is powerful and sophisticated, requiring more knowledge of fonts than is possible to supply in this book. You will need to be very familiar with fonts or to read books about fonts. Producing professional-looking fonts requires some studying.

Average Macintosh users will not need the application, but the desktop publishing professional and businesses will want to give Fontographer a serious look.

Downloading Fonts

One thing that can save time if you have one or several repeatedly used fonts that are not stored in the memory of your printer is to download the font to the printer. This downloading stores the information needed to generate the font in the printer's temporary memory and saves you time by skipping the automatic download the Macintosh performs every time it needs a printer font is present but not in the printer's memory.

This is one time you do not have to purchase a utility. The LaserWriter Font Utility is included in the System 7.0 and 7.1 System Software disk sets on the Tidbits disk. The utility downloads a printer font to your LaserWriter and stores it in the printer's temporary memory.

NOTE

Downloaded fonts are stored in the printer's RAM, which means that the fonts disappear when the printer is turned off. They must be downloaded for each session. This is not true if you have a LaserWriter capable of storing fonts on an external hard drive and have the hard drive attached to the printer.

Remember that you are taking up printer memory when you download fonts. This can cause your printer to slow down when printing or even to be unable to handle large documents. You will want to download only the one or two most-used fonts. Otherwise, you may lose time, not save it.

The utility also enables you to display a listing of the fonts in the printer's memory (both permanent and temporary) and to print font samples.

The LaserWriter Font Utility is misnamed. The utility also has options that enable you to format a hard drive attached to the LaserWriter, download a PostScript file to be printed, set the LaserWriter's startup page options, and remove TrueType from the printer's temporary memory. The utility might more appropriately be called the LaserWriter Printer Utility.

Adobe also has a font downloader and includes the utility with many of the type libraries offered by the company.

Previewing Fonts

System 7 users can easily preview bit-mapped screen fonts and TrueType fonts. Simply double-click the Font file icon and a window opens to display the font (see fig. 8.9). Click the close box of the window when you have finished your preview.

Using Font Utilities

The Macintosh is known for its font capabilities—not only for the built-in capabilities, but also for those available from software companies in the form of utilities. There are a number of utilities that enable you to work with fonts and create spectacular documents.

Fig. 8.9

Viewing the Courier
TrueType font.

Type Enhancement Utilities

Several packages are available that enable you to enhance and add
special effects to type to create logos, headlines, advertising, and other
such materials that need eye-catching text.

One excellent example is TypeStyler by Broderbund. This utility enables
you to create special effects with fonts. With TypeStyler, you can bend,
squeeze, shade, size, and change the appearance of type, as well as add
shading, drop shadows, and other effects. Figure 8.10 shows the dialog
in TypeStyler that enables you to choose the shape and style of a line of
text. Figure 8.11 shows the results of the settings in figure 8.10.

Fig. 8.10

Setting a line of text to arch
and use gradients.

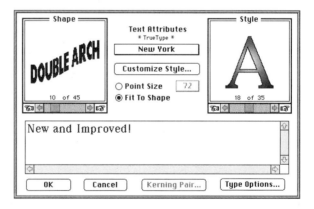

Fig. 8.11
The arched and shaded
line of text.

TypeStyler can create a variety of three-dimensional effects and can use 64 shades of gray and 256 colors. It has 128 patterns available, and each can be edited as needed. You need to have a monitor capable of displaying at least 256 colors or shades of gray (8-bit depth) to take advantage of the utility.

Those users who create newsletters, booklets, pamphlets, advertisements, and so on will want to give this package a close look. Broderbund is known for high-quality software, and I don't hesitate to recommend their products. TypeStyler includes the Adobe Type Manager (ATM) and 13 Adobe typefaces (ATM is covered later in this chapter).

In a similar vein, Adobe TypeAlign is available from Adobe. TypeAlign can create skews, curves, perspective, and other effects with text. The utility is meant to be used with Adobe Type Manager, covered in the Font Manager section of this chapter. The available effects are not as extensive as TypeStyler, but the utility is worth a look for those on a budget.

The text enhancement utility addDepth is available from Ray Dream, Inc. This package adds depth and perspective to type and illustrations. You can create illustrations in the utility or import from packages such as Adobe Illustrator.

Typestry by Pixar can move, resize, and rotate text, but its distinguishing features include the ability to add marble, gold, glass, and other effects. Typestry might be comparable to calligraphy, the art of illuminating letters and words, although it uses an electronic form.

Font Conversion Utilities

With all the different font types floating around the Macintosh universe these days (including two types of PostScript fonts and the TrueType font standard), the serious font user will probably want to consider a conversion utility.

Altsys is one of the premier font utility companies (see "Creating Fonts" earlier in this chapter) and offers a font conversion utility named Metamorphosis Professional. The utility converts Type 1 PostScript fonts to Type 3 or TrueType for use on Macintoshes or IBM PCs. You also can convert to editable EPS (Encapsulated PostScript) or PICT (the standard Macintosh graphic file format) files that can be imported into most all graphics applications (see Chapter 16, "Using Graphics Software").

Incubator Pro 2.0 by Type Solutions enables you to convert between Type 1 PostScript fonts and TrueType, as well as to change the descender, tracking, x-height, and other attributes of the font. This package is appealing for users who have to deal with TrueType after they have built a PostScript font collection.

Font Managers

When it comes to installing or removing fonts, two packages stand out, although they are not solely for use with fonts. Both MasterJuggler by ALSoft and Suitcase by Fifth Generation enable you to install and remove fonts with greater ease than any of the System Software versions offer. With the utilities, you can turn fonts on and off easily and use fonts that are stored in locations other than the System Folder.

Because these two utilities are full-resource management systems— enabling you to manage sounds, desk accessories, function keys, and other items—they are covered in Chapter 19, "Using Utility Software." The utilities are mentioned here because of their excellent font-handling capabilities.

Adobe Systems Font Utilities

Adobe Systems offers several software solutions that no serious user of fonts should be without. The first among these is the Adobe Type Manager (ATM). ATM is a software item that should have been integrated right into the Macintosh System Software a long time ago. ATM eliminates the constant problems (caused by the differences between the type on-screen and the type on your paper) that you encounter when you use PostScript fonts. Figures 8.12 and 8.13 illustrate the difference.

Fig. 8.12
Without ATM, fonts appear
jagged.

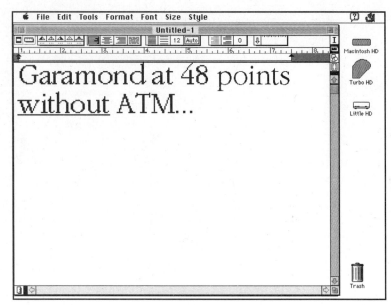

Fig. 8.13
Using ATM produces
smooth characters.

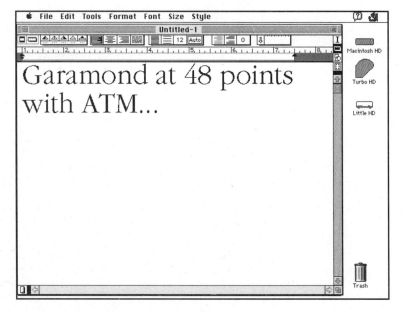

The obvious winner in this case is ATM. ATM not only matches your screen display to the printer more precisely, but also enables you to use PostScript fonts on non-PostScript printers and to improve print quality dramatically. Also supported are Bitstream fonts, a popular alternative to PostScript fonts.

Adobe Type Reunion is another must-have for serious font users. Type Reunion organizes your Font menu by font families and creates a more orderly menu. Compare figures 8.14 and 8.15.

Fig. 8.14
Without Type Reunion.

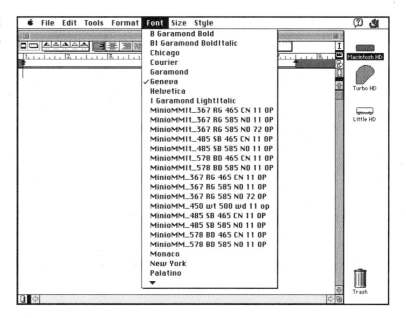

As the figures show, Type Reunion gathers the related fonts installed in your System file and gives you access to them by use of hierarchical menus.

Going even further, Adobe has introduced the SuperATM package, which combines ATM, Type Reunion, a Type On Call CD-ROM, and the new SuperATM ability to create and use substitute fonts.

Substitute fonts can aid you in solving the problem often encountered when Macintosh users share documents. Suppose that a colleague gives you a document to edit that was created with the Garamond font, which you do not have. Normally, the Macintosh substitutes an available font that probably does not match the original font's spacing. The result is that documents edited on one Macintosh do not line up properly on another Macintosh. The usual solution is to install exactly the same fonts on the Macintoshes on which the document will be used. This is not always possible, however. You might find that a document contains a font that you do not have, for example, on the same day that you need to complete the work, and—overnight delivery service notwithstanding—you may not have time to acquire the font.

Fig. 8.15
With Type Reunion.

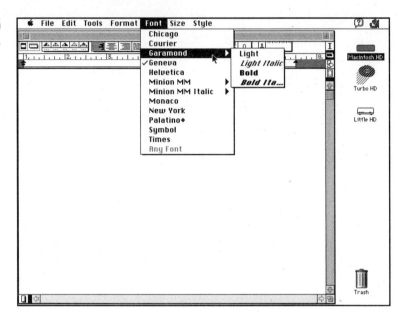

The SuperATM package creates substitute fonts that have the same basic measurements as the orginals. The substitute font will not have the same display or print quality as the original, but will enable you to edit or create a document that will have the same spacing when the document is opened or printed with the original font.

SuperATM also enables you to manually create a substitute font that can be permanently installed in your System Folder. Figure 8.16 shows a sample of the Charlemagne substitute font about to be created. Creating a permanent substitute font and then installing the font in the System enables you to create documents that will display and print properly on Macintoshes that have the actual font, even though you do not have the font available.

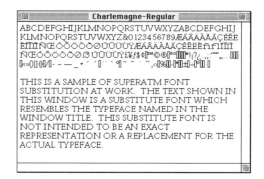

SuperATM also includes the Type On Call CD-ROM that contains bit-mapped screen fonts and printer fonts of over 1,300 fonts (font packages 1–265) from the Adobe Type Library. This enables CD-ROM player owners to sample any of the Adobe fonts available. (See Chapter 3, "Managing Disks," and Chapter 26, "Expanding the Macintosh," for more on these players.) Several printer fonts are included in the price of the disk, but the rest must be purchased. They are encoded and can only be unlocked by a key you purchase from Adobe (or through a mail-order source). The bit-mapped screen fonts are not locked and can be installed in your System at will.

In other words, you can view or even use in documents any of the over 1,300 fonts on-screen. To have access to the excellent display of fonts at any size that ATM offers and the high quality of printing afforded by PostScript fonts, however, you must purchase the printer fonts. The biggest advantages of the Type On Call CD-ROM is that you can see the font before you purchase it, and you can obtain the printer font immediately by purchasing and receiving the key to unlock the font over the phone. (Adobe and many mail-order companies such as MacWarehouse take Type On Call orders over the phone and—if you have a credit card—can issue the key immediately.)

As a bonus, the SuperATM package includes the Bellevue, Cottonwood, Madrone, and Zapf Dingbats PostScript fonts for free.

Adobe has put the multiple master technology to use to provide users with even greater font flexibility. Multiple master fonts can be customized to a far greater extent than previously. Simply put, a multiple master font is installed by placing a set of base fonts in the System and installing font metrics files on the hard disk. The *metrics files* describe the font and its measurements, hence the term *metrics*. The user then can alter the font along designer-specified axes and alter the attributes of the font. An example of this kind of font can be found in the Adobe Minion font, as shown in figure 8.17.

Fig. 8.17

Changing the attributes of the Minion font.

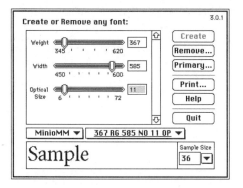

This figure shows the dialog of the program Font Creator, which enables you to alter multiple master fonts. With the Minion font, you have control over three attributes: the weight, the width of the characters, and the optical size.

You alter the font by dragging the sliders or entering the numbers for the attributes in the fields to the right of the sliders. You can see both a display of the font in the bottom of the dialog and the affect of your changes. When you are satisfied with the font, you click the Create button to generate that version of the font. The font then becomes available to the applications that start up after creation of the font. You can choose the available multiple master fonts from the left pop-up menu (displaying MinioMM in the figure) and the standard, supplied sizes from the pop-up to the right. This enables you to find the font you wish to edit and then match it with a master font. You also can set the two font menus to the font and style you wish to remove and then click the Remove button to remove the font from the System. (If you create or remove a font while an application is running, the font menu may not reflect the change unless you quit and then restart the application.)

Multiple master fonts show promise of greater font flexibility, enabling you to become almost your own font designer by customizing fonts to suit your purposes. Multiple master font technology has become quite a buzzword in the font world, but the interest seems justified.

Some Tips for Font Use

One very important point to remember about fonts is the font ID numbers. When a new font is developed, it must be assigned an ID number so that the new font can be accessed and used. These numbers range from 0 to 32,767. A problem occurs when these numbers get used up or when two manufacturers develop different fonts and assign the same number. (This is not likely, but it can happen).

A font conflict has occurred when you see fonts in your documents changing appearance for no apparant reason. The Macintosh has requested the font in your document but received the wrong font because the numbers conflicted.

The best solution to the problem of font conflict is to use MasterJuggler or Suitcase. You then can switch between font sets, using the fonts of one manufacturer at a time. Alternatively, these utilities (covered in Chapter 19, "Using Utility Software") can resolve font conflicts by renumbering fonts.

With all the fonts available, how do you make a decision about which one to use and in what combination with other fonts? The following general guidelines may help you make those decisions:

- Use a serif font for text and a sans serif font for headlines. This tried-and-true combination almost always works well.

- Match the font with the text to get your message across. Each font has a set of characteristics and a feel all its own. Some are bigger than life and yell "Read me!"; others are more refined and quiet.

- Avoid working with more than two families of fonts. If you use Helvetica and Times, don't add a third. Too many fonts (or styles of fonts) in one document gives a cluttered feel or can draw attention to the characters in a message rather than to the message itself.

- Do experiment. The beauty of the Macintosh is that you can change the font of an entire selection with just a few mouse clicks. Don't leave the changes on-screen. Print them and compare them. Better yet, print them and leave them while you get a cup of coffee. After a break, you will be better able to judge whether the fonts you selected do the required job.

Table 8.2 offers some suggestions about which fonts can be used together. Keep in mind that mixing fonts is a project-by-project decision and must be evaluated in light of the message you are trying to convey. You cannot go wrong if you stick to one font.

Table 8.2
Mixing Fonts

	Bodoni	Bookman	Courier	Garamond	Helvetica	New York	Optima	Palatino
Bodoni	1							
Bookman	1	1						
Courier	2	2	1					
Garamond	3	3	2	1				
Helvetica	1	1	2	1	1			
New York	2	2	2	2	1	1		
Optima	1	2	2	1	2	1	1	
Palatino	3	3	2	1	1	1	1	1
Schoolbook	2	3	2	3	1	1	1	3
Times	3	2	2	2	1	1	1	2

1 = go well together   2 = may be acceptable   3 = don't use

The Big Mac Recommendation

If you have only modest font needs, you will probably want to consider TrueType. System 6 users can obtain the System extension that enables them to use TrueType or, better yet, upgrade to System 7 (see Appendix A, "Using System 6," for more on System upgrade issues).

System 7 users already have TrueType. These fonts print well on any printer and can greatly enhance your printed documents.

Users with more extensive font needs will want to consider Adobe's PostScript fonts. The SuperATM package is a must for the professional desktop publisher, and multiple master fonts are worth serious consideration because of their flexibility in customizing.

Part II

Macintosh Software

Includes:

9   Buying Software
10 Working with Word Processors
11 Using Spreadsheets
12 Using Databases
13 Using Integrated Software
14 Using Finance and Business Applications
15 Desktop Publishing
16 Using Graphics Software
17 Using Communication Software
18 Using Multimedia
19 Using Utility Software
20 Learning and Having Fun

CHAPTER NINE

Buying Software

T here are some important considerations involved in selecting software packages for your Macintosh. The first of these is to understand the categories generally used to group software packages. Understanding the categories enables you to find the kind of packages you need in catalogs and from dealerships, as well as to follow magazine reviews of software.

Knowing about the sources of software also is important, especially if you are new to the Macintosh world; there are several sources that you may not know about. Evaluating software is crucial. You need to understand how to determine whether the software works on your Macintosh, whether you have enough memory to run the software, and other considerations that can help you avoid inappropriate purchases and the hassle of returns.

Types of Software

The categories in Part II of this book cover the main types of software available to you. This category list is not exhaustive, due to the enormous variety of software on the market today; however, it covers the main types of packages most users need.

Word Processors

Word processors are programs that help you work with text and, in more sophisticated packages, graphics. Chapter 10, "Using Word Processors," is primarily concerned with applications that aid in creating, editing, and formatting text. Word processing applications also enable you to create reports, form letters, memos, and even entire books. Chapter 10 also covers optional applications such as thesauruses, spelling checkers, and sophisticated dictionaries.

Spreadsheets

Chapter 11, "Using Spreadsheets," covers packages that enable you to work with numbers in a tabular form. Spreadsheets primarily are used in financial planning; however, people use them in other areas in which they want to tabulate and manipulate numbers. Chapter 11 explores the graphing feature of many spreadsheets, as well as the *macro* capability—the recording of steps for later automatic execution. Optional "add-ins" are also covered.

Databases

Databases are covered in Chapter 12, "Using Databases." These programs store and manage lists of information such as mailing lists, client records, inventories (for businesses and households), and other such collections of data. They are good choices when you have large amounts of information to store, sort, and report. The chapter explores the less expensive, easy-to-use applications suitable for home and small business use, as well as the higher-end databases that enable you to write your own applications in their programming languages.

Integrated Packages

For those who need a variety of application types but don't need all the features of a dedicated software package or who have limited disk or memory space (PowerBook users and owners of smaller Macintoshes such as the Classic or Performa 200), Chapter 13, "Using Integrated Packages," covers the "Swiss army knives" of the Macintosh world. These packages generally include a word processor, spreadsheet, communications program, and so on—all combined in one package that works consistently. This consistency helps you quickly learn and use the applications.

Financial and Business Programs

Personal finance management, tax planning and preparation, and business accounting packages fall into the category covered by Chapter 14, "Using Finance and Business Applications." In this chapter, you see applications that help you manage money and plan expenditures.

Desktop Publishing

Applications in Chapter 15, "Using Desktop Publishing," help you with page layout and document design for such items as newsletters and advertisements. Desktop publishing applications usually offer methods of integrating text and graphics from a variety of sources into a single document.

Graphics

Drawing tools and painting applications are covered in Chapter 16, "Using Graphics Software." The chapter discusses available collections of ready-made artwork you can purchase, as well as utilities that help you create graphics documents. You also see the *computer-aided design* (CAD) software available to Macintosh users that aids in the design of floor plans, equipment, and other items that require drawn plans and specifications.

Communications

Communications applications connect your Macintosh to other computers by modem to enable you to access on-line computer services. Chapter 17, "Using Communications Software," discusses the software you use to connect your Macintosh to on-line services, as well as the available services. The chapter also discusses modems, with the goal of giving you access to on-line systems.

Multimedia

Multimedia is the new buzzword of the personal computer industry. This category of software, which is discussed in Chapter 18, "Using Multimedia," enables you to create animation, slide shows, and overhead presentations. You can also integrate music, sounds, pictures, videos, and text into museum-quality instructional materials.

Utilities

Chapter 19, "Using Utility Software," is a catch-all chapter that explores various Macintosh-enhancing software. This category includes hard disk tools, data recovery programs, Apple menu enhancers, Finder enhancers, security systems, data compression, macro utilities, virus protection, and other programs. You learn about many utilities that enable you to work faster, smarter, and safer.

Learning and Fun

This category includes computer games and other leisure-time items, as well as many programs that aid learning. Chapter 20, "Learning and Having Fun," discusses educational software for children and adults, as well as sounds, music, and other available "just for fun" materials.

Sources of Software

You can obtain software from several different sources. Appendix E has a product listing, and Appendix F has a listing of vendors; both can be useful in your search for software.

Software sources generally are divided into the following three categories:

- *Commercial sources.* Your dealer, software stores, and mail-order houses all offer the latest from commercial manufacturers.

- *On-line services.* These electronic services offer many free or inexpensive software choices that you can download by using a modem. Some, such as CompuServe, offer electronic "shopping malls," where you can order commercial software. See Chapter 17, "Using Communications Software," for more about on-line services and how to access them.

- *User groups.* These informal gatherings of Macintosh users often have free or inexpensive collections of software.

Software that is offered by individuals or small groups rather than corporations falls into two categories: *freeware* and *shareware.* Freeware programs are those packages an individual has written and distributed but chosen not to charge for. Remember, however, that freeware *is* copyrighted and cannot be sold or altered without the author's permission.

Unlike freeware, shareware has a price—but it's usually small. You pay for shareware after a trial period in which you decide whether you want to keep the package. Shareware is a good source for inexpensive but useful software. You can do well investigating this source by joining a Macintosh user group or accessing one or more on-line services. However, remember that the software—although inexpensive—is not free, and you are obligated to send a payment if you continue to use the software. If you try out shareware and find the program to be useful, remember to send your payment. The authors of these programs generally receive no compensation other than the voluntary payments.

You can try out some shareware programs by purchasing Que's *Big Mac Secrets*, which includes over 4 megabytes of useful shareware programs, as well as instructions for using the programs. You also receive valuable information about the Macintosh.

Remember that all software—even that offered by major corporations—is the product of someone's effort. Copying software without permission is the same as stealing and undercuts the livelihood of the authors. (Yes, the author of this book is a former programmer and gets a bit touchy about the subject of software piracy.) In any case, taking the work of others not only hurts them and their ability to make a living, it is a federal crime.

Evaluating Software

You should choose carefully when you purchase software, especially from a mail-order source. Although mail-order companies and many dealers generally have liberal return policies, the hassle of buying and installing a software package, only to have to remove and return the program, is something you want to avoid. Before buying software, carefully consider the package's requirements in memory, Macintosh type, System Software version, and other basics.

Memory Considerations

When you purchase software, consider the amount of memory you have. All manufacturers state the amounts of memory needed to run their software. This information is on the box of the software package or listed in mail-order catalogs.

When you think about a manufacturer's memory requirement statement, don't forget that your System Software also requires memory space. An application program that requires 2 megabytes of memory does not have enough room on a 2-megabyte Macintosh because your System Software requires part of the memory space.

You can find the amount of memory that your System Software normally requires by choosing the About this Macintosh command from the Apple menu. (If you are using System 6, choose About the Finder.) This command also tells you the amount of memory you have left for running application software.

Macintosh Type Considerations

Software is generally rated as running on a particular machine or higher, for example: *runs on the Macintosh Plus or higher.* This means that the software is designed to run on the Macintosh Plus or any machine introduced after the Plus (which was introduced about 1986).

At other times, you might see specifications by the microprocessor chip—the central part of the Macintosh (or any personal computer, for that matter). These specifications are written as: *requires 68030 or higher.* The Macintosh uses chips from the Motorola 680x0 series. This series is 68000, 68020, 68030, and the 68040. Each chip is more advanced than the last and has special features that the previous one does not. Hence, if your Macintosh uses an older chip than the one specified, you cannot use the software. You can check Appendix C to determine which microprocessor chip your Macintosh contains.

Sometimes you see specifications such as *requires an FPU.* An *FPU* (or *floating-point unit*) is a special chip that processes numeric calculations faster than the *CPU* (*central processing unit*—the 680x0 chip). Some software requires the FPU because of intense mathematical calculations. Such software does not run on 68000 machines, and runs only on 68020 and 68030 machines that have the FPU chip. The FPU chip is an option on many 68030 machines, such as the IIsi. On some machines, the chip is already included, as in the IIci. 68040 machines such as the Quadra series have the FPU built in.

Some software may require a *PMMU* (*paged memory management unit*). This is built into machines that use the 68030 and 68040 chip. It is not available to 68000 and 68020 machines. If you use a Mac II, which uses the 68020 chip, you can get a PMMU chip for the computer. Most 68000 and 68020 machines can also be upgraded to a 68030 or 68040 machine through hardware upgrades.

Software that requires an FPU or PMMU is rare and should not be a problem for the average user. You might want to double check, however, before purchasing expensive software. In fact, the more expensive packages usually have more stringent requirements.

System Software Version Considerations

Differences in System software versions are not usually a problem. Most applications were written under earlier versions of the System Software than the most commonly used version due to the lead time inherent in writing and distributing software.

The System Software version requirements are usually stated, as in *System 6.0.5 or higher*. You can check your System Software version by choosing the About this Macintosh command from your Apple menu. (If you are using System 6, choose About the Finder.)

The exception to this rule is System 7, which was a *major* rewrite of the System Software. Consequently, some packages are written to take advantage of System 7's enhanced features and therefore will run *only* with System 7 (or higher)—not with earlier versions. Most current software, however, is written to operate with both System 7 and System 6.

All new Macintoshes are shipping with System 7. If you have a recent machine and have System 7, you should make sure that the application you are buying is at least *System 7 compatible*, which means it should work with System 7. Ideally, the application should be *System 7 savvy*, which means it takes full advantage of the power of the System Software.

Understanding Version Numbers and Compatibility

Application software version numbers can seem mysterious. The first release is the easiest to understand, because this version is Version 1. After that, however, the numbers can do some strange things.

In general, the way software version numbers work is that the first digit indicates the major rewrites. Version 1 indicates a first release. Version 2 is the second release—a major rewrite that usually includes enhanced features. The major version number can skip numbers at times. I've seen Version 1.5 followed by Version 4.0. You usually see such skips when a manufacturer decides to synchronize the version numbers of its Macintosh and IBM products. In any case, the higher the number, the more powerful the program, because it has been rewritten and features have been added.

Manufacturers have two different ways to tackle the digits following the decimal. One approach is to use the first digit *after* the decimal to indicate "bug fix" releases. In other words, problems found in the software are fixed, and a new release with the same features—hopefully without the problems—is shipped. Hence, Version 1.0 is followed by 1.1, with the latter being the fixed version of the former. (It's inevitable that not all the problems in software are discovered until after shipping begins, regardless of how good the testing is; it's the nature of software.)

Apple has taken a different approach, as have many manufacturers. The System Software consists of three digits, as in *Version 6.0.8*. In this case, the first digit indicates major rewrites, the second indicates a feature enhancement, and the third indicates fixes of problems found after shipment. Hence, Version 7.0 of the System Software was followed by Version 7.0.1, then 7.1.

Some manufacturers use letters and other numbers. You might see *Version 3.4v2*. Others use a numbering system that means something only to them. Generally, the first digit is consistent, but later numbers and letters can vary in use from manufacturer to manufacturer.

In any case, the trend is always upward. The version numbers increase as problems are found and fixed and as features are enhanced. You will want to watch this process carefully because it can affect you in some interesting ways.

One of the most important ways you can be affected by version differences is if you upgrade your System Software. Your application software was written on a machine running a particular System Software. The programmers had this System's capabilities in mind when they wrote the software. Hence, your application software might not be able to run under a newer System Software. You might need to upgrade—purchase a new version of the software.

Other situations can arise. Version 2.3 (for example) of a particular software package may not run with Version 4.1 of another software package. The two versions may conflict. Many times, the manufacturer is already aware of the problem and might have a newer version that does not conflict with other software packages.

You should be aware of your software versions. This is especially important because the version you purchase may not always be the most recent. This happens because the inventory of a store or mail-order company may have older versions in stock and is only recently receiving the newer one. Generally, manufacturers automatically upgrade your software in this situation or offer a free or low-cost upgrade. Sending your registration card is important because you can then be notified of newer versions of the software.

You can find the version number of your software in one of a couple of ways. When the software is running, you can choose the About command from the Apple menu. The software displays a dialog box that usually contains the software version. You can also use the Get Info command, which always displays the version number. (See Chapter 2, "Understanding the System," for more on finding information about application program icons.)

Finally, if you need to contact a manufacturer about a problem with your software, you need to know the version number of the package you are having trouble with, as well as the version number of your System Software. Technical support departments are aware of many problems and solutions based on these numbers alone. (When I worked in a technical support department, I had a chart of version numbers and problems; if a user had version numbers on-hand, we could often shorten the call to a few minutes.)

Understanding Warranties and Return Policies

In the early days, software was sold "as is." In other words, after you bought it, you were stuck. Recently, however, the industry is moving to the more acceptable position of money-back guarantees and liberal return and exchange policies.

You are probably already familiar enough with return policies in cases of non-computer-related items to easily understand how they apply to software. A 30-day, money-back policy means about the same thing in software as it does with a toaster. If the software does not satisfy you, you can return it for your money in the first 30 days.

This is no longer uncommon in the software industry and is a welcome change. You should determine the exact warranty and return policy for a given item of software. Some warranties enable you to return only defective items. Some enable you to return items that do not satisfy you. Each company determines its own policies.

Your best bet is to purchase software created by manufacturers with the most liberal return policies. This is not only safer (because you can return software that does not work out for you), but also rewarding (because the liberal policies encourage more manufacturers to follow suit).

Understanding Technical Support

One important consideration you should weigh is the support you receive after the purchase. All software companies (as well as many dealers and mail-order companies) offer technical support. These departments are devoted to solving the problems users have with software packages.

At one time or another, we all need technical support. Even the most experienced Macintosh users (the "power users," as they are called) run into problems they cannot handle without help.

Various companies offer differing levels of technical support. In addition to the question of whether a company offers quality support, there is the question about how long the support lasts, whether it costs money, and what you have to do to obtain support.

The most common form of technical support is the telephone call. You dial a number and talk to a company representative who can help you with technical problems. The only cost is the cost of the phone call (many of these calls are long distance). Because long distance is relatively inexpensive these days, you can get quite a bargain—you receive help much more cheaply than if you had turned to a free-lance consultant (who might charge $50 to $100 per hour or more).

Companies offering free support usually require you to send in your registration card. This enables the company to aid only legitimate purchasers of the product and, at least to some degree, ward off software pirates. (Usually pirates copy only disks, not manuals; some software thieves attempt to use technical support in place of a manual.)

Some companies offer registered users a limited amount of free support—to help them get started—then charge for further support. This is often necessary with large, powerful packages because companies must pay higher salaries to the more technically proficient in the software industry. Generally, the cost to you is still far less than if you hire an individual consultant.

A valid concern about purchasing expensive software is the quality of support you will receive. You should investigate this matter before making a major purchase. You can do so by reading Macintosh magazine reviews, talking to other users, or talking to your dealer.

On smaller purchases, you most likely get free technical support. However, expect the phone lines to be jammed; many users call and it can be difficult to get through to the support department. A good alternative is to determine whether the company uses any of the on-line systems such as CompuServe and enables you to request help by posting an electronic message to the support department. This kind of support is among the best, in that it is very cost effective for both you and the software company.

Some companies offer their own bulletin board systems that enable you to call in by modem and post electronic messages to the support department. Again, this is very cost effective for you because transmitting a letter-length message is much faster than speaking over the phone.

On more expensive software items, you should not be surprised to find a charge for extended support. How cost effective this is depends on your needs. If the software package is critical to you, the cost is worth the quick response time and quality assistance of paid support. At the same time, if you pay for support, you have the right to demand that it be of the highest quality with quick response and knowledgeable technical personnel.

The Big Mac Recommendation

Become a smart software shopper by following a few simple rules:

- Acquire low-cost or free software by joining a user group or using on-line information systems.

- Be aware of your Macintosh's capabilities so that you can match the memory, hardware, and System requirements of your computer to the software you are considering.

- Be aware of version numbers of software as an indicator of bug fixes and feature enhancements as well as compatibility with System Software and other software packages.

- Watch for and reward liberal return policies.

- Send in your registration card as soon as you can so that software companies can notify you of new versions.

- Watch magazine reviews of software for information about whether a package is reliable and has the features you require.

- Determine the support policy of the manufacturer. Determine how much support you receive, how much it costs, and how you obtain support after the purchase.

CHAPTER TEN

Working with Word Processors

The word processor began as an electronic version of the typewriter. The only unique feature was its revolutionary capability to edit text *before* it hit the paper. Before word processors gained general acceptance, however, they were held back by limits imposed by early personal computers. The only inexpensive storage medium was cassette tape, which was maddeningly slow; printers were slow and noisy. The dot-matrix printers of the time produced grainy-looking letters, and word processors (such as the early WordStar) had to accommodate limited keyboards with no function keys, no Alt or Command key, and, certainly, no mouse.

But the potential for word processors was obvious to many people. Editing text on-screen and then printing only finished copy was a feature that held a promise of increasing productivity enormously.

Today, that promise has been fulfilled beyond the wildest dreams of many of us who worked with those maddening keyboards and convoluted control sequences. Word processors save uncounted hours of retyping; they can decrease the production time of a report or a manuscript, and you can exert great control over the appearance of your completed documents.

Word processors come in all shapes and sizes, ranging from specialized word processors designed to produce mathematical formulas to the full-fledged workhorses that have become the mainstay of many businesses. You even find powerhouses that approach the level of desktop publishing.

Currently, the most popular word processors include Nisus, Microsoft Word, WriteNow, MacWrite (both II and Pro versions), and WordPerfect for the Mac. This chapter discusses these word processors (as well as some others), and recommends which one might be best suited to your needs.

With prices of word processors ranging from $50 to $500, almost everyone can find a program that fits his or her budget. Price, however, is not the best guide to the usefulness of or ease of learning a word processor. MacWrite Pro, which retails for around half of Microsoft Word's price, compares favorably with the feature-laden (and sometimes obstinate and difficult) Microsoft Word. Both programs do an excellent job of managing text and files, but Word offers extras such as a grammar checker, the capacity to create tables of contents and indexes, and other features, including a toolbar you can edit for frequently used commands. Word and other higher-end word processors such as WordPerfect are closer to desktop publishing packages than word processors. If you produce professional documents, you probably need one of the larger packages. Home users and small businesses will probably prefer one of the less expensive programs, such as MacWrite Pro, for easy use.

In this chapter, you learn about the capabilities of these programs and about the way most basic features of all word processors work. You learn about entering, editing, and deleting text; formatting pages; printing; using special features such as a spelling checker and a thesaurus; merging to generate form letters; and constructing tables. You also see specialized add-on programs that can aid you in word processing; for example, you can add on quote programs, grammar checkers, large thesauri, and dictionaries.

Creating Documents

Although a word processor's most general function is to manipulate text, this task can be broken into five basic steps: entering text, editing text, saving text, accessing stored text, and printing text. From the most basic memo-writing tool to the most advanced and complex program, all word processors can perform these five tasks.

When you use a word processor, you first enter the information you want to work with. As you are probably aware, the most frequently used input device is the keyboard; however, other input devices exist, too. You can use a drawing tablet that has been "taught" to recognize your handwriting, for example, or you can use voice-recognition software to enter your text by "talking" to your computer. You also can scan text to disk from paper.

After you enter the text, you then edit as necessary. Editing involves a variety of different operations, ranging from the simple insertion of new text to checking the spelling or even correcting the grammar of your document. Many existing utilities automate these operations.

After you edit, you probably want to save your work as a file. Saving your work enables you to use the same information again (perhaps in a form letter) or to continue editing the file. Many people save at regular intervals as they edit, to ensure the safety of the document as they work. The information that appears on-screen exists only in temporary memory (RAM); when you turn off your computer, the memory that holds your document loses its contents. To keep a copy of your document, therefore, you have to save your work to disk.

If during your next word processing session you want to work with the same text you saved, you must retrieve, or open, the saved file.

The last step in the process is printing. You print a document so that you have a permanent copy to share with others or to keep for your files.

For Example...

The best way to illustrate what a word processor can do is to explain the various steps in a typical work session. The following example uses Nisus to write an article.

The first step is to create a file. Choose the New command from the File menu to produce the opening window you see in figure 10.1. After you open a file, you are free to use your Mac as a typewriter to enter text. The title bar indicates that the file has not been named. Nisus provides a name consisting of "Untitled" and a number (which depends on the number of new documents you have created in the current session) for your first new document.

Fig. 10.1
Creating a file in Nisus.

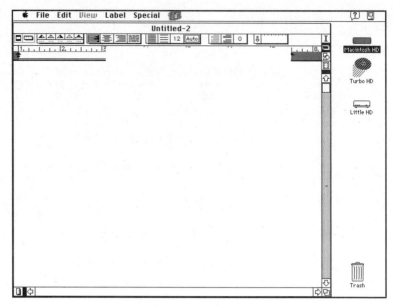

Next, save what you entered—regardless of how the text reads or how many typing mistakes you made. To save (and name) a new file, choose the Save command from the File menu or press ⌘-S. When you choose the Save command, a Save dialog appears and prompts you for a name for the file (which can be up to 31 characters) that you created (see fig. 10.2).

Fig. 10.2
Naming a new file in Nisus.

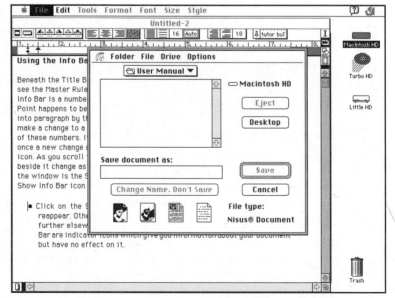

elements appear in most other word processors.) At the top of the Save dialog, you can see that the active folder is User Manual. From this pop-up menu, you can choose any folder that contains the current folder. You can also click the Desktop button to display your disk drives and then select one by double-clicking its name in the list box.

In the Save document as box, enter the name you want to assign to the current document. After you enter a name (*Chapter 1*, for example) and click the Save button (or press the Return key), the file you are working on is saved under that name.

You use the following four buttons:

- Save saves the file under the name you assign.

- Cancel cancels the save operation and returns you to your document.

- Eject ejects the disk whose files are listed in the list box.

- Desktop displays the disk drives attached to your Macintosh so that you can choose one to store the document on. (System 6 users see a Drive button, which switches from one disk to the next with each click.)

You can see the format buttons at the bottom of the dialog. From left to right, the format buttons enable you to save the document as a Nisus document, a Nisus stationery document, a Microsoft Word document, or a text-only document.

Nisus also uses the XTND technology to enable you to save in many common formats. This capability is now common among Macintosh word processors. All the high-level word processors enable you to open and save documents created by other word processors (even those documents created by IBM PC programs) and other application programs. Even many of the lower-end word processors now include the capability to work with the more common formats of other applications. However, if you need to translate to and from other formats frequently, a higher-end word processor is a better choice. (Also, consider the suggestions of Chapter 29, "Using Connectivity Software," which explores transferring, translating, and sharing information between different computers.)

Now that the file is saved, you can edit it at your leisure.

Macintosh word processors offer many features—from the most basic insertion of a space to the use of a spelling checker and thesaurus to help you with your writing.

Suppose that you want to add a sentence at the end of a paragraph. You simply do the following:

1. Move the mouse pointer to where you want the new text to appear.

2. Click the mouse button.

   This places the insertion point where the mouse pointer is located.

3. Type the text.

The location of the insertion point shows where new text (whether typed or inserted by the Paste command or other insertion command) appears. When you open a new word processing document, the insertion point appears in the upper left corner.

To change the location of the insertion point, move the I-beam (over text that can be edited, the mouse pointer becomes the I-beam) to the desired location and click once. The insertion point moves to that location, and any text you enter appears there.

If you don't like a sentence, word, or even a paragraph, you can delete it easily by selecting the text and then pressing the Backspace key. You select text by dragging through all the text you want to select. To drag through text, place the I-beam at the beginning of the text you want to select. Click the mouse button and hold it down. Then drag over the text you want to select, highlighting the text.

If you want, you can also choose the Cut or Copy command from the Edit menu, place the insertion point in the new location, and choose the Paste command from the Edit menu. The text appears in the new location. Some word processors, such as Nisus and Microsoft Word, enable you to take a shortcut in this procedure by dragging the text to a new location instead of using the Edit commands.

Different word processors have different selection capabilities. All enable you to select just one word by double-clicking that word. Others go beyond that level. WordPerfect, for example, enables you to select sentences or paragraphs by using menu or keyboard combinations. The Nisus word processor enables you to select a line, sentence, or paragraph—depending on the number of times you click. To select an entire document in Word, move the cursor to the left until it turns into an arrow that points to the upper right, and then press the command key and click once.

A document looks better when it is dressed up a bit. To boldface the document's title, select the title and choose the Bold command from the Style menu (see fig. 10.3), or use the keyboard equivalent to invoke the command. You should note that the keyboard equivalents shown in the figure are mine—Nisus, Word, WordPerfect, and other high-end word processors offer a great number of customization options, such as the capability to change your keyboard equivalents for menu commands.

Fig. 10.3
The Bold option in the Style menu.

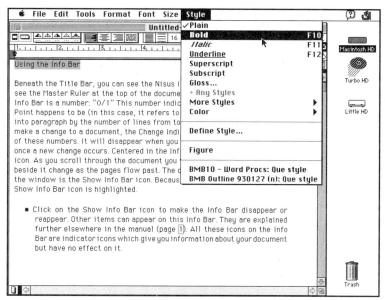

Next, select the entire document and choose a font from the Font menu. Remember that to make any changes permanent and part of a file, you must save the file after the changes are made. Now you're ready to print.

To print the document, choose the Print command from the File menu, and then click the Print (or OK) button in the Print dialog that appears. You start the printing process the identical way in all Macintosh applications. Be sure that you selected the appropriate printer driver by using the Chooser.

Opening Documents

Word processors would not be much good if you could create a file but not use that file later. After you save a file, you easily can access it the next time you need to. Choose the Open command from the File menu (or use the ⌘-O key combination), and choose the file by name (see fig. 10.4). Generally, files that cannot be opened by your word processor appear with their names dimmed.

Fig. 10.4
Choosing your file
by name.

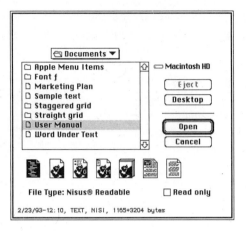

To speed up file selection, enter the first few characters in the file name as soon as you select the Open command. The word processor highlights the name of the file that matches those characters.

Another command on the File menu, New (⌘-N), sometimes confuses users new to word processing. Choose New when you want to begin an entirely new document—not when you want to recall a previously saved document. A new document initially is called *Untitled*, followed by a number that indicates whether it is the first, second, third, or so on new document created this session. In Nisus, for example, the first new document appears as *Untitled-1*. You can open as many untitled new documents as your computer's memory supports.

Saving Documents

One basic step in word processing (and in most other Macintosh applications) is saving a document as a file. Saving is an essential step, and you should be aware of the many components of the saving process.

First, on the File menu, you can choose the Save As command. The Save As command enables you to save the active document under a different name. Suppose that you create a letter and want to modify it slightly. You can save the original letter as *Letter/Main*. You can make the necessary changes to the letter and save the newer version as *Letter/ Modified*. If you use the Save command to save a file that already has been named and saved, the word processor saves the file under its existing name. To save the same document under a different name, you must use the Save As command.

Some word processors offer handy features that go along with the save process. In figure 10.5, for example, you see how WordPerfect enables you to set an automatic backup feature so that the program saves your document every five minutes and makes a backup of the file under a different name. You can imagine how valuable this feature can be if you accidentally delete a file or if a drive crash destroys your original as you work.

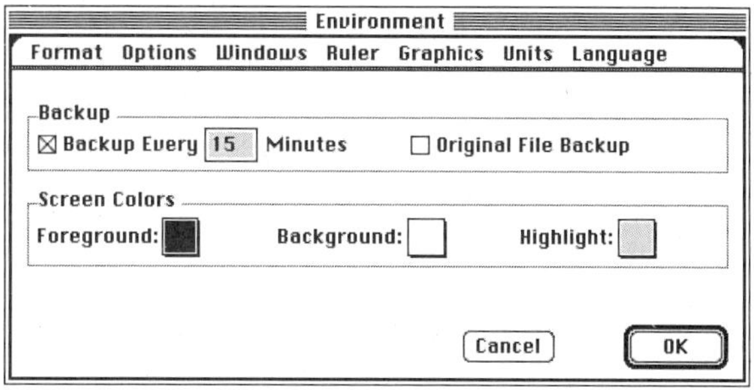

Fig. 10.5
WordPerfect enables you to set an automatic backup feature.

```
╔══════════════════ Environment ══════════════════╗
║ Format  Options  Windows  Ruler  Graphics  Units  Language ║
║                                                  ║
║  ┌─Backup ──────────────────────────────────────┐║
║  │ ⊠ Backup Every │15│ Minutes   □ Original File Backup │║
║  └──────────────────────────────────────────────┘║
║  ┌─Screen Colors ───────────────────────────────┐║
║  │ Foreground:▓   Background:□   Highlight:▒    │║
║  └──────────────────────────────────────────────┘║
║                                                  ║
║                          ( Cancel )   ▐ OK ▌     ║
╚══════════════════════════════════════════════════╝
```

Nisus is another program with a helpful save feature. With the Saving Files Preferences dialog shown in figure 10.6, you can create a backup file (with the same file name and BAK extension), save after a certain number of keystrokes, and save to two disks at once. To save to two disks at once, simply check the Secondary Disk Save box and specify where you want Nisus to save your second backup copy. For absent-minded folks, that feature is reason enough to choose this word processor.

Fig. 10.6
The Nisus Saving Files Preferences dialog.

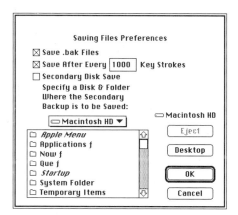

Microsoft Word also offers the capacity to set a timed backup of your document, but is unable to save according to number of keystrokes.

For a writer, the keystroke feature is superior because writing rarely moves by minute—10 minutes of work may be ten keystrokes or 5,000—but any automatic backup feature is helpful.

WriteNow has a Save/Compact command that saves your file in the smallest form possible.

Editing a Document

The capacity to edit and manipulate your text is probably the most important feature of a word processor. This section discusses the features that affect the way you edit your documents. In MacWrite, for example, you can insert the date into the text with an Edit menu command, and in WordPerfect you can manage files without returning to the Desktop.

Deleting Text

Unless you turn out perfect copy every time, you need to edit text. Most commonly, editing involves deleting mistakes or unneeded text.

To delete a large amount of text, select the unwanted text and press the Delete or Backspace key. Also, with all word processors, when you select text and then type new text, the newly typed text replaces the selected text. This latter feature enables you to replace a single word quickly by double-clicking a word and then typing a new one.

If you make an error and delete text that you really meant to save, you can use the Undo command, usually located on the Edit menu. Undo reverses the results of your last keystrokes and restores the deleted text. Undo works beautifully; in some word processors you can set the number of levels of Undo. (Nisus can handle up to 32,767 levels of Undo!) You could undo a deletion even after you complete 10 different operations.

Keep in mind, however, that every deletion you save by using the Undo option uses precious memory and deprives you of operating speed. If you use Nisus, keep the number of Undo levels low. (I keep my Undos set to about 20—more errors than that and I rewrite.)

Inserting Text

In addition to the times you need to delete text, you will certainly need to insert text sometimes.

Any text that you enter always appears at the location of the vertical insertion point. To move the insertion point, you move the I-beam to where you want to insert text and then click. Inserted text appears to the left of the insertion point.

In all word processors, you can also move the insertion point with the arrow keys. Various word processors make use of other keys to enable you to move quickly through text. Microsoft Word has one of the most extensive sets of keyboard controls for the insertion pointer. You can move by line, word, sentence, paragraph, page, screen of text, and other options by using key presses. Word enables you to change these key settings to suit your needs. Nisus offers the ability to use keystrokes to move the insertion pointer by word, line, sentence, screen, and page. Other word processors offer similar features, with Word and Word-Perfect offering the greatest flexibility in configuring these keystrokes (though Nisus users can always use macros to change key meanings).

Moving Text

Moving text is perhaps one of the most useful features of a word processor. When you move text, you use the Cut, Copy, and Paste commands, located on the Edit menu. When you select text, the highlighted area is called a *block*. These commands place the block on the Clipboard.

You can paste as many different things as you like keeping in mind that the Clipboard can store only one item at a time. When the second item is cut, the first item no longer is available.

I n most Macintosh applications—including all the word processors discussed in this chapter—you can paste the same Clipboard contents repeatedly by selecting the Paste command or by using the ⌘-V key combination.

The Clipboard is a temporary storage place for text and graphics. When you select the Copy or Cut command from the Edit menu, the cut or copied material is placed into the Clipboard. Because this feature is part of the Macintosh operating system, all word processors have the Clipboard; it is not really a separate word processor feature. After an item is cut or copied, the only way to get it out of the Clipboard is to use the Paste command on the Edit menu.

WARNING

Y ou can cut, copy, and paste any amount of text, but beware. Always save your document before you do any extensive cutting and pasting. Better yet, work on a copy of your original document. If you save your document, you can more easily recover from errors. For example, you might accidently paste material into the wrong place. Or you might cut two blocks of material and then discover that the first block is gone forever—the Clipboard can hold only one thing at a time.

At least one high-end word processor enables you to use more than one Clipboard. Nisus provides a total of ten. To choose one of the ten Clipboards, use the Set Clipboard submenu in the Edit menu (see fig. 10.7).

Clipboard 0 is the main Clipboard, the one you would use to transfer text and graphics in and out of Nisus. Use the other nine Clipboards for storing frequently used text or graphics, or for communicating information to and from macros.

Fig. 10.7
Setting Nisus to use Clipboard 4.

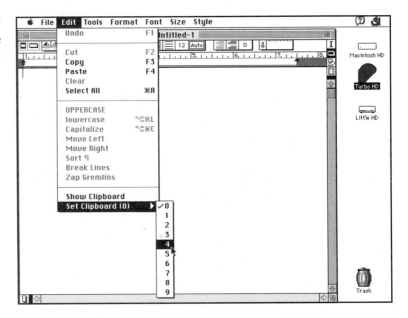

WordPerfect offers a variation on the use of the Clipboard by enabling you to perform a Paste Special command that copies the formatting of selected text. You can then paste that formatting on another selection of text (see fig. 10.8).

Fig. 10.8

Pasting text formatting in WordPerfect.

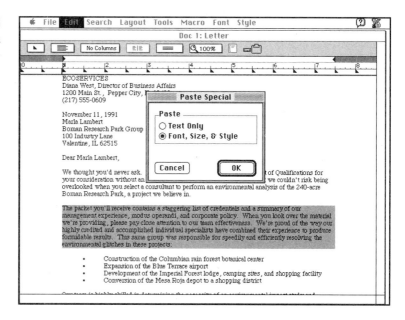

Microsoft Word offers a similar function through the use of the Copy Formats command.

One of the newest variations on moving text is the "drag and drop" of Microsoft Word and the "intelligent cut and paste" of Nisus. These are two names for the same basic feature. In either word processor, after text is selected, the I-beam pointer becomes the familiar mouse pointer arrow, indicating that you can now drag the selected text to a new location in your document.

This feature is worth its weight in gold. As a writer, for example, I constantly move words or phrases. With this new intelligent cut and paste (or drag and drop) feature, I only need a double- or triple-click to select and drag. And if you drag out of the window, the window scrolls automatically. The feature offers a quick and easy way to move a word, sentence, or paragraph short distances in your document (for longer distances, the traditional cut and paste is usually easier). Nisus offers the option of requiring the control key for the drag to work; both word processors offer the option of switching this feature off.

I expect this form of moving text to become a standard in word processing in the near future.

Searching for and Replacing Text

The search-and-replace features come in handy, particularly when you deal with a long document. The search feature (called Find, Find/Change, or a similar variation) enables you to hunt through a document for a string of characters or formatting. The search-and-replace feature (called Replace, Find/Change, Change, or a similar variation) can save you a great deal of typing time. Suppose that you are writing a report. Instead of entering the full phrase "economic advantages of lower tax rates," you can enter the letters **ETX**. When you finish typing your report, you can use the search-and-replace feature to replace each occurrence of ETX with the full phrase.

Often, word processors enable you to search for an item capitalized in a certain way, or to search for the word regardless of its capitalization. For example, you could search for CAT, cat, Cat, or any occurrence of the three letters. This is called "case matching" or "case-sensitive." Here "case" means uppercase or lowercase.

In figure 10.9, for example, you can see how Word enables you to search for whole words, or to match upper- and lowercase letters and replace them with text you enter by using the Replace command. (You can also simply search by using the Find command.) The Format menu enables you to search for formatting—you can locate each occurrence of the boldfaced word "special" and replace it with the italicized word "fantastic," for example. The Special menu gives you the capacity to search and replace special characters, such as the end-of-paragraph carriage return, the tab, the hard space, and so on. Word even enables you to search through saved documents on disk.

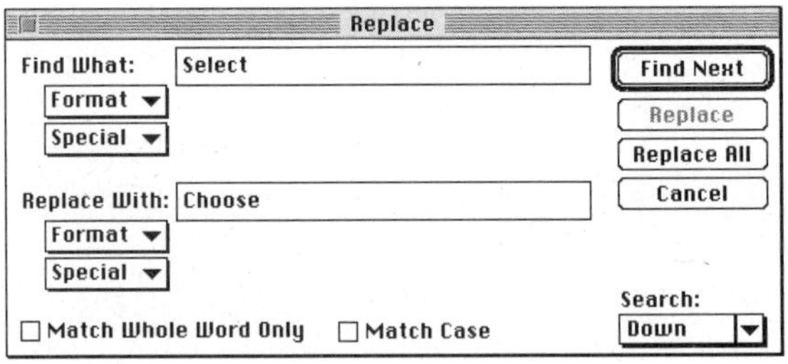

Fig. 10.9
The Replace dialog in Word.

WordPerfect has a sophisticated search-and-replace capability. The Find/Change command brings up a dialog that contains a series of menus from which you can choose options to tailor a search (see fig. 10.10).

Fig. 10.10
WordPerfect offers
sophisticated search and
replace options.

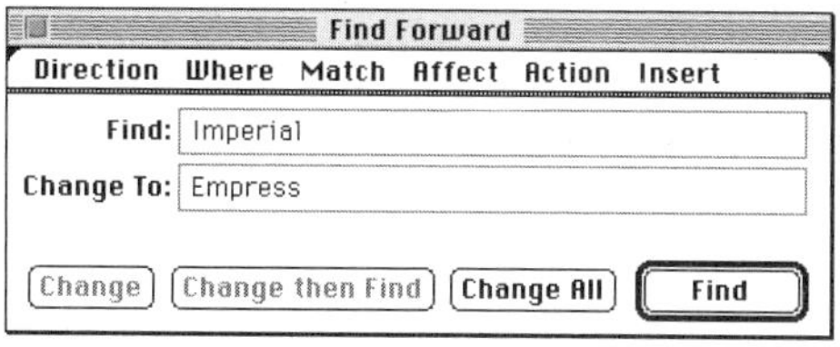

You can narrow the search to certain parts of the document (such as the headers and footers); you can also set the search to match and affect only the case, text only, font, font size, or style of the searched for or matched text. You can set the result of the search to be a replacement, to position the insertion pointer, or to extend your selection to the matched text. When text that matches your criteria is found, you can insert special characters.

Nisus comes with a thorough set of search-and-replace tools. For those with considerable text manipulation needs, this program is the winner in the search-and-replace category. Nisus uses the concept of GREP from UNIX to enable you to do incredibly powerful searches and replacements with PowerSearch (see fig. 10.11).

Fig. 10.11
An example of
PowerSearch.

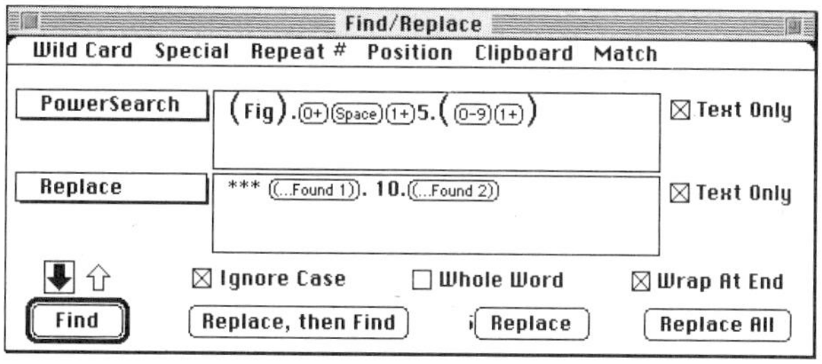

Consider the following situation: You are writing a manual with figures that contain the chapter number, followed by a figure number, as Que books do. For example, you might have Fig. 5.12, which would be Chapter 5, figure number 12. If you move a chapter—say that you change Chapter 5 to Chapter 10—you can search and replace with "Fig. 5" as the match text. But what happens if sometimes you forget to type the period at the end of "Fig," or if you insert extra spaces by accident?

This example of the figure searches for figure references in the text of a book, locating any text beginning with "Fig" and followed by zero or more periods; then the program searches one or more spaces, and then the number 5 and a period followed by a number of one or more digits. The text is replaced with a more regular figure notation and changed to reflect a new chapter number, Chapter 10.

This search is so inclusive that incorrectly typed figure references would be located and corrected as well as updated to the new chapter number. Fig... 5.34, for example, would be caught despite the bizarre typing.

PowerSearch can require you to experiment, and it can be a bit difficult to learn, but the power is enormous. If you need to edit text heavily, PowerSearch is worth the trouble of learning. And no other word processor comes close in text search-and-replace power.

Another fortunate aspect of Nisus is the large number of undos. PowerSearch is so powerful, you may scramble your document unmercifully as you learn to use it. But Nisus can undo so many changes in your document that you can experiment without fear.

MacWrite Pro cannot be left out of a discussion of sophisticated search and replace. This program has an easy-to-use but powerful search and replace that enables you to search not only for strings of text but for particular fonts, formatting, and even text color and language—in support of Apple's new "world ready" System 7.1. (For example, you could find all red-colored French words.) Although the MacWrite Pro word processor is a less expensive word processor, it offers tremendous search-and-replace power that's easy to use. You could, for example, locate all words in Helvetica font boldface and change them to New York font italicized.

Formatting Documents

The appearance of documents is often as important as their message. Although the form is not the message, the form can make the difference between a message received with pleasure and one that is just tolerated. Good spacing, carefully selected fonts, and other formatting features can make your documents stand out.

Setting Margins

You can change the top, bottom, left, and right margins of documents to achieve the effect you want. With all Macintosh word processors, you use ruler increments to help you change the margins. Figure 10.12 shows two paragraphs in Microsoft Word. The top paragraph uses the default margin settings, and the bottom paragraph has a 0.5-inch left margin setting and a 3.5-inch right margin setting. In this example, the margins were adjusted by dragging the small triangles on the ruler. For more precise adjustments, you can use a dialog. The new margin settings are in effect where they are inserted in the document.

Fig. 10.12
Using default and set
margins in Microsoft Word.

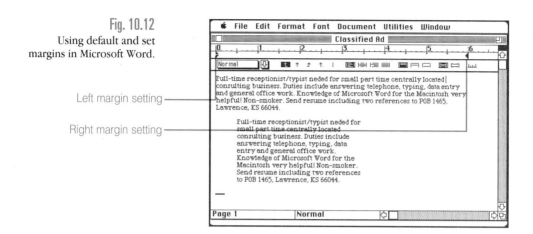

Left margin setting ──────

Right margin setting ──────

Note, however, that adjustments made in the Document dialog are for the entire document and not for one paragraph. Word processors usually enable you to set a default margin for the entire document, and then change the settings for lines or paragraphs as you see fit.

Setting Tabs

Where would we be without tabs? Imagine trying to construct columns of figures or text by pressing the space bar again and again! That method is time-consuming and often inaccurate. Like almost every Macintosh word processor, Nisus uses tabs that can align text to the left, to the right, in the center, or along a decimal. That's the function of the small triangular tab indicators below the Edit menu in figure 10.13. To set these tabs, drag the tab indicator to the place on the ruler where you want the tab. The left tab aligns text with the left margin, the center tab centers text, the right tab aligns text with the right margin, and the decimal tab aligns text with the decimal point.

All the major Macintosh word processors offer at least the tab options of left, center, right, and decimal. All the higher-end and most of the lower-end word processors offer tab leaders—characters such as periods that fill the space between the left margin and the tab. Some, such as Nisus, add special tabs, such as the justify tab. Text justification is covered shortly, in the section "Justify Text."

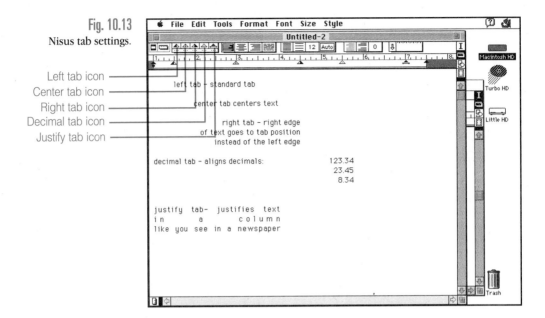

Fig. 10.13
Nisus tab settings.

Left tab icon
Center tab icon
Right tab icon
Decimal tab icon
Justify tab icon

Creating Tables

With Word, you easily can create and customize tables. This has always been one of Word's strong points, and in Version 5.1, the feature has improved.

WordPerfect can also handle tables, and has some powerful macros that relate to table-making. Word and WordPerfect are a bit ahead of Nisus in this area, although you can use Nisus to create tables and emulate many of the built-in table-handling features of the other two word processors.

The Pro upgrade of MacWrite handles tables well, and continues the Claris tradition of being easy to use. Though perhaps not as powerful as Word or WordPerfect, MacWrite Pro's capacity to handle tables is suitable for almost any application, and is easier to use than in the two larger word processors.

Justifying Text

Depending on your needs, you can align or *justify* text in several ways. The text in most books is fully justified, which means that words are spaced so that all lines are of equal length. Text can be left-justified, right-justified, centered, or fully justified.

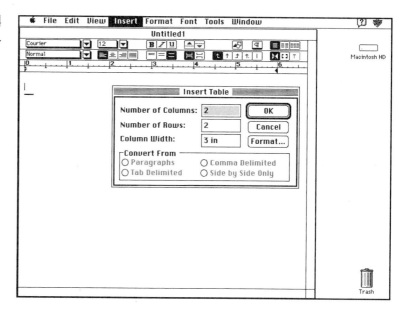

Fig. 10.14
Creating a table in Word.

Figure 10.15 includes four sample paragraphs in Word that show each type of justification. Which type should you use? Most documents are left justified because people are accustomed to reading documents that have a straight left edge—that's where your eyes are trained to return when you finish reading a line. A fully justified document can look very attractive, but unnatural spaces often are included to make all the lines even. You can alter these forced gaps with manual spacing changes, but the trouble often is not worth the effect. Center justification is useful for titles and headings. Right justification is often used when you need to align text to a graphic (for example, in a figure reference where the figure or picture is to the right of the text).

W ord processors have limited controls for adjusting the spaces between letters or words. If you are making business cards or flyers, you may want to look into purchasing a page-layout program such as QuarkXpress or PageMaker, which are popular programs for the Mac.

Most documents should be ragged right (left justified) or fully justified. Often, however, full justification produces awkward-looking lines. On some word processors, such as WordPerfect, you can adjust the spacing between letters. This action is called *kerning*, and adjusting the spacing between words is called *tracking*. Word enables you to do kerning by using the Expanded and Condensed styles; the spacing of those styles can be adjusted by using the Commands command.

Fig. 10.15
Four types of justification.

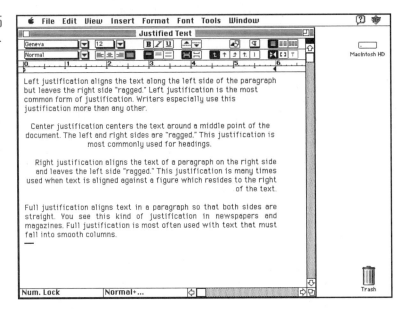

Using Fonts, Sizes, and Styles

When it comes to using fonts, the Mac can offer you an almost unlimited number of choices. A *font* is a family of characters, numbers, and symbols with the same characteristics. Examples of these families include Times Roman, Helvetica, Cooper, Palatino, Geneva, and Zapf Chancery Dingbats. Chapter 8, "Using Fonts," discusses fonts in greater detail.

Fonts come in different styles, such as underline or boldface, and in different sizes. In most word processing applications, the sizes range from 1 to 255 points. The most common sizes are between 6 and 72 points. A *point* is approximately 1/72 of an inch. The point size of a font refers to the vertical height of the letters—from the tops of letters with ascenders (such as b and h) to the bottoms of letters with descenders (such as p and q). Sometimes a particular font style is a family, such as Palatino Italic, but these fonts can be styled further.

In general, avoid fonts smaller than 4 points on a laser printer or 6 points on a dot-matrix printer. These machines usually do not have the resolution to reproduce the character clearly at such small sizes.

Usually, you change fonts, styles, and sizes by selecting the text you want to change, and then selecting the font you want to use from the appropriate menu. WordPerfect offers the style, font, and size options on one menu. Other word processors arrange the options differently, but all word processors have menus for setting size more precisely than on-screen mouse changes. If you use Adobe's Type Reunion (see Chapter 8, "Using Fonts"), the organization of fonts is even easier to use—fonts are organized by font type, style, and size.

On the Font menu, MacWrite Pro displays the fonts as they appear when they are printed. By viewing the Font menu, you can be sure of a font's appearance before you choose it for your document. This feature is an enormous help to people who like to try different font combinations, because font names don't usually indicate what the font looks like.

WordPerfect makes it easy to change font styles; you can set the word processor to display letters that show style changes at the bottom of the screen. To make text bold, select the text and click the B at the bottom of the screen. Follow the same process for the Plain, Underline, Italic, Outline, Superscript, and Subscript styles. Microsoft Word also has a similar feature in the new toolbar in Release 5.1. You can place commonly used font styles on the toolbar as a button, where those styles are available at the click of the mouse.

WriteNow's Size menu contains Larger and Smaller commands, which you can use to increase or decrease the size of the font in 1-point increments. Simply select the text and then choose the appropriate command. Nisus and Word offer a similar option with Increase and Decrease and Up and Down commands, respectively.

You may notice in a Font menu that some font sizes are outlined and others are not. The outlined fonts are installed in your System Folder. You can select and use the other fonts, but the clarity and resolution on-screen are not likely to be as good. You resolve this problem by using TrueType fonts or ATM with PostScript fonts (see Chapter 8, "Using Fonts").

Beware of font clutter. Using every font feature the Mac offers can overwhelm your document, drawing attention away from the message and to the characters themselves. Choose just one or two fonts per document to avoid the distraction of too many fonts on a page.

Adjusting Line Spacing

All word processors offer you an easy way to change from single to double (and sometimes to triple) spacing. Some programs also offer a dialog from which you can adjust spacing precisely. Typically, business forms (and typewriters) use a 6-lines-per-inch setting.

Working with Pages

In addition to changing line width, spacing, and fonts, you also can make changes to the entire page by using the Page Setup command, which is often located in the File menu.

As you can see from the dialog shown in figure 10.16, you can make changes in the orientation of the printed copy and enlarge or reduce your final output. You can enlarge an image up to 400 percent, or reduce it to as little as 25 percent of its original size on a LaserWriter (other printers may offer different options for enlargement and reduction).

Fig. 10.16
Using the Page Setup dialog to change a document's orientation.

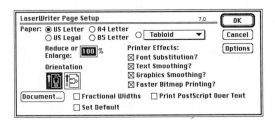

Some people enter text in a size larger than they eventually want the text to be printed in. When the text is reduced, the image on the printed page is more dense; however, this method involves some trial and error. When 12-point text is reduced 25 percent, it prints as 9-point text—but the text is more dense and blacker than regular 9-point type. Sometimes laser fonts don't scale well, but fully scalable fonts are a feature of System 7.0 and Adobe PostScript fonts.

Another feature is page orientation. In the Page Setup dialog, you can find the Portrait option (which prints the contents of the page vertically) and the Landscape option (which prints the contents of the page horizontally). The choice of page orientation is as much aesthetic as practical; however, if you want to keep long lines of type together, Landscape may be the better option. A document can contain only one page orientation.

Most word processors have the Print Preview option in common. By using Print Preview, you can see how the pages of a document will appear when printed. Figure 10.17 shows facing pages as you would see them in Microsoft Word's Print Preview option. Print Preview shows you how the document will appear when printed.

In figure 10.17, the icon with the parallel vertical lines is a margin icon, which you can use to set margins. You can switch from a one-page to a two-page display by clicking the third icon.

Most programs enable you to change margins and view two pages simultaneously in the preview mode.

Fig. 10.17
Using Word's Print Preview feature to see facing pages of a document.

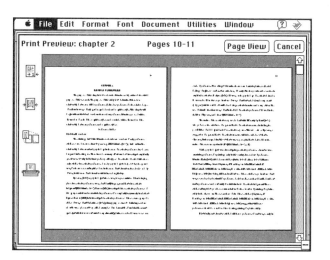

Understanding Special Functions

All word processors can perform the editing and formatting functions described in preceding sections, but some special features really add power and versatility to your word processing chores. Although these features may not be for everyone, they certainly can make performing highly specialized tasks much easier and less time-consuming.

Using the Spelling Checkers and Thesauri

Most spelling checkers work similarly—they go through your document word by word, looking for words or strings of text that don't match text contained in an internal dictionary. When the spelling checker finds a word it doesn't recognize, the program stops on that word, highlights it, and prompts you for a decision.

You can perform one of several actions at this point: you can ignore the spelling checker and proceed with your check, or you can correct the word if it is misspelled. The spelling checker often offers a suggestion for the unrecognized word. You can choose the suggested spelling, or you can have the program add the unrecognized word to a supplemental personal dictionary. In some cases, you even can look up the meaning of the word. MacWrite Pro has a feature that can alert you to spelling errors as you type.

In figure 10.18, you can see how Nisus highlights a word it does not recognize. The program then searches through its dictionary and picks an alternate spelling. Now the decision is in your hands.

Fig. 10.18
The Nisus spelling checker highlighting unrecognized words.

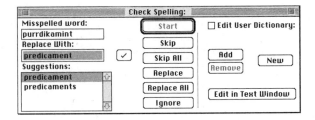

One warning: spelling checkers cannot detect improperly used words. In other words, you may be spelling a word correctly, but using it improperly. For example, I tend to transpose the middle letters of the words "form" and "from"; both are correct spellings, but produce meaningless sentences when interchanged. Some spelling checkers now detect when the first word of a sentence is not capitalized, and can flag doubled words, but the spelling checkers still cannot check word usage.

Using Merge

The merge feature can be a real lifesaver. Imagine writing 2,000 personalized letters. Wouldn't you rather write one letter, and then merge the letter with a file of addresses? That method certainly is more efficient.

That's exactly what the merge feature enables you to do. You create a main document (a letter or contract, for example), and merge other information into it. Then you create a data document that contains the information to be merged into the main document. Figure 10.19, for example, shows a main document (in MacWrite Pro), with merge variables (surrounded by <<>>) that will be replaced with data from a data document.

The variables (such as <<First>>) instruct the word processor to look for the information in the data document, which you create separately.

The merge feature, which is available on all major word processors, has more uses than you can imagine. You can use this tool for many different applications, such as the following:

■ Modify letters containing the same basic structure but different information.

■ Maintain mailing lists.

■ Advertise and perform marketing research.

■ Use the conditional features offered by programs such as Word to select files with certain characteristics—for example, you could find clients who are 30 or more days late with a payment, and print one document for them and another type of document for those whose payments are current.

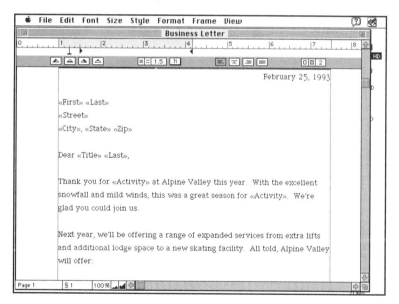

Fig. 10.19
A main document ready for mail merging.

You can use established databases to read in a set of names and addresses to use with your own letter or form. Many word processors enable you to export this information in a quick and useful way.

In addition to simple data fields, you can do some conditional logic in many word processors with commands embedded in the text.

You are by no means limited to print merging letters. You can use the merge feature for documents, such as direct mail advertisements in which certain factors are varied, or contracts with client-dependent clauses.

Using Sort

Although sorting is largely a database feature (see Chapter 12, "Using Databases"), most word processors offer simple sort functions. With the sort command, you can sort lists of items alphabetically or numerically; some programs also can sort in ascending and descending order.

Word processors generally sort information based on the first character encountered, and bring along all other information that goes with that word or paragraph. Most word processors offer paragraph sorting. WordPerfect offers an extensive sort capability with up to nine different keys (see fig. 10.20).

Fig. 10.20

Preparing to sort a file in WordPerfect.

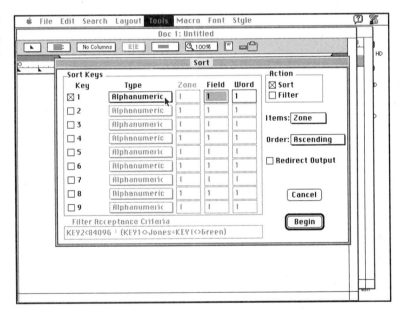

362 Macintosh Software II

Using Glossaries

A *glossary* is a word processing feature that enables you to store text or graphics, which you then can insert into a document with little effort. You may, for example, store a stationery heading logo or a paragraph from a contract. Whenever you need the insert, you simply go to the glossary and pick what you need.

Some word processors, such as Word, automatically store the date as a glossary entry. To insert the date, you open the glossary, and then just click the glossary entry named date. In figure 10.21, for example, you can see the Glossary dialog. To enter the date (as has been done in the upper left corner of this new document), you just double-click. The dialog shows formats of the glossary date entry in abbreviated, long, and short forms.

Fig. 10.21
Word's Glossary window.

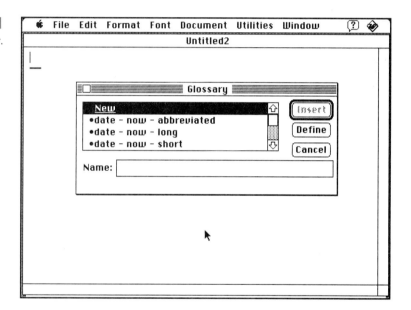

You also can create your own glossary entry by highlighting the text or graphic, selecting the Glossary dialog, assigning the entry a name, and clicking the Define button. Next time you go to the Glossary dialog, the entry is there, ready to be double-clicked and inserted in your document.

Nisus enables you to enter abbreviations, which then appear in your Glossary menu. You can then expand the abbreviations with a keyboard command.

Using Macros

Some word processors (including Nisus and WordPerfect) have built-in macro features. A *macro*, which many users believe is the most useful feature of a word processor or any application, is a set of stored keystrokes that acts like a tape recorder. You record what you want the macro to do, and then you play the macro back.

For example, you can have Nisus memorize a set of keystrokes that selects and then changes the font of an entire document. Suppose that you name this macro CF for Change Font. Each time you want to change a document's font, you invoke the macro named CF. You even can create a macro that pauses to enable you to insert or select the font.

You can create macros to do almost anything. You can use macros to select your document's headings, and then the headings for a table of contents. Perhaps you need text formatted for your paste-up project. No problem. You can create a macro to format the text into two columns two inches wide on an eight-inch page. Macros can simplify most actions that you can perform with your word processor.

Figure 10.22 shows the WordPerfect window that appears when you begin recording a macro.

Fig. 10.22

Defining a macro in WordPerfect.

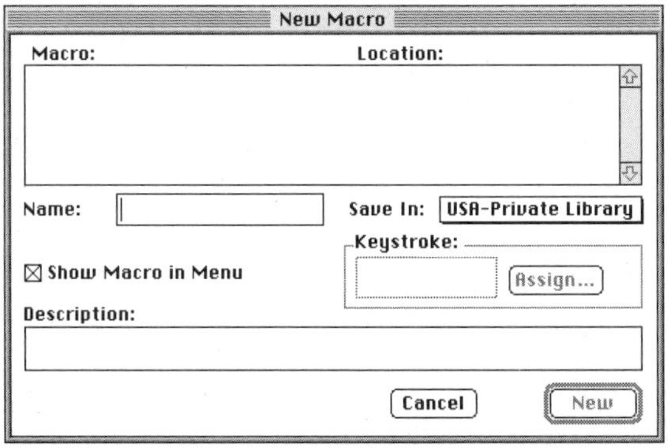

But the word processor winner in the macros category is Nisus. The macro language that Nisus uses is powerful and sophisticated, but the macros are almost as easy to edit as regular text. Nisus also has a language in which you can go further than macros and write programs to manipulate your documents. Or you can use the basic record function to duplicate your steps. The level of complexity is up to you.

Using Tables of Contents and Indexes

Generating a table of contents or an index is a great timesaver. All the word processors discussed in this chapter (except WriteNow and MacWrite Pro) can create both.

To create a table of contents or an index, mark the text that you want to include, and then indicate the level of entry for a table of contents or the type of entry for an index. After you follow this process for all the text you want entered, you generate the table of contents; it is placed at the beginning of the document. To create an index, you mark terms, and then use the Index option on the Utilities menu to define the type of index you want.

Figure 10.23 shows some text marked with Word header codes to show the headline entry level in the table of contents. Figure 10.24 shows the table of contents that Word generated. In Word, you can designate up to nine levels of entries. In WordPerfect, you select the text and use the Mark Text command to assign it to a table of contents or an index. This process is a bit less cumbersome than Word's.

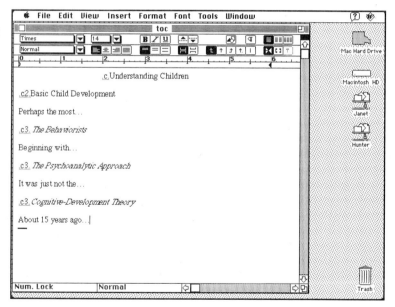

Fig. 10.23
Marking text for a table of contents in Word.

Notice that all page numbers for this sample table of contents are 1s; in this case, all the headings appeared on Page 1.

Want to speed things up? You can create a macro that automatically marks your text for a specific table of contents level, such as 1, 2, or 3.

Fig. 10.24
A Word table of contents.

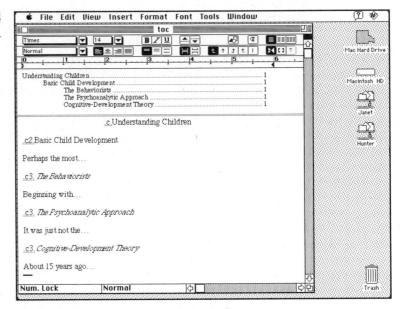

Using Graphics

It was only a matter of time before graphics became integrated with word processing. Now many word processing programs offer both. Dedicated graphics packages and word processors, however, perform their respective tasks best.

For the most part, you can create a graphic by using one of the many available graphics programs (see Chapter 16, "Using Graphics Software"), and then insert the graphic into a document. You can use the cut, copy, and paste operations quite effectively.

You can insert graphics just as you would insert any other piece of information cut or copied from another source. You simply cut or copy the graphic from its home location, go to the document in which you want to insert the graphic, and then paste it.

Nisus, MacWrite Pro, and WordPerfect include a draw feature as part of their programs. Using these graphics tools, you can create a graphic right in your document (see fig. 10.25).

Fig. 10.25

The Nisus graphics tools.

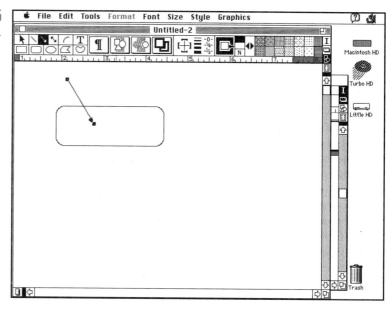

Word enables you to import graphics from other sources and place them in your document as well as draw object-oriented graphics with tools accessed from the Ruler.

One surprise is finding that MacWrite Pro—an inexpensive word processor—can "flow" text around a graphic (see fig. 10.26).

Fig. 10.26

Text flowing around the graphic of the skier in MacWrite Pro.

You would generally find this feature only in more expensive word processors such as Nisus, Word, and WordPerfect, or in desktop-publishing programs such as Aldus Personal Press.

Using Document Translation

Suppose that you create a document at home in Microsoft Word and then want to work on it at the office in WordPerfect. What are your options?

Many word processors can save in other formats so that other programs can read these files without losing any formatting codes and characteristics. If you have to use different word processors at home and the office, you may want to look for this capability.

Various options usually are available for file conversion. All word processors can save standard text files, which all other word processors can read.

The XTND technology used by MacWrite Pro and Nisus affords a wide variety of file translation formats (see fig. 10.27).

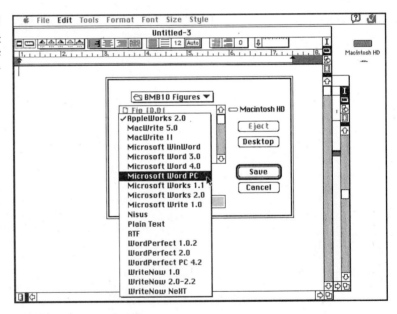

Fig. 10.27

Saving a Nisus document for use by Microsoft on the IBM PC.

Microsoft Word offers a large number of file translations. Additional file translations can be obtained by using the translators created by DataViz in the MacLink Plus file translation utility (see Chapter 29, "Using Connectivity Software").

Using Specialized Word Processors and Add-Ons

Any of the word processors discussed in this chapter probably can meet most of your needs. You may, however, need special capabilities these programs don't offer. Several special-function word processors may fill your needs. These applications are not full-fledged word processors in the same sense as the packages discussed previously.

Spelling Checkers

You don't have to rely on your built-in spelling checker—several operate independently of your word processor. These other tools many times are faster, have larger dictionaries, and offer additional features.

Spellswell 7 from Working Software offers additional specialized dictionaries, including the Spellswell Medical Dictionary, Legal Dictionary, Science Dictionary, Geographical Dictionary, Business Dictionary, and Expanded Dictionary. Spellswell 7 is a thorough checker, detecting punctuation errors, words run together, incorrect spacing, and the like (see fig. 10.28).

Fig. 10.28

Checking a document's spelling with Spellswell 7.

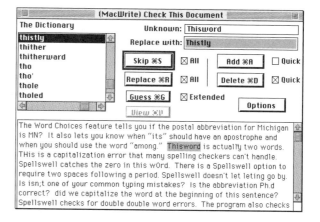

Thunder 7 by Baseline is a highly rated spelling checker. This System extension/control panel combination offers interactive spelling checking (checking as you type).

Spelling Coach Professional by Deneba is highly rated, though noted as somewhat difficult to learn. This program can perform check-as-you-type spelling checking. The Big Thesaurus—which is truly big—accompanies the package.

Microsoft Word users can purchase additional spelling dictionaries for specific uses. TechWords by Geocomp is a set of seven dictionaries covering terms in chemistry, computer science, physics, and the like. Alki Software offers foreign language dictionaries for Word. You can purchase French, Italian, Spanish, and others.

Thesauri and Dictionaries

A thesaurus is a tool that helps you find the word that's on the tip of your tongue. In a typical thesaurus, such as the one from Nisus, you highlight the word for which you want to find a synonym, and then select the Thesaurus tool from the Tools menu (see fig. 10.29). You see the word's definition along with the substitutes that the word processor offers. Double-click the word that you want to use.

Fig. 10.29
The Nisus thesaurus
at work.

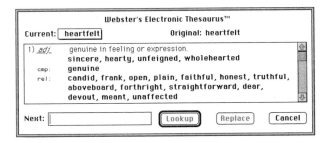

Deneba's Spelling Coach Professional comes with the Big Thesaurus, which is rated as one of the best.

Word Finder Plus by Microlytics is a good, solid thesaurus, but not one that completely takes the place of your printed Roget's. Before you purchase the thesaurus, check the one in your word processor. Microlytics has licensed Word Finder to many word processor manufacturers; you may already have Word Finder in your word processor.

The American Heritage Electronic Dictionary by WordStar International has over 100,000 entries, which you can access through your Apple menu as you are work in your word processor. Roget's II Electronic Thesaurus is included.

Inside Information, a dictionary program by Microlytics, includes a feature worth noting—the "reverse dictionary" enables you to search for words based on a definition you enter.

Grammar Checkers

Grammar checkers are not high on my personal list but then, I have an advantage you may not—editors. My grammar is checked—often. Grammar checkers tend to irritate me because I've become accustomed to skilled people reviewing my text to catch blunders. But if you don't have an editor (and can't afford to hire one), what do you do?

First, keep in mind that *no* grammar or style checker can replace a human editor. Computers simply do not have the power to understand the written word as human beings do. A grammar checker is useful only if you already understand grammar and style. This may sound contradictory, but a grammar checker goes through your text mechanically and tests the text against a set of rules. A grammar checker does not understand context, and may offer suggestions that you should reject. However, if you are aiming for a certain level of grammar usage and style, a grammar checker can help you catch errors you overlooked.

One example is the infamous "split infinitive." The rule states that it is proper to write "to run quickly," but not "to quickly run." However, this rule is changing in less formal language. In this example, you can see the two-edged sword of a grammar checker that flags split infinitives. It does no good to try to educate a grammar checker in the finer points of linguistics. When I test a grammar checker, I split infinitives with impunity to quickly drive them mad if possible.

At the same time, nonsense or not, the rule *is* accepted generally. If you write a formal paper or letter, you may want to adhere to the rule. A grammar checker can help you identify this usage, especially in this kind of case, as it has become more common in English to split infinitives and to end sentences in prepositions.

You cannot take the advice of a grammar checker on faith. You must be able to take the advice as suggestions, and depending on the context of the writing, suggestions may be good or bad. So you must be reasonably proficient in grammar to use a grammar checker. If you do not know what an infinitive is, you cannot evaluate the advice of the grammar checker.

RightWriter by Que Software, Grammatik Mac by WordPerfect Corp, and Correct Grammar by WordStar International are all good style tools, and all function in basically the same way. You start the style application and select a document to check. The style checker applies its rules (see fig. 10.30) and completes the operation by providing you with a special summary document that informs you about the education level your writing is reaching, suggestions on how to strengthen the writing, and other grammar and style related information.

Fig. 10.30
RightWriter chastises the
author about word usage.

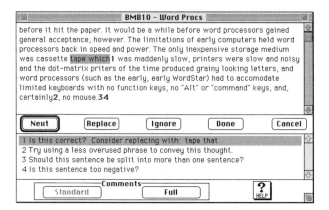

Along the way, you can tell the style checker to change the rules it uses for checking, such as the audience's grade level or the type of writing.

Grammatik Mac from WordPerfect Corp. comes with 10,000 rules. A strong feature of Grammatik is its interactive nature, which you can select as an option. As you can see in figure 10.31, Grammatik uses a split screen, stops at the first error it encounters, and gives you advice that you can follow or ignore. Figure 10.32 shows the document summary Grammatik generates.

Fig. 10.31
Grammatik as it begins
checking.

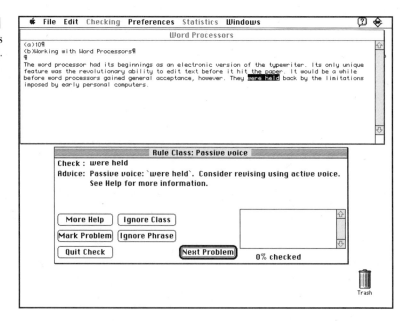

Fig. 10.32
Grammatik's style statistics.

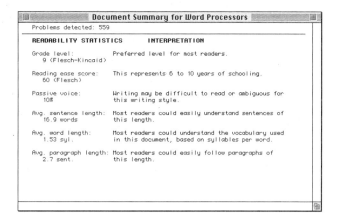

Grammtik Mac has been getting good reviews and does have the advantage of being customizable. RightWriter also has extensive customization features, which are important for grammar checkers. You need to be able to adjust the checking and application of the rules to fit your writing style.

Correct Grammar checks spelling along with grammar, and can use Microsoft Word's user dictionary in the spelling checking.

Microsoft has incorporated Grammtik Mac in Version 5.0 and higher of Word.

Writing Assistants

One interesting application is Writer's Dream Tools by Heizer Software. These HyperCard stacks—you must have HyperCard 2.1 to use the stacks—give you sets of cliches, catch phrases, slang, events, and more.

Correct Quotes by WordStar International (see fig. 10.33) is a HyperCard stack that contains a great number of quotations that you can view by topic or author indexed or searched for by any string of text.

EndNote Plus is worth a look if you write papers that require references. The application enables you to create and search databases of references. You can paste the citations into documents, and format the citations (you can customize the formatting). EndNote Plus comes in three forms: a full application suited for use in System 7 and under System 6 MultiFinder; a desk accessory you use in System 6 or 7 when you have limited memory or are not running MultiFinder; and a plug-in module you use with Microsoft Word 5.0 or higher (see fig. 10.34).

Fig. 10.33
Looking for a quotation in
Correct Quotes.

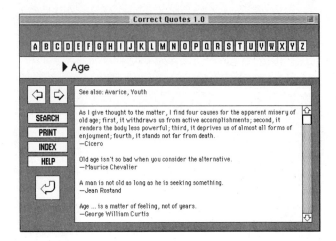

Fig. 10.34
Searching for references
with the EndNote Plus in
Word.

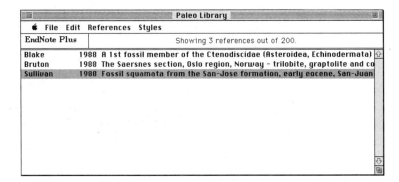

EndNote Plus is a worthwhile investment if you need to write papers
with citations. Students and scholars will appreciate being able to create
citation databases, sort them, search through them quickly (using
multiple keywords, if desired), and paste formatted references into a
word processing document.

EndNote Plus is compatible with Nisus, Word (the plug-in module with
Version 5.0 or higher), WordPerfect, WriteNow, MacWrite, and any
processor that creates ASCII text.

Using Equation Generators

MathType from Design Science is a word processor that enables you to
enter complex formulas without worrying about fonts or the Option
and Shift keys. MathType comes with a macro utility, a strip of often-
used symbols, and more than 100 templates that you can set up for
frequently used equations. MathType also provides a set of tutorials.

Expressionist from Prescience is another equation generator that has an easy-to-use interface and more logically arranged symbols. Expressionist enables you to change the structure of a formula quickly. In addition, Expressionist's convert-to-text feature enables you to switch from Expressionist to a word processing format.

Even though these specialized equation editors are available, don't forget that the latest versions of Microsoft Word (3.0 and higher) also offer an equation editor.

Predesigned Documents

A new wave of word processor add-ons provides you with already-written documents. One such add-on is ResumExpert (from A Lasting Impression). ResumExpert consists of templates that provide different resume formats—you can just pull up the format on-screen and insert what you want. This add-on enables you to be well-versed when you put together a document so that you have an advantage when looking for a job. You can use the templates with Word, MacWrite, or WriteNow.

A Lasting Impression also offers cover letter templates for everything from layoffs to career changes to follow-up letters. You cannot use these examples right out of the can, but they do provide a great beginning. If you know Word, you can use these documents as a basis for formulating style sheets that make your own creations easier.

Another resume helper is ResumeMaker from Individual, which automatically prompts you for relevant data and enables you to put together your own letter from a collection of different headings, paragraphs, and salutations. ResumeMaker also contains a word processor and an appointment calendar. With ResumeMaker, you have everything you need to get that job!

WillMaker helps you prepare your will. You can specify up to 28 separate bequests, name an executor, create a trust, and name a guardian for minor children. You can update WillMaker any time, as you can with any text document.

Correct Letters by WordStar International provides a source of model business letters. You can edit within the program itself, or in your word processor.

Text Editors

In addition to Nisus, NISUS Software offers QUED/M, a powerful text editor. QUED/M doesn't have all the high-powered features of Word or

Nisus; you can't use QUED/M to place borders around memos or to place graphics in headers, for example. QUED/M takes you straight to the task of text editing, which is very useful when you write programs or prepare a document to send via some telecommunications tool. The text editor is aimed primarily at the programmer, and offers many programming tools, such as the ability to balance parentheses.

Desk Accessories

With a word processing desk accessory—the small, mini-applications that reside in the Apple menu of System 6—you can edit a document without actually working in the application in which the document was created.

Vantage from Preferred Publishers is perhaps the most comprehensive desk accessory (DA). Vantage enables you to access and manipulate text created with other applications; it contains a dictionary, macro capability, an Undo command, and an icon grabber that enables you to capture icons and move them to the Clipboard. In addition, you can open up to 16 windows simultaneously, sort, reverse the order of lines, form paragraphs, and convert spaces to tabs; the feature list goes on and on.

ExpressWrite from Exodus is a DA particularly well-suited for letters and correspondence. On the opening screen is an envelope icon you can use to place text in the correct position for printing. Although ExpressWrite is not a full-fledged word processor, its features (including the envelope printer) make it quite handy.

Specialized Word Processors

Maitreya's miniWRITER is a shareware desk accessory word processor—you need only make a small payment to David Dunham, the designer, if you choose to use it. You select miniWRITER from the Apple menu and enter text as you like. With such features as smart quotes, search-and-replace functions, and formatting tools, miniWRITER rivals some low-end word processors. For ease of use and power in a DA word processing tool, miniWRITER ranks highest.

If you use Scriptor from Screenplay Systems, you made it big in Hollywood or New York—or you intend to. Scriptor is a highly specialized word processor that enables you to create a script following the highly formatted guidelines that a script demands. Specialized style sheets, pagination, placement of text, scene numbering, and so on make script writing much easier than it would be with a typical word processor.

Finally, if you save text in ASCII format to export to another application, or if you import ASCII (or text) files from another application, you may find hard returns at the end of every line. This situation is especially likely if a file is transmitted over a telecommunications setup. When you import such a file, each line is like a paragraph; you have to go in and delete each hard return so that the text flows together.

To avoid this problem, you can use Word Wrapper, a neat tool that automatically replaces these hard breaks with soft returns, making the file much more usable. You just identify the file, open it, and then wrap. Even big files take practically no time at all. If you ever saved a large file as a text file and found hard returns all over the place, you will love what Word Wrapper has to offer.

Choosing a Word Processor

When you're ready to buy a word processor, keep the following points in mind:

- If at all possible, try the package before you buy it. See whether your local dealer has different packages, or perhaps your local user group can help. Your dealer may have demonstration packages you can try out.

- Know what you need before you start looking. Don't pay for bells and whistles that you will never use.

- Read reviews of different word processors in popular computer magazines to learn what others think about a particular package.

- Be sure to consider such factors as the programs ease of use and the amount of memory it requires. (WriteNow uses about half a megabyte, Word can use four or more times that.)

- Keep in mind the integrated packages, which include a word processor, a spreadsheet, a database, and communications software—all at a relatively low price. ClarisWorks is the best, in my opinion; see Chapter 13, "Using Integrated Packages." The word processors included in the integrated packages may not have the power of the high-end programs, but one of them certainly may fit your needs.

- Finally, keep in mind what you already know. If you use WordPerfect on a DOS machine, maybe you should consider WordPerfect for the Mac. The same is true for Word users. In addition to being familiar with the general command structure, you also will find that most Macintosh word processors have easy-to-use transfer utilities so that you can go from Mac to DOS and back again.

The Big Mac Recommendation

Do you want to write a memo? Or a letter to the editor? A school paper? Any of the word processors discussed in this chapter do just fine for short documents, including letters and simple reports.

If you are a recent convert from an MS-DOS system, and you are accustomed to Microsoft Word (especially Word for Windows), you may want to use Word for the Mac, because the transfer is easy and many of the commands will be familiar. Word is good for the professional who creates large documents such as manuals with graphics, tables, tables of contents, and the like.

If you are accustomed to WordPerfect DOS (or WordPerfect for Windows), you may want to switch to WordPerfect Mac. WordPerfect's toll-free number and excellent support always offer a big plus. Offices may want to consider WordPerfect Mac because WordPerfect DOS has long dominated that market. Compatibility between the DOS and Macintosh versions of any two word processors is excellent now, and you can transfer files easily, though you may need additional inexpensive software (see Chapter 29, "Using Connectivity Software").

With its powerful word processor, Nisus has much to offer and should be high on your list, along with WordPerfect and Word. If you do text-intensive writing and edit extensively, your choice narrows to Nisus. The program's superior text handling (with PowerSearch) makes it perfect for text-heavy work, yet graphics are not at all neglected. Word and Nisus are often compared in the Macintosh journals as the top word processors in the Macintosh market—and for good reasons.

In my opinion, Word and WordPerfect are both migrating right out of the word processing category into desktop publishing, which is fine for those who need this kind of capability. But professional writers and those who deal with text more than formatting are left in the cold as the programs grow to massive size and devour disk space with formatting features that lie unused. I personally abandoned Word when I was throwing away unused modules of the massive program. At the same time, I had to do rewrites because of the weak search-and-replace in Word.

Those who need to deal with more than one language, which is becoming more common in today's world, have their choices narrowed to Nisus and WordPerfect. Both programs accommodate the multilingual world by adding the capacity to work with the alphabets and scripts of any language. Nisus is rapidly pulling ahead in this arena, which is a brilliant move in my opinion, given many current events. Nisus takes full advantage of Apple's move to a world-ready System for the Macintosh (Version 7.1).

MacWrite Pro and WriteNow are more reasonably priced programs. They are quite acceptable and especially easy to learn. The beginning Macintosh user will want to look at these packages, avoiding the confusion of first-time learning and the expense of the larger, power packages. MacWrite Pro is my personal pick for the new Macintosh user. Claris is known for maintaining high standards in ease of use and support, and the program is powerful enough for even small business users who need to create ads, flyers, newsletters, and the like.

CHAPTER ELEVEN

Using Spreadsheets

N o business, whether a small "mom and pop" shop or a multi-national manufacturer, does its bookkeeping, invoicing, and inventory tracking without the help of computers these days. In many (if not most) businesses, the preferred tool (after a word processing program) is a *spreadsheet program*, a kind of electronic ledger used to help manage and organize information and to generate graphical representation of that data.

In this chapter, you learn what spreadsheet programs are and how they work; what some of their special features are, including functions, formulas, and charting; and where you can buy this type of program.

Understanding Spreadsheet Programs

A *spreadsheet* is an electronic ledger in which you organize information into worksheets that consist of rows and columns. A spreadsheet program is the actual application, such as Lotus 1-2-3, Excel, Resolve, or BiPlane, which creates a worksheet—the file or document into which you enter numbers, formulas, text, and the like. Just as you do with other Macintosh applications, you can create a worksheet and then save it for later editing or output. A spreadsheet program consists of these basic components: worksheets, graphics features, charting features, a database, and macros.

Understanding Spreadsheet Components

A spreadsheet program enables you to work with and manipulate numbers and text by providing you with a worksheet containing a "grid" of rows and columns. You can enter numbers or text into the intersections, called *cells*, of these rows and columns and then perform a variety of operations on the information—such as sorting, mathematical calculations, and more.

Many spreadsheet programs offer graphics features that enable you to draw on the worksheet. These features can be used to highlight particular parts of the worksheet, drawing attention to charts, numeric values, or text of particular importance.

Another feature, charting (or graphing), enables you to represent numerical data in the form of a chart (or graph) automatically—the program draws the chart for you. The most popular spreadsheet programs offer pie, line, area, column, and bar charts. More spreadsheet programs now provide three-dimensional charts.

The database component of a spreadsheet program enables you to organize data in the form of records. You then can use the information in the records to search for and to select particular records.

Macros work with spreadsheet programs as they do with word processing programs: they automate keystroke and mouse operations. By pressing one or two keys or key combinations, for example, you can open a worksheet, go to a specific location, enter a particular formula, reformat the worksheet, and then exit the worksheet.

Considering Uses of Spreadsheet Programs

Although word processing programs are probably the most frequently used applications, spreadsheet programs are almost irreplaceable in the business community. Any or all of the following operations are possible with the use of spreadsheet programs:

- Create a monthly budget for all your income and expenses, and then compute the difference between the two values, as shown in figure 11.1.

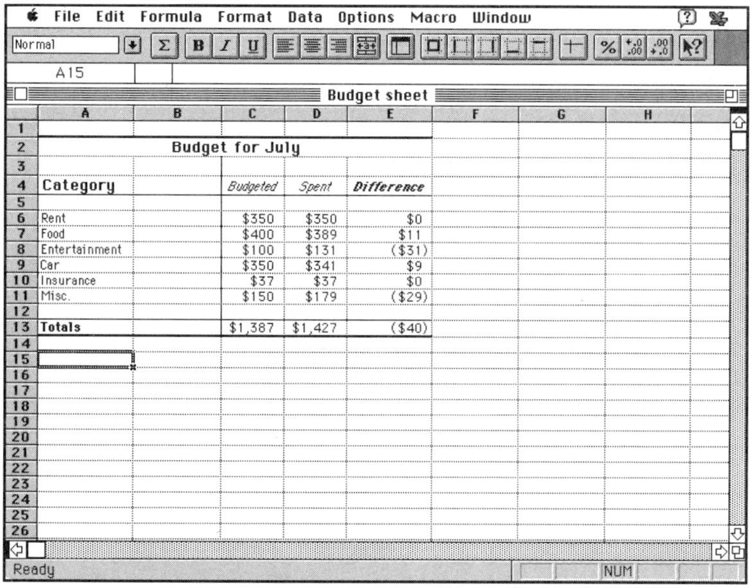
File Edit Formula Format Data Options Macro Window
Normal
A15
Budget sheet
Budget for July
Category Budgeted Spent Difference
Rent $350 $350 $0
Food $400 $389 $11
Entertainment $100 $131 ($31)
Car $350 $341 $9
Insurance $37 $37 $0
Misc. $150 $179 ($29)
Totals $1,387 $1,427 ($40)
Ready
NUM

Fig. 11.1
A monthly budget with actual and budgeted amounts.

- Perform what-if calculations to test numerical hypotheses and to do break-even calculations.
- Use the built-in functions to figure the monthly principal and interest payments on a loan.
- Produce charts showing information such as employee ownership in terms of years on the job (see fig. 11.2).
- Create a database of clients and search the file to find names of those who are interested in a new product.

All these possibilities and more are available to you. The spreadsheet program is as easy to work with as any other Macintosh application.

Fig. 11.2
A three-dimensional chart.

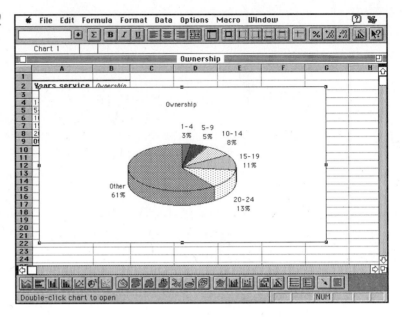

Considering Benefits of Spreadsheet Programs

Spreadsheet programs are fast and reliable, and they do not make mistakes. In fact, these programs are perfect for the person who has always been afraid of math yet needs to work with large sets of numbers, or for anyone who hesitates to tackle big number jobs. These programs are logically organized and give you the wrong results only if you give them the wrong information.

Macintosh spreadsheet programs are especially useful because they take advantage of the Macintosh's friendly graphical interface and use the mouse to help speed up your work and increase your efficiency. Although the IBM world has been far ahead in the development of spreadsheet programs and their application to business problems, Macintosh programs such as Excel, Resolve, and Lotus 1-2-3 have surpassed their DOS cousins in some ways.

Of all the functions that spreadsheet programs serve, their most important use springs from the days of VisiCalc (for visible calculator), developed in the 1970s as the first spreadsheet program. VisiCalc was the brainchild of then-Harvard graduate student Dan Bricklin who, in 1977, had the idea of using an electronic ledger for business forecasting. VisiCalc was written for the Apple II computer; this combination of the computer and the program is what made the personal computer a viable business machine.

A vital part of forecasting is a procedure called *what-if analysis*. Suppose that you own a store and you just purchased 100 items at 50 cents each. What is your profit if you sell each one for 52 cents? This example is an easy one, right? But imagine that you have 300 products to sell at prices that vary according to the season and the number of each product you purchase, and that you also must include tax rates and other variables. A spreadsheet can assign values to each variable and be set up in such a way that any one variable can be changed, and then reflects the effects of that change on all variables.

The power in a spreadsheet program lies in its capability to recalculate all entries when only one entry is changed. You can have the spreadsheet recalculate manually (when you indicate) or automatically (each time the spreadsheet is updated). This capability means that you also can see the effects on several different variables when you change only one variable. This power applies to small changes (such as one number in a simple list and the effect it has on the total) as well as to large changes (such as hundreds of variables all dependent on one another in a large spreadsheet). In both cases, the power of the spreadsheet is easy to see because the spreadsheet saves you endless hours of recalculating values.

Using Worksheets

To show you some of the ins and outs of a spreadsheet program, the example in figure 11.3 uses the leading Macintosh program, Excel, to create a simple loan analysis worksheet.

Any loan analysis takes into account the amount of money being borrowed, the interest rate, and the period of time for which the money is loaned. In figure 11.3, you can see how one of Excel's financial functions (shown in the formula bar at the top of the spreadsheet) calculates the monthly payment. *Functions* are predesigned computation tools in which you substitute certain values in the equation. In this example, the interest rate, number of months of the loan, and the amount borrowed are entered into columns called Interest Rate, Period, and Value, respectively. The formula determines the amount of the payments. (Parentheses usually mean a negative number because a payment is a negative transaction.) You can see that as the period of the loan changes (the number of months decreases), the payment increases.

This example uses the what-if capabilities of Excel to manipulate one factor and to display the results immediately.

Fig. 11.3
Using a spreadsheet for
loan analysis.

Formula bar

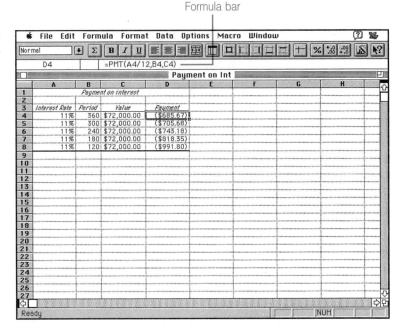

	A	B	C	D	E	F	G	H
1			*Payment on interest*					
2								
3	*Interest Rate*	*Period*	*Value*	*Payment*				
4	11%	360	$72,000.00	($685.67)				
5	11%	300	$72,000.00	($705.68)				
6	11%	240	$72,000.00	($743.18)				
7	11%	180	$72,000.00	($818.35)				
8	11%	120	$72,000.00	($991.80)				

Understanding the Worksheet Screen

A blank worksheet, such as the Excel worksheet you see in figure 11.4, consists of many separate features.

The most obvious component of any worksheet is the large number of squares, or cells, making up the grid. The grid is composed of rows, designated by numbers, and columns, designated by letters of the alphabet. These rows and columns also have *headings*. Each cell has an *address*, which is determined by the headings of the intersecting column and row. In figure 11.3, you can see how the cell address B4 (representing column B and row 4) holds the value 360.

Different spreadsheet programs hold different numbers of cells. An Excel worksheet can contain as many as 16,384 rows and 256 columns (for a total of 4,194,304 cells), for example.

Fig. 11.4
A blank worksheet in Excel.

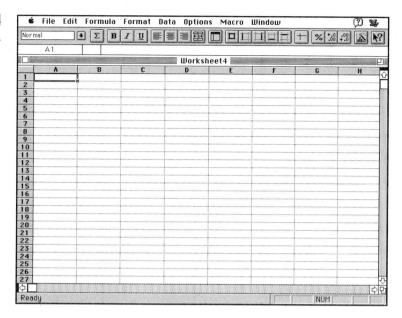

NOTE

Large worksheets have some significant disadvantages. First, navigating a large worksheet can be trying for the beginner. Additionally, the larger a worksheet gets, the more slowly it performs calculations. You cannot see the difference between a worksheet with 10 rows and 10 columns and one with 20 rows and 20 columns, but you can see a difference if the larger worksheet has 100 rows and 100 columns and continues to get bigger—especially if you have many formulas and calculations to do. Fortunately, large worksheets do become easier to work with as your experience and confidence increase.

Spreadsheet programs are smart programs, however, and in general can handle large amounts of data. You can include whole units of information on one sheet, such as a month's schedule or a year's budget. This capability saves you the work of going other places to find information. In addition, most spreadsheet programs enable you to link one worksheet with another worksheet—giving you access to large amounts of information in a relatively small space.

Notice the usual menu names across the top of the window in the blank Excel spreadsheet shown in figure 11.4. Each menu contains commands that perform specific functions, such as opening and saving files (on the File menu) and changing the way the worksheet's contents look (on the Format menu). If you compare this menu to the one in figure 11.5, which shows a blank Lotus 1-2-3 worksheet, you see that they have some things in common yet differ from each other as well. The File, Edit, Format, and Window menus perform many of the familiar Macintosh commands (opening files, cutting, copying, pasting, formatting text, etc.), for example. Options—in Excel—is a catch-all menu for everything from displaying formulas to protecting worksheets from outside eyes. The more familiar menus such as Macro and Data for Excel and Graph and Tools for 1-2-3 are product-specific. They have many similar functions, however, even though the command names and the menu locations may be different.

Fig. 11.5

A blank worksheet
in Lotus 1-2-3.

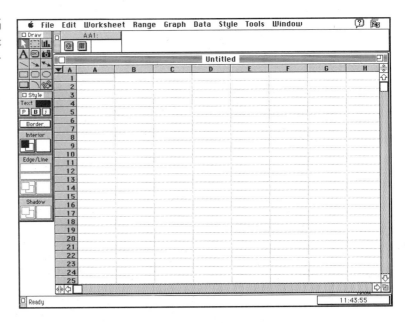

In figure 11.4, you can see the formula bar (or entry bar) just below the menu where you can edit and enter information. The address for the active cell, such as cell A1 in this case, always shows in the left of the bar. The active cell is the one that is selected. As you see later in this chapter, you can select one cell or a group of cells (called a *range* of cells).

In figure 11.5, you see a blank worksheet in 1-2-3; the console just below the menus performs a similar function to Excel's formula bar but also contains two menus from which you can choose a formula or named range for entry into a cell. One big difference between these programs is that 1-2-3 enables you to edit directly in a cell rather than having to do edits solely in the formula bar as you must do in Excel.

Creating a Worksheet

In all spreadsheet programs, you choose the New command from the File menu to create a new, blank worksheet. Note, however, that most spreadsheet programs (as most word processing programs) open a new, blank worksheet for you when the program first starts up, and you can skip making the menu choice. Any time other than startup, you must choose the New command to create a new, blank worksheet.

Excel requires an additional step after you choose the New command. You must specify the kind of document you wish to create (see fig. 11.6).

Fig. 11.6
Creating a new worksheet
in Excel.

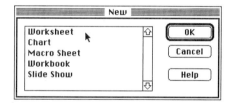

You can choose a Worksheet, Chart, Macro Sheet, Workbook, or Slide Show. Excel separates these different functions— worksheets, charts, macros, and slide shows—but they can be combined into a workbook document which acts as a binder of sorts. To complete the steps for creating a new worksheet, merely double-click on Worksheet in the list box.

Entering Data in a Worksheet

Entering data into a worksheet is as easy as entering data into a document in a word processing program. Just type the data and then press the Return key to move the mouse pointer to the next cell down. You may use the direction keys on the keyboard—the Tab key to move one cell to the right, the Enter key to stay at the same cell—or you can click elsewhere in the sheet and then move to the selected cell to enter the data.

If you make an error before you pressed the Enter or Return key to insert the entry into the worksheet, just use the mouse to place an insertion point in the formula bar and correct your mistake by using the Backspace key; then make your changes. Editing in the formula bar follows standard Macintosh conventions.

If you notice your error after entering the data, click the cell containing the error first to place the data in the formula bar and then edit the data.

I n Lotus 1-2-3 you can edit a cell's contents by double-clicking the cell and then using the standard Macintosh editing techniques rather than resorting to the console. You may find it convenient to use the console for editing, however, if the cell contains a long string of text or a complex formula; you can see long entries more easily in the console than in the cell.

Formatting a Worksheet

A great deal of spreadsheet work has nothing to do with numbers; worksheets are also used to construct charts, for example. As with other types of Macintosh applications, you can use various tools to change the appearance of the information you are displaying. Spreadsheet programs provide the same basic types of formatting options (alignment, fonts, presence of grid lines, and other features) as word processing programs, and in some cases you can do even more.

Aligning Cell Entries

Spreadsheet programs offer a variety of ways to align cell contents. In figure 11.7, for example, the Excel dialog provides several alignment choices. As with other Macintosh applications, you first highlight the cell entries you want aligned and then select under the appropriate menu the type of alignment you want. The Left, Right, and Center options do what their names indicate. The default General option aligns text on the left margin and numbers on the right. The Fill option repeats a value within a cell until it is full. If cells are blank to the right of the active cell and are formatted by the Fill option, repetition continues in those cells. You also can see that Excel has the capability of centering text across a selection (a useful feature for headings) and of rotating text. These formatting choices are specific to Excel 4.0, but other spreadsheet programs have similar options.

Fig. 11.7
Excel's alignment options.

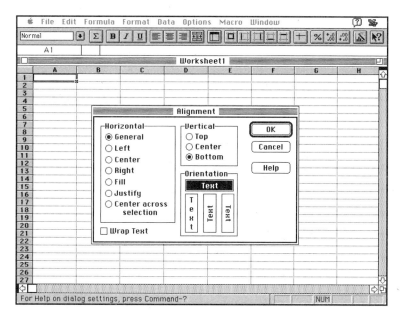

Column headings look best centered, and the General format option will suit most of your needs—except when you have particular design requirements, such as using your worksheet to design an organizational chart where you want all the text centered.

Formatting Numbers

Most spreadsheet programs offer a variety of formats for numbers (such as $7,390.82, 7390, or $7,390). They offer variety not only in the way that the values appear in the worksheet but, just as important, in what the values represent. In figure 11.8, for example, you can see the Range menu from Lotus 1-2-3, which contains the Format command, followed by common formats. (You can add your commonly used formats to the menu as well.) Figure 11.9 shows the Format Number dialog in Excel.

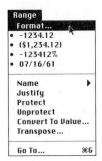

Fig. 11.8
One set of formatting
options for numbers in
Lotus 1-2-3.

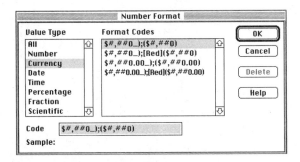

Fig. 11.9
The Format Number dialog
in Excel.

Your choices in the Format Number dialog range from Currency
($32,067), to D-Mon-YY (19-MAR-88), to a format you can custom define,
such as 0003.26 or 3.26000-82 for special purposes.

When you choose the Format command from the Range menu in Lotus
1-2-3, you see the Range Format dialog, similar in function to the Format
Number dialog of Excel (see fig. 11.10).

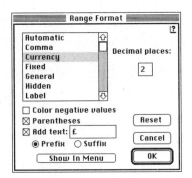

Fig. 11.10
The Range Format dialog.

You can customize the formats by changing attributes such as the number of decimal places, by adding parentheses or color (or both) to negative numbers, and by prefixing or suffixing text (useful as in the figure for dealing with other currencies such as the British pound). You then can add the custom format to the Range menu.

Lotus 1-2-3 puts the Format command in the Range menu because you can format a range of cells at one time. You also can do this in Excel, but 1-2-3 is geared towards handling ranges of cells than single cells, and the menu names reflect this.

Such formatting options are common in spreadsheet programs; however, some programs offer different and unique variations.

Working with Fonts

Numbers are not the only elements for which you can change the format in a spreadsheet. You also find the tools you need to style text.

In figure 11.11, for example, you can see text before and after font and other format changes. (The grid lines have been removed from the worksheet so that you can see the changes more clearly.) The middle set of cells uses italic to emphasize the headings. The lower set of cells uses a feature of Excel's that is worth noting and applauding, the AutoFormat. With the click of a button on the Tool bar (or by a menu command), you can format a table without having to make a series of menu choices. You can customize AutoFormat to suit your tastes.

Fonts and other text formatting can add style and emphasis to a spreadsheet as much as they add to word processing documents. However, use formatting sparingly. Too many fonts, font styles, colors, and so on can detract from the message of the spreadsheet, drawing attention to the formatting itself.

Fig. 11.11

Changing the style of text.

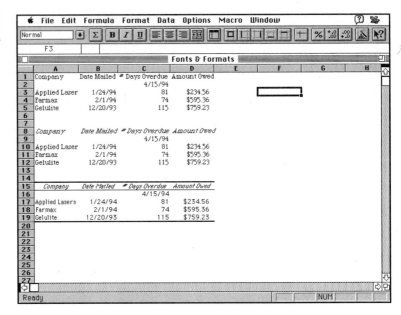

Using Formulas

Formulas (and functions) are the true workhorses of any spreadsheet program. By using a formula, you can manipulate information to meet your specific needs. Formulas are equations you enter to perform various mathematical functions on the data in your worksheet.

Entering Formulas

In figure 11.12, you can see the open and close prices for a variety of stocks. If you want to find the amount that the value of the stock increased or decreased, you can use a simple formula (shown in the formula bar) that subtracts one value from the other. Figure 11.13 shows the result of a formula that computes the gain or loss in percentages. What is so useful about a spreadsheet program is that you can change any value in the equation to see the effects that change has on other values. This what-if capability makes spreadsheet programs valuable planning and prediction tools.

Fig. 11.12

A formula to find the change in stock prices.

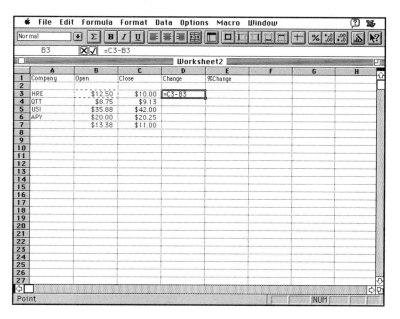

Fig. 11.13

Computing the percentage change in stock prices in 1-2-3.

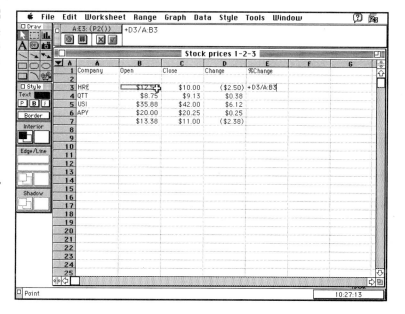

Excel recognizes that a formula is being entered when the entry is preceded by an equal sign (=) while Lotus 1-2-3 uses a plus (+) sign (although 1-2-3 courteously permits you to use an equal sign and then automatically converts it to a plus). The formula shown in figure 11.12 uses some cell addresses and performs a specific operation. In this case, the formula subtracts the value in cell B3 from the value in cell C3.

Figure 11.13 goes further to compute the percentage of change by dividing the result by the value in B3. Note that the formulas use whatever values you place in these cell addresses, whether they are 12.50 from 10.00 or 8.75 from 9.13, for example.

Figure 11.13 illustrates an important principle in entering formulas in most spreadsheet programs. Rather than having to type the addresses of the cells you need, you may click on the cell and the program enters the address into the formula for you.

Another important feature in entering formulas is the Copy Down command (or Copy Right command) that enables you to duplicate formulas as well as repeat data entries. The change in price and percentage formula will be the same for each row, for example, and entering the formula repeatedly is tedious. Instead, you can drag through cells to select the ones that you want the formula to be copied to and then choose the Copy Down command from the Edit menu (see fig. 11.14).

Fig. 11.14
Copying the formula to other cells.

Excel 4.0 has an innovative feature called AutoFill to do the same, but you do not have to use a menu command. You can simply drag the cell's selection box by the lower right corner to copy the formula or data to other cells (see fig. 11.15).

Cell addresses are adjusted automatically in both programs.

Fig. 11.15
Using Excel's AutoFill to
duplicate a formula.

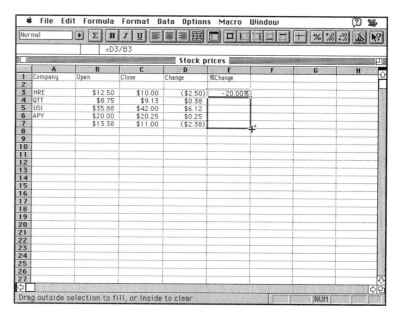

You have almost unlimited options for your formulas. They can be simple or complex, depending on your purpose. You are limited in the size of the formula, however, to usually no more than 255 characters; you need to be creative and divide complex formulas into smaller segments so that they fit into the formula bar. This limitation is not a hindrance. Long formulas should be broken up to aid you in keeping them simple and in making changes and corrections to the formulas.

Using Operators

Operators are such things as add (+), subtract (–), multiply (×), divide (/), and other such operations that you must have in order to create formulas. All spreadsheet programs give you the basics, but many go much further.

Excel gives you comparison operators (equal, greater than, less than, and so on), for example, as well as text concatenation (joining). Most spreadsheets also have logical operators such as #NOT#, #AND#, and #OR#, to enable you to do logical comparisons.

If you are familiar with math (as you must be to utilize a spreadsheet), you will already know most of the operators. You will only have to learn the characters used to represent them in the spreadsheet programs (for example, "not equal to" is often represented with "<>," which is not common in mathematical notation but is common with computer programs).

Using Functions

A *function* is a special component of formulas. A function is a predesigned formula; all you need to do is inset the function and the values (or the cell addresses of the values). Spreadsheet programs offer many different types of functions in areas such as business, date and time, and statistics. Functions are incredible timesavers and enable you to compute sophisticated values quickly and easily.

The amortization computation chart shown in figure 11.16 demonstrates the Excel function PMT. All functions have a syntax that requires special values placed in a special order. The syntax for the PMT function is

$$=PMT(rate, nper, pv, fv, type)$$

PMT (the function) is the payment due on a loan. The arguments and their meanings are as follows:

> *rate* is the interest rate.
>
> *nper* is the number of periods.
>
> *pv* is the present value of the loan.
>
> *fv* is the future value of the loan.
>
> *type* is the type of loan.

Do you think that you may have a difficult time remembering all the functions and what they do—let alone what each one requires for input? To make using functions easier, some spreadsheet programs, such as Excel, enable you to paste the function, and its needed arguments are then inserted into the cell so that you can see what information is required. In figure 11.17, the function PMT, which computes loan payment amounts, has been selected with the Paste Arguments option turned on. The formula appears in the formula bar as well as the cell itself. You then can edit the function in the formula bar or—in Lotus 1-2-3—in the cell, replacing arguments with cell addresses or numbers. This feature enables you to pick up almost any function and at least know what arguments are needed to make the function work.

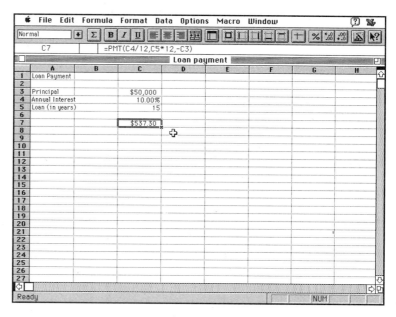

Fig. 11.16
Example of the use of a
function in Excel.

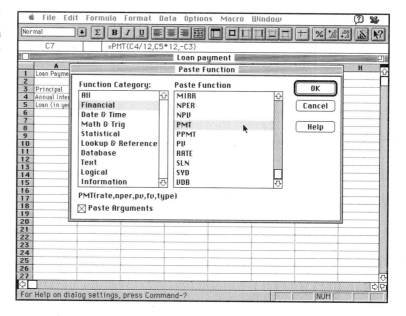

Fig. 11.17
Excel's Paste Function
dialog.

The big challenge of functions is to understand your needs and to identify which of the many functions can be of assistance to you. To understand functions, you have to use your spreadsheet program for every possible task you can think of and then practice with it all the time. Read the software manual and get acquainted with the functions. An overlooked function that most spreadsheet programs have is DATE in Excel (other spreadsheet programs may use a different name), for example, which is used to compute the number of days between two dates. This function is handy for billing, scheduling jobs, and so forth, but many people don't use the feature because they don't know that it exists.

Creating Charts

Charts (also called *graphs* in many spreadsheet programs) are indispensable for making data in a worksheet more understandable. They can add pizzazz to a presentation and make information that can be confusing crystal clear.

Spreadsheet programs offer a variety of chart types. Figure 11.18 shows the Toolbar (the buttons along the bottom of the screen) containing some of Excel's 17 available chart types. Lotus 1-2-3 offers 16 different types of graphs.

How do you choose a chart? When should you use a chart? For the most part, what looks right to you may be best. When you are representing the number of sales over a period of time, for example, a line chart is best. When you are dealing with categorical information, such as percentage of sales by category, a pie chart is best.

Figure 11.19 shows a sample graph from 1-2-3. You select the type of graph from the Type submenu of the Graph menu (you also can tear off this menu, converting it into a palette as has been done in the figure).

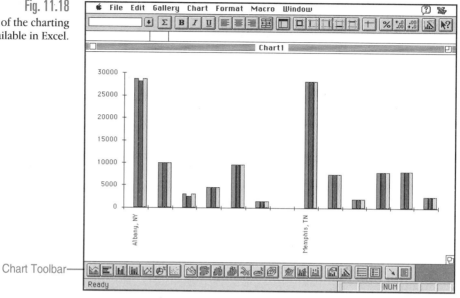

Fig. 11.18
Some of the charting
options available in Excel.

Chart Toolbar

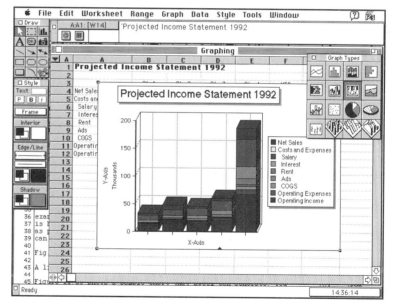

Fig. 11.19
A 1-2-3 bar graph and
Graph Type palette.

Creating a Chart

To create a chart in Excel, highlight the data and then select the New command from the File menu. A dialog with five choices (Worksheet, Chart, Macro Sheet, Workbook, and Slide Show) appears. Double-click on Chart. A column chart, the default chart type, appears.

Other spreadsheet programs, such as Lotus 1-2-3, require the same basic steps, but with 1-2-3 you can draw the graph on the worksheet by selecting the data, choosing the Graph tool, and then drawing a box to define the graph's size and location. The graph then appears.

After the chart is generated, you can add legends, rescale axes, and change fonts through a set of new graph-specific menus that appear at the top of the window.

Adding Text

Charts (or graphs) by themselves contribute greatly to the understanding of a set of data. You can improve on the chart's visuals, however, by using text added to the chart in the form of legends, titles, notes, and more.

Charts are easy to customize. Suppose that you want to point out a particular quarter of sales by attaching text to the chart. You also can add an arrow to an Excel chart to emphasize the point, as shown in figure 11.20.

Excel enables you to add text to any place on a chart by entering the text and then using the mouse to position the text where you want it. You enter the text from the keyboard. When you press the Return key, the text appears in the middle of your screen. You then can drag the text wherever you want it. You also can change the font, its size, and its style just as you can with the other major spreadsheet programs.

Formatting Charts

After a chart is finished, you can fancy it up by using some of the formatting tools that are usually available. For example, some of the things that you can do are

- Change the patterns and colors used to represent different series of data

- Enclose added text, titles, or other information in boxes to highlight it

- Remove or add boxes around certain parts of the chart

- Create three-dimensional effects

- Change the scale of the x- or y-axis for more emphasis

- Emphasize the title by changing the style and font (to Bold Helvetica, for example)

These effects were achieved using Lotus 1-2-3 in the chart you see in figure 11.21.

Fig. 11.20
Adding text to an Excel chart.

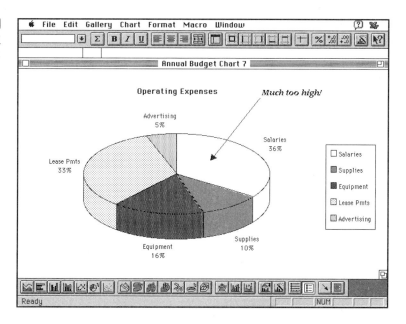

Using the Spreadsheet as a Database

A spreadsheet can do many different things, such as arranging and working with numbers as well as producing impressive graphs. Another valuable purpose the application serves is to act as a database where records (and not just values) can be manipulated.

Why would you want to use a spreadsheet as a database rather than use a database program? First, if the data is already in a spreadsheet, why not work with it as it stands rather than transfer the data to a database? Working in the spreadsheet is more convenient, especially if the operations you need to perform are relatively simple ones, such as finding and extracting records rather than relational activities (which you learn about in the next chapter).

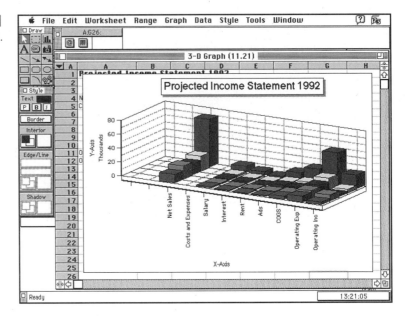

Fig. 11.21
A 3-D Lotus 1-2-3 graph.

Second—and this reason may be a bit of a lazy response—you may not want to go to the trouble (or the expense) of learning a database program if your spreadsheet can do all that you need.

Keep in mind that a spreadsheet application is not a database. The primary feature you sacrifice when using a spreadsheet rather than a database is flexibility in the way you can display and manipulate your data. You cannot easily change the order of how columnar information is presented in a worksheet, for example. With a database, all you need to do is create a new layout screen. If your major tasks are numerical analysis and manipulation, use a spreadsheet. Otherwise, use a database.

Creating a Database

Figure 11.22 shows an Excel spreadsheet used as a database. The records (one each for five people) are organized by fields (Last Name, First Name, Age, Gender, and Years at the company). A *record* consists of a set of fields and corresponds to a row in the spreadsheet. *Fields* are the columns of the spreadsheet.

Fig. 11.22
A simple Excel database.

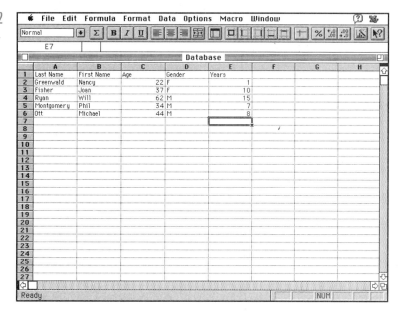

Databases are usually established by first entering and selecting the data (including the column labels) and then selecting a database command on the appropriate menu. In the case of Excel, the menu is the Data menu and the command is Set Database (see fig. 11.23). After you select this command, the database is automatically defined.

Until the database is defined, you cannot perform any database operations. Any time new records are added to the database, it must be redefined.

Sorting a Database

Sorting is an often-used tool that is not limited to databases. In figure 11.24, the records that are part of the Employee Records database are highlighted and then sorted alphabetically by selecting the Sort command from the Data menu. Most databases automatically sort on the first field (in this case, Last Name), but most can sort on any field, or they can "nest" sorts within fields. You can sort the field Years at the company within the field Gender, for example.

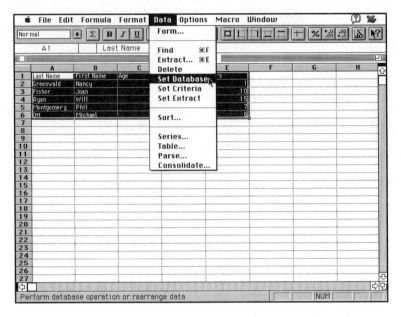

Fig. 11.23
Defining a database after selecting the cells in the worksheet.

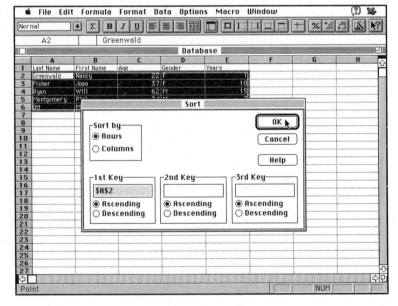

Fig. 11.24
Sorted records and the dialog for choosing sort criteria.

W hen you highlight information in a database, make sure that you highlight only what you need to use. If you are defining the database, you must select column headings because you need these headings if you want to find and extract information. If you are sorting a column, however, you do not want to sort the column heading and therefore do not want to include the column heading in the selection.

Finding and Extracting Information

After your database is established, you can use spreadsheet tools to find specific records. In the Employee Records database, for example, suppose that you want to find all the records for females. To find these records, you have to select all the records that have an F in the Gender field.

All search efforts through a database require that you tell your database what the criteria are for the search. A criterion can be thought of as a filter through which you pass the data. Data is allowed to pass through if it meets certain conditions, such as listing the first name as Joan or listing time as more than 5 years. A criterion can be located anywhere on the worksheet outside of the database range. In this case, you add a criterion in another location on the spreadsheet, as you see in figure 11.25. In the same figure, you can see that the criterion range is selected and then designated as the criterion for searching through or extracting records. The criteria range includes headings drawn from the database headings; the headings must match those of the database although you do not have to use all of the headings, only the ones you need. The criteria range also includes some values (such as F), as you see in figure 11.26. After this criterion is entered, you then can choose the Find command from the Data menu to select the first matching record.

When the criteria are designated and the Find command is chosen, Excel highlights the first matching record. You then can use the up and down arrows to move to other matches in your database.

You can combine criteria as well. What if you want to locate the records of the men who have worked for the company for more than 10 years, for example? You use two criteria: Gender is equal to M and Years is more than 10 (written as >10). Excel then selects the records that fit the criteria (see fig. 11.27).

Fig. 11.25
Selecting and defining a criterion range in a database.

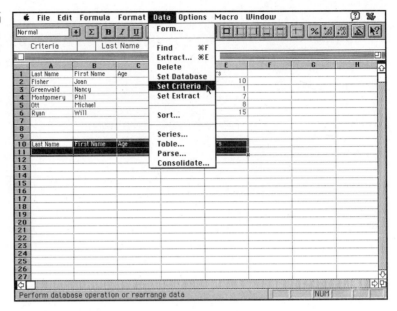

Fig. 11.26
The first record matching the criteria is highlighted.

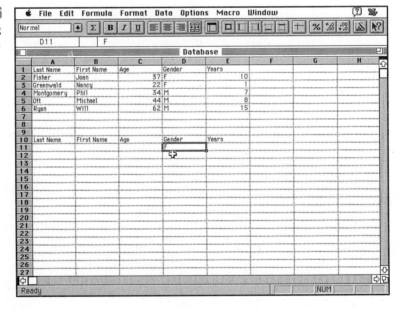

Fig. 11.27
The record is highlighted.

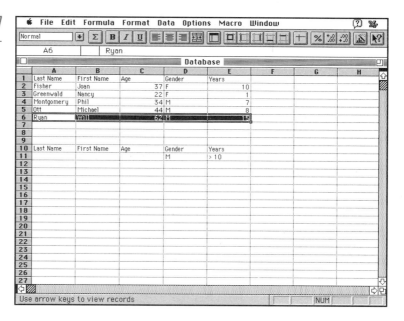

Finally, in figure 11.28, a new area (the extract range) is defined where records that meet the criteria can be extracted.

Fig. 11.28
Extracting information
based on the criteria range.

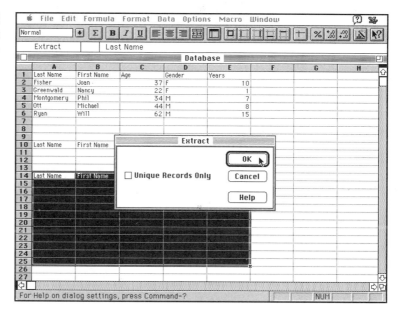

You choose the Extract command as in figure 11.28 and the records that meet the gender criteria of Female are reproduced in the extract range. Data is extracted by Excel when you reproduce the exact name of the field in another part of the worksheet. Excel looks for the records that meet the criteria, selects the fields of the records that match the criteria, extracts these records, and places them in the area you have previously defined in the worksheet.

Creating Macros and Using Macro Languages

As spreadsheet users' demands for more flexibility have increased, the designers of spreadsheet programs have tried to meet these needs by including "languages," which you can use to have spreadsheet programs perform specific tasks.

The designers of Lotus 1-2-3 developed a language, for example, that allows you to use commands to have 1-2-3 perform certain functions. Figure 11.29 shows a script that automatically labels columns A, B, and C with the names of the three months in the first quarter.

Fig. 11.29

A simple Lotus 1-2-3 script.

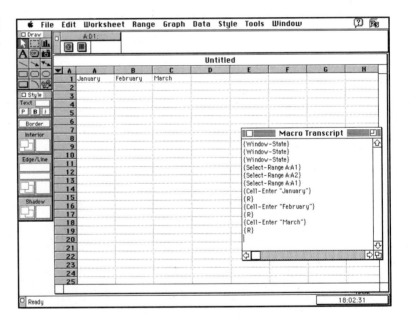

The command {Select-Range A:A1} selects cell A1 in sheet A (1-2-3 is able to handle three dimensional spreadsheets and labels them alphabetically). Then {Cell-Enter "January"} enters the text "January" in the cell. Finally {R} moves to the right one cell. This example is simple but can easily be applied to other situations.

Lotus maintains the Macro Transcript at all times. You can view the commands you have performed while working with the worksheet. You also can copy the desired commands into your worksheet to build a macro.

Having the Macro Transcript makes learning the macro language of 1-2-3 easier. You can perform the commands you wish to incorporate into a macro, and then view and copy the macro commands for the operations you performed.

Excel also has a comprehensive macro command language that enables you to customize a worksheet to fit some very specific needs. You can enter text to create a prompt into a macro sheet, for example, and then run the macro. While these kinds of operations are more advanced, all you need is the commitment to use them and practice. You will be amazed at what you can do.

Several stand-alone macro packages also are available. Individual's Power macros for Excel, for example, allows you to do such things as the following:

- Automate databases
- Create mailing lists and invoices
- Automate charting
- Eliminate errors
- Generate loan payment schedules

These macros and many others are available at the touch of a key combination, making Excel (or other spreadsheet programs and macro sets) even more powerful than the program can be alone.

Assessing Compatibility among Spreadsheet Programs

Like word processing files, you can transfer worksheet files from one spreadsheet application to another, but you may be limited by the export capability of the program itself. You might want to take a table you created in Excel and use it in WordPerfect, for example.

Because Lotus 1-2-3 for DOS is so popular, many Macintosh applications allow you to import and translate 1-2-3 DOS worksheets—especially 1-2-3 for Macintosh. You can always save a spreadsheet as a text file, of course, and then transfer the file to another application.

Translating the format of a worksheet file most often consists of selecting a command from the File menu. In the case of Excel, the Save As command leads you to the file formats you see in figure 11.30. With the worksheet active, selecting any one of those file formats saves the file in the new format. The file is now ready to be "read" by another application, depending on the format that application can read.

Fig. 11.30
Choosing a different file
format in Excel.

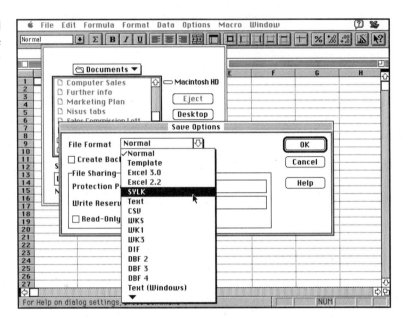

More and more spreadsheet developers also are building these tools so that they can read files created with other spreadsheet applications. Lotus 1-2-3 for Macintosh can easily read Microsoft Excel files, for example. The latest versions of many spreadsheet programs also can communicate to entirely different platforms, such as Excel's support for DEC, UNIX, Windows, and OS/2 systems. This feature may not seem important for the hobbyist, but being able to share data with established business equipment such as a VAX or PC is a long-awaited blessing for the people who have Macs on their desks.

One of the problems you can encounter in any file transfer is that functions and formulas may not always stay intact. That is, although the cell entries may transfer, the actual contents of the cell may not. Make a practice of testing a newly transferred spreadsheet to ensure that it works properly.

Excel for the Macintosh and Excel for Windows are remarkably similar. Microsoft, the developer of Excel, provides a file format that enables you to go directly from one to the other and preserve most, if not all, formula and function entries. Users of Lotus 1-2-3 in DOS also will appreciate the compatibility between the DOS and Macintosh versions.

Considering Smaller Spreadsheet Programs

This chapter has concerned itself primarily with the two largest spreadsheet programs. Most users of spreadsheet programs are business oriented and looking for the power of the larger packages. Many home users may want to make use of spreadsheet programs, however, but do not want to have to invest in high-powered and high-priced programs. Fortunately, many lower-end packages are avaiable.

You also can consider an integrated package such as ClarisWorks (see Chapter 13 "Using Integrated Software"). These packages contain smaller, easy to use spreadsheet modules that have all that the power home or small business users need without all the high-powered features—and high-powered price—meant for larger offices. Another inexpensive alternative is BiPlane (see fig. 11.31).

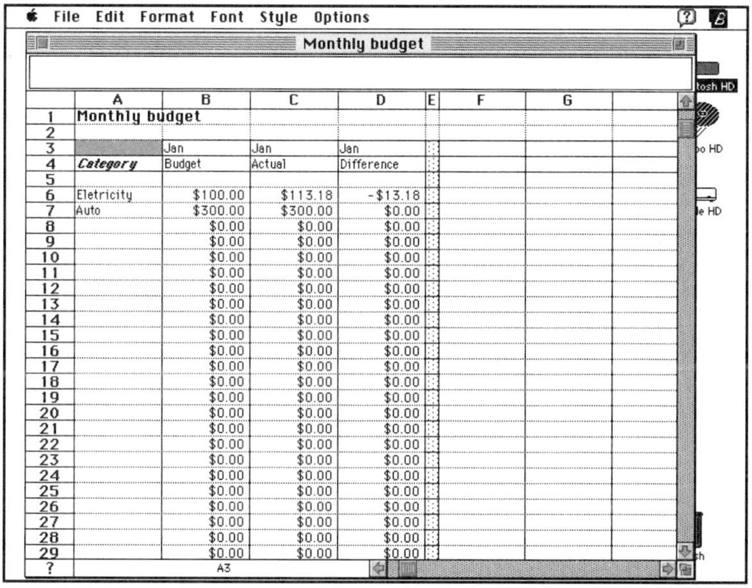

Fig. 11.31
A monthly budget being prepared in BiPlane.

This spreadsheet program started as shareware but is moving towards being a full commercial package in power. BiPlane has over 100 functions, 8 customizable charts, and full support of Macintosh fonts and font styles. This inexpensive package by Night Diamonds Software is well-suited for the home and home business user who needs a basic spreadsheet but does not need all the "bells and whistles" of the larger packages.

The Big Mac Recommendation

Perhaps the most important factor in choosing a spreadsheet program is that more than 70 percent of people using a spreadsheet program on the Macintosh use Microsoft Excel. This means that Excel has more support, more articles written about it in popular periodicals such as *MacUser* and *MacWorld*, more available add-ons (such as task-specific spreadsheet utilities), and more competition for sales (meaning lower prices for you).

On the other hand, Lotus 1-2-3 offers graphics capabilities that Excel cannot touch, plus a programming language that can be very useful for personalizing applications and making the program highly user-responsive. Also, if you are a business user who is adding Macintoshes to a previously all-PC installation using 1-2-3, you can reduce the amount of time your employees spend learning the new system by choosing 1-2-3 for the Macintosh. 1-2-3 Macintosh offers several features to make the transition easier, such as the capability to call up and use the DOS version's command menu in the Macintosh version. File sharing between the DOS and Macintosh version is very easy.

Home and home business users might want to look at ClarisWorks (an integrated package) or BiPlane. Both programs are easier to use than Excel and 1-2-3 Macintosh, but are quite powerful.

CHAPTER TWELVE

Using Databases

ustomers' names, addresses, purchase records, buying habits, and sales dates represent just a small part of the information that businesses need to track. Fortunately, software tools called *database management systems* (sometimes abbreviated DBMS) can help. These systems range from simple to complex.

Although you can keep track of large sets of data with a spreadsheet program, a database program has one major advantage: a database treats each collection of related data (called a *record*) as an independent unit. This feature provides great flexibility when you are formatting, searching, sorting, and manipulating data.

Understanding Databases

A database is a list of information organized into functionally related files that facilitate manipulation and retrieval. Your telephone book, for example, is a database of names, addresses, and telephone numbers. The phone book is organized by name. Your real estate agent also has a database—a list of properties, organized by address. The real estate agent's database uses the same information that's in your telephone book, simply arranged in a different way.

The term *database* refers to the data itself; the database management system is the tool that binds or organizes the data. Although database management systems differ (examples include Acius's 4th Dimension, Microsoft's FoxBase+/Mac, Helix Technology's Double Helix, Blyth Software's Omnis Seven, and Claris's FileMaker Pro), you can use—and program—the systems for specific purposes, such as generating payroll reports or keeping track of baseball batting averages. (In fact, you can keep track of batting averages in a database and include a picture of the third baseman!) The *database form* is a skeleton into which you can incorporate information from a particular record.

Understanding Fields, Records, and Files

A database management system enables you to organize information in a logical fashion so that you can manipulate it as necessary. All databases are organized into three levels: fields, records, and files. A *field* is an individual piece of data, such as a last name, a first name, an address, sales per year, or the name of a student. A *record* is a collection of fields, such as the last name, first name, and address of a client. A *file* is a collection of records. You can manipulate each record individually. This characteristic distinguishes a database from a spreadsheet.

NOTE   Some database management systems use different terms. These systems call files *relations,* and they call a set of relations a *collection.*

Suppose that a kite shop owner needs to keep track of the following information:

> Account number
> Name
> Street address
> City
> State
> ZIP code
> Phone number
> Type of kite preferred
> Date of last purchase

This example contains nine different fields. Entries for one customer in the nine fields make up a record. In turn, a set of customer records makes up a file.

A calculated field's contents are a function of an operation involving two other fields (for example, balance due multiplied by interest rate). Calculated fields are similar to spreadsheet cells that contain formulas.

Not all the fields in a record have to contain information. Figure 12.1, for example, shows the format for a record from a sample database.

Fig. 12.1
A record form in a database.

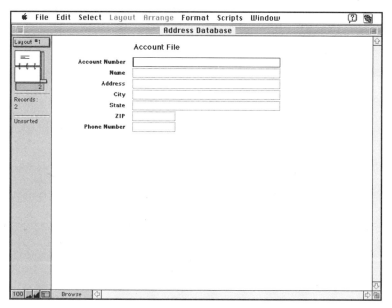

The essence of a database is that it can take information contained in fields and records and manipulate that information in a variety of ways, including sorting, extracting information to be used in another file, setting criteria that identify certain records, and so on.

Database management systems can hold enormous amounts of data. Acius's 4th Dimension, for example, can hold millions of records.

Comparing Flat-File and Relational-File Databases

Different types of databases enable you to keep track of information in various formats. The two database types covered in this section are flat-file and relational-file. The names refer to how the databases can handle information.

Flat-file databases enable you to work with just one file at a time. In a *relational-file database*, you can work with more than one file at a time—in essence, relating one file to another. Flat-file databases have been around longer than relational-file databases, but the latter are more powerful and flexible. Most of today's stand-alone database programs are relational.

Flat-File Databases

A flat-file database consists of individual files with no connections to any other files. Consider a standard manila file folder that contains invoices. In database terminology, the individual items in each invoice are fields, each invoice is a record, and the manila file folder is the actual database file. Flat-file databases tend to be less complicated and generally easier to use than relational-file databases are (see fig. 12.2).

Fig. 12.2

A flat-file database.

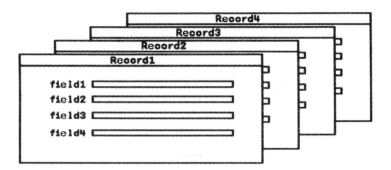

The two types of flat-file databases are memory-resident and disk-based. A *memory-resident database* keeps your data file in RAM (hence, the database is memory-resident). You can access memory-resident data files quickly. A *disk-based database* tends to be slower than a memory-resident database, because a disk-based system constantly is reading from and writing to your disk. An advantage of using a disk-based database, however, is that you can create and use large files. In a memory-resident database, file size is limited to what your available RAM can hold.

Two examples of good flat-file database programs are the Microsoft Works database application, which is memory-resident; and FileMaker Pro (from Claris), which is disk-based. Both databases are easy to set up and use. FileMaker Pro even enables you to use a picture as a field. Imagine a household inventory or a sales catalog that displays items as well as describes them.

Relational-File Databases

Unlike a flat-file database, a relational-file database contains multiple files with one or more linked fields, enabling you to update or add information to many files at the same time. For this linking to take place, you need a key field. A *key field* is a field that is common to all records and that keeps track of the related records (see fig. 12.3).

Fig. 12.3
A relational-file database
containing key fields.

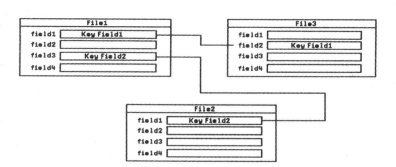

You may want to use a relational-file database instead of a flat-file database for several reasons. The main reason, of course, is that you can relate files to one another. Another reason is the flexibility of relational-file databases. Generally, these databases also provide a scripting language with which you can create a program to automate the database and provide special menus.

The current big hitters among relational-file database programs are 4th Dimension, FoxBase+, Omnis, and Double Helix. Omnis and 4th Dimension are not as easy to use as flat-file database programs are, but they can do almost everything that you need a database package to do. In addition to performing the standard database functions, 4th Dimension and Omnis can access a mainframe's database, download the data, perform complex mathematical analysis, and generate graphs of the result.

One measure of a product's success is the number of add-ons that the product inspires. *Add-ons* are programs that work with other programs, and 4th Dimension seems to have its own following. TrueForms (from Adobe), for example, enables you to print forms from within 4th Dimension. After Hours Software offers Quickhelp for 4th Dimension, an on-line reference guide for 4th Dimension's powerful programming language. Other companies offer tools that you can use to develop relational-file databases. One such product is Easy4D (from Natural Intelligence), which simplifies and speeds development of 4th Dimension databases.

For this kind of power, you can expect to pay a price. The main price (other than the cost of the package) is the complexity of using a powerful database program. Over time, however, database programs have become easier to use; Double Helix and Omnis Seven have improved dramatically and now are rated as easy to use, and 4th Dimension was developed specifically for the Macintosh. In all three programs, however, the term *easy to use* is relative. Any sophisticated package will have a learning curve with which you must deal.

Because of the power and expense of relational-file database programs, sharing them on a network, where everyone in an office can use them, makes sense. If you find that relational-file database programs such as 4th Dimension and Omnis Seven are too big, you have alternatives such as FileForce from Acius.

When you look at FileForce, you get the impression that it is intended to compete with FileMaker, one of the easiest-to-use flat-file database programs around. Unlike FileMaker, FileForce is relational-file (although not as powerful as 4th Dimension). Also unlike FileMaker, FileForce enables you to search by example; to store to 511 fields per file and up to 16 million records per file; and to access eight types of built-in business graphics.

FileForce's screens are clear and to the point; creating a database is as simple as selecting fields and naming them. The program comes with extremely well-written documentation and includes a large tutorial that actually is a program demo. FileForce is not a watered-down version of 4th Dimension; FileForce can stand on its own. This program is highly recommended if you want to go beyond a flat-file database program but don't need all the power of a really big DBMS. FileForce is intuitive in design and sure to please.

Choosing a Database Program

Following are some questions you should ask about a database management program before you purchase one:

■ *How easily can you integrate files in the database?* A relational-file database program should enable you to integrate existing data files easily, which saves you the trouble of reentering information. You may run a business, for example, in which you have several different files that contain information about clients. If you have a relational-file program, you can identify each file by account number rather than by name, address, phone number, and so on. Efficient database programs enable you to relate information among files so that you need not duplicate data.

■ *How easily can you import and export data?* Suppose that you have taken over a business whose 6,000-record mailing list was created with Microsoft Works, and you want to import that mailing list into your new DBMS program. If the 6,000 records are in a form that your database program can understand, you surely will save time.

■ *Does the program provide sufficient security?* Security most often is provided through the use of a password. Does the DBMS program offer different levels of passwords with different levels of access? (You might want one level for the average user, another for whoever enters and edits data, and still another for the administrator of the database.)

■ *Does the relational-file database program reduce data redundancy?* If you don't have to include the same information in a variety of files to access and integrate data, you save time. Highly integrated database programs also reduce complexity by reducing redundant entries.

■ *Does the database come with a supply of templates and predesigned forms?* (Even better, can you customize these templates for your own purposes?) Predesigned forms can help you quickly create the database you need by providing a format that already contains needed information and formatting.

■ *How simple is the programming language?* Programming language is the downfall of many new database users. Double Helix is said to be a database management system for nonprogrammers.

Because Double Helix is in part graphically based, developing a database in this program is easy. Another easy-to-use, graphically oriented program is Easy4D, which you can use to create 4th Dimension databases. Acius also offers development aids such as 4D XREF.

■ *Can you edit and add records easily?* After you create a database, you may find that you need to add a field. A good DBMS enables you to add that information without disrupting the organization of existing records.

■ *How well does the program manage data entry?* A good database program facilitates the formatting of input and output files, simplifying data entry and enabling you to match your database reports with other documents.

Creating a Database

This section discusses points that you should consider in creating a database, using FileMaker Pro as an example. Although FileMaker Pro databases may appear to be simple, the steps you follow to create them apply to all database management systems. In general, the only two steps are designing the form (including all the fields you want to use) and adding the records that make up the file. After that, the power of the database takes over.

Designing a Database

Many people make a good living designing databases. Designing a database, however, is not easy, even if you have some experience. You must be sure that you have organized your information so that examining the relationships among various elements is easy.

Whether you are designing your first or your fiftieth database, your job will be easier if you adhere to the following guidelines:

■ *List the information that you want to include in the database.* Be sure to include all information that you may want to use, such as first name, last name, street address, city, state, and ZIP code. Although you can add items at any time, including them when you create the database is preferable. Keep in mind, however, that the more information you add, the larger the database becomes and the more processing power your program and machine need to work in an efficient manner.

■ *Use as many fields as you need, but not so many that the data becomes confusing and unmanageable.* If you have too few fields, you cannot break down the information to perform necessary analysis. If you have too many fields, managing all the information can be an overwhelming task. You want the balance to be just right. You need enough fields to enable you to get what you need from the database. If, for example, you need to sort by size preference, don't place size information in a field called Preference that also includes color. Create a field called Size so that the information has a unique place in the database.

■ *Use specific terms for field names.* A bookstore owner, for example, might want to keep track of customer preferences. The owner might organize a database with the following fields:

Field	Entry
Name	Linda Frankel
Address	4401 Widge Way
City	Queens
State	NY
ZIP	12345
Preference	Mystery

A more complete database, which requires more fields, could be as follows:

Field	Entry
Last Name	Frankel
First Name	Linda
Address	4401 Widge Way, Queens, NY 12345
Preference	Mystery
First Author	Paretsky
Second Author	Andrews
Editions	First American

■ *Use graph paper (or a spreadsheet) to create a table of the fields you want to use in your database, in the order in which they should appear.* This procedure helps you organize your database, because you can check the table to make sure that your data is organized logically. The City field, for example, should follow Street Address, and fields that you use only occasionally should be listed last. Although the Macintosh is by nature a visual machine, and although all good databases walk you through the process of creating a database form, a little planning never hurts the process.

If you are creating a relational database, also consider the following:

■ *Create as many tables as you will have files that you want to relate to one another.* These tables should show you the relationships among parts of various files.

■ *Avoid entering the same data in more than one file or in more than one place in a file.* Data redundancy is a waste of space and energy.

■ *All files that will be linked should have common fields.* You can use the common field in each data file to link the files.

Creating a Database File

The first step in creating a database is creating the file in which records will be stored. You then can begin to create fields in the database records.

Figure 12.4 shows a FileMaker Pro Entry Options dialog, which enables you to set the attributes of the field you are creating.

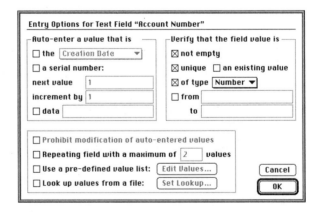

Fig. 12.4
The FileMaker Pro Field Options dialog.

Notice that in this example, the Not Empty, Unique, and Of Type options are selected and that the Number type has been chosen from the pop-up menu next to the Of Type option. These selections mean that the field in question is a required field (must contain text) and that entries in this field can consist only of numbers.

The next step is to create all the other fields that you will use in the database. You most likely would want to create a Client Name field to hold customer names, for example.

A client's name in this example is not as important a piece of information because this information will not be used for searching or any other organizational task, so the entire name is included in one field. If you want to sort by last name, the database needs to have separate fields for each part of the name.

Entering Data

After creating the data form, you enter data into each of the fields. Remember that a database is designed to enable you to access information at any time and in the form you need.

After you finish creating records in the form that you designed, your database is complete. You can begin using your database to search for particular records, to create custom programs, and to generate reports.

Searching for Records

When you need to locate records, you can use either the Find or Browse feature of a database program. Browse enables you to "flip" through the records, viewing each in turn. FileMaker Pro uses this metaphor for browsing by providing a flip-file icon that you can use to page from one record to the next (see fig. 12.5).

In figure 12.5, you see the number of records in the database (6) as well as the number of the record you are viewing (3).

The Find feature enables you to specify criteria that match certain records, narrowing the number you have to page through. In the bookstore example, you might want to find all customers who prefer science fiction. You could set up the Find feature as shown in figure 12.6.

Figure 12.7 shows the results of the search. Notice that the program displays the first record found and indicates that two records were found that match the criteria. You can flip through these records, using the flip-file icon.

Flip-file icon

Fig. 12.5
Choosing to view the next
record.

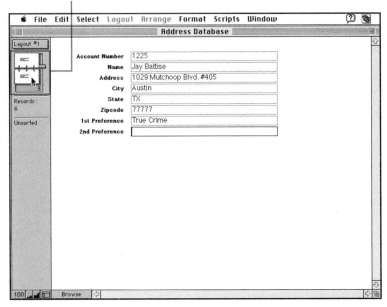

Fig. 12.6
Searching for science-
fiction customers.

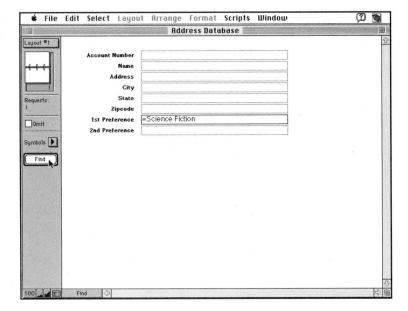

Fig. 12.7
The first record located is
displayed.

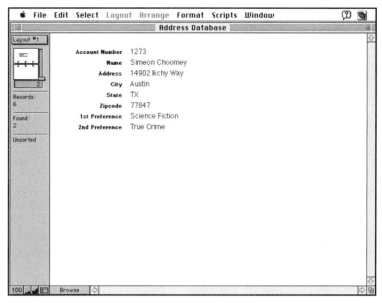

Creating a Layout

If all you could do with a database was search through records and view
them, the database would be of little use. Fortunately, layouts enable
you to print your data in various forms. To continue the bookstore
example, now that you have found the records you need, you decide
that you want to notify these customers of a new book that might be of
interest to them. You could use the Layout command to create a form to
print their name and addresses on envelopes (see fig. 12.8).

The example program, FileMaker Pro, provides many tools that help you
create layouts. Figure 12.8 shows several tools, including graphics tools
(rectangles, lines, and ovals), a text tool, and color and pattern tools.

Moving fields around in a layout is easy; you merely drag them on-
screen. The fields automatically align to a grid, which makes creating the
layout simple.

Importing and Exporting Records

If you have a word processing program with mail-merge capability, you
can use your database to create a merge file that places your customers'
names and addresses in a letter.

Fig. 12.8
Creating a layout for
envelope addressing.

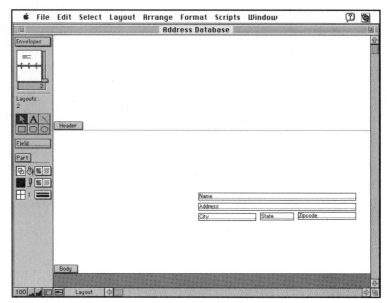

The import feature can perform the reverse operation. If you have been using the mail-merge feature of a word processing program to maintain a client list, you can create the necessary fields in your database program and then import the mail-merge file, so that you don't need to type the information into each record.

Using Small Databases

An alternative to a full-fledged database management system is a desk accessory such as QuickDEX from Greene, Inc. QuickDEX is billed as a "random data organizer" that you can use to organize and retrieve information quickly. (You can search through 1,000 records in fewer than 2 seconds.) If the information for which you are searching is a telephone number, and if you have a modem, QuickDEX can retrieve and then dial the number for you. If you don't have a modem, you can hold the telephone receiver to the Mac speaker and let the tones do the dialing for you. This feature is not a DBMS function but a nice convenience nevertheless.

Figure 12.9 shows a screen from another database desk accessory: Preferred Publishers' DAtabase, which contains several modules and a tutorial. DAtabase enables you to create a complete flat-file database.

Fig. 12.9

The opening screen of a
stock-analysis database
created by DAtabase.

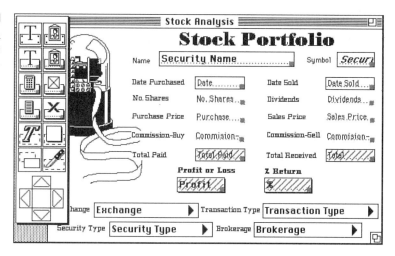

DAtabase contains worthwhile features, including a complete and friendly graphic interface, phone-dialing capability, and HyperCard-like design options for designing backgrounds and linking records. Unlike HyperCard, however, DAtabase has no scripting capability.

Retriever II from Exodus is an exceptionally easy-to-use desk accessory for database management. Retriever II comes with several sample files, including a mortgage-analysis calculator (see fig. 12.10), conversion databases for distance and temperature, and a database of the moons surrounding the planets in our solar system.

Fig. 12.10

A sample Retriever II
database.

Retriever II

File : Calculator – Mortgage

Rec	✓	Principle	Interest Rate	# of Pmnts	Payment	Total Payout
1		100000.00	5.0000	360	536.82	193255.78
2		100000.00	5.5000	360	567.79	204404.04
3		100000.00	6.0000	360	599.55	215838.19
4		100000.00	6.5000	360	632.07	227544.49
5		100000.00	7.0000	360	665.30	239508.90
6		100000.00	7.5000	360	699.21	251717.22
7		100000.00	8.0000	360	733.76	264155.25
8		100000.00	8.5000	360	768.91	276808.85
9		100000.00	9.0000	360	804.62	289664.14
10		100000.00	9.5000	360	840.85	302707.51
11		100000.00	10.0000	360	877.57	315925.77
12		100000.00	10.5000	360	914.74	329306.15
13		100000.00	11.0000	360	952.32	342836.42

13 | 0 |

Using Specialized Databases

Many people need a particular data-management tool and don't want to fuss with creating their own database management systems. Several programs are available that enable you to manipulate specific kinds of information rather than create a database from general database tools.

Graphical Databases

Filevision IV from TSP Software offers an interesting approach to data management. The package is sold as a business tool—a multilayer integrated database and drawing program. Filevision differs from other database packages in that it enables you to work with information presented as pictures as well as numbers. At heart, Filevision is a database; its capabilities include sorting and adding records. You can use Filevision's drawing feature, for example, to create a housing plan in which you click buttons to indicate a house model, which in turn produces a floor plan of a particular house.

Bibliographical Databases

EndNote Plus from Niles Associates stores and manages bibliographic references. For users such as researchers, lawyers, and academic types, who spend much of their time dealing with such information, EndNote Plus is a worthwhile investment. EndNote Plus comes as a desk accessory, as a full-blown program, and a plug-in module for Microsoft Word users.

A competing product is Pro-Cite by Personal Bibliographic Software. Pro-Cite, however, is a high-priced program that is noted for being difficult to use.

Another specialized database from Niles is Grant Manager, a checkbook-like database-and-spreadsheet combination that helps you manage private and federal grants by keeping track of accounts, payments, and related activities. When the month (or year) is over, you can print a record of all transactions. With Grant Manager, you can manage up to 32,000 references (for those long papers), and you can format your references in any of nine formats (such as American Psychological Association style or *The Chicago Manual of Style* format).

Contact Managers

Name-and-address managers (often called *contact managers*) seem to have caught on well. Don't be surprised to find specific contact-management packages such as MacPhonebook (from Synex), Address Book Plus from PowerUp), and TouchBase 2.0 (from After Hours Software).

MacPhonebook provides import and export capabilities, a label-printing feature, a calendar, personal-information trackers, and dial tools for modems (see fig. 12.11). You also can print in a variety of formats, including output that fits the little black book that Synex provides, making it very easy to keep your daybook up to date. You even can print in a format that fits those wonderful DayTimers, FiloFaxes, and similar books.

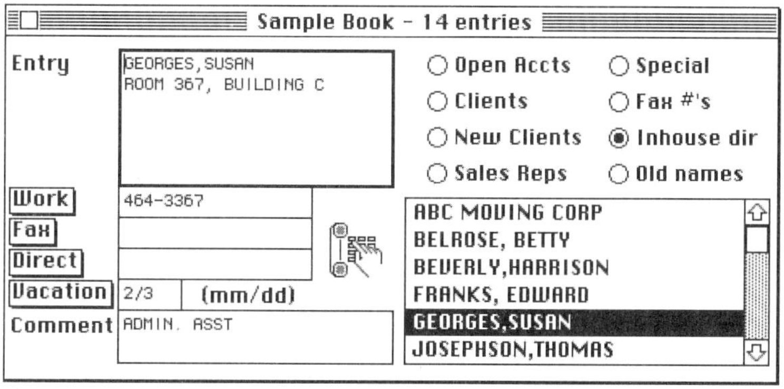

Fig. 12.11
A MacPhonebook screen.

Address Book Plus enables you to enter a comprehensive collection of vital information (see fig. 12.12).

Address Book Plus is extremely useful, especially because you can use the Dialer desk accessory to dial anyone listed in Address Book Plus files from within another program.

Appointment Managers

Personal computers have made generating reports and filing data easier, but people sometimes forget where they are supposed to be—and when. *Appointment managers* are specialized database programs created to correct that problem. These programs are similar to the three-inch-thick day planner you carry around to remember when to feed the kids. With this type of Mac program, however, you don't have to buy a new day planner every year.

Fig. 12.12
An Address Book Plus
screen.

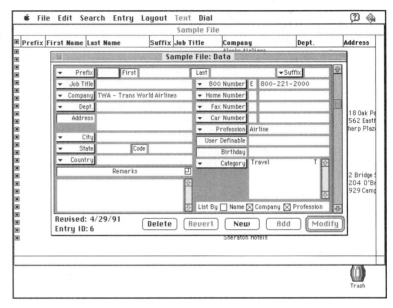

Now Software offers one of the best appointment managers available: Now Up-To-Date (see fig. 12.13).

Fig. 12.13
Adding an appointment in
Now Up-To-Date.

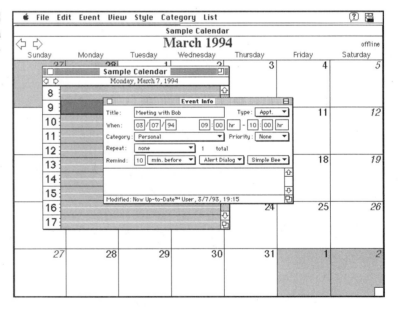

The program enables you to create various categories for your appointments, enter "to do" items that are carried forward automatically until you mark them done, enter repeating appointments, and even set an alarm to warn you of an appointment's approach.

Business users whose office Macintoshes are networked will want to take a close look at this package. Now Up-To-Date enables you to maintain a public calendar that all network users share. A department meeting could be scheduled and set to appear in the calendars of all department members. Employees could enter off-site appointments (or even days off) and the public calendar would notify everyone. A Reminder System extension is included to announce appointments even when the calendar program is not running.

CE Software offers Alarming Events, a personal scheduler in the form of a desk accessory. Alarming Events uses single-day, five-day, and calendar windows to organize and keep track of appointments. You can use the program to remind you about an appointment later (if you're busy the first time it reminds you), to keep detailed notes of diary entries, and to import and export files. To remind you of appointments, Alarming Events can be programmed to bark like a dog or sound like a cuckoo clock.

Visionary's First Things First, a System extension, is interesting and useful. The extension's icon can "float" on your Desktop, so as to be available at all times, or you can have the extension place its commands in the menu bar along with a calendar/clock. To open the calendar, you can press a command-key sequence, double-click the floating icon, or double-click the menu bar.

Sometimes, great things come in little packages, as is the case with MTM (MyTimeManager). This scheduler offers some terrific tools, including a clock and cyclical tracking of tasks.

Another appointment manager is FastTrack Scheduler (from AEC). This comprehensive program facilitates scheduling projects and appointments. You can organize project charts by date across the top axis and by task along the side axis.

Grade Managers

If you're in the grading business—as a teacher, trainer, or boss—several database programs can help you. Teacher's Rollbook (from Blyth Software) covers the entire range of activities involved in managing student records, including grades, addresses, attendance, and follow-ups. You can sort grades, assign weights to different assignments, create composites, and even roll the information over into a new file.

Figure 12.14 shows MicroGrade (from Chariot), another powerful grade-management tool that enables you to work with data in a variety of formats.

Fig. 12.14
A sample MicroGrade screen.

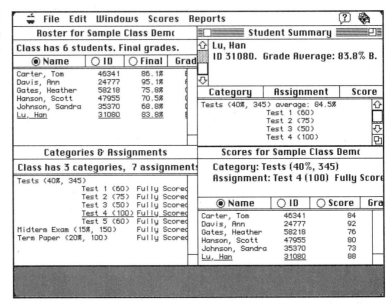

Chariot also offers MicroTest, which enables you to create and manage test items, as shown in figure 12.15. If you're in the business of creating tests that you have to revise repeatedly, MicroTest can be a valuable tool.

Client and Employee Managers

You can use any flat-file database or one of the name and address tools described in this chapter to manage your files, but ABRA 2000 (from Abra MacDabra) can do a better job. This program is a full-fledged database program that runs under FoxBase (which you don't need to buy, because ABRA 2000 comes with a run-time version of FoxBase).

ABRA 2000 also comes with a slew of features, including the capability to generate reports. As you work, the program takes you through a series of menus. ABRA 2000 also enables you to sort by date, name, salary level, department, and so on.

Also from Abra MacDabra is AbraTrak, which you can use to track job applicants. AbraTrak's many features include estimating costs associated with hiring, searching applications for specific skills, generating form letters, analyzing referrals, and completing affirmative-action reports.

Fig. 12.15

A sample MicroTest screen.

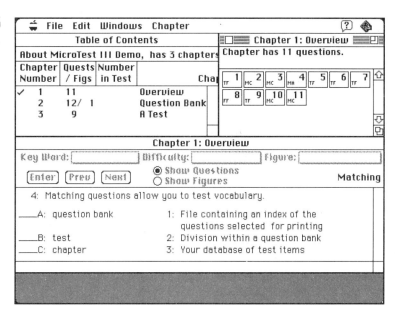

Managing employee information certainly is enough of a headache, but on top of that, you have to keep track of client information. CLIENTmac from Software Complement can help. CLIENTmac (like more and more programs) comes compressed and decompresses when you start it. CLIENTmac uses StuffIt, which is licensed by Aladdin Systems. (For more information about disk compression, refer to Chapter 4.) With CLIENTmac, you can set up a client database and then use search tools to find what you need, manipulate files, print reports, and write form letters.

The Big Mac Recommendation

Home and small-business users should consider FileMaker Pro, which is easy to use yet provides considerable power, and files can be shared with Microsoft Windows users. You can use this program to create and maintain client lists, employee records, or household inventories, and to produce reports of various kinds.

Larger businesses will want to look at larger programs. Currently, the leader is 4th Dimension. Without doubt, 4th Dimension is the database program of choice for the Macintosh. You can use utilities such as Easy4D with 4th Dimension to develop databases quickly.

Users in mixed PC-and-Macintosh environments might want to take a look at FoxBase+ by Microsoft. FoxBase+, which is well known on the IBM PC side, may be a good choice if you use dBASE III or FoxBase databases on PCs and need to transfer those files to Macintoshes.

CHAPTER THIRTEEN

Using Integrated Software

Y ou just reviewed the features and flexibility of the big three: word processors, spreadsheets, and databases. Not everyone, however, needs to create a spreadsheet that contains hundreds of thousands of cells, and not everyone needs to search through 500 records to find a specific piece of data, such as the names of all men over 20 years of age. Nevertheless, most users require some combination of the features offered by the big three.

For these users, integrated software packages offer a set of applications that work together seamlessly. In addition, integrated software packages usually cost less than any of the big software packages discussed in the preceding three chapters. That may be an important reason why integrated packages such as ClarisWorks, Microsoft Works, and WordPerfect Works have become popular. This chapter introduces you to some of these packages and shows you how an integrated package works.

The Idea behind Integrated Packages

Often, you do not need all the features found in the three most powerful types of software: word processors, databases, and spreadsheets. You may be better served by an integrated package that contains several *components* of each type of software. These components are often referred to as *modules*. Each module performs a specific function. The word processing module, for example, enables you to work with documents. The characteristic that distinguishes an integrated package from other software is that the sharing of information among modules is seamless. The term *seamless* indicates that you can move easily from one module to another without worrying about file formats, memory restrictions, menu changes, and general compatibility.

Figures 13.1 and 13.2 show the interface for ClarisWorks and Microsoft Works, from which you can select one of several modules. You already know what the word processor, spreadsheet, and database can do. The communications module enables you to use your telephone lines to share data with others or to access bulletin boards. The drawing and graphics modules (in Microsoft Works and ClarisWorks, respectively), enable you to create drawings and other graphical documents.

Fig. 13.1
The opening ClarisWorks screen.

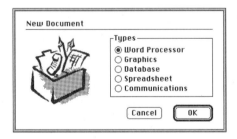

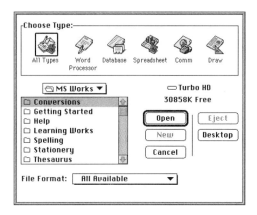

Fig. 13.2
The opening Microsoft
Works screen.

Integrated packages have the following benefits:

■ *The capacity to share data among modules.* Suppose, for example, that you create a database file of names and addresses. You
can then easily use a print merge feature to incorporate those
records into form letters that you created in the word processor
module.

■ *The ease of learning one interface.* Because the interface for each
module is the same, you don't have to learn three separate
programs—you can learn just one.

■ *File compatibility with high-end products.* Some products
maintain file compatibility with other Microsoft and Claris products, such as Microsoft Works and Excel, and ClarisWorks and
Resolve. Most users find that these integrated packages are a good
introduction to the products' more powerful "aunts" and "uncles."

ClarisWorks

ClarisWorks is an excellent integrated software package. This section
uses ClarisWorks as an example of a typical integrated system.
ClarisWorks includes the following five modules:

■ *Word processor.* A mid-level word processor, similar to MacWrite
Pro, that offers standard editing and file features such as Cut and
Paste. It also offers a spelling checker, automatic reformatting, and
automatic pagination.

- *Graphics.* A mid-level, object-oriented graphics module that enables you to create logos, floor plans, hierarchy charts, basic presentations, and other graphical documents.

- *Database.* A mid-level database, similar to FileMaker Pro, that lets you create records and perform such basic database functions as sorting and selecting. Various formats for reporting database information are available.

- *Spreadsheet.* A mid-level spreadsheet with mathematic, trigonometric, logic, and finance capabilities. Also includes capabilities for date, time, and special operations. You can then present the data in line, bar, stack, or scatter charts.

- *Communications.* A basic telecommunications program that enables you to share data with other computers, including on-line information services, other Macs, DOS-based machines, and even mainframes. ClarisWorks provides the conduit through which you communicate. The communications module also offers Hayes modem compatibility.

ClarisWorks can copy information from one module to another with little effort. The most common way to transfer information among documents is the familiar Cut-Copy-Paste routine via the Clipboard.

C larisWorks runs in about 900KB of memory and takes up about 750KB of disk space. (Auxiliary files stored in the System Folder such as the XTND translators, the Help system, communications tools, and the like can take over a megabyte, but these files are optional and can be discarded.) The compactness of the program makes ClarisWorks a good choice for users of smaller machines, such as the LC Macintoshes and PowerBooks. Compactness is a feature of integrated packages that you should consider if you have limited disk and memory space.

Transferring Information

Suppose that you have database information that you want to use in a letter you are writing. The beauty of an integrated package is that applications are constructed so that transferring data from one module to the other is simple and accurate. As an example, this section walks you through exporting database information to the word processing module.

Figure 13.3 shows the sample database that comes with ClarisWorks. This database displays information in a layout called Quarterly Sales by Category. Notice that ClarisWorks indicates a database by displaying (DB) in the title bar. This module includes the search, sort, and other functions that you would get in a stand-alone database package.

Fig. 13.3

The Quarterly Sales by Category layout in the sample database.

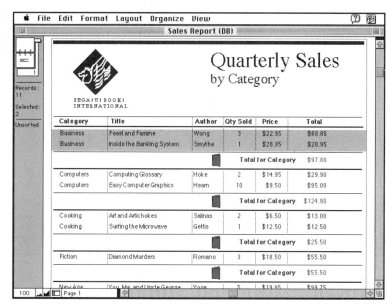

Suppose that you wrote a letter in the word processing module and want to include the database information in the letter. Figure 13.4 shows the open database (with DB in the title bar) and word processing document (with WP in the title bar). Figure 13.5 shows a letter that combines the word processed text with the database records.

Transferring data among modules, then, can be done by copying and pasting. Because you don't have to leave one module in order to enter another, the procedure is much easier—a significant benefit of any integrated package.

You can also access the database by the word processor through mail merge. You can select database fields to insert into a word processing document and then print letters, drawing information from a database without having to copy and paste the information (see fig. 13.6). The advantage to using the merge is that if you change information in the database, the word processing document is also updated automatically.

Fig. 13.4
Preparing to copy database
information into a letter.

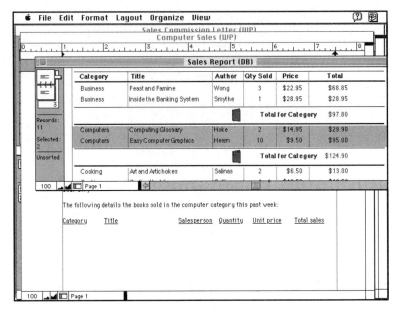

Fig. 13.5
A letter after database
material has been copied.

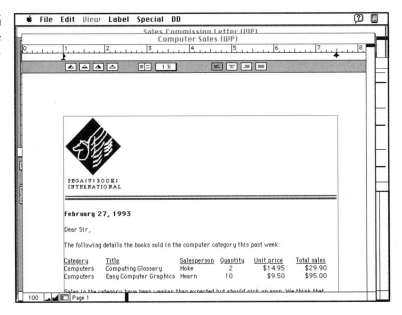

Figure 13.6 shows the Mail Merge dialog in ClarisWorks, which enables
you to choose which database fields you want to pull information from.

For example, to insert information from the Invoice Data field of the database into the letter, you click the name Invoice Date, and then click Insert Field.

Fig. 13.6

Inserting a database field
into a word processor
merge letter.

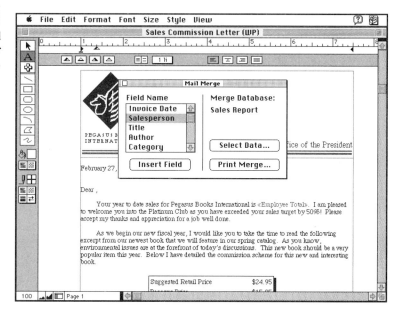

Considering Module Integration

The word processing module of ClarisWorks is similar to MacWrite Pro, Claris' main word processing program. Figure 13.7 shows a sample letter derived from one of the examples included with the program.

Look at the tools along the left of the screen in figure 13.7. You may already notice a similarity between the tools in the figure and others you saw in previous chapters. At the top is the Selection tool, indicated by the arrow. Then the Text tool, indicated by the letter A. Then the Spreadsheet tool. Below these three main tools, you see a collection of graphics tools.

Notice that the word processing module has tools from other modules. For example, you can add a small spreadsheet to the letter by clicking the Spreadsheet tool and drawing the spreadsheet on the letter (see fig. 13.8).

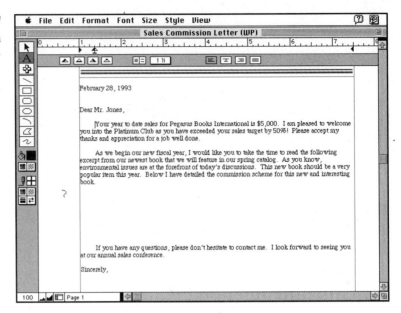

Fig. 13.7
A letter written in ClarisWorks.

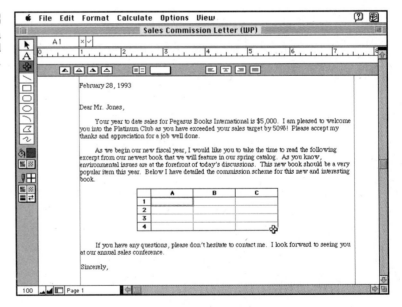

Fig. 13.8
A spreadsheet added to a letter in the word processing module.

To improve the aesthetic appearance of the spreadsheet, you might want to remove the column and row headings. You can make this change while still within the word processor. Notice that the menus in figure 13.8 are different from the menus in figure 13.7—you are now working with the spreadsheet module, even though you are working with a word processing document. Consequently, you can access spreadsheet menus such as Calculate and Options without ever leaving the word processor.

The Options menu contains the command you need to remove the row and column headings. Now you might look at the spreadsheet and decide that you want to add a graphic to further enhance the appearance of the letter. You can add a "shadow" by using the Rectangle tool (see fig. 13.9).

Fig. 13.9

Adding a shadow to the spreadsheet.

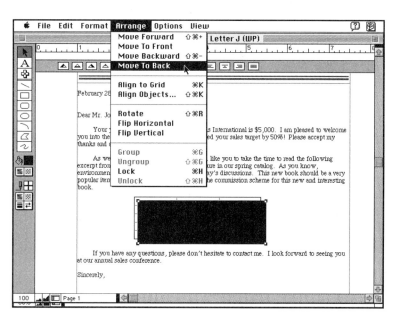

You can see that the menus change again. Now they contain graphics module menus, such as Arrange.

Throughout the modules, the same commands aid you in learning and working with the different modules. Figures 13.10 and 13.11 show the command for invoking the spelling checker in two different modules.

As you can see, the Spelling menu in the Edit menu is identical whether you are in the spreadsheet or word processing module. And the procedure for checking spelling is identical, too, regardless of which module you are using. This consistency is a hallmark of a high-quality integrated package and is the main advantage of owning one—especially if you are a new Macintosh user.

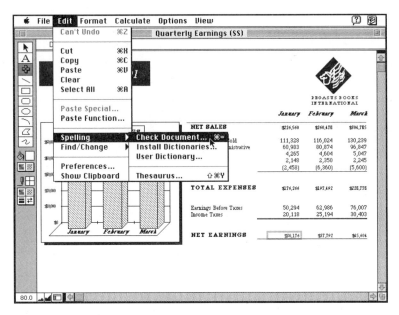

Fig. 13.10
Accessing the spelling
checker while in the
spreadsheet module.

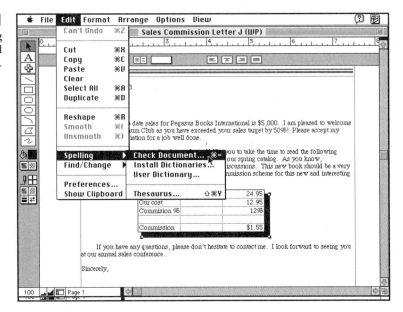

Fig. 13.11
Accessing the spelling
checker while in the word
processing module.

Surveying the Modules

ClarisWorks consists of five modules: word processor, graphics, database, spreadsheet, and communications. These modules are fairly representative of the different kinds of Macintosh software, and typical of integrated packages.

The word processing module is similar to the MacWrite Pro word processor offered by Claris. The word processor is mid-level in power, but sufficient for the beginning to average Macintosh user. This point would be especially true for the home user, but also for the small business user. Some features include a spelling checker and a thesaurus. The module supports multiple columns—up to nine. The ClarisWorks Mail Merge feature, as you have seen, enables you to pull information from the database as well as another word processing document.

The graphics module is an object-oriented environment and has seven object tools: Line, Rectangle, Rounded Rectangle, Oval, Arc, Polygon, and Free Hand (see fig. 13.12).

Fig. 13.12
The graphics module enables you to jazz up your documents.

Object tools—

The graphics module supports the use of color for the fill and pen patterns, and has 64 patterns from which you can choose, as well as several line widths and arrows. The menus for these items are *tear-offs*, which means that you can make the menus into palettes that float over your document (see fig. 13.13).

Fig. 13.13
The color, pattern, and
width tear-off palettes.

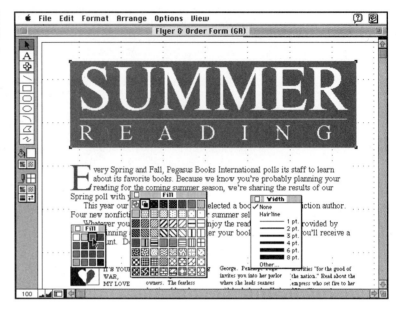

The spreadsheet module is a basic spreadsheet program with some 90
functions that you can use in formulas. The spreadsheet module also has
seven different chart types that you can create quickly (see fig. 13.14).
Figure 13.14 shows the dialog that enables you to create one of the
seven chart types.

Fig. 13.14
Creating a chart in the
spreadsheet module.

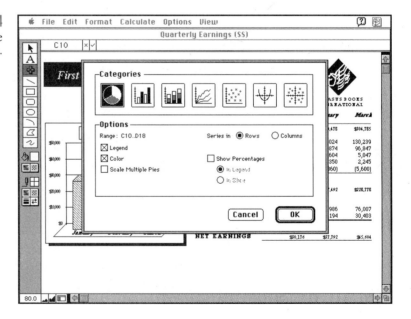

The database module is similar to FileMaker Pro and has the same ease of use as that program. You can create multiple layouts to display and report data in different ways, browse and enter data easily, match records by criteria you set, and sort records with multiple keys. Figure 13.15 shows the Sort Records dialog, which enables you to choose sort keys to use in sorting database records.

Fig. 13.15
Setting sort options in the database module.

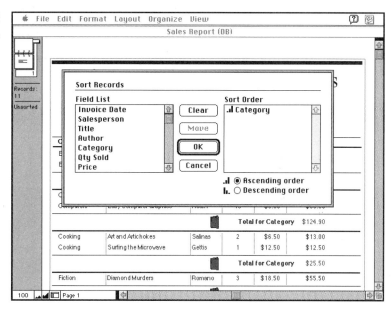

The communications module works with a modem, AppleTalk, or the serial port, enabling you to connect with other computers. Usually, you use the communications module with a modem. For example, you could use the communications module to connect with the CompuServe Information Service (see Chapter 17, "Using Communications Software").

You can, however, use the communications module to connect with another ClarisWorks user on an AppleTalk network. You can also connect to another Macintosh by connecting the serial ports (though you need a cable from your dealer to do this). In either case, you can transfer files back and forth (either over the network or over the cable), as well as with another computer user by typing.

Sharing Information with Other Programs

This book has explained how you can share information between the different ClarisWorks modules. ClarisWorks uses the XNTD technology to import and save files in many other program formats, including such popular programs as Microsoft Word, Microsoft Excel, Nisus, MacPaint, Microsoft Works, and others.

The Open, Insert, and Save As dialogs contain a pop-up menu from which you can choose several file formats (see fig. 13.16).

Fig. 13.16

Some file format options, with the PC format selected.

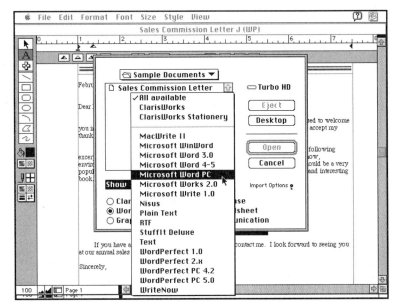

Moving to Stand-Alone Packages

One advantage of a good integrated package such as ClarisWorks is that you become familiar with the company's products and can transfer what you learn to the separate, larger packages if and when you need to move up to a more powerful program.

For example, if you start with ClarisWorks and learn how to use the word processing module, you can easily transfer what you know to the MacWrite Pro word processor offered by Claris. In only a short time, you will use the full potential of the program, because you do not have to relearn the entire program. Instead, you can concentrate on learning the more powerful features. Your files also are easily transferred to the new program because Claris assures that all programs manufactured by the company are compatible and can work with each other's file formats.

In the area of graphics, you can easily move up to MacDraw II or MacDraw Pro, both very powerful, object-oriented graphics programs. (MacDraw Pro is the more powerful of the two packages.)

The information that you learn in the database module can easily be applied to FileMaker Pro, which is just as easy to learn, because of the strong similarities between FileMaker Pro and the database module of ClarisWorks. (Of course, these similarities didn't just *happen*; the packages were designed to be similar.) Again, your files transfer easily.

With spreadsheets, you can move up to Resolve, Claris' full spreadsheet program, bringing your experience and files with you while adding more powerful features.

Any well-planned integrated package offers this kind of "upward compatibility," but Claris has gone to great lengths to assure consistency between products. This is one reason I always recommend Claris products—especially to the new user, who wants the introduction to the Macintosh to be a smooth, uncomplicated learning process without the hair-pulling that would occur with feature-laden, massive stand-alone packages.

Microsoft Works

Microsoft Works is one of the leading integrated packages, probably because of the Microsoft name.

While I find that some other products are more in line with my personal needs, there are reasons to consider a package such as Microsoft Works. Primarily, those who use Microsoft products at work may want to have a compatible program at home (although ClarisWorks has XTND translators that can make this a moot point in file sharing).

If you are already familiar with Word or Excel, for example, you may want to take advantage of your knowledge by purchasing a similar product for home use. And Microsoft Works may fit the bill perfectly.

Microsoft Works runs in about 1MB of memory, but takes up almost 4MB on disk. Almost 1MB of this disk space is consumed by the Help system, and the sample files are responsible for approximately half of 1MB. The sample files are optional and can be deleted to save disk space. Whether you delete them depends on how proficient you are in using the package.

Surveying the Modules

Like ClarisWorks, Microsoft Works has five modules. When you choose the New command from the File menu, you can choose to create one of the file document types (see fig. 13.17).

Fig. 13.17

The five modules in
Microsoft Works.

If you click the Show Stationery check box, the dialog in the figure expands to display a list box that shows stationery documents (predesigned documents) that you can open and use.

When you want to add graphics to a word processing document, you first need to switch to a draw layer. To switch quickly, you can click the Draw button in the tool palette, available at all times in both the word processing and drawing modules (see fig. 13.18).

Fig. 13.18

The Works word pro-
cessor has a separate
drawing layer.

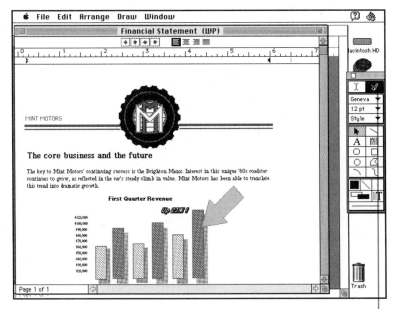

Draw
button

As you can see in the figure, the menus switch to the menus of the drawing module when you choose a drawing tool in the word processing module. Figure 13.19 shows the menus and tool palette of the drawing module, showing you the similarities that aid you in working with the different modules.

Fig. 13.19
Menus are consistent
between modules.

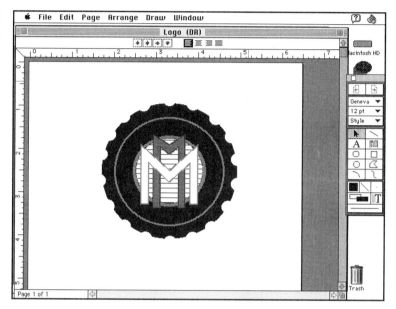

The spreadsheet module in Works offers a drawing and charting layer. The charting layer includes five types of charts, and you can customize those charts (see fig. 13.20).

The spreadsheet module in Works contains an impressive feature. You see that the available functions are grouped, and you receive automatic help—right down to manual page number references. Figure 13.21 shows how the Paste Function dialog displays a description of the selected function (NPV), even providing the page number in the manual where the function's description is found.

The communications module of Microsoft Works is exactly like the communications module of ClarisWorks and has the same features, probably because Apple's communications tools are used in both.

Unfortunately, the modules are not completely integrated. You cannot use the word processor's spelling checker and thesaurus while working in other modules.

Fig. 13.20

The five available chart types in the spreadsheet module.

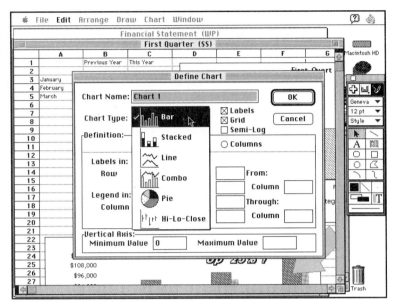

Fig. 13.21

The Paste Function dialog displays a description of NPV.

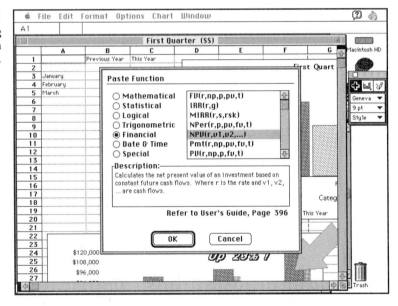

The word processing module, on the other hand, can include draw information from the database module for the mail merge function. This feature means that you can maintain a mailing list or client database in the database module and create customized form letters from that database (see fig. 13.22).

Fig. 13.22
A mail merge letter that will include information pulled from the database module.

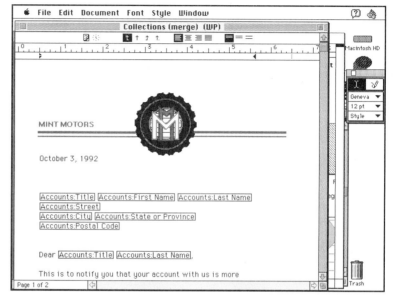

Works Add-Ons

As with many other Macintosh applications, Microsoft Works enables you to purchase and use add-ons that increase its effectiveness. Lundeen & Associates, a company involved in the development of Microsoft Works, has created WorksPlus Spell and WorksPlus Command. Almost every review of these products praises them and recommends these add-ons as essential improvements to the basic Macintosh Works program.

WorksPlus Spell performs the following tasks, which are not included with Microsoft Works:

- Checks for duplicate words, as well as capitalization and spelling errors.

- Remembers words that have been skipped or checked previously so that the program doesn't have to stop and query you every time it encounters the same questionable word.

- Enables you to use *glossary terms*, which are short blocks of text that you use repeatedly and can enter quickly.

- Uses Smart Spelling to check spelling as you type (if you choose). A beep tells you that the word is "pieces," not "peices," for example. The program cannot, however, tell you when a typographical error resulted in another word; for example, WorksPlus Spell does not beep if you type "form" when you meant "from."

- Enables you to view and edit the contents of the dictionary.

- Quickly checks your documents; WorksPlus Spell can check more than 24,000 words a minute.

Although Works contains a macro feature, WorksPlus Command offers you a higher level of macro performance. Using this add-on, you can create programs in the WorksPlus Command macro language. You also can access built-in macros for different Works modules. The following list outlines several of these macros:

- For all Works modules, macros for dialing a phone number, converting text, and saving all open files.

- For the database or the spreadsheet modules, macros for searching and replacing data and transforming values.

- For the word processor module, macros for creating multicolumn documents, defining and using styles, resizing and repositioning pictures, and generating tables of contents and indexes.

- For the database module, macros for entering data down a column and importing a database from another program.

The primary difference between the macro features that accompany Works and the WorksPlus Command add-on is that the add-on is programmable. Lundeen & Associates even provides an extensive programmer's reference manual.

The latest version of WorksPlus Command enables you to resize pictures, add recorded macros to the WorksPlus Command menu for easy selection, and play back macros in any application—not just Works.

Other Integrated Packages

WordPerfect Corporation just released WordPerfect Works, a package similar to ClarisWorks that offers additional features such as Balloon Help and support for Apple Events. Most impressive, and potentially most useful, WordPerfect Works supports hot links between documents. Suppose, for example, that you use a spreadsheet to create a chart in a word processor document. If the word processor document and the spreadsheet are linked, any changes that you make to the spreadsheet are automatically reflected in the chart. In addition, you can wrap text around an object and place grid lines anywhere in a document.

Several companies offer products that can share information. The products are not *integrated*—that is, these are packages of separate programs instead of a single program with integrated modules. Still, the products are very similar in design and interface. For example, Microsoft Corporation offers the Microsoft Office, consisting of Word, Excel, PowerPoint, and Mail at a price well below what you would pay to purchase these programs individually. Although these applications are not intentionally integrated, they do work together very well.

WordPerfect Corporation offers a product called WordPerfect Office, which contains Mail, Calendar, Notebook, File Manager, and Forms Maker. This package is different from Microsoft Office, however. WordPerfect Office is intended to *enhance* productivity for WordPerfect users; you must purchase WordPerfect separately.

Symantec offers GreatWorks 2.0, which contains eight applications: Write, Database, Spreadsheet, Chart, Draw, Paint, Outline, and Communications. The programs use the same core technologies for a consistent interface.

The Big Mac Recommendation

Integrated software may be just what you need—especially if you run a small business or if you want to have all the tools you may need without spending an exorbitant amount on any one. As always, try before you buy and find a friend who uses an integrated package. You may find that such sets of applications fit your needs nicely.

For new Macintosh users, I recommend ClarisWorks. The package is by far the easiest to learn and best integrated. Before the introduction of ClarisWorks, I consistently recommended against *any* integrated package. This one, however, changed my mind.

I am somewhat prejudiced in favor of Claris products; but I feel this prejudice has a solid foundation. Claris consistently works toward maintaining ease of use and consistency between products. Once you learn one Claris product, you have a great start on learning any other Claris product. I applaud this intentional consistency.

Even as I tout Claris products, however, I recognize the dominance of Microsoft products and the popularity of Microsoft Works. If you work in an office environment that uses Microsoft Word and Excel heavily (either Macintosh or PC versions), consider purchasing Works for the home or PowerBook. There is much to be said for compatibility.

My only major complaint about Microsoft Works is that the program requires considerable disk space to install (almost 4MB), and you are not given the option to choose which disk drive to install the program on.

CHAPTER FOURTEEN

Using Finance and Business Applications

Y ou may want to spend the money to buy a personal computer so that you can manage your finances. Whether you are a member of an ordinary household, a small business, or a division of a corporation, the Macintosh can help you watch over your dollars.

Businesses of all sizes, as well as individuals, manage information with general accounting software, tax management software, and checkbook accounting software. Whatever the task, business people, academics, and scientists find themselves dealing with numbers and needing to manipulate numerical information. With the Macintosh and some of the available software discussed later, data analysis becomes easy.

Using Personal Finance Programs

Geared for the home user and the home professional, personal finance programs can handle both family finances and small business finances. Personal finance managers are not full, true accounting systems, but perform many of the same functions on a smaller scale. A "must have" for the Macintosh user, a personal finance program is well worth the price. If properly used, these programs can save you money by helping you budget your finances, balance your checkbook with much less trouble, and even plan your taxes.

Understanding Accounts

The basis of all personal finance packages is the account. An account might be a checking account, a savings account, a money market account, and other accounts familiar to you. These accounts hold money you can withdraw as needed (though some accounts have limitations, the idea is basically the same).

Personal finance packages also use a broader definition of the word account. You can have a *cash account*, which is the amount of cash you have on hand at home or in petty cash. You can have an *asset account* that tracks the value of your Macintosh and peripherals or your household inventory. You can have *liability accounts* that represent money you owe on a car loan or other debt.

In a personal finance package, the basic idea of an account is that money is owned by you or owed to someone (see fig. 14.1).

Some personal finance packages also consider factors such as your income source and your expenses to be accounts. Others call these "categories." The basic idea is the same. Income accounts or categories show sources of money. Expense accounts or categories show money spent (a Groceries account or category, for example).

Fig. 14.1

A checking account register
in Quicken showing the
money you have.

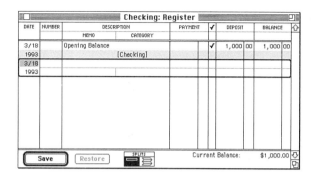

Creating Accounts

As one of your first steps in using the personal finance package, you create accounts. Keep your checkbook (or books) handy and all your loans nearby.

Figure 14.2 shows the Set Up New Account dialog in Quicken 3.0.

Fig. 14.2

The Set Up New Account
dialog in Quicken.

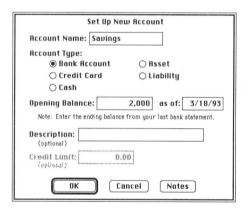

As you can see in the figure, Quicken provides five different account types: Bank Account, Credit Card, Cash, Asset, and Liability. Bank Account, Cash, and Asset are all actually asset accounts; they track assets you own (your money or possessions of value). Credit Card and Liability are liability accounts—tracking money you owe to someone else. Like other personal finance packages, Quicken offers you some special versions of the standard asset and liability accounts with features that aid you in tracking the accounts. For example, the Bank Account enables you to print checks from bank accounts, and is aware of check numbers. The account register uses familiar bank terms such as "payment" and "deposit" instead of the more general "increase" and "decrease" of plain Asset accounts.

Entering Transactions

Each time money moves from one place to another, you have a transaction. A check written to the grocery store is an example of a transaction. You provide the personal finance manager with information by entering transactions. That information can later be used to create reports, balance your accounts, and print checks.

Before you can enter transactions, you must be aware of categories (or accounts, as they are called in some programs). You track your income or expenses—where the money comes from and where it goes—by using categories.

Most personal finance packages enable you to add a predefined set of categories (or income and expense accounts) when you create your financial data file. Quicken has this ability and offers you a set of home or business categories. Figure 14.3 shows you some of the home categories in Quicken.

Fig. 14.3

Some of Quicken's home income and expense categories.

Many familiar items appear in this list: Clothing, Groceries, Interest Earned, Medical, and so on. Note also that either Income or Expense type is listed for each category. Some categories are indented beneath another name; these are subcategories. Insurance, for example, has two subcategories: Auto and Home. This subcategory system enables you to individualize expenses in reports (you can have a report on your auto insurance payments for the year, for example). At the same time, however, you can group related expenses and income.

A transaction defines an action that occurs between an account and one or more categories or another account (the latter transaction type being such things as transferring money from savings to checking). If you keep a checkbook, you are already familiar with entering transactions. Each line in your checkbook is a transaction. To make entering transactions easier, personal finance packages imitate a checkbook (see fig. 14.4).

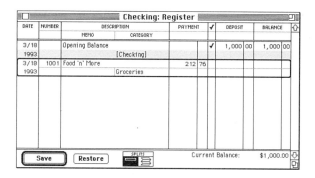

Fig. 14.4
Entering a grocery check in Quicken.

To understand transactions in personal finance managers, you need to know that you can "distribute" or "split" transactions between categories or accounts. For example, you deposit your paycheck, splitting the deposit between the checking account, your savings account, and some cash that you spend on an evening of entertainment (it's Friday, let's say). The transaction might look like figure 14.5 in Quicken.

Fig. 14.5
A split transaction in Quicken.

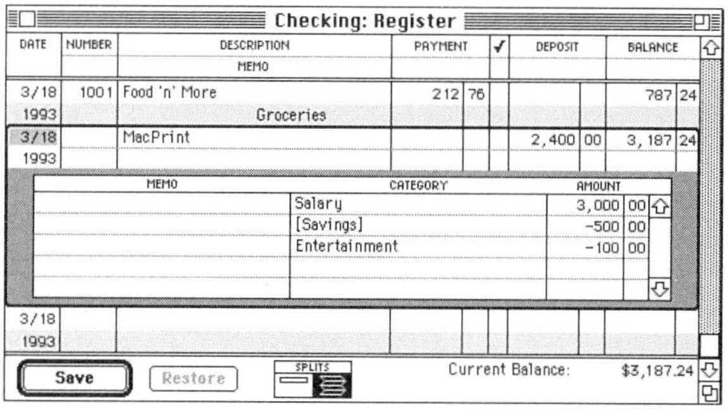

This ability to split transactions can help when a single check covers more than one expense or account, or a deposit from more than one income source.

Creating Reports

Without reporting capability, personal finance packages would be only as useful as checkbook balancing programs. An important feature of personal finance packages, reports can tell you a variety of things. For example, consider the kinds of reports provided by Quicken 3.0:

- Budget
- Cash Flow
- Itemized Categories
- Net Worth
- Balance Sheet
- Tax Summary
- Income Statement
- A/P by Vendor
- A/R by Customer
- Job/Project
- Payroll
- Reconciliation
- Transaction Detail
- Transaction Summary

You can customize reports in many personal finance packages. You can define the date range the report covers, the accounts involved, the kind of transactions reported on, and so on. Figure 14.6 shows the dialog in Quicken that enables you to customize the Transaction Detail report.

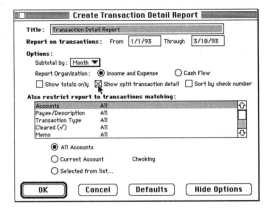

Fig. 14.6
Customizing the Transaction Detail report in Quicken.

When you choose a personal finance package, consider the number of reports offered, the kinds of reports, and whether you can customize the reports as you choose.

Choosing a Personal Finance Program

This section covers three major personal finance packages, including the industry leader, Quicken. This section also discusses the features of these programs that enable you to choose the program best suited to your needs.

Quicken

One of the best buys in software, Quicken, from Intuit Software, is in-expensive; the street price is about $45. Quicken is an intuitive and easy-to-use program. At its simplest level, Quicken is a checkbook manager. Quicken presents you with screens that look just like your real check-book ledger or the checks that you need to write and print every month. You also can use Quicken to generate reports of tax-deductible items, write and print checks for recurring transactions, and track expenses. You can even use it to do some fairly sophisticated business accounting.

Quicken offers an actual checkbook register that the program maintains for you, enabling you to keep your balance up-to-date as you make transactions. Quicken also stores payee names and amounts due, and reminds you of upcoming payments. Of course, *you* put the check in an envelope and mail it, but this method is far better than those tedious once-a-month check-writing blues.

Quicken can print checks (which you special-order; details come with Quicken) and generate reports you can print or show on-screen, as shown in figure 14.7. In this figure, a transaction report is generated from 1/1/91 to 11/26/91 for all transactions in the account.

To avoid licking stamps and addressing envelopes, consider the Checkfree service that works with Quicken. Your Quicken package provides details but, essentially, Checkfree is an electronic bill-paying service that eliminates the need for checks in many cases. To use Checkfree, you must have a modem; you are also charged a monthly fee.

Fig. 14.7
A Quicken report on
categories.

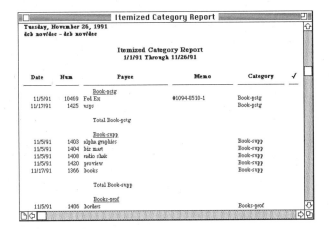

Managing Your Money

Managing Your Money 5.0 (from Meca) has an extensive set of features
for investing, planning for tax benefits, analyzing income versus expenses, working with your net worth, and more. The opening screen in
figure 14.8 shows you how Managing Your Money can handle different
facets of your financial records. If you are a bit negligent in keeping your
records up-to-date, for example, Managing Your Money reminds you
(through an on-screen message) when it is time to transfer files and
make backups (all of which the program guides you through).

Fig. 14.8
The Managing Your Money
opening screen.

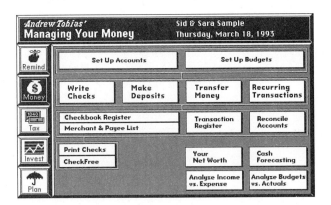

In Managing Your Money (MYM), "navigators" lead you through the
steps needed to do your financial planning. One of the navigators is the
Tax Navigator. This navigator can lead you in estimating your taxes (see
fig. 14.9).

Fig. 14.9
Estimating your taxes with
Managing Your Money.

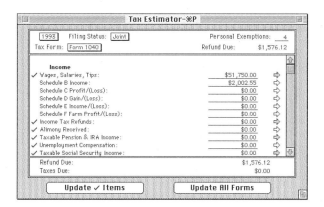

The categories shown are in a previously constructed finances file that
includes your accounts and transactions. Managing Your Money even
computes the tax you may or may not owe. The Managing Your Money
manual is good. This program seems to capture the wit and wisdom of
well-known popular financial writer Andrew Tobias in an easy-to-use
program.

One way Managing Your Money eases your transaction entries is by
imitating a check. MYM can print checks or use Checkfree to transmit
payments electronically. (Checkfree is a separate service. You must sign
up for it and pay a monthly fee.) MYM has a great number of reports.
There are 17 money reports—that is, reports dealing with your transactions—which you can customize (see fig. 14.10).

Fig. 14.10
Choosing a Check Register
report in MYM.

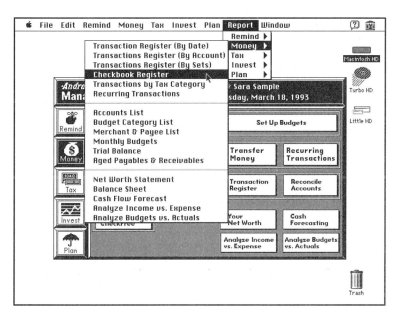

Other reports are available for tax planning, investment planning, retirement fund planning, and more.

MYM 5.0 is a well-respected, overall financial tool for the home user and small business.

Dollars & Sense

Once the dominant personal finance and small business package, Dollars & Sense (by Business Sense) has not kept pace in sales with other packages, but even after several years, it remains one of the better personal finance packages. I have to confess that I have a weak spot for this program because I was one of the members of the development team back when the original developer and owner of the program—Monogram—was in business.

Despite the program's flaws (users report some irritating bugs at times), the program remains a solid personal and small business finance management package. The program offers true double-entry accounting (though scaled down for home use) and the ability to handle equity accounts. Figure 14.11 shows part of the predefined home set of accounts in the account file creation dialog.

Fig. 14.11
Creating an account file in Dollars & Sense.

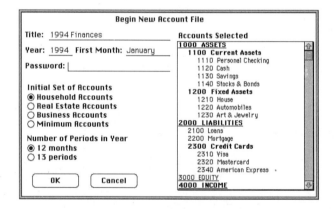

Dollars & Sense offers some features still not seen in other personal finance management packages—a customizable icon interface, the ability to graph your finances (see fig. 14.12), and the ability to handle equity accounts with ease.

Dollars & Sense is still a good value for the money. But since the demise of Monogram and the company's subsequent collapse, the program has not been managed well. Business Sense recently purchased Dollars & Sense and expressed definite interest in marketing and supporting the program.

Fig. 14.12

Graphing net worth in
Dollars & Sense.

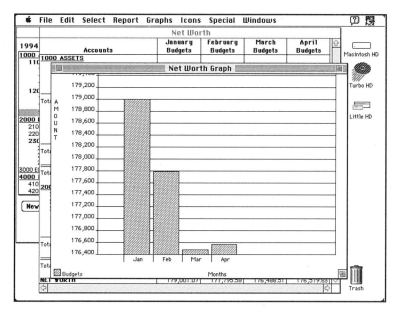

Using Tax Preparation Programs

MacInTax, from Chipsoft, is one of several programs that can help you prepare your tax returns. MacInTax forms look just like Internal Revenue Service forms. MacInTax even prints the forms exactly as they would appear if you completed the actual IRS forms. The IRS accepts the signed printed output.

MacInTax is a large, well-thought-out spreadsheet program that links many smaller spreadsheets (representing tax schedules) to produce one final accounting. Figure 14.13 shows a MacInTax screen, including a copy of an actual tax form. You can access any one of more than 70 schedules from this main screen. As you enter data on a schedule or the main form, all the information is tied together into the bottom line, meaning that any information you enter into any of the schedules or forms enters automatically into any other form that might list that schedule as a source of input.

Programs like MacInTax have a group of very well-designed tax worksheets that are linked to one another. The worksheets are not independent of each other; what happens in one affects the others. The MacInTax package also comes with an excellent Federal Tax Highlights book, produced by the accounting firm of Arthur Young.

Fig. 14.13

A MacInTax screen and
menu.

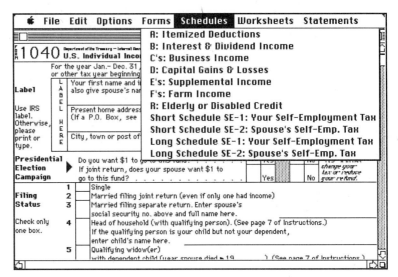

CAUTION

F or the simple 1040 EZ form, nothing beats a program like
MacInTax. After you receive your W-2 form, you can complete
your taxes easily in less time than it takes to print the return. If you
have a complicated and detailed tax situation, MacInTax certainly
can handle the numbers—but do you know which numbers go
where?

Perhaps—but don't assume that because you use a computerized
tax-generation system, your decisions about deductible items are
acceptable to the IRS. The IRS accepts what tax laws allow, not
necessarily what your Macintosh can generate. The first time
around, you may want to have your return checked by a tax
accountant so that you can save yourself quite a headache.

Like some other programs, BottomLine (by CompuCraft) requires
HyperCard (used as the front end) and Excel to run. BottomLine
contains all the short and long forms you need to make the IRS happy,
including individual forms, corporation forms, partnership forms, estate
tax forms, and several miscellaneous forms. Need to tap into form
1065.GEN? You can see part of it in figure 14.14.

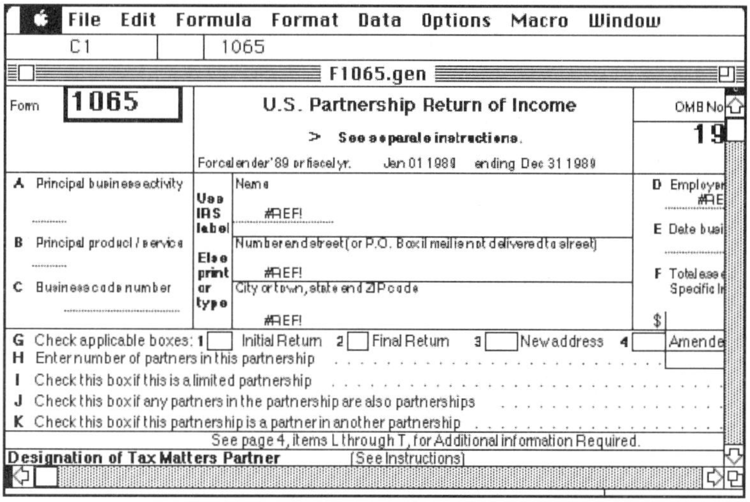

Fig. 14.14
IRS form F1065.GEN
produced by BottomLine.

Using Other Financial Programs

One financial program worth mentioning is Wealth Builder by Reality Technologies. This program can help you determine your investment and financial planning strategies. WealthBuilder can read directly from Quicken, MacMoney, and MYM files, and can then calculate your net worth and aid you in defining financial goals.

WealthBuilder creates charts and reports that aid you in tracking your finances. An OnLine Link feature (which requires a modem) enables you to download current stock, bond, and other financial information.

Using Accounting Software

Most of the accounting software available for the Macintosh helps people with the everyday jobs of running a business. Some programs, such as SBT (from SBT Corporation), handle many different functions, such as general ledger, accounts payable, and sales order processing; others, such as Quicken (from Intuit), serve a single purpose, such as balancing checkbooks. Many of these programs are configured to use spreadsheets or databases as their "engines." SBT modules, for example, run on Foxbase+/Mac—a dBASE clone.

Before you shop for accounting assistance, you must determine your needs. If you are the owner of a business with frequent and complex financial transactions, you may need to seek additional assistance from an accountant to determine which program fits your needs best. If you own a small business, or if you want some help with your taxes, the program that your friends use and like may be adequate. Almost all business users need the following basics:

■ *A general ledger program* contains a set of accounts and keeps track of transactions in the accounts as the transactions occur. It also reconciles each account activity with overall balances, and is the basis of a business's balance sheet.

■ *Accounts receivable and accounts payable features* give the business manager information about what is coming in and what is going out, as well as whose accounts are overdue and by what amount.

■ *Payroll features* record data such as hours worked, overtime, hourly rate, Social Security and other tax information. Payroll also generates checks.

CAUTION

When you consider accounting, tax preparation, and other such software, keep in mind that the program does not "know" whether what you enter into it is valid. Financial and statistical applications can give meaning to the saying "garbage in, garbage out."

Understanding Accounting Programs

Accounting is the process of measuring economic information and using it to make decisions about budgets, payments, and financial planning. To get an idea of what a comprehensive accounting package can do, examine the capabilities of a popular accounting package. The SBT Database Accounting Library (Mac/Series Six Plus) was written using the dBASE database system. This program consists of 14 modules that are linked together. Figure 14.15 shows how some of these modules are linked. SBT is relational; the balance due on an account can appear in several different modules, for example, even though you enter the information about the account only once. (See Chapter 12, "Using Databases," for a discussion of what relational means in data management.) SBT provides the source code and other development tools so that you can develop programs to meet your specific needs.

Fig. 14.15
Linking modules of one
accounting package.

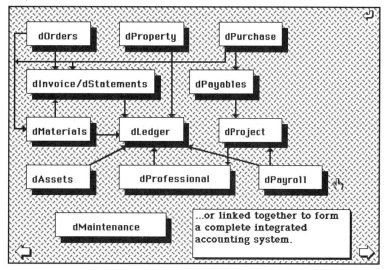

SBT's modules perform a variety of functions:

■ The dLedger module gives you information about journal transactions and helps you manage balance sheets and income statements. Figure 14.16 shows an SBT general ledger. This module can compute more than 20 different business ratios.

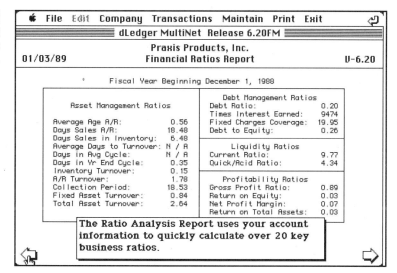

- The dInvoice/dStatements module keeps track of inventory; it also produces sales analysis and accounts payable and accounts receivable reports.

- The dPayables module writes checks and keeps track of business expenses.

- dOrders tracks inventory and maintains sales orders. Because modules are linked (as in a relational database), dOrders enables you to create an invoice automatically when a product is shipped.

- dPurchase updates vendor and inventory account balances.

- dPayroll makes it easier to compute different types of payroll checks—for example, for employees who are hourly, those who are salaried, and those who are on commission. This module also generates W-2 forms and other IRS documents.

- dAssets can help you profit from the depreciation of equipment and other assets, and traces loan activity.

- dProject is one of the what-if modules of SBT. It examines how changes in categories can affect overall budgets.

- dBy tracks the use and cost of materials; dMaterials helps forecast the costs of manufacturing.

- dProfessional helps manage a business by providing billing and accounts receivable capability, as well as reporting how time is being spent.

- dProperty can help you manage everything from your office building to apartments and commercial real estate.

- dMaintenance helps you keep up with the maintenance schedule of equipment you sell or lease.

- dScanner reads information generated from bar code readers to help speed up tasks such as inventory, purchasing, and billing.

- dMenu/Backup is a file management system that helps you manage files (move, delete, back up, and so on), and ensure against the loss of important data.

You purchase only the SBT modules that fit your needs. For basic accounting, for example, dInvoice/dStatements, dPayables, dPayroll, and dLedger are sufficient. If your company grows, you can add easily modules.

Considering Other Accounting Packages

Other excellent accounting programs, such as Great Plains Software, offer many of the same features as the SBT library. Like SBT, Great Plains has the following features:

- General ledger
- Accounts payable
- Accounts receivable
- Payroll
- Inventory
- Purchase order
- Order entry
- Job cost
- Printer's Ink
- Executive Advisor
- Network Manager

Great Plains also has some other features well worth noting, especially the Executive Advisor, which uses tables or graphs to analyze business performance. This module also includes 70 business ratios to help you understand your current financial position and determine adjustments that you may need to make. Printers Ink estimates printing costs and tracks jobs from inception through completion. Printers Ink also produces schedules and invoices.

Great Plains also offers a Network Manager, with various security levels and file protection; several people can use different Great Plains modules simultaneously. This networking arrangement is an attractive alternative to the larger, more powerful computers that you would otherwise need so that several people can access the software at the same time.

Great Plains introduced Cash Management with Checkbook Reconciliation. These two products do the following three important business tasks:

- Provide reports of cash position, enabling business managers to make short-term borrowing or investment decisions
- Generate deposit slips, pulling information from all the modules in the Great Plains accounting series
- Reconcile bank accounts

Another Great Plains product is ImportManager, which imports data from databases and spreadsheets into the Accounting series.

Unlike some programs, which were created for DOS systems, Insight Expert (from Layered) was designed for the Macintosh. Therefore, this program has features like multiple windows and uses double-clicking to add entries to a field.

Insight Expert has many of the same capabilities as SBT and Great Plains. These modules are easy to use. Insight Expert includes sets of templates for constructing entry forms, and control logs to assist in tracking expenses. For example, figure 14.17 shows an opening screen. The customer's logo has been clicked, and the screen for the first customer displays from a database of customers. When you click ITEM CARD, a description of items in the inventory and information about stock numbers and the like appears (see fig. 14.18).

Fig. 14.17
Selecting customers from
the Insight database.

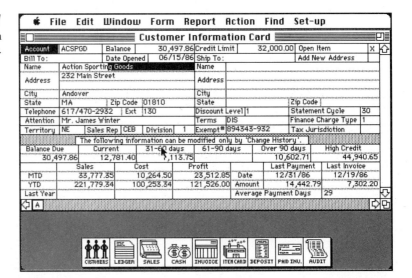

A complete training package that takes you from setting up to using the programs accompanies the modules, and several companies offer a variety of printed forms to use with Insight Expert. Layered established a network of CPA firms and consultants who are trained to implement the Expert system for businesses. The cost of this service depends on the installer and his or her hourly rates.

Accountant Inc. Professional (from SoftSync), designed expressly for the Macintosh, is another high-end package that offers financial management tools as well as integrated accounting modules. The eight disks that accompany the program contain tutorials, HyperCard stacks, sample businesses to examine, plus password security, printing of forms, and more than 100 financial reports that you can export to spreadsheet applications.

Fig. 14.18
Selecting an item
(a product) to work with.

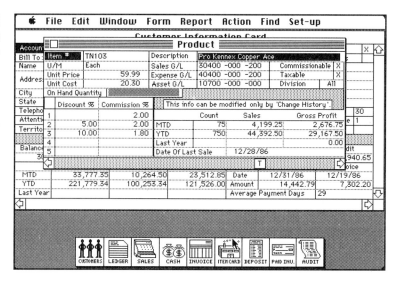

Finally, there's Champion's Accounting, a whopper of an application that is competitive with Expert, SBT, and Accountant. The most outstanding features of Champion's Accounting are a data-recovery feature (which surely can save the day) and the source code for applications so that you can customize the programs to fit your needs.

Layered also offers a new mid-range accounting product called AtOnce!, a bundled program of modules. AtOnce! appears to be designed especially for the small business or novice accounting user. This easy-to-learn program includes on-line help, automated data entry, four fully linked modules (general ledger, accounts receivable, accounts payable, and payroll), password control, inventory, and more. AtOnce! is not a child of Insight's Expert, but a stand-alone product in design and purpose.

The Great Plains low-end entry is Plains & Simple, a fully stocked accounting system for businesses on the small side. The Great Plains people, incidentally, are known for their terrific product support. You cannot go wrong with either AtOnce! or Plains & Simple.

Besides AtOnce! and Plains & Simple, other contenders are available in the low-end range. A one-disk package organized by multiple ledgers and journals, ACCPAC Bedford (from Computer Associates) offers help files, lots of examples, and the accounting records for Universal Construction (a sample company) to help you learn the ropes.

A unique approach to accounting, Fiscal Knowledge (Mathesis, Inc.) takes advantage of Excel's powerful number manipulation and charting features. The program offers the standard accounting procedures, and also offers a powerful set of macros, such as Trial Balance and Create Account, which speed up and simplify your day-to-day activities. An additional bonus is a well-designed and well-written manual that includes information about basic accounting procedures (plus a great T-shirt along with the package!).

Another popular program, SuperMOM, or Super Mail Order Manager, (from National Tele-Press), is often compared to general ledger programs, but it can do much more. SuperMOM has the general ledger and accounting features, but specializes in helping to manage mail-order businesses by offering features like the following:

- Customer tracking by group and marketing efforts
- A variety of shipping charge methods
- Preparation of shipping manifests
- Inquiry tracking

The Tele-Press people offer exceptional support and even will help you customize SuperMOM to meet your requirements. Figure 14.19, for example, shows an address file for a customer, including information about dates catalogs sent, pricing, tax codes, and involved salespeople.

Fig. 14.19
A sample screen from SuperMOM showing direct-mail information.

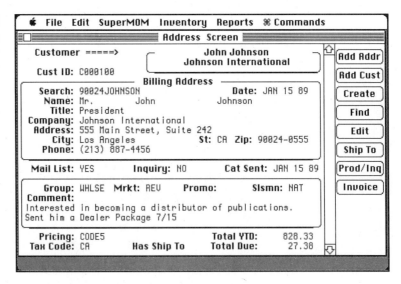

This highly specialized vertical-market tool (dealing with products in various ranges for various worksheets) contains the standard material for accounting, combined with a powerful marketing tool and is recommended for people in the catalog and direct-mail business.

ShopKeeper (from ShopKeeper Software) is a less elaborate accounting system designed for easy use and especially suited for smaller businesses. Although ShopKeeper does not consist of linked modules, it does a nice job of keeping track of inventory. This program prepares bids and billing and other accounting "regulars," such as accounts payable and accounts receivable. ShopKeeper can do floor planning (for sales per square foot, for example), produce mailing labels, and read bar codes, which can be incorporated into point-of-sale management. ShopKeeper even reminds you to back up your file when you quit the present session. You can order specially designed checks and forms that ShopKeeper can print for you.

If you're looking for a good buy and a package to handle your financial planning and forecasting needs, try Up Your Cash Flow (Granville Publications Software). This package makes routine financial planning tasks painless, and comes with a business-planning guide rated as a top-10 book by *USA Today*. The features in Up Your Cash Flow include standard profit and loss, cash flow forecasting, and ratio analysis. Also standard is their What If feature, consolidated forecasts, and planning business strategy.

All this high-powered accounting doesn't need to be just for accountants or even owners of small businesses, however. Millions of folks who run small businesses, tradespeople, and so on, need small applications designed for the individual, such as Service Industry Accounting from Brown-Wagh Publishing. SIA is unique because the transactions take place as though you are working out of a book (see fig. 14.20). Just click the company you want to work with. To set up a new company, the New option on the File menu guides you through the process and enables you to find everything from credit limits to code numbers.

Programs like these are a bit more manageable than the huge accounting programs, but do have their limits. For most people running small businesses—and especially those who need to keep track of their clients and customers in a relatively simple fashion—SIA and other applications can be a great help.

A more specialized accounting package is P.O.S Macintosh, a point-of-sale system (which some other accounting packages offer as a module) that works on a run-time version of Omnis 3. Any good point-of-sale system has the features that P.O.S Macintosh offers, such as floor planning, audit trails, customer mailing lists, seven levels of security, price quotes that convert to invoices, and tracking of advertising revenues.

Fig. 14.20

The book format used
by SIA.

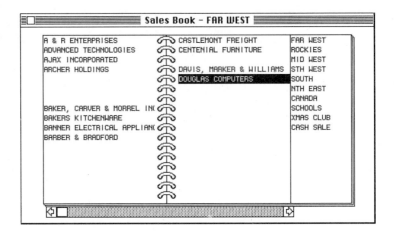

Other neat point-of-sales tools are available as well. From E.E.S. Companies comes Credit Card DA, which enables you to dial up and confirm the validity of a sale, determine credit limits, and answer all those other questions that you wonder about when you charge that meal with your MasterCard or Visa. If you are really into automating your point-of-sales system, inventory, and so on, you can generate bar codes by using PrintBar (from BearRock). Bar codes are the thin and thick black lines on merchandise that stores use for inventory control and other business "housekeeping" tasks.

In addition to the accounting concerns already mentioned, a key component of any business is keeping track of costs. Unfortunately, you don't just jot down the amount of pocket change you have left at the end of the day and the cost of nails at the lumberyard. You need to include many factors, including an estimated cost of a job. Cost Management System (from Softouch Software) can help tremendously by breaking down cost management into estimating, costing, and maintenance. Cost Management System provides a continuous window on the costs of a project as variables change and help you develop a comprehensive plan for staying within costs.

TimeSlips III (from NorthEdge) also helps you track time (which is money) and expense as part of job costs. This tool is ideal for people who bill by the hour (psychologists, auto-body repair people, or plumbers, for example). You must eventually consolidate all those little slips of paper on desks, in appointment pads, or even in the back pocket of that recently cleaned suit or skirt. TimeSlips offers a nice DA, named TSTimer, that generates time slips. By providing time slips that give you a clear picture of how you spend your time, TSReports produces bills that you can use for as many as 250 users (your employees) and 2,000 clients. You also can generate and print information—for example, you can determine which client generates the most billable time, the type of activities that produce the most billable hours (perfect for lawyers), and actual versus estimated time spent with each client.

Other accounting packages you may want to investigate include Rags to Riches, BPI General Accounting, Strictly Business, Simply Accounting, and Back to Basics Accounting. You also may want to look into Aatrix modules, Accountant Inc., CheckMark, MultiLedger Payroll, Flexware Accounting System, or In-House Accountant, M.D.A.

Considering Forecasting and Planning Programs

Much of the material in this chapter discusses how to organize business information after it is generated. What if you want to predict outcomes on the basis of previous sales or employee information? Or design a business plan? Or think more creatively about a business problem?

Tim Berry of Palo Alto Software designed a set of forecasting and planning tools that enable you to design a business plan and make predictions based on previous sales or employee information.

Forecaster, for example, enables you to make a forecast not by using numbers, but by drawing a line (by clicking points along a scale). The program fits the numbers to the line. Figure 14.21 shows a line drawn using the cursor; the values of the points appear in the Forecast data window.

Fig. 14.21
Using Forecaster to draw a forecasting line.

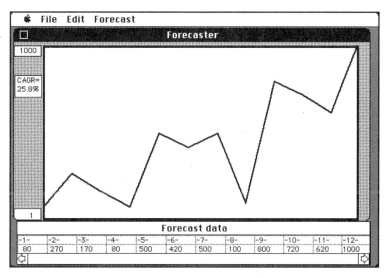

The Business Plan Toolkit (from Palo Alto Software) is compatible with Excel (which you need in order to run many of Business Plan Toolkit's features) and almost all popular word processors. This planning tool helps you design a business plan and use it in forecasting. Business Plan Toolkit is easy to use. As you can see in figure 14.22, you use a HyperCard Stack to generate a business plan. (See Chapter 30, "Using HyperCard," for more information about HyperCard.) Through this stack, you answer questions about business plan categories (see fig. 14.23).

Fig. 14.22
Generating a business plan using the Business Plan Toolkit.

Fig. 14.23
Questions for generating a business plan.

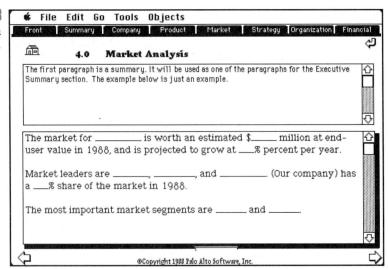

Some of the categories used from the HyperCard stack follow:

- Executive summary
- Mission (goals of the company)
- Company history
- Company locations and facilities
- Product description and features
- Present and future products
- Market analysis
- Financial plan

After you enter the answers to the questions, you simply create a text file and put all the information in it, as you do in an actual business plan.

The Sales Marketing Forecasting Toolkit is designed for Excel and comes with Excel templates and macros for producing forecasts using customer polls, market share, the chain method, and several other techniques.

Considering Creative Problem-Solving Programs

Products now available can help you generate new ideas, solutions to problems, and more. These applications are called *thought processors*, or *idea processors*, or even *idea generators*. They cannot create a corporate image or help you design a business plan unless you do your homework and thinking, but after you have some direction, these applications can help you a great deal.

IdeaFisher is the brainstorm of the same person who brought us Century 21 real estate, Mel Fisher. After a few short years and a not-so-small fortune, he used his energy and enthusiasm to develop a tool, IdeaFisher, to help harness Century 21's creative potential. Most applications come with an envelope containing the application disks; IdeaFisher comes with a box.

IdeaFisher is similar to a game of associations. As you click through and answer questions, IdeaFisher tries to determine the direction of your responses. For example, you might be brainstorming an approach to solving a particular problem, such as coming up with a slogan or a trademark for your business. IdeaFisher steers you toward alternatives, given your response to questions.

All nine of the disks (containing more than 7MB) contain more than 60,000 ideas, phrases, words, and cliches. These individual entries are cross-referenced, so the entire application offers more than 700,000 cross-referenced items in some 28 major categories (such as Things/Places or People/Animals). Like one giant hypertext, IdeaFisher supplies the facts; you supply the brains to pull these facts together. IdeaFisher is fun to use, and you can count on new insights into your problem as a result of using the program.

MindLink (from MindLink) is structured differently from IdeaFisher. The program is based on the theory that when you look at the same question from a variety of perspectives, a thread common to the answers becomes the solution. Through a HyperCard stack, you are asked a series of nested questions. The application guides you to a place to which your responses point. You begin with a decision to enter the Gym, Idea Generation, Guided Problem Solving, or Problem Solving (see fig. 14.24). After you make your selection, you go into different exercises (as questions).

MindLink helps you solve problems by using an already-established library of creative thinking tools and techniques. You can see in figure 14.24 how you start your journey. The Gym provides you with exercises to strengthen your creative skills. For example, one of the 18 Gym rooms asks you to enter a list of as many diverse activities as you can think of, or to think up as many ways as possible to use a newspaper. This package is nice, and a great many of the exercises are based on success with real companies.

Fig. 14.24
The MindLink map.

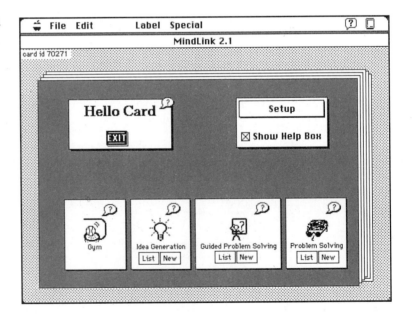

Synchronicity (from Visionary) is not in the same category as IdeaFisher or MindLink, but it is a valuable addition to the problem-solving tool box. Billed as "stress-reduction" software by many reviewers, the application uses graphics and sound to reduce stress associated with decision-making, and provides an on-screen environment that encourages creative thought.

Synchronicity reduces the stress associated with making decisions under difficult, and sometimes unbearable, pressure. For example, in the opening screen you see and hear a brook babbling by a small gazebo. A gentle gong follows as the opening message (What's on your mind, Neil?) invites you to relax and use Synchronicity as a game as much as a tool. You enter your question; the program follows with suggestions for breathing and relaxing exercises. You then move to the keyboard-focus process for getting to the answer to your question. As your question rotates around the screen, questions and quotations from the *Book of Changes*, an ancient work guiding individuals toward personal fulfillment, appear (see fig. 14.25).

Fig. 14.25
Sample question on the Synchronicity screen.

Does all this sound like too much for a simple Macintosh application? Perhaps, but the program does provide you with stimulus for insight into your problem. It cannot give yes or no answers and does not want those types of questions.

Using Spreadsheets as Financial Tools

Even though there are specific programs for accounting and other financial uses, don't forget what your spreadsheet can offer. You already saw how certain products are designed specifically to be used with spreadsheets such as Excel. You can perform other accounting activities with spreadsheets.

Whether you use Excel, Resolve, Lotus 1-2-3, or ClarisWorks, you can use the built-in functions to easily program the spreadsheet to produce exactly the output you need. With their ease of programming, scripting, and other features, spreadsheets can be especially useful for business owners. In the "Using Tax Preparation Programs" section earlier in this chapter, you saw how BottomLine uses Excel, so you know that spreadsheets have the power and the graphics to do just about anything you can imagine.

Figure 14.26 shows an Excel worksheet—Balance Sheet and Ratio Analyses—for the four quarters of a business year. With only a few formulas, this worksheet is relatively easy to construct. You can even execute what seem like complicated computations with simple planning. The payroll ledger in figure 14.27 shows the total amount due after calculating overtime and tax contributions (using simple formulas).

Some developers combined the power of spreadsheets with specific user demands to create spreadsheet-dependent templates for tasks such as the preparation of taxes. These products contain all the formulas and categories you need to complete the returns. You simply enter the numbers in the appropriate places.

One of these companies, EZWare Corporation, produces EZTax-Prep 1040 and EZTax-Plan Business for the preparation of federal income tax returns. EZWare runs under Excel. EZTax-Plan has some nice features. It prepares your present schedule of taxes and can help you plan for the future by predicting what your taxes will be for the next 45 years. Perhaps EZTax-Plan's most valuable feature is its side-by-side comparison of different tax strategies, where you can finally see the advantages of giving your nephew Bruce that $1,000 or keeping it for yourself.

EZWare includes information about recent changes in the tax laws, free first upgrades, and an increasing number of software packages that prepare certain state returns. EZWare also includes acetate templates to help prepare batches of returns for professional return preparers.

Fig. 14.26
Using a spreadsheet for calculating a balance sheet.

Balance Sheet/Ratio Analysis

	A	B	C	D	E	F	G	H
1	BALANCE SHEET AND RATIO ANALYSES							
2								
3					J&R Manufacturing			
4					101-598 W 57th Street			
5					Seattle, WA 12345			
6					(314)-878-2400			
7								
8				Quarter 1	Quarter 2	Quarter 3	Quarter 4	Total
9	ASSETS							
10								
11	Cash			$899,354	$1,876,453	$987,096	$994,097	$4,757,000
12	Market Securities			$298,576	$372,645	$172,645	$253,456	$1,097,322
13	Bonds			$98,465	$101,987	$100,987	$99,067	$400,506
14	Treasury			$20,000	$40,000	$30,000	$20,000	$110,000
15	Accounts Receivable			$286,756	$354,676	$325,676	$298,765	$1,265,873
16	Inventory Value			$789,465	$867,543	$657,486	$657,887	$2,972,381
17	Prepayments/Taxes			$150,987	$104,987	$135,768	$107,987	$499,729
18								
19	Total Current Assets			$2,543,603	$3,718,291	$2,409,658	$2,431,259	$11,102,811
20								
21	Equipment			$645,978	$645,978	$645,978	$645,978	$2,583,912
22	Property			$1,500,000	$1,500,000	$1,500,000	$1,500,000	$6,000,000
23	Depreciation			($62,800)	($67,196)	($71,900)	($76,933)	($278,828)
24								
25	Total Fixed Assets			$2,083,178	$2,078,782	$2,074,078	$2,069,045	$8,305,084
26								
27	TOTAL ASSETS			$4,626,781	$5,797,073	$4,483,736	$4,500,304	$19,407,895
28								
29	LIABILITIES							
30	Notes Payable			$65,748	$67,345	$90,867	$87,456	$311,416
31	Employee's Retirement			$2,345,756	$2,978,654	$2,876,456	$2,313,453	$10,514,319
32	Taxes On Income			$89,675	$78,454	$84,567	$91,243	$343,939
33	Wages			$213,453	$241,234	$231,456	$243,453	$929,596
34	Mortgage			$5,968	$5,968	$5,968	$5,968	$23,872
35	Loans			$87,456	$65,375	$54,768	$45,654	$253,253
36	Long Term Debt			$354,674	$453,123	$543,234	$453,654	$1,804,685
37								
38	TOTAL LIABILITIES			$3,162,730	$3,890,153	$3,887,316	$3,240,881	$14,181,080
39								
40	STOCKHOLDER'S EQUITY							
41	Common Stock			$1,134,222	$187,657	$165,467	$176,789	$1,664,135
42								
43	TOTAL EQUITY			$1,134,222	$1,875,641	$1,654,345	$1,231,232	$5,895,440
44								
45	TOTAL LIABILITIES AND EQUITY			$4,296,952	$5,765,794	$5,541,661	$4,472,113	$20,076,520
46								
47	RATIOS							
48	Current Ratio			1.46	1.49	1.15	1.39	1.37
49	(Assets/Liabilities)							
50	Equity Ratio			0.25	0.32	0.37	0.27	0.30
51	(Equity/Assets)							
52	Debt/Equity Ratio			2.79	2.07	2.35	2.63	2.46
53	(Liabilities/Equity)							

Considering Statistical Analysis Programs

The statistical analysis, or number crunching, software available today is quite incredible. The capabilities of programs such as Systat, Mathematica, and SuperAnova mimic the capability of mainframes. In some cases, these programs exceed the mainframe's features because of the control you have.

14 Using Finance and Business Applications **487**

Fig. 14.27

Using a spreadsheet to calculate wages due.

Payroll Ledger

	Name	# Ded	FIT Rate	Hourly Wage	Hours Worked	Over-time	Over-Time ($)	Base Salary	Total Wages	FICA	FIT	State Tax	Total Deduction	Total Payment
1	PAYROLL LEDGER													
2														
3	FICA value		0.08											
4	State Tax		0.00											
5	Overtime Rate		1.50											
6														
10	J.K.	2	0.33	$11.50	51	11	$189.75	$586.50	$776.25	$44.05	$193.55	$32.26	$269.85	$316.65
11	H.G.	2	0.15	$7.50	42	2	$22.50	$315.00	$337.50	$23.66	$47.25	$17.33	$88.23	$226.77
12	W.B.	1	0.15	$8.50	45	5	$63.75	$382.50	$446.25	$28.73	$57.38	$21.04	$107.14	$275.36
13	R.T.	4	0.15	$8.00	41	1	$12.00	$328.00	$340.00	$24.63	$49.20	$18.04	$91.87	$236.13
14	I.O.	2	0.28	$8.50	42	2	$25.50	$357.00	$382.50	$26.81	$99.96	$19.64	$146.41	$210.59
15	F.D.	2	0.28	$7.50	44	4	$45.00	$330.00	$375.00	$24.78	$92.40	$18.15	$135.33	$194.67
16	W.E.	1	0.28	$11.00	48	8	$132.00	$528.00	$660.00	$39.65	$147.84	$29.04	$216.53	$311.47
17	H.T.	2	0.28	$12.00	40	0	$0.00	$480.00	$480.00	$36.05	$134.40	$26.40	$196.85	$283.15
18	W.Q.	2	0.28	$10.00	50	10	$150.00	$500.00	$650.00	$37.55	$140.00	$27.50	$205.05	$294.95
19	T.F.	0	0.28	$8.50	44	4	$51.00	$374.00	$425.00	$28.09	$104.72	$20.57	$153.38	$220.62
21			TOTALS		447				4181.00	313.99	1066.69	229.96	1610.64	2570.36

NOTE

Don't be put off too much by some of the following terminology. Readers who need programs that analyze data will have no trouble following the terminology. Those who are unfamiliar with these types of programs will find some new words, but the ideas and concepts are fairly consistent across many disciplines.

Statistics is the science of reducing data to a form that can be analyzed and more easily understood. General classes of analysis are available in different programs. Your choice from the variety of available statistical programs depends upon what you need. The following descriptions of the general classes of statistics and the examples of what they do can help you determine the best programs for your needs.

Considering Features of Statistical Programs

A good statistics program should have at least the following features:

- *Ability to transfer data between applications easily.* You can create your data file, for example, by using Excel, and then save it as a text file, and easily import it into MYSTAT (from SYSTAT).

- *Ease of use.* Most users of statistical analysis programs know what they want to do, so the options should be easily available.

- *Graphic output.* Even the simplest data becomes more powerful when illustrated. Histograms, stem and leaf charts, box charts, and other charts and graphs should be available as well. Now dedicated graphics software for statistical analysis is available.

- *Data transformation.* Many times, data needs to be transformed or recoded to make it easier to understand. A good statistics program should have the capacity to assign weights, recode, or transform special types of standardized scores.

- *Easy-to-understand output, including probability levels associated with the results.* A user should not need to search through tables of significance levels—that information should appear in the output.

SYSTAT offers three levels of programs: MYSTAT (used to be free, but now is $5), FASTAT ($195), and SYSTAT ($395). SYSTAT handles the most complex operations. To get MYSTAT for $5.00, send the company a letter of request; the company hopes that later you will buy FASTAT or SYSTAT. SYSTAT offers Version 6.0 (new)—a powerful and very popular data-analysis program. SYSTAT also has complex statistics, graphing, and additional modules (such as LISREL and path analysis), plus great technical support. With SYSTAT on your hard disk, your options for data analyses are almost unlimited.

Most programs begin with some kind of data screen, such as the ones shown in figure 14.28. On the data screen, you enter the data you want to use and then go on to choose from a variety of dialog boxes the type of analysis with which you want to work.

MiniTab (from MiniTab) finally came around to a Mac-like interface. A program that has been around for years and years, Minitab has more than 4,000 devoted followers on university and corporate campuses. Minitab comes with 170 commands, regression and time series analysis, graphics galore, and miniWRITER, a DA word processor (see Chapter 5, "Configuring the Macintosh"). Minitab also comes with a nice workbook, useful for those of you who teach and have Minitab on your mainframe.

Descriptive Statistics

Descriptive statistics describe the characteristics of a sample or a population, and usually fall into the categories of measures of central tendency (sometimes known as averages) and measures of variation. To use FASTAT to find the average values for sales, for example, you select the Stats command from the Stats menu and ask FASTAT to compute the mean. Figure 14.29 shows how the variable SALES was selected; the mean and standard deviation were computed, as shown in figure 14.30. You also could select a grouping variable (such as GROUP), and compute the descriptive statistics for sales by group.

Fig. 14.28

Part of a StatView data screen with 25 cases and 18 variables.

	Name	sex	Age	Weight	Cholesterol	Chol -
1	S. Kaufman	female	24	123.0	177.0	
2	L. Aycock	male	25	158.0	135.0	
3	G. Lucas	male	22	160.0	152.0	
4	B. Jones	male	22	201.0	188.0	
5	M. Little	male	24	187.0	155.0	
6	R. McClendon	male	21	175.0	166.0	
7	W. Rogers	male	21	146.0	161.0	
8	A. Wright	male	25	177.0	159.0	
9	H. Timms	male	22	167.0	253.0	
10	L. Henry	male	22	156.0	151.0	
11	G. Regular	male	23	162.0	192.0	
12	Walker	male	23	139.0	172.0	
13	B. Hill	male	24	163.0	188.0	
14	D. Smith	male	24	153.0	130.0	
15	C. Norman	male	24	136.0	191.0	
16	G. Oakman	female	23	192.0	167.0	
17	D. Whitsel	male	25	162.0	182.0	
18	J. Williams	male	23	191.0	167.0	

Menu bar: File Edit Font Vars Describe Compare View Tools Σ
Window title: Demonstration Data

Fig. 14.29

Selecting the variables to be analyzed.

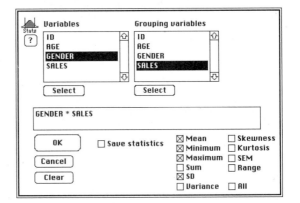

Variables: ID, AGE, GENDER, SALES
Grouping variables: ID, AGE, GENDER, SALES
GENDER * SALES
OK Cancel Clear
Save statistics
Mean, Minimum, Maximum, Sum, SD, Variance, Skewness, Kurtosis, SEM, Range, All

Group Differences

You commonly use group difference statistics when you compare one group's performance to another group's performance. You can compare more than two groups, and the groups can be the same people tested at more than one point in time. The most common of these techniques are the t-test and analysis of variance, which examine differences between the means of different groups.

Fig. 14.30
Simple descriptive
statistics.

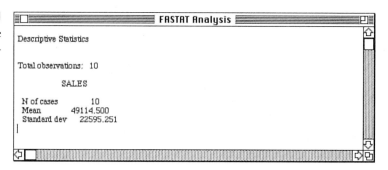

With Minitab (and some Minitab-provided data), for example, you can examine the difference between the means of two samples (see fig. 14.31). You can examine the average preference score for two types of cereals, for example, and determine whether the difference is due to the actual preference people have for the cereal, or to some other factor (which statisticians call chance).

Fig. 14.31
Using Minitab to compare
the difference between the
means of two samples.

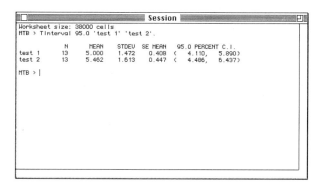

You can extend these statistics techniques by controlling such factors as analysis of covariance. This control makes equal any initial differences between groups. You may want to know the effectiveness of a sales training program, for example, but you don't want years of experience to be a factor. You can use ANCOVA (analysis of covariance) to reduce statistically the influence of years of experience.

SuperAnova is one such program dedicated to the examination of group differences.

Measures of Association and Prediction

Often, questions arise about the relationship between variables. For operations of this type, statistics such as correlation (for examining association) and regression (for examining prediction) are indispensable.

The simple Pearson Product Moment correlation, for example, analyzes how much two variables share—such as sales and number of hours spent in training. The result of this analysis can be direct, where both variables move in the same direction at the same time (see fig. 14.32).

Fig. 14.32

The relationship between two variables in FASTAT.

Or the result can be indirect, where the variables move in opposite directions. These types of analyses give you information about the association between events and say nothing about any type of causal relationship. Just because two variables are related does not mean that they cause one another. Increasing the number of hours spent training salespeople, for example, does not necessarily result in increased sales.

Regression

Regression uses one or more variables to predict another variable. Regression is a common tool used in financial markets to predict prices and other variables. To perform a regression analysis, you enter a series of predictor variables. Based on the variables' relationships to one another and their relationship to what you want to predict, you get a value reflecting the power of the prediction. Figure 14.33 shows the StatView 512+ analysis of the extent to which age, weight, and sex (in a multiple-regression analysis) contribute to cholesterol level.

Nonparametrics

Researchers often find that the samples they work with are too small to truly represent the population from which they were drawn. In such instances, researchers often use nonparametrics, or distribution-free statistics, to enable them to perform tests of significance that would otherwise produce potentially misleading results. Unfortunately, few of these statistical packages teach you anything about how to choose the test that may be appropriate for your research design.

Fig. 14.33
StatView's regression output.

View of Demonstration Data

Multiple Regression Y₁ :Cholesterol   3 X variables

Beta Coefficient Table

Parameter:	Value:	Std. Err.:	Std. Value:	t-Value:	Probability:
INTERCEPT	200.285				
Age	-1.009	3.923	-.054	.257	.7995
Weight	-.132	.296	-.099	.444	.6616
sex	15.692	18.017	.194	.871	.3936

2

Considering Graphical Presentation

Even relatively simple programs like FASTAT can produce powerful graphics like the one shown in figure 14.34, which is a three-dimensional view of sales, training, and grouping. Such graphs can sometimes confuse rather than clarify a situation, however. Because generating the graph is so simple, draw the graph and then decide whether you want to use it. Recently, some very powerful dedicated graphical statistical packages became available for the Macintosh, such as Mathematica, Theorist from Prescience Corporation, and Igor.

Fig. 14.34
A three-dimensional graph in FASTAT.

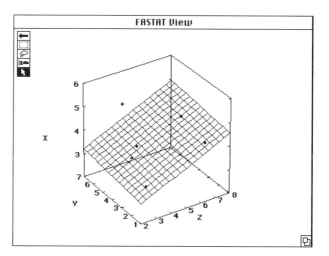

Considering Some Specific Statistic Packages

In addition to full packages such as SYSTAT, MiniTab, and StatView, several fine specialized tools address one procedure or perform one function very well. Sometimes you may need only one very powerful function instead of several less powerful ones.

SuperAnova (from Abacus), for example, is dedicated to univariate and multivariate analysis of variance—perhaps the most common statistical test performed in the social and behavioral sciences. SuperAnova also is very flexible, offering several "canned" models from which to choose (such as repeated measures). You can also design your own model, given your particular needs (nested factors, for example), by using a blank ANOVA table (for "analysis of variance"). People wince at the thought of designing their own models, so this blank screen is about as unfriendly as you can get.

Just for starters, SuperAnova offers analysis of covariance, Latinsquare design, nested designs, planned comparisons, post-hoc comparisons, repeated measures, split-plot designs, and even unbalanced designs. The last option is particularly useful because an assumption of analysis of variance in general is that the cell sample sizes are equal, or at least the cell variances are homogeneous. When this is not the case, such an unbalanced design option can compensate. SuperAnova is a fast program that is intuitive in its design and easy to use. Like the other programs in this section, however, this program is not a general statistics package. SuperAnova is highly specialized; you should know what analysis of variance you're doing before you buy it.

Being able to visualize the way something looks is always a great asset to learning, especially when that something can be quite complex, as in the relationship between three variables. JMP (from SAS) is a subset program of SAS's major statistical package.

With JMP, you can perform statistical analyses, and you can view them by using one of the available graphs. You provide the names of your variables and their level of measurement (nominal, ordinal, and so on), and JMP provides you with paths to take for the analysis—for example, the distribution of Y variables or the fit of one Y by several Xs. After you enter the data into the spreadsheet-like grid, you simply click the mouse to see things such as a graph that helps you figure out just what amount of oil and which type of popcorn yields the most popcorn.

A very sophisticated program from WaveMetrics, called Igor, also helps you visualize the relationship between variables. Igor is based on a data structure that the authors of the application call a wave or a one-dimensional array of numbers (such as scores on a test or number of people who were interviewed). Although Igor does data analysis, its strength is in the quality and information-laden graphs it can produce. Figure 14.35, for example, shows you a graphic representation of some sample Igor data.

Igor provides more than 100 math and utility functions, as well as macro capabilities and a list of options for laying out pages. Igor is not as easy to use as JMP or some other statistical packages (particularly for beginners), but as far as customizing graphs to fit into other manuscripts is concerned, Igor may be the most flexible program—Igor's graphs are easily exportable. And yes, the icon for Igor looks like—you guessed it—the Igor from *Dracula*. But relax; it doesn't say "Yes, Master" (yet, anyway).

Fig. 14.35
A graphical representation of sample Igor data.

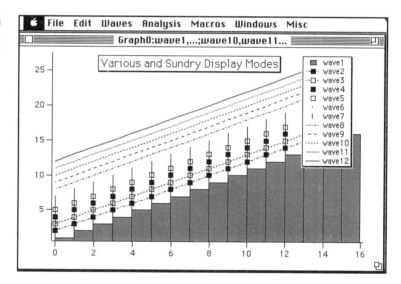

Considering Project-Management Packages

Using multiple time frames and other features, several Macintosh programs can help you with project management. The type of program you need depends on what tasks you have ahead of you. Do you want a simple time line or a complex chart that tracks what gets done and when? In any case, project managers can perform these functions:

■ Outline the tasks involved in a project, organizing those tasks as a sequence of events or as sequence within major topics. (Remember that many word processors have outlining capabilities as well.)

- Generate planning charts that include such important information as project milestones (such as the beginning or end of a project) and the task associated with the milestone (begin construction, or move into a new building).

- Identify the critical path that a project, or a part of a project, needs to take to see completion.

- Allocate and track resources.

- Track tasks, a function that includes supplying information about the task or milestone at hand and the time frame within which a certain task should occur.

- Help you manage a defined set of tasks. If a specific task needs to be rescheduled, your project manager should be able to do it quickly and easily.

Word processors don't speak English, equation solvers don't speak math, and project managers don't speak management. Remember that the people who use the software need to acquire these skills through training or experience. Project managers help you balance resources and needs for meeting the dates or other restrictions on the project.

MacProject

A project-management package is a combination outliner, draw program, and database. The package uses functions from all of these tools, incorporates the tools, and takes a few hundred dollars out of your pocket—but it's well worth the expense. No project management package can meet everyone's needs, but of several available, MacProject illustrates the common characteristics of many of the packages.

MacProject offers eight types of management charts. You can have all charts open simultaneously, but, as in other Macintosh applications, only one window can be active at any one time. The following brief descriptions of each chart and table demonstrate how they are linked.

The Schedule chart's information informs you about conflicts that may occur in the planning and execution of a project. Figure 14.36, a sample chart from MacProject, shows a part of this project chart. MacProject uses different types of visuals to represent different parts of a project; for example, the square-cornered boxes represent tasks (such as Talk to real estate agents), and the rounded-cornered boxes represent milestones (such as Start project).

Fig. 14.36

Part of a schedule chart
generated by MacProject.

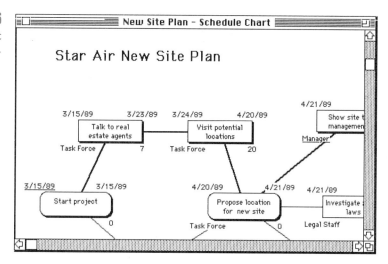

The Resource Timeline and Task Timeline charts include horizontal
bands. Each band represents the amount of time for a particular task,
and the chart can include expected and actual time durations by task.
Figure 14.37 shows the Task Timeline for the information presented in
figure 14.38. The diamond denotes a milestone; the bars represent time
needed for tasks. If you select a task, the information about the task
appears in its own window, where you can edit it. Talking to real estate
agents, for example, is scheduled for a duration of seven days with a
priority level of 100.

Fig. 14.37

The Task Timeline.

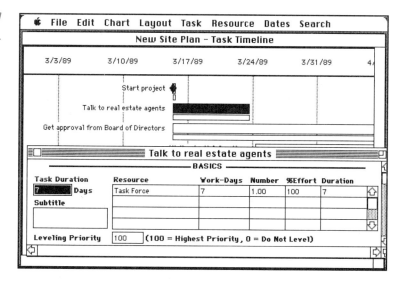

Fig. 14.38

A project table.

Name	Earliest Start	Latest Finish	Slack	Actl
Start project	**3/15/89**	**3/15/89**	**0**	
Talk to real estate agents	**3/15/89**	**3/23/89**	**0**	
Get approval from Board of Directors	3/15/89	4/20/89	7	
Visit potential locations	**3/24/89**	**4/20/89**	**0**	
Propose location for new site	**4/20/89**	**4/21/89**	**0**	
Show site to management	**4/21/89**	**5/18/89**	**0**	
Prepare offer	4/21/89	5/18/89	5	
Investigate zoning laws	4/21/89	5/18/89	10	
Make presentation to New Site Commi	**5/19/89**	**5/26/89**	**0**	
Negotiate contract	**5/29/89**	**6/9/89**	**0**	
Sign contract and begin escrow	**6/9/89**	**6/12/89**	**0**	
Get land-use permits	6/12/89	8/4/89	32	
Inspect landscaping	6/12/89	8/18/89	46	
Make structural repairs	**6/12/89**	**8/18/89**	**0**	
Arrange financing	6/12/89	8/18/89	32	

The Task Cost Entry table shows the cost of each project activity.

The Resource table shows resources assigned to the project.

The Cash Flow table shows the income and expenses associated with the project.

The Project table shows what project tasks happen when, including their beginning and ending dates and the amount of slack time available, if needed. Tasks critical to the project appear in boldface, as shown in figure 14.38. (Tasks appear in red if you have a color monitor.) Because these letters can be large, MacProject includes a condensed version of this chart and can output it to a large plotter for wall charts.

The Resource Histogram displays the amount of work for one resource.

The MacProject structure is similar to that of a relational database. Changes in subprojects are linked to the larger project, and any related scheduling entries update automatically.

As with other complex software, when you use project management software, keep in mind several points:

- Sketch your ideas on paper before you begin to work at the keyboard.

- Talk to the people involved in the project to be sure that you define tasks and responsibilities accurately.

- Use the Subproject option available with many project managers. This feature enables you to schedule several projects as part of a larger one, and helps you organize and manage aspects of the project more efficiently.

- Let your management responsibilities drive the software, not the opposite. Just because a feature is available doesn't mean that you must use it. For example, maybe you have seen documents that use every font, style, and size imaginable—and look horrendous.

Other Project Managers

A terrific project manager, FastTrack Scheduler (from AEC) is a comprehensive application that enables you to work with people and appointments, and schedule projects, too. In page-preview mode, you can see how project charts can be organized by dates across the top and tasks along the side axis. There's even a hard hat thrown into this construction project example. FastTrack doesn't miss a whole lot; it includes a very understandable manual, outlining capability, color, Gantt charts, and more.

Any talk about project management usually ends up with at least the mention of the word flowchart. After all, managing anything is a sequential act (even if at various levels), and the flowchart's primary design (from the top down) lends itself to understanding the order of events. It should be no surprise, therefore, that the leading flowchart design tool is TopDown (from Kaetron). Through a series of tools on an extensive palette, you can create, move, and resize symbols; work with text through a variety of options; and create what TopDown calls Notecards—information that contains as many as 32,000 characters attached to a symbol (see fig. 14.39). When you can create your own symbols, you can really customize your diagrams.

MacInUse, from Softview, can help you track when and how your Macintosh is being used. Some of the possible uses for this program include the following:

- Keeping track of time for client billing

- Tracking the use of resources

- Tracking the use of machines and specific software

MacInUse is simple to install; it records usage data in a separate file named MacInUse Data. At any time, you can examine how your Macintosh is being used. The advanced features of MacInUse enable you to edit existing information forms to meet individual tracking needs. You can keep track of personal use, business use, time spent on work for a specific client, and so on.

Fig. 14.39
Examples of symbols
created in TopDown's
Notecards.

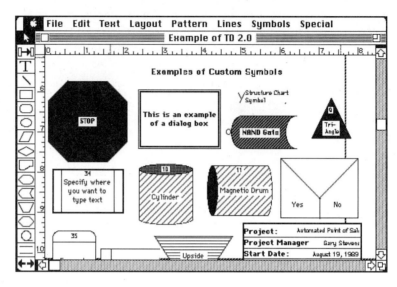

The Big Mac Recommendation

For a personal finance package, Quicken is the most popular choice for good reasons. Managing Your Money has more investment and other financial planning features, and is very popular. Dollars & Sense is a high-quality product, but has suffered from lack of support. Still, it is worth considering.

The decision to buy a certain application depends your needs (and your pocketbook). You can find an application to do just about anything you want. To make the best use of your application, however, you need to remember that most software packages do not teach you what you need to know to understand the results. If you don't know the difference between accounts payable and accounts receivable, for example, it is unlikely that any package will teach you. With some knowledge of the content, however, you can use these tools to increase your output and efficiency, to say nothing of your enjoyment.

CHAPTER FIFTEEN

Desktop Publishing

I n the earlier days of publishing, there was the printer's tray—about two feet by three feet with 89 different compartments, each compartment designed to hold a type character, such as the numeral *1*, the capital letter *A*, or the bracket *]*. The printer's tray stored complete sets of characters. Then each individual piece of type was placed into a composing stick, which held the type while it was composed into lines. The lines of type then were placed into blocks, and these blocks were placed on the press where pages would be printed.

Today, with the advent of desktop publishing (DTP), the tasks of design, composition, paste-up, and other traditional printing steps are performed by computers like the Macintosh and desktop publishing software. Typesetting is still a precise and delicate operation that requires patience, skill, speed, and precision.

Understanding Desktop Publishing

Desktop publishing is the application of desktop computer systems to all phases of the publication process from the entering of text to the production of final camera-ready copy. Desktop publishing has given birth to a new industry: the manufacturing of desktop publishing products and desk accessories; the creation and development of page description languages such as PostScript, and graphic images and clip art; and the production of books, magazines, and newsletters.

Desktop publishing also has helped create a whole new generation of graphic artists capable of producing on their $10,000 or less home systems impressive work that 20 years ago would have required $100,000 or more worth of equipment. The samples in figures 15.1 and 15.2 were composed using PageMaker, the market leader. These pages look almost as good as any professional printer could produce with the most sophisticated equipment, but PageMaker produced the material at a fraction of the price of the more sophisticated equipment.

Consider the range of products that can be produced using desktop publishing techniques. Not everyone has the skill or desire to be a graphic artist, but almost everyone can learn to use the available software and do an acceptable job on

Fliers	Enclosures
Magazines	Manuals
Invitations	Posters
Catalogs	Bulletins
Books	Booklets
Brochures	Charts and graphs
Newsletters	Advertisements
Reports	In-house mail and other publications

CAUTION

R emember that, as some sage once said, "Paint and a canvas do not a Rembrandt make." This comment is as true of desktop publishing as of any other activity that takes training and skill. Some people naturally have a better sense of design than others; but if you have little talent for or experience in design, you probably need to consult a professional designer for desktop publishing projects.

Fig. 15.1
A page produced by desktop publishing.

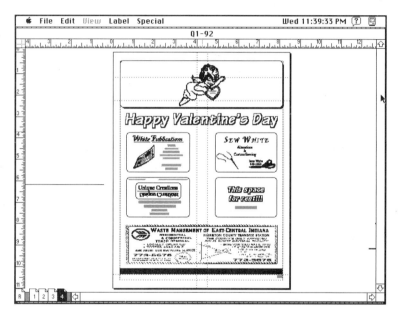

No matter how good your sense of design, you still need instruction and practice using the tools described throughout this chapter. If you need help learning about equipment or software, you can go to your local dealer, read magazines and newsletters, or take a trip to Boston and visit the SIS Applied Technology Center. SIS is a training center with all the available new scanners, software, printers, and more so that you can see how they work together.

This extra effort may not be worth the trouble. If you run a small business that produces invoices once a month and a letter or two a week, you probably don't need to go to the extra expense. Buy a good accounting package that takes care of the invoice forms and a simple word processing program. If you need to produce ads, mail out flyers, create newsletters or such, however, a desktop publishing system may be just what you need. Don't jump into the desktop publishing arena unprepared. Read, talk to others, and look at all the alternatives. In any case, try to do as much as you possibly can with your word processor before you buy a desktop publishing package. Documents produced with even the simplest word processor can have significant impact—especially when it is in the hands of someone who understands the basics of design (which you can learn on your own).

Fig. 15.2
A newsletter template with graphics produced by desktop publishing.

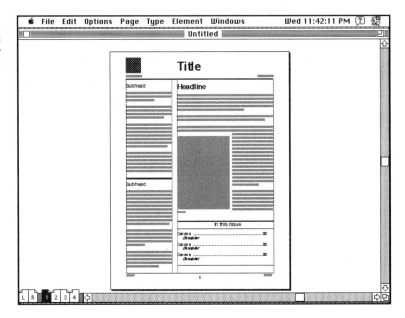

Using a Service Bureau

Service bureaus also are a tool you should have in your arsenal. Service bureaus usually are well-equipped businesses that do everything from design to printing at a page-by-page or hourly rate.

B e sure to shop around. The quality and cost vary widely. In addition, never send your 450-page manuscript for printing without first getting a sample printed.

Service bureaus also have software that home publishers and copy centers can use to send the bureau their files for final output on a high-resolution printer. One such product is ServicePro, developed by softDev, Inc., for $1,995; it is worth every penny.

One book that was published using a Macintosh is *Whale Song, A Pictorial History of Whaling and Hawaii* by MacKinnon Simpson and Robert B. Goodman, published by Beyond Words. The story goes that the authors could not find a publisher. When they said that they would publish the book themselves, they were laughed at and told that they could not afford to publish a book. They did publish it, however, and the book is quite good. Some of the pictures were pasted in, but most were generated on the Macintosh. Now *Time* and *Life* magazines, *The New York Times*, and *National Geographic* do much, if not all, of their prepublication work on the Macintosh. Furthermore, this book, *Que's Big Mac Book*, was written on a Macintosh, and the production department of Que uses Macintoshes to do the layout and design of their books (even the IBM books).

Comparing Traditional Publishing with Desktop Publishing

The use of desktop publishing as a tool to produce printed materials can be appreciated only if you have some understanding of the traditional way that printed materials were designed and then printed.

Don't get the impression, however, that if you don't desktop-publish your newsletter or book you are stuck with lead type and manual printing presses. Today, a good deal of traditional publishing is done using advanced technology, such as the production of inexpensive plates for printing. But rather than literally cutting and pasting images, desktop publishing enables you to store and paste text and graphics electronically. Table 15.1 summarizes the steps taken in both traditional and desktop publishing production and the degree to which desktop publishing tools can help.

Table 15.1
Desktop Publishing in the Publishing Process

Publishing step	Desktop publishing help	How step is accomplished
Develop ideas	None	Read, study, be creative
Write text or copy	A great deal	Desktop publishing packages or word processor
Proofread text	Somewhat	Spelling and grammar checkers
Draw graphics	A great deal	Draw and paint programs, clip art

continues

Table 15.1
Continued

Publishing step	*Desktop publishing help*	*How step is accomplished*
Shoot pictures	A great deal	Scanners
Design page layout	A great deal	Desktop publishing packages
Lay out pages	A great deal	Desktop publishing packages and templates
Produce rough draft	A great deal	Roughs not necessary
Review	None	Personal review
Set type	A great deal	Desktop publishing packages
Print proofs	A great deal	Desktop publishing packages
Print document	A great deal	Desktop publishing packages

Clip art is a collection of drawings, such as automobiles, a child playing, a baseball, and other common objects, that can be cut out of the publication and then pasted into your work. Today clip art (now sometimes called click art) is provided on disk or CD-ROM. You can click (with the mouse) the graphic you want to use and import it into your document. Figure 15.3 shows examples of clip art.

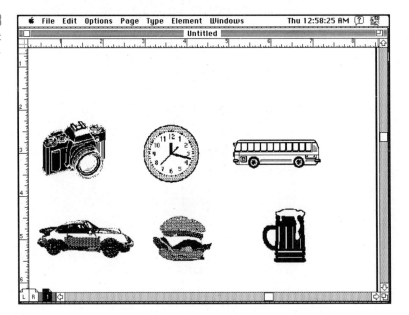

Fig. 15.3
Examples of clip art for the Macintosh.

So much clip art is available that drawings of standard artwork are almost unnecessary. If you want original art, however, try one of the many available paint or draw programs, such as Aldus SuperPaint or IntelliDraw.

Learning Design Basics

Although you may think that all you need for desktop publishing is some software and the right hardware, you must keep in mind certain basic principles of art. Regardless of how you intend to produce your documents, certain basics are essential to success. Following are brief descriptions of some important design principles. The ease of using the Macintosh and the versatility of the software make following these principles a fairly easy task.

Balance dictates that the different areas and elements of the page, chart, or graphic be balanced with one another. In other words, everything of importance should not appear on one page of a two-page spread while the other page contains trivial or visually unappealing material. One way to ensure that visuals are balanced is to place things symmetrically. The problem with anything that's balanced, however, is that it can be so balanced that it becomes boring. For that reason, many designers create elements that are asymmetrical, not symmetrical.

Proportion establishes a sense of relationship among different elements in a design so that objects, sections, types, and sizes of text appear to belong with one another. When elements are in proportion to each other, their size is congruent with their relative importance. If you keep in mind that the subordinate elements are always smaller than the primary, or key, element, you will do fine.

Perhaps the most often stated rule of proportion is the golden section: the ratio of the smaller dimension of an object to the greater dimension of that object is the same as the greater dimension is to the whole. In numbers, this statement means that the ratio of small to large is about 3 to 5, a ratio on which the design of many books is based. Most clip art you see advertised maintains that ratio.

Size is directly related to proportion. Even though items can be proportionate to themselves (remember the 3:5 rule), they may be under- or oversized.

Sequence and *direction* provide for a flow of the information and help keep the reader's interest. Have you ever been bothered by having to turn to three different pages to finish a four-paragraph article? Or have you actually not known where to begin on a page to make sense out of the advertisement or text? We naturally view (and read) from left to right and expect the sequence of items to appear in that order (see fig. 15.4).

Fig. 15.4

Using sequence and
direction to help
the reader.

Emphasis and contrast enhance the meaning of the message you are trying to convey, and white space is the most common element used to achieve these ends. (White space is a blank area in or around your text or graphic.) In any design, the major elements in a design should be emphasized. This emphasis is often accomplished through location, size and weight of type, or use of techniques that help draw attention to the item you want the reader to notice. In figure 15.5, you can see a stationery heading that uses white space effectively by placing elements (the graphic, lines, and so forth) close to one another without crowding.

Fig. 15.5

Emphasizing elements
through the use of
white space.

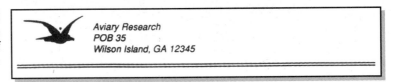

Sink is another technique in which white space is used for emphasis. Sink is extra white space used at the top of the page to provide a bit of interesting imbalance.

The capability to produce color output is available in the high-end desktop publishing packages now. Look at almost any popular Macintosh magazine, such as MacWorld or MacUser. Much of the actual design of these magazines is desktop produced and includes extensive color. A complementary design basic, tone, can almost be thought of as monochromatic color. Tone is used to add fades to designs to highlight a particular element.

The principle of unity dictates that a printed piece convey only one major theme or idea. For example, an advertisement for a certain product should emphasize the advantages the product has over competitors, not elements that are irrelevant to the potential consumer.

Consistency is found in a document in which elements are similar to one another, regardless of their location (unless intentionally different for design reasons). In a consistent document, for example, all first-level headings may be 18-point Helvetica and all text 12-point New York; text begins at the same place on each page, and graphics have the same type of border. The more consistent the elements are within a document, the more weight emphasized elements can have.

Considering Design Techniques

Desktop publishing can help you produce documents that are "clean" and that communicate an important message effectively or convey information in the format you think best fits the task. Putting letters on paper is often not enough, however. Using the following design techniques can further enhance the quality of your productions. Although some techniques (such as kerning) are basic to good presentation, others are fancy flourishes, enabling you to increase the design quality of your letterhead, newsletters, or the simplest memo form.

When you are choosing a desktop publishing package, look for features that support these techniques.

Kerning is the adjustment of space between letters. Most desktop publishing packages automatically kern between certain combinations of letters, depending on the font and the style being used; even then, certain combinations of letters may not look right. As with other characteristics of type, the degree of kerning is determined by appearance, which, after all, is an important test of any document. Figure 15.6 shows a series of letters, for example, that have decreasing amounts of space between them. Several examples of positive and negative kerning are shown to make the point.

Most desktop publishing applications (and word processing programs) enable you to add or subtract space between letters by using a kerning option or keyboard combinations to "step" the space between letters up or down. What you know as expanded type and condensed type are built-in kerning that the application automatically imposes on the letters in selected words. If available, these options usually can be found on the Font dialog box of several word processors. Ligatures are letter combinations, usually used in foreign languages. For example, æ is a combination of the letters a and e.

Fig. 15.6

Different kerning settings.

```
abcdefghijklmnopqrstuvwxyz  -10 kerning
abcdefghijklmnopqrstuvwxyz  -5 kerning
abcdefghijklmnopqrstuvwxyz  0 kerning
abcdefghijklmnopqrstuvwxyz  +5 kerning
abcdefghijklmnopqrstuvwxyz  +10 kerning
```

Desktop publishing applications kern by first drawing an imaginary square around the letters that are to be kerned and then adjusting the space between letters, based on that square. The space between letters is expressed in em spaces. An em space is a square that is the width in points (with 72 points to 1 inch) of the typeface being used. If you are working in 12-point Times, for example, an em space is 12 points wide. Normal spacing, or autokerning, provides about the same-size square for each letter. When you begin adjusting the kerning setting, the space increases or decreases in increments based on the value you enter in that application's dialog box for kerning.

Certain letters (such as *W* and *Y*) need more space; if you begin a word with a capital *W*, for example, you will find that the next letter is spaced more widely than you expect because the *W* takes up a good deal of room by itself. Other letter combinations can give you similar problems and necessitate kerning. Be especially careful with words that begin with the capital letters *W*, *T*, and *Y*.

Although most word processing programs and desktop publishing applications incorporate kerning into their design, third-party kerning tools that are more precise in their adjustments are becoming available. MacKern from ICOM Simulations and LetrTuck Plus from EDCO Services are kerning editors, for example. LetrTuck Plus enables you to adjust the kerning by scrolling in a window. MacKern enables you to view multiple fonts and to see the results of any kerning changes.

Tracking is similar to kerning but is applied to all the letters in selected text rather than to individual pairs of letters. When you tighten the tracking in a selection, the type becomes more dense (see fig. 15.7). Be careful before you apply a tracking correction to a large selection of text because you may be adjusting spaces that would better be left alone.

T he best bet is to allow your application to do most of your kerning and tracking and then manually adjust spacing as necessary.

Before Tracking

You have to be careful if you alter the spacing between letters for an entire selection that you have not changed combinations of letters that should have been left alone.

After Tracking

You have to be careful if you alter the spacing between letters for an entire selection that you have not changed combinations of letters that should have been left alone.

Leading (rhymes with "bedding," not "bleeding") is another type of adjustment. Leading refers to the space between lines of type. When your local printer friend tells you that the type was set 9 on 11, he or she means that the size of the text itself is 9 points and the spacing between the baseline of the letters is 11 points. Most desktop publishing applications automatically set leading at 120 percent of the size of the type, so 10-point type is set with 12-point leading. Figure 15.8 shows you some examples of leading: no leading, or "solid" leading (with the same space between lines as the size of type); the program's automatic leading; positive leading (with more space between lines than the size of type); and negative leading (with less space between lines than the size of type).

Why should you attend to leading? Following are two good reasons:

- When you have slightly more space between lines than the size of the type, the page looks less monotonous.

- Text broken up by white space is easier to read and therefore makes communicating your message easier.

Headlines sometimes look better (an important criterion), for example, when they are set with some positive leading, as you see in the top example in figure 15.9. Line spacing is really leading in disguise.

TIP

D on't get stuck in the leading game and feel that you have to apply different leading to every instance of type.

Runaround, or *wraparound*, is a technique that adds style to the most mundane graphics and text combinations. A runaround is the use of irregular lengths of text with a graphic (see fig. 15.10). Runarounds are usually quite easy to produce with almost any software designed for desktop publishing. They effectively close up white space that might unintentionally draw the reader away from the message.

Fig. 15.8
Examples of different
leading.

Solid Leading

Leading is the amount of white space that is between lines of type. Leading is the amount of white space that is between lines of type. Leading is the amount of white space that is between lines of type. Leading is the amount of white space that is between lines of type. Leading is the amount of white space that is between lines of type. Leading is the amount of white space that is between lines of type. Leading is the amount of white space that is between lines of type. Leading is the amount of white space that is between lines of type.

Auto Leading

Leading is the amount of white space that is between lines of type. Leading is the amount of white space that is between lines of type. Leading is the amount of white space that is between lines of type. Leading is the amount of white space that is between lines of type. Leading is the amount of white space that is between lines of type. Leading is the amount of white space that is between lines of type. Leading is the amount of white space that is between lines of type. Leading is the amount of white space that is between lines of type.

Positive Leading

Leading is the amount of white space that is between lines of type. Leading is the amount of white space that is between lines of type. Leading is the amount of white space that is between lines of type. Leading is the amount of white space that is between lines of type. Leading is the amount of white space that is between lines of type. Leading is the amount of white space that is between lines of type. Leading is the amount of white space that is between lines of type. Leading is the amount of white space that is between lines of type.

Negative Leading

Leading is the amount of white space that is between lines of type. Leading is the amount of white space that is between lines of type. Leading is the amount of white space that is between lines of type. Leading is the amount of white space that is between lines of type. Leading is the amount of white space that is between lines of type. Leading is the amount of white space that is between lines of type. Leading is the amount of white space that is between lines of type. Leading is the amount of white space that is between lines of type.

Fig. 15.9
Leading and headlines.

The Role of Preventing Injuries in Young Children
The Final Report

The Role of Preventing Injuries in Young Children
The Final Report

Fig. 15.10

Text flowing to the side of
a graphic.

One of the nicest features that many desktop publishing packages offer is the ability to wrap around a graphic. One of the nicest features that many desktop publishing packages offer is the ability to wrap around a graphic. One of the nicest features that many desktop publishing packages offer is the ability to wrap around a graphic. One of the nicest features that many desktop publishing packages offer is the ability to wrap around a graphic. One of the nicest features that many desktop publishing packages offer is the ability to wrap around a graphic. One of the nicest features that many desktop publishing packages offer is the ability to wrap around a graphic. One of the nicest features that many desktop publishing packages offer is the ability to wrap around a graphic. One of the nicest features that many desktop publishing packages offer is the ability to wrap around a graphic. One of the nicest features that many desktop publishing packages offer is the ability to wrap around a graphic.One of the nicest features that many desktop publishing packages offer is the ability to wrap around a graphic. One of the nicest features that many desktop publishing packages offer is the ability to wrap around a graphic.

Another type of text and graphics combination is the insertion of the graphic into the text itself (see fig. 15.11). A significant distinction among different desktop publishing tools is whether the text can be made to flow around the graphic or is aligned on one side of the graphic.

Fig. 15.11.

Text flowing around a
graphic.

Another feature that many desktop publishing packages offer is a type of runaround where the text flows around the entire graphic, usually when the text is formatted in columns as you see here.Another feature that many desktop publishing packages offer is a type of runaround where the text flows around the entire graphic, usually when the text is formatted in columns as you see here.Another feature that many desktop publishing packages offer is a type of runaround where the text flows around the entire graphic, usually when the text is formatted in columns as you see here.Another feature that many desktop publishing packages offer is a type of runaround where the text flows around the entire graphic, usually when the text is formatted in columns as you see here.Another feature that many desktop publishing packages offer is a type of runaround where the text flows around the entire graphic, usually when the text is formatted in columns as you see here.Another feature that many desktop publishing packages offer is a type of runaround where the text flows around the entire graphic, usually when the text is formatted in columns as you see here.Another

is formatted in columns as you see here.Another feature that many desktop publishing packages offer is a type of runaround where the text flows around the entire graphic, usually when the text is formatted in columns as you see here.Another feature that many desktop publishing packages offer is a type of runaround where the text flows around the entire graphic, usually when the text is formatted in columns as you see here.Another feature that many desktop publishing packages offer is a type of runaround where the text flows around the entire graphic, usually when the text is formatted in columns as you see here.Another feature that many desktop publishing packages offer is a type of runaround where the text flows around the entire graphic, usually when the text is formatted in columns as you see here.Another feature that many desktop publishing packages offer is a type of runaround where the text flows around the entire graphic, usually when the text is formatted in columns as you see here.Another feature that many desktop publishing packages offer is a type of runaround where the text flows around the entire graphic,

Hyphenation and *justification* features provide several choices for how your words align on a page: ragged right, ragged left, and justified (even margins on both sides). You also can center lines of text. Although each of these has its own place, ragged right is frequently chosen because many desktop publishing programs (and people) don't know where to hyphenate words. In addition, ragged right enables the whole word to be printed without your being concerned with any adjustment between characters and words, which is necessary if justification is in effect. Figure 15.12 shows ragged-right text; figure 15.13 shows the same material set in justified lines; and figure 15.14 shows centered text.

Fig. 15.12
Ragged-right text.

This is ragged right text. This is ragged right text. This is ragged right text. This is ragged right text. This is ragged right text. This is ragged right text. This is ragged right text. This is ragged right text. This is ragged right text. This is ragged right text. This is ragged right text. This is ragged right text.

Fig. 15.13
Justified text.

This text is full justified. This text is full justified. This text is full justified. This text is full justified. This text is full justified. This text is full justified. This text is full justified. This text is full justified. This text is full justified. This text is full justified. This text is full justified.

Fig. 15.14
Centered text.

Please Join Us To Honor

Michael Morely

On The Opening Of His New Business

Line length is one of the rarely mentioned, yet important components of a well-designed page of text. If lines are too short, they look choppy and unreadable (imagine a column one word wide). If lines are too long, they become tedious and boring. As a guideline, a printed line should contain about 70 to 80 characters or about 8 to 12 words. Another way to judge the correct length of a line is that it should be about 2 1/2 alphabets long:

abcdefghijklmnopqrstuvwxyzabcdefghijklmnopqrstuvwxyzabcdefghijklm

Keep in mind, however, that the length of a line and the number of characters in that line depend largely on the size and font you are using.

Adding Special Effects

Reverse type prints white on black (see fig. 15.17). This technique is used to emphasize a particular part of the text and is available on the Page Setup menu of many applications under the Invert Image command. Here are some cautions about using reverse as a technique for emphasis:

- Use reverse only on short phrases; otherwise, it loses its effectiveness.

- Limit the use of reverse to large fonts; otherwise, the little letters get lost in the black.

On many paint and desktop publishing applications, you will find on the same menu that contains the Reverse command other effects such as slant, distort, free rotate, stretch, and perspective. You can see examples of some of these in figure 15.18.

Fig. 15.15

Justified text in a narrow column.

Many people ask me, "Should I buy my computer equipment from some mail order company rather than from a local dealer?" My answer to them is usually, "yes and no." Although this might confuse them even more, there are both pluses and minuses to buying "out of town." Here's a discussion of some of them.

There are several reasons that you might find buying through the mail to be a real advantage.

First, and probably most important, is the significantly lower price that you will pay for the same equipment that you could buy locally. Mail order discounts usually run up to 30 to 40 percent, allowing you to save a significant amount on a system. For example, in my area, the best price that I could get on a complete system looks like this:

Fig. 15.16
Unjustified text in a
narrow column.

Many people ask me, "Should I buy my computer equipment from some mail order company rather than from a local dealer?" My answer to them is usually, "yes and no." Although this might confuse them even more, there are both pluses and minuses to buying "out of town." Here's a discussion of some of them.

There are several reasons that you might find buying through the mail to be a real advantage.

First, and probably most important, is the significantly lower price that you will pay for the same equipment that you could buy locally. Mail order discounts usually run up to 30 to 40 percent, allowing you to save a significant amount on a system. For example, in my area, the best price that I could get on a complete system looks like this:

Fig. 15.17
Reverse is an effective
technique for emphasis.

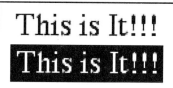

Fig. 15.18
Some other special effects.

Distort

Slant

Perspective

Stretch

Screens, whichare areas of color or shading, are another way to add emphasis and to increase the contrast in a presentation. Most applications enable you to set the density of the screen from 0 percent (white) to 100 percent (black) and provide you with some interesting effects. In figure 15.19, for example, you can see that a 25-percent screen adds to the effectiveness of the presentation.

Fig. 15.19
Using a screen to
emphasize text.

25% shading adds an extra element to text

A *drop cap* is a large letter that drops below the baseline of the line of type. If drop caps are used sparingly to begin a paragraph, article, or advertisement, they are effective for drawing the reader to the starting point of the text. As you can see in figure 15.20, drop caps also enable you to combine what might otherwise appear to be incompatible fonts. Some programs offer variations, such as raised caps, hanging caps, and contoured caps.

Fig. 15.20
A drop cap.

Right after Richard realized that he had left the car door unlocked, he was already in the house.With the lashing winds and rain he was not going back out there for anything, including the map that he found earlier in the abandoned mine shaft. The last time he found himself in this kind of situation, he was sorry that he didn't stay in. But this would be different...or would it?

Manipulating Text

Manipulating text refers to a variety of techniques that can be used, mostly under the control of PostScript language (see Chapter 7, "Printing"), to manipulate text to achieve different effects. In figures 15.21 through 15.26, for example, you can see several screens from SmartArt, which comes in three volumes. You can work with the individual components of each effect you want to incorporate and see the effect before you print or save the image. All these effects are accomplished through the use of PostScript commands.

Fig. 15.21
The SmartArt half-circle text effect.

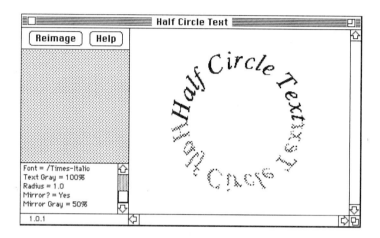

Fig. 15.22
Removing the mirrored effect from the half-circle text.

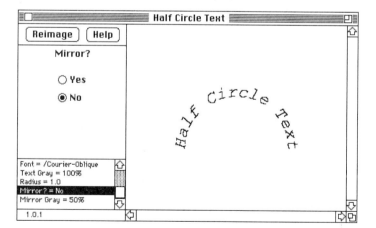

Fig. 15.23
Using the SmartArt
angled text effect.

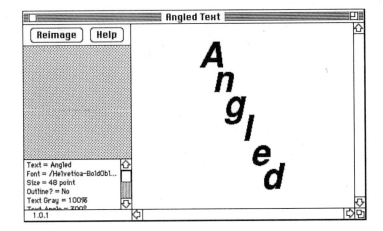

Fig. 15.24
Using the distance text
effect to give perspective.

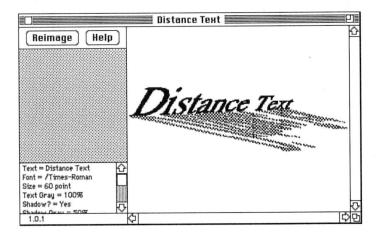

Fig. 15.25
Rotating text by using
SmartArt.

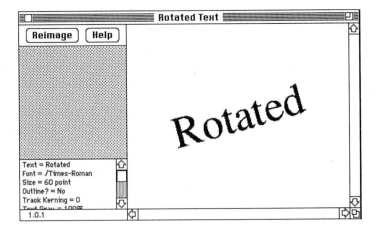

Fig. 15.26

The SmartArt oblique
effect gives text an
interesting slant.

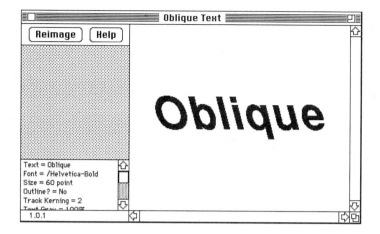

The good part about using programs such as SmartArt is that you don't have to know the PostScript language; you just have to be able to adjust any of the parameters as you want. In figure 15.21, for example, you can see the effect screen for half-circle text with a mirrored effect. In figure 15.22, the mirrored effect was removed and the font changed to Courier. Figure 15.23 shows an example of angled text. You see an unusual shadow effect in figure 15.24. Figure 15.25 shows rotated text, and figure 15.26 is an example of oblique letters. In the figures, you can see examples of different types of effects you can accomplish with PostScript commands or through the use of tools such as SmartArt from Adobe. These techniques fit in a variety of settings and can add a dramatic touch to the final document.

If you can't beat 'em, buy 'em. Adobe did just that when it purchased SmartArt and TypeAlign from Emerald City Software. TypeAlign is a powerful, easy-to-use utility that enables you to flow and manipulate text—adding special effects such as skewing, perspective, and curves—for use with any application.

Another type-enhancing program is TypeStyler by Brøderbund. TypeStyler enables you to create and manipulate decorative type using Brøderbund's SmoothFont technology. TypeStyler is a tool especially useful for designers and advertisers because the images you create with TypeStyler can be exported in many different file formats. The TypeStyler window looks like a page-design application with a drawing area and a set of tools. Creating designs is as simple as using the text tool to enter the text and then applying one of the many (35) predefined shapes and predefined styles. (See Chapter 8, "Using Fonts," for some TypeStyler examples and more details.)

Filling objects with text is another advanced text-manipulation technique. The text fits into an invisible object (an object that is there but that you can't see).

Using Style Sheets and Templates

Another technique to consider in desktop publishing is the use of style sheets and templates. Some programs use style sheets; others use templates.

A *template* is a model for a specific kind of production or graphic. You use the preset formats and specifications and provide your own content. A *style sheet* consists of type specifications for all the elements in a production. You simply enter the codes, and the text is printed in the correct fonts, styles, and size. The idea behind style sheets and templates is to save you time and energy when you reproduce the same design with different words or graphics.

Suppose that you produce a newsletter and, after a great deal of experimentation and hard work, have finally come up with a design you love. The size, style, and font selection are exactly what you need to make the text itself work well with the graphics. For illustrative purposes, here are the steps you follow to create a simple style sheet using QuarkXPress. This procedure is about as easy as it can get, although other applications offer more powerful styling features.

To create a style sheet for a newsletter, follow these steps:

1. Create the newsletter as you want it to appear. Use all the features you want to incorporate, including text characteristics such as size and style, borders, position, and so on.

2. Select the text you want to use as a pattern for defining the style.

3. Choose the Styles command from the Edit menu. When you do this, the dialog shown in figure 15.27 appears.

4. Name the style sheet and click Save.

You have just created a style sheet in the dialog. As you can see, QuarkXPress has assigned particular sizes, styles, fonts, lines, and other attributes to each part of the newsletter. The next time you want to produce another month's newsletter in the same format, you just recall this style sheet and enter the new text or graphic. Everything you enter will appear as you want it. In QuarkXPress, you can even assign a keyboard equivalent to retrieve the style sheet.

Fig. 15.27
The QuarkXPress Styles
dialog.

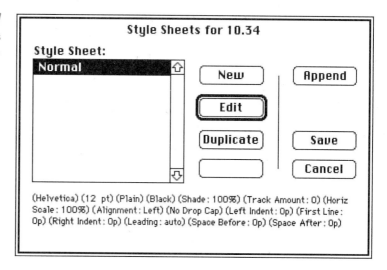

Style Sheets for 10.34

Style Sheet:

Normal

New   Append

Edit

Duplicate   Save

Cancel

(Helvetica) (12 pt) (Plain) (Black) (Shade : 100%) (Track Amount : 0) (Horiz
Scale : 100%) (Alignment : Left) (No Drop Cap) (Left Indent : 0p) (First Line :
0p) (Right Indent : 0p) (Leading : auto) (Space Before : 0p) (Space After : 0p)

Using Default Pages

Another way that some desktop publishing packages create style sheets
is through the use of default pages, called *master pages* in PageMaker.
QuarkXPress enables you to set up a default page, for example, and
enter on that page any information you want to appear on every page,
such as a logo, a heading, certain graphic features, and so forth.

It would be silly for you to have to enter the same design
elements, including lines, white space, styles, and sizes, for each
weekly issue. Why not just design a template? Then you can simply
read the text into the template form and have your finished design.
If your desktop publishing package doesn't have this facility, you
should look around for another package.

Using Predesigned Style Sheets and Templates

Several entrepreneurs came up with style sheets and templates to meet
the need to perform time-saving tasks and to fit existing applications.

Publishing Packs from Adobe are sets of document and font combinations that take the guesswork out of which fonts to use and when.
Publishing Packs contain Optima, Franklin Gothic, and Galliard typefaces, with sample documents showing the use of these fonts, for

example. Publishing Pack versions are available for newsletters, forms and schedules, and presentations. In addition to the examples for creating different types of documents, a good deal of information, including interviews with noted designers, also is included. It's not exactly like having the expert there with you, but, if you can see good examples of what you need to do and read the rationale for why they appear as they do, you're well on your way to learning how to recognize good design.

Aldus, the maker of PageMaker, offers three sets of templates: Designs for Newsletters, Designs for Business Communications, and Designs for Manuals. You wouldn't expect the programs such as QuarkXPress and PageMaker to appear for too long without the introduction of a complement of templates. The designers of these commercial templates do all the work, and you impress your boss (until he asks you how you did the layout). What could be better?

QuarkStyle from Quark is a set of templates for producing publications such as newsletters, fliers, invitations, calendars, and advertisements. Each of the more than 70 templates was developed by a group of noted designers and comes as a part of QuarkStyle. You just enter your own text in the corresponding locations in a copy of the template, and the format is maintained.

CAUTION

Style sheets and templates are great time-savers, but remember that they are limited because they are somewhat fixed in how they prescribe the way your work should look. You can change the elements to better suit your taste, of course. Just don't save the changed style sheets and templates under their original name or the original format will be gone forever.

Annual Reports, Inc. in Franklin, Indiana, has developed templates for corporate annual reports that save corporations time, hassle, and money. The templates work with a desktop publishing system, and after being produced on the Mac, the files are sent to a phototypesetting machine for final output—including color separations.

On the low-price end, Publish It! Easy from Timeworks offers an entire disk of ideas as templates that you can use to design your own documents such as advertisements, coupons, fax forms, invitations, memos, and newsletters.

Surveying Desktop Publishing Applications

Desktop publishing has become one of the most widespread applications of the Macintosh computer. Newsletters, magazines, and even complete books and daily newspapers are designed, prepared, and published using programs such as QuarkXPress, PageMaker, and the like. This section gives you an overview and a comparison of their different features.

D esktop publishing packages are different from one another in terms of what they can do. Be sure to read the section "Buying a Desktop Publishing Package" before you go out and spend many dollars on something that may be too much or too little for what you need.

The packages examined in this chapter are PageMaker; Ready, Set, Go!; QuarkXPress; Interleaf; and several low-end packages (which often offer everything you need at a much lower price). These packages were chosen because they are the market leaders in sales. As you will see throughout this discussion, however, many of the effects achieved by desktop publishing also can be achieved by the word processors discussed in Chapter 10, "Working with Word Processors."

PageMaker

Apple is responsible for the term *desktop publishing*, but PageMaker from Aldus was the first full-featured product to be marketed aggressively as a desktop publishing package. PageMaker is absolutely filled with features that enable even novice users to produce documents that look decent even at their worst; in the hands of a capable designer, this program has almost no limitations.

Using a pasteboard, you drag text and graphics to the pages on which you are working in order to complete your design. The pasteboard allows for the storage of frequently used text and graphics and the easy movement of elements to pages. PageMaker has all kinds of capabilities to make your desktop publishing easier. These capabilities include the following:

- Automatic conversion of regular quotation marks (") to "smart quotes" ("")

- Story Editor that enables fully integrated word processing within PageMaker
- Complete control over type, including rotation of text and expanded and condensed text
- Extensive use of style sheets
- Expanded color capabilities
- Automatic table of contents and indexing
- Search-and-replace features
- Spelling checker
- Automatic flow of text from one page to the next until all the text is incorporated into the PageMaker document
- Wrapping of text around graphics and even through a graphic for interesting effects
- Adjustment of brightness and contrast in scanned and bit-mapped images
- Flexible grid system for alignment of text and objects
- Differently-sized views of the drawing
- Object-oriented drawing tool

If PageMaker leaves you anything to complain about, it's the program's complexity which makes it difficult to learn and use. But the product continues to set the standard; Aldus has made some changes and has greatly enhanced the word processing capabilities of the program.

Ready, Set, Go!

Ready, Set, Go! from LetraSet is also a popular desktop publishing program. It offers gray-scale enhancements and a word processor with several advanced features (including glossaries, case conversion, and search and replace of both formatting and text). This program also offers design grids and color-separation capability. Ready, Set, Go! is relatively small compared to giants such as PageMaker.

As with other programs, like QuarkXPress and PageMaker, you begin Ready, Set, Go! with a master page. Into this form you enter any text or graphics you want to appear on every page.

This program is usable and priced below Pagemaker and QuarkXPress, but it is not as powerful in its control over page elements. Ready, Set, Go! offers conversion of quotes and importing of graphics, for example, but does not enable bit-map editing, or offer on-line help or automatic rules with paragraphs.

QuarkXPress

QuarkXPress from Quark is an excellent choice for its capability to work with type specifications. QuarkXPress has been a contender for the number-one position in sales, and now the program's capabilities have really begun to shine.

QuarkXPress is designed so that the boxes you create for text and graphics can be manipulated as you see fit. Creating separate boxes for everything from a visual to a drop cap allows you great flexibility in page design. In addition, boxes can be linked easily so that text flows from one part of the document to another. This feature is especially helpful for magazine and newsletter publishers, who need to keep readers on track about where text in one column picks up again in another column. QuarkXPress also has extensive and easy-to-use full-color features and color-separation tools.

QuarkXPress really shines in its typography capabilities. Kerning is precise (up to 1/200 of an em space, which for a 12-point letter is .0006 of a point). QuarkXPress has excellent word processing capabilities and can import text files from more word processors than any other desktop publishing package. The package imports files from Word, WordPerfect, WriteNow, MacWrite, and others. Like Ragtime, QuarkXPress also allows for searching and replacing of words based on their attributes.

Interleaf Publisher

Interleaf Publisher is a desktop publishing package that does everything and more. In addition to multiuser capabilities, Interleaf Publisher offers superior handling of long documents; compatibility with a variety of operating platforms, such as Macintosh, UNIX, and DOS; and many tools for dealing with long documents, including automatic figure numbering, cross-referencing, column balancing, drawing, and graphics.

Interleaf is a tremendous tool for desktop publishing, but this program comes at a price. The price is an interface that is very "unMac-like." The nonintuitive interface does not always make sense to Macintosh users.

The program requires some relearning of procedures. In addition, Interleaf does not work well with Adobe and other PostScript fonts, and Interleaf uses its own page-description language, again complicating matters. For example, Interleaf does not print on non-PostScript printers. Interleaf is a workhorse, however, and may be what the large publisher requires if many people need access to the software at the same time.

Other Packages

Another desktop publishing package worth mentioning is Multi-Ad Creator from Multi-Ad Services. Although it is not a desktop publishing package in the same genre as those already discussed, Multi-Ad Creator offers an extensive selection of tools for creating high-quality documents. This program is graphically oriented (as most advertisements should be), as you can see by the opening screen. Multi-Ad is ideal for graphically based productions such as coupons and layout-intensive tasks. The program also can check spelling but was not designed for large text-oriented tasks such as books or even long newsletters. Some of its notable features are design sheets (like style sheets), customized layout sizes, and rotation of objects. Multi-Ad Creator costs just under $1,000.

Don't get bowled over by the cost of these high-end desktop publishing packages. Sooner or later, companies catch on and start producing lower-cost (but not disproportionately less powerful) packages. Some of these programs are discussed next. These programs are the middle ground between word processing programs and the full-fledged desktop publishing applications.

Publish It! Easy is one such package that provides power at a low cost. This program is a stepchild of the Timeworks full package, Publish It, and has many of the same features. Some of its best features are as follows:

- 112,000-word spelling checker and 240,000-word thesaurus
- Advanced page-layout capability
- Built-in drawing and painting tools
- Hyphenation
- Mac-like word processing
- Tons of templates

One of the basic differences between packages such as Publish It! Easy and high-end programs such as PageMaker is that Publish It! Easy, although a great start, lacks the multitude of typographer tools that characterize PageMaker and make it so popular.

Recognizing that PageMaker is not easy for the average user to learn, Aldus released Personal Press. Personal Press offers many of the features of PageMaker but at a much lower cost (about a fifth of PageMaker's price) and in a much easier to learn format. Personal Press offers an AutoCreate feature that leads you through a series of dialogs to create a document quickly and easily.

Although it is a scaled down version of PageMaker, Personal Press is not lacking in features and is suitable for small businesses or even individuals needing to create flyers, newsletters, and other smaller publications. The program has the following features:

- Text-wrapping around graphics—an important DTP feature

- Copy Fitting that automatically adjusts your text to fit

- AutoFlow that adds pages as needed automatically

- Features such as drop caps, bullet text, smart quotes, and other text enhancements

- Full drawing capability including free rotation of graphics, scaling, cropping, shadows, halftones, and more

The AutoCreate feature is very impressive and recommends the package to the new user. AutoCreate takes you step by step through the creation of a publication. Although I never had seen the package before, I was able to easily create a fictitious publication using the tutorial sample graphics and text (see fig. 15.28).

The Writing Center from The Learning Company might be the easiest to use of all these packages. It allows for some sophisticated page-layout tools, a 100,000-word spelling checker, more than 200 professional-quality color and black-and-white images, wraparound text, and easy movement of graphics. It can even import PICT drawings you create with other applications.

These less-expensive applications are not substitutes for the top-of-the-line models, but they can meet the needs of many desktop publishers who feel that they need more features but really don't.

Fig. 15.28
A newsletter created with
Personal Press.

More and more desktop publishing tools are becoming available. One of these tools is UltraSpec from Publication Technologies, a HyperCard stack dedicated to computing copyfitting calculations for design and layout purposes. The opening screen shows the UltraSpec menu bar. This program also comes with an audiotape that talks you through the program and helps you get started. You select typefaces, sizes, leading, scaling, and so on as you tell UltraSpec about your document. The program then tells you the amount of space you have available.

Buying a Desktop Publishing Package

Suppose that you're about to go into business for yourself. The subject of buying printers and so forth is covered in Chapter 25, "Choosing a Printer"; this chapter focuses on desktop publishing software.

Following are some tips to keep in mind:

■ Know your projects. If you are a newspaper publisher planning to switch to Macintosh software, your needs are certainly different from those of the publisher of a simple newsletter printed on a laser printer and sent out from home. Start itemizing the tasks you need to do but can't do with your word processor.

- Don't forget about word processors and what they can do. Top products such as Microsoft Word, WordPerfect, and FullWrite can often match the capabilities of the more sophisticated desktop publishing packages.

You probably already know that a decent desktop publishing package costs from $100 to $500 or more. Some desktop publishing packages come with word processing and graphics capability, and some of them do not. If you do not have a word processor, the question is whether you should invest in a desktop publishing package rather than a word processor such as Microsoft Word, WriteNow, or Nisus.

Stand-alone word processors have many features that make them similar in function to desktop publishing systems. Most can do page layout, print preview, margin settings, and so on. If you can create columns, for example, is that desktop publishing or word processing? Such an argument can go on and on, but the fact still remains that word processing programs such as Microsoft Word and Nisus have some extraordinary desktop publishing features:

- Capability to print back-to-back pages

- Capability to import standard graphics formats

- Use of sidebars that contain graphics or text (important in the production of magazine formats)

- Ease in setting leading

- Selection of measurement units including lines, inches, centimeters, picas, points, and even pixels

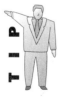

Get some of the popular books on these word processors and see whether you can find examples of what you can do with their desktop publishing features. If you find that you are too limited, then consider purchasing a desktop publishing package.

When you are purchasing a desktop publishing package, consider the following:

- Be sure that the desktop publishing package you are selecting can read files created in your regular word processor, or the text may have to be reentered or read as a text file (and you lose all your formatting codes).

- Try to meet two goals—word processing and desktop publishing—with only one application.

- Keep in mind updates, service, and support; these can make all the difference in the world.

Using Desktop Publishing Utilities

Now that desktop publishing is in full swing, there are a great many utilities available that can be welcome additions to your favorite DTP program. A brief description of some utilities that may make your desktop publishing more enjoyable follows:

SmartScrap from Solutions is a desk accessory that enables you to organize multiple scrapbooks.

Now Scrapbook—part of the Now Utilities package—also enables you to manage several scrapbooks and hold a variety of different types of items from text to graphics as well as sound and QuickTime movies.

The Clipper, also from Solutions, enables you to clip and insert images so that they fit.

DeskPaint from Zedcor gives you full power as a DA painting tool to fix up images within an application that may not have the full power you need.

ImageGrabber from Sebastian grabs screen images and saves them.

Exposure Pro by Baseline also is an excellent screen shot tool and was used in the writing of this book.

Capture! by Mainstay is yet another good quality screen shot tool and was used to capture some of the figures of this book.

MathType from Design Science inserts mathematical expressions into a document.

DiskTop from CE Software cleans up files and general all-around Finder stuff.

OnLocation from Go Technology finds files and text in files for you.

Capturing Screens

You don't realize it when you begin a project, but you may often need to have an exact duplicate of what you see on your Macintosh monitor. You may need the image for teaching purposes or for capturing a screen for printing in another document such as a manual or a third-party book like this one.

All image-grabbing programs work basically the same way. You invoke them to "snap" a picture of the image on-screen. Many of these programs have a time-delay feature that enables you to set a certain number of seconds before you invoke the capture program that takes the picture. Others (such as Exposure Pro) take over the screen and give you a palette of editing controls.

You can use the Macintosh Command-Shift-3 key combination to take a picture of the screen and save it to disk. Unfortunately, this built-in screen dump has little power and no options. Camera, a 1984 shareware utility, was great until Version 4.2 of the Macintosh operating system became obsolete. Camera then died a slow death (but we owe the concept and what we have to its developer, Robert Esau).

Capture from Mainstay can save files in PICT or other graphic format and the latest version can capture the cursor on-screen. Capture was the program I used for quite a while in the production of screen shots (and some in this book were done using the latest version), but lately Capture has slipped to my second choice due to the lack of on-screen editing capability.

ImageGrabber from Sebastian enables you to frame in any part of the screen you want. It has a time-delay option and can then save that image to the Clipboard as a Paint or PICT file, or it can print the image (see fig. 15.29).

Fig. 15.29
The ImageGrabber
screen options.

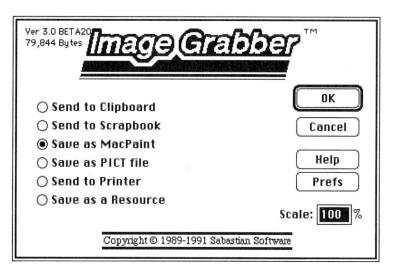

A tool that many desktop publishers find invaluable is Partner from Salient. This INIT helps integrate graphics applications into word processing or page layout and desktop publishing applications such as Word, PageMaker, QuarkXPress, or RagTime. These graphic insertions then can be edited but remain linked to the original application through which they were created.

Exposure Pro from Baseline was used in the creation of this book. Exposure Pro enables you to edit the screen with standard drawing tools before the screen is saved. You can save to disk, to the Scrapbook, to the Clipboard, as a Macintosh resource for incorporation into an application, or as a StartupScreen.

Baseline also offers a smaller, less powerful screen shot utility called—appropriately enough—ScreenShot for those who do not need such features as the capability to edit the screen shot.

Learning Desktop Publishing

Many companies offer desktop publishing assistance. Be sure to read the hints about participating in these programs before you schedule your time to do so. Other companies offer programs that teach you about the procedures of desktop publishing.

One instructional software package is DTP Advisor from Brøderbund, which consists of a bunch of HyperCard stacks that take you through the steps of planning, management, design, typography, art production, and printing. DTP comes with master forms that you can use for your own desktop publishing projects, as well as typography and printing-specifications forms that make your desktop publishing life much easier.

Also important are the printed materials (books, newsletters, and so on) that can offer you substantial help. Two books by Roger C. Parker are easy to read and full of good information. *The Make Over Book* shows you before and after examples of advertisements, brochures, newsletters, and more. *Looking Good in Print* is a basic guide to good design. Both books are available from Ventana Press. Remember that good desktop publishers are not born—they're made.

The Big Mac Recommendation

Again you're faced with a choice. PageMaker is the leader in the marketplace and for good reason. Tons of articles and books about the product are available, and Aldus supports the program strongly. PageMaker does not, however, come with as powerful a word processing feature as does the other contender, QuarkXPress.

QuarkXPress is the choice of many for typography because it has many fine-tuning tools to set attributes such as leading and kerning and because you can work with graphics so easily. In fact, Quark's word processing has so many features that you may be able to skip purchasing a word processor altogether, especially if you do not need advanced features such as index generation.

PageMaker and QuarkXPress have been the top two packages for some time now. The gap in features between them has closed as each has been upgraded. Serious users such as businesses should consider both to determine which will best suit their needs.

For the small business and the individual, Personal Press is the clear winner, especially with AutoCreate. Although the complete novice will have to do some reading and learning, the user familiar with the Macintosh but new to DTP should be able to put the program to use quickly.

This chapter has given you some idea of the possibilities of desktop publishing. The information about the packages available should help you get started with desktop publishing.

There may be no other type of application that has so quickly thrust the Macintosh into the hands of the business world. The savings are immediate, the technology is relatively easy to use (given the complexity of the old cut-and-paste and typesetting by hand that required years of study and work to master), and the outcome can be nothing short of fantastic. Whether you do the school newspaper or an investment magazine sent to 50,000 readers, you can't go wrong by investing in Macintosh equipment and software for desktop publishing.

CHAPTER SIXTEEN

Using Graphics Software

T he most distinctive feature of the Macintosh is probably the graphical user interface, sometimes called a GUI. This interface is what makes the Macintosh so easy to work with; you simply manipulate the appropriate visual symbol, or icon, on-screen to accomplish a task. This interface also makes producing Macintosh graphics simple.

Graphics routines (such as a routine for drawing a circle) are embedded in the Macintosh's ROM, and graphics programs can access these routines directly. Not only does Macintosh approach the goal of providing a match between the screen display and the printed output, but it enables you to create graphics intuitively. If you want to draw a circle, for example, you select the icon that looks like a circle. If you want to paint an area, select the paintbrush. This simple, straightforward approach is largely responsible for the Mac's success.

This simplicity does not sacrifice power, however. With graphics programs such as FreeHand, Adobe Illustrator, Super 3D, Mac3D, MacroMind, IntelliDraw, and a host of others, you can create visual images of almost anything imaginable.

The wonderful images you see reproduced in Macintosh publications were produced on a Macintosh. The first MacPaint image (circa 1984) shown to the world on a Macintosh 128 startled some, excited others, and started a revolution in creating and printing graphics.

This chapter discusses the many different types of graphics programs that are available: paint and draw programs, programs with pre-drawn images (often called clip art), utilities to manage clip art, three-dimensional graphics programs, and enhanced draw programs known as CAD (computer-aided design) programs. This chapter also covers charts, color graphics, and scanners—hardware that turns hard copy into a screen image.

Understanding Graphics Software

Macintosh graphics programs are usually divided into one of two categories: paint or draw. Some programs, such as Canvas from Deneba and SuperPaint from Aldus, can create images of both types.

Paint programs draw with bit-mapped images, filling in individual dots, or *pixels*. MacPaint II creates a circle in a pattern you control, for example. You can manipulate the shape of the circle by using paint tools to add or delete pixels. The major advantage of paint programs is their flexibility; you can add, delete, or change the appearance of single pixels. A disadvantage is that the resolution of these bit-mapped paint files may not be precise enough for finished artwork. Some applications have gone beyond the 72 pixels per inch (the Macintosh screen resolution) of the original MacPaint and can produce more fine-tuned graphics. SuperPaint 3.0, for example, offers 300-dpi images that you can edit.

Draw programs, which are object-oriented, do not create an object as a configuration of dots. These programs generate a mathematical expression (sometimes based on vectors) that produces the outline of the object. Each mathematical expression is represented on a separate physical layer, so you can draw one object (a circle, for example), and then place it over another object (such as a square). One measure of the power of a draw program is the number of layers the program can manage. You can reverse the order of the objects by rearranging the layers on which they are drawn.

Because you are dealing with objects, you cannot edit the object as you can with a paint program, but you can resize it. Graphic images have "handles" surrounding the item that enable you to resize the object.

The major advantage of draw programs is that they produce a higher-resolution image with smooth, rather than jagged, curves. You see jagged curves on-screen because of the monitor's limitations.

Vector graphics are based on a set of points and the rules that are used for connecting them. Like object-oriented graphics, a line between two points is the unit for drawing and manipulation. Although generally very fast, vector graphics don't have the richness of paint graphics.

You notice graphics first in a design, and you can learn much by spending a few extra minutes examining designs that occur all around you. Look at the cereal box, the newspaper, the latest issue of a sports or fashion magazine, the newsletters you receive, and even the junk mail that you think is ugly. Ugly material can teach you what not to do. The more you look, the more trained your eye becomes.

Using Paint Programs

This section describes several popular paint programs. A good paint program should have the following features:

- Intuitive tools and design
- Adjustable grids
- Sufficient drawing area
- Printing capability for your needs
- Tools to enlarge parts of a painting
- Adjustable grids with optional rulers

- Skew, distort, and perspective capabilities
- Edge tracing to fine-tune fill patterns and to smooth jagged lines
- Brush and spray cans that can be edited
- High-resolution bit-mapped editing
- Color (which is quickly becoming a necessity)

In addition to all these features, paint programs are relatively cheap compared to what you pay for traditional art supplies. FullPaint and MacPaint cost much less than a good drafting or drawing table alone.

MacPaint 2.0

MacPaint, the first paint program for the Macintosh, has to be one important reason why the first Macintosh screens received such good reviews. On what other desktop machine could you draw with the mouse as you do with a pencil, fill in the drawing, erase mistakes with a few clicks, and save the result? MacPaint was the preferred program for some time.

MacPaint 2.0 from Claris is still very popular. MacPaint 2.0 is an up-graded version of the original, and the newest version does offer the following enhancements:

- The capability to open multiple documents
- Tear-off menus that you can remove from the menu bar and place on-screen anywhere you want
- The capability to save preferences you select with the file
- Auto scrolling when a drawing or selection tool reaches the edge of the screen
- The capability to view and edit documents at reduced or enlarged sizes
- The capability to take a snapshot of a screen and refer to it as you work

As an added advantage, MacPaint 2.0 shows Claris's devotion to making easy-to-use software with a consistent user interface.

Other Paint Programs

Three other programs deserve mention and your attention if you don't want to spend hundreds of dollars. Color MacCheese from Delta Tao is inexpensive. The program's manual begins with the sentence, "This manual was designed to be useless." That statement reflects the ease with which the program works. Color MacCheese comes with unique tools such as The Rake (for making edges fuzzy), The Water Drop (for smoothing edges), and the Transmogrifier (a ray gun icon that adds realism and texture to selections). Standard tools such as those of the venerable MacPaint and many other features well worth exploring also are available.

Crystal Paint from Great Wave is a unique paint program that enables you to create intricate images such as the one you see in figure 16.1. Crystal Paint resembles the original Brush Mirrors from MacPaint but has many more options.

Fig. 16.1
A Crystal Paint image.

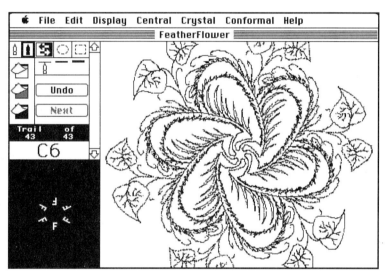

Finally, there is a paint program that is as beautiful to look at (packaging, manual, and entire presentation) as it is intriguing to use. MacCalligraphy from Enzan-Hoshigumi even comes with rice paper to print on and includes specialized tools to create drawings (see fig. 16.2). A reduced image always is available in the lower right corner.

KidPix (Brøderbund) is indeed the "new kid" on the block. This award-winning paint program for children allows for many of the same features found in MacPaint and MacDraw, but the interface is kid-oriented. It has an option for "little kid" displays, for example, that relies heavily on pictures rather than words, a great way to introduce children to art and the Macintosh as well. This program is discussed more in Chapter 20, "Learning and Having Fun."

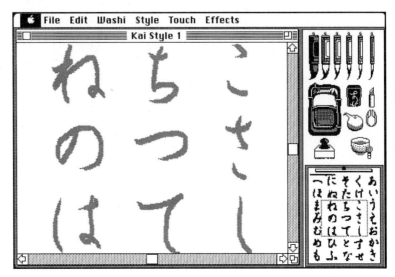

Fig. 16.2
You can use your Macintosh to do high-quality calligraphy.

Paint Desk Accessories

Another category of paint programs includes programs that can be used as desk accessories as well as stand-alone applications. You install these programs as desk accessories by dropping them into the Apple Menu Items folder in System 7, or by using the Font/DA Mover utility provided by Apple in System 6 to install the accessory in the System file. If you have access to your paint program as a desk accessory, you simply call up the program when you are working on a document and need to fine-tune or create a graphic. This category includes programs such as DeskPaint from Zedcor and Canvas from Deneba. DeskPaint and Canvas offer the same basic tools that most paint programs offer. Canvas is discussed in more detail in the "Using Programs with Paint and Draw Capabilities" section.

Using Draw Programs

This section describes the features that some popular draw programs offer. Although draw programs have become less popular because of their editing limitations, the technology used in these programs has provided a basis for such expanding areas as computer-aided design (CAD).

Among other things, a good draw program does the following:

- Includes intuitive drawing tools
- Can group and ungroup objects (the primary unit you work with)
- Can align objects with one another
- Can change the order in which objects appear
- Can work with bit-mapped images created with paint programs
- Offers Bézier-curve capability
- Offers gray scaling
- Defines ruler settings
- Creates arrows and special lines
- Saves to different file formats
- Has full font, style, and size control
- Locks and unlocks object arrangements
- Provides 2-D drop shadows and 3-D shadowing
- Has word wrap

Draw programs differ from each other in the extras they offer and the special things they can do to set your creations apart from the ordinary.

MacDraw Pro

MacDraw Pro is a new and different version of the old standby MacDraw that originally came packaged with the Macintosh (as did MacWrite and MacPaint). Now produced and marketed by Claris, MacDraw Pro offers a variety of tools suited for users who need to draw with precision: designers, architects, and engineers, for example. MacDraw Pro is almost as easy to use as the original MacDraw, so it is suitable for users who have used the Macintosh interface and prefer to stay with the familiar. This familiarity makes the program easy to learn and use.

Although more sophisticated draw programs are available, such as Claris CAD (a kind of grown-up MacDraw aimed at the professional design market), MacDraw Pro is relatively inexpensive and often produces quite acceptable graphics. The program provides 500 layers and 3,200 percent enlargement features and can produce complex designs. Figure 16.3 illustrates an advertisement created with MacDraw Pro; figure 16.4 shows a neat flow chart illustration. Both of these designs are included as desktop publishing templates with MacDraw Pro.

Fig. 16.3

An advertisement created
with MacDraw Pro.

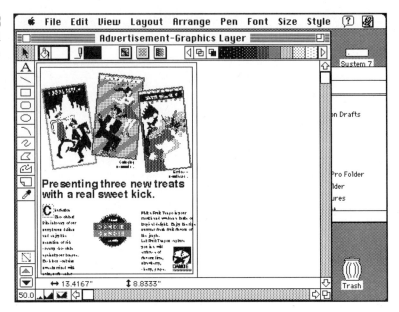

Fig. 16.4

A sales document created
with MacDraw Pro.

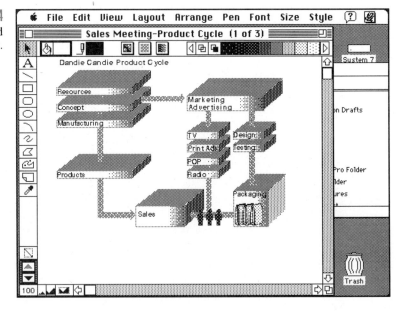

The latest version of Claris CAD increases the flexibility of MacDraw Pro with add-ons to the existing draw features. These new features include the following:

- The capability of creating slides and preparing presentations

- Notes that can be attached to certain parts of a drawing

- Smoothing, grouping, aligning, rescaling, and more

When you add these features to MacDraw's capability of enlarging an area 32 times or reducing it to 3 percent of its original size, you can see why many users need only this graphics program.

You also can customize MacDraw Pro for your specific needs. You can design your own patterns, for example. When you double-click an existing pattern, you see a dialog that enables you to customize the pattern by changing its contents (see fig. 16.5). Figure 16.6 shows a solid white fill pattern transformed into a diagonal line pattern. This pattern is available as a fill; it replaces the solid white square.

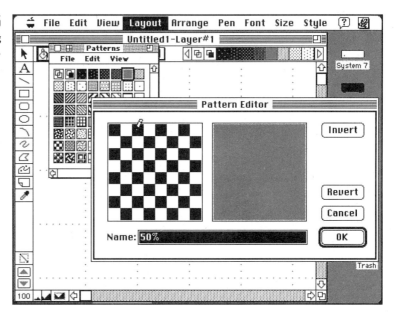

Fig. 16.5
The Pattern Editor dialog in MacDraw Pro.

You also can add color to the available patterns. When you create a color pattern, it appears on the pattern bar as an entirely new entry.

Fig. 16.6

Applying a pattern in
MacDraw Pro.

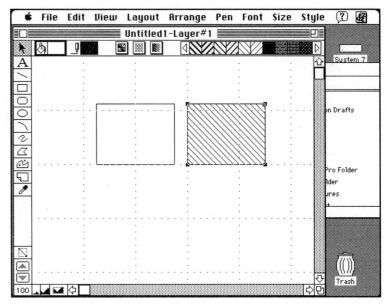

Illustrator and FreeHand

If you need to produce all types of graphics from simple graphic images
to the most complex you can imagine, consider purchasing either
Illustrator from Adobe or FreeHand from Aldus graphics package.

Adobe Illustrator and Aldus FreeHand are competitive, with only slightly
different features. Either program should meet your need for an advanced PostScript drawing tool. Both programs have the following
features:

- Blend tools that enable you to blend shapes and colors

- Autotrace tools that enable you to convert an imported image into
  an object image

- Pantone matching system (the standard system used to match
  printer's ink colors from screen to printed job)

- Customizable patterns

- Capability of converting paint files to object-oriented PostScript
  files

- Utilities for creating color separations

Illustrator was the first of the two programs on the market, and Adobe has worked hard to stay competitive. The following features characterize Illustrator:

- The precise FreeHand drawing tools—important for illustrators who produce detailed work
- Preview capabilities for viewing the artwork, the template, or both on-screen
- Multiple windows
- A color separator
- An autotrace feature
- Full use of the Adobe Type Manager

FreeHand offers these features:

- Outstanding type features and type control, such as the capability of mixing fonts, styles, and sizes in text blocks
- Familiar user interface
- Multiple text blocks
- Automatic and manual kerning
- Text "on a path"
- As many as 100 levels of Undo
- Grids for helping to align and size objects in your drawings
- As many as 200 layers
- Clip art library

You can achieve stunning effects with Illustrator and FreeHand. You can create the same special effects (such as arced letters) with these PostScript drawing tool packages as you can with SmartArt, discussed in Chapter 15, "Desktop Publishing."

The Illustrator versus FreeHand contest continues with the differences between the two diminishing with each successive version. As the competition becomes more intense, users benefit by getting a better product with more features.

If you use much text in your illustrations and want flexibility, FreeHand may be your best choice. If you want increased precision and control over the basic drawing tools, however, Illustrator probably should be your choice.

Using Programs with Paint and Draw Capabilities

Canvas and SuperPaint 3.0 have both paint and draw capabilities. With these programs, you can create and work with object-oriented or bit-mapped images, translating them back and forth simply by switching between a paint brush and a drawing tool icon. The paint and draw tools are used in separate layers, but the output appears as one layer. In SuperPaint, you can switch from paint to draw and back again by checking the appropriate icon.

Canvas

Canvas was one of the first programs to combine paint and draw capabilities. Canvas is remarkably versatile, and it can produce a hard-copy image up to 9.3 feet square (in sections, of course). Canvas works best on a Macintosh II series machine, which enables you to take advantage of its color features. One of the most helpful features of Canvas is its Object Manager, which enables you to keep information about a particular object—such as foreground and background colors, height, type of object, and dpi—in one place for easy access. Canvas is particularly helpful if you design and work with more than one complex graphic at the same time.

Another Canvas feature is the Layer Manager, similar to the file managers found in many applications. The Layer Manager helps you manage the different layers a draw program creates. As you manipulate these layers, the Layer Manager keeps you informed of the status of the layer you are working with. In addition, Canvas has Ruler, Pen, Arrowhead, Pattern, and Color Managers that give you a high degree of control over its features.

Power users appreciate Canvas's capability of producing a MacroObject. Macros are small programs that enable you to store keystrokes and replay them at a later time. The keystrokes you store to create a MacroObject represent objects that can be stored in libraries. Another convenience is that you can store these MacroObjects as tools to facilitate their selection later.

SuperPaint 3.0

The original SuperPaint was a major step up from the original MacPaint, offering a combination of painting and drawing layers. You could use both pixel-based paint objects and object-based graphics objects in the same document.

Aldus now owns SuperPaint and has upgraded the program to Version 3.0 and added a great many features, making it one of the more powerful graphics programs around. SuperPaint 3.0 offers the ability to work in 8-bit, 16-bit, and 32-bit color or black and white with multiple color palettes (see fig. 16.7).

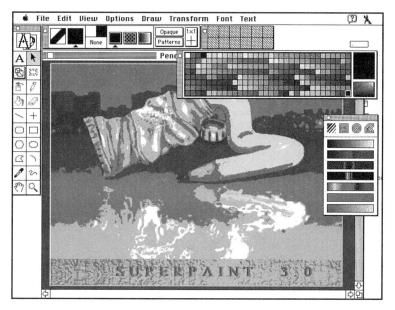

SuperPaint is the most popular paint and draw program available. It's easy to use and combines the best of the MacDraw and MacPaint programs. The toolbox contains two icons that enable you to switch between paint and draw layers with a click, each mode displaying the tools that are appropriate for drawing or painting. You don't spend time clicking a tool that will not do anything, as can happen with other paint and draw programs.

With SuperPaint, you can do the following:

- Autotrace bit-mapped images and convert them to objects in the draw layer

- Tile (arrange in small squares) multipage documents

- Edit bit-mapped objects in the draw layer with no restriction on size

- Customize airbrushes for pattern and flow

- "Plug in" a paint tool, such as the calligraphy brushes, for special effects
- Create precise drawings with a Bézier tool
- Store frequently used forms on templates

Storing Graphics Images

You can save paint and draw files in the same way you save any other file—in a variety of file formats. (A *file format* is the structure the program uses to save the data.) For example, figure 16.8 shows the Save dialog for SuperPaint 3.0, which can save files in the SuperPaint, MacPaint, or PICT format. Every paint program you learn about in this chapter can save files in the PICT format, the original MacPaint format. If your graphics program reads PICT files, you can use it to work with any PICT file, regardless of the application used to create the file.

Fig. 16.8
The SuperPaint
Save dialog.

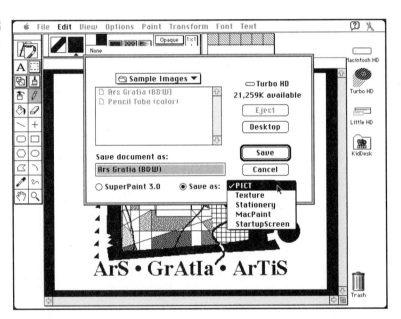

PNT or PNTG (paint) files are old standbys that many graphics applications can create. These files print at 72 dpi and are not much more than black-and-white dots arranged in a pattern.

PICT files are a generic file format for storing graphics on the Mac. PICT files are generated by using QuickDraw routines. They are bit-mapped or object-oriented graphics.

TIFF (for tag image file format) files store images in bit-map format and are used to store photographs and other high-resolution images that have been scanned. TIFF was designed to capture and store the subtlety of the many shades of gray that appear in photographic material. The same precision can be applied to files with color images; TIFF has the capability of working with and storing many colors. Images stored as TIFF files usually take up a large amount of disk space.

EPS (Encapsulated PostScript) files are compatible with PostScript devices such as printers. The highest quality clip art comes in an EPS format you can manipulate easily without sacrificing quality. Not every program can read and work with EPS files.

Graphic Image File (GIF) format is used by CompuServe, the on-line information service, for transferring graphics between different systems.

T he format you use to store your images depends on how you create the image and what you plan to do with it. If you scan a photograph, you must save it in TIFF format. If you use advanced graphics tools, such as FreeHand, you need the flexibility of an EPS file format.

You can imagine what kinds of problems can occur when an application cannot save a graphic document in a format that is readable by other applications. The graphic becomes limited in its usefulness.

Fortunately, converting between formats is becoming easier and utilities are available that can transfer your files between computers and different file formats (see Chapter 29, "Using Connectivity Software"). Many programs also enable you to save in different formats. Claris products, for example, come with the XTND translators that enable you to open and save in a variety of file formats.

Working with Color

The color capabilities of the Macintosh family have made the Macintosh an excellent tool for graphic artists. This section discusses the use of color graphics and reviews some of the graphics applications that produce color images.

Color monitors work in an interesting way. All monitors (monochrome and color) are coated on the inside of the picture tube with a phosphor that is sensitive to energy in the form of electrons. This energy is directed toward the coating and shows up as black and white (charged and uncharged pixels) on a monochrome monitor, and as a combination of three colors (red, green, and blue) on a color monitor. The various combinations of these three colors determine how each pixel is colored on-screen.

1, 2, 4, 8, 16, 24, and 32 bits means how many bits each pixel uses to display colors. If each pixel uses 1 bit, it can be either black or white (on or off). 2 bits can produce four colors. 4 bits yields 16 colors. 8 bits enables you to use 256 colors. 16 bits can produce 32,786 colors. 24 bits (the maximum on the Macintosh) gives you a choice of 16 million colors.

In 32-bit QuickDraw, only 24 bits are used to describe the color. This is still enough for over 16 million colors, which is photographic quality. The other 8 bits are reserved for other uses.

If you have an 8-bit video board, the Macintosh can display 256 different colors on-screen at one time (each pixel can be on or off, so 2 raised to the 8th power is 256). With a 24-bit video card (see Chapter 26, "Expanding the Macintosh"), the over 16 million colors of the palette are available. At this level, you can do high-quality photographic work on-screen.

Selecting Color Applications

Color paint programs are designed specifically to display color on-screen and produce color output. The most popular color paint programs are PixelPaint from SuperMac, Modern Artist from Computer Friends, and Studio/8 from Electronic Arts. These programs are all at, or moving towards, 24-bit color. Studio/8 now supports 32-bit color.

A new color paint program, UltraPaint from Deneba, is worth looking at. UltraPaint combines black-and-white painting, 8-bit color painting, grayscale image processing, and drawing tools. Because so many tools are loaded on the palette, UltraPaint's power is always accessible.

A good color paint program includes the following:

■ All the tools offered by conventional paint programs, such as paint brush, fill, shape drawing, and so on

■ Bézier curves and fractal lines (geometric forms derived from complex mathematical equations)

■ Object masking

■ Light source shading and positioning

- Dithering (the capability of mixing pixels of various colors)

- Smoothing where colors meet

- Color separations (necessary for color printing)

- Color mixing on-screen

- Airbrush capability

- Color editing

- Importing files from color scanners

Producing Color Documents

You can produce color in your documents in many ways, all of which have their advantages and disadvantages.

One inexpensive way to print color is to use a color ribbon on your printer to produce color output (see Chapter 7, "Printing"). Many programs output in color to an ImageWriter II's four-color ribbon, which is black, yellow, blue, and red, similar to the CMYK model. If you have a laser printer, however, you can change the color of your toner cartridge. Toner refills are available in red, blue, and brown, as well as black. Of course, changing the color of your toner for just one printout is impractical, and running a sheet through the printer several times for more than one color would be very time-consuming.

Color printing is becoming less expensive. Inkjet printers can be purchased for less than $1,000. Even the higher priced thermal wax transfer printers are dropping in cost. See Chapter 7, "Printing," and Chapter 25, "Choosing a Printer."

Another option is to use a presentation program such as PowerPoint from Microsoft to generate color slides and then send them by modem or disk to a developing service. Although this method is quick (usually overnight if you pay for the faster service) and accurate, it also is expensive—you pay anywhere from $10 to $15 per slide, and the services usually require a minimum number of slides.

The color separation process is the most accurate method of duplicating a color image. Most color-separation software (such as the software that accompanies Adobe Illustrator and Aldus FreeHand) uses the traditional four-color publishing method to produce four different separations, or images in cyan, magenta, yellow, and black. Each image is "shot" to produce a plate of the particular "color"—a given combination of hue, intensity, and value—that then is used to produce the printed image. A color image is actually printed four times, from each of the four plates, before it is complete. The beauty of the whole desktop publishing revolution is that the available software enables you to produce these color separations yourself. QuarkXPress produces the separations you need, for example, when you select the Make Separations option from the Print dialog.

Using Color Utilities

A number of utilities are available that enable you to work with color images in a variety of ways. Colorizer from Palomar, for example, contains four programs that enable you to do the following:

- Establish a palette of colors, using a control panel called Colors

- Add color to existing PICT2 files

- Capture a color image as a PICT file by using an FKEY utility (necessary for much desktop publishing work)

- Print to a color printer

The Colors component comes with 39 predefined color schemes, but you easily can modify them to fit your own needs.

Using Clip Art

For users who are not artists but need graphics to enhance their documents, clip art—predrawn images in every imaginable category—is the solution. The term *clip art* refers to the large collections of images often sold in book form; when graphics artists need a graphic, they clip it out of the book and glue the graphic into the document. The computer files of clip art today are much like these books; they contain holiday symbols, animals, food, business images, architectural symbols, and almost anything else you can imagine. You load your application and select the picture you want to use. Many of these images have been drawn using paint programs, or they are scanned and saved in a format that can be read by a variety of programs. Recently, Macintosh users witnessed a great expansion in the quantity and type of clip art available.

Artbeats, for example, offers the Full Page Images Library with background images for ads, flyers, brochures, and other publications in EPS format. The company also offers the Marble & Granite collection, which is a set of TIFF images of stone textures—good for backgrounds—on CD-ROM. T/Maker has ClickArt, collections of various images such as business, cartoons, religious, and more.

Desktop Graphics has collections in PICT format of sports images, borders and graphics for publications, business forms, education, and more.

Cliptures by Dream Maker Software is an extensive collection of different sets of business, sports, world flags, borders, and other images.

Many companies—too many to list—offer different collections of images you can import into your document. Metro ImageBase, 3G Graphics, and MicroMaps Software are just a few, in addition to the previously mentioned ones.

The collections of MicroMaps are worth considering. These collections are maps of the world, countries, states, metropolitan areas, and so on that can be imported.

The BMUG (Berkeley Macintosh User's Group) and the Boston Computer Society Macintosh User's Group produce CDs (compact discs) that hold hundreds of clip art pieces. And more CD clip art will be available in the future. ProArt (and its ProArt Trilogy) features borders and headings, food, and people as part of its collection. On this CD-ROM are many terrific clips. The food folder contains folders on baked goods, dairy, the four food groups (chocolate, chocolate, chocolate, and chocolate), fruit, meat, prepared foods, and vegetables, for example.

EduCorp is also a good source for clip art. They offer a catalog filled with CD-ROM and disk-based collections of clip art.

Creating Your Own Clip Art

Producing your own clip art is not difficult. You can use public domain art, a fruitful source for images. Thousands of Macintosh images are available for pennies apiece through organizations that offer public domain and shareware artwork. If you have access to a scanner (they are available for rent at some photocopying stores), you can just scan an image and then edit it with a paint program to produce a piece of clip art. (Scanners are discussed later in this chapter.)

Scanning takes much time, however, from actually setting up and scanning the image to cleaning up the image after it is scanned. The scanned images may not turn out as well as you had expected, and you will need to use a traditional paint program to work with the individual elements if you want a better picture.

CAUTION

R emember that not all software can accept all types of images; some software will not work with EPS, for example. Most graphics programs can accept PICT images however.

Tracking Clip Art

A variety of tracking applications can help you organize your clip art so that you can make some sense out of your collection. One such tracking application is PictureBase from Symmetry. At startup, PictureBase displays a set of icons representing the PictureBase libraries on the current disk (see fig. 16.9). You can open these libraries to reveal information about the individual graphics.

Fig. 16.9
A library of art organized
by using PictureBase.

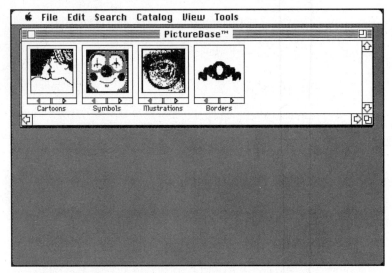

Figure 16.10 shows an open library with the name of the library, the page number where the image can be found in the library, the name of the image, key words (which help you search through libraries to see what's available), and a description. This system makes tracking images easy. You then can cut and paste the images as needed and even place them directly into the Scrapbook without going through tedious cut and paste operations for each one. You also can organize the images into libraries.

SmartScrap II from Portfolio Systems is a popular art manager. SmartScrap II is an enhanced Scrapbook that enables you to resize graphics to fit the space where you want to insert them. SmartScrap substitutes for your regular Scrapbook on the Apple menu.

One of SmartScrap's best features is the thumbnail sketch it displays of a file's contents. This feature is handy when you are searching for a particular image. Figure 16.11 illustrates one of these table of contents. SmartScrap even comes with some sample clip art from T/Maker,

DublClick, and a wonderful utility called ScrapMaker, which creates multiple Scrapbooks from images without cutting and pasting. SmartScrap also can print a Scrapbook to get a hard copy of your clip art, search by file name, and use multiple Scrapbooks.

Fig. 16.10
An open PictureBase library.

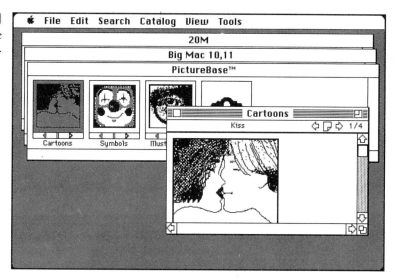

Fig. 16.11
A visual table of contents from SmartScrap.

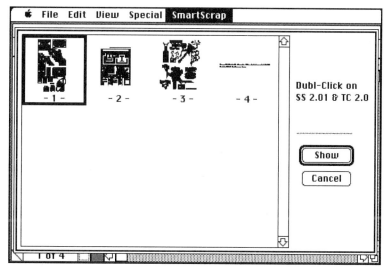

Also from Portfolio Systems is SuperGlue II. SuperGlue II enables you to share graphics and other information between Macintoshes, regardless of application. SuperGlue II creates a specialized file format for saving images that can be viewed (but not changed) using SuperViewer, SuperGlue II's companion program. SuperGlue II files also can be transmitted by modem, and the recipient then can use the Scrapbook desk accessory to view the transferred files (if he or she does not have SuperViewer).

Creating Three-Dimensional Graphics

You now can create graphics that represent our three-dimensional view of the world by using applications such as Super 3D from Silicon Beach and Mac3D from Challenger. You can design a jet plane in three dimensions, for example, and change the viewer's perspective by rotating the axes of the object on-screen.

If you are familiar with simple graphing, you know that the x-axis is horizontal, and the y-axis is vertical. Three-dimensional graphics also use a third "in and out" axis, the z-axis, that provides the dimension of depth (see fig. 16.12). This third dimension enables you to produce incredible images; in the right hands, the artwork generated borders on phenomenal.

Fig. 16.12

A 3-D graphic using three axes.

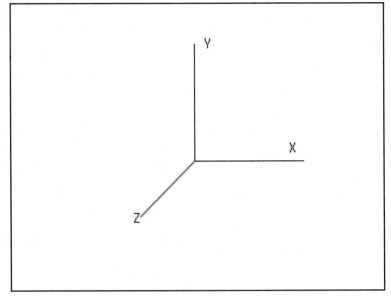

A good 3-D graphics program includes the following features:

- Wireframe views to reveal the understructure of the object
- Light shading
- Adjustable light sources and intensity
- Capability to work with text and lines
- Animation to rotate the object and change the viewer's perspective
- Zooming to enlarge a part of the picture
- Ready manipulation of the position of an object in any of the three dimensions
- Capability to reshape objects by dragging different parts
- Extruding, taking a two-dimensional object and projecting it into the third dimension

Figure 16.13 shows a right triangle drawn with Super 3D's polyline tool. The Revolve command from the Tools menu transforms the triangle into a 3-D image called a *wireframe*. Selecting the Display As Solid command from the Options menu and using the Spin Wheel option fills in the wireframe image to create the solid cone rotated toward the viewer, shown in figure 16.14. Some shading completes the image.

Fig. 16.13

The beginning of a cone in Super 3D.

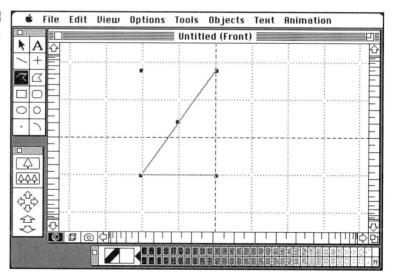

Fig. 16.14

The solid cone in
Super 3D, rotated
toward the viewer.

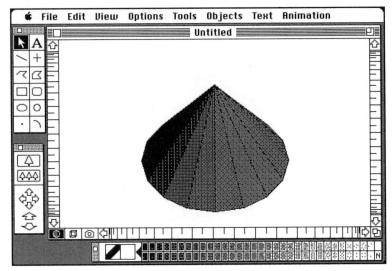

No matter what you draw, creating 3-D images can be a slow process because the software has to refresh, or "rethink," and then redraw much of the image each time you ask it to make a change.

Mac3D has many of the same capabilities as Super 3D, plus some other exciting features. Mac3D comes with a set of 28 basic 3-D shapes on the tool palette. Another nice feature is the capability of selectively reshaping a drawing simply by dragging part of it so that only that portion is redrawn.

Mac3D also handles rotation through a dialog that enables you to change the degree of rotation of an object in one of the three dimensions and then see the results before the object is actually rotated.

StrataVISION 3D from Strata has amazing rendering tools. You can purchase attribute libraries such as Wood Grain and Decorative Stone to enhance StrataVISION. The only shortcoming is that StrataVISION cannot animate, as several other 3-D programs can.

For the best deal, however, you can turn to Zing from Enabling Technologies. At $200 (compared to thousands for some programs), you get a well-designed and easy-to-use modeling and drawing tool.

DynaPerspective is a 3-D surface modeling, design, and presentation package that allows unbelievable power in designing images.

Animation Works from Gold Disk is a wonderful graphics tool that enables you to combine graphics, text, and sound into colorful "movies" that really do work! Although it is not yet the quality of true animation such as the kind you see in TV cartoons or Disney movies, Animation Works is an effective tool for creating storyboards for advertising, to say nothing of the educational applications for students learning about the process of animation.

Using Computer-Aided Design (CAD) Programs

Computer-aided design (CAD) programs are to designing what word processing is to writing: they transform your computer into an electronic drafting table. Their cousins, computer-aided manufacturing (CAM) programs, are electronic project managers that assist in every phase of the manufacturing process. Although CAD/CAM programs are true application programs, they resemble very fine drawing instruments and therefore have been included with this chapter on graphics.

Interest in CAD began during the late 1950s and early 1960s when designers realized that automobiles, household appliances, and rockets were more complex than the designers' physical design skills and tools could possibly handle. The Macintosh II's present capability of running CAD/CAM programs with its faster processors, larger screens, and larger RAM have made the Macintosh almost indispensable for engineering applications.

CAD programs take drawing to a new level of power and precision. They contain not only basic drawing tools but also sophisticated statistical analysis capabilities and highly specific modules for particular projects such as electrical circuit design, aerospace engineering, and architecture. One popular and inexpensive (about $100) CAD program, Real CAD Level 1 from AutoDesk, has the following symbol libraries:

- Basic Home Design
- Kitchen Design
- Electronics
- Home Landscaping
- Flowcharts and Schedules
- Industrial Pipe Fittings
- Heating and Air Conditioning
- Commercial and Residential Furnishings

You can use these symbol libraries with Real CAD Level 1 or Level 2 to expand the usefulness of the basic program. For example, architects depend on symbols in their drawings to represent everything from commodes to stairs. These symbol libraries avoid the necessity of duplicating the symbols in a paint program and then pasting them in; the symbols are ready to be used in the CAD application right away.

Experienced users of paint and draw programs can be very precise in their work and depend on 2-D and 3-D programs to do their design work. There's no substitute, however, for the vector graphics that can be produced by using CAD applications. The detail can be finer and the precision greatly increased because these programs have tools that help the user achieve these goals.

More than 50 different CAD programs now exist for the Mac. A good CAD program should contain all the features found in a draw program, plus the following:

- Assignment of objects to multiple layers

- Zooming capability

- Different names for different views

- "Snap" to objects in the window

- Autodimensioning (the program adds dimensions)

- Symbol libraries (with some programs, such as ClarisCAD, you can create and store your own symbols)

- Multiple preferences for units (use inches and centimeters in the same drawing)

- Floating-point decimals

- Capability of printing to various types of printers and plotters to scale, when necessary, for blueprints and other plans

ClarisCAD

ClarisCAD, one of the market leaders, is a powerful CAD program with many options. ClarisCAD offers the following features:

- 25 drawing tools, including those for fillets and chamfers

- Dimensioning tools that automatically calculate and display dimensions in the units you select

- Flexible drawing strategies (from corner to corner or from center to corner)

- Precise size and location specifications
- Zoom control
- Color option

AutoCAD

The most popular CAD program is AutoCAD. AutoCAD's popularity has generated more books and training tools than any other CAD program. After AutoCAD documents are completed, you can use AutoShade to render the final document.

Other Programs

Many times a major application, such as a CAD program, inspires similar programs that incorporate many of the same features but aim at a different audience. Such is the case, for example, with Design Your Own Home Architecture and Design Your Own Home, both from Abracadata. These draw programs include dozens of sample plans for dream houses and vacation homes.

Both programs include architectural shapes such as stairs, doors, and windows, and you can use add-on libraries as well. The programs give you a high degree of flexibility in designing your own plans. Figure 16.15 shows the tool palette and a sample architecture plan.

Fig. 16.15
Design Your Home—Cape
Cod or Tudor?

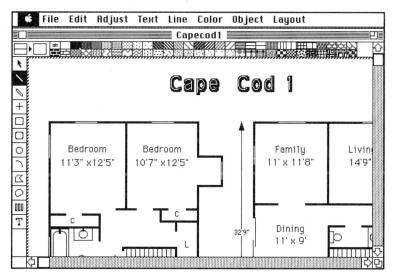

Design Home-Interiors (Abracadata) enables you to create renderings of what an interior will look like, color and all. With Interiors, you can use hundreds of to-scale furniture shapes, and you can even create wallpaper effects. MacInteriors from MicroSpot is another room layout application with similar capabilities.

MiniCad Plus from Graphsoft, one of the most popular CAD programs, has the features of the high-end programs plus others, including a spreadsheet and programming language that can be integrated into a CAD drawing. Figure 16.16, a sample file from MiniCad Plus of a boat design, illustrates the intricate detail that is possible.

Fig. 16.16
A sample file from
MiniCad Plus.

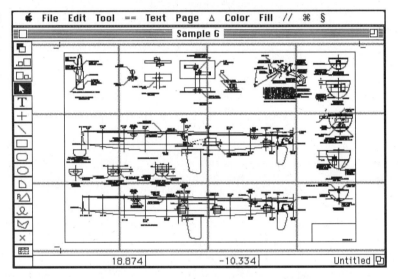

Figure 16.17 shows a portion of the boat design that has been zoomed by double-clicking the zoom icon in the toolbox or using the ⌘-1 or ⌘-2 key combinations. Writing that was barely recognizable as text is now clearly legible.

Graphsoft also offers Blueprint, an inexpensive drafting tool that competes with other high-end CAD packages (such as ClarisCAD and Dreams). Blueprint, designed for the architectural drafting community, is loaded with drawing tools and specialized menus.

Some CAD programs with limited capabilities sell for as little as $150, but the more powerful programs are much more expensive, ranging around $500 to as much as $2,000. If you create technical drawings for a living, however, a good CAD program is indispensable.

Fig. 16.17
A close-up of a portion
of the boat design
from figure 16.16.

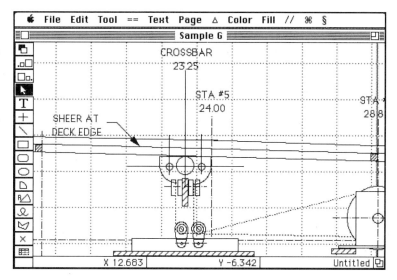

Creating Graphs and Charts

The graphing (or charting) capability of the various spreadsheets is discussed in Chapter 11, "Using Spreadsheets." Some of the math programs can create good charts as well, such as those produced by Igor and Mathematica. The distinction between a chart and a graph is minor, especially because both types of programs can produce just about the same type of outcome. A good charting program (or any program that can do charts) should offer the following features:

- Import data from other applications or have the program read data from other applications such as Excel

- Work with the data after it is imported to see how the change affects the finished graph

- Redraw the graph without having to exit the application

- Work with text, both of the fixed (such as axis label) and nonfixed (or free-floating) kind

- Have style and size options for text

- Offer many different types of charts

- Have symbols available as part of a library and be able to work with clip art and other graphic features

Picking the Appropriate Chart Type

The charting program you select should be able to generate all the types of charts in the following list. This list also suggests the purpose for each chart type.

- Text charts are used to present information that is nominal or categorical in nature, such as an organization chart in a company.

- Pie charts enable you to examine the relative proportion of one category of information to another, such as the percentage of total expenses spent on entertainment.

- Line charts enable you to reflect changes over time such as trends in financial markets.

- Bar charts are similar to line charts but use vertical bars, rather than points, to mark values on the y-axis.

- Area charts represent the relationship between two series of data points by looking at their relative proportions.

- High, Low, and Close charts are used in the stock and futures markets (and anywhere else where a high, a low, and a close needs to be visually represented).

Picking a Graphing Package

With CricketGraph from Computer Associates you can create scatter, line, area, bar, column, pie, stacked bar, stacked column, polar, QC, double Y (axis), text, and combination graphs. As you can see in figure 16.18, creating a graph in CricketGraph begins with a spreadsheet-like matrix (with 100 columns and 2,700 rows) into which you insert values.

After you insert the data, you need only to select the graph type and to set the variables you want graphed. You can export this graph to many applications. Because CricketGraph can import and export data, you don't have to reenter anything. Just transfer the information and go to work.

Other features include multiple graphs per page, color graphs, plot symbols, and as many as 2,000 data points per chart.

Another excellent charting program is KaleidaGraph from Ablebeck. KaleidaGraph offers 16 types of graphs and is packed full of features. These features include as many as 80 open data windows, undo, a programmable calculator with 100 memory registers, least squares regression, nonlinear curve fitting, and on-line help, to name a few. In figure 16.19, you can see some sample data in the spreadsheet-like matrix that characterizes KaleidaGraph.

Fig. 16.18
Starting a CricketGraph
with a matrix form to
enter numbers.

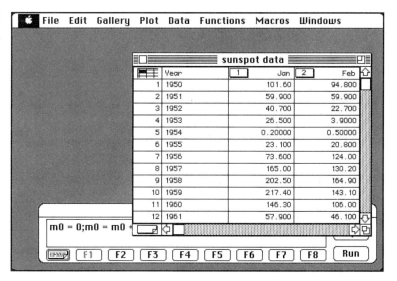

	File	Edit	Data	Graph	Curve Fit	Goodies	Formats	Windows	

Science Data

	1	2	3	4	5	6	
	Time	Signal #1	Signal #2	Column 4	Column 5	Column 6	Colu
1	0.5	2.7	0.733				
2	0.6	7.5	1.343				
3	0.8	4.5	2.132				
4	1.0	9.3	3.067				
5	1.2	8.1	4.127				
6	1.4	3.3	5.299				
7	1.5	8.7	6.573				
8	1.6	14.7	7.942				
9	1.8	8.1	9.400				
10	2.0	9.3	10.941				
11	2.2	19.5	12.561				
12	2.4	14.7	14.256				
13	2.5	17.7	16.024				
14	2.6	12.9	17.861				
15	2.8	17.1	19.765				
16							
17							
18							
19							
20							
21							

Fig. 16.19
Beginning a KaleidaGraph.

	File	Edit	Gallery	Plot	Data	Functions	Macros	Windows

sunspot data

	Year	1	Jan	2	Feb
1	1950		101.60		94.800
2	1951		59.900		59.900
3	1952		40.700		22.700
4	1953		26.500		3.9000
5	1954		0.20000		0.50000
6	1955		23.100		20.800
7	1956		73.600		124.00
8	1957		165.00		130.20
9	1958		202.50		164.90
10	1959		217.40		143.10
11	1960		146.30		106.00
12	1961		57.900		46.100

m0 = 0;m0 = m0 +

	F1	F2	F3	F4	F5	F6	F7	F8	Run

You use the Gallery menu to select the type of chart you want to create.
In figure 16.20, you see a linear graph for the sunspot activity from 1950
through 1968 for the month of June. This graph was created from the
data in the matrix in figure 16.19. Notice the toolbox on the left side of
the screen; you can use these tools to dress up the graph.

Fig. 16.20

A graph created with
KaleidaGraph.

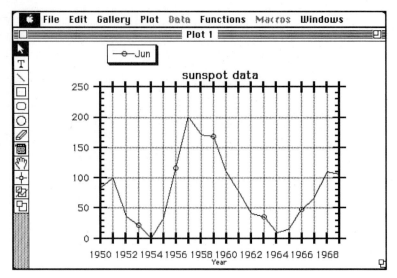

Although you cannot create area graphs with KaleidaGraph, the program does have a good macro feature, a spreadsheet with 256 columns and 32,000 rows, a text file import feature, and the capability to plot as many as 20 dependent (or outcome) measures at a time.

DeltaGraph from DeltaPoint is the competition. DeltaGraph includes both 2-D and 3-D charts, a spreadsheet-like data form (called a Note-book), a full tool palette, and 256-color support. When you revise the data, the graph changes just as some spreadsheets change as the data changes.

If you need graphs (and need them fast) to insert into your documents, you should consider Cheshire, a new tool from Abbot. Cheshire is easy to learn, fast, and is surprisingly complete for a desk accessory. Even if your graphing needs are complex, Cheshire may be the only graphing program you need.

To use Cheshire from within any application, you select the data you want to graph. Then you use the Cheshire hot-key combination (⌘-Option-C) and double-click the graph type you want (from more than 20). You can choose from many options for graph formatting. You can see in figure 16.21 the thumbnail sketch that Cheshire provides.

Fig. 16.21

A graph created with
Cheshire, a resident
graphing program
that works with many
different applications.

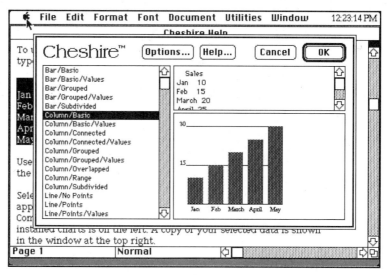

Using Scanners

If you often need to enter previously printed text or graphics into a file to be edited, a scanner can save you hours of tedious work. Scanners are hardware devices that convert an image into a series of digital signals, which then are translated into an electronic file. Using advanced digital image-processing programs, such as Digital Darkroom and ImageStudio, you then can edit this file just as if you had scanners organize pixels so that your document can become a representation of the original. The number of bits per pixel determines the quality of the image produced: the more bits per pixel, the better the image because more shades of gray can be produced. Flat scanners read only on and off signals (blacks and whites) and allow less precision.

The most expensive scanners, flat scanners, are similar to early copying machines. You place the document to be scanned on a sheet of glass and start the scanner. A bright light moves across the scanner face. More than 2,500 photosensors in the moving part of the scanner capture changes in the image, which are recorded by the scanner as "ons" and "offs." These scanners can come in the form of a sheet feeder, an overhead (similar in appearance to a typical overhead projector), or a flatbed configuration in which you place the book or paper on the surface that is scanned.

Another group of scanners, print head scanners, are mounted on the print head of the ImageWriter. As the print head moves across the page to be scanned, it transmits the "ons" and "offs" directly to your Macintosh.

The best known of these print head scanners is ThunderScan from ThunderWare, which is one of the cheapest scanners available. It is discussed in more detail in the next section.

Finally, relatively inexpensive hand-held scanners also are available; with these scanners, you move the scanner manually across the area to be duplicated.

One of these hand-held scanners is Caere's Typist, a beautifully designed hand-held tool that you pass over material that you want to scan. It's easy to use, comes with OCR software, reads about 500 words per minute, and even enters information in special formats such as spread-sheets.

To use a scanner, you need specialized software that matches the type of scanner you are using. In many cases, the best combination of hardware and software may come from different companies, so you should explore a variety of options. The remainder of this chapter discusses some of your choices.

Using ThunderScan

ThunderScan from ThunderWare deserves special attention because it is inexpensive and easy to use. ThunderScan places the power of a true gray-scale image at your fingertips, but it is very slow. You must be very careful to align your picture properly; ThunderScan now comes with an alignment tool, but it does not work particularly well with glossies.

ThunderScan enables you to adjust brightness and contrast, it supports all popular file formats, and it produces acceptable images. It comes as a package with a digitizing cartridge (the scanner), an adapter box, software, and more.

With ThunderScan, you can scan half-tones and line art, select printers (ImageWriter I or II), change speeds, and even use different ports (modem or printer). ThunderScan cannot give you the same quality image as the flat scanners mentioned earlier, but its images are highly acceptable. ThunderScan also can be useful for importing low-resolution images into HyperCard.

Because the ThunderScan is really a printer of sorts in disguise, it scans at 72 dpi, which does not produce very precise printed images. To offset this weakness, magnify the image to be scanned to 400 percent and then, after you have scanned it, print it at 25 percent by adjusting the Page Set Up options on your Mac. The resulting image will be of better quality. Enclosing the images you want to scan in clear, nonreflective plastic also may produce a better ThunderScan image with higher resolution.

Using Optical Character Recognition (OCR) Software

Optical Character Recognition (OCR) software is the "brain" of the scanner. The OCR software enables the scanner to read and translate characters into text files you then can manipulate with your favorite word processing program. OCR software can make your life easier, especially if you deal in desktop publishing. Suppose that you want to take your old documents and redesign them, but you no longer have the disks that contain the original files. You can just scan the text. If you have a large body of text created before personal computers were around that you want to convert to a word processing file, just scan it.

Three basic types of OCR software are available:

- Nontrainable software, which is limited to the specific type of text and printers for which it has been designed. Nontrainable OCR software is fast, but you cannot change fonts or printers without changing the software as well.

- Trainable software, which can be "taught." You actually provide the software with the set of rules that you want it to follow by building a template, a reference to which the software compares the scanned image, character by character.

- Automatic software, which includes some artificial intelligence and is designed to read text with no "training." Of course, these software packages are considerably more expensive.

Even the most sophisticated OCR software is not perfect. Its accuracy may be affected by the hardware being used, the cleanliness of the scanning surface, and the quality of the print it is reading. Therefore, you can never assume that a scanned file is the exact duplicate of the original printed material.

OCR software registers two kinds of errors: errors of omission and errors of commission. When an error of omission occurs because the software cannot read the text, it leaves out the character and enters a nonsense character, such as ~ or •. Errors of commission occur when the software reads the text incorrectly; for example, you may get sotfware rather than software. The only way to locate errors of commission is to use a spell checking program or manually proofread the document.

Buying OCR Software

Keep the following suggestions in mind when you buy OCR software. Remember that, whether you are scanning text or graphics, you need to purchase software and hardware.

- Be sure that you know how much memory the software uses. The way the OCR software compares and matches characters determines the amount of memory needed. On scanners with insufficient memory, the software may run at an unbearably slow speed.

- Be sure that the hardware matches the software requirements. Some OCR software runs only with specific hardware, especially when the same manufacturer produces both.

- Ask about the accuracy of the software for a given system configuration. Remember that the more characters the OCR software misses, the more editing you have to do.

- Try before you buy. OCR software is sensitive to font, style, size, and every other characteristic of the printed page. Your 150-page document in 12-point Times Roman may not even be readable. Take a sample of the type of material you will be scanning to the dealer for a trial. Then go back to your computer and edit the text with your word processing software just to be sure that you understand the system.

- Before buying, determine whether you need nontrainable, trainable, or automatic OCR software.

- Find out whether the software enables you to edit scanned images or whether you have to import them to another program before editing. Be sure that you can control such qualities as brightness, contrast, and hue.

- Select software that enables you to print according to the capabilities of your printer. If you have a Linotronic, for example, you need better resolution of the scanned image than the resolution offered by a 2-bit machine that can read only black-and-white images.

- Be sure that you need the software! It may be cheaper to pay someone to reenter text than to scan it, size it, read it into your word processor, and then have to edit the text again.

- Be sure that the software you are considering can save the scanned files in the format you want. You may use Word as your word processor, for example, and although all software can save text as an ASCII file, wouldn't it be easier to go straight to Word and not have to reenter those format codes lost when you go to ASCII?

Using Gray-Scale Scanning

OCR software can read text quite accurately and in a sense does not have to work as hard as software and scanners that scan graphics. As you know, graphics are rarely simple line art; they often include a variety of shades of gray. These shades, or levels of gray, and the sensitivity of the software determine the quality of the image resulting from the scan.

The number of bits per pixel determines the precision of a scanned graphic image and, to some extent, the price of the scanner. The Apple scanner lists for about $1,800, for example, and can reproduce 16 different gray levels. On the other hand, Microtek's MSF300Q, which can scan as many as 64 gray levels, lists for almost $8,000.

Fine-Tuning Scanned Images

After you have scanned an image and edited it using the software tools provided with your scanning software, you still may need a more precise image. Two popular programs that enable you to do precise fine-tuning are Digital Darkroom from Silicon Beach and ImageStudio from LetraSet.

These programs enable you to edit a gray-scaled image to produce the half-tones necessary for incorporating high-quality photos in your documents. You also can cut and paste as you want; for example, you can take a photo of a model and paste on clothes, airbrushing to make the elements fit together nicely. In addition, you can retouch a photo, incorporating special effects to create a completely different picture. This technology can be a great boon to artists, but remember that you must know the programs and have some knowledge of how to use the "real life" tools (such as an airbrush) to get the results you want. These programs are packed with features and are not overly expensive ($300 to $500), but be sure that you are familiar with retouching before you invest in them.

Using Color Scanners

Color scanners are special for many reasons. They offer incredible options for working with scanned material but at significant expense; they cost about four times as much as the average gray-scale scanner, and they occupy a great deal of memory. You need a Macintosh II series computer or higher (Centris or Quadra) with 4 or 5MB of RAM (or virtual memory) to view your work while reproducing color images.

Some color scanners can scan more than just flat images. The Barneyscan system from Barneyscan, for example, offers hardware for converting 35mm color slides into images. You simply insert the slide into the scanner, and minutes later you have on file an image that you can edit using tools from an extensive set provided with the scanner. You also can use the software to produce four-color separations.

After you scan the images you need, you can transmit them by modem. Photos from last year's World Series were sent, for example, from Los Angeles to New York through a modem after first being scanned with the Barneyscan XP. Although the photos were black and white, this example illustrates the possibility of transmitting photos over telephone lines in order to be included in a document at the other end, where they can be cropped and adjusted.

The Big Mac Recommendation

The world of Macintosh graphics only now seems to be opening. Starting with what now seems to be a simple and small 128KB MacPaint, tools have grown in size and complexity and can match the technical accomplishment of any skilled draftsperson. Along with scanners, OCR software, color capability, and public domain libraries full of clip art, anyone can have the needed tools. You probably cannot go wrong no matter what software package you buy. Although SuperPaint 3.0 may lead the crowd, FullPaint and MacPaint 2.0 also can provide you with much, if not all, of what you need.

Experience is a different story—learning to use these tools has become simple with the abundant aids available (such as the videotape that comes with Illustrator), but using them well often takes further training. Many community colleges and universities are now offering classes in the area of computer-aided graphics and graphic design, even though such classes may simply be called Design or Desktop Publishing. Seek out these classes, practice, and look around for the print and screen designs you like.

CHAPTER SEVENTEEN

Using Communication Software

T housands of people today use personal computers to work from home offices. With your computer at home, you now can access information on almost any subject, check your stock prices, order your travel tickets, "talk" to a colleague in Tokyo, download a new desk accessory, and even share your frustrations with the president of a software company. With the new system and sufficient memory, you can even download files as you work on another task, such as writing a report or playing a game.

How can you do all this? Through telecommunications—the interaction and exchange of information using the personal computer over the telephone lines. If you haven't caught the bug yet, you will, because telecommunications is one of the next frontiers of personal computing.

This chapter introduces you to the world of telecommunications. First, you learn the basic equipment you need. Then you receive more detailed information about modems and software and a survey of electronic mail (E-mail) and bulletin boards. Finally, you learn about information services.

Reviewing Telecommunication Requirements

To use your Macintosh computer for telecommunications, you need three items:

- A modem
- Communications software
- An open phone line

The Modem

A *modem* is a device that modulates and demodulates electronic signals that represent information. The modem connects to the computer and to the telephone line.

In your Macintosh, data is formatted as digital signals. Because telephones are designed to transmit sounds, however, telephones work as transmitters of analog signals. A modem converts the digital signal to an analog signal; this process is called *modulation*. The modem converts digital data (such as the 10000001 that represents the letter A in ASCII) to tones in order to transmit information to another computer. *Demodulation* is exactly the opposite process—the conversion of analog signals to digital. The modem converts tones to digital data in order to receive information. In other words, the modem acts as a translator.

Communications Software

To use a modem, you also need communications software, which changes data into a form the modem can use. This software plays another important purpose—it begins and helps to manage your session. With the software, you set the rules you use to communicate with the other computer (through what is called a *protocol*), and you configure your system to match that of the computer with which you want to connect.

S ome software even helps you accomplish certain tasks, such as automatically logging on at a specified hour of the night when rates are cheapest, saying good-bye, and disconnecting.

The Phone Line

The telephone line you use may be a line dedicated to telecommunications, or a regular line that you also use for voice communications. If you have only one line for both voice and data, your voice line is tied up when you transmit data. Because most transmissions don't take very long, this situation may not be a problem for you; however, some transmissions, such as downloading an entire new Macintosh System release, can take a long time. You cannot use a modem on a party line; also, other special services, such as call waiting, may give you trouble.

If you do have call waiting, disable it before you begin your work session. Follow these steps:

1. Lift the receiver.

2. Press the * button.

3. Press **70**.

I n some areas, the pound key (#) or two number ones (1) replace the asterisk in step 2. Check with your local phone company for more information.

Many serious users of telecommunications have two phone lines, one for voice and one for data communications. One line is connected directly to the modem, and the other to the telephone. You can connect the phone lines directly to your modem with standard phone cables available at electronics and even discount stores; the modem connects to your computer modem port with an Apple cable, similar to the cable that connects your printer.

An alternative to two phone lines is one of the newer modems, such as The Home Office by Prometheus. This sophisticated modem/fax combination detects the type of incoming call and responds appropriately. The modem even gives voice callers a voice mail-style message, and enables callers to leave messages for you.

The Connection

At each end of the connection, you have a computer, telecommunications software, and a modem. The two modems are connected by telephone lines. With telecommunications, you can share information directly with others, or, for a fee, you can gain access to information providers such as GEnie, CompuServe, Delphi, and America OnLine. These services are huge on-line databases and electronic mail networks you tap into with your telecommunications hardware and software. After you log on to one of these services, you can access any information the service has available.

There are also literally thousands of computer *bulletin boards* (*BBS* for Bulletin Board System) throughout the world to which you can link without paying anything more than the costs of the telephone call.

I n effect, when you connect to an information service, your modem is connected to a file server, which provides the information you request. In some cases, the BBS or information provider you use may be able to connect you to a service such as Telenet, a nationwide network of local phone numbers that connects you to the main computer at the information provider. Though you can save long distance charges, be aware that services of this kind usually have their own charges.

Defining Terms

Telecommunications has evolved into a kind of buzzword central, with specialized terms for everything. Before discussing what your Macintosh should be capable of doing to join in the fun, you need to know the definitions of some basic terms. You encounter the following terms throughout this chapter, where they are discussed in more detail.

ASCII file: A file consisting of characters that are universally readable as defined by the American Standard Code for Information Interchange. ASCII files contain no formatting information—such as boldface or underlining.

Baud: A unit of measure of the transmission of information. A 1200-baud modem transmits 1,200 pieces of information each second, or 1,200 *bps* (*bits per second*).

Bit: A piece of information, such as one of the eight 1s or 0s that make up a unit of information called a *byte*.

Bulletin Board System (BBS): An electronic cousin to the bulletin board, on which you tack messages. On an electronic bulletin board, you leave and get messages, upload and download files, and access information over telephone lines.

Downloading: Transferring a file from another computer to yours.

Dumb terminal: A device that acts as a receiver and transmitter of information but has no computing power of its own. A dumb terminal is sometimes referred to as a *TTY terminal* (short for teletype).

Full duplex: A protocol in which data simultaneously flows in both directions over transmission lines. (See the definition for protocol.)

Half duplex: A protocol in which data flows in only one direction at a time over transmission lines.

Host: The computer or system that controls access to and management of the system. If you transfer a file from a bulletin board to your computer, the bulletin board is the host.

Information service (or provider): A service containing information in various large databases that you access through telecommunications.

Modem: An electronic device that modulates and demodulates information at different speeds (called the *baud rate*) to enable you to communicate with other computers.

Node: A specific device along a network, such as a computer or printer.

Null modem: A cable device that directly connects two computers (without the use of modem), allowing one computer's output to become another computer's input.

On-line: A computer's status as it is in communication with another computer.

Protocol: A set of conventions that make possible the transfer of information between different sites. Some popular protocols are XMODEM, YMODEM, and Kermit.

Terminal emulation: The state in which a computer acts as a terminal capable of receiving information.

Uploading: Transferring a file from your computer to another.

Using a Modem

The Macintosh uses external and internal modems. An *external modem* sits outside the computer. External modems are usually small boxes filled with electronic devices; this type of modem has two phone jacks: one for your Macintosh and one for the phone. Some modems need an external source of power (they must be plugged into an electrical socket), but many run off the power the Macintosh draws. As the name suggests, *internal modems* are installed inside the Macintosh and use the computer's internal power supply.

The first generation of modems were acoustically coupled, meaning that you needed to place the telephone handset on a platform with round receptacles to "speak" to another computer and then to "listen" to what that other computer had to say. Today, most modems are the direct-connect kind described in this chapter; they connect directly to the phone line.

Always check downloaded files with a good virus detection program such as Disinfectant or SAM (the latter by Symantec). Viruses are often passed by BBS systems inadvertently, though efforts are made to prevent this occurrence. The larger systems, such as CompuServe and America Online, go to great lengths to safeguard their files, but you can never be too careful.

Modem Protocol

With any modem and the transmission of data, you must follow certain conventions in order to share information. These conventions are settings, which you make either directly on the modem, or through the use of the communications software that may come with the modem.

A *protocol* is the set of rules that dictates how the parties on the two ends of the telephone line communicate with each other. When you speak with someone else in person, the protocol includes such rules as looking at each other, speaking the same language, not interrupting, and so forth. A telecommunications protocol consists of the same kinds of rules for communication. Protocols often are set by *de facto* standards, usually those being used by the majority of the users. A frequently used protocol is XMODEM, an error-correcting protocol.

In an effort to establish some consistency across protocols, the International Standards Organization (ISO) developed a telecommunications model with seven layers, each of which is important (but not critical) to successful communication between computers. To communicate with another computer, some of these layers, but not all, must be compatible. Which layers are compatible depends on both your hardware and your telecommunications software.

Here are the layers and a brief description of each:

> The *physical layer* consists of the hardware itself, including the modem, cables, and telephone lines.

> The *data link layer* handles the way information is organized and sent from one location to another, including what is sent and when.

> The *network layer* controls the actual sending of the data and its routing from location to location.

> The *transport layer* confirms that the information sent is the information received.

> The *session layer* deals with the way different computers use protocols to ensure that they coordinate their activities so that both are not sending at the same time.

> The *presentation layer* works with the format of the communication to ensure that it is understandable when received.

> The *application layer* formats data so that it can be used by an application.

A variety of protocols is used, but you will most likely run into two kinds when you make decisions regarding telecommunications. A *half-duplex protocol* enables information to flow in both directions between the sender and the receiver, but data can be sent in only one direction at any one time. Most communications systems use a half-duplex system. A *full-duplex protocol* sends information in both directions simultaneously.

The full-duplex protocol method is fast, but can run into problems, just as two people might during a telephone conversation when both talk at the same time. With this type of protocol, coordinating simultaneous sending and receiving can present some difficulty.

Finally, there's *echoplex*, an add-on to a full-duplex system. (Ever see the ECHO ON message on your computer screen?) Echoplex lets you know that the data has been transmitted and checked for the accuracy of the transmission. In other words, the data is echoed to enable you to see that what was sent was what arrived.

Software controls protocols. The protocols used in telecommunications vary, depending on the type of information you want to transfer. For example, MicroPhone II offers several protocols used for different purposes. The Text protocol enables you to transfer files saved as ASCII or text files; the XMODEM and MacTerminal protocols are designed for the transfer of specific file formats.

Modem Speed

Baud (bits per second) is a measurement of how often information goes from digital (1011100) to analog (sounds) and back again. (The term is named for French communications expert J. M. E. Baudot.) The faster the modem (higher the baud rate), the faster you can send information and the less time you spend transmitting. Modems can communicate at a variety of speeds, which are measured in *baud rates*. The most common speeds are 300, 1200, and 2400 baud, with 9600 fast becoming the dominant standard and 14,400 becoming popular. But the faster the rate, the more information services charge to transmit.

To communicate with another telecommunications source, your modem's speed and your computer's baud rate setting must match those of the computer with which you are communicating. This process is known as *handshaking*. Any modem can receive transmissions at baud rates that are lower than the modem's setting. For example, a 1200-baud modem can adjust to receive a 300-baud transmission, but the reverse is not true. A 300-baud modem cannot receive 1200-baud transmissions.

The most common rates at which information is transmitted have been 300 and 1200 baud, but those rates have been surpassed by 2400 baud. In turn, 2400 baud is now being replaced by 9600 baud. And as soon as the price comes down and compatibility between senders and receivers is established, the standard rate will increase to 14,400 baud. Table 17.1 compares different baud rates with file sizes.

Keep in mind that baud rate alone does not determine completely how quickly (or accurately) data is transmitted. The protocol the modem uses and the compression of the data also affect transmission speed.

You can send more information when it is compressed by using a utility such as Stuffit Deluxe (from Aladdin Systems). Compressing a file reduces its size, creating a smaller file that contains the same amount of information. To use the file after transmission, of course, it must be "unstuffed." Most people who telecommunicate and send files on a regular basis compress files before sending them, and most files on services (such as CompuServe) are compressed to save space and download time.

Table 17.1
Baud Rates versus File Sizes

Baud	Text Document	Transmission Time (approx)
300	10 pages	2 minutes
	20 pages	4 minutes
1200	10 pages	30 seconds
	20 pages	1 minute
2400	10 pages	15 seconds
	20 pages	30 seconds
4800	10 pages	10 seconds
	20 pages	20 seconds
9600	10 pages	< 10 seconds
	20 pages	< 10 seconds
14,400	10 pages	< 5 seconds
	20 pages	5 seconds

Error Checking

The efficiency with which modems check for errors in the information they send and receive also differs. A transmission is sent in blocks, and your modem or telecommunications program verifies that the transmission is complete and accurate.

Parity checking, often referred to as *parity*, is one method that a modem and the associated software use to check each data bit (all the 1s and 0s) to see whether any erroneous information (such as interference on the telephone line) is being passed on. The parity is selected by the users at both ends of the telecommunications link and has to be the same. In the simplest terms, parity involves totaling the digits of the binary transmission on both ends. Parity can be odd, even, or none. For the most part, parity is usually set at none because communications software usually includes sophisticated error-checking routines to ensure the clean transmission of data.

Start and stop bits indicate when a character is beginning (start bit) and when it is ending (stop bit). The start bit tells the computer that information is coming and helps the computer prepare for the transmission. The stop bit is the last bit in a character and defines its end. The type of communication in which characters are preceded by start bits and followed by stop bits is known as *asynchronous communication*.

Synchronous communication does not use start and stop bits and is used primarily to move data between mainframe computers. It does not use the start and stop signals because the mainframe's software precisely times the transmission of the data, a feat that requires more complex circuitry than is available (or affordable) in asynchronous modems for computers such as the Macintosh.

Although starting with telecommunications and working on-line are not difficult, you can't just plug in and play. To work with a modem and telecommunications software, you must be aware of the points just mentioned. For both ends of the line to "shake hands," they must be able to communicate with each other in the same language and at the same speed, always checking that what they are "saying" makes sense. Telephone your BBS or on-line service or check their documentation to find the correct settings for communications with the service.

A good setting to try first is eight data bits, one stop bit, and no parity. Most systems use this configuration now.

One of the biggest problems with modems is that they communicate over phone lines. These lines are often old and not very reliable in terms of digital communications. Before the breakup of the AT&T monopoly on U.S. communications, there was little to no incentive to improve the quality of phone lines or switch systems. Even if your phone connection was not of the highest quality, you could still communicate verbally in most cases.

Digital communications require connections of far higher quality than connections needed for ordinary verbal communication. The pressure is now on to switch the entire U.S. telephone network to digital quality. And, because of competition, the long distance carriers are leading the way with fiber optic and digital switches.

Unfortunately, state-mandated local phone monopolies have no competition and continue to strangle local communications connections. In response to this situation, the free side of the market produced modems that utilize some of the latest developments in information theory to overcome the disruptive noise of old, unreliable connections.

For compression and error correction, the newest innovations are V.42bis and MNP-5. Modems with these features can communicate faster and more reliably over unreliable connections. Also, these features are common now and quite inexpensive. Purchasing a modem with these features will ensure that you are up-to-date when the near-future day of widespread use of the features arrives.

Look for V.42bis and MNP error correction features on a modem, even though not all information services and bulletin boards are equipped to utilize them (the protocols must be on both ends to work effectively). Even if you communicate with systems that do not offer these features, you can communicate at least as effectively as a modem without the features. And, when you do connect with systems using these features, your connection will have superior quality and speed (effective speeds can reach as high as 57,600 baud with these features in the modems at both ends).

MacBinary

After most of the bugs are out of any new movement, people realize that a standard set of rules is needed to allow further development to take place. *MacBinary* is a standard communications protocol for the Macintosh, first proposed by Dennis Brothers in 1985.

MacBinary is intended for communication between connected Macs that may not be running the same terminal programs. MacBinary's primary advantage is that it can transfer documents directly from one location to another without converting the file (as long the file is a Macintosh file). Because no conversion is necessary, you save time and money, and the whole process becomes more efficient. In addition, MacBinary is not dependent on the type of telecommunications protocol you are using, so MacBinary works with many available programs.

Facts about Fax

Because the facsimile machine or fax is so similar to the modem, it was easy for manufacturers to add this feature to modems. The fax modem is now common and inexpensive.

Fax modems transmit documents from your Macintosh to fax machines, just as if you printed the document and then used a fax machine. Fax modems that can receive faxes can store a fax transmission on your Macintosh disk; then you can print or view the document. Because having a fax in your modem is so inexpensive, consider a fax modem combination instead of just a modem.

Fax modems come in two configurations—send-only, and send-and-receive. Send-only fax modems can only transmit faxes, not receive them. Send-and-receive fax modems can send faxes as well as receive them.

The standard fax protocol is Group III. The early Group I and II are so uncommon that most fax modems do not support them. You should encounter no problem with this, as Group III is the dominant (and probably by now, only) fax standard.

When you choose a fax modem, be aware of one confusing point. Commonly, the baud rate for fax is higher than the baud rate for the digital data transmission. Ads for "9600-baud" modems may refer to 9600 baud for the fax part of the modem and a lower speed (usually 2400 baud) for the digital data transmission part. You should be aware of this point so that you do not inadvertently purchase a 2400-baud modem when you want a 9600-baud modem. Commonly, the highest speed is advertised, but the smaller print informs you that the higher speed is for the fax component instead of the modem component. When you choose a fax modem, you must often deal with two speeds: one for the fax, one for the modem.

Choosing a Modem and Modem Software

Modems range in price from around $89 to several thousand for the fastest and most sophisticated. What do you need? Consider the following points:

> *What will you use the modem for?* If you plan to hook up during the evening just to find out how the Yankees did yesterday, get the least expensive model that does what you want. If you plan to transfer huge quantities of data, you may want to consider the fastest modem you can afford (at least 9600, if not 14,400 bps).

What features does the modem offer? Some modems automatically call, answer, dial, and redial (given the proper software). With such a modem, you can have a colleague in another city transmit a large data file to you during the night when long-distance rates are lower and your machine is not tied up with other work. Some modem packages, such as the PowerUser 24/96 Send/Receive FaxModem with Voice Messaging (the first product with an ad for a name) by PowerUser, can even take voice messages. The Home Office by Prometheus can also take voice messages and even has a voice mail-type system with private mailboxes and customized messages. With the prices falling, the day may come when you hear "Thank you for calling the Jones residence. Press 1 for the living room, press 2 for Johnny, press 3 for..."

Is software included with the modem? Some modems come packaged with communications software, so don't let the modem be the sole consideration in your decision. You can use some communications software to set modem capabilities. Such software is more flexible than the modem; software packages differ markedly in the options they present. In recent times, however, the trend is toward including only basic communications software with the modem. More sophisticated packages are sold separately.

For fax modems, check reviews in magazines such as *MacUser* and *MacWorld*. Though improving, fax modem software can be irritatingly difficult to use (mine is a constant annoyance, as it is quite finicky). Ask for a demonstration at your dealer.

Considering Some Guidelines

When you have decided to purchase a modem, here are some guidelines to consider:

Be sure that the modem you buy is Hayes AT Command Set compatible. Hayes began manufacturing modems in the early 1970s, and set the standard by which other modems are designed. Hayes and Hayes-compatible modems are compatible with the modems used by all the large on-line databases.

The advantage of full Hayes-compatibility means that often, you can simply plug in the modem and use it without learning the command set at all (unless you choose to do so in order to configure the modem to your personal taste). Less-than-compatible modems often require some tinkering and manual reading to work effectively.

B e wary of "Hayes-compatible" claims. Make certain that the modem is 100 percent Hayes-compatible. Otherwise, you may find yourself dealing with headaches coming from that 10 percent of not-so-Hayes-compatible.

Purchase the fastest modem that you can afford. You can expect to pay more for a faster modem. But for the higher price, you get faster sharing of information. When you download large files from an information provider and want to minimize the on-line telephone charges, speed is most important. Some information providers charge more when you use a faster modem, but you still may save money in the end because you are on the phone less. For example, CompuServe charges about twice as much for a 9600-baud connection as for a 2400-baud connection but 9600-baud connections take roughly only one quarter as much time as 2400-baud connections. You end up paying roughly half as much in connect time fees.

Also, modems can work at slower speeds than their fastest rate if necessary. But modems obviously cannot exceed their fastest speed. A 9600-baud modem can handle a 2400-baud connection. But a 2400-baud modem cannot speed up to match an available 9600-baud connection.

Considering Available Modems

Modems for the Macintosh have different features; some modems have outstanding capabilities. The section discusses some available modems.

The Hayes family is the "Mercedes" of modems. For the Macintosh, you can choose from the Hayes Ultra 24, Ultra 96, and Ultra 144, which has Smartcom software tools that enable you to control features like speaker volume, transmission mode, and phone number memory. Those units are 2400, 9600, and 14,400 baud, respectively. Those units also carry "Mercedes" prices, but Hayes modems are the highest quality and offer the best reliability. The Ultra series can be shared over networks, connect with packet-switched networks, and offer other, more business-oriented features. In addition, Hayes now offers the Optima series of modems. These modems offer the same quality, but they are less expensive, offering fewer of the high-powered features of the Ultra.

You can find 2400-baud modems (some with software) for as little as $90 from other manufacturers. Send/receive fax modems (9600 for fax, 2400 for modem) run about $150 to $200, but through special deals, you can get them for less (I bought mine at $120).

At 14,400 baud, some of the fastest modems around also are becoming more affordable. Only a few years ago, they cost thousands. Now they cost right around or under $500, and many different models are readily available. For example, Prometheus Ultima Home Office has all the features mentioned—V.42bis, MNP-5, send and receive 9600-baud Group III fax, and voice messaging—for just under $500.

Global Village Communications has the Teleport series, which has costs that range from $199 to $450. These modems attach to the Apple Desktop Bus (ADB), which is used to connect your mouse and keyboard to the Macintosh. The modems draw their power from the ADB, are fully Hayes-compatible, and offer the features of remote access (you can even turn on your Macintosh over the phone). The PowerPort series by the same manufacturer consists of internal modems for the PowerBooks.

Just as you can share peripherals such as laser printers, you can share modems. Shiva offers modems that enable you to network a single modem by using AppleTalk. After the modem is set up, you select it from the Chooser and begin telecommunicating. The price is fairly steep, unless your business needs to have more than one computer with modem capability. In that case, the price is much more reasonable than buying individual modems for each user.

The budget-conscious will want to look at the Zoom series of modems. I've used a Zoom 2400-baud fax modem for some time now with great success. Zoom offers a 14,400-baud data modem with send and receive fax (also at 14,400 baud) with V.42bis and MNP for $300 (without fax, the unit runs about $255). Zoom modems carry a warranty of an amazing seven years.

Assessing Telecommunication Costs

To determine whether it's worth it for you to get into the telecommunications race, consider the following variables and weigh them against such express mail services as Federal Express, UPS Blue Label, and the post office's overnight delivery:

- File size
- Number of files (or amount of data) transmitted
- Cost of transmission
- Frequency of transmission
- Cost of equipment

The more you use your telecommunications equipment, the more you receive your money's worth, but unless you telecommunicate regularly, the equipment may not be worth the expense or trouble involved. At the same time, consider the kind of information you regularly handle. Overnight mail can be more expensive than long distance charges if you regularly send documents. Other information simply cannot be sent through the mail. For example, CompuServe enables you to access the Books in Print database to search for currently published books, which Federal Express does not offer.

The deregulation of telephone companies has brought the benefits of reduced prices. You can take advantage of these rates. For example, MCI and Sprint, as well as AT&T's other big competitors, have services for data transmission, including *dedicated data lines* (also called *leased lines*) at reduced cost.

Even if you do not have a dedicated line for data transmission, your costs are still reduced if you use a company that rents lines instead of using the company that owns them (AT&T).

When you need help getting set up, decide for yourself which company is the most helpful and has the "cleanest" lines. Over the years, I've found that Sprint has some of the best connections and has customer service so superior that I regularly throw popcorn at absurd AT&T "I-dialed-Phoenix-and-got-Fiji" ads.

When telecommunicating, you can save money by using data compression programs such as Stuffit from Aladdin Systems (the standard in the Macintosh world, though Compactor Pro is widely used also). Some text documents can be compressed to 50 percent of their original size. See Chapter 19, "Using Utility Software," for more on data compression and translation.

Buying Communications Software

Of all the components of a telecommunications system, the software is probably the most flexible. All these software packages enable you to send and receive files. But good programs go beyond this simple function. The following list describes features better programs offer:

- A command language, such as macros, customizing telecommunications functions (often called *scripts*).

- On-screen buttons that control functions.

- Support of multiple protocols so that you can communicate with as many different modems as possible.

- Support of all major protocols, especially Text, MacBinary, XMODEM and YMODEM, and Kermit.

- Terminal emulation (so that your Macintosh can act like a "dumb" terminal. Some packages support a wide variety of terminals, including those used with mainframe computers).

- Transmission of graphics.

- Transmission of color.

- On-screen timing with billing to help you keep track of the time you spend on-line with an information provider and of the basic on-line phone charges.

- On-screen help.

- Automatic answering, dialing, and redialing.

- Interactive telecommunications (you work with another computer).

- Filters to remove "garbage characters" that are incidental to the transmission.

This list is not all-inclusive, but it should give you some idea of what features are desirable. Keep in mind, however, that you may not need all these features in the same program, even if those features are available. As with other purchases, buy what you think best fits your needs.

With telecommunications software, there is a tradeoff between the number of features available and the program's power and user-friendliness. Unlike word processors and spreadsheets, telecommunications software is not particularly intuitive; for many people, it is downright alien. This lack of user-friendliness stems partly from the complexity of the telecommunications process and from the many variables, such as speed, parity settings, and other settings.

The leading communications packages are MicroPhone II, MicroPhone Pro, and White Knight. These packages share the top spot. They are so full of features and so well designed that if only one existed, you would never miss the others. With these packages, you cannot miss. (Many prefer MicroPhone because the package is slightly more user-friendly.)

MicroPhone II and Pro

MicroPhone II and Pro (from Software Ventures) offer a good balance of power and user-friendliness. MicroPhone II is based on MacTep, written by Dennis Brothers, the author of the original MicroPhone, and is one of the most successful commercial telecommunications programs available.

MicroPhone offers special features, such as multitasking support (for System 7 as well as System 6 MultiFinder) and a sophisticated scripting language for customizing your telecommunications operations. You can also launch an application from within MicroPhone, so you can download a file and continue working with another application. The software includes a series of setup files you use to communicate with telecommunications services such as GEnie, CompuServe, MCI Mail, and Dow Jones. In fact, these files are really scripts already written for you. You just click the appropriate icon and you're ready to go.

Figure 17.1 shows the set of commands for the log-on script for CompuServe. These prepared scripts save you time because you do not need to know the command language to use them.

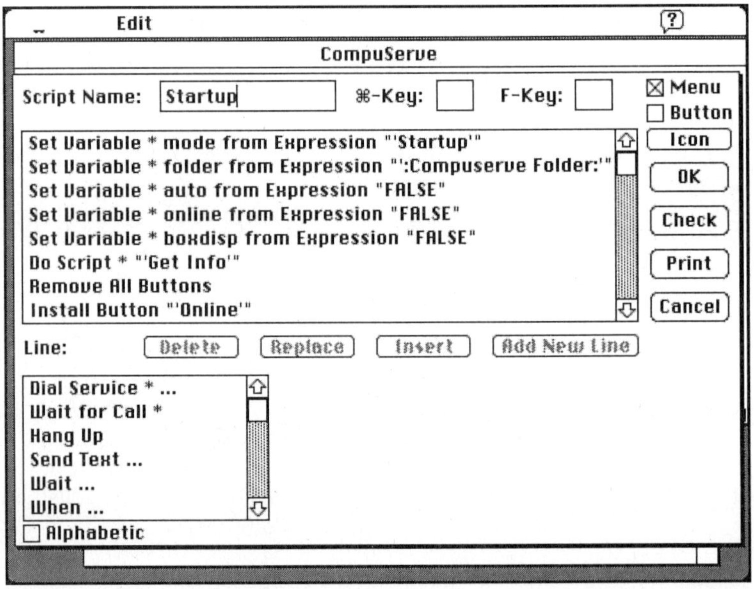

Fig. 17.1
A MicroPhone script for logging on to CompuServe.

With MicroPhone, you can easily log on to an information provider such as CompuServe, one of the largest electronic information providers in the world. The following instructions assume that you already set up your modem, and that you are using MicroPhone to log on to CompuServe.

First, double-click the icon marked CompuServe in MicroPhone's folder window (see fig. 17.2). The menus across the top of the resulting screen show the options available with MicroPhone. The Settings menu enables you to set all the important parameters necessary for your modem, which takes out the headaches and stumbling blocks of getting started. Figure 17.3 shows the Communication Settings dialog. Here you specify settings such as baud rate, stop bits, parity, and so on, depending on your telecommunications software.

Fig. 17.2
The MicroPhone product displayed on the Desktop.

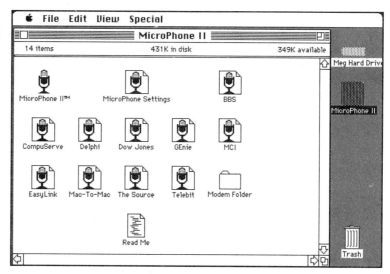

Fig. 17.3
The Communication Settings dialog used to set modem features.

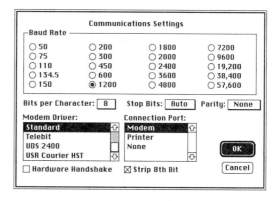

To dial the service you want to use, choose the Create Service command from the Phone menu. You see the screen shown in figure 17.4. Now dial the service you want to use.

Fig. 17.4

The Create Service dialog.

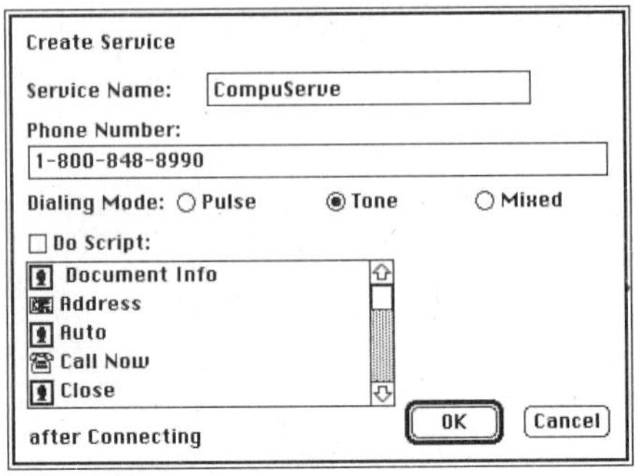

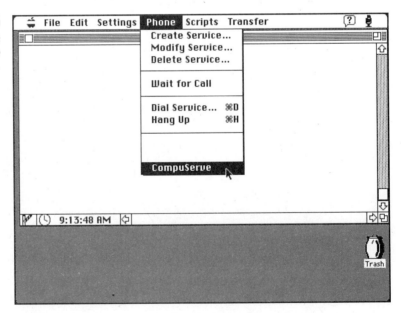

Enter the requested information—the name of the service, the phone number (which the service provides), and the type of phone service that you have—touch-tone or pulse (rotary). "Pulse" is the old rotary service; it has nothing to do with your actual phone. When you finish, click the OK button.

Now you are ready to connect. Choose the CompuServe command from the Phone menu (see fig. 17.5). Through your Mac's modem speaker, you hear the number being dialed. Next you see a message from CompuServe, which indicates that you are connected and ready to go and that the meter is running (you are being charged).

Fig. 17.5

Selecting CompuServe after setting up communications.

The first time you sign on to any telecommunications service, you have to supply all kinds of information, especially instructions for billing. Most services require you to use a major credit card, such as MasterCard or VISA. Some services, such as GEnie, enable you to sign up on-line; others, such as NewsNet, require a completed application form.

All telecommunications programs ask you to enter the name and phone number of the service or person you want to connect with. When you select the service you want, MicroPhone enables you to skip the tedious work that other programs require.

MicroPhone Pro is the latest version of the MicroPhone program. The added features include support for System 7 Publish and Subscribe, aliases, connection to TCP/IP hosts, and fax modem support. Another feature includes Apple Events, which enables you to automate program operation, especially with macro utilities such as QuicKeys.

White Knight

Another popular program, White Knight, is based on Red Ryder, the first terminal emulation program for the Macintosh. The first nine versions of Red Ryder were shareware; Scott Watson, the author, finally released the software of Version 11 commercially and renamed it White Knight.

White Knight (from FreeSoft) is a tremendously powerful telecommunications package. You can tell by its version number (currently Version 11—Red Ryder went through 10 upgrades) that it has been around for some time. For half the cost of MicroPhone, this program is a steal.

With the introduction of the commercial package, White Knight now has full scripting and records your actions so that you don't need to know the procedural language to create a script. Just use the Write a Procedure for Me command and go about your business. White Knight remembers. The program has three levels of password support, can operate in color, works as a mini-bulletin board to exchange messages, supports all the important protocols, and includes Okyto. Okyto is a simple transfer tool you can use to identify the files you want to send or retrieve. You can then send or retrieve the files with a few simple clicks.

For those of you who really want to get into the telecommunications game, White Knight offers a set of commands (called RCMDs) for its scripting language. This feature may be beyond the grasp (or interest) of many novices, but if you are interested, you can use this feature to fully express White Knight's power. However, with a more than 270-page manual that goes through many complicated processes step by step, White Knight has been responsive to beginners' needs. Here are some other White Knight features well worth noting:

- Works in the background under the Finder.

- Has user-defined macro keys.

- Can track service use with multiple phone books.

- Saves time and money with a buffered keyboard.

- Tells you with on-screen menus how much time and money your call is costing you.

- Supports 300 to 57,600 baud.

Smartcom II

Smartcom II for the Mac (from Hayes) has a scrollable buffer that enables you to read through previous on-screen information that has been saved. Smartcom also supports full color. Other programs use scripts or macros; Smartcom uses autopilots, which are basically the same—a set of stored instructions that you invoke through the click of a button. Like MicroPhone, Smartcom includes autopilots to get you started with many of the major on-line information providers.

Smartcom II uses icons for major functions and has a simple interface for the sophisticated functions of Hayes modems. Many Hayes modems come with a version of Smartcom. Obviously, if you purchase a Hayes modem, you know that Smartcom will work fully with the modem, because the program is manufactured by the same company. Even if your modem is from another manufacturer, however, you will have one of the best packages available. However, be certain to use Smartcom with a fully Hayes-compatible modem for best results.

Specialized Software

CompuServe and America Online both offer specialized communications software to use with their information systems. CompuServe now includes the CompuServe Information Manager with all new subscriptions. America Online also provides software to new subscribers. Other services are rapidly following suit, and as the result, telecommunications is becoming easier.

CompuServe can also be accessed through Navigator, which automates so many common functions of using the service that no CompuServe user should be without the package. Navigator sells through mail order for about $50 now, and pays for itself after you use it for only a session or two. The program quickly and effectively handles electronic mail and forums (electronic gathering places that evolved from the BBS system). A typical Navigator session can last as little as five minutes, accomplishing tasks that would take a couple of hours without the program. At CompuServe connection prices, using the information system without Navigator is affordable only for Ross Perot types.

Using Electronic Mail

Telecommunications software is frequently used to create electronic mail, or *E-mail*, the electronic equivalent of letters and memos. E-mail creates an electronic mailbox, a central storage system in which people can access mail left for them and leave mail intended for others. For central mailboxes, many E-mail users rely on telecommunications software—White Knight or MicroPhone, for example, or MCI Mail and CompuServe on the large services. Such arrangements are called *public E-mail*.

With programs like CE Software's QuickMail, other people establish *private E-mail*—E-mail networks within their own organizations. Suppose that you come to your office at 8 a.m. You log on to your E-mail system and find three messages waiting for you. You select the message that appears to be the most important (it's from the boss), read it, and send your answer. You can respond to messages from the boss upstairs or from a company halfway around the world. E-mail is inexpensive and as quick as a phone call. Today's popular software makes E-mail easy as well.

Public E-Mail Services

Public E-mail is big business. Leaders such as MCI and AT&T have hundreds of thousands of subscribers. Public E-mail is easy, inexpensive, and, best of all, reliable. When you send a message, you can tell whether it has been received; several services can even let you know when your message has been read.

Like all information providers, most services offer a starter kit that includes your ID number, instructions, and sometimes a certificate for free time to encourage you to use the service. Generally, you have to give the company a credit card number so that the company can bill you automatically. Established businesses (with appropriate credit ratings) can often be billed directly.

To use an E-mail service, you sign on, give your password, and check for mail. E-mail systems differ from one another, but in all cases, you usually check your mailbox for any messages first.

Public E-Mail Software

Several products are designed exclusively for use with E-mail systems. One popular program, Desktop Express (from Dow Jones), includes MCI Mail service. Desktop Express uses MCI Mail to transfer documents from one Macintosh to another without any concern for matching protocols and other modem parameters, making this software especially easy for beginners to use. But what happens when you send your partner an Excel Impact spreadsheet and he or she does not have Excel? Even though the partner can't edit the file, he or she can receive it and view it because Desktop Express comes with Glue. With Glue, you can read any file, regardless of the application that was used to create it.

One major shortcoming of Desktop Express is that it is not a total communications package, so you cannot go on-line to other data services or to another Macintosh. You are limited to MCI Mail and the Dow Jones news service.

Private E-Mail

Private (sometimes called corporate) E-mail has some distinct advantages over an E-mail service. First, private E-mail is under your control. You set it up, choose who is on the service, and decide what options will be available. When things go wrong, you fix them.

Second, security is almost guaranteed, although no system is truly impenetrable. Messages on public services can be read by people other than the intended recipients. Although the public companies would probably be reluctant to admit it, the more people who have general access, the higher the likelihood (no matter how small) for a potential leak.

Third, over a long period of time the cost of private E-mail can be much less than that of public E-mail. With most private E-mail programs, the cost of the software is your only expense.

Private E-mail has drawbacks, however. Someone must be the administrator, or the custodian, who makes sure that each computer or other device attached to the network works as it should. In addition, if hardware must be dedicated for the mail system's storage places, you must consider that added cost when you decide whether to set up an E-mail system.

For more information about private E-mail, see Chapter 28, "Networking."

Exploring the World of Bulletin Boards

```
5/1/92 1:20AM

Please provide your ID: Wacky Wordman

Please remember our rules and tell a friend
about the WordPerfect Forum. What's your question?

*How can I get WordPerfect to do a headline and then
do columns?
```

It's after 1:00 in the morning, and Wacky Wordman signed on to an electronic bulletin board to ask a question about WordPerfect. Tomorrow morning, he will sign on to the bulletin board again and probably find 10 to 20 answers to his question. The information is free, and the telephone connection charges at that hour are minimal.

In addition to big commercial information providers, noncommercial information sources, commonly known as bulletin boards, are available. A *bulletin board system (BBS)* is an electronic bulletin board that contains memos, real-time conversations, programs that can be downloaded, games, and every type of electronic information you can imagine. All this information is made accessible to others through their telecommunications systems.

Bulletin boards, which come in virtually all sizes and are targeted toward different types of computer users, are a labor of love. Usually, system operators (*Sysops*) run bulletin boards, and sometimes (but rarely) charge a membership fee. By all measures, BBSs are shining examples of the personal computer's power and the ways people can share information. Most bulletin boards have three divisions:

- E-mail for sharing private messages

- Public messages for sharing information with other BBS users

- Public-domain and shareware files that can be accessed by BBS users

The third division is the most important, for here the entire shareware market is open to thousands of people beyond the circle of friends of the developer. This division is where the advertising for new products takes place; you can easily download to your own hard disk the thousands of programs available from a BBS.

Some Sysops charge for their services, some request a donation, and others don't charge anything. How any stay in business is always a mystery; it is no surprise that few survive the day-to-day rigor of uploading and downloading files, answering mail, and cleaning up files, to say nothing of the cost of dedicating a Macintosh and a hard drive to the BBS.

Each bulletin board is different, and all display some kind of introductory statement the first time you sign on in order to acquaint you with what they do. Here are some rules of bulletin board etiquette that you need to follow:

- *Don't* sign on and download hundreds of files in one sitting. Many boards enable only one person to sign on at a time.

- *Don't* abuse the BBS system by uploading commercial software.

- *Don't* use anything you download unless you are sure that it is virus free. Use a virus detection program to check the downloaded file.

- *Don't* use abusive or profane language or insult other people on the line.

- *Do* make a contribution if it's called for.

- *Do* share the BBS with other friends who use the Macintosh, and encourage them to join.

- *Do* be sure to follow the rules of the BBS on which you are working (sign-on and sign-off procedures, downloading, bug testing, and so on).

- *Do* respect other users' privacy. Many people use code names for anonymity and don't want others prying.

Using Information Services

The commercial information services focus on providing information on every conceivable topic through telecommunications. From the standpoint of Macintosh users, commercial information services fall into three categories.

First, many services, such as CompuServe, America Online, and GEnie, have forums, or sections devoted solely to Macintosh users and Macintosh products, as well as sources for general information.

Second, others, such as MacNet, are devoted exclusively to Macintosh interests.

Third, some services, such as Dialog, provide information from hundreds of databases. Your modem, telecommunications software, and Macintosh can easily access each type of service. All you need to do is to subscribe to the service, call it, and pay. You can often subscribe on-line. Several computer periodicals contain advertisements for these services; many list toll-free numbers you can call to sign on.

When you sign up with some services, you receive some free connect time. To open your account, you have to supply a credit card number and you have to give the company a billing address. If you are a novice, be sure to find out what kind of support (preferably toll-free) the companies offer.

CompuServe

CompuServe offers on-line activities such as news, weather, sports, travel, shopping, E-mail, and financial information. It also provides access to other information services, including massive bibliographic databases and thousands of abstracts (or brief summaries) of articles about personal computers, product reviews, and noncomputer topics. The system is quite extensive. For example, at one point I used the service to locate papers and a book on the grammar of an American Indian language spoken by fewer than 1,000 people.

For Macintosh users, CompuServe offers several forums. Answers to questions, reviews, and even on-line discussions with famous Macintosh personalities are offered. The following list shows some topics for forums:

- Some forums focus on increasing your productivity with your Macintosh in applications such as word processing, desktop publishing, and programming.

- Arts and entertainment forums provide information for people who want to use their Macintosh to explore topics about music and art.

- Business user forums discuss business and software useful in running a business (accounting programs, for example).

- CompuServe also offers games, including multiplayer "game shows." Be forewarned that on-line games are very expensive to use.

- You can also participate in on-line discussions in various forums with Macintosh programmers and Apple officials.

Personal Bibliographic Software offers a package called Pro-Search, which enables you to tap into a specific database, Dialog. You can choose the search method and the database you want to search, auto-mate connections, and subscribe to updated Dialog database information sources.

CompuServe is my personal favorite and a long-time "stomping ground." With all that it offers, the service is quite addicting. With over a million subscribers and an almost overwhelming array of services, CompuServe is fast becoming an electronic universe all its own. Word has it that even members of the Clinton campaign had a log on and frequented the service. Currently, the White House is setting up a CompuServe account to enable users to send mail to the Administration electronically. Speaking of politics, CompuServe offers the CongressGram service that enables you to send quick messages to your congressperson.

New users can find CompuServe overwhelming and should consider a "map" to the service. Que offers *Que's Quick Guide to CompuServe* to help you make sense out of the massive service. (Yes, this is a blatant plug for my book, but if you're new to CompuServe, a book by someone who's been around the service some five years or more can help.)

GEnie

The main advantage of GEnie (from General Electric) is its reduced charges. GEnie is less expensive than many other services. It offers the Macintosh RoundTable, which has thousands of files ready to be downloaded, as well as a Macintosh bulletin board to keep you informed of what's happening in the Macintosh community. GEnie also offers Business & News, Comp-U-Store (home shopping), on-line travel assistance, and on-line reference to travel guides.

America Online

A relatively new service (1989), America Online is run by Quantum Computer Services, a company that has extensive experience with Commodore on-line services. America Online has a Macintosh interface, is easy to use, and even has a digitized voice that guides you through the sign-up procedure.

One of the most outstanding features of Online is the real-time "talking" you can do with other on-line users. Although other services (most notably CompuServe) also offer this feature, America Online's feature is more user-friendly and makes accessing other people easier. The hourly rates are significantly cheaper than other services. Quite a few on-line conferences have occurred, and other conferences with famous Macintosh experts are planned. The service also has a respectable

Macintosh library from which you can select files to download. Finally, CE Software and other mail products support America Online.

Apple and America Online recently announced plans to work together. Most likely, America Online will become the main service that disseminates Macintosh information and support in the near future, though CompuServe certainly will not ignore the challenge.

Dialog

Dialog contains many individual databases that give you access to on-line abstracts of important articles in several different disciplines. For example, Dialog includes databases in business and chemistry, as well as in the humanities and social sciences. Dialog has access to more databases than any other similar service. At a cost to the user, Dialog also offers Telenet and DIALNETZ, Dialog's own telephone system.

BRS

BRS (for Bibliographic Retrieval Services), which consists of several different products, is similar to CompuServe but not as comprehensive. BRS consists of BRS/Search service with access to 150 databases, BRS/Colleague, which contains the same information as BRS/Search, and BRS/After Dark, a reduced version of BRS/Search available during off hours (about 6 p.m. to 8 a.m.).

Search and Colleague differ in the type of interface they use. Search is command and menu driven; Colleague is just menu driven. Although commands are quicker and more to the point, menus don't require as much training and enable you to explore, even if you don't know the intricacies of the system.

Orbit

If you need technical and scientific information, Orbit is one place to look. Like other information providers, Orbit uses on-line English commands to help you find what you want. Orbit's many databases include the following:

- LitAlert
- Chemical Economics Handbook
- Aqualine

- Inspec
- ACCOUNTANTS
- Ceramic Abstracts
- FOREST
- LABORDOC

Dow Jones News/Retrieval

Business and finance information is available from Dow Jones News/Retrieval. Dow Jones claims to be the only provider devoted exclusively to business information. The service has the complete edition of the *Wall Street Journal* on-line, and also contains text from such publications as *Barron's*, *Business Week*, *Forbes*, and *Money* magazine. Dow Jones offers a complete line of financial analysis software, such as Market Manager PLUS, which you can use to perform stock analyses after you download market prices from one of the databases available on Dow Jones News/Retrieval.

NewsNet

NewsNet offers access to more than 360 newsletters that deal with topics such as metals and mining, investment, energy, travel, chemistry, education, and defense. In addition, NewsNet offers NewsFlash, a clipping service that scans more than 3,000 articles and selects those with the key words you identify. NewsFlash "looks through" the information on 10 major national and international news wires—which means that you can get information before it appears in the newspaper.

Prodigy

Prodigy is a joint effort of IBM and Sears. Though oriented primarily towards shopping services, it offers many of the same services as America Online and CompuServe. The service, which is fairly easy to use, is aimed at the beginner and home user, but it is slow and somewhat limited in its capability. Recently, a controversy surrounding Prodigy is that the Sysops have been censoring and editing the electronic mail they find offensive. Other users complain about the constant advertising encountered on the service. Prodigy is not popular among Macintosh users.

CONNECT

CONNECT is an information network, not an information provider; it is devoted to transmitting information as quickly and efficiently as possible. CONNECT is the gateway through which you access information from other databases. This service is especially nice for Macintosh users, because the MacNet software used for communicating with CONNECT has familiar Macintosh interfaces and enables you to transmit Macintosh information and graphics easily.

CONNECT has the lowest charges of any of the services examined here.

The Well

The Well (for Whole Earth Lectronic Link) is the brainchild of Stuart Brand, the person who brought us the Whole Earth Catalog. Although you can do many of the same things on the Well that you can on the larger services (such as accessing different networks), the Well is one big conversation between people participating in different conferences about everything from flying to design to UNIX. You cannot read last Thursday's *New York Times* on the Well, but someone on-line will probably know about the article you want and mail it to you.

How to Choose an Information Provider

If you are new to the telecommunications game and are considering signing up with one of the services, the following tips may help you avoid some pitfalls.

Send for an information packet or a subscription kit. Then you can study the information and call the service with your questions (most have toll-free numbers).

Note the different types of charges for the different baud rates at different times. CompuServe no longer charges different rates for different times. Now it charges solely on the basis of modem speed, but it also offers a flat-rate package that combines some of the more popular services.

Check the availability of local connections to save connection charges. If a phone number is not local to you, consider the charges for connecting through your long-distance provider. Depending on the local phone carrier, it can be cheaper to call an out-of-state number instead of a relatively local number.

For example, I found that Southwestern Bell charges outrageous prices inside the state of Texas, making it cheaper to connect to Louisiana CompuServe numbers through Sprint instead of calling the number in a city only a 45-minute drive from where I live.

See whether the service you want to use has Telenet available. Owned by General Telephone and Electronics, this data communication service enables you to use a local number to link into the service you want to use. This option may save you money. Other connection options are also possible; check with your local phone company.

Learn as much as you can about the different services before you actually go on line. Again, call for printed information, which can save you time and aggravation.

See whether the service has a software tool. Some services offer software tools to steer you through the many menus and commands to get at what you want. CompuServe has the Navigator, for example, which helps you cut down your on-line time. Navigator costs extra but saves enough money to pay for itself.

Don't read long documents on-screen. Instead, download the documents, print them, and read them at your leisure.

Develop a general feel for where the information you need may be located. For example, if you want to know the win-loss record of the San Diego Padres, don't try to find the answer in Orbit, which is primarily a scientific database.

Don't use a BBS or an on-line information provider for information available elsewhere for less. You could sit at your computer and find out the population of Tangiers, but you can get the same information from an encyclopedia or from the library, which saves both time and money.

On-Line Addiction and Billing Problems

A word of warning is in order. On-line services like CompuServe can be quite addictive. With so many services available, so many people to communicate with, and an entire electronic world to explore, connection fees can add up to frightening sums ($200/month was not unusual for me).

If you are on a strict budget, you can easily bankrupt yourself before you realize what's happening. This point is especially true when you consider the electronic debit system used by CompuServe and America Online, which transfers funds out of your checking account or charges your credit card automatically.

Watch your connect time carefully. Even with Navigator or a similar software tool, you could run up expensive monthly charges. And, it should be noted, I've waged several battles with CompuServe over billing problems encountered by friends. (To date, my only problem was solved rather quickly by the system.)

When you deal with the larger systems, remember that these services are—according to CompuServe officials—completely unregulated. You have no recourse to a regulatory body (at least I haven't found one yet; I'm still looking). You must protect yourself.

Take strict steps to safeguard your account. One important point is to make your password complicated, and something no one could easily guess. Follow these rules:

- Never use easily discovered passwords, such as your birthdate, your name (or your dog's name even), your phone number, address, and so on. Use something obscure, made up, and convoluted. Preferably, your password should be something you can remember yourself but in case you forget, the services can change your password for you, though it means that you are locked out of the system for a while.

- Use nonalphabetic characters in your password.

- Never write down your password.

- Never give your password to anyone.

- Never type in your password while you are on-line, except when you first log on. That is the *only* time a service asks for your password. If you are in the middle of a session and receive a request for your password, someone is trying to steal your account. Report it to the Sysop, and then change your password immediately.

- Change your password frequently, at least once a month, and more frequently if others have access to your computer.

- If you use any automated systems that store your password, such as Navigator, remember that *anyone* who has access to your computer can log on to the system or copy your communications software and log on from another Macintosh.

  Recently, a friend of mine discovered that someone was logging on to her account every few minutes. Apparently, someone copied her Navigator software and then passed it around. She's now facing CompuServe, which is demanding over a thousand dollars before turning her account back on, even though she can demonstrate that she wasn't anywhere near her computer when many of the log-ons occurred.

- Whenever possible, use a credit card to pay for the service. Federal law enables you to refuse to pay for services you did not receive.

  If you have problems and refuse to pay, you will most likely be cut off from the service (as my friend was), but at least you do not have to pay the charges.

  If you use the direct checking account debit service, determine the exact date that the service draws on your account. Then check your charges before that date. If all else fails, you can instruct your bank to refuse the debit.

- When you deal with on-line service customer service departments, take down names. This tactic is one of my favorites. When an individual knows that his or her name will go up the chain of command (all the way to the president of the company, if necessary) along with a service complaint, that person has a stronger motivation to solve problems.

  Conversely, a compliment for a problem solved directed to a supervisor encourages customer service departments and improves relations.

- Never forget, you are a paying customer. And never let your service provider forget, either. If you receive poor service, report it to publications, such as *MacUser* or *MacWorld*. Publicity is a great motivator.

A great many people use on-line services for years with no problems at all. But horror stories do exist. Practice "defensive computing" at all times.

Using Fax Modems

A fax modem is a modem that enables you to send files rather than hard copy to a fax machine or to another fax modem. The recipient prints the file when he or she chooses. Fax machines use phone lines, as modems do. If you send or receive faxes on a frequent basis, you should have a dedicated phone line.

Fax modems are driven by software. BackFax (from Solutions International) enables you to using a fax modem to transmit in the background as you continue to work on other files. For example, you could write a letter to one client as you fax another letter to another client. Another outstanding feature of BackFax is that it enables you to set up address books (names, addresses, fax numbers, and so on) and specify delivery instructions for when you want certain files sent. The background feature works whether or not you are running under Finder. You can even send messages larger than fax paper because BackFax can send messages in strips the recipient can assemble.

Some fax machines can also can be used as a fax modem; by plugging into your Macintosh, you can fax files instead of hard copy. You can print the fax files you receive on your printer if you want a hard copy other than the copy the fax machine produces. Fax modems store information as files; they do not automatically print the files.

The Relisys RA2110M fax/fax modem can store more than 200 fax numbers. The machine is easy to set up, and the ease and speed with which you can obtain information is incredible.

Relisys has just released a model called the Telax System that is not only a FAX machine but also a scanner, printer, copier, and modem.

The Big Mac Recommendation

For information services, the Big Macintosh recommendation is CompuServe and America Online.

CompuServe offers a fixed rate of $8 per month for basic services, no matter how much time you spend on the phone. Additional services are charged at different rates. CompuServe's offerings are far more extensive than any other general information service.

America Online is rapidly becoming the premier Macintosh on-line service. With the Apple-America Online deal, this point should become even more true. America Online has also announced drastic price reductions for use of the service. The new pricing should be implemented by the summer of 1993.

Many people use both services. Both contain a wealth of information services and features.

More than likely, you will want to avoid Prodigy. Some Macintosh users do like the system, but a great many more report problems (such as the "censorship" fiasco), and complain of the overt sales and marketing that goes on incessantly.

Regardless of the service you use or BBS you access, always protect your password religiously. Even if you use a free system, there are those people who steal passwords, and then cause trouble in your name.

Always check downloaded files with a good virus detection program such as Disinfectant or SAM (the latter by Symantec).

CHAPTER EIGHTEEN

Using Multimedia

Multimedia is an idea that is both praised and vilified at the same time. Supporters say it is the next computer revolution while detractors insist it is simply another slick, high-tech way of saying nothing. The truth probably lies somewhere in the middle.

The idea of multimedia is to combine different medias into a whole—to use video, sound, graphics, and other technology to transmit a message. Multimedia is not a new concept. At trade shows or museums you've probably seen high-tech presentations using a wall of video screens or combining animated graphics and sound to sell a product or to educate.

These two different uses probably illuminate part of the multimedia flap. Although a good, high-tech presentation with sounds, music, video, and special effects can captivate an audience, the presentation simply may be a slick way of making a mediocre product seem spectacular. On the other hand, only one thing is certain about marketing a product: if you don't catch your audience's attention, you won't sell the product.

On the other side of this multimedia flap lies kids being fascinated by a history presentation when a textbook and a droning teacher may put them to sleep. Few people can argue against multimedia when a child's imagination is captured by a museum presentation. (Some still do. The old learning-is-drudgery nonsense is still around, and demonstrating that children learn in stimulating and overtly "fun" environments falls on deaf ears when you deal with the I-suffered-horribly-but-persevered-to-get-MY-education crowd.)

An excellent warning in the area of multimedia is the phrase *content-free presentations.* Multimedia can be visual chewing gum as much as television. Presentations can be slick, full of animation, music, spectacular effects, and still transmit little to no information.

As multimedia moves to the Desktop, you're sure to see an increase in content-free presentations—spectacular looking nonmessages that leave you with only a vague feeling that you learned "something." But this event simply is the high-tech version of the captivating speaker with nothing to say—something not lacking.

Computer technology multiplies and amplifies. Multimedia in the hands of people with nothing to say or no talent simply is an animated, narrated, music-scored waste of time. But in the hands of people with a message worth hearing—even with no technology at all—and the talent to translate that message into video, music, sound, graphics, and the like, multimedia can be a powerful force.

After all, the power of video, sound, music, and special effects is already established. Have you counted the number of television sets owned and sold in this country lately?

Understanding Multimedia

Multimedia has already been defined as combining different medias into a single presentation to transmit a message. But what does this definition mean in terms of the Macintosh computer?

As a graphically oriented computer, the Macintosh is well suited for multimedia. Before the term became a buzzword, users found that they could create presentations more easily on the Macintosh; they could create and edit pictures and graphics more easily because of the Macintosh's graphic orientation. Music and sound have been on the Macintosh for some time, and video is basically graphical in nature. But before putting video on the Macintosh, developers had to wait until hardware technology became fast enough to handle the number of frames and until storage media became large enough to store them all.

All of these different medias came together to fuse into multimedia. Software that could integrate the different medias into a single, cohesive whole appeared then. Users at a Macintosh Desktop could manipulate a variety of medias in one program rather like DTP packages (see Chapter 15, "Desktop Publishing"), enabling them to integrate text and graphics into a single publication.

Multimedia software and hardware enable you to draw from different medias, edit and manipulate the sound, graphics, video, or other data, and integrate them all into a single presentation document.

This chapter surveys the various items to which you have access that enable you to create presentations that once required a team of specialists. None of the hardware or software gives you talent or takes its place. But if you have something worth saying and have the talent to make use of the power available today, your message can have a tremendous impact—much more than was possible for users only a few years ago.

Using Sound

Sound is an important part of multimedia. Visual images, video, animation, and the like are fine, but without sound are rather flat. The Macintosh is known for its sound capabilities. Even earlier models had the capability of storing and playing a wide variety of sounds. Later models are capable of playing stereo, and upcoming models promise even more sound capability.

If you plan to work with multimedia, one of the medias you may work with is sound. You may want to record, store, and play back sounds. The Macintosh has sound-playing capabilities, but they are limited without additional software. Basically, you're limited to using the included microphone (which comes with all sound recording–capable Macintoshes) to add alert sounds to your System file.

To go beyond this point or to add sound to a Macintosh that does not have the built-in sound-recording capability, you must add hardware and software. See "Choosing Multimedia Hardware," later in this chapter, for more on the hardware and "Using Multimedia Utilities," also in this chapter, for more on the software.

Sound is *analog,* meaning that it consists of waves that vary continuously, rising and falling in strength (amplitude) as well as increasing and decreasing in pitch (frequency). Computers, on the other hand, are *digital.* Digital equipment deals with discrete items—in this case, numbers consisting of ones and zeros (the binary, or base two, system).

For digital equipment to deal with sound, a conversion must take place. The Macintosh, like the CD player and DAT recorder, digitizes sound—turns the continuous waves into discrete numbers and back. The Macintosh uses an *analog-to-digital converter*—a chip that converts analog information into digital and back. This conversion is done by sampling the analog information (the sound in this case) very quickly, taking "snapshots" of the sound and recording as a number the value of the sound wave at a particular time. Figure 18.1 illustrates this idea in simplified form.

Fig. 18.1
Sampling a simple sound wave.

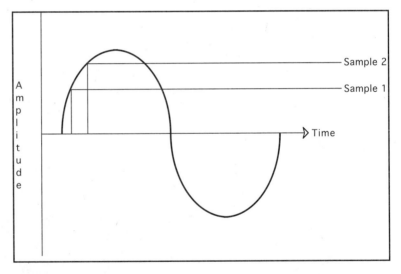

In the figure, Sample 1 and Sample 2 indicate points at which the sound is "listened to" and measured. The value of the sound (measured in a positive or negative number) is recorded.

By sampling sound very quickly, the Macintosh builds up a series of numbers that represents the sound. The *sampling rate* is the number of times that a sound each second is sampled. The typical minimum rate on the Macintosh is about 11KHz, or 11,000 times per second. The normal rate of sampling is 22KHz, or 22,000 times per second.

Sound waves are measured also in hertz (a standard measure of changes per second—frequency). KHz is the abbreviation for kilohertz, or thousands of hertz—thousands of changes per second.

Because of the way sound sampling works, you can digitize frequencies at twice the sampling rate. An 11KHz sampling rate, for example, digitizes sounds of up to 22KHz in frequency, and 22KHz sampling rate digitizes sounds of up to 44KHz, in frequency.

For average sounds such as speaking, 22KHz (an 11KHz sampling rate) is sufficient (the telephone carries sounds of only up to about 4KHz, and you can still recognize voices). The best quality sound, however, is produced with a 22KHz sampling rate recording up to 44KHz, which is actually higher than the human ear can hear. The typical CD player uses this sampling rate to produce high-quality stereo sound.

The only drawback to a 22KHz sampling is that it requires about 22KB per second of recording; 11KHz takes about half that. Generally, if you use voice or simple sounds, you can save disk space by using an 11KHz sampling rate. But if you need quality sound effects or music, 22KHz is the only way to go.

Several sound formats are used on the Macintosh. They are as follow:

- System 7 sound files. These files are used for sounds in the System file and are of the type "snd."

- SoundEdit files. SoundEdit is a widely used sound utility that has created something of a standard on the Macintosh.

- AIFF files. These files are the standard sound-recording files on the Macintosh, as defined by Apple.

You probably deal more with the latter two sound-file formats in multimedia. Usually, you see the first only in the System file.

Using Video

Like sound, video is an important part of multimedia. For example, being able to record, store, and manipulate video can help you add a great deal of impact to a presentation.

QuickTime is the Macintosh system for handling video on the Macintosh (see the following section, "Using QuickTime"). It is the System Software side of the process, giving you the ability to perform the standard Macintosh cut, copy, and paste operations with video movies.

With the proper setup, you can import video from a video camera, VCR, video disc, or other video source. You also can "print" to video or send the video movie to a VCR for recording. These features require software in addition to QuickTime, however.

Following are some considerations to think about if you must work with video:

■ Although the Macintosh with QuickTime can play and edit video movies, you cannot record your own movie from a video source to disk, or to a video recorder from disk, without hardware to translate the video signal. You need a video digitizer (see "Choosing Multimedia Hardware").

■ Video movies need a fast Macintosh to run well. Running QuickTime movies on an average 68030 machine can produce rather "jerking" movies. For best results, you need considerable processor speed and video display speed. Consider a fast 68040 Macintosh or various CPU and video acceleration cards (see Chapter 26, "Expanding the Macintosh," and Chapter 24, "Choosing a Display").

■ Video in the U.S. (and some other countries) uses the *NTSC standard* for defining frame rate, screen resolution, and so on. QuickTime is most compatible with this standard when displayed in at least 16-bit color (32,768 colors). Less than this amount of color depth results in a poor display. Increasing to the 16-bit level, however, increases the amount of memory and disk space you need to work with video.

■ QuickTime movies take a great deal of storage space. One of the sample movies Apple supplies with the Starter Kit, for example, is only 11 seconds long but takes 722KB of disk space, even with compression—an average of about 66KB per second. Another movie of only 10 seconds (from the American Media disk) takes 1.5MB, for an average of 150KB per second. The size of movies varies depending on various factors (such as the number of changes from frame to frame), but each one takes large amounts of storage space.

Using video on the Macintosh takes hardware and software that can cost considerable money. You should consider your needs carefully.

Using QuickTime

QuickTime is Apple's support for video on the Macintosh. QuickTime enables you to take video recordings, store them on the Macintosh, play them back on the Macintosh screen, and edit them. To take full advantage of QuickTime, you need software. Apple provides the QuickTime Starter Kit, which gives your Macintosh the ability to play QuickTime movies and use the Macintosh's familiar cut, copy, and paste editing with video.

The QuickTime Starter Kit sells for about $150. To use QuickTime, you need at least a 68020 and 4MB or more of memory. To play movies, you need 8-bit color (256 colors), but for best results, you need a minimum of 16-bit color (32,768 colors). A CD-ROM player is not absolutely required, but because of the sheer size of the movies, QuickTime is no more than a novelty without one. Without a CD-ROM, your computer needs a massive amount of hard disk space. (You need a great deal of space *with* a CD-ROM, but the amount without one would be prohibitively high.) Also, CD-ROM is the main distribution method for QuickTime materials.

The QuickTime Starter Kit installs the following on your hard disk:

- The QuickTime System extension

- Movie Player for playing QuickTime movies

- Picture Compressor for accessing compressed images and compressing pictures you create

- Movie Converter, which can create QuickTime movies from other movies (or selected parts of them) or from still video frames

- Movie Recorder, which creates QuickTime movies from a video source. You must have video digitizing equipment to use this software.

- Scrapbook, which is an enhanced version of the Macintosh Scrapbook that can hold QuickTime movie frames, selections of movies, or entire movies

- A set of Corel Converter System extensions that gives you access to pictures created on the IBM PC in DOS, Windows, or OS/2.

- Sample movie files on floppy disk and an entire collection on the QuickClips CD-ROM

After you install the QuickTime Starter Kit, simply double-click the movie's icon to play QuickTime movies. A window opens, displaying the first frame of the movie (see fig. 18.2).

Fig. 18.2
Starting a QuickTime
movie.

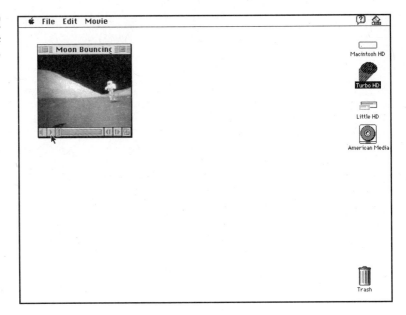

The QuickTime movie player can play movies and step through them frame by frame, enabling you to copy frames to the Clipboard for use in graphics programs.

The QuickTime Starter Kit is a must if you want to work with QuickTime movies, because you need the capabilities the Starter Kit provides. You also can begin a basic exploration of QuickTime with the kit. To go further, you will definitely need more software and probably more hardware. The Starter Kit is just that: a starting point. But if you are wondering whether QuickTime is worthwhile, the kit is an excellent starting point and should be your first multimedia purchase.

Using Multimedia Software

Several multimedia software packages that enable you to integrate different medias into presentations have been introduced. You need at least one of these packages to create multimedia presentations. Following are a few packages you might consider.

Macromedia is the leading company of multimedia software. If you've seen animated demos of Macintosh software, you most likely saw a dialog at the end of the demo announcing that the presentation was created using Macromedia Director by Macromedia.

Macromedia Director 3.1 is the leading multimedia presentation product. This powerful program integrates QuickTime, graphics, sound, music, and other medias into presentations you can edit, play back, or export easily. Macromedia Director enables you to write "scripts" to give you greater control over your presentation. You also receive the Macintosh Player, which you can use freely to distribute your presentation.

Macromedia Director represents the high end of multimedia presentation software. The program is powerful but, as with all high-end software, has a few drawbacks. The memory overhead can be quite high, and you need a fast and powerful Macintosh to take full advantage of the program. The price is also high at about $800. This program is not an impulse purchase by any means. If you need to create presentations of the highest quality, however, Macromedia Director is the way to go.

For a less expensive alternative to integrate video with graphics, animation, sound, and music into a presentation, consider MediaMaker at about $480. This mid-level presentation program is not as powerful as Macromedia Director but is quite sophisticated. Using a section of the program called "Collections," you can create a database of media elements—segments from video sources, CDs, sound files, and more. You then can reference the elements of the database by *picon,* a kind of icon, and integrate them into a full presentation.

If you need a good, basic presentation system for business, Macromedia has released Action! for the Mac. Action! is one of the easiest-to-use presentation programs around. You work with scenes that can be as long as one minute each.

In figure 18.3, you see the Action! tool palette (to the left) and the control panel (to the right). Using the tool palette, you can add text, draw graphics, add a button, change colors and line types, edit object actions, add sound, and create links between objects and scenes.

The control panel displays the name of the current scene. From a pop-up menu, you can choose the scene you want to work with (see fig. 18.4).

The buttons in the control panel enable you to step through a scene (you can adjust the amount of time each step consists of), play, stop, and rewind the presentation. You also can move through the scene by using the slider in the control panel or by clicking the up or down arrows to the right of the time indicator.

Action! also has a Scene Sorter that aids you in creating your presentation by enabling you to view and change the order of the scenes (see fig. 18.5).

Fig. 18.3
Adding a button to a scene
in Action!

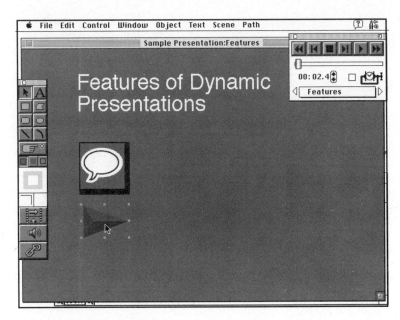

Fig. 18.4
Choosing the Introduction
scene.

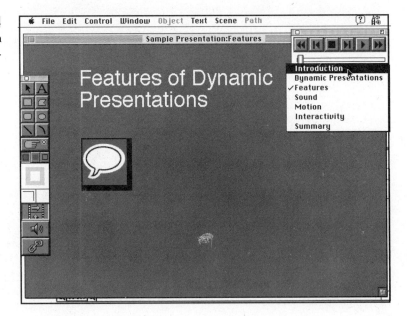

Fig. 18.5

The Scene Sorter shows you the order in which scenes are played.

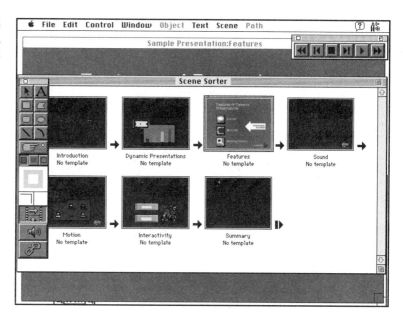

The Timeline shows you the timing of each object in the scene and enables you to edit objects and adjust their entry, hold, and exit times, (see fig. 18.6). The timeline of each object shows you when the object first appears on-screen (the left edge of the timeline), when the entry action is completed (the first white line in the timeline), the amount of time the object stays on-screen (the middle section of the timeline), when the exit action begins (the second white line in the timeline, as in the "summary" text timeline of figure 18.6), and when the object disappears from the screen (the right edge of the timeline).

You can adjust any aspect of the timeline by dragging one of the bars or part of a bar that represents an object. Double-clicking the timeline opens the Edit Object dialog, enabling you to change the object's attributes. The visual timeline is extremely useful because you can see the timing of each object in the scene and adjust it as needed.

Action! comes with a set of templates that consists of predefined layouts such as an introduction, bullet chart, chart, paragraph (for a block of text), and others (see fig. 18.7).

Action! is an excellent choice if you are a business professional who needs to create presentations quickly and easily. With very little effort you can build basic presentations by using the templates. You can create more sophisticated presentations by importing sounds and pictures and adding animation, and you also can "print" your presentation to video (with a video output card installed in your Macintosh).

Fig. 18.6
The Timeline shows all objects and the amount of time each object is on-screen.

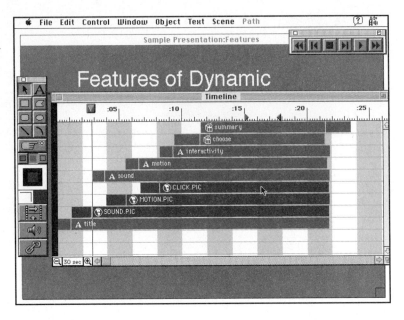

Fig. 18.7
The Action! World Map bullet chart template.

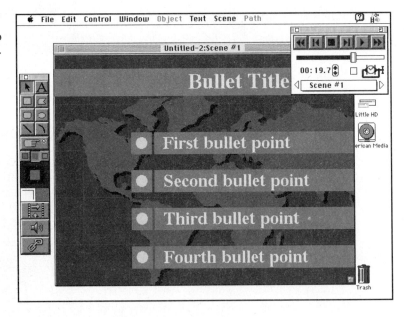

Action! at $350 is well worth the price if you need to create presentations but don't have the time to spend learning more complicated programs.

Another small, easy-to-use program by Macromedia is Magic. Using Magic, you can create animated presentations by drawing objects that become "actors" on a stage. Animating the objects consists of drawing lines. Magic costs about $280.

Although Macromedia produces more multimedia products than anyone, other companies offer presentation products as well. Adobe offers Premiere 2.0, which you can use to create QuickTime movies and videos, integrating digitized video, audio, and graphic animation. Premiere has a wide variety of effects for transitions. This program costs about $440.

The MovieProducer Bundle by Computer Friends/DiVA enables you to create presentations that combine video, graphics, sounds, text, and animation. The bundle has hardware and software, including the ColorSnap 32+ video image capture board and VideoShop by DiVA. You need add only a VCR, camcorder, laserdisc, or other video source to begin creating your own QuickTime movies. This package sells for about $780.

Using Multimedia Utilities

Multimedia utilities aid you in various ways to create multimedia presentations. Rather than being full-blown packages such as Action!, utilities enable you to work on specific aspects of a presentation. SwivelMan by Macromedia consists of two software programs, and it enables you to create three-dimensional models in photorealistic color (full 24-bit color), for example, and then animate them. This $620 program can create full presentations, or you can integrate the three-dimensional objects with a full presentation program.

MacroModel and MacroMind Three-D, multimedia utilities both by Macromedia, work with three-dimensional objects. In MacroModel, you create two-dimensional objects with CAD accuracy and then convert them into three-dimensional objects. You can create working models of three-dimensional mechanisms.

MacroMind Three-D creates photorealistic three-dimensional stills and animations that you can use with a multimedia presentation program. This program creates "three-d" type (letters, numbers, and symbols) from TrueType fonts and offers an unlimited number of animated objects, lights, and cameras.

Both of the preceding packages sell for just under $1,000 and are for the professional who needs to create three-dimensional illustrations and presentations. If you're an engineer who needs to create accurate, working models, MacroModel is good. MacroMind Three-D is oriented more toward creating presentations, providing three-dimensional objects for use with a multimedia presentation program.

Macromedia offers a less expensive option in Swivel 3D Professional, which costs about $480. This program is for three-dimensional modeling. For three-dimensional architectural design, ModelShop II is a good choice at $620.

Cinemation by Vividus Corporation can animate existing PowerPoint or Persuasion presentations, or it can create new presentations by using buttons, text, animation, paint, QuickTime, and more. A player is included, as is 12MB of clip media. Cinemation costs about $370.

CameraMan by Vision Software is a screen-recording utility you can use to make movies of the action on your Macintosh screen. This $100 package is a good, low-cost alternative to a full presentation package when you need to demonstrate Macintosh software or teach users about a package. You can edit your movies and add sound effects and music.

For playing, recording, and editing audio, one low-cost utility is AudioShop. You can create your own system beeps or add sound to QuickTime movies and HyperCard stacks. You can add special effects such as reverse sound, flange, reverb, and others. AudioShop also enables you to play audio CDs in a CD-ROM player (you can use this program without a CD-ROM player). Two disks of sounds come with this $70 program.

If you have a CD-ROM player, you often can avoid purchasing a video card by buying *clip media.* These CD-ROM disks come with a wide variety of QuickTime movies ready for pasting right into your presentations. The American Media ClipTime series by ATG Inc. is an excellent choice. Volume II, for example, includes movies from NASA, nature scenes, U.S. presidents, and more, for a total of 300 movies. Scenic photos are included, as are some 75 sound effects.

Macromedia also offers two clip media disks: "Business and Technology," ClipMedia 1 and "Industry at Work," ClipMedia 2. Both contain royalty-free QuickTime movies, graphics, sounds, animations, and more.

Using Photo CD

Kodak has created a system by which you can have your pictures developed to CD. Developing is available where Kodak developing is offered. To access the photos on the Macintosh, you need the Kodak Photo CD Access Software, which costs about $35. With the Access Software, you can use your CD-ROM player to view and import your photos (see fig. 18.8).

Fig. 18.8

Viewing a Kodak photo on
CD-ROM.

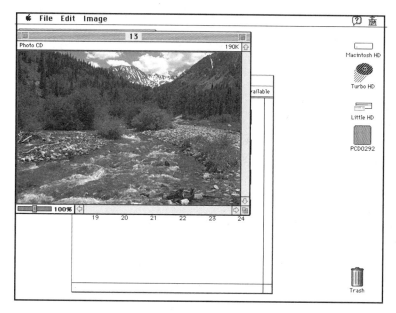

Figure 18.8 shows a smaller photo viewed with 8-bit grayscale (256 levels of gray). For superior quality, you need a Macintosh capable of at least 16-bit color, and for photorealistic work, you should have a 24-bit color video card. Unless you need photorealism, 16-bit color is sufficient—the pictures look realistic enough to the eye at that color depth. At times, 8-bit color or grayscale leaves something to be desired in quality.

Programs that accept EPS, PICT, or TIFF files can import photos. Photos are available at five different resolutions running from 192 × 128 to 3072 × 2048.

Photo CD is an excellent tool if you create ads, flyers, or other publications that use photographs. With this software, you can bypass the scanning process and import photos directly from CD. You should check the price for film development, however; it's rather high (about $25 per roll). One advantage of Photo CD that you should consider is the durability of CDs as opposed to negatives and pictures. CDs can last for decades without deteriorating significantly. If you work in a museum or restore old photos, you should consider switching to Photo CD, as should publications needing long-term archives.

Choosing Multimedia Hardware

Hardware for multimedia is not cheap. You should consider your needs carefully before you buy. If you need to import video, you at least need hardware that can convert video signals to a form that the Macintosh can handle. Following are descriptions of some hardware you might consider.

Computer Eyes Color/RT Frame Grabber for the Macintosh is one hardware option. This frame grabber interfaces with your SCSI port instead of taking up a slot in your Macintosh. Using Computer Eyes, you can capture images to PICT, TIFF, MacPaint, or QuickTime movie format. This $480 system can capture 24-bit color at 640×480 screen resolution.

For about $3,300, Cannon offers a still-image camera that yields 450-line resolution (television screen resolution), has a 3X power zoom lens, shoots up to 2.5 frames per second, and has auto focus and exposure. You need a NuBus interface card, which costs about $3,900, to use this camera with your NuBus-capable Macintosh.

A less expensive still camera is FotoMan by Logitech. For about $639, you can take up to 32 pictures that are stored in the camera's memory for later download to your Macintosh through a serial port. You can save the snapshots in 1- or 8-bit TIFF, PICT, PICT2, or EPS format. FotoMan includes Digital Darkroom for editing pictures.

For sound, you should consider MacRecorder Sound System Pro by Macromedia. It is the industry's leading sound recording and editing system. You can record from almost any source and add special effects. SoundEdit is included, enabling you to edit your sounds. You can save sounds in 8-bit or 16-bit (CD-quality) format with sample rates up to 48KHz (far more than the human ear can hear). This $240 system includes all the hardware and software you need to get started with sound.

The VideoVision System by Radius is an all-in-one audio/video interface card that installs in a NuBus slot. VideoVision captures images and sound from almost any source (video camera, VCR, and the like) and converts them to QuickTime movies. VideoVision supports 24-bit color depth and costs about $2,200.

Video Spigot by SuperMac also enables you to input video and sound from a VCR, video camera, television, or other video source and convert them to digital format, which you can import to QuickTime movies. SuperMac offers an si and LC version (at about $380 and $270 respectively), as well as a $400 NuBus version.

The Big Mac Recommendation

If you are ready to move into the world of multimedia presentations, your choices are wide open. This chapter surveyed only some of the basic aspects of this relatively new and growing field.

Macromedia's products lead the multimedia industry, and for good reason. You have a wide choice from which to choose in levels of power, and every product is high quality. For recording sound, the industry standard is MacRecorder Pro. It is a worthwhile investment. Action! is excellent for basic presentation needs, and you can get started quickly with the templates. Action! also provides easy editing (a video is included to help you learn the program quickly).

If you need powerful presentations that use a wide variety of media, Macromind Director is the way to go. This program has become the industry standard and is widely used.

For bringing video into your Macintosh, VideoSpigot and VideoVision System are both good choices. VideoSpigot is by far the less expensive, but VideoVision System is more powerful.

You at least must start with the QuickTime Starter Kit from Apple. It gives you QuickTime movie capability and "gets your feet wet."

CHAPTER NINETEEN

Using Utility Software

U tilities are the housekeeping software on the Macintosh. These programs cover a broad range of functionality, including such things as backing up hard drives, recovering accidentally deleted or damaged files, guarding against virus infection, diagnosing problems with hardware or software, and more.

Some utilities help you become more productive. They can locate files you've misplaced on your hard drive, partition large hard drives into smaller, more manageable sections, keep track of your most recently used folders and files and then give you quick access to them, enhance your Apple menu, and more.

A great many useful and some necessary utility software programs are available. This chapter explores the software and discusses some that you definitely need.

Essential Utilities

This section covers utilities that you definitely should have: not necessarily the exact program—although I point out some—but rather the kind of utility and why you should have one. In particular, this section covers such essentials as hard disk backup programs, data recovery and hard disk maintenance programs, virus protection programs, and diagnostic programs.

Backup Programs

If you have a hard disk, you should back up the data on the disk. You can back up with floppies, copying the essential files to disks for safe keeping. But many users find that backup programs, such as the ones covered here, are time-savers. Also, if you have a very large hard disk or a network with hard disk servers, you may find a backup program to be a necessity.

Dantz Development is one of the leading manufacturers of backup utilities. Dantz offers a choice of four different utilities: Retrospect Remote, Retrospect, DiskFit Pro, and DiskFit Direct. Each is intended for different Macintosh configurations.

The utility that is best for the average or beginning user is DiskFit Direct. It is designed to be easy to use (see fig. 19.1).

As you can see by the initial screen of the utility in figure 19.1, DiskFit Direct makes backing up easy by giving you simple options: restore data or back up data. DiskFit Direct backs up your entire hard disk the first time you run the program. After the first time, DiskFit Direct backs up only changed files. This backup utility, therefore, is good for the new user.

If you need more options than are offered by DiskFit Direct, DiskFit Pro may suit your needs better. DiskFit Pro is a more advanced version and offers more options (see fig. 19.2).

Fig. 19.1

DiskFit Direct's initial
screen.

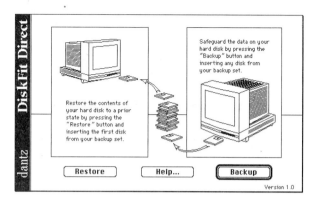

Fig. 19.2

Preparing to back up the
hard disk Macintosh HD
using DiskFit Pro.

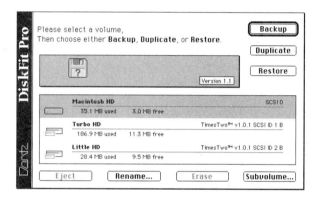

DiskFit Pro retains DiskFit Direct's ease of use but adds features that give
you more control over the backup process. You can duplicate a disk
using the Duplicate button and even erase or rename a disk. DiskFit Pro
gives you options that can speed backup by using faster copying,
reducing the amount of safeguards during a backup (an option to be
used carefully), excluding folders from the backup process, giving you
the ability to designate a folder as a subvolume so that it can be backed
up separately, and more. You can set DiskFit Pro to shut down your
Macintosh after a backup if you have a tape or other backup system that
enables you to do unattended backups (using floppies requires that you
stay with your Macintosh and insert the floppies as needed). DiskFit Pro
is for the more advanced user who needs greater control over hard disk
backup.

The DiskFit utilities create Finder-readable backups. This feature is well
worth considering because backup disk sets can potentially become
damaged, and you can recover your data from a Finder-readable backup
more easily.

Retrospect is the advanced backup option. Users who have large hard disks and back up to tape or an optical drive will appreciate the ability to schedule automatic, unattended backups to tape, optical disk, or removable hard disk. The network version—Retrospect Remote— enables a network manager to use a calendar to set backups to occur at designated times. Retrospect Remote supports 11 users on a network. You can add more by purchasing Retrospect Remote 10 or 50 packs.

The Dantz backup utilities have received excellent reviews and have won awards. If you have a hard disk, you should have a backup system of some kind; one of these utilities would be an excellent choice.

Two of the major utility packages—Norton Utilities 2.0 and MacTools— also contain backup utilities. See the section "Utility Packages" later in this chapter for more information.

Data Recovery and Hard Disk Maintenance Programs

No matter how careful you are, you're bound to lose data at some point. Perhaps you place a file in the Trash and empty the Trash only to discover that the file was an important one. Or you have a system crash that does strange things to your hard disk, and you are unable to access your data.

To reduce hard disk problems and recover from them when they occur, you should have a utility package that can protect your data. One of the best of these packages is provided by Symantec. Peter Norton, well known in the IBM PC world for Norton Utilities, and Symantec have jointly created Norton Utilities 2.0. I use this utility package regularly to guard my hard disks from problems.

Norton Utilities 2.0 contains—along with other items—the Norton Disk Doctor, which can check your hard disk for problems and repair them. Norton Disk Doctor is extremely easy to use. You simply start the Disk Doctor and then choose the hard disk you want to be checked. The Disk Doctor then scans for problems (see fig. 19.3).

When the Disk Doctor finds a problem, it gives you the option to fix the problem (see fig. 19.4). You don't have to understand the problem; Norton Disk Doctor can fix it with a click of the Yes button.

Norton also includes a System extension that aids you in recovering both accidentally deleted files and crashed hard disks. You can set the FileSaver to keep track of recovery information for up to 500 deleted files. You then can use Norton UnErase to recover deleted files (see fig. 19.5).

SYMANTEC.
THE NORTON DISK DOCTOR
Diagnosing "Turbo HD"
Checking Volume Info
Analyzing Directory
Checking Hierarchy
Checking Allocation
Looking for Lost Files
Analyzing Files
Pause
Cancel

Fig. 19.3
The Norton Disk Doctor looking for hard disk problems.

SYMANTEC.
A problem has been found on "Turbo HD"
A problem was found in the disk's directory
Description:
A problem was found with a file or folder on this disk (alias name mismatch). The file(s)/folder(s) in question are:
#1715 "progress"
#1715 "Progress".
801:1710
Do you wish to correct this problem?
Yes
No
Quit

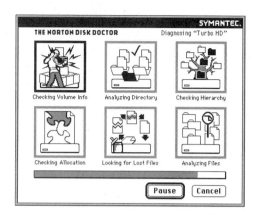

Fig. 19.4
Disk Doctor has found a problem on the hard disk.

Norton UnErase™
Macintosh...
» UnErase »
2K selected
Macintosh HD
View File
Get Info
Sort
Name Data Rsrc Modified Date Type Creator Recoverability
Now Profile 51K 10/28/92 12:58 APPL NSPU Excellent
Now Scrapbook 165K 3/04/93 21:33 APPL PBA+ Excellent
PATHS.DOC (Word4) 11K 6/17/92 22:02 SPSU SIT! Poor
PC Exchange 138K 4/27/92 12:00 cdev dosa Poor
Port.dat 4K 3/18/93 23:12 CTRE ???? Excellent
Port.dat 4K 3/18/93 23:11 CTRE ???? Poor
Port.idx 2K 3/18/93 23:18 CTRE ???? Excellent
Port.idx 2K 3/18/93 23:12 CTRE ???? Poor
Print File 19K 3/16/93 15:26 PFIL PSYS Excellent
PubUtilTemp 1K 3/21/93 23:03 ???? ???? Poor
QL II Fax 1K 2/20/93 14:53 adrp QLSR Poor
QLIIFax CM.001 1K 2/22/93 13:04 Qcmd QLSR Poor
QLIIFax CM.002 22K 1K 2/22/93 14:19 Qcmd QLSR Very Good
QLIIFax CM.003 22K 1K 2/22/93 14:17 Qcmd QLSR Poor

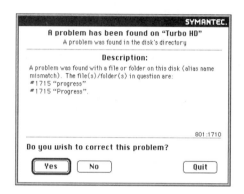

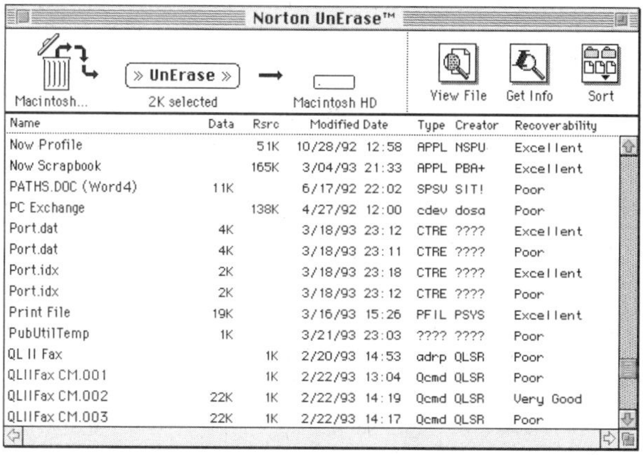

Fig. 19.5
Norton UnErase's listing of files that can be recovered.

Not all files can be recovered easily. You usually can bring back your most recently deleted files with ease, however. Norton tells you the chances of recovering the file.

FileSaver also keeps your hard disk format information in a file that you can use in case of a crash to restore your data more readily. This file is updated at periods of time (such as shutdown, every few hours, and so on) that you set.

Norton Utilities comes with an emergency disk that you can use to start your Macintosh and attempt repairs should your startup hard disk crash.

Central Point Software also offers a similarly capable package in MacTools. MacTools includes a disk scanning and repair utility called DiskFix (see fig. 19.6). The package also includes an undelete utility to recover deleted files.

Fig. 19.6

Preparing to scan Macintosh HD for problems.

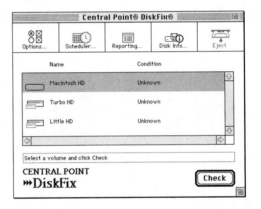

Both Norton Utilities and MacTools are utility packages and contain several utilities. See the section "Utility Packages" later in this chapter for more information.

A recent entry into this category is Safe & Sound by Central Point Software. This utility is meant for the new Macintosh owner who should have a hard disk recovery program but who needs an easy-to-use utility. Safe & Sound is a scaled-back version of the full MacTools package but offers you the ability to diagnose and repair hard disk problems, check for viruses, and recover deleted files (see fig. 19.7).

Fifth Generation Systems Inc. offers Public Utilities. This utility set includes the capability to scan for and repair hard disk problems, recover deleted files, and optimize your hard disk (see fig. 19.8).

Fig. 19.7

Scanning a hard disk with
Safe & Sound.

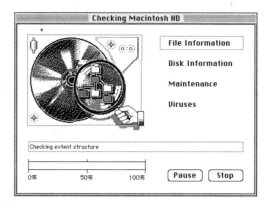

Fig. 19.8

Ready to scan for problems
in Public Utilities.

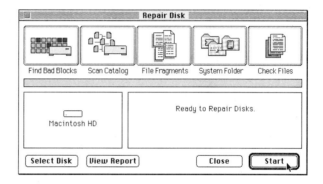

Microcom offers two programs of interest. Complete Undelete helps you
recover deleted files while 911 Utilities recovers data or disks.

Virus Programs

Although virus infections actually are relatively rare, one virus is too
many. The loss of data and time that a virus infection can cause is
something to avoid. And you can do much to avoid an infection by
having a virus protection program.

A *virus* is a series of computer program lines designed to alter
the normal functioning of a computer by destroying data,
corrupting system files, locking you out of the computer, or
flashing messages on-screen at predetermined times. In many

continues

continued

cases, you may be unaware that a virus exists in the system until it is too late to protect the existing data. A virus is generally passed from disk to disk and from computer to computer through disk sharing or telecommunication file transfers.

I use Symantec Anti-Virus for the Macintosh (SAM) by Symantec. SAM consists of both a System extension and a utility. The extension checks your disks for viruses at user-set times such as startup or shutdown and can be set to scan floppies or other removable media (see fig. 19.9).

Fig. 19.9
The SAM Virus Clinic utility scanning for virus infections.

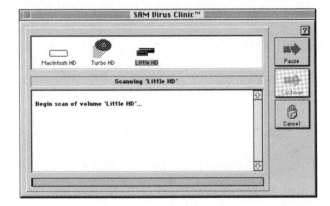

In many cases SAM can repair virus infections. Symantec offers to registered users free updates that come in the form of postcards with the necessary information for updating your virus definitions file when new viruses are found. Also, Symantec offers a BBS that enables you to log on and report problems, acquire help, and download the most recent version of the virus definitions file. You can also acquire help and the latest virus definitions file on-line through CompuServe.

Microcom offers Virex, which can detect and repair many viruses and is widely used. The Central Point Software utility packages MacTools and Safe & Sound both check for viruses as well.

Your least expensive option is Disinfectant by John Norstad. This program and System extension combination is free and widely available through on-line services and user groups. You must keep track of the most recent version, however, and acquire it yourself. No notifications of upgrades are mailed as with the commercial packages. Disinfectant is an excellent choice except for this drawback.

I switched to SAM primarily because Symantec mails updates to registered users on a regular basis. Being notified that a new virus has been found and receiving a card with instructions on updating SAM are worth the cost to me. SAM also offers the most extensive options I've seen in a virus protection program, enabling you to set the level of protection you want.

Diagnostics

Diagnostic programs are a relatively new category of utilities. Diagnostic programs that can help you detect problems in hardware and software and potentially avoid them have begun to appear recently.

One item of software in this category that is receiving much attention is Help! by Teknosys. Help! scans for and detects software problems, notifying you of potential conflicts, installation problems, and other helpful information (see fig. 19.10).

Fig. 19.10
A Help! report.

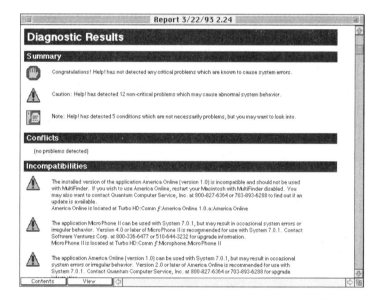

Help! is a worthwhile program for the professional using a Macintosh for business purposes or the person responsible for the Macintoshes in an office. Although average users can benefit from Help!, they may not use enough software to justify needing the program.

Help!'s only drawback is that the program relies on reports from manufacturers concerning problems. If a problem is not known or reported, Help! offers no help in that area. Help! also can run behind in software versions (I found that I had more current versions in many cases than the ones Help! was aware of).

If, however, you must maintain your Macintosh for business use or must oversee several Macintoshes, Help! definitely can be of aid to you. Businesses may want to consider the program to maintain their Macintoshes in working order and take some burden off the technical people in the company by automating checking for incompatible software, for example. Teknosys offers a subscription service to update Help!'s database.

One Help! feature that may be of benefit is the capability to simulate a Macintosh System configuration. If you or your company is considering an upgrade to a new Macintosh, Help! can do its diagnostics as if the machine were already present. This feature can alert you to problems that might arise when you move your software to the new Macintosh.

On the hardware side of diagnostics utilities is MacEKG II by MicroMat. This extension runs diagnostics on your Macintosh hardware and reports not only problems but potential slowdowns from System extensions and control panel devices. If you're an individual user who must have a perfectly functioning Macintosh for professional purposes, you may want to consider MacEKG II to help locate hardware problems. Businesses with many Macintoshes may want MacEKG II because the extension can help save time and money by diagnosing the Macintosh before the service personnel are called (perhaps a hardware problem can be ruled out, saving a service call entirely).

MacSleuth by Dariana Inc. also checks your System configuration on both the hardware and software side. MacSleuth provides you with detailed information about your Macintosh that can be of benefit should you need to call technical support or service personnel.

Useful Utilities

This section covers utilities that can help you be more productive. You learn about utilities that compress the data on your hard disk to give you more room; manage your hard disk files; enable you to control your System extensions and control panels; manage fonts, desk accessories, sounds, and other resources; enhance the Finder to make it easier to access files and applications; secure your hard disk from access by unauthorized persons; and other useful functions.

Data Compression

No matter how big your hard disk is, you will run out of room at some point. Rather than purchase a new disk, you can consider various schemes of data compression to squeeze more data onto the disk. Data compression also is useful if you must transmit files by modem, you can reduce the size of files and the transmission time.

Stuffit Deluxe 3 by Aladdin is the premier compression program in the Macintosh world. This program started as shareware and became a full-feature file and disk compression package that has few peers.

Stuffit Deluxe can compress your files into archives (see fig. 19.11). You can cause an archive to become a self-extracting archive, enabling you to send compressed files to Macintosh users who may not own Stuffit Deluxe. You also can create archive files that are encrypted with passwords and cannot be accessed by anyone without the password. Stuffit Deluxe can handle a great number of compression formats including AppleLink packages, DiskDoubler files (although you must own the DiskDoubler extension), and even the IBM PC ZIP format.

Fig. 19.11
An archive file 59 percent smaller than the decompressed files.

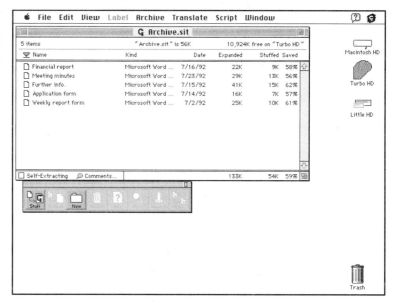

Stuffit Deluxe 3.0 comes with an automatic disk compression system that enables you to compress files in the background and save space on your hard disk. You also can designate folders or labels that cause files to be compressed automatically, as well as create archives by simply renaming a folder.

My only complaint about Stuffit Deluxe comes in the automatic compression area. The system is so extensive that it slowed my Macintosh's performance (most likely because I installed it along with a number of other extensions). But few compression systems can beat Stuffit Deluxe.

Competing with Stuffit is DiskDoubler and AutoDoubler by Salient. DiskDoubler places on the menu bar a menu that enables you to compress files on demand. You simply click to select the file, group of files, or folder and then choose the desired compression (or expansion) command from the DD menu (see fig. 19.12).

Fig. 19.12
Compressing files with
DiskDoubler.

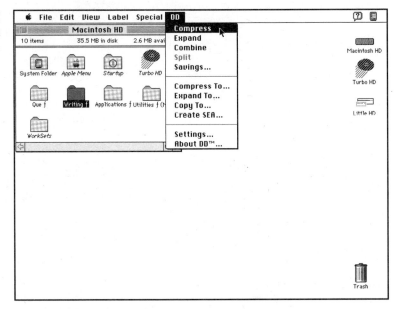

DiskDoubler also can create self-extracting files as well as archives; however, the extension does not have the extensive archiving features of Stuffit Deluxe.

AutoDoubler is the automatic compression companion for DiskDoubler. AutoDoubler compresses files on your hard disk to give you more room for storage.

More Disk Space and SuperDisk! by Alysis Software can also give you more space on your hard disk. More Disk Space compresses files and has the added feature that it automatically can replace duplicate files with System 7 aliases. SuperDisk! gives you more options and control over compression options.

The best solution to running out of disk space, in my opinion, is TimesTwo by Golden Triangle. Using the same technology as Stacker on the IBM PC, TimesTwo effectively doubles your hard disk space by installing a new disk driver. After you install TimesTwo, your hard disk is effectively twice as big, and you need no compression routines at all (except for use with a modem perhaps). TimesTwo eliminates the wait for a compression routine to unpack your file. You notice no difference between the operation of your hard drive in any way except that it holds about twice as much as before. As this book is being written, a 100MB hard disk (formatted at about 98MB) is holding just over 188MB of data—impressive performance in my book.

Startup Managers

If you use a number of System extensions and control panels, you may start running into problems. The bane of Macintosh users is the System extension conflict. One way you can get your extensions and control panels under control is through a startup manager. These utilities enable you to turn extensions and control panels on and off, create sets of extensions, and even define links that prevent conflicting extensions from being turned on at the same time.

My personal favorite is Startup Manager, which comes with the Now Utilities package (see "Utility Packages" later in this chapter). Using Startup Manager, you can create sets of extensions and control panels, change the order in which the items load simply by dragging, and turn items off and on with ease (see fig. 19.13).

Fig. 19.13
Startup Manager enables you to turn extensions off and on with a click.

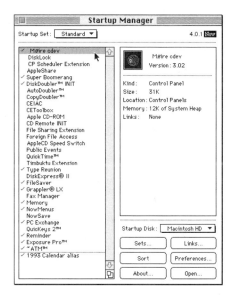

You can create links that prevent incompatible extensions from being turned on at the same time, as well as define forced load orders when one extension must be loaded before another. Finding extension and control panel conflicts is much easier with Startup Manager, and Startup Manager even turns off crashing extensions automatically. You can open Startup Manager as your Macintosh starts up and switch extension sets easily.

INIT Manager by Baseline also enables you to turn your extensions and control panels on and off, as well as change load order. INITPicker 3.0 by InLine Design gives you control over your extensions and control panels, enabling you to switch them on and off.

Startup managers are very much alike, and choosing between them is difficult due to their similarities. With the other items in the Now Utilities package (see "Utility Packages"), however, I think the scale tips toward Now.

Resource Managers

One of the Macintosh's more popular aspects is your ability to customize the Macintosh with resources. Resources are items such as fonts, desk accessories (mini-applications), fkeys (single function programs invoked by key presses), and sounds. As the number of these items grows on your hard disk, however, you may find that they are difficult to manage and use greater and greater amounts of memory (despite my best efforts, my System Software now needs at least 3MB of memory to run).

There are two resource managers of note in the Macintosh community. The first is Suitcase 2.0 by Fifth Generation Systems. Suitcase is the oldest and longest lived of the two and still offers some of the best value. You can add or remove resources with ease by turning on and off suitcases containing the resources (see fig. 19.14) rather than dragging things in and out of your System file (in System 7) or using Font/DA Mover (in System 6).

Fig. 19.14
Adding a font resource with Suitcase 2.0.

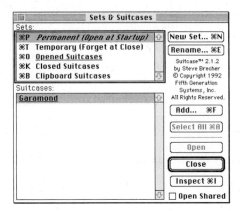

Suitcase is easy to use and can set resource suitcases to be opened temporarily or every time you turn on your Macintosh. The resources don't even have to be on your startup disk—much less in your System Folder or System file.

MasterJuggler by ALSoft, the second notable resource manager, also enables you to turn resources on and off without bothering with Font/DA Mover or dragging things in and out of the System file. MasterJuggler and Suitcase are close in functionality, and about the only thing that tips the scale in the direction of Suitcase, in my opinion, is the more coherent organization of the utility. MasterJuggler has added features such as KeyChains, which enables you to start up groups of applications, but the additional features are rather "patched in" and feel like afterthoughts. Still, either utility is an excellent choice.

Finder Enhancers

No matter how many times Apple updates the Finder, Macintosh users always find themselves thinking, "Now why doesn't it do *that?*" The answer to such pondering is found in one or more of the existing Finder enhancement utilities.

DiskTop 4.0 by CE Software enables you to bypass the Finder for many basic operations. You can create folders; check AppleShare access privileges; copy, move, delete, and rename files; search for files; and perform other Finder actions without switching to the Finder itself.

Hand-Off II by Connectix Corporation eliminates that annoying `application not found` message by opening files in the application of your choice. You also can create groups of files that can be opened simultaneously, automatically hide things you're not using to keep Desktop clutter to a minimum, and enhance the Apple menu.

CanOpener 2.0 by Abbott Systems performs a function similar to Hand-Off II by opening any file, even when you don't have the application that created it on your disk. You then can browse and copy the file's contents.

On Cue II by ICOM Simulations manages your files and applications by creating a menu that enables you to launch or open any application or file. You also can assign keystrokes to files and applications or groups of the same. Your most recently used files are easily accessed.

In the area of enhancing the Finder, one utility stands out as one that should have been incorporated into the Macintosh System Software a long time ago. SuperBoomerang enhances the rather annoying Save and Close dialogs, making them powerful and easier to use. Your most recently used files and folders are added to menus in both dialogs. You can choose one from the menu, assign a keystroke to the file or folder, or add the file or folder to the menus permanently (see fig. 19.15).

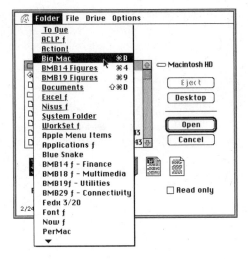

Fig. 19.15

Opening a folder in the
Open dialog of Nisus.

SuperBoomerang also adds to every application's Open command a
submenu from which you can choose your most recently used files,
bypassing the Open dialog entirely. If you've already opened the Save
dialog and discover you need a new folder, you can create one without
having to close the dialog. Your most recently used file or folder is
remembered and "rebounded" to. If you cannot locate a file, you can
open the Find dialog without having to close the Open dialog.

SuperBoomerang is one of those utilities I cannot live without. This
utility is part of the Now Utilities package, and even if the rest of the
package were useless—which it definitely is not—it would still be worth
the price for SuperBoomerang.

System 7 users may appreciate another part of the Now Utilities package—Now Menus—for its enhancement of the Finder's Apple menu.
Now Menus turns the Apple menu into a powerful, hierarchical command center (see fig. 19.16).

Using Now Menus, you can set the order that items appear in your Apple
menu simply by dragging them. You can add separators to divide
different sections of your menu. Also, you can open folders on the menu
up to five levels of nesting. A submenu is attached to applications, and
you can use it to access your most recently used documents (as in figure
19.16). To any item in the menu, you can add keystrokes.

Now Menus not only enables you to make these changes to the Apple
menu but also to three other menus: one in each of the upper corners of
your screen and one optional menu that appears on the Desktop with a
mouse click.

HAM (Hierarchical Apple Menu) by InLine Design performs a similar function to Now Menus by making the Apple menu become hierarchical (that is, submenus display the contents of folders on the Apple menu to several levels of nesting).

Fig. 19.16
An Apple menu using
Now Menus.

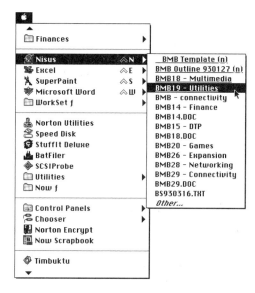

Security Utilities

Perhaps you work with sensitive materials: trade secrets, government contracts, personnel files, or maybe love letters and poetry. In any case, you often don't want others to see or have access to what is on your hard disks. In such cases, you can use any of the several security utilities.

FolderBolt, NightWatch II, and MacSafe II offered by Kent Marsh give you several options in security. FolderBolt enables you to lock individual folders, "bolting" them so that they cannot be opened. NightWatch II locks entire drives, preventing your Macintosh from being started up— even from a floppy disk—without the proper password. NightWatch II includes a screen saver that locks your Macintosh after a specified time and requires a password to reopen. MacSafe II enables you to create "safes" on your hard disk that encrypt files when the files are placed in the safes. A safe can have a "drop box" that enables others to drop files into the safe but not have access to the files inside.

Citadel with Shredder by Microcom uses a password to lock your hard disk and prevent access by unauthorized persons. The encryption capability is included. Shredder, which is included, is an electronic version of the paper shredder, eliminating files completely from your hard disk so that even the most technically skilled snoop cannot recover them.

SafeLock by Fifth Generation Systems offers automatic locking at shutdown and includes a desk accessory for short periods of time without shutting down your Macintosh (say, during lunch), automatic locking after a specified idle time, and locking of individual folders.

CAUTION

S ecurity software can be tricky to install and use. If you have System extension conflicts with security software, you could be in for some harrowing moments.

Security software does some strange technical voodoo with your hard disk. You should exercise caution in using it. When first installing, make sure you have a backup of your data. And if you need to use security software, you should not install System extensions and control panels into your System Folder left and right. If extensions conflict with your security system, you could have some traumatic hard disk problems.

Go slow. Proceed cautiously.

Of the products listed here, I think FolderBolt and NightWatch II are my favorites. For less expensive security, consider that Norton Utilities and Stuffit Deluxe both have encryption capabilities to encode your files in such a way that only you can access them.

Macro Utilities

Macros can automate your work to a great extent. With a macro utility, you can record keystrokes and mouse actions and store them so that they can be invoked by a single key combination.

Two major macro systems exist for the Macintosh: QuicKeys 2 by CE Software and Tempo II Plus by Affinity. Tempo used to be *the* macro system for the Macintosh but has not seemed to do well lately. To be honest, I haven't been able to get any version of Tempo to work on my Macintosh for a year or so now. Tempo used to be and probably still is a very powerful system, but after receiving a couple buggy versions that never worked properly, I gave up and haven't bothered with Tempo for a while.

The clear winner these days is QuicKeys 2. The only drawback to this system may be that it is too powerful. You may begin to wonder what the Macintosh needs you for when it has QuicKeys. Fortunately, a simplified system that steps you through creating basic macros has been added to the latest version.

If you find yourself repeating the same basic steps over and over, consider purchasing QuicKeys 2. Learning the powerful package may take a bit of experimenting, but in the long run, QuicKeys 2 can save you a great deal of time and effort.

Utility Packages

Utility packages incorporate several items of utility software in one package. You can acquire considerable functionality with a single purchase.

Now Utilities 3.0 by Now Software has won more than one award and for good reason. This package includes seven powerful items that enhance your Macintosh in useful ways. At least two of them I could not live without. Now Utilities includes the following:

- *SuperBoomerang.* This extension is worth the price of the entire package. SuperBoomerang adds functionality to your application program Open commands as well as the Open and Save dialogs. You can choose folders and files from menus, search for files, create folders, and add key commands to files and folders you use often.

- *Startup Manager.* You use Startup Manager to control your extensions and control panels (see "Startup Managers" earlier in this chapter).

- *Now Menus.* This utility enhances the Apple menu and adds three more. It also gives you the ability to add key commands to *any* menu, including the Finder menus. See "Finder Enhancers."

- *Now Scrapbook.* This utility replaces the Apple-supplied scrapbook. It enables you to have more than one scrapbook. You can store sounds, pictures, text, and QuickTime movies (you need the QuickTime extension for this).

- *WYSIWYG Menus.* You can use WYSIWYG Menus to display font menus in their actual typefaces, making font selection much easier.

- *Now Save.* This utility automatically saves your work at preset times. It is worthwhile if you want to avoid losing data.

- *Now Profile.* A rather technical item, Now Profile displays information about your System Software. It is good for when you call technical support.

Norton Utilities 2.0 for the Macintosh is a joint effort between Peter Norton and Symantec, incorporating Norton Utilities for the Macintosh and Symantec Utilities for Macintosh II (SUM II). This package includes the following:

- *Norton Utilities.* Enables you to check your hard disk and repair problems, as well as recover deleted files and recover from hard disk crashes.

- *Speed Disk.* A hard disk optimizer. Fast and functional.

- *Norton Encrypt.* Encodes files so that they cannot be accessed without a password.

- *Layout Plus.* Enables System 6 users to alter the appearance of various items in the Macintosh System.

- *Floppier.* Makes copying floppies easier by creating images on a hard disk and then enabling you to make multiple copies.

- *Norton Backup.* A backup utility that can have automatic scheduling and notification.

- *Wipe Info.* A utility that erases deleted files completely so that they cannot be recovered by even the most technically oriented.

- *KeyFinder.* An enhanced replacement for KeyCaps, shows you the characters in a font and which keys you press to access them.

- *Fast Find.* A file finder that moves quickly. Many times I prefer it to the Finder's Find command.

- *Norton Partition.* Enables you to subdivide large hard drives into smaller parts. You can encrypt the partitions so that they can be accessed only by password.

- *DiskLight.* Flashes as disks are accessed.

- *FileSaver.* An extension that saves your hard disk formatting information and watches over deleted files. Works with Norton Utilities to aid you in recovering deleted files and crashed hard disks.

- *Directory Assistant.* A Save and Open dialog enhancement that adds a menu from which you can choose files and folders.

MacTools by Central Point Software is another well-known utility package. It includes the following:

- *CP Anti-Virus.* A virus checking program to help you watch for infection.

- *CP Backup.* A backup utility for saving your hard disk data.

- *CP DiskEdit.* For the more technical, a disk editor that gives you access to the contents of files.

- *CP DiskFix, FileFix, and Undelete.* A disk and file repair system that can aid you in recovering from hard disk crashes as well as recovering deleted files.

- *CP Optimizer.* A hard disk optimizer that speeds your hard disk's performance.

The Big Mac Recommendation

Without question, my first recommendation for utility software is Now Utilities. You cannot go wrong with this package and will probably find in short order that you are unable to live without it.

Norton Utilities also is a good choice. With regular use, Norton Utilities has saved me from having major hard disk problems and has recovered many files I threw away without thinking.

You should have a backup system. Backups are necessary insurance that you will wish you had if you find yourself facing a crashed hard disk. For backups, consider the Dantz products.

A virus protection program also is a good investment. Viruses are not as common as the media makes them out to be, but it takes only one infection to ruin a great deal of data. Businesses without virus protection have experienced week-long work slowdowns (and outright stops) because of viruses.

Diagnostic programs are mostly essential to businesses that must keep their Macintoshes running well to save money and time. Help! and MacEKG II are a good combination.

CHAPTER TWENTY

Learning and Having Fun

This chapter is about serious fun—the many games and other sources of entertainment available for the Macintosh family of computers. This chapter also includes educational applications that show what the Macintosh can do to teach the ABCs or even the basics of calculus and physics.

Discussing all the Macintosh's possibilities for fun is impossible. Many of the programs mentioned in this chapter—all chosen subjectively—are called games because they are fun, whether they land you on the moon or help a child to learn the basics of addition and subtraction.

Not all games run on all Macintoshes. Before you buy a game, make sure that the game runs on your model Macintosh. See the game box, which details the model, color requirements, and memory requirements of the game. If you order by mail, the description in the catalog should tell you the same information, or you should ask before you order.

Considering Educational Software

For reasons that I've never been able to make sense out of, many people believe that what is fun is not education. More than once I've seen the attitude that kids "playing" on the computer are not learning, just playing. To those, I answer in two ways.

First, studies repeatedly show that "play" is an educational process. I would go further personally and assert that evidence exists that "play" is the only true educational process.

Second, I point out repeatedly to those who discourage kids from playing on the computer that a great number of people in the computer industry started by "playing" on the computer. Bill Gates started by playing with computers, and his "game" made him a multibillionaire before he reached middle age.

Elementary Skills

The best time to start children playing on the computer and learning is in early childhood. Children seem to be naturally drawn to the computer and spend hours mastering complex skills during their play.

Before considering educational games, however, you should address the issue of kids on your computer. As children explore, they can scramble your hard disk easily, maybe wiping out your thesis or your financial files. To address this potential problem, EdMark Corp. has created KidDesk. KidDesk is a Desktop for kids that you can use to hide your data and applications from youthful exploration while still enabling children to explore freely. KidDesk presents a screen that looks like a desk (see fig. 20.1).

Fig. 20.1
The KidDesk Desktop.

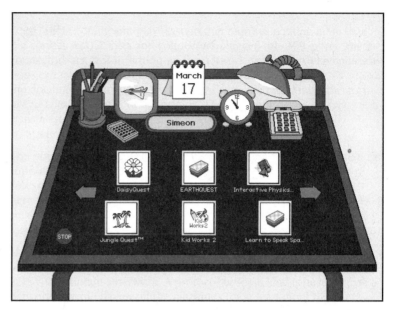

You can configure the Desktop to include icons of the applications you want your child to have access to. You also can set options such as a screen saver, an audio welcome, different desks, and even import a scanned picture of your child to be placed in the picture frame. Educators may be interested in this program because they can create more than one child Desktop with different sets of applications and set time limits for using the computer.

The desk accessories on the kids' Desktop are functional. The calculator—when clicked—opens to a working calculator. The telephone can produce "hellos" in different languages, the calendar opens to display a kid-style appointment calendar, and so on. If you have kids using your Macintosh, you can appreciate this program for enabling them to use the Macintosh but at the same time protecting your important adult applications and information.

A great number of educational games that teach your child already exist. One of the best examples is DaisyQuest by Great Wave Software (see fig. 20.2). DaisyQuest teaches basic language skills such as rhyming words and beginning, middle, and ending sounds. The program has a teacher mode that enables an educator to guide the adventure by assigning different classes and students different exercises in the game.

Fig. 20.2
Starting a DaisyQuest
adventure.

The game is an adventure type. The child explores a mythical medieval landscape and finds treasures that can be gained only by solving different puzzles involving word skills. The game is won when all the treasures are found and then Daisy, the dragon, is located. This program is part of the Adventure Learning Series, which has different modules that you can plug into the overall control center which uses a time-travel motif.

JungleQuest is an animated HyperCard stack that leads kids through various territories of Africa, quizzing them on mathematical skills as they progress (see fig. 20.3). JungleQuest is good for elementary-level children who are learning addition, subtraction, multiplication, and division.

Millie's Math House, another game, teaches math skills at the lower elementary level with animated scenarios like the cookie factory (see fig. 20.4). Millie's Math House is by EdMark, which has some of my favorite educational software. It uses sounds, music, and animation to make counting and other math skills fun.

If your child is a fan of Sesame Street, Muppets On Stage is a perfect choice for young beginners. This program by Sunburst uses the voices and animated images of familiar friends Kermit, Miss Piggy, and others to teach letters, numbers, and counting. Preschoolers will enjoy this program and learn quickly as they play (see fig. 20.5).

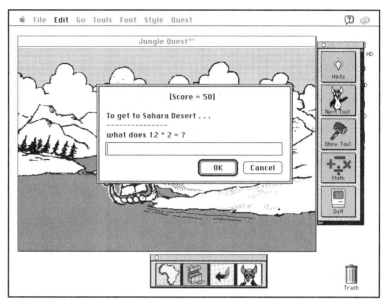

Fig. 20.3
Solving a problem to get to the Sahara desert.

Fig. 20.4
Making a cookie for Millie.

Fig. 20.5
Learning numbers with
the Muppets on
Stage program.

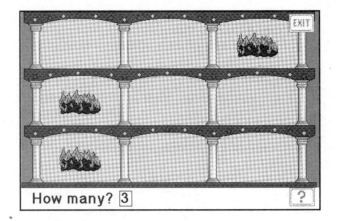

Kids Works 2 by Davidson is good for the budding writer in the family.
This program is recommended for ages 4 to 10 and enables children to
write, illustrate, add sound to, and otherwise create stories of their own
(see fig. 20.6).

Fig. 20.6
Beginning a new story
about a cat.

Kids Work 2 uses pictures extensively, and the program can read the
words and story so that your child learns words quickly. Children just
learning to read and write can create stories with pictures and then hear
the words read to them or click to see the written word. This program is
sure to capture a child's imagination yet teach reading and writing (and
typing as well) at an early age.

In a similar vein, Kid Pix by Brøderbund (another excellent source of kid's software) is a painting program for kids. Each painting tool has sound effects. Children have a choice of drawing lines, circles, squares; stamping various images such as dogs, trees, televisions, and others; and using many other tools. This program is good for the young artist.

One of my all-time favorite programs is the HyperCard stack Spelunx by Brøderbund. It contains a cave children can explore. In the cave are various rooms that contain educational games such as the player piano shown in figure 20.7.

Fig. 20.7
The player piano teaches basic music and programming.

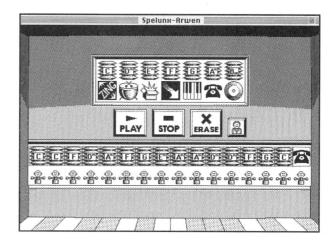

In Spelunx children also learn about the solar system, some basic physics skills, and basic biology. You can customize the cave and add modules as they are developed. Spelunx is one of the best and most entertaining uses of HyperCard I've seen yet. The only drawback to this interesting software is that it's very large and takes up to 4.5MB on disk. But the space is worth it when you see children learning about the planets, lightning, and metabolism as they play.

Turbo Math Facts by Nordic Software enables your child to earn money to purchase a race car by doing basic addition, subtraction, multiplication, and division. The better your child does with the math problems, the more powerful race car can be bought and the race won.

WordQuest by Nordic Software, another adventure-type game, leads your child through a quest to find magic words that can be used to break the spell of an evil witch.

One of the best uses of the CD-ROM I've seen so far comes from Brøderbund. Arthur's Teacher Troubles is an animated story that the computer reads to your child, and it enables your child to explore at will. Story time will never be the same. If you don't have a CD-ROM player, Brøderbund's Living Books series is an excellent argument for purchasing one. The Living Books require 256-color mode.

The preceding listing is only the tip of the iceberg of the elementary-level educational products. Companies such as Brøderbund, Nordic Software, Great Wave Software, Sunburst, Toucan/Queue, Quantum Leap Technologies (which also produces CD-ROM stories), CompuTeach, Davidson and Associates, and others offer a wide array of educational games that teach while being fun.

Secondary Skills

For the more advanced students from junior high and high school are several offerings worth noting. Following are brief descriptions of software targeted for this educational level or for educators who work with these students.

Interactive Physics from Knowledge Revolution is a physics laboratory on computer. You create experiments by using available objects and then investigate the effects of velocity and kinetic energy. In figure 20.8, you can see the actual screen used in a car-crash experiment where you can vary velocity, force, and acceleration factors and examine the impact on the dummy that crashes when the car hits the wall. Interactive Physics comes with nine folders of experiments, including Pendulum/Energy, Spring/Linear Energy, and Spring/Velocity.

Fig. 20.8
A car-crash experiment using a dummy.

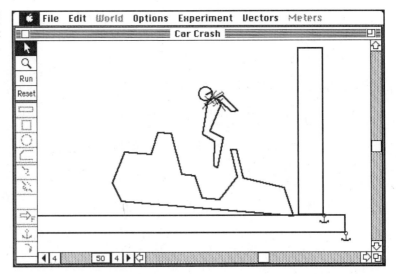

Another company is hard at work helping students learn difficult material. True Basic produces a line of applications that teaches everything from algebra to discrete mathematics. These programs don't just drill students, which has been the model most program developers have offered. Instead, True Basic products teach concepts. In figure 20.9, you can see how the equation for a simple line is illustrated, including the points that form the line, a graphic illustration, and a message.

Fig. 20.9
True Basic illustrates an equation for a simple line.

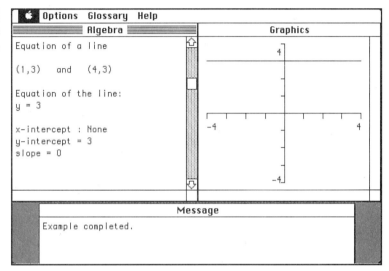

True Basic applications (Algebra, Pre-Calculus, Statistics, Probability) are not textbook- or course-specific, so they can be used in various settings.

The best program from True Basic is ASKit, the authoring tools that help you generate tests. You can construct a set of questions and a set of alternatives, including feedback for each answer chosen. You then can print each test and review a student's performance using the ASKit Reporter.

User signs keep track of which questions are chosen, how often they are answered correctly, and student performance. ASKit takes a great deal of the tedium out of being a teacher and constructing multiple-choice tests. The next step for this program is to measure difficulty and discrimination indices.

Another good educational game is American Discovery by Great Wave Software. It quizzes students on state names, capitals, and facts (see fig. 20.10). This program is good for overcoming that much-lamented failure of schools to teach geography.

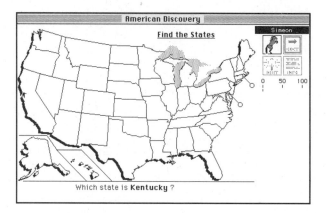

Fig. 20.10
The state name quiz in American Discovery.

Another program that can attack the same deficit is the excellent Swamp Gas series. Swamp Gas Visits Europe, for example, gives younger students—around junior high age—incentive to learn the names and locations of European nations by giving them a mission to go to a set of named countries or capitals in a flying saucer (see fig. 20.11).

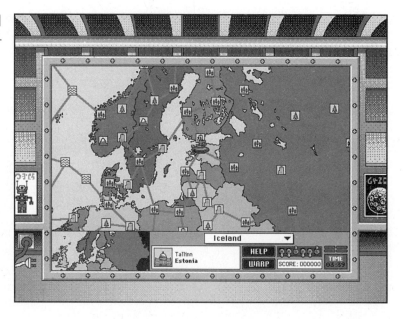

Fig. 20.11
Searching for Iceland.

When the mission is complete, the student can play a video game as a reward. I found my nephew playing this game repeatedly to get to the video game portion and—rather unwittingly I must confess—learning names and locations of European countries. Swamp Gas Visits the USA is also available. Other versions are sure to follow.

Time Treks by EarthQuest pits you against a time tyrant. You must answer questions about history to beat the tyrant and save time (see fig. 20.12).

Fig. 20.12
Exploring history with
Time Treks.

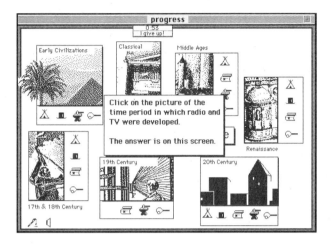

No discussion of history and geography games would be complete without mentioning the acclaimed Brøderbund Carmen Sandiego series. These programs have you gathering clues throughout history or across Europe, through the U.S.A., or other places to catch Carmen Sandiego. The games are challenging and probably best for older students or even adults who like mysteries or have an interest in the world.

Headline Harry by Davidson and Associates works in a similar vein but puts you as a reporter gathering information to file a story. Headline Harry is an excellent concept, but I found it difficult to win even though I'm well read in history and current events. The program also takes up a great deal of space on your hard disk (the program comes on nine double-sided disks). I'm not sure about recommending this one. At least consider it only for more advanced students with an interest in history.

Simulation games also have become very popular. These games teach through enabling you to create cities, worlds, or other systems of your own. SimLife by Maxis, for example, enables you to create creatures and environments. You manage your ecology and discover how biological systems interact (see fig. 20.13).

A-Train, also by Maxis, simulates economics. You are in charge of running a train transportation company and can build factories, train stations, hotels, and other items. Your success or failure depends on how well you run the train company.

Fig. 20.13
Simulating a salmon run.

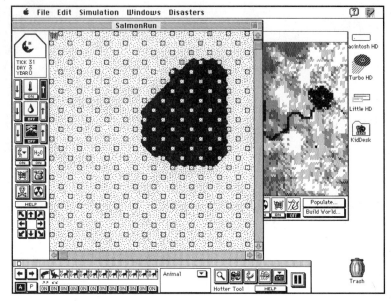

These programs are probably best for the more advanced students at the high school level at least. Simulation games are complex and have a great deal of depth but teach important concepts in systems theory—the theory of how systems work, a foundational concept in economics, management, and sciences.

Software Instruction

If you need help with your Macintosh, you now can turn to your Macintosh. With instructional software, the Macintosh can teach you how to use applications such as Microsoft Excel, QuarkXPress, HyperCard, and a great many others.

Companies such as Personal Training Systems and Individual Software offer programs that instruct you in using many popular applications as well as the Macintosh itself. The programs show you on-screen how programs are run and quiz you to reinforce knowledge. Personal Training Systems includes audio cassettes to help you along almost like a private tutor.

Language Instruction

With the Macintosh's audio and visual capabilities, you should not be surprised to find that the computer is being put to use in teaching languages. HyperGlot offers courses in Spanish (see fig. 20.14), French, German, Japanese, and others. You need HyperCard and a CD-ROM to make use of this series of programs.

Fig. 20.14

Beginning a Spanish lesson with HyperGlot.

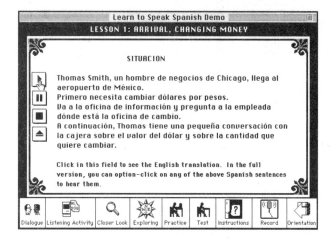

The well-known Berlitz company also offers a CD-ROM based series of language courses. Spanish, French, German, and others are offered.

Penton Overseas offers language courses for the young in Picture it! The VocabuLearn series builds vocabulary for any language student. These programs do not require a CD-ROM although the VocabuLearn series has a CD-ROM version.

One important language to learn, of course, is English. Franklin Electronics, known for the compact electronic dictionaries the company sells, has an Elementary Spelling Ace and Spelling Tutor to boost spelling skills for elementary users and any English language user. The Language Master Speaking Dictionary pronounces words by using the Macintosh's audio capabilities.

Typing Programs

Using a computer of any kind is much easier when you can touch-type. If you or a member of your family or business is lacking in this skill, programs that can help are available. You also can use some of these programs to retrain for the Dvorak keyboard. (The Dvorak keyboard is a more recent keyboard arrangement that reduces the amount of finger movement needed for typing.)

One such typing program is Mavis Beacon Teaches Typing by Software Toolworks, which is the one I use to practice the Dvorak keyboard. This game-like teaching program is also good for younger students. I've often found kids having races with the program, competing with each other, and increasing their typing skills as a result. Mavis Beacon supports the Dvorak keyboard.

Typing Instructor Encore by Individual Software is another typing program that offers advanced diagnostics to enhance your typing skills. The optional Type'n'Discover disks also enhance your general knowledge as you type.

When you've finished enhancing your skills and learning a new language, you may want a game that's purely for fun. The next section discusses these games.

Considering Games

Obviously, a good game provides one of two things: hours of challenging and engaging fun or a vicarious experience you cannot have otherwise—such as playing in the Masters golf tournament or piloting an F-16 in dog fights with enemy aircraft.

Good games also do some, if not all, of the following:

- Enable you to pick up where you left off. Often, you cannot finish the game in one sitting (unless you're ready for a 12-hour session).

- Keep track of the highest scoring players.

- Adjust the difficulty level. Some games are so complex that if users can't get the feel for the tasks at hand, they lose interest.

- Have excellent and unusual audio and visual effects. You also should be able to adjust the game for volume and playing speed.

- Provide hints or even the solution. Otherwise, you can go crazy with frustration.

- Enable you to change game characteristics. You should have the chance to change point values, the types of monsters you shoot and their point value, the story ending, and so on.

When you're considering a game, find out whether the company offers any kind of technical support because at times some games can become unnerving. You can struggle for hours to find the clue you need to rescue the princess or reach the castle, only to find that your efforts are to no avail. A small hint can mean the difference between spending all night trying to figure out what went wrong and the ultimate feeling of beating the machine.

Games are relatively inexpensive; commercial products rarely cost more than $40, and the shareware games available cost significantly less. In most cases, commercial games are worth paying the extra $20 or $30 because developers of commercial games have more incentives for current design and updates—incentives that shareware may lack.

On the other hand, hundreds of shareware games are terrific and readily available. Some shareware sources are BMUG, BCS Macintosh, and Educorp.

The following sections discuss some games available for the Macintosh.

Athletic Games

The great American pastime is on your Macintosh. These games are so real that you may think that you're right there ready to play with the best. You can have the All Stars versus the Champs in a nine-inning face-off. With Accolade's Hard Ball, you control everything from the type of pitch you want to throw to the positions of the players.

After you click to make the pitch, you field the ball and throw to a base (unless the hit screams out of the ball park). Options include designating home and visiting teams, exchanging positions, substituting players, moving outfielders and infielders, and intentionally walking the batter. With nine pitching zones to throw to, you can be a Cy Young winner in no time, without suffering a sore arm.

If golf is your game, you can be on the 18th hole at Augusta in a playoff with your arch rival. Accolade's Mean 18 Ultimate Golf opens with the sound of a golf club swinging and hitting a ball down a fairway. From there on, the course of the game is up to you. You choose from six different clubs, swing, and putt through one of five courses. As many as four players can play. You can choose expert or beginner's level, save a game to resume later, and even change courses in the middle of a match.

Figure 20.15 shows you the first hole at Pebble Beach, with the par and the course lengths for beginners or experts. Figure 20.16 shows you the beginning screen for this shot. You swing by using the mouse and the scale on the left side of the window.

Fig. 20.15

Mean 18 Ultimate Golf, first hole at Pebble Beach.

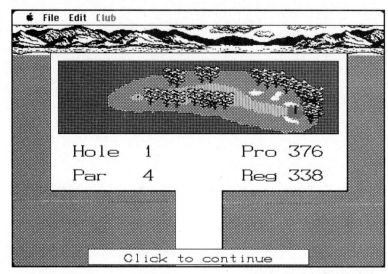

Fig. 20.16

Beginning screen for the shot at the first hole.

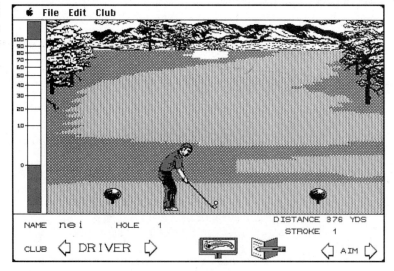

The screen has several icons that make the game realistic. You can select the club you want to use and change your aim by clicking the right or left arrow on the lower right side of the screen. You also can click the score pad to see where you stand or click to get an aerial view of the hole you're playing.

You hit the ball by moving up the Power Meter (the scale on the left side of the window) with the mouse. Each shot takes three clicks. The timing of the clicks determines how accurate your shot is. Click once to begin the back swing and again to control the distance of your shot. The final click strikes the ball, and whack! you're off to the next shot.

Accolade also brings to your Desktop Jack Nicklaus's greatest 18 holes of golf, including Augusta, St. Andrews, and Oakmont.

You also can play the great courses through Leader Board (from Access), where you can play St. Andrews, Doral Country Club, or Cypress Creek. One outstanding feature of this golf program is that after you make a shot, your Macintosh is ready for the next one very quickly. The animation of the trees and shrubs is lifelike, and the ball soars like a real golf ball—it even casts a shadow.

If you want to play racquetball, MacRacquetball (from Practical Computer Applications) is fast and quite competitive. This game is realistic with 3-D effects. Using the mouse, you control one of two competitors who actually run around and hit the ball. You even can play over a modem between two Macintoshes. A voice tells you "Side out," "Ball," or "Point." Except for the sweaty clothes, this game is the real thing.

Finally, a football game where the coaches and players actually plan a strategy. Macintosh Pro Football (from Avalon Hill) comes complete with a master disk, the relevant season's statistics for all teams (on disk), and a team disk that you use to construct your own lineups. You control everything: the toss of the coin to start the game, weather conditions, the month of play, and the selection of a team to play against, such as the 1968 Jets or the 1968 Kansas City Chiefs.

So much information goes into each move in Macintosh Pro Football that you need 1MB of RAM to work the game. If you love football, however, the game is well worth the RAM.

Another football game, 4th and Inches (from Accolade), makes you feel as though you are ready to "Start buttin' heads with the big boys," as the game's package says. The game begins with "The Star Spangled Banner" and reasonably attempts a 3-D display of the playing field, where players run, score safeties, and then react wildly to various displays.

As an add-on, you can get Accolade's Team Construction set with which you can create any team and any type of player to play with. You even can name your team and choose the jersey colors, just like an owner does.

Flying and Driving Games

You can play Ferrari Grand Prix (from Bullseye Software), a racing game so realistic that you may think you can smell the gas and oil your first time around the track. Begin in your Formula One car, the most popular type of race car in the world, and choose one of several courses and the opponents you want to race against. Figure 20.17 shows the opening screen.

Fig. 20.17
Driving a Ferrari in
Ferrari Grand Prix.

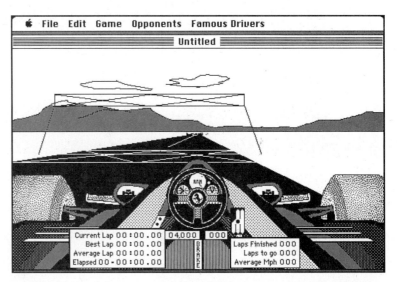

Figure 20.18 gives you an aerial view of the track, which you can change to fit your needs. This screen shows your car's current position and how you can change the track by inserting various shapes and sizes of track from options located in the lower left corner. You also can use a curve direction tool to change the direction of the curves around the track.

Another fine racing program is The Duel-Test Drive II, which pits a Ferrari F40 head to head against a Porsche 959. You can race Ferrari against Ferrari, Porsche against Porsche; race against the clock; avoid road hazards; and deal with cops. And yes, at 200 mph, the screen can become a blur. If you crash, you lose—just start up again and have fun.

Fig. 20.18
Aerial view of Ferrari
Grand Prix track.

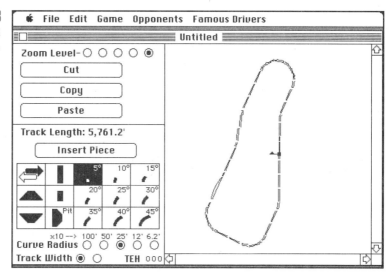

Now that you're going so fast that you are probably off the ground, imagine flying from New York to San Francisco—with the popular Flight Simulator from Microsoft. This game has such realistic sound effects that you may find yourself looking for an exit. Flight Simulator offers a realistic cockpit screen, 39 different flight characteristics, and instrumentation exactly like the real thing, be it a prop-driven Cessna 182 or a million-dollar Lear jet.

This package comes complete with airport and runway maps and other important goodies, such as aviation maps for destinations such as New York, Boston, Seattle, and San Francisco. You set the clouds, the view (cockpit, control tower, and so on), and the automatic pilot, and then take off. You even can fly over the Statue of Liberty (which really looks like her).

Get out your silk scarf and your leather flight helmet. It's June, 1944, and you're flying a P-51 Mustang with the U.S. 275th Fighter Group. After you try this experience—brought to you by P-51 Mustang Flight Simulator—you keep returning for more. The game even provides convoys of trucks, houses, and German airplanes to attack during your flight. You also can bail out and so forth.

To add to the realism, author Donald Hill Jr. has included in the manual a reprint of material contained in the original flight book that came with every real P-51. The manual also contains a list of readings you can consult if you want to learn more about the plane and military flying in general.

If you want sheer speed, try Falcon, the F-16 flight simulator from Spectrum Holobyte. You shouldn't have a hard time imagining yourself at 20,000 feet and still climbing, ready to flip on the afterburner as you increase your speed far beyond Mach 2. This game is a highly realistic simulation of one of the top-level fighter jets flown today.

Although you need some time to get used to the controls and cockpit, the game is enormously fun. You find yourself dive-bombing to avoid surface-to-air missiles, such as Sidewinders and Mavericks, while listening to great music from the Top Gun soundtrack. You are more than ready to meet the enemy MiG-21s after enduring some training sessions and practicing some predesigned flights and fights.

Now, imagine yourself entering the dark stratosphere—beyond where the F-16 can go—while flying the space shuttle. Spectrum Holobyte's Orbiter is dedicated to the Challenger's flight crew, who died on January 28, 1986.

This game doesn't have many sound effects, but it is a great learning and teaching tool. You configure your launch, orbit, and landing and decide on the mission, such as training or satellite repair. Then you see a series of screens. Control sends you a verbal message telling you what to do, and you continue through a sequence of commands until you are launched. The fun and the learning really begin when you maneuver the Manned Maneuvering Unit to repair a satellite or to make some other adjustment outside the ship.

War Games

In GATO (from Spectrum Holobyte), a real-time simulation of a World War II attack submarine, you operate the periscope, chart your course, control fire damage, and—if you're really good—sink enemy ships. You choose from a variety of missions and then act as a captain as you try to rescue downed seamen or destroy cargo ships located somewhere on your radar scope.

If you're intrigued by war games, Bomber (from Deadly Games) is technically sophisticated and quite realistic. Complete with earphones, stereo sound, and terrific visuals, you get the enemy in your bomb sights and, at 20,000 feet, you fire away.

Next, you may be in the PT-109 (also from Spectrum) that GATO is trying to destroy, although with your speed, this destruction is unlikely. With 435 different missions to choose from, enemy planes and ships to confront, and a choice of four theaters of action (such as the Philippines or the Mediterranean), you can be the John F. Kennedy on your block. The fast boat launches torpedoes (which is the T in PT). This game even gives you the splashes and the sounds of the sea.

Another ship-shape game is Battle Stations (from TimeLine), with opening voices and Klaxons telling you to man your stations, as though attack is imminent. Terrific voice effects make this grown-up Battleship fun.

Detective and Adventure Games

It's no surprise that detective and mystery games are among the best sellers, along with detective and mystery books. People must like the intrigue.

Put on your Sherlock Holmes hat and start looking for those bad guys. Moriarity's Revenge (from Bull City Software) is coupled with a geography challenge. With a pocket atlas in hand, you can try to find the location of various secret societies and the criminals they harbor.

You need a great deal of help to defeat the spooks in Beyond Dark Castle from Silicon Beach, but with fireballs and stones against bats, rats, and mutants, you can win. This animated game is a great and addictive arcade-style game.

Brain Teasers

Games that tease the brain, challenge, and provide fun are few and far between. Even under the guise of fun, they can be teaching important skills that are related to problem solving and creativity. Welcome to the Fool's Errand (from Miles Computing), which begins with a scroll and a tale about a light-hearted fool. You finish the tale by solving puzzles filled with clues of every kind. To get from the opening screen to the end, you must solve 42 puzzles of all shapes and sizes. You can get so caught up in the puzzles (which don't have to be solved in order) that you can enjoy doing them as much as solving them.

In figure 20.19, for example, you see a word-search puzzle. The jigsaw puzzle in figure 20.20 should keep you busy for a few hours. These puzzles all contain the clues you need to solve the mystery. If you find yourself going a little nuts, you always can order the Hints and Answers book to help you maintain your sanity.

The Puzzle Gallery (also from Miles) is another winner that offers 180 jigsaw puzzles that no mere mortal can come close to solving. Don't start this one while waiting for your spouse, significant other, or kids. No matter where you're going, you're sure to be late.

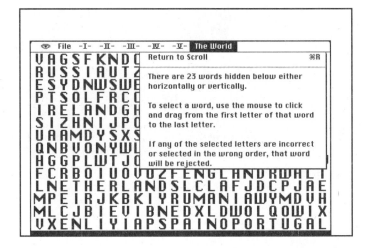

Fig. 20.19
A Fool's Errand word
puzzle screen.

Fig. 20.20
A Fool's Errand jigsaw
puzzle screen.

Arcade and Board Games

Conceived by two Soviet programmers, Tetris (from Spectrum HoloByte)
has 10 difficulty levels, random generation of pieces that must be placed
correctly, help screens, terrific graphics, and enough room for you and
all your friends.

Tetris is serious game stuff that only players with large blocks of time and perseverance should pursue. The object is to stack the tiles that fall through the air and make them fit together. Background graphics of Russian scenes and music make this game enjoyable as well as challenging (see fig. 20.21).

Fig. 20.21
The challenge of Tetris.

From the author of Tetris comes Welltris, which is sort of a 3-D version of Tetris (see fig. 20.22). The object is to align the falling pieces so that the floor of the cube is covered. Again, great sound and great visuals.

A more challenging game is Go-Man-Ku, otherwise known as Go Master from Toyogo. The national game of Japan is based on an ancient game that originally was played with shiny stones on a checkerboard pattern. The package even comes with a membership application to the American Go Association.

The object of Go is to capture the most prisoners. The game often is compared to chess in its analogy to life and the way in which the game reflects the players' personalities.

Figure 20.23 shows you a game in progress between two famous Go Masters. The game includes three types of boards with various levels of difficulty (including different-sized boards) so that if you are new to this game, you have plenty of room and time for practice. Toyogo also offers a Go Tutor study program if you really want to get into Go.

Fig. 20.22
Covering the floor of
the cube in Welltris.

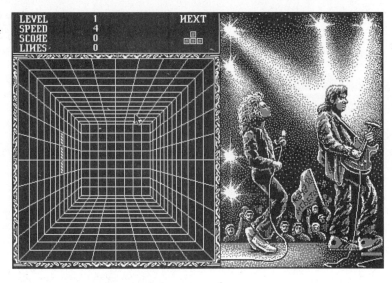

Fig. 20.23
A classic Go board.

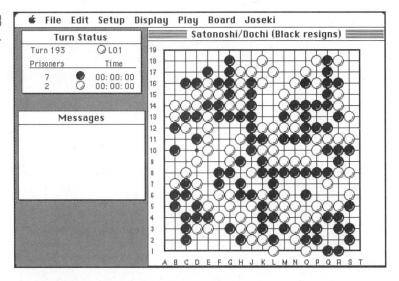

One of the most addictive games around is Crystal Quest from Cassady and Greene. Crystal Quest has been around for a long time and enjoyed justified success. The game has you gathering crystals on different levels and shooting down critters that threaten you.

Cassady and Greene has hit it big again with Glider, which won 1992's Macintosh best game award, by a great game designer, John Calhoun. Straight from Kansas and filled with "Wizard of Oz" images and ideas, Glider takes you on a tour through a 60-plus-room house on a paper airplane. You can create your own rooms, but when you fly, look out for everything from balloons to air vents to 'copters to wall sockets and a paper shredder. Probably the best nonviolent game ever and one of the best of games ever, this entry should see much success.

Brøderbund has another hit in its successful game and education line (at least a hit with me) in PinBall (see fig. 20.24). This game simulates a pinball machine so realistically, you may have to restrain yourself from jostling your Macintosh as if it were a pinball machine. (You actually can tilt this game by using the space bar—but not too much!)

Fig. 20.24
Playing PinBall by
Brøderbund.

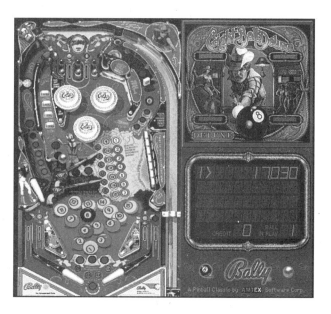

Card Games

You select the card game and SoftStream has the Macintosh version. Around for about two years, this distributor of Macintosh software offers a variety of playing card programs such as Solitaire, Cribbage Tutor, MacRummy, and 22nd Street Whist Tutor.

Solitaire is a desk accessory you can play anytime as Klondike, Canfield, or pyramid—fun variations of the standard card game.

In MacRummy, you play against the computer and can select straight or gin rummy. In figure 20.25, you can see the standoff between the Macintosh and a smart 14-year-old who is just about to draw a 10 of diamonds and defeat her Macintosh SE again. This fun game offers novice and expert levels and shows the basics while it entertains.

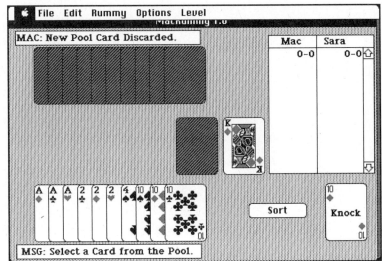

Fig. 20.25
A winning MacRummy
hand.

Other Games

Some of the names in the following list may appeal to you or sound
familiar because they are all public domain or shareware. Many of them
are the same as or very close relatives of some of the games described in
this chapter, such as GoMoku and Lunar. These games are available from
on-line systems, shareware distributors (such as Educorp), and user
groups:

1863	BMX	Daleks
3D Checkers	Bouncing Balls!	Death Mall
AdVent	Brickles	Donkey Doo
Adventure!	Bridge Baron II	Dungeons of Doom
The Adventures of Snake	Canfield	Enigma
	Carbon Copy	Explorer
Animals	Castle of Ert	Fifteens
Artillery	Colony	Fire Zone
Ashes	Concentration	Fortune Cookie
BashBB	Connect Four	GoMoku
BattleMacintosh	Continuum	Halloween Night
BillBoard Parlous	Crossword	Hangman
Blackjack	Crystal Raider	Hex Puzzle

IAGO	Mines	Space Adventure
Investigator	Mini Golf	Space Aliens
Karth of the Jungle	Missile Command	Spacestation Pheta
King Albert	Mouse Craps	Star League
Klondike	Mystery Box	Stock Market Crash
Lucky Lotto	NewWizfire	Story Maker
LunarLander	Nim	StuntCopter
MacFootball	Orion	SwampLord
Macintosh Bugs!	Ozone	Tablut
MacLotto	Pai Gow	Towers of Hanoi
MacPente	Periapt	Valleyball
MacSeven	Pharaoh	Wargle!
MacYahtzee	Pong	Wator
Maps	Radical Castle	Wave 15
Master of Middle Earth	Schmoozer	WordScrambler
MasterCues	Seven Blocks	Worm
Maze	Sitting Duck	WumpusPRO
Megarods	Social Climber	Wyrm
Mike's House	Solarian II	

Best Game Ever

I've saved the best game for last. In the category of my personal favorite Macintosh game to date is Lemmings by Psygnosis. Run—do not walk—to your dealer for a copy of this game. Lemmings has to be the most entertaining and fun game I've seen on any computer, and it is already gaining a number of awards although only recently released.

Lemmings has 120 levels in which your mission is to save hapless, green-haired lemmings that walk to their deaths, falling off cliffs, drowning, and generally going to their reward blindly (see fig. 20.26).

Lemmings runs best on a Macintosh with 256-color capability although it supports black and white. The program takes quite a bit of memory (at least 2MB) but is worth a memory upgrade to play.

There are only two problems with Lemmings. One is the copy protection scheme. Occasionally, when you start the program, it requests a number from a list in the manual, so you have to keep the manual handy. But even this is worth putting up with to play this game.

Fig. 20.26
Saving the lemmings from
horrific fates.

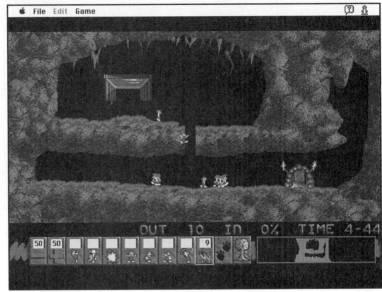

The other problem? Lemmings is too fun. Much too fun. Having it on your hard drive may tempt you to lose time from work, from balancing your checkbook, or from housework. And you'll end up staying up too late, telling yourself you can quit if you can just get past that next level.

Considering Music Programs

Although music programs are not games—like the ones you've just read about—they are entertaining and useful. They are sophisticated enough to write music using the traditional notations.

ConcertWare+ (from Great Wave Software) combines a Music Writer, Instrument Maker, and Music Player in a highly sophisticated package. You use programs like this one to create sheet music, design instrument sounds, and play back what you compose or to play one of the many samples, such as "The Blue Danube" and Beethoven's Fifth Symphony. This package, which has won awards from *MacWorld* and *MacUser*, enables you to use slurs, repeats, and first and second edits, and is as easy to use as any well-designed Mac-interfaced program can be.

Practica Musica (from ARS Nova) is an interactive tutorial that contains games and activities to teach you everything from simple notation to ear training. The program tracks your learning on a score sheet so that you can see your progress.

Figure 20.27 shows the major scales screen where you are expected to click the music staff representing the major scale beginning with the note F. Practica Musica even can help train your "ear"—or at least improve what you may not have.

Fig. 20.27

Learning major scales with Practica Musica.

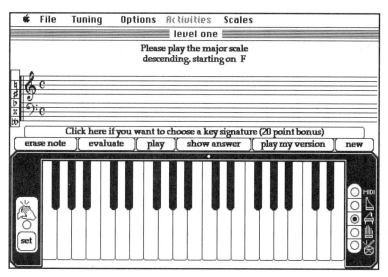

The world of computer music is driven by Musical Instrument Digital Interface (MIDI), a musical-industry protocol standard suited for synthesizers and other musical applications. In a sense, MIDI is like a programming language where the entries are not notes but directions.

Passport's sophisticated applications are definitely high-level Macintosh programs geared to the professional. Trax, an entry-level sequencer that can import MIDI recordings, enables you to create and edit your own MIDI works. Pro4, a high-end MIDI sequencer, offers extensive editing capabilities (including a kind of global search and replace), a song play list (like a jukebox), and integrated windows that enable you to edit as your creation is playing.

With Passport's Encore, you can play musical notes on a MIDI device (such as a synthesizer), and the program transcribes the notes as you create. You then can edit, add lyrics, and change what you need, however you want.

Passport also sells MIDI recordings, which you need a sequencer to play. These recordings include oldies, classical pieces, and big-band jazz tunes.

An entry that is receiving a great deal of attention and acclaim is Software Toolwork's Miracle Piano Teaching System Bundle. This program teaches you how to play the keyboard (which is included). Included with the software are 128 digitized instruments and two free song collections. This program sells for about $350 and is receiving rave reviews.

You also can find plenty of shareware programs that enable you to bang out a tune. These applications—high-tech programming at its best—enable you to use your creative skills and exemplify that computers can do what was once only visionary.

Considering Posters and Calendars

After examining all the educational software and playing games, everyone has occasion to draw a poster or make up a calendar of some kind or other. PosterMaker Plus from Brøderbund and CalendarMaker and MacBillboard from CE Software offer enjoyable utilities to accomplish these tasks.

PosterMaker Plus is a Desktop sign maker that offers features far beyond the capabilities of simple paint or draw programs. PosterMaker Plus has sophisticated options—such as different file formats, templates, smooth fonts, kerning, and scaling—so that you can achieve what you used to accomplish only with powerful graphics programs such as Illustrator and FreeHand. Although not a toy, this program is fun.

Figure 20.28 shows you the working screen for the Mickey-Lu Bar-B-Que poster created on PosterMaker Plus. You can use this program to create posters to use as is or adapt for other uses, such as printing on acetate for silk-screening or for designing signs to be used to create printing plates.

If you want a billboard up to 19 by 26 feet in size that screams Happy Birthday! or Mazel Tov!, for example, MacBillboard can create one for you in a snap. You also can create banners and greeting cards with MacBillboard (see the template in fig. 20.29).

With this program, you also can import scanned images to include in your masterpieces. In fact, CE Software calls MacBillboard a graphics machine because it imports graphics you create and enables you to reproduce them as needed. MacBillboard has a series of tools, like a good painting and drawing program, and can print copy for iron-ons and banners.

Fig. 20.28
Fig. 20.28
Mickey-Lu's ad, with the
screen used to design it.

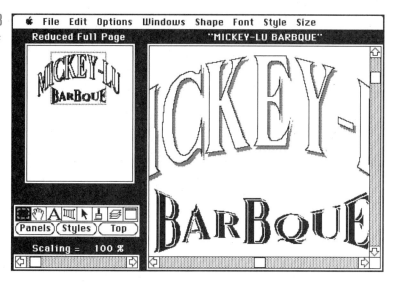

Fig. 20.29
The greeting card template
from MacBillboard.

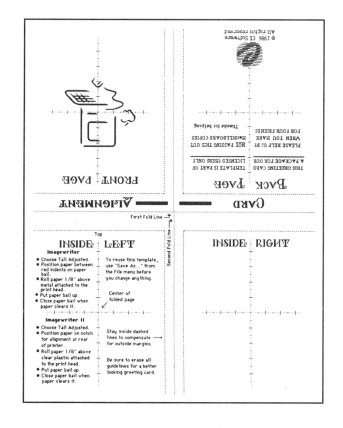

If you don't like the selection of calendars available at the store, you can make your own calendar with CalendarMaker (also from CE Software). In figure 20.30, you see the opening screen, from which you choose icons. To remember that business trip on the 18th or the weekly card game on Wednesdays, drag the appropriate icon over the day. To remember an anniversary or the dog's monthly heartworm pill, use the heart icon.

Fig. 20.30

Making your own calendar.

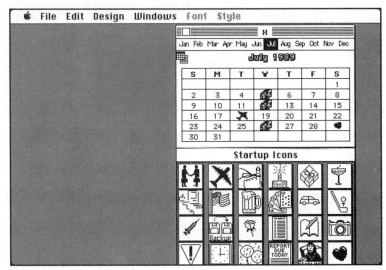

Figure 20.31 shows you a finished calendar, which does not include the notes you can attach to cells to remind yourself of appointments.

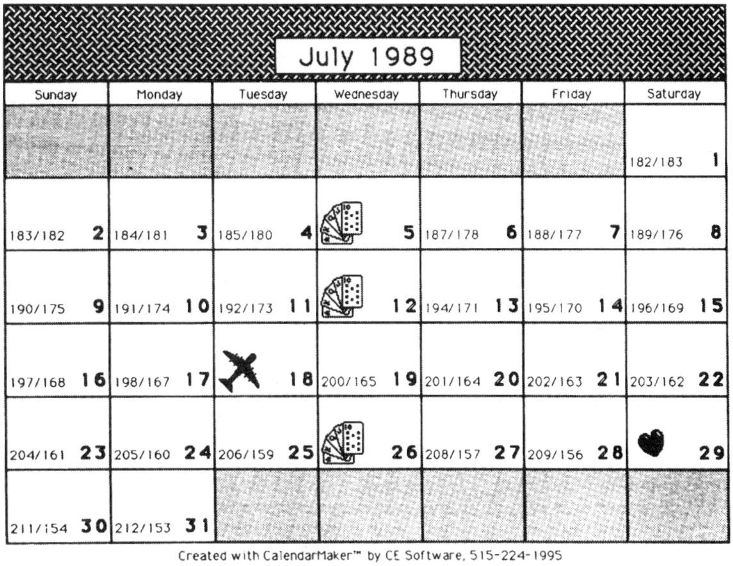

Fig. 20.31
A finished calendar from
CalendarMaker.

July 1989						
Sunday	Monday	Tuesday	Wednesday	Thursday	Friday	Saturday
						182/183　1
183/182　2	184/181　3	185/180　4	5	187/178　6	188/177　7	189/176　8
190/175　9	191/174　10	192/173　11	12	194/171　13	195/170　14	196/169　15
197/168　16	198/167　17	18	200/165　19	201/164　20	202/163　21	203/162　22
204/161　23	205/160　24	206/159　25	26	208/157　27	209/156　28	29
211/154　30	212/153　31					

Created with CalendarMaker™ by CE Software, 515-224-1995

The Big Mac Recommendation

Games on the Macintosh are great fun. As I explored the ones described here, I constantly asked myself how they can be rated or compared. I think that the fairest method is not to talk about one or two mice or however many awards a game has won. Rather, I find it easiest to judge these games on how easy they are to play and how engaging after play started. If I can get a game up and running quickly and am intrigued by what I see, I stay and enjoy it. If not, I tend to move on.

A recommendation here? One word: Lemmings. Buy it. Now.

Part III

Macintosh Hardware

Includes:

21 Buying Hardware
22 Reviewing Macintosh Models
23 Choosing Input Devices
24 Choosing a Display
25 Choosing a Printer
26 Expanding the Macintosh
27 Adding Accessories

CHAPTER TWENTY-ONE

Buying Hardware

This chapter covers the various hardware issues that you will encounter in purchasing a Macintosh or other hardware to work with your materials.

Chapters 22 through 27 cover various hardware options for the Macintosh and discuss the various Macintosh models (both current and discontinued).

Chapter 22 surveys the Macintosh models that were available either new or used at the time of this writing and discusses some of the upcoming Apple offerings. If you are considering purchasing a Macintosh for the first time or as a replacement for your current machine, you can get a good introduction to the machines available by reading that chapter.

You learn about the different input devices in Chapter 23—keyboards, different kinds of mice, mouse substitutes such as trackballs, and graphic tablets for drawing. Scanners and video cameras also are covered.

Chapter 24 covers display units and cards. You learn about the different kinds of displays for the Macintosh, review video terms to help you understand how to choose a display, consider the number of colors you need, and whether or not you need a video card. The chapter discusses adding video to early PowerBooks and compact Macintoshes and using overhead displays to aid you in making presentations to groups.

Chapter 25 discusses the different kinds of printers, how they work, the printers offered by Apple, and non-Apple printer options. Some basic care guidelines are also discussed.

Expanding your Macintosh with various cards and add-ons is covered in Chapter 26. You learn how to add power to your computer by adding hard disk storage, CD-ROM drives, memory upgrades, and accelerator cards. You may find that you can upgrade your computer for less money than you might spend in purchasing a new Macintosh.

Accessories such as power surge protectors, disk cases, carry cases, screen glare filters, and wrist rests are discussed in Chapter 27. Many accessories are available to enhance your work environment, and the chapter gives you a survey of them.

Sources of Hardware

One of the primary sources of hardware additions for your Macintosh is your local dealer. While mail order often has lower prices, dealing with a local store offers many advantages—you can view hardware, try it out, and get advice. Also, many dealers are service centers and can offer off-site or on-site service on your hardware, including service contracts, if your Macintosh or other hardware fails.

At the same time, the experienced Macintosh user can save a great deal of money by purchasing through mail order. The better mail order companies such as Hardware That Fits, MacConnection, MacWarehouse, and others often can guide you in making hardware purchases, offer technical support, and still provide low prices.

You should be careful of mail order, however. There have been some major disasters in Macintosh history. One company that sold hard drives went bankrupt with pending orders, leaving many who had placed orders in a limbo that—for some—is still ongoing.

How do you avoid mail-order disasters? Consider these points:

- *Look for longevity.* MacConnection, for example, has been advertising in Macintosh magazines for years now. They have been around probably longer than any other Macintosh mail-order company. MacWarehouse also has been around for some time now.

- *Talk to other Macintosh users.* All experienced Macintosh users have one or perhaps even a few mail-order companies they deal with regularly. This is why I can safely recommend Hardware That Fits, MacConnection, and MacWarehouse. I deal with these companies on a regular basis and have had nothing but success with them. This is not to say that these are the only good mail-order companies, only that these are the ones I know are reliable. Other Macintosh users may be able to point you to other reliable mail-order companies with whom they have been dealing over time.

- *Read Macintosh publications.* The previously mentioned hard-drive company had been reported as being in trouble in Macintosh publications such as *MacUser*, *MacWorld*, and *MacWeek* early enough that I avoided a contemplated purchase with that company before they ended up in bankruptcy court.

- *Use CompuServe, America OnLine, or another on-line service that many Macintosh users rely on.* The on-line community often knows before anyone which companies are best and which should be avoided. Also, on-line service users are quite vocal about their experiences. Asking about a company or product in one of the many Macintosh forums will bring many comments and give you some knowledge of the quality of service.

- *If possible, use a credit card to purchase mail order.* Credit purchases come under certain federal guidelines that protect consumers. You often can reject a charge for defective merchandise if a company does not remedy the problem. Always deal with companies that charge your card when the product ships. Better mail-order companies adhere to this policy.

Evaluating Hardware

One of the best ways to evaluate hardware is to go to your dealer and see the hardware in action. If you are considering buying a new display, the best way to choose one is to go to your dealer and see how it looks. Actually having a "hands on" experience with the hardware often is the best way to evaluate it.

You can gain a great deal of information through publications such as *MacUser* and *MacWorld*—especially *MacUser* because it offers many series on hardware items, running tests, and doing extensive evaluations. You must be fairly knowledgeable with the Macintosh, however, in order to understand the evaluations. In selecting a display, for example, you can evaluate it by reading a series in a magazine if you understand pixels, dots per inch, refresh rates, and other criteria used in the evaluation. If you are a new user, you may finish reading a review more confused than when you started. You still may need to make a trip to your dealer to see the hardware in action.

Reading Macintosh magazines can give you expertise in choosing hardware. *MacUser* often evaluates hardware in terms that you can relate to easily. An accelerator card may be evaluated, for example, by expressing how fast your Macintosh will perform when you add the card to it. A chart may show you that a particular card will make your IIsi run as fast as a Quadra 900, for example. This information tells you that you can have Quadra 900 power by adding the card to your IIsi for much less money than you would spend if you were to purchase that particular machine.

Macintosh magazines also provide articles to educate you about various aspects of the Macintosh. Over time, you learn such arcane things as the fact that a 50MHz 68030 is roughly as fast as a 25MHz 68040 or that the 68030 accelerator card is less expensive and more compatible with current software than the 68040 accelerator card. This information can prepare you to choose between 68030 and 68040 accelerator cards, for example, because you can understand the trade-offs between the two cards. In the end, you may save some money and headaches.

The two larger magazines, *MacUser* and *MacWorld*, and many of the small ones also offer advice columns with questions from users. You may find your answer in the column, or you can write for advice.

Understanding Warranties and Return Policies

Related to evaluating hardware are warranties and return policies. If you have purchased a piece of hardware but soon find that it simply does not perform as expected, what do you do?

Concerning the Macintosh itself, Apple currently has one-year warranties on hardware. At the time of this writing, Performa Macintoshes have one year of free, on-site service. Apple is now adding a year of free, on-site service for all desktop Macintoshes, although the details were not set as this book went to press. According to industry sources, the warranty will be applied to most hardware purchased in 1993 and beyond.

Details about the new Apple warranty will be available at Apple dealers. You definitely should inquire about the warranty and how it works before you purchase a Macintosh.

Many dealers have excellent warranties of their own. Hardware That Fits has built its business on the policy of making every customer a repeat customer. All hardware has a 30-day, money-back guarantee (except, of course, consumables and special order items). The company goes to great lengths to satisfy a customer and has liberal return policies.

Ask questions.

- If the hardware does not perform as you expected, can you return the hardware? How do you go about returning the hardware, and how many days do you have before you lose this option?

- If you need to return the hardware, can you obtain a refund, or can you exchange the hardware for something more appropriate?

- What happens if the hardware breaks down? Do you have to bring in the hardware to the service center, or will the repair person come to you? If you must mail or carry the hardware in, where is the service center? Many times service centers are not located at the dealership. The service center of the dealer down the street may be across town or even farther away.

Remember to *always* keep the original packaging of your hardware. Most dealers require that you return hardware in original packaging, right down to the last bit of Styrofoam. Annoying and space-consuming as it may be, *never* unpack your Macintosh or monitor or other hardware and toss the box. Keep the box and all packing materials.

CHAPTER TWENTY-TWO

Reviewing Macintosh Models

A pple introduced the original Macintosh computer in 1984. Since then, an almost overwhelming number of models have been introduced, with more on the way. How have models changed? Appendix B, "System Specifications," gives you an idea of the technical improvements that have taken place among Macintosh models and the peripherals. More to the point, however, is how these improvements enable you to use the machine to accomplish what you want.

The following list includes just some of the improvements Apple has made to Macintoshes over the years:

- *An open architecture.* With the introduction of Macintosh models that had expansion slots, Apple began an era of abundant Macintosh enhancements. The NuBus standard was adopted and is still used in the middle and higher-end machines. Processor direct slots (PDS) are common now and enable many models to be expanded with special cards such as accelerators and video cards (Chapter 26, "Expanding the Macintosh," discusses many of these options).

- *Increases in speed.* The speed of a computer depends on the speed of the central processing unit (CPU), which is measured in megahertz (MHz). Speed also depends on the data bus and the input/output (I/O) architecture. Macintoshes (as all computers) become faster as later machines are introduced.

- *Price decreases.* Since the success of the original, low-cost Classic and LC, Apple has pursued an aggressive pricing scheme that puts Macintoshes more in line with IBM PC and clone competitors of "comparable" ability.

- *Increased connectivity and compatibility.* With the 1.44MB SuperDrive (also called FDHD), all new Macintoshes can format, read from, and write to IBM PC disks as well as other formats (such as that for the older Apple II series ProDos operating system).

- *Increased software availability.* The development and availability of programs about everything from complex business databases to arcade-style games have blossomed to the point that keeping track of all programs is nearly impossible. Many programs once used only on MS-DOS machines have now been successfully "ported" to the Macintosh. These programs include the word processing giant WordPerfect, Norton Utilities, dBASE, 1-2-3, and Ventura Publisher. In addition, the ease of connecting the Macintosh to other Macintoshes, PCs, and peripherals has made it more attractive to businesses.

- *Increased visibility.* For years, Apple computers have been the ones seen most often in the public elementary and junior high schools in this country. At the high school and college level, Apple had taken second place to IBM. The same situation is even more prevalent in the business world. As a result of an aggressive campaign targeted at higher education and business, however, Macintoshes are showing up everywhere. Apple now provides excellent discounts to faculty and students at colleges and universities and offers large equipment grants to help increase the presence of Apple computers on campus. Apple is now shipping more Macintoshes than IBM is shipping PCs.

Apple continues to introduce new models and to discontinue others. In addition, new advanced models have been announced for future release. Of these, the machines often referred to as the Mac IIIs and the PowerPCs are the most exciting, and hold promise to radically change the Macintosh universe.

The current Macintosh models fall roughly into four categories: compact, modular, laptop, and tower.

Compact Macintoshes

The Macintoshes in this category are contained in a single casing (except for the keyboard and mouse), and are styled after the original Macintosh. The compact Macintoshes are the least expensive.

Macintosh Classic II/Performa 200

The Classic II—and the consumer version, the Performa 200—superseded the original, low-cost Classic, offering twice as much speed and power. The Classic II has built-in sound capability, the internal hard drive is standard, and the CPU is the 68030. The 68030 runs at a higher clock speed than the 68000 in the Classic, making the Classic II twice as fast. The PMMU is built-in, and you can expand the memory up to 10MB, as opposed to the Classic's 4MB limit.

Classic IIs have been selling for less than $1,000 for the 4MB memory, 80MB hard disk configuration. This machine is an ideal student or family computer. The compactness enables the Macintosh to fit easily in small places; however it has enough power to run educational programs, games, word processors, and other software that interests home users.

No expansion slots are offered on these machines; however, other companies have found ways around this and offer expansion options.

Color Classic

Sure to be a major hit, color has come to the Classic. The Color Classic comes with 4MB of memory that you can upgrade to 10MB. The Color Classic also has a 68030 CPU running at 16MHz (essentially, the LC II has been put in a compact case). The basic configuration supports 256 colors on-screen (8-bit color) at 76 dpi resolution (which is described as "very sharp"). You can upgrade the video memory to enable 16-bit color for 32,768 colors on the internal screen.

The Color Classic includes an easily-accessible LC-style expansion slot. Expansion boards are sure to be offered for this machine by Apple and the other hardware manufacturers. Apple is pricing this machine at $1,389; however, you will probably see slightly lower prices in mail-order catalogs and larger computer stores.

This machine is an even better choice for the home user than the Classic II and Performa 200. Color makes a world of difference.

Modular Macintoshes

The Macintoshes in this category have separate monitors, enabling you to choose the one you prefer instead of settling for the built-in screen. These machines are desktop units, and they generally have greater expandability than the compact models.

Macintosh LC III

The latest entry in Apple's most popular Macintosh series runs faster than the LC II that it replaces (with a 25MHz 68030 processor and a 32-bit data bus, the LC III is about twice as fast as the LC II). It can be expanded to as much as 36MB of memory. You can add a math coprocessor for speeding up mathematical calculations.

The LC III can display up to 256 colors at one time on 16-inch screens; it can display up to 32,768 colors at one time on smaller screens (12 to 14 inches). You must add some video memory (the LC II comes with 512K, but you can expand it to 768K) to obtain more colors. The standard is 4MB of main memory, and you can expand it to as much as 36MB.

A single PDS (processor direct slot) enables you to add an expansion card. Apple has maintained compatibility with LC and LC II cards.

The LC III is positioned as a home machine; however, it runs almost as fast as Apple's longtime standard business machine—the IIci. The machine is a perfect desktop home computer—especially with a list price around $1,400 to $1,500, depending on hard drive size (without the monitor). Yet it has the speed and power to be a solid small business machine. The standard internal hard drive can be 40MB, 80MB, or 160MB.

The LC III is my top pick for the home user. The LC has been a successful series for good reason. The machines are well-suited to running educational software and games, as well as the more serious software such as word processors, spreadsheets, and databases. I can't think of a

Macintosh model more ideal as a general-use computer for the entire family. And with Apple's new, aggressive pricing, you can have a complete system (including a printer, such as the StyleWriter II) for around $2,500. You are assured of owning a Macintosh with a large *install base* (in other words, the number of units being used), and software and expansion options will be available to you for some time to come.

Performa 400

The Performa 400 series Macintoshes are consumer versions of the LC II. This includes the 400, 405, and 450. The difference between the machines are such features as memory and hard disk sizes. The machines are similar to the LC III, except that they run at about half the speed, can be expanded only to 10MB of memory, and support 32,768 colors only on 12-inch monitors (and then only with a video memory upgrade).

The Performa 400 series Macintoshes come bundled with software, so you can save some money here; however, I think the LC III is still the better buy. More than likely, Apple will soon upgrade the Performa 400 series as they have replaced the LC II.

Performa 600

The consumer Macintosh's speed approaches that of Apple's longtime standard business machine (the IIci), but does not quite catch it. The Performa 600 is, however, a good home computer, especially for those who work out of their homes or bring work home from the office. The computer comes with a standard 160MB hard disk and 4MB of memory. It has a slot for an accelerator card, as well as three NuBus slots for later expansion. The 600CD version has a built-in CD-ROM drive to give you access to the wealth of information and software available on CD, as well as access to the Kodak PhotoCD.

The 600 comes with 512K of video memory standard, but you can upgrade it to 1MB. The standard configuration gives you 256 colors on up to 14-inch displays. The 600CD comes with 1MB of video memory, giving you 32,768 colors on displays up to 14 inches.

The 600 and 600CD are "high end" home machines. They are good for a combination of home and home-office use. If you are looking at this machine, you will want the CD-ROM option. Being able to access the wealth of information and software on CD is a primary reason to own this more powerful machine over the Performa 200 or 400.

Macintosh IIvx

The IIvx is something of a puzzle. Apple introduced it recently, but almost immediately "merged" the machine into the Centris line.

The IIvx is about as fast as a IIci, making it a good choice for those who need a low-cost business machine (especially with the recent price cut of the IIvx). The computer has 4MB of memory standard, and is expandable to 68MB. The standard video memory on machines without the CD-ROM drive is 512K; the standard for machines with the CD-ROM drive is 1MB. The former gives you 256 colors on monitors up to 14 inches, whereas the latter yields 32,768 colors on the same size monitors.

The IIvx is a faster version of the Performa 600 and has the same expandability: an accelerator expansion slot and three NuBus slots. The IIvx strikes me as more of a home business machine. Business users will more likely want to look at the Centris line. Home business people will appreciate the power and speed of the IIvx for the low price that Apple recently set. However, note that Apple provides no upgrade for the IIvx. This may not be a problem for you, though, because third-party upgrades are already available for this still fairly recent machine.

Centris 610/650

The new, midrange desktop machines—Centris 610 and Centris 650—offer 68040 processors running at 20MHz and 25MHz, respectively. The 610 and the minimal version of the 650 use the 68LC040, which lacks the floating-point unit (FPU), which speeds up mathematical calculations. The 650 has the 68RC040 with the FPU.

Both models come with 4MB of main memory standard (on the motherboard, so that all SIMM expansion slots are available). You can upgrade the 610 to 68MB, and the 650 to 132MB; the maximum is 32MB SIMMs (single in-line memory modules). The 610 has two memory expansion slots; the 650 has four. Both machines use the newer, 72-pin SIMMs, which Apple claims is a configuration compatible with PC memory SIMMs. Apparently, businesses running PCs and Centris Macintoshes should be able to purchase a single type of SIMM for both.

Deviating from previous Macintoshes, you do not have to add SIMMs in pairs or quintuples. You can add them one at a time. You can also mix and match the SIMMs. In a 650, for example, you could have a 4MB SIMM, add an 8MB, then later add a 16MB SIMM without removing the old SIMMs. In the 650, however, it is best to add pairs of identical SIMMs in adjacent slots. The computer automatically interleaves the memory and speeds memory access (about twice the normal speed).

Both machines can have CD-ROMs built-in if you desire, and optionally you can order Ethernet (you should order the 610 with Ethernet if you need it—no way to add it later currently exists) for networking.

The machines have hard drive options ranging from 80MB to 500MB. Both support 256 colors on up to 16-inch displays (32,768 colors on 12-inch displays) and can be upgraded to show 32,768 colors on displays up to the same size.

The 610 has a single PDS slot for expansion. Apple offers an adapter for NuBus cards; however, the casing has room for only 7-inch cards. The 650 has one PDS slot and three NuBus slots, as well as a socket for a math coprocessor.

The 610 is about twice as fast as the IIci and IIvx. The 650 is about three times as fast. Both are excellent choices for business users. The primary difference between them is the number of expansion slots. Business users usually want upgrades in the form of NuBus cards. The 650 offers greater expandability, along with an increase in speed over the 610.

It seems that the 610 will become the business "workhorse" machine. The 610's price runs about $1,859 in its minimal configuration of 4MB of memory and an 80MB hard drive. The 8/80 with Ethernet configuration is listed at $2,149. With Ethernet and a CD-ROM, the 8/230 configuration is about $2,959. (All prices are for only the computer—the monitor is extra.)

The 650 is about $800 to $1,000 higher for similar configurations. For that difference, you get an additional boost in speed (roughly two or three times as fast as the speed of a Mac IIci) and the three NuBus slots. Unless you expect to expand your machine greatly with NuBus cards and want that extra speed, the 610 is probably the better value, especially for businesses purchasing quantities.

Laptop Macintoshes

After a relatively unsuccessful attempt with a portable Macintosh, Apple introduced the PowerBooks, a series of small, light laptop Macintoshes. The machines were (and still are) so popular that demand far outstripped the supply when they were first introduced.

The PowerBooks offer all the standard Macintosh features and do so with the convenience of transportability. They come with standard Macintosh ports, an internal hard drive, and an optional internal modem.

Color has come to the PowerBooks. There are also new Duo Dock versions that enable you to use the machine as your desktop unit as well as your laptop. All PowerBooks have optional internal modems and (with the exception of the 165c color laptop) last about 2 to 3 hours on battery power (you can swap battery packs if you need more time than this).

PowerBook 145

The PowerBook 145 is the low end of the laptop series. The machine comes with 4MB of memory that you can expand to 8MB. An internal fax modem is available as an option. The screen is a passive matrix LCD, which is not as high-quality or as fast as the active matrix of the more expensive units; however, it is of good quality. The display is mono-chrome (black and white).

The 145 has the power of a IIci, essentially putting a desktop business computer in your lap. The unit can have a 40MB or 80MB hard drive, which has sufficient room for basic business use and is well-suited for writers.

PowerBook 160

Moving up from the 145 to the 160 adds 16 shades of gray to the display, room for up to 14MB in memory (4MB is standard), and up to a 120MB hard drive. The lack of an FPU (floating-point unit) to speed mathematical calculations increases battery life a touch, but makes the price difference between a 145 and 160 a bit questionable when the speed of the units is close. More than likely, the 160 will soon be Apple's low-end laptop and will replace the 145 entirely.

The 160 is as good for basic business use as its near cousin, the 145.

PowerBook 165c

This color laptop runs the same processor (68030 at 33MHz) as the top-of-the-line 180, and it has the math coprocessor to speed numeric calculations. The display is passive matrix and can show up to 256 colors at the same time. There is room for up to 14MB of memory and hard drive options up to 120MB.

The 165c, like the 180, is faster than the IIci. The color screen quality is excellent, but it drains the battery quickly. Expect about an hour of use (two hours at best, according to Apple). An extra battery pack is almost a necessity; however, you should note that if you run the 165c in gray scale, you get the normal PowerBook battery life.

The 165c is best suited for business people who want to do presentations at remote sites.

PowerBook 180

The top-of-the-line 180 gives you a 33MHz 68030 and better than IIci performance. Sixteen shades of gray are displayed on an active matrix display, which is faster and more crisp than the passive matrix displays of the other PowerBooks. Unless you need color or want to use your laptop as your desktop unit as well, this is the power laptop for business travelers.

PowerBook Duo 210/230

The newest versions of the PowerBooks enable you to "dock" the laptop with a desktop unit, turning the laptop into a desktop. With 25MHz and 33MHz 68030s, respectively, the Duo units turn in performance a bit faster than the PowerBooks 160 and 180. They also offer more memory expansion room (up to 24MB, with 4MB being standard). Both display 16 shades of gray on passive matrix screens. The 210 ships with an 80MB hard drive. The 230 has either an 80MB or 120MB hard drive. Neither unit has an internal floppy drive.

Three docking options are sold separately. The first is merely a floppy drive adapter (called Duo Floppy Adapter), although this adapter also provides an ADB port (for a mouse or keyboard).

The Duo MiniDock has the standard Macintosh ports. You can attach a monitor, keyboard, mouse, and floppy drive.

The best docking option is the full Duo Dock, which has the standard Macintosh ports but also gives you room for optional video memory (to display 32,768 colors on standard-size screens), room for an optional FPU to speed numeric calculations, two NuBus slots for expansion, and a bay for a hard drive in addition to the one in the Duo laptop. A Duo Dock (with keyboard, mouse, and monitor) gives you a full desktop machine when you insert your Duo 210 or 230.

The Duo Dock system pulls in the laptop automatically, like a video machine does a tape. You cannot accidentally disconnect the laptop and lose your data. You must press an eject button that causes the Duo to execute a shutdown sequence—including the usual Macintosh dialogs asking you whether you want to save your work—before ejecting.

A docked Duo 210 or 230 comes close to a IIci or IIvx (the 230 is within 10 percent in performance), making this configuration perfect for business and professional users who travel. For slightly more than the price of the desktop equivalent, you have both a desktop and laptop machine.

The Duo system is one of the most amazing products Apple has produced. Going from being almost unable to produce a laptop (the Portables were anything but) to delivering some of the most innovative laptops anywhere is a rather stunning achievement. The Duo system is sure to be one of the most popular Apple products ever.

Tower Macintoshes

The Quadra series is the powerhouse of the Macintosh world. Based on a 68040 central processor, these tower Macintoshes are very fast and powerful. They support built-in Ethernet hardware for networking and have room for several hard disks, which makes them ideal for network servers. With their power, speed, and support of 24-bit (16 million colors) color, these are also the "workstation" Macintoshes—the choice for high-quality imaging and graphics as well as computer-aided design (CAD).

Quadra 800

The Quadra 800 minitower is the fastest Macintosh in the current line; however, this might change in the summer of 1993 with the Mac III introduction. Although it uses a CPU that is not much faster than any other top Macintosh (the 68040 at 33MHz—same as the 950), the 800 has enhanced memory use, a faster QuickDraw (the Macintosh graphics system responsible for all you see on your screen), and consolidated system chips (more functions are handled by fewer integrated circuits).

The 800 is an excellent workstation machine with room for up to 136MB of memory (8MB standard), three NuBus expansion slots, and one PDS expansion slot. The 800 supports 16-bit (32,768 colors) color on displays up to 16 inches, but it supports only 8-bit (256 colors) color on 21-inch displays. Of course, you can easily add a video display card for up to 24-bit color on 19- and 21-inch displays.

The power supply has 200 watts available to support almost any hardware options. The drive bays support one standard 3.5-inch drive included, a 3.5-inch removable-media drive, and a 5.25-inch half-height drive.

Apple offers a 230MB, 500MB, or 1,000MB hard disk and a CD-ROM drive.

Quadra 950

The Quadra 950 can accommodate as many as four types of drives, such as different size floppy disks, tape drives, and additional hard drives or even a CD-ROM (one drive bay is taken by the floppy drive, which leaves room for you to add three). The 950 is a workhorse; it's perfect as a file server connected to other Macintoshes on a network with built-in Ethernet.

The 950 runs a 68040 at 33MHz and comes with 8MB main memory and 1MB of video memory. You can upgrade the main memory to as much as 64MB, whereas the video memory can be upped to 2MB. The 1MB video configuration supports 32,768 colors on up to 16-inch displays, whereas the 2MB configuration yields 16 million colors on up to 16-inch displays. You need a video card for millions of colors on displays larger than 16 inches.

You have a choice between a 230MB, 500MB, or 1000MB hard drive. The power supply is 300 watts, which is more than enough for most configurations. Five NuBus slots are available for expansion options (or you can install a PDS card, disabling one of the NuBus slots).

This machine is largely intended to be a network server, doling out hard disk space or other resources to other users. Because the Quadra 800 has more speed and power, those who have massive spreadsheets or work with three-dimensional graphics or photo-realistic color should look at the smaller machine.

Older Macintoshes

Home users and those on budgets have no reason not to look at older Macintoshes. The used Macintosh market has grown as machines are replaced. Although the machines are out-of-date technically, many still have life in them and might be suited to your needs. The used market (or inventory clearance sales at dealers) can net you a machine that meets your needs at a rock-bottom price.

Recently discontinued machines are one of the best buys. The IIsi has been dropped, as have the IIci and Quadra 700. Dealers will be slashing prices to move them. Older machines are even cheaper. When a machine is discontinued, the bottom falls out of the used market, especially with Apple cutting prices left and right to make way for new, more powerful machines. For example, used Classics—which sold new for about $1,300—are practically garage sale items now that twice-as-fast Classic IIs sell new for $999.

If you shop through the classifieds of your newspaper, you should first do some homework. Check the backs of publications such as *MacUser* and *MacWorld* to see the prices of used machines through companies that recondition and warranty them. A used machine sold without warranty should cost a bit less. Beware of users trying to sell machines at prices intended to recover their investment in the machine. Many users do not understand just how fast computer equipment devalues. Recently I heard of someone trying to sell an old SE for close to purchase price. Considering that you can now purchase a new, faster Color Classic for about half the original price of the SE, this sale will exist only in the mind of the seller. If I had a used SE, I think a better disposal of the unit would be a charitable donation to an organization or making it the kids' computer. The resale value is almost nonexistent.

Macintosh Classic

The Macintosh Classic offers a 68000 processor at 8 MHz, a 9-inch monochrome screen, and 1MB of main memory (expandable to 4MB maximum). The machine had an optional 40MB hard drive, and many of these units are still around. When the Classic was introduced, Apple could not produce it fast enough to satisfy demand. Apple's audience was the educational, low-end user market, and it seemed to have hit the target.

The Classic is still an excellent machine for the student or home. I still have my Classic and use it to keep visiting nephews and nieces away from my work machine. Although it is slow in comparison to newer machines, the Classic still does admirably in the basic areas. My suggestion would be an immediate upgrade to the full 4MB of memory and an integrated package such as ClarisWorks. With Classic IIs selling new at about $1,000, you shouldn't pay more than half that price for a used Classic, probably less without a hard drive.

Macintosh IIsi

The Macintosh IIsi was a one-slot (PDS), entry-level 68030 modular system now discontinued (and rather abandoned) by Apple. The IIsi offers a 68030 processor running at 20MHz, an 8-bit (256 colors) color display, and a 1MB main memory (expandable to 17M). The PDS can be adapted to NuBus. The machine was positioned as an inexpensive business machine and aimed at professionals.

Although Apple has dropped the machine like a rock, not offering an upgrade path of any kind, the machine has support from other vendors and can still be a good buy. The IIsi is a recently discontinued machine, so dealers will be trying to sell their stock. Prices for the base model through mail order are around $1,500.

Although orphaned by Apple, the IIsi is not dead yet. Companies such as DayStar Digital offer accelerator cards that can increase the machine's speed enormously (with the Turbo 040 card from DayStar, you will speed laughingly past your Quadra 950 friends).

Macintosh SE/30

The Macintosh SE/30 was based on the old SE but added a 68030 and a PDS expansion slot. The SE/30 is older than the recently discontinued IIsi but is essentially the same machine; however, it runs a bit more slowly and has only the 9-inch black-and-white built-in monitor.

The SE/30 appears in the used market frequently and is an excellent buy if you want a powerful compact unit. Many accelerator cards and expansions are still available. You can expand the memory on this machine to as much as 32MB.

Macintosh IIcx

The IIcx was the predecessor of the IIci. It offers a 68030 at 16MHz, which is slower than the IIsi's 20MHz but has more expansion possibilities with three NuBus slots. Expansion options and accelerators exist for the IIcx, making the machine still upgradable. However, this Macintosh is an older machine. You might do well to purchase through a reputable used Macintosh dealer rather than through the classifieds in a newspaper. Still, a IIcx in good shape should go for rock-bottom prices and give you considerable computing power for little money. The IIcx does not have built-in video, so you will want to be certain the video card is installed in the one you purchase.

Macintosh IIci

The IIci offers everything the IIcx has to offer, and it also is faster, running a 68030 at 25MHz—near IIvx speed. It has built-in color video capability with 256 colors on monitors up to 14 inches. The included FPU increases the speed of numeric calculations.

This machine was long the flagship of the Macintosh line. The IIci had a long life and is only just now being discontinued. Expect dealer prices to be low on new machines as stock is cleared. Also expect support to last quite a while on this machine. I would choose a used IIci over a IIcx. The used and reconditioned market for the IIci should become good over the next year, with low prices and sellers wanting to unload the older machine for a newer one. (Macintosh users have a habit of wanting the latest and greatest. This trend can give others good deals in the used market as the "power users" move up to new machines.)

Macintosh IIfx

The IIfx used to be the fastest kid on the block, with a 68030 running at 40MHz and a built-in math coprocessor for handling the numeric calculations. Although the Quadras are faster, the IIfx can operate considerably faster than the IIci. The IIfx does not have built-in video and, hence, must have a video card. If you are buying a used IIfx, check to see which video card is included and how many colors the machine can display. The used prices on this machine have been good for a while now and—although it is aging—the machine is still powerful and expandable.

Macintosh LC/LC II

The Macintosh LC and its replacement, the LC II, are among Apple's best-selling machines. The LC III and the Performa 400 series continue the success story of the original LC.

The LC was based on the 68020 processor running at 16MHz. The LC II used the 68030 at the same speed (but even at the same clock speed, the 68030 runs faster than the 68020). The LC II has a built-in PMMU, which the original LC lacked. Standard memory was 2MB or 4MB with an upgrade limit of 10MB.

Standard configurations of both machines support 16 colors on displays up to 14 inches. With an optional upgrade to 512K of video memory, the machines support up to 256 colors on the same size displays and up to 32,768 on monitors such as the Apple Basic Color Monitor.

Either machine makes an excellent choice for a home computer; this has been the area of the LC series' success. You may, however, find these machines difficult to locate in the used market. Owners of these Macintoshes have been quite content to keep them. However, if you do find a used LC or LC II and the price is no higher than about one half the cost of a new LC III, you should seriously consider the machine. A great number of options and upgrades are offered for these machines and should continue to be offered for some time to come.

Quadra 700

The Quadra 700 was the first in the Quadra line and was aimed at the "tower" or "workstation" market. Running a 68040 processor with PMMU and FPU built in and at 25MHz, the 700 was a machine suited to high-powered number-crunching (large spreadsheets with large amounts of formulas and data, for example), graphics-intensive work (computer aided design, for example) and resource serving (sharing large hard disks on networks, for example).

The Ethernet networking option appeared first on this machine, keeping with the market's needs for fast connectivity. The 700 came with 4MB of memory standard and an upgrade limit of 68MB.

The 700 supports 256 colors on displays as large as 16 inches and 16 colors on displays as large as 21 inches. 16.7 million colors on the former size displays and 256 colors on the latter size displays could be reached with video memory upgrades (the standard is 512KB, the maximum 2MB).

Two NuBus slots are provided for expansion. The 700 shipped with an 80MB, 160MB, or 400MB hard disk drive.

A used 700 would make an excellent choice for a home professional graphics artist or a consultant working with large spreadsheets. Small businesses could save money with this fast and expandable machine in the used market.

Quadra 900

The Quadra 900 is identical to the 950 with only two exceptions. The 900 runs at 25MHz instead of the 950's 33MHz and supports only 256 colors on displays up to 21 inches in size, opposed to the 950's support of 32,768 colors on displays of the same size. With the 1MB video memory upgrade (bringing the 900 to its maximum 2MB of video memory), the 900 and 950 support the same 16.7 million colors on displays up to 16 inches in size (they diverge on 21-inch displays; the 900 supporting up to 256 colors while the 950 supports up to 32,768 colors with the maximum video memory).

A used 900 would be a good purchase for a small business user in need of a high-powered Macintosh. However, if the price of the used unit is close to a new 950, the 950 with slightly more speed and slightly more video capability would be the superior choice.

PowerBook 100

The PowerBook 100 was positioned as the entry-level portable. Essentially a Macintosh Portable re-engineered and shrunken considerably, the machine runs at about Classic II speed. It has no internal drive and comes with only a 20MB hard drive. No Apple upgrade is possible. But for simple text tasks, it might be ideal.

PowerBook 140

The PowerBook 140 has an internal floppy disk drive, and runs a 68030 at 25MHz. The standard is 2MB or 4MB of memory; however room is available for a maximum of 8MB. Although slower than the 145, the machine is ideal for those who do more word processing than graphics or "number crunching." A used 140 is an excellent buy for a writer or journalist who travels.

PowerBook 170

Until the introduction of the 180, the PowerBook 170 was the top of the line. The 170 comes with a math coprocessor, internal modem, and terrific screen display. The 170 is fast enough to use as your only computer. The processor is a 68030 running at 25MHz. Memory is 2MB or 4MB standard, and is upgradable to 8MB.

The 170 is a good buy at a clearance sale or in the used market for the self-employed traveler. Apple has just discontinued the machine, so prices in the used market should continue to fall through 1993 (if old patterns hold).

Obsolete Macintoshes

Several machines should not even be considered if you are in the market for a used Macintosh. There are various reasons for this. Some are simply too old. Some cannot be expanded enough to handle today's software.

Others had some problems you want to avoid. The only exception to this rule is the *original* Macintosh—not to use it as your computer, but to save it as a collector's item. Remember those old Superman magazines?

The Original Macintosh

The first Macintosh introduced in 1984 came with 128K of memory, no expansion slots, a 9-inch black-and-white monitor, and a single 400K disk drive.

Many upgraded old Macintoshes are probably around, and you might even run into one for sale; however, you should steer clear unless you are a collector.

Macintosh 512K/512Ke

Apple's first upgrade was to quadruple the Macintosh's memory, creating the "Fat Mac." The 512Ke added new ROM (read-only memory) that could handle the "new" 800K disk drive, and this drive was included. Again, unless you are collecting old Macintoshes in the hope of auctioning them off in the year 2043 to a museum, these Macs are most useful as planters (although there was an aquarium kit around once).

Macintosh Plus

RAM could not be added to the original 128K Macintosh up through the 512K model. Software developers soon reached the limits of how much they could fit into such a small space. (The original MacPaint was a marvel considering its capability in spite of RAM limitations.) With the Plus, you could have as much as 4MB of RAM installed, but because these models contained the same processor (the 68000), there was no increase in processing power. The Plus did see the introduction of the SCSI bus, which enabled users to add hard disks.

The Plus became the workhorse for Macintosh users and Apple's first big hit. The machine enjoyed an incredibly long life span (although the Plus has been long since discontinued, Apple still includes it in the Macintosh Compatibility Chart and states that System 7.1 can be run on the machine—something that makes me giggle hysterically).

No figures are available to show how many Pluses are around today, but it was a great machine. Many people chose to keep their Pluses and upgrade the memory and other parts rather than invest in a new machine. But the Plus is reaching the end of its life span and should be avoided in the used computer market.

Macintosh II

The Macintosh II was the first Macintosh to use the 68020 chip, which gave the computers increased speed and power. The Macintosh II has six slots for expansion and color capabilities.

The Macintosh II offered increased speed, which many welcomed. Its unportability, however, is one of the things that has made it increasingly less attractive. The Macintosh II was the top of the line until the IIx series was introduced. The IIx series was aimed primarily at the business community and its need for a more powerful machine (with greater processing power and better memory management).

I can see little reason to buy a Macintosh II in the used market when more powerful machines are available. A used IIsi or IIx would be a better machine. However, companies such as DayStar Digital still offer accelerators and expansion cards for this machine.

Macintosh IIx

The Macintosh IIx is newer than the II and has six expansion slots. The machine runs a 68030 at 16MHz, putting it below the IIsi in speed but above the IIsi in expandability. Memory can be increased to 32MB. The PMMU (paged memory management unit), which becomes increasingly necessary in today's Macintosh world, can be added (or may already have been added to the used machine).

A IIx at a low price would not be a bad machine. However, the install base of the machine was never that large. Expansion card manufacturers might drop support for this machine in the near future.

Choosing a Macintosh

If you bought this book and don't even have a Macintosh yet, you've come to the right place. The two factors you should keep in mind when choosing a Macintosh are price and your needs. The best advice is the following:

■ Read as much as you can about the Macintosh in general, especially in the area in which you intend to use it. *MacUser* and *MacWorld* as well as books such as this one are great sources of Macintosh information.

- Find out the types of software you will be using and the system requirements for this software. If you want simple drawing tools (for example, MacPaint), you can use the low-end machines. If you plan to use one of the more advanced computer-aided design (CAD) packages, however, you need a more powerful machine that can work more efficiently. Otherwise, you will find yourself staring at your screen waiting, or the application you are using will crash because of memory limitations.

- Always keep your intent in mind. If you're a graphics designer, color is essential. Thus, you will need one of the Centris or Quadra machines. If you are buying a Macintosh for your children, for an occasional game to play yourself, or even for access to some sophisticated software, the Classic II, Color Classic, or an LC series machine might be your best choice.

- Try out the machine and the keyboard. Determine whether the screen is large enough. Do you need to consider a full-page monitor?

- What about cost? The space you have available for your new Macintosh? A printer? The memory you need?

Here's a list of questions you should try to answer before you go shopping; finish those you cannot answer with the information you gain on your shopping expedition. These questions will help you make some decisions about which of the many Macintosh models is best for you.

- What do you plan to do with your Macintosh?

- What types of software do you intend to buy (word processing, graphics, page layout, and so on)?

- Do you need a specific Macintosh model to run the software, or will the software work on any Mac?

- How much money do you have available for the complete system purchase?

- What's the most important feature to you? Speed? Expandability? Reliability?

- Do you need color?

- What kind of printing will you be doing? Drafts? Finished work? Envelopes? Mailing labels? How much printing will you do?

- How much disk storage do you need? What will you save and for how long?

- How much money can you afford to spend to back up your data? Tape drives? Backup hard disks?

- Do you need to work away from the office or on the road?

- What kind of storage device do you need? You need a hard disk at least, but do you need a large one? A tape backup? Perhaps an optical drive for long-term storage of large amounts of data?

- Will you be on a network and have access to other files?

- Do you plan to telecommunicate, and will you need a modem? What speed and features do you need?

- Will you be working primarily with text and numbers, graphics, or both?

- Will you need full-page capabilities?

- How flexible do you want your Macintosh to be? One year down the line, will you be wondering why you didn't buy the Quadra 800 rather than a Centris 610? As hard as it is, try to buy a Macintosh that can grow with your needs.

- What about memory? This question is a tough one because you may not know the demands of the software you will be purchasing. But you can never have too much memory. The minimum now is 4MB. A good size is 8MB. You need more for business use.

On the Horizon

Apple is threatening a major jump in computing power with an entirely new Macintosh (or perhaps the replacement of the Macintosh?). The PowerPC project holds the promise of Macintoshes that will make everything obsolete (including IBM PCs and clones). These are sci-fi computers that respond to plain English, enable you to write on-screen in ordinary scribble yet be understood, and display lifelike video images in real time. Sounds like Scotty may be beaming us all up later this decade.

In all seriousness, the PowerPC—which is supposed to make its initial debut in 1994 or so—will first yield Quadra power or more for prices around the LC series. As the decade wears on, Apple promises computers that will offer the following:

- *True preemptive multitasking.* This will eliminate those irritating hesitations when background processes are executing.

- *Multithreading.* This is the ability to run different parts of applications at the same time. For example, currently when you start a process in the Finder (such as copying files), you must wait for the Finder to finish before executing another Finder command. Each application can execute only one command at a time. Multithreading would enable you to execute more than one command (for example, start a long copy then open folders and launch an application) without waiting for the first to finish.

■ *Interprocess messaging and shared libraries.* Processes on the PowerPC will be able to communicate and share information. This will enable software manufacturers to create more focused applications instead of layering on tons of features. You will be able to pick and choose and customize more readily. For example, you could combine your favorite word processor with your favorite graphics program and favorite spreadsheet program, yet have all three work on the same document without switching between them.

Future computers will run at such high speeds and process so much information that current Quadras will look like kids' computers (and they may very well be by the end of the decade). In the meantime, Apple is close to introducing the Mac IIIs (although the name may change before the summer 1993 introduction).

The high-end machine will run a 68040 CPU at 40MHz, have three enhanced NuBus slots, and be expandable to 128MB of memory. It will support up to 2MB of video memory to display 24-bit (16 million colors) color on displays up to 16 inches. The lower-end machine will run at 25MHz, have one slot, and support 32,768 colors on displays up to 16 inches.

The major differences with the new machines include direct memory access on peripheral buses including SCSI, the new NuBus 90, faster serial ports, and a modem port that can emulate various telephone standards and—with an adapter—be connected directly to the wall, eliminating the need for a modem.

The direct memory access, faster NuBus, and faster serial ports should result in a significant increase in speed, although the CPUs of these machines are not dramatically faster than current ones.

The AT&T 3210 DSP (digital sound processor) will be built into these machines, giving them audio CD quality sound, enabling voice recognition (the machines will ship with Casper voice recognition), and speeding data compression. Video will be easier to handle and can even be passed through to the Macintosh screen (making you wonder whether the next big problem at offices will be dozens of Macintosh users watching "Oprah").

In any case, these machines will be ideal for video and sound processing, increasing multimedia power dramatically.

Choosing Input Devices

ith any computer, the input devices (the keyboard and mouse, mainly) and the screen are of major importance.

When they first use an Apple keyboard, some people fall in love; others seek more (or less) key responsiveness, bigger (or smaller) keys, a smaller (or larger) overall size, and so on.

Many Macintosh users find that the standard mouse is fine; some prefer a trackball or other input device. Specialized use sometimes requires input devices, such as drawing tablets.

Choosing a Keyboard

Like other system parts that you set up, your keyboard choice is personal. You can use the mouse to move around, but when you enter information, you're stuck with the keyboard. Because more than half of all personal computer activity relates to word processing, the keyboard quality is an important link to productivity.

A good keyboard should have some of the following qualities:

- A solid, not light, feel when you press the keys

- Adjustable key resistance; some people like a lighter touch than others

- Sufficiently large keys, especially for important keys such as Return and Shift

- Ergonomic design, so that the face of the board is slightly tilted in the user's direction

- Audio feedback when you press the keys—an especially handy feature for touch typists

- Numeric keypad for fast entry of numerical data

- Function keys that you can program to perform special application-intensive tasks, such as getting help and saving files to disk

- Macro software that enables you to automate keyboard activities

On the early Macintoshes, the keyboards that Apple supplied were small and did not offer extras like a numeric keypad or function keys. Although these keyboards took up very little space on the desk, many people complained about the lack of true keyboard feel they remembered from their typewriter days.

The Apple Extended Keyboard offers a full range of keys plus 15 function keys, arrow keys, and a numeric keypad. This keyboard offers many features already mentioned, but it doesn't come with any documentation or software, and you cannot adjust its position relative to the user. This keyboard is in the style of the IBM PC keyboard.

Apple recently introduced a keyboard worth noting. The keyboard can split in half, and the two halves of this split keyboard can be angled up to 30 degrees, matching the natural positioning of your wrists. The ergonomic design of the keyboard promises to ease the threat of repetitive stress injuries. The keyboard lists for $219. You can add an ergonomic mouse—the Apple Desktop Bus Mouse II—for about $80.

An attractive alternative is the Mac-101e Keyboard from DataDesk International. Many people find this keyboard much easier to use than Apple's Extended Keyboard, especially for extended periods of time. The Mac-101e Keyboard is found by many users to be more responsive than Apple keyboards. You also can adjust it, which reduces the strain associated with a keyboard that remains flat.

Many people's favorite keyboard by far, however, is the MacPro from KeyTronic. The keyboard that "feels" better always requires a subjective judgment, but this keyboard does offer some very nice features, such as adjustable resistance for the keys, 15 function keys, an ADB port in the back, and more.

DataDesk also offers the Switchboard keyboard. You can rearrange this keyboard as you choose. You can place the numeric keypad on the left or right side, or put a trackball in the keyboard (replacing the numeric keypad). You can place the arrow keys in different locations.

Many times PowerBook users want a separate numeric keypad so that they can enter numeric data quickly. These users have several alternatives.

Kensington offers the NoteBook KeyPad. The company is noted for Macintosh accessories, such as trackballs, keypads, and other items. The NoteBook KeyPad is well suited for PowerBook use, as it includes arrow keys as well as the regular numeric keys. This KeyPad is only just over an inch thick and weighs only nine ounces.

The Plusware Numeric Keypad is low power and small (5x4.25x0.6). The keypad includes an L-shaped array of arrow keys, six mathematical symbols, and programmable function keys, as well as Clear, Home, Page Up, Page Down, End, and delete keys.

The PowerPad by Sophisticated Circuits is a 10-key keypad that includes a hard cover that protects the keypad and serves as a support base when open. A desk accessory called 10Key Tape is included to give you a record of your work.

Choosing a Mouse or Trackball

Many people like the standard mouse, but others prefer different versions, including the popular trackball. This section discusses various options available to you.

You can purchase alternatives to the standard Apple mouse, such as the A3 Mouse by Mouse Systems. The A3 Mouse uses optics instead of a rolling ball to track (you use a special mouse pad). Accuracy is higher than the standard Macintosh mouse. This mouse has three buttons instead of one, and a System extension enables you to assign functions to the other buttons.

The Little Mouse by Mouse Systems is 22 percent smaller than the regular Macintosh mouse and 38 percent lighter. This mouse offers higher accuracy than the standard Macintosh mouse.

MouseMan offers greater accuracy than the standard Apple mouse and has three programmable buttons.

Users with children may want to consider the Kidz Mouse. This kid-sized mouse fits a child's hand and offers mouse "ears" for buttons. You can install this mouse without removing your own.

MousePenPro by Appoint seems more like a pen than a mouse. When drawing, graphic artists may prefer this tool, as it feels more natural than working with the mouse or a trackball.

Many users prefer trackballs to mice. The *trackball* looks like a mouse turned upside down, with the ball on the top. Instead of moving the unit around, you roll the ball to move the mouse pointer.

One of the most popular trackballs is from Kensington, the TurboMouse 4.0. The TurboMouse includes Brilliant Cursor, which enables you to jump to user-defined areas on-screen with little effort. You can program the two buttons to perform up to seven different commands. You can customize mouse pointer acceleration and mouse performance. You can add different colored balls to the TurboMouse. Kensington offers four colors: blue, purple, red, and black.

The Stingray by CoStar is a low-profile trackball curved to fit your hand. The Stingray comes in two colors: platinum and black.

MacTrac 2.0 by MicroSpeed is a three-button ergonomically designed trackball. You can assign left- or right-handed operation to the buttons, or assign up to eight different commands to them. The MicroTrac version fits in the palm of your hand—good to use with PowerBooks.

For a truly small trackball, ideal for PowerBook users, consider the Thumbelina Mac, a palm-sized trackball that you can operate with your thumb. This trackball is good for presentations.

Choosing a Tablet

Graphic users and other artists may want to consider a *graphics tablet*. These tablets offer an alternative to a mouse, enabling you to use a pen-like tool to draw on a surface. Then drawing is translated to the graphics program and can be edited on-screen.

A cross between a mouse and a graphics pad, the UnMouse is an interesting alternative. You can use your finger to move the mouse pointer or draw in a graphics program. A tap of a button changes the pad into 16 programmable keys.

DrawingPad Graphics Tablet, offered by CalComp, has a 7.5-inch square drawing area. The pen imitates drawing tools, enabling you to draw thick or thin lines using pressure.

The Wacom series of tablets are well known in the Macintosh community. The prices are higher than many pads, but for the serious artist or graphic designer, the cost is a worthwhile investment. The pads respond to variations in hand pressure, translating the pressure into effects in programs like Aldus FreeHand, Photoshop, Electronic Arts, and others. Wacom offers pads running from 6×9 inches to 12×12 inches. The prices range, depending on size and quality.

Choosing a Scanner

The *scanner* is an important alternative to keyboard and mouse input. Instead of typing or drawing into the Macintosh, you scan an image or text into the computer. Scanners perform rather like copy machines but transfer printed images to disk files rather than to other sheets of paper.

Apple has introduced the Color OneScanner. This relatively low-priced scanner includes a color version of the successful and highly useful Ofoto scanning software, which automatically aligns and corrects scans. (You do not have to worry about positioning the document to be scanned exactly; Ofoto does the adjustment for you.) This single-pass scanner yields a maximum of 256 gradients for each hue and corrects color problems automatically.

ScanMaker IIXE is a color scanner with 600 dpi vertical and 300 dpi horizontal resolution standard. With software options, you can achieve 1200 by 1200 dpi resolution. The scanner can work with black and white or up to 24-bit color and has a display-matching system to adjust the scanned image. You can save some money by dropping the color separation feature and purchasing the ScanMaker II. An optional automatic document feeder is also available.

The Animas True-Color Hand Scanner enables you to pass a device over your document once and scan it into the Macintosh. Resolution runs from 100 to 400 dpi and up to 12-bit color at 200 dpi or 16-bit color at 400 dpi.

Hewlett-Packard offers the ScanJet series of scanners. The IIp scans at 300 dpi resolution (same as an average laser printer prints) and can handle 4-bit or 8-bit gray scale. Typical scans take only about 10 seconds. The unit runs about $800. The IIc version handles 24-bit color at a single pass. The settings are simplified for new users, but experienced users can still gain greater control over the scanning. This unit can use an automatic document feeder.

If you scan text more than graphics, consider the Typist Plus Graphics, which is oriented towards text (or more appropriately OCR—Optical Character Recognition). This scanner is suitable for scanning in text documents. Typist scans two inches per second and stays aligned even if your hand drifts as you draw the hand-held unit across the page. You can also scan graphics, but this unit is best for those who have a great deal of text to import and want to avoid typing it all.

The LightningScan 400 by Thunderware is a competing product for Typist. This hand-held unit includes software that converts your scanned document into individual characters for import into word processing documents. This unit is highly rated. Thunderware also offers the LightingScan Pro 256, and offers 256 levels of grays at resolutions of up to 400 dpi. The LightningScan Compact, a less expensive unit that attaches to a floppy drive port, can scan graphics as well as text.

Choosing a Video Camera

One more interesting input device for the Macintosh is the video camera. Because of the rise of multimedia (see Chapter 18, "Using MultiMedia"), users often need ways to input video images to the Macintosh.

Canon offers the UC1 8 mm video camcorder kit. This small, light camera has a menu system to easily control its functions, and has a detachable remote control panel. Fuzzy logic technology eases focus control. This unit can record up to two hours on an 8 mm video tape.

Canon also offers the Hi8 Stereo 8 mm camera, with 400 lines of resolution and stereo sound. Users who want to record movies to use in QuickTime might consider this camera. You can also consider the H850 Insertable Graphics Clips, which add special effects.

Canon has a still video imaging system that you can use to take pictures on reusable floppy disks as single frames of video. You can use the RC-250 camera as a 35 mm camera, but you can import the images directly into Macintosh documents with the optional video digitizer. The camera itself is reasonably priced, but you need to add one of the two digitizer options: black and white or color. Extra floppy disks are rather expensive, but you can reuse them.

The highest quality Canon still camera is the RC-570. This camera offers 450-line resolution, auto focus, 3K power zoom lens, and a 2.5-frame per second field mode (two frames per second in frame mode), picture-taking rate. You must connect this camera to a Macintosh with a separate NuBus card. This is not a small investment, but the serious graphics artist or business may want to consider it.

The Big Mac Recommendation

Overall, keyboards, mice, trackballs, and other input devices are a matter of taste and necessity. Consider your needs carefully when you choose one.

Obviously, you need a keyboard and a mouse (or trackball) to use a Macintosh. The type of keyboard depends on your own tastes. Try keyboards at a dealership to determine the "feel," and see if the keyboard is for you.

With all the concern about carpal tunnel syndrome (a legitimate concern, as many writers attest), you may want to take a close look at the new Apple keyboard. The split design of the keyboard may seem strange at first, but your wrists are at their natural angle, which eases the stress on them.

Mice come in many varieties—again, try out a mouse to see which one you think is most comfortable in your hand and easiest for you to use. Also, consider the trackball. Many users like trackballs, but if you are accustomed to a mouse, they take some time to get used to. A trackball needs little desk space, as it does not move.

Artists might consider the graphics tablet. The average user normally has little need for one. For serious artwork, the Wacom series is probably the best choice.

If you must input a great deal of text or graphics, you may need a scanner. The Apple Color OneScanner is an excellent choice, especially with the Ofoto software and its automatic alignment feature.

Video cameras are a new input device for the Macintosh. With the advent of multimedia, the need to input video images has arisen. As yet, video cameras are not an option the average user will want to casually purchase (and the price is too high for us average souls to buy on impulse anyway). But the serious multimedia artist and businesses that do extensive presentations might call for these.

This chapter only briefly surveyed the number of input devices available for the Macintosh. Many more input devices exist and others are being introduced. Sound input is coming fast (for example, you can purchase the Voice Navigator II now if you want, but it is rather limited in use and very expensive). Over the next few years, a great number of command systems that use English will be introduced and become more common.

The pen-based systems may become prevalent, though they are more likely a niche item—suited for specific use rather than widely useful. Handwriting recognition is rapidly improving, and notebook-sized computers that you can use scribble notes on-screen will become fairly common later in the decade. It isn't likely that the keyboard will be replaced; rather, this additional device will add another method of communicating with your Macintosh.

CHAPTER TWENTY-FOUR

Choosing a Display

I n the early days of the Macintosh, users were given no choice in the matter of displays; the Macintosh came with an internal, 9-inch black-and-white monitor. No other option was offered.

Today purchasers of many Macintosh models can choose between a wide variety of displays, depending on need and taste. Apple offers several different monitors to choose from, ranging from 12-inch monochrome to 21-inch diagonal full color displays.

While compact Macintoshes and PowerBooks still have built-in displays, more of these units also can be used with external monitors.

Understanding How Monitors Work

Monitors are essentially the same as televisions in the way they are put together. Monitors lack the tuner, however, that enables the television to pull in broadcast signals.

Generally, monitors include an electron gun device that streams electrons at a phosphor coating on-screen. When this coating, which is sensitive to the energy projected onto it, is charged, it emits light. The stream of electrons strike the phosphor in specific places called *pixels,* which are essentially dots. Only one dot is illuminated at one time. The gun sweeps across the screen, drawing a line, and moving from top to bottom. Televisions go through this sweep of the entire screen about thirty times each second. For computer monitors, the rate may be higher in order to produce a better display with less flicker.

The term *resolution* refers to how clear the image appears on-screen; the higher the resolution, the crisper the image. The resolution of an image on-screen depends on two things: the number of pixels and horizontal scan rate.

First, resolution depends on the number of pixels, or picture elements, which are measured both horizontally and vertically. The Apple 21-inch display has 1152 pixels by 870 pixels for a total of 1,002,240 pixels. That number of picture elements can produce a very high-quality picture. The shape of the pixels also can have an effect on how an image appears. Pixels can appear as round or square elements. Square pixels produce sharper images because they fill the screen more completely than round pixels.

The density of the pixels is expressed as dots per inch (dpi), the same measurement as printer resolution. The standard Macintosh resolution has long been 72dpi, but recent displays have higher resolutions. The new Color Classic has a 76dpi display, for example.

Resolution also depends on the frequency with which horizontal lines are drawn across the face of the screen (as described previously). This frequency is called the *horizontal scan rate*. A television scans at the low rate of about 16 KHz (the standard measure). The medium rate is in the range of 25 to 50 KHz, and the high is more than 50 KHz. The faster the scan rate and the more pixels on-screen, the better the image on-screen.

The refresh rate of a monitor also is an important characteristic. This rate is the speed at which the screen can bring its light level up to full capacity. Flickering often is the result of a slow refresh rate because the human eye is sharp and notices even the most subtle change in the energy level. For a clear image, you need a refresh rate of at least 60 hertz (Hz) (or times) per second.

Perhaps the most obvious problem for people who sit in front of monitors for long periods of time is eye strain, which often is attributed to the glare generated from light sources. Although you can buy an antiglare screen to place on your monitor, several monitors come with an antiglare coating, and more are being designed with flat-picture screens that reduce glare and increase resolution.

Understanding Displays

The original Mac monitor was 4 1/2 by 7 inches with a diagonal measurement of about 9 inches. As the hardware requirements of software have become more demanding, new types of monitors have been developed.

Monitors now come in differing sizes. The standard external monitor is usually 12 inches diagonally. Larger displays can be 13, 14, and 16 inches diagonally. The largest Apple displays are 21 inches in size.

You should be familiar with a few terms. A *portrait* display is taller than it is wide, displaying a full page of a document at one time. These may also be called *full-page displays*. The opposite of portrait is *landscape*; it is wider than it is tall. You also will hear of two-page displays, displays that are capable of displaying two pages of a document side by side at actual size.

Black-and-white displays are called *monochrome*. *Mono* means single and *chrome* means color, so monochrome means single-color displays. Current monochrome displays are actually capable of varying shades of gray, however, which could be considered another color if you split hairs. *Grayscale* monitors can display black, white, and shades of gray, but cannot display color.

RGB, a term used for color displays, is a reference to the three primary colors of light: red, green, and blue (though technically these colors are actually magenta, green, and cyan). The name Macintosh 12" RGB Display for the 12-inch diagonal color monitor comes from these colors.

Finally, to make a good decision about a monitor choice, you should know something about color on the Macintosh. The number of colors displayed by any Macintosh computer depends on the amount of memory available for the display. Remember that the number of pixels on the screen of a monitor is quite high. For each of those pixels, a certain amount of memory is required.

For black-and-white displays, the only information needed is whether the pixel is on (white) or off (black). This mode is called black-and-white mode, monochrome mode, or 1-bit mode (the first term is the most common in the Macintosh universe). A byte is a collection of eight bits, so one byte can describe the state of eight pixels. A kilobyte (KB) is 1,024 bytes and thus can describe the state of 8,192 pixels.

The Macintosh 12-inch RGB display uses 512 by 384 pixels—196,608 pixels total. If 8,192 pixels can be described by 1KB of memory, about 24KB (196,608 divided by 8,192) describes the entire image on the screen—not so bad a sum.

Now consider the display of an image in 16 colors. Because of the number system used by computers, 16 different items require 4 bits (one half a byte) to describe. While a black-and-white image requires one bit per pixel, 16 colors (or different shades of gray) require 4 bits per pixel. That same 1KB describe only 2,048 pixels. The same 12-inch RGB display then requires 196,608 divided by 2,048 or 96K—four times as much memory.

To display 256 colors requires 8 bits per pixel. On the same monitor, you are now using about 192KB of memory. 32,786 colors requires 16 bits or 384KB and, finally, 16 million colors requires 24 bits or 576KB—in reality, 24-bit color uses 32 bits of information for each pixel (although this extra 4-bit alpha channel is not currently utilized by the Macintosh System Software), so the memory use is more like 768KB.

On a 12-inch display, you only use up to about a megabyte of memory—not a bad cost in memory for the benefits of millions of colors. But what happens when you step up to a 13-inch display with 640 by 480 pixels? That's 307,200 pixels or 37.5KB for black and white, 150KB for 16 colors, 300KB for 256 colors, and 1.2MB for 16 million colors. A 21-inch display with 1152 by 870 pixels has 1,002,240 pixels, taking 1MB for black and white! 256 colors would require about 8MB; and 16 million colors, around 32MB of memory.

Therefore, your choice of display has much to do with the video memory (called VRAM) in your Macintosh. A Macintosh IIvx with a maximum VRAM of 1MB isn't capable of driving a 21-inch display at all. (Well, your display may have room for black and white, but why would you spend that much money for black and white?)

Most newer Macintoshes are capable of 8-bit color (256 colors) on displays of up to about 14 inches diagonally. To purchase a larger monitor size or increase the number of colors, you will usually run into an upgrade of some kind (more VRAM or a video card). 8-bit color (or grayscale) is quite pleasing to the eye, so you will probably want a monitor in the 12- to 14-inch range unless you need more color for specific uses.

Choosing a Display

Which kind of monitor do you need? This decision depends on your use of your Macintosh. The average user will be fine with the lower-cost, standard-sized display such as the Macintosh 12" Monochrome or Macintosh 12" RGB Display. These monitors can display about half an average 8.5 by 11 page of a document. They are wide enough to be comfortable and—on most modular Macintoshes—display 256 shades of gray or 256 colors.

Ask yourself a few questions:

- *Do you actually need color?* Color is a wonderful thing, but the more color your monitor delivers, the more expensive your display system is and the slower your Macintosh will perform. Running a 24-bit, 16-million color system is possible with a IIsi, but the screen draws slowly and the Macintosh performs much less quickly. Your best performance speed comes with a black-and-white display.

- *How many colors do you need?* 8-bit color that yields 256 colors or grays at one time is a good average for most current Macintoshes. All newer Macintoshes perform well at this color depth, and you will not sacrifice much performance unless you drive a very large monitor (such as a 21-inch). Unless you need color for graphic art, presentations, or other work that demands thousands or millions of colors, going above 8-bit color may be overkill—pleasant to look at perhaps, but you sacrifice a great deal of memory and speed for a nice display.

- *What size monitor do you need?* A writer or desktop publishing specialist may want to opt for a portrait (full-page) display. These displays enable you to view an entire page of your document at one time. The only drawback is that, unless you are willing to go the extra money (and it can be considerable), you will have to settle for monochrome.

Graphic artists and desktop publishing specialists will be more interested in the larger displays of 14, 16, even 21 inches in size. The latter, largest size, is capable of displaying two pages of a document side by side.

Remember that as the display size increases, however, memory requirements increase. The more colors you need and the larger your monitor, the more likely that you will need additional VRAM or a display card.

■ *Will you need a display card or VRAM upgrade?* Your dealer can tell you this, or you can consider the technical specifications of your Macintosh (or the Macintosh you are considering purchasing). Read Appendix B, "System Specifications," and Chapter 22, "Reviewing Macintosh Models," for more information on the color capabilities of the Macintosh.

Considering Apple Monitors

Apple currently offers several different monitors. All are worthy of consideration for your Macintosh whether you are making a new purchase or upgrading.

The Macintosh 12" Monochrome Display shows up to 256 shades of grays on most Macintosh computers (although the LC and LC II need a total of 512KB of VRAM for this amount). The monitor is of good quality, but color monitors have come down in price, making this one less attractive.

The Apple Macintosh Portrait Display is a full-page display that displays 256 shades of gray on most Macintosh computers. (The LC, LC II, and IIvx cannot use this display without a video card, and the Quadra 700 needs at least one VRAM upgrade of 512KB to display more than 16 grays.)

The Macintosh 12-inch RGB display is a solid display that the average user will most likely want. Nearly all Macintoshes that use separate monitors can display at least 8-bit color (256 colors) on this display. The LC and LC II display up to 16-bit color (32,768 colors) with their full VRAM capacity. The Quadra 900 and 950 display 24-bit color (16 million colors) with their built-in videos. Even the PowerBook 160, 180, Duo 210, and Duo 230 deliver 256 colors on this monitor with built-in video (although the Duos do require a docking unit).

The AppleColor High Resolution RGB Monitor is 13 inches diagonally. Again, nearly all recent Macintoshes can drive this display with 256 colors, although the LC and LC II require their full VRAM capacity to deliver more than 16 colors. The Quadra 900 drops to 256 colors without a display card and the Quadra 950 falls to 16-bit color (32,768 colors) without a display card. The PowerBooks and Duos mentioned still hold at 256 colors.

The Macintosh Color Display is 14 inches diagonally but—interestingly enough—affords no more of a display area than the 13-inch High

Resolution RGB Monitor (both offer 640 by 480 pixels). Comments about the previous display also are true for this one.

When you move up to the Macintosh 16" Color Display, you begin to run into the area of needing display cards. The LC and LC II drop out entirely, unable to handle this display; the LC III can deliver 256 colors, however. The PowerBook 160, 180, Duo 210, and 230 continue to deliver 256 colors. The Quadras begin to fall to 256 colors or 32,768 in the case of the more recent 950 and 800.

Finally, when you reach the Macintosh 21" Color Display, the built-in video of all but the Quadras and Centrises drop out entirely. You simply must have a video card to handle this display on any model but a Quadra or Centris model Macintosh. Even the Centris and Quadras fall to 16 colors on this display, however, without a display card (except the 900 and 950 which hold at 256 colors).

Usually those who need the larger displays such as the 16-inch or 21-inch displays are working with high-powered graphics such as photo-realistic images. These users will probably want to purchase a display card when they purchase their monitors.

Considering Non-Apple Displays

A great number of displays are available for the Macintosh from sources other than Apple. My system, for example, uses a Seiko SII 13-inch diagonal display (with a 12-inch display area). Most Macintoshes can drive this display at 256 colors and produce a quality image.

The diagonal size of a monitor can seem a bit misleading. To achieve the best display, a black border of unused space is left around the display area of any monitor. Hence, a 13-inch diagonal monitor may only yield a 12-inch diagonal display area, as in the case of my monitor. The display area is more accurately expressed in pixels (640 by 480, for example), and you should use these numbers for display area comparison purposes. Consider that the AppleColor High Resolution RGB Monitor and the Macintosh Color Display both yield a 640 by 480 display area.

To get a better idea of the display area size, determine the monitor's resolution. For example, a monitor with 72dpi resolution and a 640 by 480 display area displays an image of about 8.8

inches by 6.7 inches (640 divided by 72 and 480 divided by 72, respectively).

The High Resolution monitor has a higher number of dots per inch. The same 640 by 480 pixel area fits into the 13-inch diagonal screen, but the higher dpi yields a sharper display than the Macintosh Color Display with a lower number of dots per inch.

So many different vendors offer monitors that to even list them all would take another chapter, so this chapter only mentions a few representative monitors—a sampling of what is available. After you have considered the technical side of the monitor choice and whether or not it suits your needs, the bottom line of a monitor choice is this: does it look good? If the answer is yes, you have found your monitor.

Radius has introduced a unique monitor that changes the orientation of the image on-screen when you change the orientation of the monitor. If you roll the Radius pivot on the side and give the monitor a moment to refresh, the image changes. This model gives you both a portrait and landscape display in one monitor.

The 15-inch version of this monitor offers 832 by 624 pixels at 78dpi and a 72Hz refresh rate. The same rules about the color capability of the Macintosh that apply to the Macintosh 16" Color Display apply to this monitor. This monitor is very reasonably priced when you consider the two-in-one feature of being able to rotate the monitor. While the monitor is compatible with the built-in video of many Macintoshes, you may still need a VRAM expansion or video card to fully use this monitor.

NEC offers a 17-inch monitor—the 5FG Color—that offers different display areas. 640 by 480 to 1152 by 870 are offered. The monitor requires a display card; it is noted for not being compatible with the built-in video of the Macintosh. The price of this monitor does not include the video card, but NEC is known for superior monitors. I have been impressed with the display quality of several NEC monitors.

Some less expensive alternatives are available from Sony and Seiko. These monitors are the Sony 13" Color and the Seiko Instruments 14" CM1445. Both offer 640 by 480 pixels. As stated before, I have used a Seiko CM1445 for over a year now with excellent results.

The RealTech series (the private label of Hardware That Fits) offers a very reasonably priced 17-inch color monitor with 640 by 480, 832 by 624, and 1024 by 768 display areas. Of course, your Macintosh may need additional VRAM or a video card for the higher resolution displays, but the 640 by 480 resolution is supported by most Macintosh built-in video at 256 colors (definitely on more current machines). You can add a color card later (but you should discuss this with Hardware That Fits to determine if a color card is offered for your Macintosh). RealTech offers monitors up to 20 inches diagonally at better prices than most vendors, yet they use the very common Trinitron display tube that Sony, Seiko, and even Radius use often.

RealTech also offers a full-page 15-inch Grayscale monitor for about half the price of the 17-inch monitor; this 15-inch model delivers a display area of 640 by 870 and is suitable for Macintosh IIs, Quadras, and Centrises (although a video card may be needed for such machines as the IIsi—which delivers only 16 grays with built-in video—or the IIvx, which cannot use this monitor without a display card).

Choosing a Video Card

If you need more colors or shades of gray than the common 256 that is becoming an Apple standard, or if you wish to use a larger monitor, you will most likely need a video card. Unless you own a Quadra 900 or 950 with full VRAM, you definitely need a video card to use 24-bit color.

One of the less expensive alternatives is the Apple 8•24 card. This card drives 13-inch diagonal screens at 24-bit color (16 million colors) and is intended for the Macintosh II series of computers.

Apple also offers the Macintosh Display Card 8•24GC, which I have been using through the writing of this book. This card is intended for the Macintosh II series of machines and delivers 24-bit color (16 million colors) on monitors up to 14 inches diagonal and 256 colors on 21-inch diagonal screens (the IIsi and IIci can deliver 32,768 colors on monitors of 16 inches diagonal with this card). This card provides some of the fastest QuickDraw acceleration available. Accelerated video cards that deliver a great deal more speed can be quite expensive (some costing as much or more than a Macintosh itself).

SuperMac, known for displays and display cards, also offers 24-bit color at 640 by 480 resolution (same as the Apple card) with the Spectrum series. Radius offers the PrecisionColor series that delivers 8-bit color to 1152 by 882 resolution maximum to 24-bit color on 1024 by 768 resolution maximum, depending on the card you choose. The PrecisionColor series is accelerated, and the 24X is rated as one of the best low-cost accelerated video cards.

Highest ratings have been going to the SuperMac products. The Thunder/24 has received excellent reviews. This card also is one of the most expensive cards. For the graphics professional who needs colors at a good speed, however, this card may be the best bet.

Adding Video to PowerBooks and Compact Macintoshes

The most recent PowerBooks (such as the 160, 165c, 180, and the Duo series) have video output as a standard feature. For the 160, 165c, and 180, you can use an external monitor up to 16 inches diagonal (832 by 624 resolution) at 256 colors (8-bit color). Only the Duo series offers expandable VRAM that will deliver more color.

The Duo series needs at least the Apple-supplied MiniDock to connect to an external monitor. Then you can drive up to 16-inch monitors at 256 colors. With the full Duo Dock system and the optional VRAM expansion, you can use up to a 16-inch diagonal display at 32,768 colors (16-bit color).

Earlier PowerBooks have no provision for external video. Many of the early compact Macintoshes (such as the Classic) also had no provisions for external video. As is common in the Macintosh universe, however, Apple omissions are often opportunities for other companies.

The PowerBook 100, 140, 145, and 170, as well as the Macintosh Plus, Classic, and Classic II, have SCSI ports but no provisions for external video. Other companies have stepped in to provide video for these units through the SCSI ports. A few companies have provided internal video for PowerBooks.

Mirror Technologies offers an internal video system—the PowerVision—for the PowerBooks. You probably should have the card installed by your dealer; the procedure can be complicated. This card has been rated as one of fastest available.

The LifeTime Memory Products Video+ PB140/170 is less expensive, but you should still have a dealer install the card, which will add a bit to the cost.

Both units are for the PowerBook 140, 145, and 170. Both are capable of 8-bit color on screens of up to 13-inch diagonal size. The PowerVision adds the capability to switch between black-and-white, 4-bit (16 colors) color, and the full 8-bit (256 colors) color displays.

SCSI display adaptors connect to the Macintosh. The Lapis PowerBase I is rated as one of the fastest adaptors and works with a variety of monitors of up to 21 inches. This unit only provides black-and-white, however.

Aura Systems offers the ScuzzyView. This unit attaches to the SCSI port and delivers black-and-white as well as 4-bit and 8-bit color at a pixel resolution of 640 by 480. Aura has announced an upgrade to support 8-bit color on resolutions of up to 1,024 by 768 pixels.

The Radius PowerView is another SCSI adaptor at a fairly low price. This unit is rated as slower than the ScuzzyView but also costs less.

Choosing an Overhead Display

If you use your Macintosh in business, in school, or anywhere that presentations are necessary, you will want to display screens overhead. Projection hardware is now well designed, reasonably priced, and relatively easy to use. When you combine these with presentation software, you come away with a powerful set of tools for making impressive displays.

Projection tools work quite simply. They are relatively small screens that are placed on an overhead, rather like a bulky transparency. In addition to output going to the Macintosh screen, output also goes to the flat screen-like display, which often is an LCD—liquid crystal display. The overhead projector shines light through the image, casting it on the overhead screen.

Given the power of so many different types of paint, draw, and graphics software, a slide-show sequence of charts can be seen effectively by everyone in the room. With the price of slides these days, it makes even less sense to have slides made when you can use an overhead.

Many of the projection panels come with remote controls, which enable you to page through screens and control several visual cues. The Kodak Datashow is the Cadillac of overhead-projection devices. This LCD panel provides a clear and precise image.

You must consider many things when you purchase a projection panel, not the least of which is cost. You can expect to pay quite a bit for one panel, but if you or your staff make presentations often, you will find it worthwhile. If the cost of slides is about $10 each (including postage and other expenses), the average-priced panel begins to pay for itself after only 100 or so slides, which is a few large presentations—in some cases only one. You can see where the savings and the convenience come in.

When you shop for a panel projector, keep some of the following terms in mind so that you know what to ask and look for:

- Panel projectors, like monitors, have certain levels of resolution. Most levels are the same as the standard Mac, but others enable you to increase the resolution.

- Panel projectors can get very hot, so look for a fan to help cool things down.

- Make sure that the panel is designed for your computer because different models fit different types of machines.

  On most panels, you can switch between regular and reverse video, making black-on-white appear as white-on-black.

- Some panels enable you to interact with them, controlling the image through mouse movement.

- Where does the panel projector get its power? If it gets power from the Mac, you need to carry one less cord. By the same token, be careful not to overload your Macintosh power supply. If you have a number of expansion cards that are drawing power, one more attachment may push your power supply too much.

- You can choose from super-twist (blue-on-white) or double-twist for your screen display. The double-twist is black-on-white and very clear. The type of screen does not seem to be related to price.

These projection tools can be valuable assets in sharing information, especially for teachers who work with computers to generate class materials or to demonstrate programming or data-analysis techniques. Just for starters, some of the companies successfully marketing these panels are Sharp, Computer Accessories, Kodak, InFocus, and nView. nView had good reviews with features such as eight levels of gray, options for displaying on a monitor and the panel, cable lengths up to 50 feet, continuous cool (low temperature), and black-on-white screens. nView offers several models.

Protecting Your Screen

The phosphor on the inside of your monitor screen is light-sensitive; otherwise, an image could not be projected onto it. If the phosphor is energized for too long, an image can *burn* into the screen coating to give you a permanent *etching*. You have probably seen this in the screens of many automated teller machines where a ghostly image of the welcome message seems to be etched into the screen.

To avoid this problem and incur the least expense, don't leave your monitor running when you are not using your computer. If you are going to be away from your computer but need to leave it on, turn the brightness down. Normal use of your Macintosh does not do much damage to your screen because the image changes frequently. You can see that phosphor burn is not nearly as much of a problem as many would have you believe by taking a look at the average television. Despite the average American viewing some six or more hours of television a day, you don't see many TVs with ghostly images of soap opera stars or Oprah burned into the screen.

You can use a screen saver. A screen saver is a System extension or a control panel that comes into play automatically after a preset amount of inactivity. A great number of screen savers are available, but whether or not they are necessary is debatable. At the same time, they can be the source of System extension conflicts that can have you pulling your hair out as your Macintosh crashes. Even if you encounter no conflicts, you are adding one more bit of overhead that will slow your Macintosh slightly. Each System extension takes CPU time and the more you add, the slower your Macintosh will become (as I—with some dozen extensions—can attest to).

The call is up to you. If your Macintosh is on for extended periods of time (mine is turned on in the morning when I get up and off at night so playing it safe with a screen saver isn't a bad idea), you may wish to purchase a screen saver as some added insurance.

If you are worried about screen burn-in, you can save performance and avoid conflicts by keeping your screen saver simple. Personally, I've usedScreen Eclipse by ALSoft with great success for some time now. Screen Eclipse is part of the ALSoft Power Utilities Bundle which also includes the excellent disk optimizer Disk Express II. Screen Eclipse is quite simple; after a user-defined period of inactivity, it turns the screen's brightness down. Any keystroke or mouse movement restores normal brightness.

Recently, I've rediscovered a screen saver that has been around a while. Moire by John Lim displays some hypnotic moire patterns in ever-changing shapes and colors. This control panel is shareware, and the cost is quite low. Unless the price has gone up recently, the control panel is $10. Check the vendor appendix for the address. If you are concerned with protecting your monitor and want some really hypnotic images to stare at while on the phone, this is a great screen saver and is compact enough to not drag your Macintosh's performance down.

If you wish, you can use one of the more fun screen savers such as After Dark from Berkeley Systems. After Dark has a host of images you can purchase. It has been and continues to be the most popular screen saver with some great images such as the flying toasters and fish that swim across your screen.

Other screen savers are available, and several are discussed in Chapter 19, "Using Utilities."

The Big Mac Recommendation

For the average Macintosh user, a 12- to 13-inch monitor is sufficient. The built-in video of current Macintoshes provides 256 colors on such screens and provide a pleasant display that is easy on the eyes. More than 8-bit color is overkill for the average user and even for the small business users, unless graphics and color are an integral part of their work.

16-bit color provides 32,768 colors and is good for working with multimedia presentations. This level of color provides good matches to NTSC video (the U.S. video standard) with QuickTime movies and presentations (see Chapter 18, "Using Multimedia," for more on these). Presentations—especially animated ones and those using QuickTime movies—will most likely require an accelerated video card or a very fast Macintosh (a Quadra or Centris would be good).

24-bit color is for photo retouching and photo realistic graphics work. 24-bit color requires enormous amounts of memory—especially on larger displays—and processor speed. Users of this level of color are either Quadra or Centris owners or those willing to spend money on a high-speed, accelerated video card such as the Macintosh Display Card 8•24GC or a card at the level of the SuperMac Thunder/24.

Writers and DTP specialists may want to consider full-page displays that enable them to view an entire page at one time. The less expensive versions of these monitors are monochrome, but a good choice for color is the Radius Color Pivot 15".

Intense graphics users, high-level DTP users, and those doing photo retouching require a 21-inch diagonal two-page display. Keep in mind that this kind of system is very expensive, however. You will need an accelerated video card and a color matching system. SuperMac and Radius are both known for full-color systems.

CHAPTER TWENTY-FIVE

Choosing a Printer

S ooner or later, you must decide what type of printer to buy as part of your system. Although you may think that cost is the most important consideration, the purpose for which you intend to use your printer and the amount of printing you will do are more important. (See Chapter 7, "Printing," for more information about different types of printers and how the Macintosh uses them.)

The following list offers some suggestions to help you choose the best printer:

- If you print only short documents in a business or home setting, you really need to look no further than an inexpensive printer, like the StyleWriter II.

- If you print multiple-part forms (such as NCR or carbon), you need an impact dot-matrix printer such as the ImageWriter II.

- To produce high-quality text, choose an inkjet or laser printer.

- To produce high-quality text and graphics, consider a PostScript laser printer. PostScript Level 1 printers are fine for the average user, but for the business or professional user, Level 2 is a must for power and most compatibility.

- If you want color printouts, laser printers that produce color printouts are very expensive for a single user (they range in price between $6,000 and $25,000), but not for large companies that easily spend that much preparing color presentations. Color inkjet printers are a less expensive alternative.

The following sections help you understand the major considerations in selecting and using a printer. The information about using and caring for printers helps you understand the specific type of printer that you have or plan to purchase.

Understanding Printers

There are some terms you will need to be familiar with to understand a discussion of printers. These terms are defined in the glossary found at the end of this book and in Chapter 8, "Using Fonts," but this section will also define them briefly.

dpi—Dots per inch, the number of dots placed on the page per inch of paper. A higher number of dots per inch is better because more dots in each inch of printed image enables the reproduction of finer detail.

resolution—A general term also referring to dots per inch. A printer with higher resolution is able to reproduce finer detail resulting in a sharper image.

ppm—Pages per minute, maximum number of pages printed per minute.

TrueType fonts—Character sets created using the Apple-Microsoft TrueImage page description language. For more on fonts, see Chapter 8, "Using Fonts."

PostScript fonts—Character sets created using the Adobe page description language. For more on fonts, see Chapter 8, "Using Fonts."

PDL—Page Description Language, a programming language or other mathematical method for describing images to a printer.

QuickDraw—The built-in drawing routines used to create images on the Macintosh screen as well as to print images on paper with some printers. (Often these printers are called QuickDraw printers.)

ATM—Adobe Type Manager, a utility that enhances print quality on non-PostScript printers. You must use PostScript fonts with ATM to utilize the print enhancement.

best mode—The highest quality but slowest print setting of Apple's dot-matrix and inkjet printers.

draft mode—The lowest quality but fastest print setting of Apple's dot-matrix and inkjet printers.

Considering Apple Printers

Apple offers a full line of printers, from the venerable ImageWriter II dot-matrix printer to high-quality laser printers. With Apple's recent aggressive pricing, you may not need to go any further than your Apple dealer for the perfect printer.

Considering Apple's Dot-Matrix and Inkjet Printers

The least expensive printers available are dot-matrix and inkjet. But, fortunately, low cost does not necessarily mean low quality. Apple offers you some choices when your printing needs are modest and you do not want to spend a lot of money. Among these choices are the StyleWriter II inkjet printer, the old "workhorse" ImageWriter II dot-matrix printer, and the new Apple Color inkjet printer.

All but a very few printers (which are usually extremely expensive printers the average personal computer and small business user would never purchase) place an image on the page by applying dots of ink. The difference between printers is mainly the method used to apply the dots of ink. Dot-matrix printers place the dots of ink by striking an inked ribbon with rods of metal and pushing the ribbon against the paper. Inkjet printers apply the dots of ink by spraying them through a small nozzle onto the page.

Because of these varying printing methods, inkjet printers are much quieter than dot-matrix. However, dot-matrix printers are still superior if you need to print on multipart forms with carbons. Usually only business users need to worry about multipart forms, and many of them do not need this capability. Hence, the inkjet printer is becoming more popular and is rapidly becoming the standard low cost printer.

StyleWriter II

The StyleWriter II, Apple's inexpensive (around $360) inkjet printer, produces clear, sharp type and graphics with its resolution of 360 dots per inch (see fig. 25.1). The only problem with the printer is that it is relatively slow, at about 1 page per minute (ppm) in best mode and 2 ppm in draft mode.

Fig. 25.1
The StyleWriter II inkjet printer.

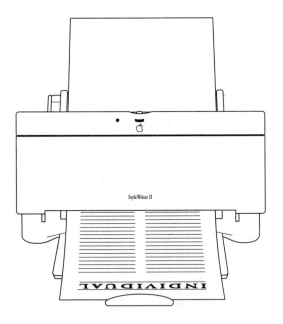

The StyleWriter II comes with Apple's GrayShare software, which improves the printer's handling of shades of grays (generating over 100 shades), and produces some impressive, almost laser-quality print. Additionally, GrayShare works with PrinterShare, which enables other

Macintoshes on the network to share one printer. The printer itself cannot be networked, but it can be accessed over a network if it's connected to a networked Macintosh.

Standard with this QuickDraw printer are 39 scalable TrueType fonts (as with any QuickDraw printer, you can use Adobe's PostScript fonts if you acquire the Adobe Type Manager). The printer's connection is serial, using the printer or modem port of the Macintosh. The multipurpose tray holds 100 sheets of paper or 15 envelopes.

ImageWriter II

The present workhorse of Macintosh printers and by far the most frequently used dot-matrix printer, the ImageWriter II has outlasted all other Apple printer models. After the introduction of the StyleWriter, the ImageWriter II began falling out of favor, but the ImageWriter II is the only Apple alternative for those who need to print multipart forms. The ImageWriter II appears in figure 25.2.

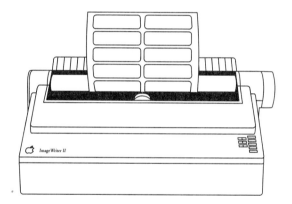

Fig. 25.2
The ImageWriter II dot-matrix printer.

The printer's resolution is 144 dpi—just under half that of a laser printer. The ImageWriter II is rather slow at 1/2 ppm in best mode (2 ppm in draft). TrueType fonts work best, as the printer uses QuickDraw, but you can use PostScript fonts if you have ATM. The interface is serial, or you can network the printer with an optional LocalTalk interface.

The ImageWriter II (and other compatible dot-matrix printers) can produce color output by using a four-color ribbon that produces red, green, blue, yellow, magenta, cyan, and black. To use these ribbons, your software must be able to recognize the presence of a color ribbon and send the appropriate control signals to the printer. Microsoft offers MacPalette II software to utilize the color ribbons and produce color printing on the ImageWriter II. Microspot sells color printer ribbons you can use with the printer.

Apple Color Printer

A better Apple alternative for color is the Apple Color Printer. This 360-dpi resolution inkjet printer runs at 2 ppm maximum (depending on complexity of the document and the processing speed of your Macintosh). This QuickDraw printer has 64 scalable TrueType fonts standard, but you can use it with ATM and PostScript fonts. Apple's GrayShare software comes with the printer to enhance gray scale printing. The interface of the printer is SCSI. A 100-sheet multipurpose paper tray can hold paper up to 11x17 inches. The printer's engine is a four-color Canon bubblejet.

This recently introduced printer is a good, low-cost color printer option that should enjoy considerable success. The only drawback is the same as any inkjet printer: paper can become soaked if you use a great deal of ink. Should you encounter this problem, special, clay-coated paper can help.

Considering Apple's Laser Printers

Laser printers are distinct from dot-matrix and inkjet in that a laser very precisely places the dots of ink on the paper. The ink—usually in powder form called *toner*—is placed with such precision that anywhere from 300 to 600 dots can be fit within a single inch of paper. This resolution results in high quality print once associated solely with professional print shops.

The prices of laser printers continue to drop. Several laser printers are now available for below $1,000, yet these low-cost printers have many features worth recommending. Apple has introduced several laser printers that are worth considering.

LaserWriter Select 300/310

The newest Apple laser printers are the LaserWriter Select 300 and 310. These 5 ppm printers are good choices for the home and home business user. Both these 300 dpi printers produce high quality print.

The Select 300 is the least expensive version—listing at a low $820—and can later be upgraded to the same capabilities as its more advanced cousin, the Select 310. The 300 is a QuickDraw printer. Your Macintosh does the image processing, which can slow you down at times, but this is true of any low-cost laser printer. If you need more speed, you must pay for PostScript. The printer comes with Apple's new built-in FinePrint technology, which improves performance over the older, 300 dpi LaserWriters by smoothing lines and curves.

A 250-sheet paper tray is included, as is background printing, which helps ease the slowness of QuickDraw. GrayShare is included to produce over 90 shades of gray.

If you start with a Select 300, you can add options as you need them. You can add optional paper trays. You can add PhotoGrade for printing high quality photographic images, graphics, and illustrations. You can also add PostScript.

The printer comes standard with 512KB of RAM, but you can upgrade to 1 or 4M for improved performance and speed.

If all the options sound good to you, consider the Select 310, which lists at about $1,080, includes Adobe PostScript Level 2 (and PCL 4+ for IBM PC connections), and has 13 scalable fonts built in. The printer works with any PostScript font as well as any TrueType font. The printer comes with standard 1.5MB of memory; you can upgrade by 1 or 4MB for a total of 5.5MB.

Both printers offer serial connections, but the Select 310 also offers a parallel connection for IBM PC compatibility.

For those who own the 300, an upgrade is offered so that you can convert your printer to the 310 at a later date if your needs increase.

Personal LaserWriter NTR

The Personal LaserWriter NTR printer is older than the Select (or Pro) series of laser printers, but it is still a good personal laser printer choice. The printer offers 300 dpi resolution at a print speed rated at 4 ppm. The printer uses Adobe PostScript Level 2 (and PCL 4+). The standard 64 scalable fonts in TrueType and PostScript format are available, and the printer works with any other TrueType or PostScript fonts. The Personal LaserWriter NTR appears in figure 25.3.

This printer offers several interfaces: LocalTalk (for networking), serial (for individual Macintosh connection), and parallel (for PC connection). All ports are active, meaning that you can connect an IBM PC and a Macintosh to the printer and print from either computer—a great feature for small offices with both kinds of machines.

Fig. 25.3
The Apple Personal
LaserWriter NTR.

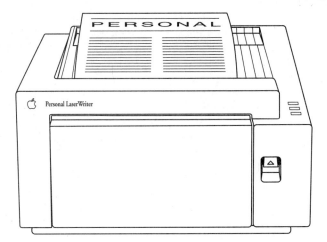

LaserWriter Pro 600/630

As the top-of-the-line Apple laser printers, the LaserWriter Pro 600/630 printers run at 8 ppm maximum and offer up to 600 dpi resolution. Both printers have 100-sheet multipurpose trays and 250-sheet trays standard, as well as 64 fonts in TrueType; all TrueType and PostScript fonts are supported. Both printers use Adobe PostScript Level 2 and PCL 4+.

The LaserWriter Pro 600 offers 300 dpi print resolution with the standard 4MB memory. To take advantage of the 600 dpi resolution this printer can use with this minimum amount of memory, you can easily—and probably should immediately—upgrade the memory to 8MB. PhotoGrade (which enhances 300 dpi printing) is an option that also requires the additional memory.

Both the printers include a LocalTalk interface (for networking), a serial interface (for direct connection to a single Macintosh), and a parallel interface (for IBM PC connection). All ports are active, which, again, is a plus for offices that have both Macintoshes and PCs.

The LaserWriter Pro 630 is essentially the same printer as the 600, but with 8MB and, hence, 600 dpi resolution printing standard. But you also receive both an internal and external SCSI interface for adding hard drives to hold large numbers of downloadable fonts. You also receive EtherTalk for networking.

Consider the LaserWriter Pro 630 if you have major networking and font needs. You cannot add the SCSI interfaces or EtherTalk to the LaserWriter Pro 600 easily—this addition would require an Apple-supplied board change upgrade. The enhanced resolution is easily gained on the less expensive 600 for only the price of a memory upgrade, but because the upgrade to SCSI and EtherTalk is much more expensive, make the 630 your initial purchase if you need or anticipate soon needing these two options. The price difference between the printers is minimal, and upgrading from a 600 to 630 would probably cost more than the price difference in the long run. But if LocalTalk meets your networking needs, and your font needs are not as extensive (meaning the 64 built-in fonts are sufficient or you need only a handful of additional fonts), the 600 with the memory upgrade is the better buy.

You can upgrade either printer to a maximum of 32MB of memory. A 500-sheet paper tray and 75-envelope feeder are offered as options.

Considering Non-Apple Alternatives

You are by no means limited to Apple printers, although Apple's current line of printers offer excellent values. But there are a great number of printers available, and prices continue to drop.

Connecting Parallel Printers

A short lesson in printer technology may help here. Computers communicate with printers and other peripherals through either a *serial* or a *parallel* configuration. In serial connections, information flows in one bit after another, as if in a line. In a parallel connection, the information flows in more than one line with the lines parallel to one another.

Your Macintosh comes with a serial port (the place where you connect the cables), so if you can find the appropriate printer driver (the software responsible for sending information from the computer to the printer), using non-Apple printers probably is feasible. Parallel printing devices are not compatible with the Macintosh without a special serial to parallel convertor.

One company, GDT Softworks, offers a collection of printer drivers that can cover over 850 different printers, including the serial-to-parallel converter. GDT also offers PowerPrint, which Apple recently chose to include in a printer package for the PowerBook series.

The PowerPoint package supports a wide variety of non-Apple dot-matrix, inkjet, and laser printers. If you switch from a PC to a Macintosh and you already have a printer (for example, you may have an Epson dot-matrix you thought you would have to abandon in the switch), consider this product. You can save some money and—with ATM—you can still have high quality printing.

Orange Micro offers the Grappler series of printer interfaces, which enable you to connect your Macintosh to parallel printers, including inkjet and laser printers. These little plastic boxes feature two cables: one for the printer and one for the back of your Mac. The Grappler LX (which I currently use with an Epson LQ-510) uses the LQ ImageWriter driver to print, and produces decent quality print on an older dot-matrix printer.

These alternatives are good for users who have functioning non-Apple printers that they do not want to replace (especially those of us on a strict budget). PowerPrint costs much less than a new printer.

Considering Non-Apple Laser Printers

Apple is not the only company that makes laser printers for the Macintosh. A great number of companies now offer printers that you may find more suitable to your needs.

HardWare That Fits offers one of the current top picks. The RealTech Laser offers Adobe PostScript Level 2 with 300 dpi resolution at as much as 9 ppm speed. 2MB memory is standard with upgrades to as much as 10MB. LocalTalk, serial, and SCSI interfaces are included, as are 35 built-in fonts and PCL 4+ support. Several paper tray options are available.

The GCC series of printers have been extremely popular, and for good reason. These low-cost printers are known for reliability. GCC was first to introduce a laser printer at less than $1,000. The BLP series uses PostScript Level 1 and runs at 4 to 8 ppm speed (the latter speed is the BLP IIS). This printer offers 300 dpi resolution and 17 built-in fonts. All BLP printers have LocalTalk interfaces; the lower-end printers also offer a serial interface and the higher-end printers add SCSI. Memory up-grades are inexpensive; you should probably add them at the time of purchase. The BLP IIS offers edge to edge printing—a feature rare in laser printers.

The Texas Instruments series of printers—the microLasers—have received considerable attention. The microLaser Plus and microLaser Turbo both run at 9 ppm maximum, and print at 300 dpi. Memory is 1.5MB and 2.5MB, respectively; you can upgrade to 4.5MB and 10.5MB, respectively. If you need to do graphics work, add memory at time of purchase. Both the microLaser Plus and the microLaser Turbo offer LocalTalk, parallel, and serial interfaces, support for PCL 4+, and 35 built-in fonts. The main difference between the two printers is that the Plus uses PostScript Level 1, while the Turbo uses PostScript Level 2.

Considering Non-Apple Color Printers

Color printers come in several varieties: inkjet, thermal wax transfer, phase change, and continuous tone. Each in turn is more sophisticated and, hence, more expensive. The level of sophistication you need depends on your printing needs. Home and small business users will want to consider inkjet, the least expensive of the technologies. As discussed in the section "Considering Apple Printers," Apple offers a low cost, good quality inkjet color printer. Other vendors offer these printers as well. Businesses and graphics artists may want to consider the main color printer standard: thermal wax transfer, or, for even higher quality, the phase change or continuous tone printers.

Outside of Apple, one of the best color inkjet printers is the Hewlett-Packard DeskWriter C. This color version of the popular DeskWriter prints 300 dpi resolution on plain paper or transparencies. The print is not photo quality, but it is good for presentation graphics. As with any inkjet printer, you obtain the best results with clay-coated paper because the ink often soaks plain paper.

The Tektronix ColorQuick received good reviews. This printer uses clay-coated paper and prints at 216 dpi on paper up to 11x17 inches. The interface is SCSI.

Seiko, General Parametrics, and Textronix offer thermal wax printers. These printers are the color technology choice of businesses and graphics artists. Print resolution is 300 dpi—equivalent to the average laser printer. These printers require special paper, though some printers can use plain paper at times. (Print quality generally suffers, however.) Transparency printing is a common feature.

The General Parametrics Spectra Star 430 accepts PostScript as well as HPGL, TARGA, and NALPS files. An optional slide printer and internal hard drive are available. The printer's PostScript is a clone, which can be slower and less reliable than actual Adobe PostScript.

Seiko offers the ColorPoint PSX Model 14 and ColorPoint PS. The PSX Model 14 offers the widest variety of printing media, including optional iron-on transfer media. The ColorPoint PS can use plain paper for printing, but the print quality is not as good as with thermal wax printer paper.

The Tektronix Phaser 200 is rated as one of the fastest, uses Adobe PostScript Level 2, and handles transparencies well. The Phaser II PXi is probably the best choice for businesses that need color printing.

The phase change Tektronix Phaser III PXi uses the newer technology for high quality print. With this printer, you receive some of the best paper printouts but lose a bit with transparencies. The printer is considered rather slow, but performance should improve as the printer driver takes better advantage of PostScript Level 2.

Phase change printers are being offered (or soon will be) by Dataproducts and Brother. Information was not available at the time of this writing.

The continuous tone Mitsubishi International CHC-S445 is the most expensive printer mentioned in this book, but it produces images near print shop-quality. The printer offers 24-bit color (millions of possible colors). For those businesses that need the best color printing, this printer would be good, perhaps as part of an in-house print shop. The per page cost of the printer runs about $5, making the printer a business printer without question.

Mitsubishi is introducing the CHC-S446i ColorStream/DS, which will include slots for the PowerPage PostScript clone and different interface options.

RasterOps is introducing a competing product, the CorrectPrint 300, with two EtherNet ports along with LocalTalk and serial ports. GCC is also introducing a continuous tone printer with 10MB of RAM and a built-in hard drive. This printer will offer an upgrade to PostScript interpreting.

Caring for Printers

The adage "An ounce of prevention is worth a pound of cure" is true for your printer. When you are finally ready to print a document that took you hours to prepare, nothing is more aggravating than getting to the Print command and finding that your printer is not functioning.

General Printer Care

The following suggestions should help you avoid unnecessary and expensive trips to the repair people:

- Keep food, liquids, and smoke away from your printer and your entire system. Keep children away from your printer, too, especially when it is operating.

- When you are not using your printer, use a dust cover to keep out the dirt.

- Use the proper weight and type of paper.

- Don't push ribbons or toner cartridges beyond the limits for which they were designed. When a ribbon begins to fray or rip, replace it immediately. When a toner cartridge begins to produce poor print, replace it. If you refill toner cartridges, do not refill them more than about twice; eventually the cartridge mechanism wears out and can damage the printer.

- Clean your printer every week.

- Lubricate the moving parts with light oil (such as sewing machine oil) every six weeks. Lubricate more often if you use your printer every day or for extended periods.

- Use a surge protector.

Surge protectors help avoid damage from the normal peaks and valleys in electricity flow. These changes in voltage can cause data loss and other problems. Surge protectors are relatively cheap (under $50), so get one when you first buy a system—or add one if you haven't already. You should be aware, however, that surge protectors *cannot* protect your computer or printer from direct lightning strikes to power or phone lines.

Lightning has the nasty habit of following the path of least resistance. If it hits your house, the electrical system naturally attracts lightning because the system acts like a huge antenna, carrying the lightning through the wiring into your machine. The *only* way to be safe from lightning damage is to unplug your machine during severe storms. Because lightning also can get into your machine through the telephone wires, disconnect your modem if you have one. Disconnecting your equipment may be bothersome, but it can save you the cost of replacing the expensive motherboard and paying $300 for five hours of labor.

Servicing Your Printer

No matter how well you maintain your printer, the time may come when it breaks down. If your equipment requires service, however, check to see whether your printer is under warranty. If your printer is not under warranty, make a few phone calls and get answers to the following questions before you take it in:

- What are the hourly rates? Even official dealers differ from one another.

- Is there a charge for an estimate, and if so, is the estimate paid as a separate cost or included in the total cost of repair?

- Is a warranty given on the repairs?

- How soon will you get your printer back?

- Can the dealer loan you a printer or rent you one at reasonable cost?

Many independent dealers repair Macintosh products. Although they may have more difficulty getting parts, independent dealers may charge less than official Apple dealers because they don't have a large overhead to pay back to the company they work for. Check your telephone book and ask for information at user groups.

Finally, if you have to mail away your printer for service, use the original cartons you saved, as you were advised at the beginning of this book. Insure your equipment for its full replacement value and get an estimate of the repair costs, if possible.

Caring for Dot-Matrix Printers

This section explains how to keep your ImageWriter (and other dot-matrix printers) running and avoiding breakdowns. To clean your printer, you need the following tools:

- Rubbing alcohol (available at any drugstore)

- A mild solution of dish detergent in warm water

- Cotton swabs

- Clean, lint-free cloths

- A can of compressed air (available at camera stores)

- A vacuum cleaner

CAUTION

When you get ready to clean, disconnect the printer. *Never* work with your printer when it is plugged in. You could damage your printer, or worse, hurt yourself.

Keep your printer and the area around it clean! Dirt is the primary enemy of all machines with moving parts; ignoring this advice accounts for more breakdowns than anything else. Vacuum your work area regularly. Also, consider buying a dust cover; it can dramatically reduce the amount of dust that gets into your printer.

To keep your printer clean, wipe down the outer plastic parts regularly with a soft, lint-free cloth dampened with warm water or a very weak dilution of a mild dish detergent (nothing stronger). Don't use plastic cleaners or solvents of any kind because they sometimes dissolve the plastic. Also, don't wipe off the print head at this point; it must be treated differently.

After you clean the outside of your printer, remove the printer cover and vacuum the inside to pick up all the accumulated bits of paper and dust. If you don't have a vacuum especially designed for computer components, use your home vacuum, but be sure to remove any attachments and hold the end of the vacuum tube with your finger on the edge—always between the tube and your printer—to avoid damaging your printer.

Moving on to the platen, the hard black rubber cylinder the paper turns around as it feeds through the printer, use alcohol on a lint-free cloth and rub the platen gently until you remove all the dirt. Do *not* use water here—water does not effectively clean ink.

Always be careful with the paper you feed through your printer. Although dot-matrix printers can generally handle quite heavy paper, including multiple forms, you can end up with ripped sprocket holes and a mess to clean out of your printer if the paper is too heavy or fed improperly. Paper that is not absorbent also can create a mess. The ink doesn't dry quickly, smears, and gets on the printer, making cleanup even more time-consuming than necessary.

Many dot-matrix printer users who print labels run into this problem: the top row of labels gets pasted onto the platen if you try to roll the labels backward. To avoid this dilemma, advance the sheet of labels so that the first row is beyond the point where it can wrap around the platen. Also, be sure that your labels are fresh. Old labels may not stick to the label sheets as well.

The most important part of your printer is the print head. Dot-matrix printers make an impression on paper when print wires on the print head strike the ribbon. To keep your printer functioning smoothly, check the condition of the ribbon regularly. The constant battering of the print head can cause a weak ribbon to fray, tear, and get caught in your ImageWriter's wheels and gears. If this happens, try using long tweezers to remove the debris, and turn the platen to drag up pieces that may be caught. If you are not successful, you will need to have your printer serviced professionally.

You do not need to clean the print head very often—only when the printed images get smudgy (the o's and 0's will appear filled, for example). To clean the print head, first remove it (check your manual for instructions on removal). Then use lint-free cloths and alcohol. You also can purchase kits for cleaning print heads—this may be a worthwhile investment.

If you re-ink ribbons instead of buying new ones each time they run dry, be careful to use the right amount of ink; otherwise, you will be cleaning more than printing. Carefully follow the instructions provided with the re-inker. Remember that more is not better; you will make a mess of your printer, the print head, and probably yourself as well.

Considering Laser Printer Maintenance

Keeping your laser printer in good working condition can be expensive, but it costs less than expensive repairs. To continue operating, laser printers need regular maintenance, as well as supplies that are a bit more complicated to install than the ribbons required by dot-matrix printers.

The most frequently-used supply is toner. You must replace toner cartridges every 3,000 to 5,000 copies, depending on your printer and the types of printouts you make. When you print graphics with solid areas, your printer uses a great deal more toner than when you print text. If your toner cartridge or refill is rated to last 4,000 copies, don't be surprised if you get only 2,000 copies if your work is graphic-intensive.

To save money on toner, turn your intensity dial to its lightest setting when you replace the toner. Then gradually turn it toward its heaviest setting as you use the toner. In effect, this action regulates the amount of toner you need.

To save money, you can purchase refilled toner cartridges. A remanufactured cartridge costs about half as much as a new cartridge. Many companies that refill toner cartridges claim they refill the originals with 20 percent more toner. If you choose not to refill your cartridges because you want to use only original cartridges, you can often sell your used cartridges to these companies.

If you use such a service, do not refill your cartridges more than about twice. The mechanisms of the cartridges eventually wear out, and a defective one can cause severe trouble with your printer.

When you replace the toner in an Apple laser printer, you also replace the drum (in a single unit). You do not always replace the drum with other laser printers, however. Texas Instruments' printers, for example, separate the toner, cleaning magazine, and drum. Other printers may require you to replace belts and developer regularly.

Because some laser printers are very large and difficult to transport, inquire about an on-site service contract. Many companies sell laser printers that include one year of on-site service. With on-site service, the service technician comes to you; you don't have to take your printer to the repair shop.

Should you purchase a service contract? Printers are amazingly reliable; for the most part, any real problem should show up well before the warranty period expires. The contracts are expensive, but they do offer peace of mind. Business users should seriously consider them—a delay for a broken printer can cost more money than you would save by skipping the service contract.

The Big Mac Recommendation

Without a doubt, the home user should consider one of two printers: the StyleWriter II or the LaserWriter Select 300. Apple definitely changed from the old days when Macintosh folk regularly recommended buying non-Apple peripherals. Today's Apple competes aggressively in the printer market, and has introduced some winning offers. The StyleWriter II is one of the least expensive printers around. To go lower in price, you must settle for a noisy dot-matrix that prints at a much lower resolution.

The StyleWriter II is slow, but the home user probably has little call for a faster, more powerful printer. However, if you do need more speed and higher quality, consider the Select 300 (or even 310). The Select 300 is a rock bottom-priced laser printer suitable for long term papers, graphics, or even that great American novel (provided you are willing to wait a while for the printout). The Select 300 is most likely my own next equipment purchase.

Business and professionals have such a wealth of choices that a single recommendation is not easy to come up with. But the Hardware that Fits RealTech series has a solid reputation for quality and speed (at 9 ppm, the printers are among the fastest). Additionally, I've dealt with the company and found that their customer service is excellent. At the same time, the Apple LaserWriter Pro 600 (with the additional 4MB or more of memory) is a great buy for the office—home or otherwise. 600 dpi resolution is twice as good as the old 300 dpi average, and the 8 ppm speed is excellent.

For low-cost color printing, the HP DeskWriter C and Apple Color Printer receive high marks for both home and office. For higher quality, the Tektronix series has received the best reviews for speed and quality.

CHAPTER TWENTY-SIX

Expanding the Macintosh

N o matter which Macintosh you purchase, eventually you need more—more storage space, more speed, more colors, more capability.

The original Macintosh came only in one configuration and never changed. While this did much to assure compatibility, it also was constraining and much-lamented. Today, so many different configurations and expansions are available for the Macintosh that choosing between them can be confusing.

This chapter will help you understand some of the terms used to describe expansion options and how to match your needs with available expansions.

Choosing Storage Devices

Storage devices range from the familiar hard disks to laser-based CD-ROM, WORM, and magneto-optical drives, as well as analog and digital tape drives. All these devices add storage capacity to your Macintosh but do so in different ways and are used for different purposes.

Understanding Storage Devices

There are three major categories of storage devices in use with computers today: magnetic, optical, and silicon. The first includes the floppy disk, the familiar hard drive, and tape. The second, optical, includes the high-capacity CD-ROM, WORM, and magneto-optical drives. The last, silicon, is a rare storage system and extremely expensive. Essentially, huge amounts of RAM are treated as a disk drive. While this is very fast, it has significant drawbacks such as the high price and the need to maintain power—and quite a bit—at all times to retain the stored information. Silicon is not covered in this book due to its extreme rareness and narrow use.

Understanding SCSI Connections

When purchasing any storage device, don't forget to check the length and configuration of the supplied SCSI cable and whether a cable is even included (some manufacturers do not include one). SCSI cables are not cheap. Having to purchase an additional one after discovering that the one included does not work is not only a nuisance but also can be expensive.

SCSI is an interface defined originally for 50 pins. That is, the plugs and cables have 50 connectors. Apple reduced this to 25 on most Macintoshes and to a smaller, square connection on PowerBooks and on some LaserWriters. There are now three different kinds of SCSI ports that you may have to deal with—not including the PowerBook Duos, which require a docking unit.

PowerBooks usually come with a cable that connects to their SCSI ports and provides a 50-pin connection at the other end. Duos require a docking unit to connect to peripherals.

If you are adding a SCSI peripheral for the first time, you will need a 25-pin connector to fit the back of your Macintosh unless you have a PowerBook. Determine the number of pins on the disk drive—does it use 25 or 50? It will most likely use a 50-pin SCSI port and include a 25-pin to 50-pin SCSI cable. Some use 25-pin ports, however, and include a 25-pin to 25-pin cable.

Most manufacturers who do include a cable assume you are connecting their drive first in your SCSI chain. If you are actually placing the drive second, third, or later in the chain, you may find yourself with a cable that will not work.

When you order any drive, be clear about which Macintosh you own and where you need to attach the drive. Ask if a cable is included and how many pins it has on each end. You may need to order a cable with the drive or specify which cable you need.

Choosing a Hard Drive

The hard drive is the storage system of choice at the present time. Hard drives are magnetic media, using magnetism to store information on a spinning disk coated with a material with a special type of metal suspension. Hard drives magnetize the coating in patterns of ones and zeros to record information.

Hard disk drives can be internal or external. If you want an internal hard disk installed in your Macintosh, you should see your dealer. Trying to install a hard disk drive yourself voids your Apple warranty and is not an easy procedure.

You can easily add an external hard disk drive by plugging one into the SCSI port behind your Macintosh. Although external drives appear to be more expensive than internal drives, this route does not entail installation costs.

The following sections deal with several features you must consider when choosing a hard disk drive.

Capacity

Hard-disk capacity ranges from as little as 20 megabytes (MB) to as much as 1 gigabyte (G) or 1 billion bytes. The amount you choose depends on your needs. Most users today find an 80MB drive to be the minimum they can comfortably live with. 100 and 120MB drives are a good starting size for many users today.

If you add a second hard disk, consider how quickly you filled the first. A second drive probably should have as much capacity, if not more, than the first internal drive. The 100MB and up drives are worth consideration.

Although hard disk capacity is advertised in round numbers, such as 40MB, no disk gives you full capacity. Formatting and invisible maintenance files require disk space. Determine how much the disk actually delivers when formatted. Many magazine reviews tell you actual capacity after formatting.

SCSI Termination and ID Selection

SCSI stands for Small Computer System Interface, a standard, high-speed method used to connect devices to microcomputers like the Macintosh. SCSI is now the dominant system used to connect hard drives and many peripherals to the Macintosh computer.

When you add SCSI devices to your Macintosh, you must deal with termination. Termination reduces the occurrence of electrical noise in SCSI connections. A SCSI chain generally must be terminated at the beginning and at the end. You may need to switch the termination of your hard drive, so you should determine how easily you can change the termination of the hard drive you are considering purchasing. Hard drives that use a plug or switch to change termination are easy to change. Internal termination is a problem that often can require you to open the drive case and move jumpers or make some other adjustment.

Each SCSI device must have a unique number. Using an external switch such as a thumb or rotary switch to set the number is the most convenient method. DIP (Dual In-line Package) switches can be inconvenient but are preferred to drives using software to set numbers.

Seek Time

Seek time is the amount of time the disk uses to locate a requested item of data. If you see 20ms (milliseconds), for example, this figure indicates that the drive requires 20 milliseconds (thousandths of a second) to locate information. The lower the number, the faster the disk drive. Seek times now range from the lower teens to as much as 50ms. The 10 to 30ms range is average.

The faster a drive is, the more the drive costs. You must decide whether the speed is worth the money. Generally, you should not go above about 20 to 30ms.

Other Considerations

You also should consider the length of the warranty offered, whether the company offers telephone support and data recovery in case of problems, and whether the drive will fit on your desk.

Many drives come with software of various types. Check to see whether the drive comes with software for backing up data. Ask whether any utilities are offered.

A front panel in-use indicator is a plus on any drive. This *LED* (light emitting diode) light flashes as the drive is accessed. Many times I've wondered whether my Macintosh has crashed or is just performing a long drive access. Unfortunately, Apple does not put an indicator on the front of the Macintosh for the internal drive.

Choosing an Optical Drive

Optical drives use a laser to read and write data. They use essentially the same kind of disk used in audio CD players; CD-ROMs use exactly the same kind of disk.

Optical drives have the same basic considerations as hard drives. Seek time is the amount of time needed to find data. This is specified in ms (milliseconds) but is generally higher than hard drives. (CD-ROMs are in the 300-360ms seek time range right now—ten times the amount of time an average hard drive needs.) The lower the number, the better. As with hard drives, however, the lower the number, the higher the price.

Choosing a CD-ROM Drive

CD-ROMs cannot store information but can give you access to a large number of fonts, graphics, and other information. Whole encyclopedias are available now on CD-ROM.

CD-ROM drives are much slower than a typical hard disk. To run, they also require special software, which usually comes with the disk drive. You may want to consult magazines and other users to see whether the software is easy to use.

Although the prices of these drives continue to fall, many of the disks themselves are expensive. Besides pricing the drive, you should check the prices of the disks you are interested in before you purchase a CD-ROM drive. Lately, the prices of disks also are falling. You can purchase a great number of disks for prices below $50 each—much better than the days of $300 or so disks (although many disks with the high prices are still around).

CD-ROM drives pose an additional consideration—transfer speed. Most hard drives have very high transfer times, many exceeding the ability of the Macintosh itself, and few users need to concern themselves with hard drive transfer speed.

With CD-ROMs, however, the transfer speeds are relatively slow and are a major consideration. The less expensive CD-ROMs generally transfer information to the Macintosh at about 150KB per second. The newer, higher priced CD-ROMs (such as the AppleCD 300) can transfer information twice as fast at about 300KB per second.

The faster the transfer rate, the better. CD-ROMs are quite slow so the more speed, the better off you are. 150KB can be almost intolerable. You should try to purchase a 300KB drive.

The CD-ROM examples of this book were explored with an AppleCD 300 drive. This drive is a worthy consideration, having the 300KB transfer rate, a front panel headphone jack for listening to audio CDs, and including the software needed to access CD-ROMs. My only complaint is that the drive is rather large—just over a foot long, although it is less than 2 inches deep and 7 inches wide. With audio CD players being so compact, I was hoping for a smaller size for a CD-ROM drive. The size has not proven to be a problem, however. You may still want to check the size of the drive when considering a purchase and think about your desk space.

Something you may want to consider when you purchase a CD-ROM drive are amplified speakers that are sold separately. Several sets are available specifically for use around the Macintosh—shielding the computer from the magnets of the speakers. Having this option can be pleasant because you then can play audio CDs as you work—if the CD-ROM drive is not in use.

You also can hook many CD-ROM drives to a stereo system or other pre-amp system through RCA jacks. You may want to check to see if these line-level RCA connections are on the CD-ROM drive you are considering.

Choosing a WORM Drive

The Write Once Read Many (WORM) drive enables you to write only once to any part of the disk. Because a laser burns tiny holes of data into the disk, information can be deleted but never truly erased. When a disk is full, you must use another disk.

Because you cannot erase the disks, these drives are best for archiving and backup. They offer high capacity and can store enormous amounts of information—in the range of 600MB per disk.

Average users will most likely not be interested in such a drive, but businesses that must keep long-term archives of large amounts of data may be.

Note that the WORM drive appears to be on the way out as the magneto-optical erasable drives fall in price. If a WORM drive sounds like it will fit your needs, you should consider a magneto-optical drive before purchasing a WORM drive. The additional ability to erase and reuse the disks may be worth the extra price (although the difference in prices is not much now).

Choosing a Magneto-Optical Drive

These extremely high-capacity drives offer the capability to erase and store information. The storage capacity is enormous. 3.5 inch drives can store over 100MB per disk. 5.25 inch drives can store as much as 600MB per disk.

Magneto-optical drives are falling in price, increasing in reliability and speed, and hinting of the day when they will threaten the standard magnetic hard drive. Pinnacle Micro began advertising the optical hard drive in about mid-1992. With a 19ms effective seek time and a high transfer rate, the PMO-650 may be a precursor of times to come when the magnetic drive is replaced.

Magneto-optical drives are still expensive—from $1,600 to $2,500 for 3.5-inch drives—but have reached a price range now to be cost effective for use in situations where you must store and transport large amounts of data. A small, 10-disk box will enable you to carry 14MB of data on floppy disks but in excess of 1,000MB if the disks are optical. A typical disk storage box that has 60 floppies contains, at the most, 84MB of data, but one with optical disks holds over 7,000MB of data—all in a space of less than a square foot and only 4 inches high.

Businesses that need to store data over the long term would do well to purchase magneto-optical drives. The media is rated as having a storage life in decades (usually rated at 30+ years as opposed to the magnetic's storage life of 5+ years) and is impervious to magnetic fields (you could stick an optical disk to your refrigerator with a magnet and never disturb the data).

In addition, media costs are comparable to removable magnetic (around $75), but the higher capacity makes the cost lower in terms of cost per megabyte.

A couple of drives to consider are the Optima Technology DisKovery 128MO at around $2,000, the PLI Infinity Optical 3.5" Drive at about $1,700, and the Procom Technology MEOD 128 at about $1,600. All three are based on Sony mechanisms and are highly rated.

Choosing a Tape Drive

Tape drives come in two varieties: analog and digital. Both are used to back up large disk drives. The difference is that the newer digital tape drives have much greater storage capacity and reliability.

The older analog tape drives can usually store about 150MB or so, which is fine for backing up smaller drives. They also are less expensive. The PowerUser Pr 160MB tape drive (with backup software) is around $800, for example. Cartridges are about $25 each.

Digital tape drives (DAT—Digital Audio Tape) are higher priced but have very high storage capacities and are more reliable. The APS Archive Python runs about $1,500, for example, but can store about 1,300MB or 2,000MB (depending on the tape purchased) on each tape. The same storage can be had with the PCPC DATStream for about $2,200, the Relax 1.2 Gig Tape Vista at about $1,500, and others. Manufacturers such as Tecmar (known for the earlier analog tape drives), Procom, PLI, FWB, Irwin, and a great many others offer DAT tape drives.

Businesses and professionals should be the groups most interested in purchasing tape drives to back up large hard drives and networks. The best approach is to buy a DAT drive—if you can afford one of these drives—because of the greater storage capacity and reliability.

One consideration, however, is that tape drives cost about what magneto-optical drives do. Magneto-optical drives also are good choices for data backup and can serve in other capacities. You may want to consider one of these drives rather than a tape drive. For backing up networks, however, DAT tape is probably the best bet. The compact tapes can store huge amounts of data and perform well for network backup.

Choosing Expansion Cards

Cards are available for increasing the power and speed of almost any Macintosh. The least expensive and most popular expansion is the memory upgrade. You can add memory for relatively little money and thereby increase your Macintosh's power and speed.

Other enhancements are available. Users who want to have more color capability can add display cards (see Chapter 24 "Choosing a Monitor," for more on color cards). Those who need more processing power and speed can add accelerator cards. Cache cards—cards that speed the processor's access of memory—can enhance the Macintosh for a less expensive investment than a full accelerator card.

Users who need more number-crunching power can add coprocessors in many cases. These chips take over the numeric calculations from the main processor and increase the speed of spreadsheets and other number-processing software.

A great many cards exist that you can add to many different kinds of Macintosh models. This chapter only surveys the main types of upgrades, the most popular and widely available ones. Before jumping in to purchase an expansion card of any kind, however, you need to understand that not all cards can be used with all Macintoshes.

Understanding Expansion Cards

Expansion cards come in three main varieties: SIMMs, NuBus, and PDS. All Macintoshes since the Plus accept SIMMs for memory expansion. Usually only the desktop models accept NuBus cards and some—like the IIsi—can only accept NuBus cards with a special adaptor. Many Macintoshes such as the IIsi, the LC series, the newer Classics (II and Color), accept PDS cards.

Understanding Memory Cards

SIMM stands for Single In-line Memory Module. These small cards contain memory chips and can be added to any Macintosh from the Plus up to increase memory capacity.

You should understand a few things about SIMMs before ordering them. First, SIMMs are used differently in different Macintoshes. A single SIMM usually provides memory with a width of eight bits—a byte. Because the Macintosh has a memory bus width of 16 or 32 bits, depending on the model, SIMMs generally have to be installed in pairs or in sets of fours.

To use the IIsi as an example, this Macintosh has a 32-bit wide memory bus. You must install SIMMs in groups of fours (8 times 4, yielding 32). You can check with your dealer, mail order company, or Apple manuals to determine how many SIMMs you must install at one time. Generally, you do not have to get too technical. Most mail order companies and dealers can tell you the number of SIMMs you need when you tell them the Macintosh model you own. To determine the maximum memory you can upgrade to, check Appendix B, "System Specifications."

Another consideration you should keep in mind is the speed of SIMMs. SIMM speed is measured in nanoseconds (ns—billionths of a second). Most Macintoshes—up to the Quadra 950—accept SIMMs of 80ns or less (less is faster). Macintoshes of less speed can use SIMMs of a higher (thus slower) rating, but the 80ns SIMM is the most commonly available now and can be moved between most Macintosh models should you purchase a newer model to replace your current one. Hence, purchasing 80ns SIMMs makes the most sense. You can find cheaper, slower SIMMs if you want to by purchasing the speed that your model accepts (see Appendix B, "System Specifications"). If you should move to a faster Macintosh later, however, you cannot move the SIMMs with you.

Some exceptions to all of this are the newer Centris models and the Quadra 800. These newer models use the 72-pin SIMMs common in the IBM PC world. These SIMMs can be added one at a time rather than in sets. They cannot be used with earlier Macintosh models.

PowerBooks are exceptions, too. PowerBooks accept memory cards that have the memory chips on them rather than the usual SIMMs.

Fortunately, dealers and mail order companies are used to all of this and offer memory upgrades, specifying Macintoshes they are intended for. You can look at the MacWarehouse catalog, for example, and find a chart that details all current Macintosh models, how much memory they can accept, which SIMMs you need to order, and how many you must install at one time.

Understanding NuBus

Apple chose the NuBus standard when the company began to move to an "open architecture," that is one that accepted expansion cards rather than one that was closed and could not be expanded or upgraded (except with periodic Apple upgrades).

NuBus is a high speed, automatic configuring, bus standard. NuBus is offered in many of Apple's desktop Macintoshes and tower Macintoshes.

Your main considerations in choosing a NuBus card are the power consumption of the card, the size of the card, and the number of NuBus slots you have available. Remember to consider future expansion. If you have a Macintosh with only one NuBus slot, you will be limiting your future expansion options by using that one slot.

Again, dealers and mail order companies can assist you in determining if a NuBus card will work in your Macintosh. Be sure to mention the model of your Macintosh when ordering or pricing a NuBus card.

Understanding PDS

The PDS (Processor Direct Slot) is common on Macintosh models. Even the LC has a PDS slot. Many desktop models that have NuBus slots also include a PDS slot that can be used for an accelerator card. PDS is a faster slot because the cards that plug into this kind of slot have faster access to the microprocessor of your Macintosh.

Some Macintosh models (the IIsi, for example) can use an adaptor to use a NuBus card. You will be giving up future expansion, however, by using your single expansion slot. Consider this carefully when choosing any PDS card.

A few companies (such as Daystar Digital) offer adaptors that enable you to use more than one PDS card in a single slot Macintosh. With these adaptors, however, you will run into possible problems with power consumption, space, and heat. Putting two cards where only one was intended may overload your Macintosh.

Whenever you consider a PDS card (as with NuBus cards), you should ask questions about the power consumption of the card and its size. Make certain to keep your dealer or mail order company aware of which Macintosh model you have and your current configuration. Ask about the size of the card, whether its power consumption is within the limits of your Macintosh model, and whether the card will be cool enough to operate once it is installed.

Choosing an Accelerator Card

Accelerator cards are available for almost all Macintosh models. The cards come in both PDS and NuBus forms, although PDS is probably more common. You can increase the speed of your Macintosh up to Quadra levels with the correct card.

Accelerator cards have different approaches to deliver more speed. The two main approaches are to use a 68030 chip at a high speed to accelerate the Macintosh. This approach can deliver near Quadra speeds but maintain compatibility with most software.

The other approach is to use a 68040 at varying speeds. The 68040 is a much faster chip than the 68030 and earlier chips and so delivers more speed and power. The drawbacks to these cards are that some software is not compatible with the newer chip (although this is much less of a problem than it has been before) and that these cards are more expensive than the 68030 cards. A 68040 card can deliver Centris or Quadra speed and power, however, for much less than purchasing one of these models.

If a Centris or Quadra seems to be the machine you would need, consider an accelerator card first. You may be able to attain the speed and power you need for much less than purchasing a new machine.

Beware of one potential problem, however. Your current memory (the SIMMs) in your Macintosh may not be fast enough to enable you to fully take advantage of your new speed. You may need to replace your SIMMs with faster ones (moving up to the 80ns range). This is usually only a consideration for owners of older Macintoshes.

DayStar Digital offers a line of accelerator cards that are highly rated and deliver a tremendous amount of power. The PowerCache Accelerators come in 33HMz, 40MHz, and 50MHz speeds, range in price from $380 to $720, and use a 68030 chip. Compare these speeds to that of your Macintosh model in Appendix B, "System Specifications." You will see that you can speed your Macintosh tremendously while maintaining compatibility with almost all software and hardware. (Because the 68030 is the most common Macintosh chip now, manufacturers are making certain that their products are compatible with this chip, making it a safe choice in acceleration.)

If you want to go to Quadra level speed and power, you can consider DayStar's Turbo 040 series. These cards have speeds ranging from 25MHz to as high as 40MHz with an optional RAM cache for even greater speed. For Quadra 700/900 performance, for example, you can purchase the 33MHz Turbo 040 for about $1,350. Adding the cache to the card speeds your Macintosh past the Quadra 950 for approximately $340.

DayStar offers more cards for more Macintosh models than just about any other card manufacturer. They have cards for almost any model that has a PDS. The PowerCache series, for example, covers the Macintosh LC, LC II, SE/30, II, IIx, IIcx, IIsi, and IIci. The Turbo 040 can be purchased for the IIci, IIsi, IIvi, IIvx, Performa 600, II, IIx, IIcx, and SE/30.

Other cards to consider are the highly rated TokaMac series from Fusion data for the IIci, IIsi, and LC. These range in price from about $1,000 to about $1,300. Radius sells the Rocket series for NuBus Macintoshes and Applied Engineering has the Transwarp series that can add speed and power to older models such as the SE, LC, and others.

Accelerator cards are an option you should consider before purchasing a replacement Macintosh. Many times you can attain the power and speed you need for a fraction of the cost of a new Macintosh.

Choosing a Math Coprocessor

Many Macintoshes accept a math coprocessor, FPU (Floating Point Unit), to speed numeric calculations. Macintoshes that can accept coprocessors are generally 68030 or 68020 models. Apple does not always provide ways to directly add the chip, but many manufacturers offer options to add the chip, usually as part of an accelerator card. IIsi owners who have now been "orphaned" by Apple will be interested in this option as they can add coprocessors to their machine without replacing it (Apple's only "upgrade" path for the IIsi is to buy a new machine). Companies such as DayStar digital offer PDS cards that have a math coprocessor on the card and still yield a PDS slot for additional cards.

If you use numbers heavily, you may want to consider adding a math coprocessor if you do not already have one in your Macintosh. Check Appendix B, "System Specifications," to see if your Macintosh already includes the FPU. If it does and you still need more speed, you will want to look at an accelerator card. If your Macintosh does not have an FPU, however, you might want to consider adding one.

Adding an Apple II Card to an LC Series Macintosh

Apple offers a card for the LC series of machines that enables them to run Apple II software. Educators will be most interested in this card in that most educational software was written for the Apple II. When you add the Apple II card to the LC series Macintosh, you have an Apple II right in your Macintosh. Educators with large collections of the Apple II software can use their software on the Macintosh and also can purchase newer, Macintosh-based packages.

The Big Mac Recommendation

The main recommendation of this chapter is for those who are considering replacing their Macintosh. Stop a moment and consider expansion cards and other expansion options. Although Apple may have replaced your Macintosh with another model, your Macintosh may still have years of life left in it and may be able to attain the power and speeds of newer models for a fraction of the newer model's cost.

Your most cost-effective expansion is a memory upgrade. Almost any Macintosh can accept a memory upgrade that will yield a large amount of memory capacity for relatively little money. Many smaller machines (such as the LC series) can be upgraded to their maximum capacity, ranging around 10 to 12MB for around $400. (See Appendix B, "System Specifications," for more on maximum memory capacity.) Reaching lower levels—such as 6MB on an LC or LC II—can be done for half that or less, depending on the model.

In any case, before rushing out and buying a new Macintosh, consider expansion cards. Read the magazine reviews such as *MacUser*'s,

MacWeek's, and *MacWorld*'s, and call a few expansion-card companies for more information.

Recently, I've been debating about replacing my IIsi with a Centris, but now I find that I can most likely surpass the Centris in speed with the new DayStar 40MHz Turbo 040 card for less money and maybe even have some money left over to buy one of Apple's new low cost Laser-Writers. Expansion sometimes makes more sense than replacement.

CHAPTER TWENTY-SEVEN

Adding Accessories

There are many accessories available to protect your Macintosh and make working with the computer more pleasant and productive. Because so many of these accessories exist, listing them all is almost impossible, but this chapter discusses several of the major options.

Power Line Protectors

One of the most important accessories is not truly an accessory, but a necessity. This is the surge protector that prevents voltage spikes from damaging your Macintosh. Although these devices cannot protect your Macintosh from direct lightning strikes on the power lines, they can protect against the common, erratic power surges from utility companies. During a thunderstorm, your best protection is to unplug the Macintosh, because lightning strikes can damage a computer that is off but still plugged in.

Surge protectors come in a variety of configurations. You find them most often in a power strip configuration with multiple outlets; six outlets is the average. Be careful not to be confused by the ordinary power strip, which is only a set of outlets and offers no protection.

You may want to look for Underwriters Laboratory certification. UL tests electrical devices to determine their safety, and a UL certification means that the device has passed several rigorous tests. UL testing is a voluntary matter, however. Not all companies participate. Companies without such certification may actually do more stringent testing of their own.

The most important standard to check on the surge protector is the *clamping voltage*, the voltage at which the protector starts to resist the increase in voltage. The Curtis line of surge protectors, for example, has a clamping voltage of 400 volts or less. Voltage of over 400 is not permitted to reach your computer. (Even if the surge protector ends up being damaged, your computer is protected.) The reaction time of surge protectors also is important but is now commonly in the billionths of seconds for almost all surge protectors.

One feature to look for is EMI and RFI protection. These filters help protect your computer by filtering out electrical noise on the line and delivering a cleaner electrical supply that can extend the life of your computer.

Another essential feature if you have a modem is surge protection for the phone line. This feature enables you to connect the phone line to the surge protector and then connect your modem to the connector, isolating the modem should a voltage spike come across the phone line.

The Curtis Ruby Plus surge protector, for example, offers EMI and RFI filtering and a modem connection. While the price is a bit high (about $70), it is actually minimal compared to the cost of repairing a Macintosh that has been damaged by a voltage spike or replacing a damaged modem.

Kensington offers several high-quality surge protectors in the PowerTree series. I use a PowerTree 20.

If you prefer, you can purchase a "command center" style surge protector. These protectors often give you individual switches for different outlets and enable you to place the command center on your desk so that you can reach the switches more easily. Curtis offers the Command Center with five outlets, full surge protection, and phone line protection. Kensington sells three different units of this type.

One interesting variation on the surge protector/command center is the PowerKey by CE Software. This system gives you four surge-protected outlets that are controlled by a soft switch, much like the power key of the Macintosh II series. The advantage of the soft switch is that the Shut Down command turns off the entire system (up to four items), rather than simply the Macintosh, and adds the Shut Down power off feature to Macintoshes that do not already have it. Your Macintosh can be configured to turn itself on at predetermined times and—with the PowerKey Remote option—can be switched on and off by modem.

One option that you should consider if you experience frequent power drops or low voltage levels (brownouts) is *uninterruptable power supply* (UPS). These units not only filter out damaging surges and line noise, but also provide a short time of backup power should the electricity fail. Kensington offers four such units that provide power from five minutes (time enough to save and shut down) up to an hour. These units are expensive, but losing important data can be much more expensive. Small business users should consider a UPS to safeguard their data.

Carrying Cases

If you need to transport your Macintosh, you may want to use one of many padded carrying cases that are available. Although they cannot protect against strong jolts, they can help reduce the effect of the accidental bump. Most cases also offer pockets in which you can carry disks and other items.

Carrying cases are not just for PowerBook and Portable Macintoshes. You can find cases for all of the compact Macintoshes (the Performa 200, the Classic series, for example) and even some of the larger, desktop machines. Cases are available for transporting the main units of the IIsi, LC series, and other desktop Macintoshes. Transporting a monitor can be difficult and problematic, but you also can purchase cases for Apple standard monitors. You can even find cases for the StyleWriter printer.

MacLuggage offers a whole line of cases from the PowerBooks to the Quadra Macintoshes. Targus offers cases for the PowerBooks, the compact Macintoshes, and Macintosh IIs.

The most important consideration in carrying cases is the protection they offer your computer. You probably should purchase this item from your dealer so that you can see for yourself how well padded the case is. Beyond this important issue, you can consider how much extra space is provided for disks and other items that you may need to carry with your computer.

Dust Covers

Another item that is probably a need rather than an accessory is the dust cover. These very inexpensive covers protect your Macintosh from dust in the air. They are generally nylon and run between $10 to $20 each. Abcom and Basic Needs offer an entire line for different Macintoshes and printers.

Keeping dust out of your Macintosh is an important preventive maintenance step. You should purchase dust covers immediately.

For extra protection in environments where the chance of liquid spills or falling objects is fairly high (a laboratory or school, for example), you can purchase hard covers for keyboards and printers from Basic Needs.

Security Devices

Computers are popular items with thieves, and, with this in mind, Apple has equipped every Macintosh with security slots. You can purchase a security system from Kensington that uses galvanized steel cable for your entire Macintosh system, including the LaserWriter, if you own one.

Kensington also offers PassProof, which locks your floppy disk and back ports to prevent unauthorized use of your computer. PassProof includes a software password system that prevents users from accessing your data when you are away from your desk.

Anti-Glare Filters

Glare screens help to reduce eye strain by reducing the glare of room lights (and sunlight) that falls on your screen. Polaroid offers several polarized filters that fit various Macintosh screens. Kensington also offers various glare filters, as does Curtis.

If you find that light reflecting off your Macintosh screen is distracting you, consider purchasing a glare screen. The distraction is only the beginning of potential eye strain; the relatively inexpensive glare screen is far less expensive than the loss of productivity and the pain (such as headaches) that can come from eye strain.

Diskettes and Disk Files

Disks are a purchase you must make frequently. You need to understand the way disks are labeled. The labeling you will encounter most often is the following:

Label	Meaning	Capacity
MF2HD	double-sided (2), high-density (HD)	1.44MB
MF2DD	double-sided (2), double-density (DD)	800KB
FDHD	floppy disk (FD), high-density (HD)	1.44MB
DSHD	double-sided (DS), high-density (HD)	1.44MB
DSDD	double-sided (DS), double-density (DD)	800KB

Note that many times disks are labeled with capacities higher than noted in the capacity column. Double-sided disks (DD) are often labeled as having a 1MB capacity and high-density (HD) disks as 2MB. In reality, they do have this capacity, but remember that the initialization process takes up some space. Also, disk drives cannot always take advantage of the full capacity of disks. The maximum capacity offered is higher than the Macintosh drives can actually use for two reasons. First, the manufacturer must accommodate several different drive types and therefore sets a maximum high enough to meet many standards. Second, the number is actually rounded to a number that sounds good on the packaging. Regardless, this discrepancy does not really affect you because the Macintosh floppy drive can only use 800KB on DD disks and 1.44MB on HD disks.

The reliability of disks has increased to such a point that few users bother with comparing disks as they once had to do. I have rarely experienced a floppy failure, and I rarely pay attention to brand name on floppy disks now and often purchase the ones on sale at the local discount store. (When places such as K Mart, Wal-Mart, and Target sell disks even in rural East Texas, you know the computer revolution is truly on.) If you are concerned about your data, however, you may want to avoid bargain-basement disks.

If you use a large number of disks, you can find disks in bulk quantities of 50 and 100—which can save you money. Alternatively, if you want to save time, you can buy preformatted disks that are ready to be used and do not have to be initialized. Also, you frequently see disks sold with plastic or cardboard storage cases included. These small, 10-pack cases make good carrying cases for transporting disks.

Disk labels are available from recognized companies such as Avery. You can find labels that can be printed in your laser printer or your dot-matrix printer.

You should definitely consider a disk file for storing your frequently used disks on your desk or shelf. You can find inexpensive cases costing around $10 that hold from 30 to 100 disks and protect them from dust (and possible coffee spills). If you prefer, you can spend a bit more (about $10 to $15 more) and purchase a wood or wood-finish case. Some even have roll tops.

You can find cases for all forms of computer media—from backup tape cartridges to CD-ROMs. All are inexpensive and are good purchases to protect your data and your drives from dust and dirt.

Stands and Bases

To reduce fatigue when you work with your Macintosh for extended periods of time, you can use a monitor stand to raise the screen to eye level. Several different stands are available. Consider MacTilt II from Ergotron, for example, a metal and heavy plastic pedestal that enables you to rotate your Mac horizontally, raises your Mac four inches, and enables you to adjust the tilt as much as 30 degrees. MacTilt holds onto your Mac with some unobtrusive clips and comes in models that support from 12 to 150 pounds. The standard MacTilt sells for about $59, and Ergotron will design one to fit any monitor or compact Macintosh.

Kensington also offers a variety of stands to make your Mac more space-efficient and easier to use. With the Macintosh II stand, for example, you can stand your Mac next to your desk so that the keyboard and the monitor are all that remain on your desk. Some people combine this stand with a wall-mounted monitor stand and keyboard drawers so that their desktop is not cluttered with computer equipment.

Kensington also offers the Keyboard Shelf, which boosts your compact Macintosh by 4.25 inches and gives you a convenient place to put your keyboard when it is not in use. Kensington sells stands for laser printers that have paper storage shelves beneath the printer.

Basic Needs has a strong, metal monitor stand for use with the Macintosh II and Quadra series Macintoshes that boosts your monitor by 5.75 inches and leaves sufficient clearance for ventilation.

Both companies also sell various useful items to go with their stands. Side pockets enable you to store your mouse, pens, and other items. Curtis offers a Keyboard Organizer that goes well with a good stand (they sell these as well) and provides not only wrist rests to enable you to type longer with less strain, but also a place to store paper clips, pens, and disks in use.

Furniture

The most important issue in furniture is comfort. Your choice of desk, chair, and other office items can contribute to your health and comfort or affect them adversely. You should carefully consider your body's most comfortable position and select furniture accordingly.

Your chair should have good back support to help keep your back straight. While a high-quality chair can be expensive, medical costs for back problems are considerably higher.

Some users find the so-called *back chair* to their liking. These odd-looking chairs actually place you in a kneeling position and cause your back to be straight. You may want to consider one of these, but keep in mind again that quality means higher cost. The less-expensive version of these chairs cannot be adjusted and hence may cause more problems than they solve. Some users also complain that these chairs cause their knees to become uncomfortable and even to hurt over long periods of time.

Your body should be relaxed when you are sitting at your desk. The height of the desk should allow your arms to be relaxed as your wrists rest on the surface; your elbows should be approximately at a right angle. A desk that is too low can cause you to hunch over as you work. One that is too high can cause you to strain slightly (keeping your arms up) as you work.

Pay attention to small amounts of strain. As you test a desk-and-chair combination, you may feel that the strain is minor. Over time, however, strain can build up.

Good tables are sturdy, made from thick, dense materials such as wood or high-quality particle board; they can be moved if you need to relocate and are attractive and easy to assemble. That's a fitting description for tables manufactured by Anthro.

Anthro's tables can be configured in a variety of ways. Their tables are made with heavy steel tubing and 1-inch thick laminated surfaces that come in a variety of colors to match your decor. The height of the table and shelves are all adjustable, and the modular nature of the design enables you to add printer tables or shelves that swing out. Mouse surfaces are attached to the top surface, and a variety of other time- and space-saving devices are available. The heavy-duty casters make relocating to another station or room easy. Anthro even includes the screwdriver you need to assemble the tables.

ScanCo is another company that manufactures high-quality, well-designed furniture specifically for the Mac. The MacTable (for about $275 and $300) comes in 48-inch and 60-inch sizes and offers independently adjustable surfaces for tilting your CPU or ImageWriter. The entire work surface tilts as well, making a welcome environment on which to move your mouse or work. A platinum melamine surface and beech trim make the whole line, including printer tables and cabinets, very attractive. The directions for assembly could be better, but still you can put the table together in only 20 minutes. It looks terrific, wears well, and is a real plus for any office.

Although you can use the MacChair (about $275) with any computer, its thoughtful design seems to be in sync with the efforts put in the design of the Mac. The MacChair is form-fitting, ergonomically designed, and, of course, matches the MacTable.

The Big Mac Recommendation

Accessories are largely a matter of taste, so I have made few recommendations. Following are a couple of important ones, however:

■ Purchase a surge protector. The cost of the protector will be paid back the first time a high voltage spike comes down the power lines. Although this may never happen, it is good protection.

■ Purchase your furniture, glare filters, stands, and other accessories with an eye to making your workspace as comfortable as possible. When it comes to spending time at a computer screen, comfort is not a luxury; it's a physical necessity.

Part IV

Advanced Topics

Includes:

28 Networking
29 Using Connectivity Software
30 Using HyperCard
31 Programming the Macintosh
32 Maintenance and Troubleshooting

CHAPTER TWENTY-EIGHT

Networking

T he Macintosh is excellent for individual use. It enhances your power to produce documents, graphics, presentations, spreadsheets, and other work that required a team of people only a couple of decades ago. But if the Macintosh can be a powerful tool in your hands, can't it also be a powerful force in groups such as offices?

The network has been around for quite some time, and users of large mainframe computers are accustomed to the idea of communicating between computers. The network also has been available to Macintosh and PC users for several years. Only in recent years, however, have networks begun to "come into their own," becoming widespread and put to work in even the smallest of offices.

The local area network (LAN) allows computers to share different devices (printers, computers, or hard drives) as well as communicate with each other. The LAN is by no means restricted to Macintoshes, nor to Macintoshes and PCs. Almost any kind of computer can be—and probably is, somewhere—hooked to a network with almost any other computer.

Understanding Network Basics

A *network* is a particular configuration of devices that are connected so that all devices on the network can share information. The components of a network are connected by cables—bundles of wires (or fiber optic) along which a great deal of information can travel efficiently with little interference from outside. The cables are attached with connectors to the various devices (or *nodes*) along a network. Some examples of networks are the following:

- A single computer and one printer
- 500 computers linked to one another
- A series of Macintoshes connected to a shared printer
- A printer and a plotter connected to two Macs

Almost any combination that fits your needs can be adequately addressed on a network. To give you some idea of the importance that the Apple people have placed on the value of communications, the Macintosh is manufactured with a built-in networking capability called AppleTalk. With other personal computers, you must buy the basic software to use a network.

Defining AppleTalk and LocalTalk

For any LAN to work, let alone work properly, a standard system of sharing information must be established (just as two people need to speak to one another in a language that can be understood by both). Apple has set this standard with the introduction and use of AppleTalk, the communications standard for Macintosh computers.

AppleTalk is the name of the protocol. A *protocol* is a set of rules to which all the computers on a network adhere so that information can be transmitted. The network that uses AppleTalk is called a *LocalTalk network*. You see references to LocalTalk connectors and cables, and you use these hardware items to hook up Macintoshes into a network.

LocalTalk is a "plug and play" system that requires nothing more than the correct set of cables and connectors plugged into Mac ports. These connectors are vital in setting up the network across which communications can take place. When you connect a LaserWriter to your Macintosh, the documents that are printed are sent from the computer's memory over a LocalTalk cable to the printer. The same holds true for any transmission of information over a network from one Macintosh computer to any other Macintosh peripheral.

The power of AppleTalk and LocalTalk is that this networking system can support the sharing of software (such as programs everyone needs to access) as well as hardware (perhaps a laser printer). The LocalTalk network consists of a series of cables used to connect different devices. A small box on each cable (a *connector*) ensures that any noise caused through electrical transmissions doesn't get into the data stream.

Although you can use and even set up a Macintosh network without understanding the AppleTalk protocol, understanding the protocol can help you maintain a network. A protocol of some kind is necessary on a network to avoid having all the machines (or at least more than one) transmitting information at one time. A protocol is rather like the *Robert's Rules of Order* for computers.

AppleTalk uses unique numbers (from 0 to 254 for a total of 255 nodes) to identify each machine on the network. AppleTalk defines how the machines address each other and how they recover from collisions. *Collisions* occur when data is being sent between two machines and another machine decides to transmit, causing data to be lost. Collisions most often occur on busy networks and can slow data transmission.

Node numbers are assigned dynamically. Essentially, when your Macintosh is connected to a network, the AppleTalk software built into the machine generates a random network number and checks the numbers of the other machines connected to the network. Finding an unused number, the AppleTalk software takes that number; otherwise, it generates another random number and tries again.

Networks are interesting beasts. Imagine one by visualizing a group of people in a dark room, all trying to communicate. They agree among themselves to take on numbers and address each other with these numbers. Only two people—one a sender, the other a receiver—can transmit a message at any one time. The people further agree that a message must be broken down into small parts—say, 10 words—so that two people cannot dominate the conversation.

Now consider that people can come in and out of the room at any time. When a person enters, he or she immediately begins trying to find out what number to use by asking for an answer from node 0. On hearing an answer, the newcomer discards that number and goes on to 1. In the meantime, other people are trying to send messages.

You can see how complicated communication could get. Node 10 may want to tell node 3 something very important, for example. At the same time, node 12 wants to talk to node 7. Node 10 starts to call out to node 3 at the same time node 12 decides to address node 7. Both must back down and try again. In that brief time, node 4 suddenly wakes up and starts to send a message to node 1, locking out 10 and 12.

A confusing situation. But without the protocol to govern message sending, chaos would result.

Defining Servers

Networking is effective because people can share resources. A distinct advantage of being on a network is being able to set up a variety of *servers*, which are devices available to all (or some) of the people along the network. For example, a file server using AppleShare—Apple's resource server system—performs two critical tasks. First, the file server acts as the storehouse for information that several people can access simultaneously, if necessary. You can establish file servers with separate sections for storage of data for individuals along the network. Second, the file server acts as a manager for the files it stores, helping to keep the disk well organized, sending information where and when it is needed, and performing other tasks that help keep manageable what otherwise would be an unmanageable amount of information on a system.

Because sharing information that is on disk is such an important part of using a network, distinguishing between disk servers and file servers is important.

A *disk server* does just what its name says. The disk server takes a section of a hard disk (containing the information the user needs) and makes that section available to users along the network. These sections usually are organized as *volumes*, which contain files and folders. Utilities (such as Symantec Utilities for the Macintosh) exist to enable you to set up your own hard drive with these volumes, or partitions. Most disk servers are set up with passwords so that not everyone has access to all information. A disk server might provide a section of storage for each of the members of a network with built-in security so that no one other than the authorized user can gain access to the information stored.

A *file server*—one of the most common of all server systems used—can share files and folders rather than share whole sections of disks at a time. You specify the location for a disk server to work, but with a file server, you specify the information itself by the file or folder name. You then can access the information you need, be it an application or a data file.

A popular file server is TOPS (Transcendental Operating System from Sun Microsystems), which allows each node on a network to act as a file server to every other node. This type of server is a *distributed file server*, and it creates a distributed network in which all the nodes are interconnected. TOPS does not require a dedicated Macintosh to act as the hardware side of the file server. Dedicated computers sit there and do only one thing: distribute and store files.

TOPS is popular and used to be the leader of the pack. Recently, however, several other companies, such as ShirtPocket Software (makers of EasyShare) and Everyware (makers of allShare), have entered the race to provide file servers without dedicated computers.

With the introduction of System 7, third-party file servers are scrambling to improve their products over and above the features offered by File Sharing, built into the new System Software. If you have System 7, you can build a small network and share disks and files between Macintoshes without any additional software.

Defining Types of Networks

Networks come in a variety of configurations, or *topologies*, differing basically in the way the different devices (nodes) are connected with one another. Following are descriptions of several different configurations.

Daisy Chain

The *daisy chain* topology is the easiest way to set up a small network. Simply put, each machine is connected to the next, as shown in figure 28.1.

Fig. 28.1
A daisy chain topology.

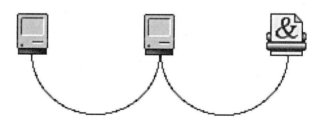

LocalTalk boxes—and third-party connectors—provide two connections on each box. In a daisy chain, the middle devices (as opposed to the ones on each end of the chain) have two cables connected to their LocalTalk box.

A daisy chain is easy to set up and is perfect for temporary networks or small work groups (for example, two Macintoshes sharing a single printer as in fig. 28.1).

You should not consider a daisy chain for use with more than about two dozen machines and peripherals, however. You can use LocalTalk only in this topology. If you need a larger network or other topology, you must move to third-party hardware.

Backbone

Backbone topology often is also called *bus* topology. A single network cable runs throughout the area to be networked with connection boxes (generally standard telephone jacks) at each location where a network connection is needed (see fig. 28.2).

Fig. 28.2
A simple backbone network.

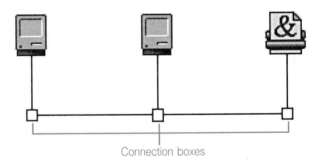

Connection boxes

This topology is ideal for small businesses. Backbone is the topology I used in setting up a software company of about 40 employees. The advantage of the backbone topology is that you can set up a decent-sized network quickly and inexpensively. You can use standard telephone jacks as well as ordinary telephone wiring. Users can plug into the network at any point to connect. Using backbone topology, you often can use existing telephone wiring. If your office has standard four-wire telephone wiring but uses only two of the wires, you can set up a backbone network by adding resistors to the two telephone jacks at either end and then plugging in your Macintoshes.

In all cases, backbone networks must have terminating resistors at either end of the network.

Star

Star networks consist of branches (rather like small backbone networks) that connect to a central wiring block (see fig. 28.3).

Fig. 28.3
A star network.

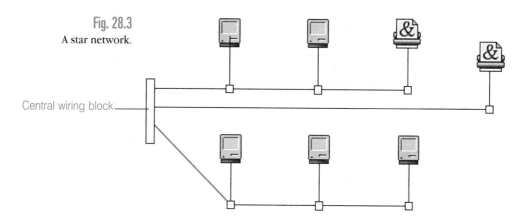

Central wiring block

Many small businesses have this kind of telephone wiring. Phones are wired to a central wiring distribution block. Two of the four wires connecting each phone to the wiring block generally are unused and can be connected quickly to form a star network.

Star networks come in two forms: passive and active. The *passive* star network has a limited number of branches off the wiring block (usually four or less). The *active* star can have more (usually around 12) but requires a controller.

O nce your small office grows beyond a dozen or more people, hiring a professional to install your network is usually wise. Although hiring an installer costs more money, it saves headaches.

The star network has the advantage of utilizing existing wiring and being expandable. The backbone also can use existing wiring, but once its limits are reached, you need to convert it to a star network in order to expand it. A business that anticipates growth may be well advised to go with the star topology in the first place.

Token Ring

One topology usually not used with the Macintosh but commonly encountered in large networks is the *token ring*. This topology is exactly as the name describes: a ring. Though not necessarily physically ring-shaped, the ring topology is like a backbone in which both ends are connected. Token ring has no definable beginning or end to the network connection.

The token ring network also has its own protocol: one in which a *token* circulates around the ring, going from one machine to another. When a machine needs to send data, it attaches the data to the token before sending it on to the next machine.

You can connect Macintosh networks to a token ring network, although doing so requires a special hardware bridge to translate the protocols.

Defining AppleTalk Zones

As you learned earlier in this chapter, AppleTalk assigns numbers from 0 to 254 to each node on the network. Node 255 is reserved for messages that are sent to every node. When a message is sent, it carries the node number. All machines at each node listen to every message but take in and use only the one addressed to them.

Until you have a larger business, 255 numbers is a decent amount. Larger businesses can have hundreds if not thousands of computers, and 255 nodes is just not enough. The solution is the *AppleTalk zone*. AppleTalk can have over 65,000 zones (in theory), each of which is a complete network in and of itself. The networks are joined by bridges (see the next section). Many businesses find it convenient to divide the complete network by floors or departments, each having its own zone. Then, up to 255 nodes can exist in each zone, or 255 total Macintoshes and peripherals in each zone.

To communicate with a particular machine, you choose the AppleTalk zone in which the machine resides and then choose the machine. Your software may choose for you, freeing you from worrying about zones.

Defining Bridges

A *bridge* is a connection between networks. When connected, each network becomes a zone in an AppleTalk internet. The people on the New York network, for example, can talk with the people on the Chicago network over a bridge; or the people in Suite A, who use LocalTalk as a networking system, can talk to the people in Suite B, who use the

EtherNet system (more about this product later in the chapter). Bridges keep track of which devices are on which network and make sure that the traffic (the information) gets where it needs to go.

A special kind of bridge, a *gateway,* connects two networks that use different protocols, or systems for communications, such as in the LocalTalk-to-EtherNet situation just described. You can connect two networks using a bridge such as those made by Hayes (InterBridge), Shiva (the NetBridge), and Solana Electronics (The I-Server).

You should know a little more about specialized bridges. NetBridge by Shiva, for example, is a bridge that links two local networks using direct connections. Shiva's other bridge is TeleBridge, which links networks connected by phone lines. With TeleBridge, you can increase transmission speeds to 57,000 baud—extraordinary for usually slower phone lines.

A second useful and easy-to-use bridge is the Hayes InterBridge, which connects two LocalTalk networks, even through a modem. Say, for example, that a law firm's Washington office has five local area networks and the Los Angeles office has three, for a total of eight LANs that need to be connected. Using InterBridge, you first can connect all the Washington LANs to one another and use another InterBridge to connect the three Los Angeles LANs. Then you need to link the Los Angeles and Washington offices, and you can make that link with another InterBridge over a dedicated modem.

Setting Up a Network

Detailing the steps for every possible configuration of a LAN would be impossible. Instead, consider the types of questions you need to ask yourself before you start the actual work, as you learn in the following sections. Then you're ready to learn the steps for setting up a simple LAN.

Planning Considerations

Before you begin work on your LAN, you have a number of elements to consider. You need to have the answers to the following questions:

1. How many computers and other peripherals will make up your LAN?

   This question is most easily answered if you are aware of the type of work that you do (large text files, frequent sharing, and so on) and the number of people who do the work. Remember that a LAN is not only computers; it also consists of printers, hard drives, modems that can be networked, and other peripherals.

2. Where will each node be located?

This information is essential for connecting the different nodes by cable. This process is done best if the entire network and all its characteristics are first drawn on paper. Remember that cables hold this whole thing together, and you must plan to run cables in places that are out of the way of feet and dogs with wagging tails. Check to see whether your phone wiring has an unused pair of wires that you could use.

3. What other hardware may be needed to make things work as you like?

If you'll be using DOS machines, you will need a special card installed in those machines so that they can communicate with the Macintoshes on the network. You will need bridges only if you have to connect to another network entirely.

Keep in mind, however, that if you start mixing DOS machines with Macintoshes, you have to take into account many other issues, such as sharing data and translating files between DOS and Macintosh formats. Check to see whether your present software already offers these features; many applications do.

4. Are the various types of hardware compatible with one another?

It's easy to get caught up in the hype of LANs and go out and buy everything you think you might need. But it's not good sense if you are just starting out. Rely on your dealer or the manufacturer to let you know whether a laser printer can be networked and accessed from a variety of nodes and if there are certain limitations. The same advice is true for software. Programs that work alone may not be accessible through a network, a fact that some people learn too late.

Constructing a Small Network

Here are the steps you would take to set up a simple all-Macintosh LAN using LocalTalk cables and connectors and the LocalTalk protocol. The components of this LAN (as with every LAN) are the cables that connect the different devices, the software that is used to send the information, and the computers. As you can see in figure 28.4, this network has four computers, one ImageWriter, and one LaserWriter, all connected to one another. Because this network is a daisy chain network, the computers are connected in a line, and all can communicate with one another. Two Mac IIcx's and two SE/30s are networked to the LaserWriter and the ImageWriter.

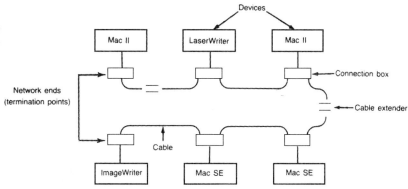

Fig. 28.4
A simple daisy chain network using LocalTalk.

You can see the following things from the simple diagram shown in this figure:

■ The devices and nodes are arranged in a line—not in a circle. No Macintosh network topology is connected in a circle. Backbones and daisy chains both have a definite end and a definite beginning. Stars have hubs with branches that end.

■ Except for the beginning and ending machines, both connectors on the LocalTalk boxes are used. You can think of a daisy chain in terms of one cable going "in" from one machine and the other going "out" to another, although transmissions actually occur in both directions.

■ Extra cables are unwanted. You have only as many cables as are needed to connect nodes, with no extra cables on the last node in the network.

Be sure that you place cables where no one can trip over them and that they are securely connected. Also, be careful of where you run them. Running LocalTalk cables (and many other brands as well) past fluorescent lights and near other electrical components can cause interference in the network. Run these cables through conduits if necessary.

First, before constructing your network, do these steps on paper; then pick up your hardware and software and get connected.

1. Determine how many cables and connector kits you need.

    For each device along the network, you need one complete kit, which consists of a LocalTalk connector box and a cable (adding cable extenders where the distance warrants). There are two different connector kits, one for an 8-pin plug and one for a 9-pin plug. Machines after the Plus use the 8-pin, which is round. Older machines use the rectangular 9-pin.

    You can get additional cables in lengths of 10 and 25 meters (or about 33 and 83 feet, respectively). Then you can combine the 2-, 10-, and 25-meter lengths to fit your needs. You also can buy a cabling kit from Apple.

2. Lay out the cables in the space where the network will be set up.

3. Don't connect your computers, printers, and other devices yet, but make the cable connections to the connecting boxes and the cable extenders. You should have a good idea where the various nodes will be located by this time and have your hardware ready to be connected.

4. Turn off each machine; then connect its LocalTalk box to the printer port and cables.

5. Turn on the hardware; then verify that AppleTalk is activated in the Chooser.

If you construct a network, small or large, you may want to consider tools offered by companies such as Farallon that help you observe what occurs on the network, such as which servers are being used to deliver which files, and so on.

Using PhoneNET

Using PhoneNET (from Farallon), you can bypass the laying of cables and use phone lines for a local area network by running the network signal through the unused pair of standard four-wire phone cabling. Not only might PhoneNET save you the expense of cable, but you can add anyone with a phone (such as a new employee) to the network—without running new cables.

PhoneNET has other advantages. First, you can have as much as 3,000 feet between nodes, whereas with LocalTalk you are limited to 1,000 feet. Second, PhoneNET uses the same type of click-in connectors you find on your phone, thereby reducing the possibility of an accidental (and data-fatal) unplugging.

Because you may have to mess around with the connections between your phone and the phone box on your wall, you may want an experienced Farallon person to assist you. Farallon has excellent technical support, so you will not be left adrift here. You also can call the telephone company to send out someone who can be of some assistance. Although the wiring is not difficult, it can be a source of trouble if not done properly.

Using EtherNet

Until a few years ago, the only way to make network connections was to use LocalTalk, which has as its primary disadvantage its lack of speed. Today, one of the most attractive alternatives is EtherNet, a fast cabling system that is compatible with the Macintosh (as EtherTalk) and meets the standards set by the majority of computer manufacturers. In fact, EtherNet is five to six times faster than LocalTalk—as much as 10 million bits per second—and you can even get it to work with an added board for the lowly Mac SE.

Other companies, Dove Computer, for example, manufacture a line of products that enhances the operation of EtherNet systems. Dove's FastNet products are communication controllers that speed up transmission along EtherNet lines.

Kinetics, another company, also produces Macintosh networking products. Kinetics products enhance connections with EtherNet systems (such as Fastpath, placed between LocalTalk and EtherNet) and increase the speed and efficiency of communications between nodes and networks by means of a bridge. Kinetics' LAN Ranger provides an easy-to-use graphical interface that logs network events, identifies network services, provides a graph for traffic, and more. Kinetics' LAN Ranger acts as a network controller, displaying loads of information about the amount of traffic, who's connected to whom, and more.

Using Shared Peripherals

There are all sorts of ways to set up a system. You may want more than one Macintosh to have access to a laser printer, for example. One of the most efficient and easiest ways to set up this kind of system is not really networking at all. The Local Connection (from Fifth Generation Systems) enables you to make connections between devices, regardless of whether they are serial or parallel. The difference between serial and parallel devices is the way they share information. *Serial* devices transmit information along a single pathway (one piece of information follows another). *Parallel* devices transmit several pieces of information along parallel pathways.

The Local Connection is a box with four serial and four parallel ports (two in and two out). It also includes a buffer so that print jobs are stacked and printed in turn, and The Local Connection contains memory-resident software, enabling you to send documents to any plotter, printer, or modem. This kind of product is an alternative to traditional networks, and if your networking needs are relatively simple, this approach is an attractive one. The price is well below the cost of a full-blown network.

Communicating by Remote Control

Consider this situation: you're working on your Macintosh at home, and you need to access a file from your office Macintosh. Or you manage all the Macintoshes for a large organization, and someone calls to tell you that he does not understand how to create a table using Word. Rather than talk him through it, you can just show him on his own Mac—even though you're five feet or 500 miles away!

You can make this connection by remotely controlling another computer through such products as Timbuktu (Farallon) or Carbon-Copy Mac (from Microcom). Timbuktu enables you to take complete control of a Macintosh remotely (see fig. 28.5).

You can control a Macintosh remotely to aid a colleague in solving a problem, for instance. You also can arrange for other users to view your Macintosh screen as you perform operations with software, having a remote class. You can transfer files to or from the remote Macintosh, enabling you to install software without leaving your office.

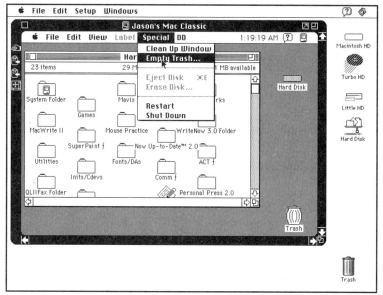

Fig. 28.5
Controlling a Macintosh
Classic remotely.

Using File Sharing

System 7 has the built-in capability to share files over a network without additional software. This easy-to-use system is good for smaller installations of up to about a dozen users. (Beyond this number, File Sharing can slow down your network and the connected Macintoshes.)

File Sharing does not replace all networking software but can perform many basic operations that can enable smaller network users to save money by avoiding additional software purchases.

Configuring File Sharing

To use File Sharing, you first must set the configuration options. You set these options through the Sharing Setup and Users & Groups control panels.

Before attempting to start File Sharing, verify that you have AppleTalk turned on in your Chooser. Also, verify that AppleShare is installed in your Extensions folder and loaded (you must restart after activating AppleTalk or installing AppleShare before either becomes active).

Setting Sharing Options

To begin File Sharing, you first must set your File Sharing options. You set these options in the Sharing Setup control panel (see fig. 28.6) located in your Control Panels folder. Double-click the control panel to open it.

Fig. 28.6
Setting Sharing Setup
options.

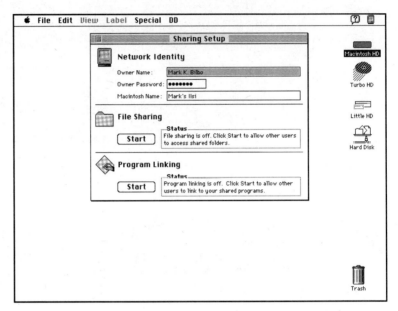

Follow these steps to configure File Sharing:

1. Type your name and then press Tab.

    You can use any name you want; this name will appear on the network to identify you.

2. Type a password and then press Return.

    You use this password to access your computer. Make it something you can remember but that is hard for others to guess.

3. Type a name for your Macintosh.

    Any name works; many users like unusual names, but I suggest you use one that identifies your Macintosh.

4. Click the File Sharing Start button.

Optionally, if you have programs that enable more than one user to link to them—use them simultaneously—click the Program Linking Start button.

5. Click the close box of the Sharing Setup window.

File Sharing is now activated. To enable others to access your shared files, you must create users and set their sharing options.

Creating a New User

To create a new user and enable a user to access your shared files, you first open the Users & Groups control panel in your Control Panels folder by double-clicking the control panel's icon. You see the control panel's window (see fig. 28.7).

Fig. 28.7
Creating a new user.

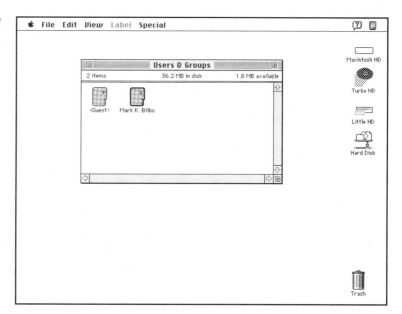

When the Users & Groups control panel opens, you already see a Guest user and your own name (the name you typed in the Sharing Setup).

To create and configure a new user, follow these steps:

1. From the File menu, choose New User.

   You see a New User icon appear.

2. Type a name for the user and press Return.

3. Double-click the user's icon.

   You see the user's window (see fig. 28.8).

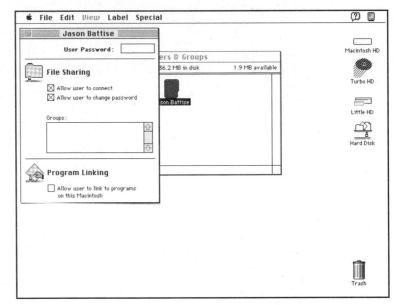

Fig. 28.8
Setting options for the
new user.

4. Type a password and press Tab.

   The user must use this password to log on to your Macintosh and access the files you've chosen to share.

5. If you want to allow this user to access shared files, leave the Allow user to connect option as is. Click this option to change it only if you want to prevent this particular user from accessing your Macintosh.

6. If you want to allow this user to change his or her password, leave the Allow user to change password option as is. If you want to control the password the user enters to access your shared files, click this option to deactivate it.

7. If you want to allow this user to link to shared programs on your Macintosh, click the Allow user to link to programs on this Macintosh option.

8. Click the close box to close the window.

Repeat these steps for each user you want to allow to access the files you've chosen to share.

Creating a New Group

You also can assign the newly created users to groups. For example, a business may want to create groups such as Marketing, Technical Support, and Sales. Assigning users to groups enables you to set access privileges for groups of users at one time rather than set each individually.

To create a group, follow these steps:

1. With the Users & Groups control panel open, choose New Group from the File menu.

2. Type a name for the group (for example, type **Sales**) and press Return.

3. Double-click the group's icon.

   You see the icon open and an empty window appear. To add users to the group, continue to the next step.

4. Drag the desired user's icon from the Users & Groups window to the new group window.

   You see a new icon appear in the group window (see fig. 28.9).

Fig. 28.9
A user has been added to the Sales group.

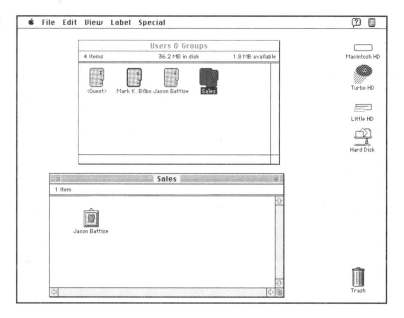

Repeat step 4 for each user you want to be part of this group. When you're finished adding users to this group, click the close box of the group's window.

Sharing Folders and Disks

Once you've set up your users and groups, you are ready to share files. To share a folder or disk and its contents, use these steps:

1. Click on the folder or disk to be shared.

2. From the File menu, choose Sharing.

   You see the access privileges window. This window is named the same as the item selected (the Shared folder window, for example, as shown in figure 28.10).

Fig. 28.10
Preparing to share Shared folder.

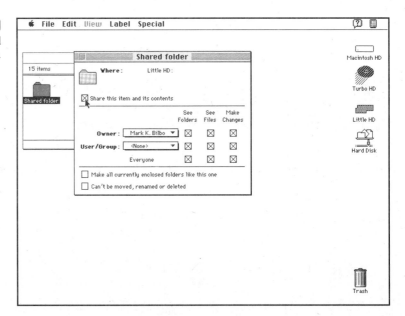

3. Click the Share this item and its contents option.

   The folder or disk is set to be shared. Its icon changes to display a network-like connection beneath the icon. If you quit here, the folder or disk is shared, but you probably want to continue and set the access privileges.

Access privileges determine how much access the user has to the shared item. You can set three privileges:

Privilege	Meaning
See Folders	This user or group can see and open the folders inside the shared item, but cannot change them.
See Files	This user can see and open files inside the shared item, but cannot change them.
Make Changes	This user can make changes to the shared item, adding files, changing files, and the like.

From the pop-up menu, you can choose the user or group for whom you want to set privileges (see fig. 28.11).

Fig. 28.11
Setting privileges
for a user.

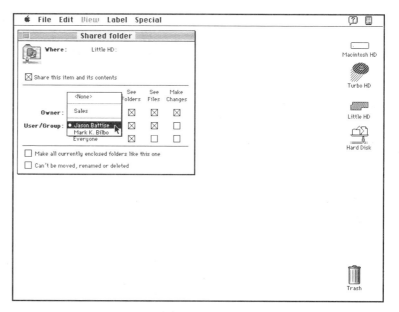

File Sharing is a bit limited in access privilege options. You can set your own options—the Owner options—and options for one other user or group as well as a general Everyone—applying to the Guest logon and any user other than the one chosen from the User/Group menu.

A single shared item cannot have different privileges for different users or groups. You set the privileges for yourself, for one user or group, and then everyone else.

Using the See Folders and Make Changes options is good for making "drop boxes" that users can copy files to, but then they can't see the files in the folder or disk and, therefore, can't open, copy, change, or delete them.

Using the See Folders and See Files options (but not the Make Changes option) is good for folders that are meant for distribution, thus creating an "out box" of sorts where others can copy files but not change them.

You can create a simple electronic mail system with these two configurations. Make an "in box" and an "out box" (better names might include your name so that users can identify your boxes better). Set the in-box folder to have the Make Changes option only for the Everyone user. This setting enables users to drop files into the folder but not see the contents (and thus not be able to change the contents even though Make Changes is on to enable them to copy files to the folder).

If you want to subdivide the in-box folder, you also must turn on the See Folders option.

You should set the out-box folder to have the See Files option on for the Everyone user. This setting enables users to copy files from the folder. You can subdivide the folder and then set the See Files option for each folder only for a specific user, enabling you to have private mail. The Everyone See Folders option can be on to enable everyone to see the folders inside the out-box folder.

Try various combinations to determine what best suits your needs.

Setting Options

You also must consider two more options in the sharing window. The Make all currently enclosed folders like this one option copies the access privileges to every folder within the currently selected folder or disk. Click this check box if you want to set all enclosed folders to the same access privileges. You don't have to set the same access privileges; using the Sharing command, you can set each folder's access privileges differently.

Click the Can't be moved, renamed, or deleted option if you want to prevent users from moving, renaming, or deleting this folder or disk.

Controlling Sharing

You should exercise control over File Sharing. You can monitor who is accessing your Macintosh, disconnect a user, or turn File Sharing off altogether.

To view who is accessing your Macintosh, double-click the File Sharing Monitor control panel in your Control Panels folder. You see who is logged on to your Macintosh (see fig. 28.12).

Fig. 28.12

Monitoring File Sharing.

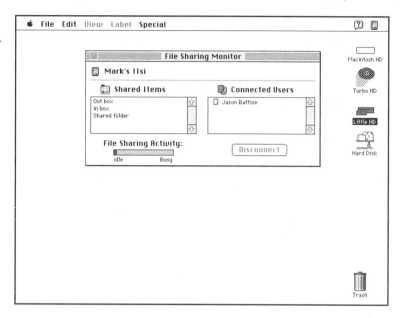

The shared items on your Macintosh are listed in the left list box. The right list box displays the users currently accessing your Macintosh. The activity monitor at the bottom shows how much activity is occurring at the present time.

To disconnect a user from your Macintosh, follow these steps:

1. Click the name of the user to be disconnected.

2. Click the Disconnect button.

   You see a dialog that asks for a number of minutes before disconnecting the user (see fig. 28.13).

3. Type a number between 0 and 999 and then press Return.

   If you type **0**, the user is disconnected immediately. A number between 1 and 999 is the number of minutes before the user is disconnected (999 minutes, by the way, is 16 hours and 39 minutes).

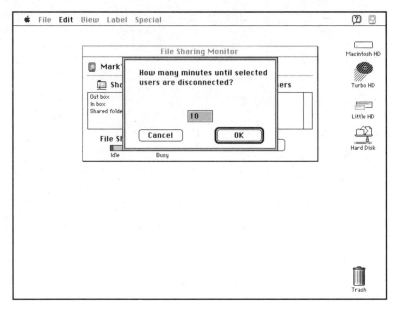

Fig. 28.13
Setting how long a user has
before disconnection.

To disconnect all users and deactivate File Sharing, double-click the
Sharing Setup control panel and click the File Sharing Stop button. You
see the same dialog as when disconnecting a single user and may set a
time from 0 to 999 minutes.

Accessing Shared Items

You have learned how to set up your Macintosh to be shared, but how
do you access others' Macintoshes? Do the following:

1. Open the Chooser.

2. Click the AppleShare icon.

   You see the names of the Macintoshes that are on the network (see
   fig. 28.14).

3. Double-click the name of the Macintosh you want to access.

   You see a screen that asks you to enter your password.

4. Type your password and press Return.

   You then see a list of the items that you can access on the remote
   Macintosh (see fig. 28.15).

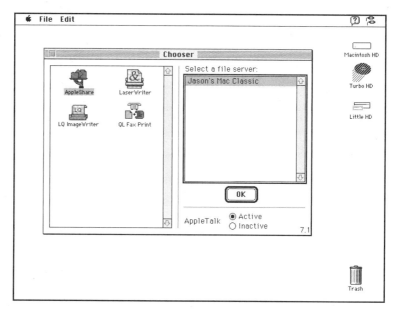

Fig. 28.14
Ready to log on to another
Macintosh.

In this window, you can click the check box to the right of the
items you want to be accessed when you start up your Macintosh.
You are asked for your password at startup unless you click the
Save My Name and Password option. Note that this option is
convenient but less secure than the Save My Name Only option.
Anyone who starts up your Macintosh has immediate access to the
shared files of the remote Macintosh.

5. Press Return.

   The shared item(s) appear on your Desktop. Note that you can
   dismount them like a floppy disk by dragging the icon to the
   Trash.

The Big Mac Recommendation

Using some of the networking technology discussed in this chapter, you
can reach out to your neighbor across the hall or across the world.
Networking with the Macintosh is becoming widespread. The concept of
work groups communicating over networks is growing fast. Expect this
trend to continue.

Fig. 28.15
Choosing an item
to access.

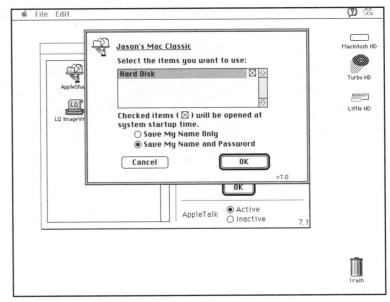

If your networking needs are modest, consider what System 7 offers in the way of File Sharing. You can set up a simple electronic mail system and share files with no additional software.

Larger businesses, of course, should carefully consider their needs in this area. EtherNet is becoming less expensive all the time and is now built into mid-range (Centris) and high-end (Quadra) Macintoshes. This much faster alternative to LocalTalk is worth consideration for large installations.

One company recommendation is Farallon. This company started out modestly with a simpler, less expensive replacement for the LocalTalk box and over the years has grown into one of the giants of Macintosh networking. Farallon has networking solutions for almost every Macintosh user.

CHAPTER TWENTY-NINE

Using Connectivity Software

onnectivity became quite a buzzword a couple of years back, but the word stands for something very important in today's Macintosh world: the capability to communicate with IBM PCs. It's not easy for a Macintosh user to admit that communicating with the arch rival is important, but connectivity is very important. The simple fact is that there are more of *them* than there are of us. Some 100 million PC standard machines have been sold—10 times the number of Macintoshes. And as the Macintosh gains greater acceptance in the business world, the chances of your needing to share files with an IBM PC increase.

This chapter surveys connectivity solutions: how you can translate files, share disks, and even run IBM software on your Macintosh. You also examine the growing trend toward software that runs the same on both machines and can share files easily between versions. The chapter also considers dealing with earlier Apple formats—ProDOS and the Apple II.

Communicating with IBM PCs and Clones

The more you compute, the more likely you are to run into the problem of sharing information between two different makes of computers. Suppose, for example, that a colleague has just completed an important report and you need a copy, but there you are with your Macintosh and she with her PC clone. You have several options when this situation happens.

The first option is to use a *file transfer* program. These programs transfer the information from a Macintosh to a PC (or vice versa) and translate the file formats to fit while doing so. You can connect the two machines by cable, modem, or network.

The second alternative is to allow the FDHD or "SuperDrive," available on the later models of the Macintosh SE, to read DOS disks directly through the use of the proper software. This option enables you to access files directly, provided your software can translate the DOS format file—as many can do now—or to use a file translation program to convert the file.

Transferring and Translating Files

Transferring files is remarkably easy to do. Two outstanding products, DataViz's MacLink Plus and Traveling Software's LapLink Pro, come with absolutely everything you need, including disks (one for your Mac and one for your PC), cables, and excellent manuals.

These products work in basically the same way. After the two machines are connected by a cable, modem, or network, you "connect" using the supplied software, and they can "talk" to one another. Then you just select the types of files that you want to send and have the software do the translation and the sending.

MacLink Plus offers almost any type of file conversion you could need and far more than any other product (now over 700 translations). Formats for the Macintosh, IBM PC, Sun workstations, and the NeXT computer are supported.

Figure 29.1, for example, shows MacLink Plus translating from Microsoft Word on the Macintosh to WordPerfect on the IBM. You select the file or files to be translated. MacLink Plus determines the file format and then considers the file translation preferences you've set. MacLink Plus then translates and sends the files to the MacLink Plus program running on the DOS machine.

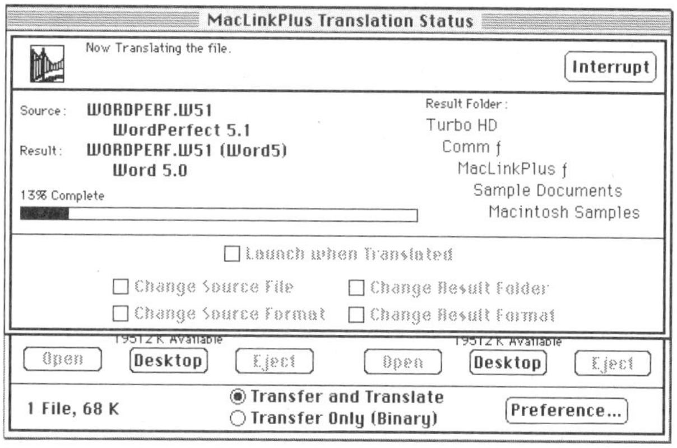

Fig. 29.1
Converting files using MacLink Plus.

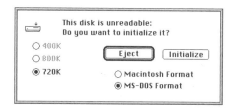

One nice feature of MacLink is that you can use the DOS Mounter System extension that allows your Mac to read and format DOS-formatted disks using the SuperDrive (see fig. 29.2).

Fig. 29.2
Formatting a disk in DOS format with DOS Mounter.

This capability enables you to avoid using the cable to transfer the file and speeds things up by placing your DOS disk with DOS files right into your Macintosh. The transfer process is much faster.

Many programs also are now able to translate DOS files. With DOS Mounter (or similar extension), you can simply insert a DOS disk and open the file. DOS Mounter even enables you to choose which Macintosh program is launched to open the DOS file when you double-click the file's icon. You do this by linking the DOS file extension to a Macintosh program on your hard disk (see fig. 29.3).

Fig. 29.3

Mapping a DOS spread-
sheet extension to Excel on
the Macintosh.

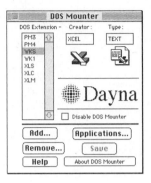

MacLink Plus/PC also has the capability to install translator files for
Microsoft Word 5. This capability allows Word to translate files directly.
You need only to open the file from within Word or choose Save As and
choose the desired file format, and the file is translated. If you are a
Word 5 user, this capability—especially combined with DOS Mounter—
is a powerful aid. You can pop a DOS disk in your Macintosh drive and
open or save in most every DOS word processing format without ever
leaving Word.

If you use Claris products, MacLink Plus/PC can link with the XTND
translation system and give your Claris programs the same capability to
open and save files in a great number of DOS formats.

LapLink is a similar file conversion program that offers some worthwhile
features:

- It uses a split screen to list files on the local and remote computer,
  making it easy to see what's going where.

- You can control the transfer process from either the PC or the
  Macintosh, whichever one you feel most comfortable with.

- Password protection at several levels, as shown in figure 29.4,
  makes sure that no one gets ahold of your Spiderman collection of
  clip art and transfers it to the PC.

Fig. 29.4

LapLink password
protection.

☐ Use Passwords	password
Personal password protection:	
Global read/write access:	
Global read only access:	
Published folders only access:	

OK   Publish Folders   Cancel

- You can get an optional Mac Accelerator that boosts Mac-to-Mac transfer up to 750,000 baud, which is very fast and makes those long documents fly through the transfer process.

A relative newcomer to the connectivity scene is Software Bridge/Mac by Argosy Software Inc. This program automatically recognizes double-clicked DOS files, loads, translates, and then launches the appropriate Macintosh program to open the file.

If you want, you can use the Apple File Exchange (AFE, from Apple) software utility. AFE is Apple's effort to increase the connections between the Mac and hundreds of other computers. The utility is not limited just to Macintoshes and PCs; it also allows exchanges between Macintoshes, PCs, and ProDOS, the operating system for the family of Apple II computers.

AFE's translators are limited, but you can extend them by purchasing the MacLink Plus/Translators. AFE can use DataViz translators for translating files. AFE is free and comes on your System Software disk set, but you must purchase the translators. You don't end up saving much money, as the set of translators costs only about $20 less than the full MacLink Plus/PC package. AFE is also harder to use than MacLink Plus. The program's only advantage is your ability to work with ProDOS disks from the Apple II.

Working with Disks

As mentioned previously, the FDHD or SuperDrive is capable of reading, writing, and formatting DOS disks. But to enable this feature, you need software. Following are several software options.

Apple File Exchange is your least expensive option in that the utility comes with your System Software disks (located on the Tidbits disk in the System 7 software set). After you double-click the AFE icon, you can insert a blank disk. Then you see a dialog that enables you to format the disk (see fig. 29.5).

Fig. 29.5

Formatting a disk in ProDOS format.

AFE has been surpassed in recent times by programs such as MacLink Plus. Now AFE's only remaining advantage is the capability to format disks in ProDOS format. But then you need the translator files to add to AFE to perform translations.

DOS Mounter by Dyna enables you to mount IBM PC disks. You also can map the extensions of DOS files to Macintosh programs that can translate these files. Although DOS Mounter is sold separately, you can obtain the extension by purchasing MacLink Plus/PC. With the full MacLink Plus/PC package, you also obtain the translator to make use of the DOS files DOS Mounter enables you to access. You might consider purchasing DOS Mounter separately if your application program has the translation capabilities you need already built in and you need to access only PC disks.

AccessPC 2.0 by Insignia Solutions also is a System extension that mounts DOS disks in your SuperDrive, as DOS Mounter does. You also can format DOS disks.

This book was written using Apple's entry into this field: Macintosh PC Exchange. PC Exchange offers the same basic capabilities as the other, previously mentioned extensions.

With any of these extensions, your Macintosh no longer recognizes a difference between IBM PC disks and Macintosh disks. Your only indication is that the disk icon appears differently to indicate that it is PC format. Other than that, DOS files appear on your Desktop just like Macintosh files. If you work in a mixed environment (Macintoshes and PCs), one of these extensions is a must.

Running IBM Software

Compatibility has been a headache for all users. But in recent years, the lines between the PC and the Macintosh have blurred—and not just because of the recent IBM-Apple alliance.

People have many reasons for wanting compatibility between the Macintosh and other types of computers. Some people who have access to both Macintosh and IBM machines and are familiar with both prefer to do their word processing on an IBM or an IBM-compatible and their graphics work on a Macintosh. Others need to run both side by side, as a computer writer (such as myself) may need to do.

Regardless of your preference, if you could use the application of your choice on the computer of your choice, that capability would be a breakthrough. Today that breakthrough is not far away. The irony is that the Macintosh is far more advanced in connecting to the PC than the other way around. But then, that makes sense when you consider which machine dominates the market. Sad but true: Macs have to be compatible with those irritating command-line beasts.

Using a Hardware Solution

Today, several products available enable you to use PC applications on your Mac. AST Research produces the MAC286.10 (for the Mac II), for example, a set of two cards installed in your Mac. MAC286.10 provides you with the equivalent of an IBM PC or AT personal computer and also enables you to exchange data between Mac and DOS computers (like the IBM). The AST card contains a central coprocessor that takes advantage of the Mac II bus, or the traffic pattern along which information is sent from and received by the computer's brains. This special NuBus architecture allows the Mac to run both Mac and DOS software applications. With this setup, you can switch between PC and Mac applications and even cut and paste between them. To make the whole thing work, you need to hook up Apple's 5.25-inch disk drive.

In a sense, MAC286.10 gives you the best of both possible worlds. The cost, however, can be restrictive—around $1,500. This price is more than you have to spend to buy a PC-clone with the cables and the software (such as MacLink Plus/PC) that you need to connect the two to transfer files and such. On the other hand, you may be in an environment where you cannot have two computers sitting side by side, or you may have a constant use for one PC application that works well on the MAC AST cards. If either is the case, then MAC286.10 may be worth the price.

Using Software Solutions

Hardware isn't the only way to go. For much less money, you can get that PC application on your Macintosh screen by using only software. Following are several options.

Insignia Solutions offers an entire line of IBM PC emulators that enable you to run PC software on your Macintosh.

Universal SoftPC 2.5 emulates the IBM PC and enables you to run DOS applications in a window on any Macintosh. You need at least 2MB of RAM (and sometimes as much as 4MB) to run the emulator. This program sells for about $200.

Keep in mind that you also may have to buy more memory if you want an emulation program on your Macintosh, which brings the costs of the software solution closer to the hardware solution but not by much, given the low cost of memory upgrades these days.

SoftAT 2.5 emulates an IBM AT with EGA graphics, LIM expanded memory, as well as a math coprocessor for PC applications for about $300. You need a Macintosh with a 68020, 68030, or 68040 coprocessor.

If you own an older Macintosh with only a 68000, you can use Entry Level SoftPC 2.5, which emulates an IBM AT and costs about $125. Be forewarned, however, that emulation tends to be a slow process. The IBM programs do not run as quickly as on a current PC or PC clone.

If you need to access a Novell PC network, you can add SoftNode 1.0 to Universal SoftPC or SoftAT for about $100. Then you can communicate with PCs through an EtherNet connection. (You need to add EtherNet if your Macintosh does not have this capability; because this addition can be expensive, consider it carefully.)

As UNIX becomes a more popular operating system, you can count on seeing Mac-UNIX marriages such as MACIDRIS (from Whitesmiths).

And don't leave graphics out of the picture. MacLink Plus and LapLink do a great job of transferring graphics files. People who use the Macintosh for producing training manuals, for example, might capture a DOS Windows screen as a PCX (Windows Paintbrush) file and then port it over to the Macintosh, where it is converted to a PICT file that can be read by such programs as QuarkXPress, Amazing Paint, Word, WordPerfect, and PageMaker.

Using Your Mac with Mainframes

Although relatively few Macintosh users need to connect regularly to a mainframe to do daily memos and budgets, big business is more intent on using the Macintosh as a connection to mainframes then ever before. The Macintosh can easily be treated as a dumb terminal, using any of the communications software discussed in Chapter 17, "Using Communication Software." (Just dial and you're talking to your millions-per-second-instructions supercomputer.) You also can use one of the specialized packages described in the following paragraphs. The obvious advantage, in either case, is that you can have your Macintosh speak to a mainframe instead of requiring a dedicated mainframe terminal located next to your Mac on an already crowded desk. Just think of it. You can use your Mac to run Excel or 4th Dimension and then turn the task over to the mainframe to run the batch job on the mainframe.

As the world gets smaller and more connected, more personal computers will talk directly with mainframes and minicomputers more often than ever before. So the name of the game is designing interfaces for the very large computers, such as those manufactured by DEC (Digital Equipment Corporation) and its family of VAX computers.

DEC has a marketing agreement with Apple, and, as you might expect, several products to link the Macintosh to the VAX computers. These products include cables, new software, bridges, and terminal emulators. The computer industry is a business of ripple effects: one move in the marketplace never occurs in isolation. Product development, more often than not, leads to new products, and so on.

One of these products is the DynaComm Asynchronous communications package from Future Soft Engineering, which produces a HyperCard stack. Using this package, you can write scripts to create buttons (and other HyperCard tools) and connect and work with the VAX family and the IBM family of mainframes. Software is even under development to enable you to take advantage of your Macintosh graphic interface when working with Cray supercomputers.

Digital Communications offers a whole line of micro-to-mainframe links, making your Macintosh compatible with IBM mainframes in an interactive fashion or through terminal emulations.

One of the products that has proved itself to be successful is the MacIRMA WorkStation, software that works in conjunction with the MacIRMA card to connect you from a variety of Macs to a mainframe.

A University of Michigan project holds promise for the development of a universal platform (everyone's ultimate wish) in which DOS, UNIX, Mac, and other system users interact seamlessly with a mainframe. This Institutional File System, or IFS, holds great promise for bringing one filing system to the world of computers.

Avatar is trying to fill the same big set of blue shoes with software and hardware products directed exclusively at Mac-to-mainframe connectivity. Avatar's MacMainframe graphics, for example, enables you to edit mainframe graphics from your Mac simply by using a mouse.

The Big Mac Recommendation

Without a doubt, MacLink Plus PC is foremost in my mind for translating files between Macintoshes, PCs, and other computers. With over 700 translations, this package offers tremendous flexibility and is the one I have used personally for more than three years.

Lately, I've found DOS Mounter to be a bit weak and have started using Apple's Macintosh PC Exchange for mounting DOS disks. This extension has the advantage of being written by the people who know the Macintosh best. But DOS Mounter and AccessPC are excellent products. You may want to forgo the cost of the additional extension. You aren't missing much at all by using DOS Mounter; the extension served me well for three years before I decided to replace it.

Before purchasing any file translation software, you should consider the translation capabilities that are built into your application programs. You may need to add only a DOS disk mounting extension to do the translations you need.

CHAPTER THIRTY

Using HyperCard

yperCard stirred quite a bit of interest when it was first introduced. The program was the first Macintosh implementation of the *hypertext* concept which had been a part of computer theory for some time. HyperCard made it possible for average users to create their own computer programs by simply linking sets of cards containing graphics, text, and actions.

NOTE

At the time of this writing, Apple and Claris had announced that HyperCard would return from Claris to Apple and be integrated with future development projects. Apple has not outlined its future plans, however.

The material of this chapter applies to the current Claris HyperCard product, which you can purchase at dealers and through mail order.

Apple will be announcing future plans as development proceeds.

Today thousands of HyperCard programs—called *stacks*—are available, and numerous newsletters, columns, books, and even clubs are dedicated to this interesting software tool.

This chapter contributes to your HyperCard knowledge by covering a number of useful topics. It outlines the basics of getting started with HyperCard, provides an introduction to HyperTalk (the HyperCard programming language), and reviews some HyperCard applications that are currently available.

The examples offered here are based on HyperCard Version 2.1, a new version of the software that offers some major improvements over the original. Some of the most important improvements include: increased speed, improved window functioning with variably sized cards, more powerful searching tools, a built-in icon editor, new graphics effects, *Hot* text with which you can assign a script to words or groups of words, user-definable menus, improved printing, and color PICT support.

If you use the original HyperCard, you might want to convert your old stacks to the new version. If you don't already have HyperCard Version 2.1, you can buy it through your Apple dealer.

Defining HyperCard

HyperCard was developed by Bill Atkinson, one of the original Macintosh software developers (and the author of MacPaint, the first graphics program designed for the Mac). HyperCard was born of a desire to create a software tool that would enable people to access and use information easily and quickly.

In the early 1980s, Atkinson worked on a program called WildCard, which was something like an advanced MacPaint program. WildCard was different from its simpler predecessor, however, because it worked with a series of pages rather than only one at a time. This important difference eventually led to the development of HyperCard, which was introduced in late 1987 and was bundled free with all new Macs until mid-1988 when a limited version was supplied with all Macs and a full version began to be sold as a separate product.

Atkinson has described HyperCard as a software erector set that can be used to build applications.

HyperCard is a tool developed so that everybody who wants to should be able to use it, regardless of experience, current ability, or aptitude for programming with the Mac. You can use HyperCard for a wide range of functions, from simply storing addresses to generating complex interplay of text, graphics, and database functions that you can design. Through the use of external commands (XCMD) and external functions (XFCN), you can access any of the Toolbox routines that were not built into HyperCard. (XCMD and XFCN are routines external to HyperCard and written in a programming language; the Toolbox contains the basic programs that run the Macintosh computer.) And you can also use programs (stacks) created by other people.

Learning HyperCard Basics

HyperCard helps you construct your own system for managing information using a handful of basic elements such as stacks, cards, backgrounds, fields, and buttons. In order to take full advantage of HyperCard, you need to be familiar with these elements and their uses. But first, you need to know how to start HyperCard and how to set the user level so that you can begin creating your own stacks.

Starting HyperCard

To start HyperCard, double-click the Home stack icon (see fig. 30.1). This action starts HyperCard and opens the Home stack.

Fig. 30.1
Preparing to start HyperCard.

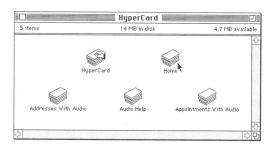

HyperCard starts up and you see the first card of the Home stack displayed (see fig. 30.2).

Fig. 30.2
The Home stack is displayed.

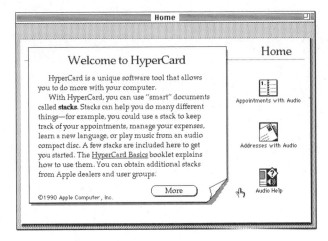

Note that the mouse pointer turns into a hand with a finger extended. This indicates that you are ready to *push* buttons on the cards.

Setting the User Level

Before you can do any serious work with HyperCard, you must set the user level. This action should be done by everyone to fully enable HyperCard. Follow these steps:

1. Press ←. (Alternatively, press ⌘-2 or choose Prev from the Go menu.)

   The Preferences card appears.

2. If five buttons appear on the Preferences card, skip to step 4. If two buttons appear, press ⌘-M (or choose Message from the Go menu).

3. Type **magic** and press Return. All five user level buttons appear (see fig. 30.3).

4. Click the button for user level 5—*Scripting*.

5. Press → or choose Home from the Go menu.

You are now ready to edit and create cards and stacks. For your general information, the purposes and privileges of the different user levels are as follows:

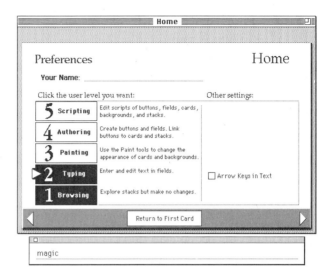

Fig. 30.3
The five user level buttons.

Level 1—*Browsing*—enables you to work your way through stacks and read their contents either by clicking a card button or by using the left and right arrow keys on the keyboard. At Level 1, you cannot alter information in any way.

Level 2—*Typing*—enables you to add text and to edit the text that is already contained in the fields of cards.

Level 3—*Painting*—provides access to paint tools, including the paintbrush, the lasso, and tools for drawing rectangles, circles, and polygons. You are probably familiar with these tools, which make up a typical MacPaint palette. You can use them to draw directly on the card layer or background layer of cards.

Level 4—*Authoring*—enables you to access and alter the basic parts of a card. At this level, the Object menu is added; you can create fields and buttons. You can also link cards and stacks to one another (an important HyperCard operation).

Level 5—*Scripting*—is the final, most complex, and most powerful level. At this level, you become a programmer using HyperCard's English-like language, *HyperTalk*.

Understanding the Building Blocks

A *stack* is a collection of units of information that have something in common, much like a set of records in a database. HyperCard does not require that the information on all cards be related, but within a particular stack this is most often the case.

A *card*—one complete screen of information—is the basic unit of information in HyperCard. HyperCard assigns a unique ID number to every card you create. Individual cards can contain various types of information including text, graphics, charts, or even sounds and animation. As shown in figure 30.4, for example, you might create a card that holds someone's name, address, phone number, and other information. Using HyperCard, you can easily build and manipulate a stack of such cards that functions like a Rolodex file. If you have a modem, you can even use HyperCard to dial clients' phone numbers for you!

Fig. 30.4

A card containing information about a client.

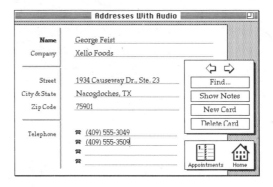

Each card is made up of three basic components: background, fields, and buttons. The *background* is the set of elements on a card that is shared by several or all of the cards in a particular stack. If you are designing a stack in which each card must contain a particular name and address, for example, you can place that information in the background for that stack. Then you don't have to reenter the same information every time you create a new card. Each card is always associated with a particular background, but you can use different backgrounds within the same stack.

You can view the background for the current card by using the ⌘-B key combination. To remind you that you are looking at the background, HyperCard places strips around the main menu. When you view the background, you can also change it; any changes you make then appear on all cards in the stack.

The *fields* on a card contain text. Text typed into fields can be formatted by size, style, and font. A field is analogous to the basic unit in a database.

Fields can be associated with a background or with a particular card only. A *card field* appears only on a single card, but a *background field* appears on all cards using that background. In a particular card you can enter text into both types of fields. The text entered in background fields is associated with those fields but appears only in that particular card.

You can move between cards and stacks by using *menu commands* or *buttons* that you place on cards. A button represents a link or an action that you define. You can design a button to take you to another stack or to another card within the same stack. Buttons also can show pop-up message fields and play sound—anything that you script.

You can cut, copy, and paste buttons. HyperCard supplies some useful buttons, and you can create your own as needs dictate.

One of HyperCard's most useful features enables you to link cards to one another. For example, you can link an address card that contains an individual's name, phone number, and product preference to a card in a different stack that indicates the date of that individual's last purchase. Then you can easily select and contact a customer on the basis of his or her last purchase date. In this sense, HyperCard works like a relational database. The section "Linking Cards and Stacks" that appears later in this chapter provides more information about linking.

Another major advantage of HyperCard is that you don't have to know how to design stacks to use them. Any stack created with HyperCard can be shared with other HyperCard users. This feature has created a major market for the development of stacks by outside parties (sometimes called third-party developers), some of which are covered in "Selecting HyperCard Applications" later in this book.

The number of buttons that you use and the way that you link cards in stacks to each other is limited only by your imagination. That's what HyperCard is all about: creating a program that fits your view of the world and the way you want it organized.

Using Commands

You can perform many tasks by using the message box to send HyperTalk commands to HyperCard. To display the message box (which you used in a previous section of this chapter called "Setting the User Level"), press ⌘-M. Then you can execute any single-line HyperTalk command by typing it in and pressing Return. If you enter the command **Go Stack Inventory** and press Enter or Return, for example, HyperCard takes you to the first card in the stack called Inventory. After a command has been entered in the message box, it remains available for repeated execution until you replace it with another command.

Working with an Existing Stack

You can begin most of your HyperCard work with a stack that has already been created. To begin with the Addresses with Audio stack, for example, move the pointing finger cursor in the Home card to the Addresses with Audio button and click once. (HyperCard, unlike the Finder, initiates actions with a single mouse click.) The first card of the Address stack appears (see fig. 30.5). The six buttons along the right side of the card have the following functions:

Button	Function
Find	Helps you find text in a stack.
Show Notes	Shows you the notes that have been created to accompany a record.
New Card	Begins the creation of a new card.
Delete Card	Deletes the current card.
Appointments	Takes you to the appointment calendar.
Home	Returns you to the first card in the Home stack.

Fig. 30.5
The first card in the
Appointments Stack.

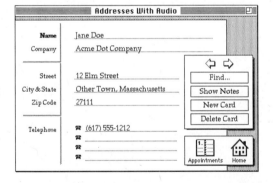

Opening a Stack

You can easily open a stack that has already been created even if no button for that stack appears on your Home card. To do so, choose the Open Stack command from the File menu. You can then make your choice from a standard Open dialog listing all the stacks that are in the current directory. Alternatively, you can open a stack from the Finder by double-clicking its icon. HyperCard starts up, the stack is opened, and the first card in the stack appears.

Adding and Deleting Cards

Suppose that you want to add a new card to the Addresses with Audio stack. To do so, select the New Card command from the Edit menu (or use the ⌘-N key combination). The screen displays a new card containing only the background information that is currently associated with each card. Now you can enter information on the new card as necessary.

Within the limits of your Mac's memory (RAM), you can add as many cards to a stack as you want and work with any number of them. When you add a new card, HyperCard places it in front of the current card in the stack and saves the card as part of the stack automatically. In fact, with HyperCard, you never need to concern yourself with saving anything. Unlike most other Macintosh application programs, it saves everything you do automatically.

Deleting a card is just as easy as adding one. With the card on-screen, select the Delete command from the Edit menu.

You can display information about the stack by choosing the Stack Info command from the Objects menu. The number of cards, the look of the backgrounds, the size of the stack, and the amount of free space available in the stack are displayed (see fig. 30.6).

Fig. 30.6
Getting information about
a stack.

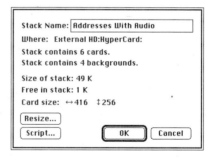

Cutting, Copying, and Pasting Data

You can cut, copy, or paste cards just like text or numerical values. A card, or part of one, can be selected using the tools on the Tools menu; the selected block of information can then be cut or copied and pasted into another location on the same card or elsewhere in the stack.

Moving through a Stack

HyperCard provides several methods for moving through a stack. The most obvious method is to use the right- and left-pointing arrow buttons located on the card. You can flip to the preceding card in the stack by clicking the left arrow; advance to the following card in the stack by clicking the right arrow.

These arrows do not appear in every stack, however, so you may need to use another method to move about. The Go menu provides you with a helpful alternative. Table 30.1 lists the commands on that menu and describes what you can do with them.

U sing the Recent command is the ideal way to find a card that you have worked with but forget where you saw it.

Table 30.1
Navigation Commands in HyperCard

Menu command	Key(s)	Action
Back	⌘-~	Moves to the preceding card in the stack
Home	⌘-H	Moves to the Home card
Help	⌘-?	Moves to HyperCard Help
Recent	⌘-R	Gives a picture of the cards you have viewed (as many as 42)
First	⌘-1	Moves to the first card in the stack
Prev	⌘-2	Moves to the preceding card in the stack
Next	⌘-3	Moves to the next card in the stack
Last	⌘-4	Moves to the last card in the stack
Find	⌘-F	Finds a card that contains certain information

When you select the Find command from the Go menu, HyperCard displays a find prompt (" ") in the message box at the bottom of the screen. Enter the information you want to find (between the double quotation marks), and HyperCard goes almost instantly to the card containing that information or even any part of it. For example, you can find the card that contains the name *Morrison* by entering **son** within the prompt's quotation marks. If HyperCard cannot find the card, the program beeps (or squeaks or boings or chirps).

Converting a Stack

To convert a stack that was created for an earlier version of HyperCard, follow these steps:

1. Make a copy of the stack to be converted.

2. Choose Open Stack from the File menu.

3. Choose Convert Stack from the File menu.

> **NOTE** The Convert Stack command only appears when you open a Version 1 stack.

4. If the stack converts successfully, delete the old copy.

Creating a New Stack

Now you know how to add a card to an existing stack. But what if you want to design your own stack? That task might seem a bit ambitious for the beginning HyperCard user, but HyperCard comes with a bunch of stack ideas that make it much easier. The stacks are like templates that enable you to create and work with personalized stacks. So building your own stack is not as difficult as it may sound at first.

Copying from an Existing Stack

Using an existing stack format to modify for your use is much easier than creating one from scratch. Let's say you plan to enter a name, an address, and some other customer information for each individual in a HyperCard customer file. You can create such a stack using a preexisting design by following these steps:

1. Open the stack you want to use as a starting point. For this example, choose the stack called Stack Ideas (from a previous version of HyperCard).

A card appears—the first of four that include different stack design ideas. Figures 30.7 and 30.8 show the first and the third of these cards.

Fig. 30.7
The first Stack Ideas card.

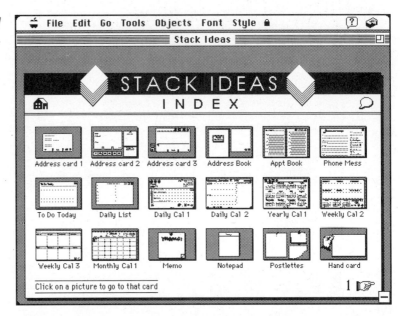

Fig. 30.8
The third Stack Ideas card.

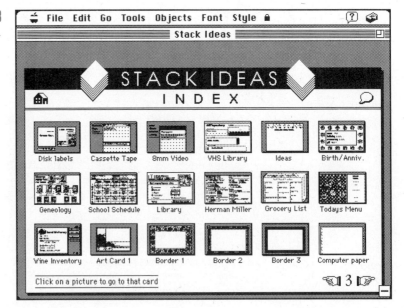

2. Select the address format you want to use as a starting point for your new stack. For this example, choose Address card 1 from the first screen.

3. With a sample card from the stack on-screen, choose the New Stack command from the File menu. A standard Save dialog appears and prompts you for a name for the new file.

4. Type a descriptive name such as **address book**. After your file name is entered, HyperCard displays the background for the new stack (see fig. 30.10).

   Remember that a card's background consists of all characteristics that the card will have in common with others in the stack. Because this stack is brand new, nothing has been entered yet and no background information exists.

Fig. 30.10
The background for the new cards.

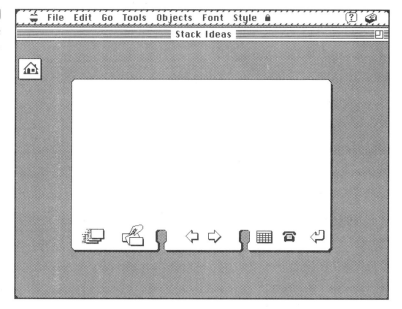

5. Place the mouse pointer in the upper right corner of the first card in this new stack and click once. The familiar flashing horizontal insertion bar appears.

6. Enter your information into the different fields.

   To change fields, use the mouse pointer or press Tab (to go to the next field) or Shift-Tab (to go to the preceding field). Key combinations enable you to see the various components of a card. To view buttons, for example, press the ⌘-Option key combination. To view both buttons and fields, press the ⌘-Shift-Option key combination.

T I P

Remember that the ⌘-B key combination toggles you into and out of the background layer of the card.

7. After you complete the first card, create the next card in your new stack by using the ⌘-N key combination or by choosing New Card from the Edit menu.

As you work, HyperCard automatically saves your creations.

You can duplicate a stack using the Save a Copy command on the File menu. This command can save you a lot of work when you want to create a new stack that is similar to an existing stack. Use it to save an existing stack under another name, then modify the new stack to meet your needs.

Linking Cards and Stacks

HyperCard would not be of much use if it did not provide you with an easy way of linking cards and stacks to one another. This section provides an example of linking cards by using a button. First, let's create a button called *More About Author?* that provides more information about the author of a quotation. This example uses a stack called Quotations, created under an earlier version of HyperCard and then converted.

To create the new button, follow these steps:

1. Begin by pressing ⌘-B. This step assures that the button is created on the background, so that it appears on every card.

2. Choose the Button tool from the Tools menu (see fig. 30.10).

Fig. 30.10
Choosing the Button tool.

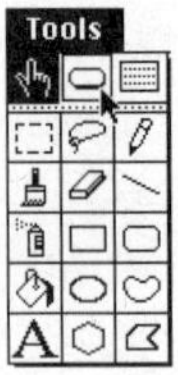

3. Choose New Button from the Objects menu. HyperCard places a selected button with the default name *New Button* in the center of the screen.

4. Double-click the newly created button, or choose the Button Info command from the Objects menu. The dialog shown in figure 30.11 appears. (In the figure the correct button name has already been added.)

Fig. 30.11
The Button Info dialog.

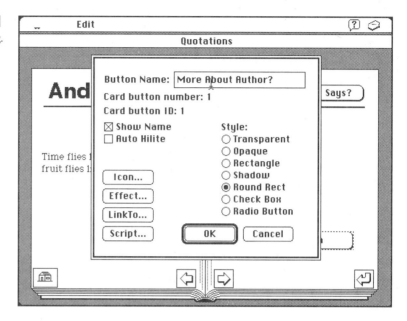

Now let's link the newly-created button to a card containing additional biographical information on an author in another stack.

To link the button with a card or stack, follow these steps:

1. While still in the Button Info dialog, click the LinkTo button to open the LinkTo dialog.

2. Move to the card that you want to link to the button or open the stack you want (using the Open command from the File menu).

   The LinkTo dialog remains on-screen, as shown in figure 30.12.

3. Click This Card or This Stack, depending on what you want to link.

   Clicking This Stack links you to the first card in the stack. In this example, click This Card to link the More About Author? button to the card. HyperCard automatically returns you to your starting card.

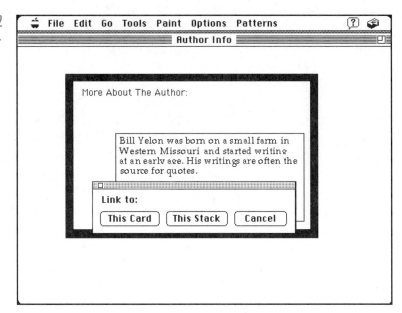

Fig. 30.12
The LinkTo dialog.

Now when you click the button named More About Author? on the card, the additional author information is produced.

The stack wouldn't be much help, however, if you could not go from the author information back to the original stack at which you started. You can create a button (labeled "Go Back To Quotes!") in the background to appear on each author biography card. Then each quotation is linked to more information about the author of the quotation, and each card that contains additional information about the author is linked to the stack named Quotations.

Printing Stacks and Cards

You can use the Print commands on the File menu or the ⌘-P key combination to print stacks and cards. As with other documents, keeping a record of your stacks for backup purposes is important. Also, you can print cards to create hard copy of your information.

Printing HyperCard cards and stacks is much like any other printing procedure. To print one card (the card displayed), choose the Print Card command from the File menu; to print the entire stack, choose the Print Stack command from the File menu.

In either case, you see the Print Stack dialog shown in figure 30.13; it enables you to handle tasks such as printing multiple copies, printing reduced versions of the cards, and including headers. You even see a print preview of the cards that will be printed.

Fig. 30.13
Printing a HyperCard stack.

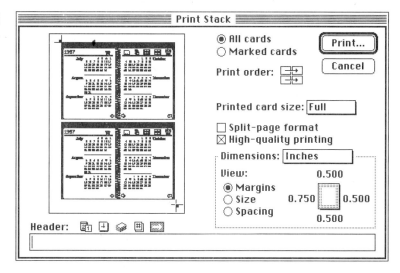

You also can print reports by choosing the Print Reports command from the File menu. This feature enables you to select the fields you want to print and to arrange them in rows or columns for your report. You could, for example, print mailing labels from a stack like the Address with Audio stack used as an example earlier in this chapter.

If you have a different sort of printing task to accomplish, try using the message box. It enables you to do things such as printing a selected set of cards from a stack. If you need to print the first 10 cards from a stack of 200, for example, simply follow these steps:

1. Go to the first card in the stack.

2. Use the ⌘-M key combination to display the message box.

3. Enter the command **print 10 cards**.

Using HyperTalk

Even if you only knew the HyperCard techniques presented so far, you would find HyperCard to be useful and applicable in many different situations. But if you want to go beyond the basics, you need HyperTalk—HyperCard's programming language. With HyperTalk, you can create and customize HyperCard stacks.

HyperTalk is a programming language that consists of 53 commands (more than 1,000 if you include all the built-in functions). As with high-level programming languages such as BASIC, Pascal, and C, these commands direct HyperCard to perform specific actions. For example, you can tell the program to go to a particular stack with the command Go to [*stackname*] or to fade from one card to another with the command dissolve. With HyperTalk commands, you can control audio and video effects, arithmetic operations, printing, sorting, and more.

Examining a Script

The HyperTalk commands that you enter are organized into *scripts*. A script is simply a list of commands that acts as a set of directions. To examine the script that is associated with a button and to find out what instructions the script gives HyperCard, follow these steps:

1. Go to the Home card by using the ⌘-H key combination.

2. Choose the Button tool from the Tools menu. The location of all the buttons on the card is shown with outlining.

3. Double-click the Appointments with Audio button to open the Button dialog.

4. Click the Script button to display the script in the script window (see fig. 30.14).

Consider what each line in this script means. The first line reads on mouseUp. All HyperTalk scripts begin with the word on, followed by some action. The mouseUp command tells HyperCard to begin this script when the mouse is released.

You may have difficulty believing that HyperCard's fancy screen tricks can be produced with only one or two command lines, but that's often the case. For example, the second line of this script—set cursor to watch—instructs HyperCard to transform the cursor into its familiar watch shape.

The go to stack... command in the third line directs HyperCard to go to the previously created stack called Appointments with Audio.

Finally, the combination of end and mouseUp in the last line tells HyperCard that this set of HyperTalk commands is ending. This script is a simple one, but it contains all the characteristics of the most complex script: a beginning statement, a set of commands that represent actions for HyperCard to execute, and an end statement.

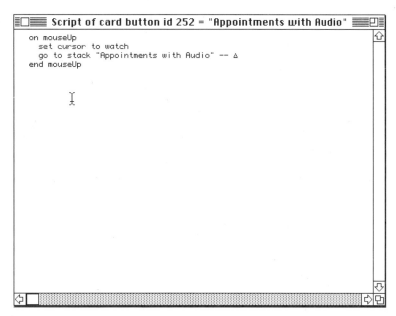

Fig. 30.14

Displaying a script for a
button.

```
on mouseUp
   set cursor to watch
   go to stack "Appointments with Audio" -- Δ
end mouseUp
```

Scripts can consist of hundreds of commands that are often organized
into smaller units called *message handlers*. A message handler is any set
of commands that begins with the command on and ends with the
command end. Each message handler is, in fact, a self-contained
HyperTalk script.

Scripts can be assigned to any HyperCard objects—buttons, fields, cards,
backgrounds, and stacks—depending on what you need to do.

Viewing Some Examples

The following sections of this chapter provide a discussion of some
HyperTalk commands and some examples of scripts and what they do.

Try these scripts, but remember that HyperTalk is not smart.
Like any other programming language, unless you tell
HyperTalk exactly what you want it to do by typing every single
character, the language cannot do its job.

Creating Music and Sound

To create sound with HyperTalk, use the Play command. The general syntax for this command is

play *<voice> <tempo> <notes>*

The *<voice>* parameter is used to choose one of the four sound generators that HyperTalk provides for you to use in scripts: harpsichord, boing, silence, and dialing tones. The script in figure 30.15, for example, plays a scale in the harpsichord voice. The c5 in the scale plays a c note in the next-to-highest octave (you can select from three). If the octave is not specified as part of the note, the default middle octave (5) is used.

If you like, you can change the speed with which sounds are played by using the optional *<tempo>* parameter. The script in figure 30.16 shows two Play commands: one that plays a boing sound fairly quickly (tempo set at 240), and one that plays a boing sound at a much slower tempo (set at 60). The tempo can be set to any value between 1 and 800.

Fig. 30.15

A simple scale that uses the Play command.

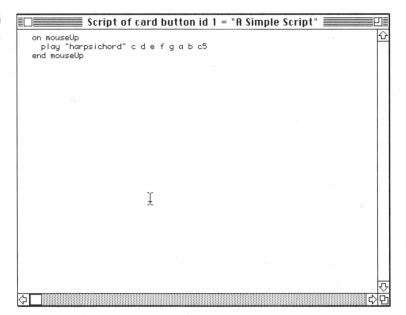

```
═══════════════ Script of card button id 1 = "A Simple Script" ═══════════════
on mouseUp
   play "harpsichord" c d e f g a b c5
end mouseUp
```

As with other HyperTalk commands, it is sometimes helpful to test the effect of your Play command by entering it in the message box before placing it into your script.

Fig. 30.16
Changing the tempo in a
Play command.

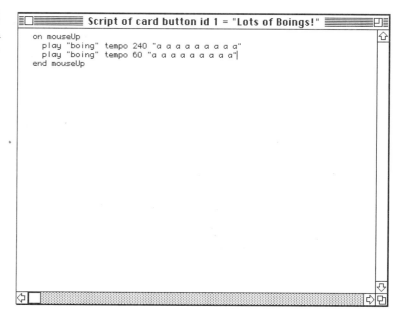

```
on mouseUp
  play "boing" tempo 240 "a a a a a a a a"
  play "boing" tempo 60 "a a a a a a a a"
end mouseUp
```

Composing with HyperCard usually takes a great deal of experimentation, but perseverance can produce some satisfying results.

Adding Visual Effects

Visual effects can be as impressive as sound effects, and HyperTalk offers a host of them. The script shown in figure 30.17 responds to the click of a button by dissolving from the current card to a linked card.

Most visual effect commands are placed before a Go command. Here are the HyperTalk visual effect commands and what they do:

Fig. 30.17

Adding some visual effects
to a script.

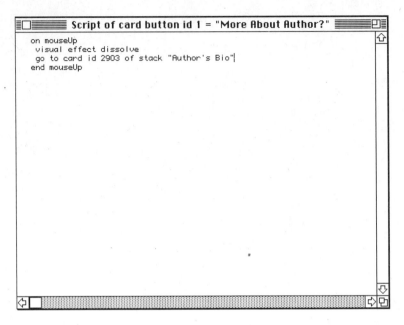

```
▤▯▤▤▤▤▤  Script of card button id 1 = "More About Author?"  ▤▤▤▯▤
on mouseUp
  visual effect dissolve
  go to card id 2903 of stack "Author's Bio"|
end mouseUp
```

Command	Effect
Barn door open	Opens to the next screen from the center out
Barn door close	Opens to the next screen from both edges of the screen in
Scroll left	Replaces the current screen with the new screen by sliding the new screen across from the left
Checkerboard	Creates a checkerboard pattern that fades into the next screen
Iris open	Opens from the center of the card
Iris close	Closes from the center of the card
Zoom open	Opens from the position of the mouse click
Zoom close	Returns to the card shown before a zoom open
Dissolve	Fades from one card to another
Venetian blinds	Goes to the next card by switching horizontal bands
Wipe left	Changes cards with wipe from left to right
Wipe right	Changes cards with wipe from right to left

Command	Effect
Wipe up	Changes cards with wipe from bottom to top
Wipe down	Changes cards with wipe from top to bottom
Scroll right	New card scrolls into picture from left to right
Scroll left	New card scrolls into picture from right to left
Scroll down	New card scrolls into picture from top of screen

Another interesting visual effect is created by the Flash command, which makes the screen flash a designated number of times. Entering **flash 5**, for example, causes the current screen to flash on and off five times and then stop.

Using Interactive Scripts

Suppose that you are constructing a script in which you need to prompt a user to supply information or to select one of several alternative answers to a question. The answer command enables you to ask such questions in a variety of ways. The syntax for the command is

answer *<question>* with *<reply>*

The message box in figure 30.18, for example, asks the question generated by the script entry **answer "What's your name?"** The figure shows how HyperTalk places the question in a dialog and presents it on-screen.

Fig. 30.18

Using the **answer** command to design interactive scripts.

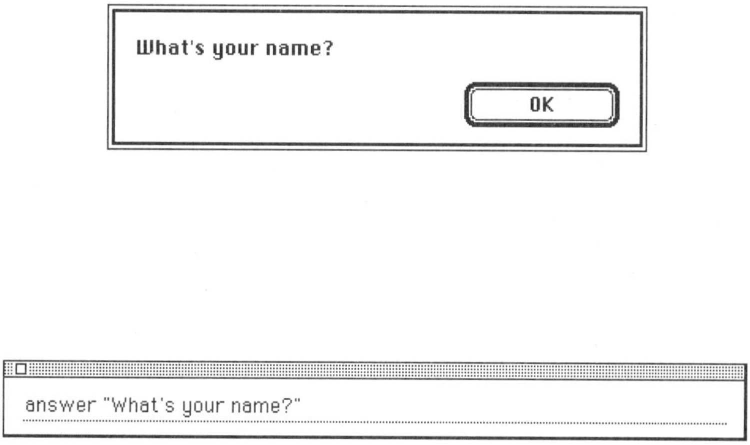

```
What's your name?

                                    OK
```

```
answer "What's your name?"
```

You can create a multiple-choice question like the one shown in figure 30.19 by using the Or command to provide alternatives. The figure shows the format of the command in the message box. If desired, you can link each button in the answer box to another card that provides feedback appropriate for the selected answer. This method is an ideal way to design a learning experience in which immediate feedback is necessary.

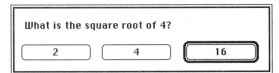

```
answer "What is the square root of 4?" with "2" or "4" or "16"
```

Using Loops

You can use the Repeat command to create command loops in HyperCard. This command instructs HyperCard to repeat a group of commands a number of times. Suppose that you want to open your stack with an important message, and you want to make sure that you bring it to the user's attention. The script in figure 30.20 combines several of the features you have read about in this chapter and repeats the sequence of events five times.

The script plays a boing while flashing the first card in the stack, waits for five seconds, and then flashes again. The End repeat command tells HyperCard when to stop repeating. The script then dissolves into the stack called Lesson 1.

Working with the Date and Time

HyperTalk provides you with a variety of ways to enter the date and time in a field. Suppose, for example, that you have designed a While You Were Out message in which the card contains date and time fields (see fig. 30.21). As figure 30.22 shows, the Put the date command is tied to the button (and field) titled *date*. When you click the Date button, the program puts the date into the date field. The Put the time command works the same way for the time field.

Fig. 30.20

Using the repeat function
to repeat a sequence of
commands.

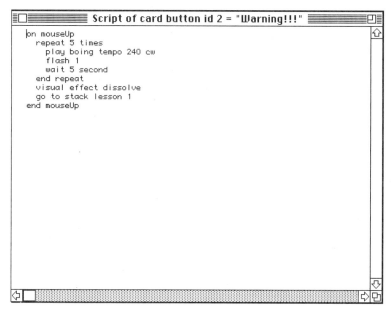

```
on mouseUp
  repeat 5 times
    play boing tempo 240 cw
    flash 1
    wait 5 second
  end repeat
  visual effect dissolve
  go to stack lesson 1
end mouseUp
```

Fig. 30.21

A While You Were Out
form with Date and Time
buttons.

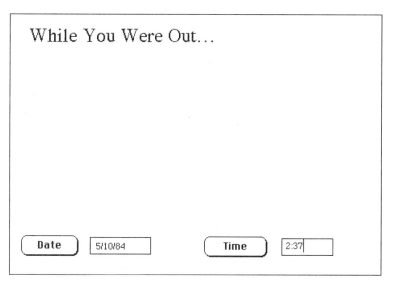

You can also choose to place other forms of the date into a field using different forms of the put command. Use *Put the long date* for a format like *Sunday, May 9, 1993*. Just want the day? Use *Put the first word of long date*. You can play some of the same tricks with the format of the time. Using Put the long time produces *2:37:45 AM* (matched to the System time); Put the time produces *2:37 AM*. You can even combine words and time and date functions. For example, you might have a document that often needs updating. The command Put "Dated" & the long date produces *Dated Friday, March 17, 1992*.

Fig. 30.22
The script for putting in the date.

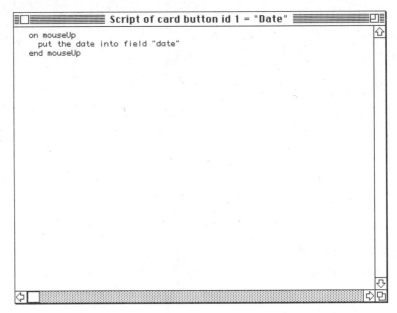

```
on mouseUp
   put the date into field "date"
end mouseUp
```

You can get some programming help with HyperTools #1 and #2 (from Trendware). This product includes 37 tools that provide you with shortcuts and well-conceived general aids for design and develop scripts. With them, for example, you can search for strings of text, leave the stack for other applications (and then return), automate the production of buttons, and edit icons.

Claris HyperCard Developer's Kit offers great user support and complete documentation. In addition, you might want to pick up the book *HyperCard 2 QuickStart*, published by Que Corporation.

Considering Alternatives to HyperCard

Silicon Beach, a subsidiary of Aldus, offers a package called SuperCard that offers you many features HyperCard does not. These features include:

- Use of full-size windows. SuperCard does not restrict visuals to the size of HyperCard cards. Draw and Paint graphics can be sized up to 34 feet by 34 feet.

- Flexible windowing. SuperCard enables you to scroll, resize, and manipulate windows just as you can in any other Macintosh application; several windows can be open at once.

- Full-color object-oriented drawing tools.

- Expanded file importation. SuperCard enables you to import many different types of files, including Encapsulated PostScript.

- Full gray-scale and 8-bit color support.

- On-line help with the scripting language.

- Complete control over menus and menu items.

- Unlimited access to as many open stacks as you want.

- Stand-alone development. With SuperCard you can create applications that will run stand-alone; the end user does not need SuperCard to use them.

- Easy addition of digitized sound.

- Compatibility with HyperCard scripts. (You can run HyperCard scripts with SuperCard.)

- AutoTrace to convert bit-mapped images to draw images.

SuperCard offers some other interesting and potentially useful features in addition to the ones listed. You can use the SuperCard cycle command to set the number of times and the rate at which a card rotates through all or some of its colors. You can use the Move command to place an object on a pixel of your choice. And perhaps best of all, you can attach a script to any object (not just words) or area of a graphic (such as a part of a machine).

These are only a few examples of the features that SuperCard offers. If you're planning to buy HyperCard, you might want to take a look at SuperCard first.

Selecting HyperCard Applications

A great many HyperCard stacks are available to choose from. This section includes some examples of HyperCard stacks on topics that you might find interesting and useful. Several periodicals offer regular reviews of new HyperCard products, so you can find additional information there.

Indexing Stacks

HyperKRS and HyperIndexer enable you to find information in any stack. To use these stacks, you prepare a regular stack (or use one already established). Then you must use HyperIndexer to index each word. Next, you install the HyperKRS engine into the stack. Finally, search and find!

The tool has all the characteristic menus of HyperCard. With such huge stacks (such as the 120,000 records in the CD-ROM National Directory), search tools are invaluable. There is even a Rod Serling-like voice on the disk to introduce you to the product!

Travel Stacks

The designs of HyperCard and SuperCard make them perfect for applications like HyperAtlas that manipulate large quantities of information. HyperAtlas is a series of HyperCard stacks that contains maps and travel information cards. Just click the location you want and HyperAtlas takes you there, providing geographic, economic, and demographic information about countries, states, and cities.

Generating Reports

Many people have complained that generating reports from stacks in HyperCard is much more difficult than it should be (and in some cases is even impossible). Applications such as Reports address this problem.

Reports provides a set of external commands (called *XCNs*) and a generic form for producing reports. You select a tool in Reports and then create the form that you want to use in the HyperCard stack you plan to print. You simply design the form you need, such as an invoice or an information form, and then let Reports do its work. Reports includes features that enable you to sort, perform simple calculations, print reports drawing information from multiple stacks, and print only cards containing selected field values. The last of these features is quite important in a business setting, for example, when you want to bill only those clients who owe $100 or are 30 days late.

Using XCMDs and XFCNs

*XCMD*s and *XFCN*s are chunks of source code written in Pascal or C and then compiled. These terms are thrown around quite a bit in HyperCard literature. An XCMD is an external *command*, and an XFCN is an external *function*. These two items act as extensions to HyperTalk scripts and enable you to access any feature of the Macintosh toolbox. They are, essentially, treated as HyperTalk commands, though they are written in another programming language (C, for example).

Some specific products now on the market consist of libraries of XCMDs and XFCNs that you can plug into your existing scripts. They enable you to do modular script design in which you simply select the external commands you need and avoid detailed scripting.

More stacks and scripts are available with 101 Scripts and Buttons for HyperCard (from Macropac International). These are predesignate scripts that you can incorporate into your existing scripts or use as stand-alone scripts to perform many functions.

The most comprehensive and useful set of XCMDs and XFCNs is Wild Things from Language Systems. This four-disk set is full of external commands and HyperCard extensions that can enhance your stacks as well as add useful functions and routines. Wild Things offers animation, statistical tools, icon design, and special effects. It also includes a full-featured icon editor and ResCopy tools. ResCopy installs resources or tools you use to change the Mac operating environment in HyperCard stacks.

With Wild Things, you have no reason to write a script to draw a curve. You can just go to the DrawCurve stack and use the Width and Height sliders to set the spikiness/smoothness and the shortness/tallness of the curve. After you draw the curve, you can cut and paste the script into a stack. You can add animation effects in much the same way. The source code for all the resources in Pascal, FORTRAN, and C is also included (for programmers). You can even use the templates that are provided to design your own XCMDs.

Authenticate is used to authenticate the contents of a field before the data is written to disk. This add-on application is basically an editing tool. Mutate is used to format or transform the contents of a field. This add-on helps you to increase the consistency of field display; it reduces the amount of code (and scripting time) required to create and use fields.

HyperBASIC from Teknosys helps you to get started designing your own programs for the Mac with external commands. HyperBASIC is a building tool that enables you to create new externals and to edit existing ones. The program gives you direct access to many of the routines in the Mac ROM called the Toolbox. Some of these routines are Font Manager, QuickDraw, and Memory Manager. In addition, the program comes with more than 30 external routines for you to use and modify as you learn.

From Heizer Software comes Dialoger, a HyperCard application that helps you create dialogs (or interactions between your program and the user). Dialoger comes with four stacks: Dialog Maker, Dialog Help, Dialog Commands, and Dialog Examples. These stacks are designed to help you create the specific dialog you need. This program is very thorough and has a host of initial menu options that can lead you through the creation of a dialog. The program also shows off the unique nature of the Mac interface and works with SuperCard and Plus.

Finding Stacks Sources

Educorp and International Data both offer a large assortment of stackware. Here are some other sources worth investigating:

> Advantage Computing
> 24285 Sunnymead Boulevard
> Moreno Valley, CA 92388
> (800) 356-4666

> HyperSource
> 2619 S. 302nd Street
> Federal Way, WA 98003
> (206) 946-2011

> maxStax+
> P.O. Box 2719
> Oakland, CA 94602

Don't forget that information services like CompuServe and America On-Line have nice libraries of stacks available for downloading. And most bulletin board services (BBSs) have large collections of stacks.

The Big Mac Recommendation

HyperCard has received a great deal of attention for providing an extraordinary array of tools that any computer user, beginner or expert, can put to good use. The HyperTalk scripting language uses clear English-like commands like **go** and **answer**, and its application is limited only by the creativity and resourcefulness of the user.

If you need to create a custom application but don't desire to learn programming in depth, HyperCard and SuperCard offer easy-to-use alternatives.

CHAPTER THIRTY-ONE

Programming the Macintosh

I n Chapter 30, "Using HyperCard," you learned how HyperTalk can create simple programs that perform tasks such as linking cards with a button, finding an item, and asking HyperCard to give the date. This chapter focuses on the more generalized aspects of programming and on some of the languages you can use.

First, however, you should familiarize yourself with some programming terminology:

- A *program* is a set of instructions that a computer uses to execute an action or set of actions. A *programmer* is a person who writes a program.

- A *language* is the syntax or grammar used to create your program. (HyperTalk, for example, is the HyperCard programming language, but you learn about many other languages in this chapter.) The actual computer words used in a program are the *code*.

- A *macro* is a small program within a program. Some macro programs—such as QuicKeys 2 or Tempo II—enable you to program by recording your keystrokes.

As application programs have become bigger and more complex, you now find that they commonly come with a programming language, such as HyperCard. FileMaker II has a scripting language, and FoxBase+/Macintosh (a dBASE clone) has an implementation of dBASE.

Getting Started

Most people use computers without ever learning or using a programming language. Most applications discussed in the preceding chapters are complex programs written in various languages (most commonly in C or Pascal). These programs are set up to shield the user from ever having to worry about the details of the program's operation.

In terms of what you can accomplish, no doubt, programming can be powerful, and learning to program can be challenging and rewarding. Programming also is a good intellectual exercise. You might want to write a simple program, for example, to compute the number of days from the present date until your next birthday or a 200-year calendar or a checkbook-balancing program. These tasks may sound difficult, but your job is really a matter of breaking down the task into smaller tasks and then linking them together. Many star programmers started just like you—with a book.

The Macintosh is unique in that a vast library of shareware programs has been created by people just like you. If you have a program that you want to distribute, you can upload the program to a bulletin board and request payment from its users.

All kinds of people program. As a high school student, Raymond Lau created Stuffit, the standard utility for file compression on the Macintosh.

One place to read about the programming mystique is the book *Hackers* by Steve Levy (published by Dell Press).

Programming for the Macintosh is not easy. Consequently, Macintosh programmers are highly sought after. Beginning Macintosh programmers commonly can make $40,000. Programmers with experience make $60,000. Experts can make six-figure salaries. If you are the proud creator of a hit program, of course, the sky is the limit.

Understanding the Programming Process

The most important part of programming is the planning stage. You must plan a program so that you can construct it efficiently. You must decide what the program must do, what features to include (if possible), and how all the parts should work together.

Programmers often use flow charts to help them outline programs (see fig. 31.1). You also can use flow charts on your Macintosh with a commercial project management program such as MacProject II (Claris), Manage That! (Varcon Systems), or MacFlow (Mainstay).

Better, more complex development tools are available for specific languages because few commercial programmers write sophisticated programs completely from scratch anymore. You can buy parts of a program—sometimes from a library of programming routines—and integrate them into your program. You also can use development tools such as those discussed later in this chapter.

At the beginning of a complex project, a programmer spends much time documenting the program, planning each stage of the program's operation. Often, teams of programmers write complex programs. Each member is responsible for one particular feature. Apple writes System Software this way, as do Microsoft and many other companies.

In many instances, however, one programmer writes a major program alone. One example is the original version of the database 4th Dimension from ACIUS. If you've ever used that powerful program, you can begin to realize just what you can accomplish.

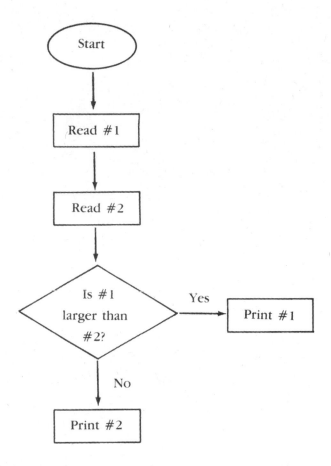

Fig. 31.1

A simple flow chart for a program that compares two numbers and prints the larger one.

Defining a Good Program

Several things differentiate a bad program from a good one (or even a good one from a great one). These characteristics are the following:

- The features the program delivers. Basically, does the program do the job it's supposed to do? If it's an accounting program, for example, you want it to be able to do general ledger business. If it's a grammar checker, you want the program to spot poorly constructed sentences.

- Ease of use. Is the program friendly? Is the program consistent with the computer interface?

An *interface* is all the things on-screen, such as menus, commands, windows, and icons, that make a Macintosh a Macintosh. Apple considers its interface so important that the company publishes a book on the subject for programmers. Apple also has sued other computer companies to protect its interface.

- Program efficiency. The speed at which the program runs indicates how well the programmer wrote the program. Long, complex programs can require that the computer go through unnecessary procedures, but programs with compact code eliminate all but the essential steps.

- Compatibility. A successful program not only runs properly but runs along with your other programs without causing problems.

Apple publishes rules for programs that use a Macintosh, and as often as possible, programmers try to follow those rules. Sometimes when programmers try to add a feature, however, they cheat a little. Often they can get by with cheating, but sometimes they get unexpected results, and the computer bombs. Writing perfect software is impossible.

Debugging Your Program

After you write a program, you must test it thoroughly to make sure that it operates correctly. The process of testing a program is called *debugging*.

You can use professional tools called *debuggers* to help you with this process. MacsBug from Apple Programmers Development Association is a machine-level debugger that is perfect for assembly language programs. TMON by Icon Simulations is one of the most used. Many programming systems, called *development environments,* incorporate debugging tools also. Think C by Symantec enables you to step through your program, executing one line of commands (called code) at a time.

Generally, debugging uses up the larger part of your development time. Using a source-level debugger, such as Think C's, can speed things a bit. But no matter how well you program, problems always crop up—and usually where you least expect them.

Understanding Computers

Learning to program well requires that you know about all aspects of your computer. Some computer languages shield you from knowing what microprocessor you have in your Macintosh or what the bus structure is. Eventually, you learn these details as you program because the commands available to you are defined by your equipment.

Understanding Microprocessors

Macintosh computers use Motorola *microprocessors*—the main processing unit of the computer—referred to as the 680x0 series. This series includes the 68000 (Macintosh 128K through the Classic and the Portable), the 68020 (original Macintosh II and LC), the 68030 (Macintosh SE/30, Classic II, Color Classic, all Macintosh II series except the original Mac II, all PowerBooks and Duos except the PowerBook 100), and the 68040 (all the Quadras and Centris Macintoshes and the upcoming Mac IIIs).

A pple may build its next machine around a *RISC,* or Reduced Instruction Set Computer, chip set. RISC-based machines run faster because they contain a less-complicated instruction set. They run more instructions overall and also run more efficiently. All members of this family of CPUs have beside them on the motherboard a ROM (read-only memory) chip, where instructions and routines (small programs) are encoded.

The 680x0 series is a *CISC* microprocessor, the initial C standing for *Complex.* CISC is the idea of adding functions that a single chip executes. Each chip in the 680x0 series added more functions and power.

RISC holds more promise because it is possible to create more narrowly focused chips that can run much faster to process different commands. Where a CISC chip executes both commands to move data as well as math functions, RISC-based computers direct the data movement to one chip and the math to another.

Any program, including the ones Apple writes to operate the Macintosh System and the Finder, is read to the microprocessor one command line at a time. The chip decodes the command and then performs the action—rather like a human being reading a set of assembly instructions. Microprocessors actually execute very simple commands such as moving a bit of data, adding two numbers, comparing an item of data with another, and then going to a location based on the test. They give the illusion of being "smart" by doing a large number of simple tasks very quickly.

Understanding Machine Language

In the early days of microcomputing, users bought a few boards, some chips (most likely including the 8008 microprocessor by Intel—the first true microprocessor introduced), some LEDs (light emitting diodes) for their display, and a few flip switches. Then they soldered all of it together and had a computer.

In those days, users "talked" directly with the microprocessor, flipping switches to indicate the machine instruction they wanted placed in memory, using *machine language*.

A CPU works with digital signals turned on or off. The language you use consists of instructions made up of ones or zeros, which correspond to on or off. This machine language was used for a brief time in the 1950s on larger computers and in the early 1970s when microcomputing first became a hobby. ("Home brewing" a computer—building one in your den—actually started before this time; once the microprocessor was introduced, however, it really took off as a hobbyist pastime.)

In figure 31.2, you see a screen from Norton Utilities for the Macintosh by Symantec. The screen shows the Microsoft Word 5.0 application open with its machine code displayed. You could change the code and any aspect of the program, but you must know how to program before this capability is useful. If you change the code incorrectly, you can destroy your file.

CAUTION

A lways work on a copy of your file and boot up from a copy of your System if possible.

As you can see in the figure, this kind of programming—dealing directly with machine language—is confusing. In the early days, you had to remember that, say, "B9" meant to add two numbers together. You usually had to keep a card or booklet of instructions handy.

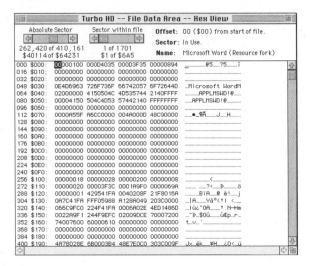

Fig. 31.2

Machine code displayed by Symantec Tools in SUM.

Different microprocessers have different instruction sets. That is, even though two microprocessors from different manufacturers might have more or less the same power, their machine language is different (usually different machine languages are not at all alike), their internal structure is different, and the way they go about executing commands is different.

Two microprocessors might be capable of doing more or less the same things, but the programs that instruct them how to operate are totally different. This difference is one of the barriers between IBM PCs and Macintoshes. They speak totally different languages at their most basic levels.

Understanding Assembly Language

The step up from machine language is called *assembly language*. This language enables you to enter commands with *mnemonics* that at least resemble the command they cause to be executed. The 68000 microprocessor, which was used in the original Macintosh and up to the Classic, uses the MOVE D1,D2 command, for example, to move data from one location to another, whereas the machine language is something like 0001 0010 0000 0010 or 1202.

Assembly language exists for each family of microprocessors, and an assembler translates computer programs written in assembly into a form that your CPU understands (a set of ones and zeros). Some programmers use assembly language to create small, compact routines that execute quickly.

Assembly language is easier to understand, but you are still faced with learning different assembly languages for different machines, and the mnemonics can still be difficult. (I ran across a good one from the old 8086—the granddaddy of the current IBM PC chips—called XLAT, which, if you try to pronounce it, sounds amusingly close to a particular over-the-counter medicine that shall remain unmentioned.) Assembly is difficult to program in and still not portable. You cannot move assembly language programs from one computer to another.

Most programmers, however, don't use assembly language to program because they can use more sophisticated languages to create complex programs with fewer lines of code. When you use Pascal or C, both high-level programming languages, you must compile your program (source code) into *object code,* or machine language. Assembly language is slightly removed from machine language. For every assembly instruction is one machine language instruction; for Pascal and C, sometimes one instruction can translate into several machine language instructions.

Using Compilers and Interpreters

All high-level languages work by using complex commands. In BASIC, you may have a PRINT command as part of a larger program, for example. When the Macintosh does a print routine using this command, the computer actually executes several functions.

To allow a language to use complex (often English-based) words after you finish writing your program, the language initiates a recoding of your instructions into machine language. This process is called *compilation.* When you buy a commercial version of a language like C or Pascal, the package is a *compiler.*

Even some macro packages require compilation to run efficiently. WorksPlus Command (Lundgren and Associates), a macro package for Microsoft Works, compiles your macro after you finish writing it.

High-level languages have the advantage of being more like English, but this measure is relative. The C language, currently used by most programmers on microcomputers such as the Macintosh and IBM PC, still uses some rather arcane commands such as *strcspn* and *wcstombs* and, one of my favorites, *fflush*.

Still, when you move from one computer to the other, you do not have to relearn the entire language—just the parts that are different. Before the Macintosh, programmers could move rather freely between computers and often even run programs from one computer on another without having to relearn languages. The Macintosh took such a different approach to computers that even if you knew Pascal, the high-level language the Macintosh was geared toward using, or C, the high-level language that became standard, you still had much to learn.

This need to learn was mainly due to the Macintosh interface—the use of graphic images such as windows, icons, menus, and the mouse, to communicate with the user. The Macintosh was part of a growing idea in computing whose time now appears to be coming. This idea is object-oriented programming.

Understanding Object-Oriented Programming

In recent times, the development of languages has taken a new turn. The very idea of a program being a set of instructions executed one by one is being abandoned. And rather quickly lately. Instead, programming is turning toward object-oriented programming.

Old programming ideas are being turned inside out. The usual way of creating a window on the Macintosh, for example, is to write a series of commands that cause the microprocessor to draw the window, giving it a title bar, adding scroll bars, and the like. Then, when the user clicks the close box, another set of commands describes how the window closes.

Now programmers are looking at things in reverse. You know what a window is. And you know windows have certain properties, such as close boxes and scroll bars. So you consider the window to be an abstract object. Then the windows that appear on the Macintosh screen are specific instances of the window object. Rather than go to the trouble of drawing each window, you can request the creation of an instance of a window object. Then you can send messages to the window object (a message such as "close" or "scroll").

It's almost as if the objects that were once created by the programming code are now in charge of the code that creates them. In a development environment such as Prograph (covered later in this chapter), you do not bother with how a window is created; you simply create an object that is an instance of a window object. Your new window object inherits methods (behaviors) of the window object type (such as opening, closing, and scrolling).

Assembly language gives you more abstract commands such as MOVE, but you still have to know which part of the chip (or computer memory) you want to move data to and from.

High-level languages have become abstract enough that you could almost move easily from one machine to the other. The PRINT command of BASIC is on every computer that runs BASIC. But you still run into idiosyncrasies that differentiate one machine from the other.

Object-oriented programming offers to give you a level of abstraction that will create truly portable programs. The program need never know whether it is running on a Macintosh, an IBM PC, or some yet-to-be-introduced computer. A window will be a window, regardless of the machine instructions needed to actually draw it on the screen of the computer.

Understanding Interfaces

Among the first microcomputers built were character-based machines such as the IBM PC. For these computers, you type commands into the computer by keyboard, and they are in text form (**Format A:**, for example, to initialize a disk).

A character-based computer normally has a prompt, which is the computer's way of saying it is ready to accept commands. This kind of interface—commonly called a *command line interface (CLI)*—is fast and powerful but very basic. CLIs also are difficult to learn—rather like assembly or some high-level languages.

The prevalence of IBM PCs and PC clones is due in part to the fact that CLIs are programmer oriented. Programmers need to exercise a great deal of control over a computer, and the basic level of CLIs gives them the ability to do so. The use of CLIs was also dominant among the room-filling mainframe computers businesses were accustomed to using.

This early use is probably where much of the prejudice against the Macintosh came from. "Real" computers were arcane behemoths with text-based interfaces that did things fast. The new Macintosh, on the other hand, was rather slow and had a simple interface based on pictures.

The Macintosh is an example of a *graphical user interface (GUI)*. Most functions on a Macintosh are accomplished by using symbols (icons) and motion-related input (like you do with your mouse).

The disadvantages of a GUI are that it uses a lot of memory and is slower than a text-based machine. The advantages are that GUI is intuitive and easy to learn. Essentially, a GUI puts much of the work on the machine rather than the user, which means that the interface has a great deal of overhead in processor time and memory use. In the earlier days of microcomputing when machines were more expensive than people's time, business was justified in many ways in preferring CLI computers, which required users to read manuals and spend weeks making mistakes and learning long, convoluted commands.

In more recent times, however, computers have become—and continue to become—less expensive than the time of a human. There is little justification to make a user learn things that a computer can handle. Why make a user remember a path name, for example, as he or she must in a CLI machine? Rather, have the computer remember the path and simply display an icon that enables the user to access a file.

Graphical interfaces are by no means unique to the Macintosh. New Wave for Hewlett-Packard computers and various UNIX shells, such as X-Windows and Open Motif, are examples of graphical interfaces, as is IBM's OS/2 operating system. The Apple Macintosh's success spurred their development somewhat, but overall the idea of a GUI has been growing for a number of years as computers have become less expensive and more powerful. And it makes progressively more sense to turn basic operations over to them, freeing the user to do other work.

The interface for Microsoft Windows for DOS-based machines also is almost exclusively graphical, and a host of applications have been developed to fit that interface. In many ways, the Macintosh and the DOS operating systems are coming closer together in appearance and functionality.

All items that appear on-screen, such as windows and menus, are built into the interface and must be included in your program. As your Macintosh refreshes the screen, it builds a new image of the screen for the next update in a part of your video card's RAM called a *screen buffer*. This buffer is emptied and rebuilt with each pass of your monitor's electronic sweep.

But if the programmer has to re-create the programming code to draw a window in each program, for instance, Macintosh programs would be enormous and require massive amounts of memory to run in. This problem is, indeed, what IBM PC software manufacturers began to run into as they began to develop programs that were easier to use. Each program had to "reinvent the wheel," so to speak. If the programmer wanted to open a window with scroll bars, he or she had to incorporate the code to draw and run the window into each program.

Programming with the Toolbox

The *Toolbox*—a set of programs used by developers to show windows, create dialogs, and much more—makes the Macintosh special. This section discusses elements of the Toolbox, the choices available for programming languages, and the way you decide which one to use.

Apple Computer, Inc., sponsors a multiple volume set of guidelines that detail all the elements of the Macintosh Toolbox. These guidelines are called *Inside Macintosh* (published by Addison-Wesley). A cross reference to the guideline volumes is published in a separate book called *Macintosh X-Ref*. These books are not the place to learn how to program the Macintosh, however. They are more like the programmer's encyclopedia to the Macintosh. When you need to know how to access a part of the Toolbox, you can look up that part. The Toolbox consists of a set of *managers*, which are each described separately in *Inside Macintosh*. If you need to know how to access the Macintosh font routines, for example, you look up the Font Manager.

A developer's tool worth mentioning for developing a Macintosh application interface is AppMaker by Bowers Development. This prototyping tool can be invaluable because the Macintosh can be difficult to program. A great deal of complex programming goes into the Macintosh's appearance to make the interface understandable and friendly. But taking the burden off the users often places it on the programmer.

With AppMaker, you click to produce items, such as windows and menus, or to take advantage of the library of routines provided with the product. You also can generate code that is compatible with several different languages such as C and Pascal. AppMaker is offered at a substantial educational discount.

Figure 31.3 shows a set of menus created by using AppMaker. The MainMenu option lists the File and the Edit menus, and the Options menu is added. The Phase 1, Phase 2, and Phase 3 items also are added on that menu. You can create any menu by using graphics, text, and sound.

Fig. 31.3
A set of menus created by
using AppMaker.

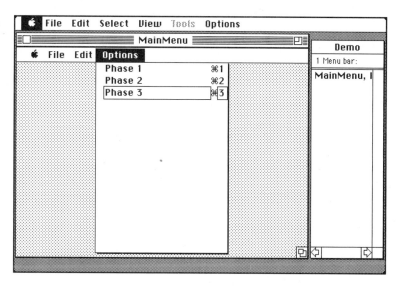

The Toolbox is organized around specific functions, such as printing, communications, events, QuickDraw routines, and so on. When your program asks Macintosh to do something, the program is placing a call to the Toolbox for a particular manager.

All paint programs on the Macintosh have similar tools, for example, and many of the same selection techniques are available in different programs like Word or Nisus because many routines were encoded into the ROM or are part of the System file. Apple encourages this uniformity and issues a set of guidelines as to how programs can work. The whole idea is to create a user experience that makes working with new, unfamiliar programs easy for the user.

Understanding the Event-Driven Environment

The Macintosh is an event-driven computer—meaning that the computer constantly checks for new input and monitors the state of the current input. The Event Manager of the Macintosh Toolbox checks such things as whether your mouse button is up or down, whether you have issued a keyboard or menu command, whether you have clicked in a window or on an icon, and so on.

The Event Manager checks conditions many times a second and passes the events to the running programs—along with other information such as which window is frontmost on the screen—and the programs must decide for themselves how to respond to the event.

 A complete explanation of the Toolbox is beyond the scope of this book. For more information, check the section "Finding Resources for Macintosh Programmers" later in this chapter.

Understanding Memory Management

Your Macintosh must do some juggling to keep several programs running at the same time. When you boot up, the Macintosh loads the Finder and System, which then run as long as the Macintosh is on. If you launch an application, that application runs also. All programs must be placed somewhere in the main memory of the Macintosh. And each program uses memory to store and manipulate data. The Macintosh has only one continuous block of memory and must portion it out between programs. This portioning is called *memory management*.

The basic principle of memory management is that your computer executes programs in random-access memory (RAM). The amount of RAM has a direct bearing on the size of your application load. Places in RAM are assigned addresses, or specific locations in a computer's RAM, which are numbered from low memory to high. Your System (which loads first) goes into low memory, and Apple assigns these address numbers so that no other programs can run in them. This part of memory is called the *System Heap*.

Applications load above the System Heap, and the addresses taken normally are not released until the application is closed. Programs (including the Finder) are loaded into the upper section of memory called the *Application Heap*. Between the System Heap and the Application Heap is the remainder of memory, and either heap can grow into this free memory as needed. (It is indeed possible for the two heaps to collide in memory and destroy one another, which leads to a crash. In fact, poor memory management by application programmers is the most common cause of crashes on the Macintosh.)

The Memory Manager in the Toolbox oversees the allocation and releasing (deallocation) of memory. The Memory Manager also does housekeeping such as reordering the blocks of memory allocated to applications to keep things tidy and to free up as much of the unused memory as possible. (One of the biggest headaches new programmers have in learning the Macintosh is knowing when the Memory Manager moves memory around behind their program's backs. You must take special pains to ensure that your program doesn't access memory that has been moved when it was not looking—another common cause of program crashes on the Macintosh.)

Understanding Apple's Human Interface Guidelines

Apple is so concerned with preserving what is called "the look and feel" of its interface and programs that it publishes a guideline called *The Human Interface Guidelines* (published by Addison-Wesley), which tells programmers how to make their applications behave.

By decree, you must have at least the Apple, File, and Edit menus, and those menus must contain certain commands, such as Open, Close, and Quit. The use of certain keystrokes, such as ⌘-O for Open, is required, and others are strongly recommended.

Apple maintains the guidelines, which discuss such things as how to use color to communicate effectively with the user, which buttons should be the "default" (should a Cancel or OK button be activated by pressing the Return key?), how to make icons meaningful, and other such topics.

I strongly recommend a thorough reading of *The Human Interface Guidelines* for all new programmers. Many programs have died in the market and been forgotten because of user rejection. One of the biggest complaints leveled against them is that they do not adhere to the Macintosh interface.

Choosing a Language

Because you are about to choose a language to learn, you probably are wondering where to start. Most people begin with a good high-level language such as BASIC, Pascal, or C. BASIC is somewhat easier—also less powerful—than Pascal, which is easier than C. In terms of use in Macintosh programming, C is used more commonly today. All serious Macintosh programmers also need to know Pascal, which is in common use and referred to often by publications you may use (especially *Inside Macintosh*). The Toolbox was originally developed in Pascal.

Schools tend to teach BASIC and Pascal. Pascal was chosen as the standard language in the College Entrance Examination Advanced Placement tests. Pascal was developed by a man named Niklaus Wirth, who had the intention of using the language to teach programming. Pascal is oriented toward good programming habits and has a clean, logical structure.

Two types of languages are used today: procedural and object-oriented programs.

A *procedural programming language* creates a command structure that manipulates defined routines in some programmed ways. Most of the common languages, like BASIC, Pascal, and C, are imperative in nature (imperative as in "print this," "read that," and so on).

The smaller—but fastest growing—class of languages is made up of *object-oriented programming (OOP)* languages. HyperTalk and SmallTalk/V Macintosh are examples of OOP. Several languages, such as C++ and Object Pascal, are rewrites of other languages (C and Pascal, respectively) with defined objects built in. In OOP, objects are pre-defined along with their properties and appropriate actions that you can perform on them.

Now entire object-oriented programming environments such as Prograph and MacApp are available. Recent trends indicate that the Macintosh is moving rapidly toward object-oriented programming.

NOTE

Symantec (owner of Think C, the dominant Macintosh programming environment) recently acknowledged that much of its original programming staff had left the Think C project. Industry observation is that the people who create the tools used by application programmers in creating Macintosh software are migrating to object-oriented environments. This migration is a sure sign that object-oriented programming is on the verge of taking over.

A language you buy generally has several pieces to it, and most languages operate with several windows open to show you those parts. In one window you program, in another you have your compiler set up, and in a third you can set up and work with your debugger. All these windows are part of a commercial package, which is why programmers frequently refer to a language package as a development environment.

Originally, the Macintosh operating system was programmed in Pascal. When you look at early editions of *Inside Macintosh,* you see Pascal examples. Over time, C became more popular so that now most serious programmers know and program in a version of C. Many programmers still use Pascal, however, and either language serves you well in your programming experience.

The term *portability* refers to the rewriting of an application in another language so that it runs on another computer. Porting an application from the Macintosh to DOS means that the application has a better chance of being commercially successful. Often, porting means that you must rewrite the program totally from scratch, but not always. Object-oriented environments such as the Macintosh, Windows, and the forthcoming systems developed jointly by IBM and Apple are object oriented. Portability will become easier as object orientation takes over.

When you choose a programming environment, keep this in mind: you probably should learn Pascal and C because of their prevalence in the Macintosh universe. But you should concentrate on object-oriented systems, which will be the dominant standard in the near future.

Understanding High-Level Languages

This section discusses several high-level languages and commercial products that are available for the Macintosh. As a worthwhile introduction to computer languages, read *Computer Languages: A Guide to the Perplexed* by Naomi S. Baron (published by Anchor/Doubleday, 1986). The McGraw-Hill *Encyclopedia of Electronics and Computers* contains a concise dictionary of technical terms.

BASIC

BASIC (Beginner's All-purpose Symbolic Instruction Code) was written in 1964 by John Kemeny and Thomas Kurtz at Dartmouth College as a simplified version of the earlier FORTRAN, for student instruction. BASIC is the most popular computer language because of its simple syntax and is the most often taught language in college. By estimate, more people know BASIC than can speak French.

BASIC—somewhat free-form in its earlier versions—has evolved into newer standardized versions that are more structured. Structured BASIC includes features such as line numbering and indentation marks for a procedure in the source code, both features found in Pascal. Microsoft BASIC and True BASIC (written by Kemeny and Kurtz) are earlier versions. Other BASIC packages include DS-BASIC (Daystar Software), PCMacBASIC (Pterodactyl Software), RBASIC (Indexed Software), and FUTUREBASIC (Zedcor). MS QuickBASIC, which is a later, more-structured version, enables you to program in one window while giving the results in a second. You also can print the results.

CAUTION

Keep in mind that most forms of BASIC are not entirely compatible with one another.

Pascal

Pascal, named for French mathematician Blaise Pascal and written by Niklaus Wirth, is a highly structured programming language. Based in part on ALGOL, Pascal is a standardized language with specifications by the International Standards Organization. Pascal is a recommended starting place for learning C, which is now the most popular development language for microcomputers. As mentioned previously, the original Macintosh operating system was programmed in Pascal.

A recent package called Just Enough Pascal from Symantec is a tutorial on Pascal on the Macintosh. In this tutorial, you program windows and create a simple game. Just Enough Pascal is a highly recommended introduction to programming.

The commercial versions of Pascal on the Macintosh include Think's Lightspeed Pascal and Turbo Pascal for the Macintosh from Borland International.

C and C++

C is the developmental language created by Dennis Ritchie at AT&T as a portable language on which UNIX is based. C, which succeeded a language called B, is structured, runs fast, and has good memory management features built in, but it is difficult to learn.

Several versions of C are available to Macintosh users, including Aztec C (Manx Software), Consulair MacC 68020/68881 (Consulair Corp.), Consulair MacC Jr. (Consulair Corp.), and Think C (Symantec Corp.).

Because of its speed, Think C is a highly regarded and popular product—the dominant standard in Macintosh programming.

Recently, C has been updated to include object-oriented features. Apple has completely rewritten the System and Finder for System 7 in this new language, called C++. The package Designer C++ is available from Oasys, Inc., and from the Apple Programmers Developers Association. Symantec's Think C supports C++ object-oriented features, also.

LISP

The LISP language works by acting on, or manipulating, lists of items. The name is an acronym that comes from LISt Processing.

Although LISP requires significant amounts of memory to run, it is a highly efficient, intelligent language with considerable power. LISP has found favor in various artificial intelligence applications, serving as the underlying mechanism, or inference engine, for programs from academics to industrial research.

Available packages include ExperCommon LISP and ExperLISP (both from ExperTelligence), MacScheme (Semantic Microsystem), and Allegro Common LISP (for A/UX) from Franz, Inc.

L ISP is a complex language that requires considerable process ing of instructions. Often people add coprocessor boards, such as the Micro Explorer NuBus board from Texas Instruments (for the Macintosh II series), to make programs run faster.

LOGO

LOGO, developed at MIT by Don Bobrow and Seymour Papert, is a favorite language to teach to children. LOGO is based on LISP. Its name comes from the Greek word *logos*, meaning word or thought (logical, logistics, and so on).

Graphics are easy to program in LOGO, which is a full programming language. Considered more difficult to create documented programs in than Pascal or C, LOGO is not recommended as a starting place. Packages available are ExperLOGO-Plus (ExperTelligence) and Terrapin LOGO for the Macintosh (Terrapin).

Forth

Forth, a less popular language than some of the others already discussed, is used by some programmers as a primary programming tool. Forth is a compact language that emphasizes the interaction between the user and the machine's capabilities.

MacForth from Creative Solutions is a leading Forth version and has been used to create a variety of interesting applications. Easy 3-D, for example, was written entirely in MacForth, taking advantage of the specific Macintosh functions that deal with menus, windows, files, and mice.

Forth has never been a popular programming language, however, and may not survive in the Macintosh world for much longer.

Miscellaneous Languages

Many other languages are available for the Macintosh. Every other day, it seems, a new one is developed. Most of these languages see very limited service, some die out, and some (like C++) become important over time. The following paragraphs discuss some of these languages but by no means all of them.

Modula-2, based on—but more sophisticated than—Pascal, offers modules and concurrent programming. In *concurrent programming*, more than one module can be executing at the same time. Programs written in Modula-2 can be compiled in modules and run separately, thus providing real-time control. Packages include MacLogimo Plus (Project Modula), MetCom Modula-2 (Metropolis Computer Networks, Inc.), and Semper-Soft Modula-2 for MPW (Semper Software).

COBOL is an early computer language that has found favor on mainframe computers for business applications. The name stands for COmmon Business-Oriented Language. Virtually no programs run in COBOL on microcomputers.

FORTRAN (FORmula TRANslator) is an old standby language used for mathematical manipulations mostly on larger computers. It remains in some use at research centers but has no impact on microcomputers. Packages include FORTRAN Converter (True BASIC), which translates FORTRAN to True BASIC; MacFORTRAN (various versions by Absoft Corp.); and Mactran Plus (DCM Data Products).

APL, or A Programming Language, is useful for manipulating numerical arrays. APL manipulates matrices, creates compact code, and uses symbols that make a program hard to understand and read. Packages include APL*Plus System for the Macintosh (STSC, Inc.) and APL 68000 for the Apple Macintosh (Spencer Organization).

VIP, or Visual Interactive Programming (Mainstay), uses the flowchart analogy, icons, and symbols to create a program. An example of a graphical language in VIP is the program itself, which is what you see when you examine the source code.

Using Object-Oriented Programming

Object-oriented programming (OOP) is the beginning of a new wave in programming languages. Unlike Pascal or C, which are examples of procedural languages, OOP manipulates defined objects in ways that the objects define themselves.

In OOP, different classes of objects are loosely arranged in an order, or hierarchy. Actions or commands flow through this structure of objects until they find an appropriate object that can handle them.

To draw a circle on-screen in procedural (imperative) code, for example, follow these general steps:

1. Initialize the Toolbox.

2. Open a window.

3. Draw a circle.

In OOP, you do the following:

1. Initialize the Toolbox.

2. Create the definition of the circle object. (This step includes drawing instructions.)

3. Tell the circle to draw itself.

The advantage of OOP is that you can change or alter the basics of an object without affecting the rest of the program. The routines that actually put the bits on-screen to draw the circle are hidden from the part of the program that orders the circle to draw itself. Hence, if you need to change the way bits are placed on the screen to draw the circle, you can change the program easily.

This approach is rather like using building blocks or interchangeable parts. The main program needs to know only that it can draw a circle by issuing a "draw circle" message. The entire routine that draws the circle can be changed or replaced without affecting the main program.

This is the object-oriented approach of the Macintosh Toolbox in ideal form. Properly programmed applications do not need to know how the Toolbox does its magic. Rather, they send messages through well-defined interfaces. To draw a circle, for example, Macintosh programs can request that the QuickDraw part of the Toolbox draw a circle on-screen. How QuickDraw actually draws the circle is unknown and unimportant. If Apple were to change how QuickDraw operates, the application could still use the routines to draw a circle, never being aware of the change.

Although the object-oriented approach described above is the ideal situation and does not work perfectly (no programming endeavor can be perfect), this approach works well. Recently, I ran across some disks from 1985. On these disks were programs written to run on the original Macintosh with the original Toolbox. Out of curiosity, I attempted to run them under System 7 on a IIsi with a Toolbox changed and enhanced by several versions from the original. Most of the programs ran without trouble. Some exhibited strange behavior, but only one crashed the Macintosh. If you try this experiment with an IBM PC, you get nothing from 1985 to run at all.

One object-oriented development environment is Prograph from TGS Systems. This visual programming language is very easy to use. You work with the familiar Macintosh interface to create a program.

Prograph is completely picture oriented. In figure 31.4, you can see the Health Monitor demo of Prograph (which comes with Prograph) and how icons are connected with each other as part of the graphical nature of the application.

Fig. 31.4
The Health Monitor program example.

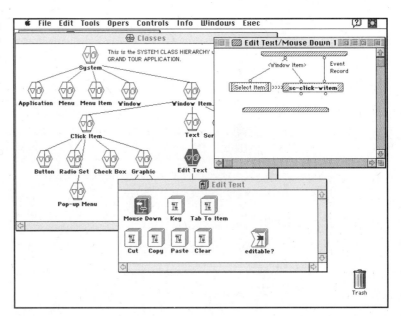

The whole point of object-oriented design is to create enough underlying structure to the program so that complex programming tasks are bundled together into simple manipulations.

Prograph enables you to create the methods of an object by linking icons together. Consider the Edit Text/Mouse Down 1 window in figure 31.4. Already you can see the flow of data even though the icons may not make sense to you. Data items (the Window Item and the Event Record) flow down the connector lines to the two rectangular icons that then operate on the data.

You create the objects you need with a single command (such as clicking the mouse to create an instance of a button in the Classes window). Object-oriented programming is easy to get started with: just understand what objects are available and how they are related, and off you go.

On further examination, you also realize that all the objects and their relationships are available to you for changes. You can change the behaviors of objects—their methods—to suit your needs. And the biggest advantage is that you can change them individually without affecting other parts of your program. For example, you can change the behavior of a button easily, often without rewriting code that uses the button.

Any OOP language is truly full featured. Because of the basic properties of the objects, the language also is highly structured. This structure makes the language logical, easy to plan programs in, and powerful.

When Steve Jobs visited Xerox Corporation's Palo Alto Research Center (PARC), where he saw the Xerox STAR, he immediately grasped the importance of its graphical user interface. The STAR served as the model for the Apple Lisa computer, which later was developed into the Apple Macintosh.

Underlying the Xerox STAR and equally as significant was an object-oriented programming language called SmallTalk, which computer visionary Alan Kay (now an Apple Fellow) created. Kay defined many of the principles of graphical user interfaces.

SmallTalk needs significant memory and speed to operate. Now that the Macintosh has grown, this language is in commercial packages. Two such packages are SmallTalk-80 from ParcPlace Systems and SmallTalk/V Macintosh from Digitalk, Inc. SmallTalk/V Macintosh has a PC 286/386 counterpart, and the vendor claims it is easily portable. People who have worked with SmallTalk say that creating a full-featured program is hard, but the program itself is easy to learn and use.

If you're interested in the early days of Apple computers and the philosophy and politics that created the Macintosh, read *West of Eden* by Frank Rose (Viking Press).

Defining Artificial Intelligence

Artificial intelligence (AI) programs, or *expert systems*, are computer programs (often written in languages like C or Pascal) that deduce solutions to complex problems based on a clear set of rules that you program in.

An AI program runs on what is referred to commonly as an *inference engine.* Many AI programs are statistically based. You supply initial conditions and any subsequent factors that are important, and the AI program does the deduction based on a clearly defined set of rules. Obviously, the AI program is only as good as the programmer who programs it. In this rapidly developing field, however, these programs are quite good.

Often, AI programs manipulate lists of objects in specific ways or deal with specific properties of objects. This capability makes AI perfect for leading-edge languages such as LISP and OOP. Many of the languages owe their existence to the solution of particular problems in the field of artificial intelligence.

Applications of AI span the entire spectrum of life from the engineering disciplines (such as optimizing the construction and operation of a microchip), to speeding up a factory floor, to distilling the knowledge of a human expert (say, in soup making) into a set of rules that others can use.

The preceding sections have discussed some languages, like LOGO and LISP, that are commonly used in AI applications. Some others include Advanced A CASE, or computer-aided software engineering, a programming tool in which you use the software to write other software. Sometimes CASE tools are endowed with AI features, but not always.

Some others include A.I. Systems' Prolog (Advanced A.I. Systems), Cognate (Peridom, Inc.), ExperFacts (ExperTelligence), ExperProlog II (ExperTelligence), Inter-Expert (Human Intellect Systems), Level5 Macintosh (Information Builders), MacSmarts (Cognition Technology Corp.), Nextra and Nextra Object (Neuron Data), Nexsus (Human Intellect Systems), and SuperExpert (Softsync).

CASE, or computer-aided software engineering, is a programming tool in which you use the software to write other software. Sometimes CASE tools are endowed with AI features, but not always.

With CASE, you can create complex computer programs logically and quickly. Although a complete discussion of CASE falls outside the scope of this book, the language is an important developer's tool and part of a rapidly advancing field.

CASE tools typically cost many thousands of dollars and require a long time to learn. Packages available include ACPVision (Andyne Computing Ltd.), AdaFlow (Iconix Software Engineering), Blue/20 and /60 (Advanced Software Logic), DEFT (Deft), Design (Meta Software Corp.), ERVision (Andyne Computing), FormsProgrammer (OHM Software), Foundation Vista (Menlo Business Systems), Iconix PowerTools (Iconix Software Engineering), MacAnalyst (Excel Software), Macintosh Bubbles (StarSys, Inc.), MacDesigner (Excel Software), MetaDesigner (Excel Software), and Silverrun (Peat Marwick).

Using ResEdit

ResEdit, the resource editor, is Apple's programming tool that enables a developer to enter a program and easily change its features, or to create the interface objects such as windows, menus, and icons for a new program. Using ResEdit is not programming, but most Macintosh users find working with ResEdit to be fun because the tool enables you to manipulate features such as layout, icons, dialogs, and a whole host of other features. Programmers also must understand resources on the Macintosh and how to work with ResEdit because they must deal with the objects ResEdit manipulates.

Understanding How a Resource Editor Works

Macintosh files are different from those found on other microcomputers. Macintosh files consist of two parts: the resource fork and the data fork. The *resource fork* contains resources such as icons, dialogs, and menu commands—the things that make a Macintosh program look like a Macintosh program. The *data fork* contains all the data you create in a file.

Some files created by applications contain only data and may have only a data fork. Separating the two parts of a file enables developers to improve the program by changing the resources without concerning themselves with the data. This separation modularizes the process.

When developers write a program for the Macintosh, their resources usually are grouped into common units. Developers normally create a template that can be viewed in the resource editor for that resource. Not all resources are mapped out this way; the developer must do it. If a developer doesn't like a particular menu command location or keystroke equivalent, he or she can use the template and ResEdit to change it.

A developer may create a template and put so much of the guts of the program out where it can be changed because the procedure greatly simplifies the development process. Few Macintosh users, however, tap into the power of ResEdit—which is probably a good thing. ResEdit is both powerful and dangerous. You can easily damage a file and cause your Macintosh to crash or behave strangely.

If you use ResEdit, work only on copies of files so that if you do ruin something, you can start over easily without damaging your system. If you do make an error, before you save anything, choose Revert File from the File menu to return to the original status.

In figure 31.5, you can see the ResEdit opening screen and icon (for Version 2.1), a playful icon that opens your Macintosh world to any changes you may want to make.

Fig. 31.5
The opening ResEdit
screen.

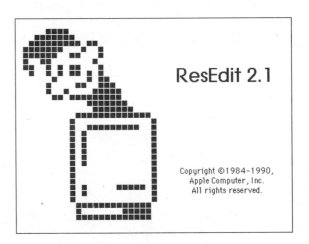

In figure 31.6, ResEdit has been launched, and the System file has been opened.

In the active window is a partial list (shown as icons) of all the resource templates available for editing. Typical resource templates are as follows:

Resource name	Refers to
WIND	Window
PICT	Picture
SIGN	Small icons
PAT	Patterns
TEMP	Templates
PAT#	Single patterns
MENU	Menu definitions
PREC	Printing
ICN#	Icon list
FKEY	Function key control
FONT	Font information
ALRT	Alert or warning boxes
DITL	Dialog text
DSAT	System start-up box
DLOG	Dialogs
CURS	Cursor
ICON	Icons

Fig. 31.6
Resource templates viewed in ResEdit for a System file.

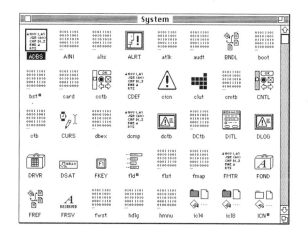

CAUTION

An important rule to remember when running ResEdit is to work on a backup copy of a file. Changes you make may crash your program. In some cases, you can corrupt your System file. Always work on copies of files, not the originals—especially if you're making changes to the System or Finder files.

Changing Icons

You can use ResEdit to change the icons that appear on your Desktop. The procedure is as follows:

1. Launch ResEdit.

2. Double-click the System file's name to open it.

3. Double-click the ICN# resource, which contains many of the main icons.

4. Double-click the icon representing the System file icon. (This icon is displayed graphically; you see the System file's icon in the window.)

You see the screen shown in figure 31.7.

Fig. 31.7
The System icon open in ResEdit.

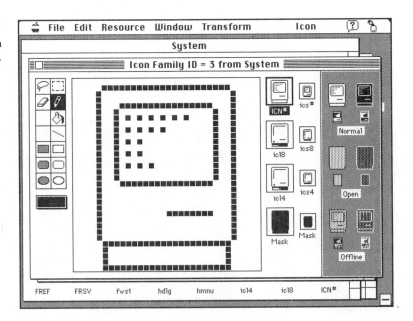

You can see how you can choose from several already-constructed substitutions and then go on to design your own for normal disk icons, ones that represent open files, and more. Icons consist of two patterns: a mask and a monitor. The actual icon on your Desktop is a composite, one superimposed on another.

To change an icon, click pixels on and off (or black and white, if you are in that mode). Figure 31.8 shows a modified System icon. You can preview what the icons look like (a big Q) on the right side of the ResEdit screen.

Fig. 31.8
A new System file icon.

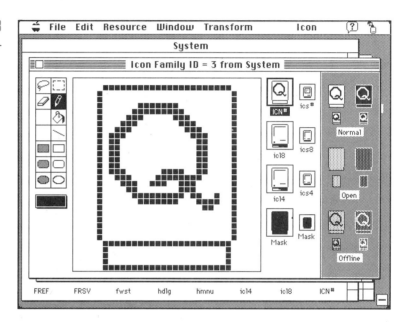

If you have a color-capable Macintosh, you can use a shareware program called Color Finder with ResEdit to create 32-bit color icons on your Desktop. The program has a color palette. Look for Color Finder in shareware and public domain collections such as BCSMacintosh and BMUG.

Cursors also are available for editing. If you don't like the arrows, wristwatches, and flashing horizontal insertion bars or anything else on-screen, go into your System file and edit them by using ResEdit. Turn your busy wristwatch into an hourglass, or be fanciful and amaze your friends.

Changing Menu Commands

If you are annoyed that your favorite command appears on the wrong menu or that the keystroke equivalent is not the one you favor, you easily can change them.

Changing menu items is identical in operation to what you have done so far with ResEdit. Just open and change the MENU template of your favorite application (of course, use a working copy).

CAUTION

Many programs do not appreciate having their menus changed behind their backs and may crash if you do so. Again, work on a copy of the application, not the original.

Changing Alert Boxes

If you don't like the message, you can edit alert dialogs; you can change the message in ResEdit. Look for the alert templates in the ALRT or DITL templates, and you can even change personalization data in start-up screens.

TIP

Be careful to use your personal copy when you try to make changes to alert dialogs because that way you don't violate the copyright laws, depending on the licensing agreement.

In figure 31.9 you can see the DITL resource for an out-of-memory message in WriteNow 3.0. You can edit the text of the message as well as the size and display location of the dialog.

Changing Fonts

You also can edit fonts in ResEdit by opening the FONT resource. A typical font screen is shown in figure 31.10.

In ResEdit you can create and edit screen fonts easily, but you need a more powerful tool to edit and create PostScript fonts (see Chapter 8, "Using Fonts").

Fig. 31.9
A DITL resource from
WriteNow 3.0.

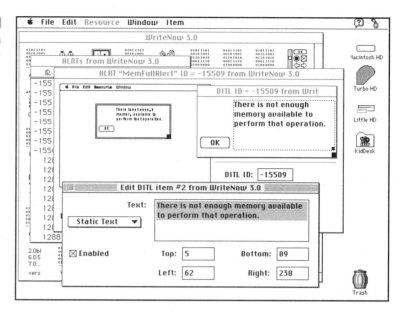

Fig. 31.10
The New York 14 screen
(bit-mapped) font.

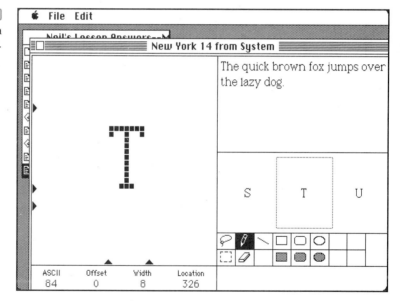

Finding Resources for Macintosh Programmers

What follows is by no means a complete list of resources, but is intended to give you a starting point. You also should get a copy of *Guide to Languages and Tools* (available from Apple Developer Services) for more information.

Apple-Related Resources

APDA, the Apple Programmers Developers Association, provides development tools and documentation. APDA also publishes the *APDALog* quarterly.

AppleLink is an electronic bulletin board service for developers. It provides access to Apple technical staff and the latest information. Developer Programs administers the Developer Partners and Associates program and supplies marketing information.

Developer University offers technical training for developers. *Phil and Dave's Excellent CD,* published by Apple, is the complete developers' documentation on CD-ROM.

Macintosh Associations

TechAlliance publishes *MacTech Quarterly* and sells development software and documentation.

The MacApp Developers Association publishes a bimonthly newsletter, *Frameworks.* It also sells source and object code libraries and books, and provides training courses.

Publications

MacTech (formerly *MacTutor*) magazine publishes technical articles on Macintosh software and hardware development. No Macintosh programmer should be without a subscription.

New Inside Macintosh, a new version of *Inside Macintosh,* collects topics (for example, *Inside Macintosh: Files* covers all aspects of files on the Macintosh) instead of having them scattered across the several volumes of *Inside Macintosh.* Available from APDA, this series is a worthwhile investment.

Macintosh Development Tools and Languages Guidebook from Apple pulls a great number of resources together into one catalog. You should acquire this publication early.

On-line Forums and Roundtables

CompuServe Information Service hosts a forum for all Apple developers. CompuServe also hosts the Symantec forum, which supports Think Pascal and Think C, and the Borland forum, which supports Turbo Pascal as well as others.

America Online has become Apple's choice for distributing Macintosh information. America Online has regular roundtables for Macintosh developers.

Delphi hosts the ICONtact Special Interest Group (SIG), which includes a programmers' group. It also hosts the NOSY SIG, which supports MacNOSY and the MacNOSY debugger.

GEnie hosts the MacPro Roundtable, which supports Macintosh developers, and the Borland Roundtable, which supports Turbo Pascal.

User Groups

Many local user groups have programming SIGs. Two of the more prominent user groups (with national memberships) are the Boston Computer Society (BCS) and the Berkeley Macintosh Users' Group (BMUG). Both groups offer public domain software, monthly newsletters, and programming special interest groups.

The Big Mac Recommendation

Programming really isn't as mysterious or as difficult as it looks. In fact, you may find programming a challenge that can lead you to creating your own Macintosh tools. If you are interested, try to find a local continuing education or community college course or someone who may be able to guide you.

If you are simply interested in programming as a hobby, you might want to start with HyperCard. The HyperTalk language is easy to learn and use, and can be used to create some very useful programs. Many average users find HyperCard and HyperTalk to be a good introduction to programming.

The more serious programmer will want to learn Pascal and C. A great number of books are available on these languages, and many universities teach courses in them.

My highest recommendation goes to Prograph by TGS. The future of Macintosh programming is object oriented, and Prograph has to be the easiest development environment to use that I have seen to date. Even when I made a living writing programs, the learning curve of a new language was about six months. Yet with Prograph (even though I wrote my last program some five years ago), I was able to begin development of a small program literally in a couple of days. The step-by-step tutorial gets you started quickly. Being able to work with objects and see their behavior graphically enables you to both program quickly and learn rapidly. Prograph is my personal development environment of choice.

CHAPTER THIRTY-TWO

Maintenance and Troubleshooting

S ome Macintoshes hum along forever without any problem. Others seem to develop a new problem every other day. Most problems are software related and not as destructive as hardware problems can be. Fortunately, hardware problems are relatively rare, and you can take steps to keep them rare.

This chapter discusses some of the problems you may have with your computer and tells you how to solve them. Although you may not be able to perform all necessary repairs and upgrades on your Macintosh, you can save time and money by following the basic rules outlined in this chapter.

Practicing Preventive Maintenance

Some of the most important things that you can do for your computer are among the most basic. Keeping your computer clean, avoiding static, and changing batteries, for example, are tasks that you easily can do to prolong your computer's life.

Many of the accessories discussed in this section are also covered in Chapter 27, "Adding Accessories." You can refer to this chapter to discover what brands and kinds of accessories are available.

Avoiding Electrical Spikes

Without a doubt, no user of any computer should be without a surge protector. This item isolates your computer from dangerous spikes of electricity that may come through from your power company. Users who are located in small towns, rural areas, or near industrial sites are particularly susceptible to this danger, but all users are at risk.

If you use a modem, you should make sure that your surge protector can filter voltage spikes that come through the phone lines. No matter how good your surge protector is, however, you should remember one important rule: do not leave your Macintosh plugged in or connected to the phone line during a thunderstorm. No surge protector can prevent damage should a bolt of lightning strike your power lines. Rather, the surge protector *and* your computer will be damaged.

Avoiding Heat

All computers are meant to operate at room temperature. You should make certain that you don't locate your computer in a location that rises much above ordinary room temperature. Computers generate a great deal of heat inside, and if the outside temperature is high also, the computer cannot cool itself. Damage to the electronic components can occur.

If you are uncomfortable in the heat, your Macintosh is doubly so. Keep the computer in a cool room and away from direct sunlight.

Avoiding Dirt

Dirt kills. It gets into little cracks and crevices, on disk-read heads, and into internal parts. To prevent problems caused by dirt, you should take the following steps on a regular basis:

- With a damp cloth, wipe down the surfaces of your Mac, printer, and work area at least once a month. Use a mild detergent only if you need to remove stubborn dirt. When you clean your monitor screen, don't spray the monitor itself; you may get liquid inside the monitor (or it may run down into your disk drives or other hardware). Rather, spray the cloth with water and then wipe the monitor.

- Every now and then (at least every month), vacuum around the keyboard to get out the little things that can get trapped underneath keys and make them non-functional. If you have a pet, vacuum more often (pet fur gets into everything).

- Keep food away from your work area. Food particles can get into everything: your keyboard, disk drives, the Macintosh itself. Liquids can spill and short out electrical equipment. Stories abound about users who spilled liquids on keyboards and attempted to dry them only to have to call a repair person (one story related to me was about someone who attempted to dry the keyboard with a hair dryer and melted several keys).

- If you smoke, do it away from the machine. Your computer's tolerance for dirt is quite low, and smoke particles can get on the head of the drive and cause a monumental crash. Smoke particles are much smaller (by an order of 4 or 5) than regular dirt and easily can infiltrate your Macintosh's vitals.

Avoiding Dust

You know what dirt can do to your machine; therefore, you should take steps to prevent the kind of damage that even the smallest particles of dust and smoke can cause. Good dust covers should be made of materials that allow your computer to breathe so that residual heat can be dissipated. At the same time, dust covers should be protective enough to stop dirt from landing on and filtering into your computer. In dirty environments (where many people smoke, the windows are open, or construction is going on nearby), protection is even more important.

Cleaning the Mouse

Your mouse gets dirty as the ball picks up dust, hair, and grime from the surface on which it rolls. You can buy cleaning kits, but you also can clean the mouse with household items. Turn the mouse over, unscrew the ring, take out the ball, and blow into the opening. Wipe the ball and the rollers inside the mouse with a cotton swab dipped in isopropyl alcohol. Then use another cotton swab to clean off the grime that accumulates on the internal rollers. You don't have to be a contortionist to clean your mouse; just take your time. When you're finished, pop the ball back in and replace the ring. Now your mouse is squeaky clean.

Almost every manufacturer of Macintosh accessories offers some kind of mouse cleaning kit, which usually includes items such as cotton swabs, isopropyl alcohol, and a lint-free cloth. If you use your mouse a lot, you're bound to need some help (either a kit or some home cleaning supplies) sooner or later.

The little feet on the Mac mouse can become worn and more difficult to slide. You can remedy this problem in several ways. You can buy Teflon feet (from International DataWares) that stick on the bottom, for example. DataWares also sells a cage with ball bearings so that you can move your mouse quickly across the mouse pad or table.

One way to help keep your mouse healthy is to use a clean surface for a mouse pad. You should clean that surface regularly. Your mouse has to spin on something—so why not provide it with a surface that it can slide across effortlessly? Many mouse pads are available.

A good mouse pad has the following characteristics:

- A surface on which the mouse ball can track easily

- A material that is dense enough so that constant back-and-forth motion does not leave a lasting impression

- An appropriate size (if a pad is too small, you can't move around the entire screen)

Avoiding Static

You never can be too careful about the effects that static electricity can have on your Macintosh and your files. The electronic components inside your Macintosh are very sensitive, and even the slightest static electric discharge from your fingers across the face of a chip can damage the chip.

You can dissipate static electricity in several ways. One method is to use antistatic sprays. Using a spray can help, if used regularly. Spraying carpet around the Macintosh and other upholstery with a good antistatic spray can help avoid static buildup. You also can clean your monitor with an antistatic spray.

Many command-center-like accessories, which have many switches for everything, enable you to dissipate static by touching a small metal part of the center that is indirectly grounded. You also can purchase accessories that come with grounds you can touch to discharge static electricity.

If you live in an area that has low humidity, you're particularly susceptible to this problem, as you can probably tell by the number of times a doorknob has "zapped" you.

Avoiding Computer Viruses

Much has been made of the infamous computer virus. The press has had a field day with viruses, making much ado about little. Many people use their computers for years without a single infection. The problem does exist, however, and one infection can be disastrous. A little paranoia now can save you headaches later.

The high risk groups for computer viruses are those who have multiple contacts with other computers. Users who make extensive use of on-line systems (especially privately run BBSs), share disks with other users, and participate in a user group are at the greatest risk.

If you are a home user who buys a commercial software package only now and then, never shares disks with other users, don't even have a modem, and has never heard of shareware or user groups, chances are that you are perfectly safe. Computer viruses cannot travel through the air as some human viruses do. They travel in files. Commercial software publishers have extremely stringent controls that assure that the chance of infection is almost nothing.

To be on the safe side, you should acquire and use a virus protection program. You can use Disinfectant, which is free and very effective. Disinfectant is widely available through user groups and on-line services.

Commercial packages also are available. I use Symantec Anti-Virus for the Mac (SAM). This package has a system extension that you can set to scan automatically for viruses when you start up, shut down, insert a disk, or at other user-controlled times. Symantec mails update cards to all registered owners, enabling them to add virus definitions. You can also call a bulletin board system to update your virus definitions.

MacTools by Central Point Software also includes virus protection. You also can consider Virex by Microcom.

Whichever package you choose, you should use it regularly to check for virus infection. It is always good to scan every new disk that you receive, regardless of source. Also, scan files that you download. You should check any file coming onto your Macintosh to be on the safe side.

You should also remember that backups are a good safeguard against virus infection. Keeping your master application and System Software disks locked at all times ensures that you have uninfected copies of the software. Regular backups increase the chance of your having an uninfected backup copy of your files should an infection occur. However, you still should use a virus protection utility to check for infections (or attempted infections). If you don't discover an infection early, you may end up with backups of infected software.

So far, viruses on the Macintosh infect only application and System files. Data files are not infected although an infection definitely can damage your data. You might want to keep separate data and application backups to be on the safer side.

Traveling Safely

If you are a PowerBook user or must move your Macintosh, you should take care to avoid potential problems from arising as you move your computer from one place to another. Consider these preventive tips:

■ Make certain that the case you transport your Macintosh in has a considerable amount of padding to protect your Macintosh from jolts and vibrations that occur on planes, automobiles, and trains.

This story may sound a bit odd but is true. Seatbelts not only save lives, they can save laptop computers. Being a rather paranoid person, I regularly belted my laptop in when carrying it in the car by running the seat belt through the carrying case handle. Many people thought this a funny thing for me to do until a car ran a red light and hit my car at between 40 and 50 mph.

Not only is the laptop still working, but it didn't fly about the interior of the car as it could have done (a PowerBook may be light, but even 6 pounds thrown at your head can hurt).

The Macintosh in my trunk was nearly destroyed, by the way, needing almost $1,000 in repairs.

- When passing through security, try to avoid passing your computer through any kind of metal detector or X-ray machine.

  The general consensus is that metal detectors definitely wipe out disks and X-ray machines might also. Many security checks at airports allow you to have your Macintosh inspected rather than passed through metal detectors or X-rays. Be aware that you most likely will be required to demonstrate that the computer is functional (and then presumably not a bomb with a laptop casing). So make certain to have a charged battery and have the laptop in sleep mode to avoid the delay of starting up.

  You should also make certain to keep your floppy disks separate from your luggage so that you can pass them through rather than let them be X-rayed or run through metal detectors. Because floppy disks are too small to conceal weapons or bombs, security personnel generally let you hand them across as you pass through the metal detector. A clear floppy disk carrying case is good in this situation because the attendant can readily see that the contents are merely diskettes.

- Always carry on your PowerBook. Never check a PowerBook as luggage. Never pack your PowerBook in your luggage. All luggage is run through security devices that may erase your data.

Protecting against Theft

In this section you learn how to keep your Macintosh computer itself secure. Macintoshes are among the most popular items for thieves.

The first concern is to make sure that your Macintosh is not stolen. One good hardware solution to keeping your Macintosh safe and preventing anyone else from using it is The Muzzle from ErgoTron. The Muzzle's 14-gauge metal collar fits around the Macintosh to cover it and prevent access to the internal floppy drive as well as to the power switch.

With The Muzzle in place, you cannot turn the Macintosh on or get to the floppy drive opening. The Muzzle, locked together by a hardened padlock, is made of heavy-duty steel that appears impossible to get through. This heavy-duty setup is good for schools or other public institutions.

Apple provides a socket on the back of your Macintosh for a security cable that you can attach to any solid fixture. This same socket is on all of Apple's peripherals as well. Kensington sells an inexpensive security system that uses these sockets; this system is ideal for the home user.

Considering Computer Insurance

Home users should check their policies to determine if their computer equipment is covered. If the computer is used for any kind of home business, it may not be covered by a home policy.

Separate computer insurance does exist, and you can find a number of ads in the back of publications such as *MacUser, MacWorld,* and *MacWeek.* But be certain to ask your insurance agent to check on these companies to verify their trustworthiness before you purchase a policy. You also should check with the Better Business Bureau.

Considering Ergonomics

In recent times, much attention has been focused on preventing problems that occur because users spend a great deal of time in front of a computer, often typing much. Various health problems have been reported, not the least of which is carpal tunnel syndrome—the fear of all writers. You can do many things to reduce the chances of ill effects to your health; following are a few ideas.

Reducing Glare and Easing Eye Strain

The best situation for working with your Macintosh is with diffused light shining from behind you onto your Macintosh screen; however, the light should not be so direct that the screen acts as a mirror and creates a harsh glare—giving you a headache. The best solution is to reposition your monitor so that you can work comfortably. When this solution is not possible, an antiglare screen can help. Kensington is one of many companies that offers antiglare screens. NoRad sells a nice mesh black screen that reduces glare and the low-frequency radiation that some people believe is a serious health hazard (more about that later).

Protecting against Radiation

If you've seen articles about VDTs (video display terminals) and the possible danger of the radiation they emit, you are not alone. For years, this danger has been discussed, but only recently has it become enough of a concern for some people to take action. This radiation is from low-frequency electronic emissions—the same stuff emitted from high-power lines, microwaves, hair dryers, and telephones. No current evidence, however, proves that using VDTs poses an imminent health risk.

You can take several steps to minimize any danger that might be presented by VDTs. First, the level of radiation decreases sharply as the distance from the monitor increases. Second, because the highest dose of radiation is emitted from the sides and back of the monitor, try to remove people from that direct exposure. Third, take breaks of 10 or 15 minutes after each hour of work. Fourth, look for a filter screening device such as the one sold by Ergonomics. In the years to come, Apple and other manufacturers of color displays (which emit the most radiation) are reducing the amount of radiation emitted from displays.

Some commercial products such as NoRad (from NoRad) also claim to eliminate the threat of radiation exposure from VDTs.

Avoiding Muscle Strain and Carpal Tunnel Syndrome

Nothing is worse than coming to the end of a day of working with your Macintosh and feeling that twinge in your back or an ache in your hands. Carpal tunnel syndrome—one type of repetitive stress disorder—can be disastrous. Typists may encounter a problem in which moving their hands and fingers becomes extremely painful. This pain comes from the stress of repeated movements of the fingers, hand, and wrists that typing incurs. Corrective surgery sometimes may be needed and is a painful and expensive process.

You should consider several points that can help you avoid these problems:

■ Keep your monitor at eye level. Use a monitor stand to raise it so that you can look straight at the monitor.

■ Keep your back straight. You may need to invest in a good quality chair to sit correctly. With all the flap over VDT radiation, you would think that people might consider that most of their health problems probably come from poor posture caused by cheap chairs. Back pillows, which can help keep you sitting up straight, are available at medical supply stores and through chiropractors.

■ Keep your keyboard at a level so that your elbows are bent close to right angles. Also, you should not have to lift your hands much to type. You can purchase keyboard holders that lower the keyboard, or you should consider a better chair that enables you to adjust the height.

■ Consider a wrist rest. These rests are widely available and enable you to rest your wrists as you type—which reduces strain—rather than keep them suspended in the air.

- Consider Apple's new keyboard. You can adjust this odd-looking split keyboard so that your wrists are at their natural angles rather than turned, as is common with ordinary keyboards.

- If you type long hours, consider switching to a Dvorak keyboard.

The preceding change is one I made a few years ago. Many articles have discussed how the Dvorak keyboard enables the typist to type faster. Whether this is true is debatable. I type faster since switching, but my increase could be a result of the fact that I type so much that my speed gradually increases anyway (the more you type, the faster you type). How much of my speed increase is due to the keyboard switch and how much is due simply to long hours of practice, I cannot determine. Since switching, I haven't been able to tell whether I've gained typing speed so much as that I can type longer periods with much less strain.

Troubleshooting

It's a beautiful day, and you're ready to sit down at your Macintosh to put the finishing touches on that book. And suddenly you feel as if your stomach has dropped out of your body! Your Macintosh goes on and on like a car trying to start with a dead battery, and that little smiling Macintosh face is nowhere to be found.

Another nightmare occurs when the disk with your dissertation or treasure map provides you with a `disk is unreadable` message. The following sections provide some solutions to problems you may encounter with your Macintosh.

Determining the Problem

If your Macintosh is not working as it should, try to determine the source of the problem. This knowledge may not necessarily help you fix the problem, but because you know your machine better than anyone else, you certainly can give the service people help by describing the symptoms. The more help you give service people, the less time they need to spend on the job, and the less money your repairs cost you.

When your Macintosh is not functioning correctly, begin by being a good detective. Take out your trusty notebook and ask the following questions:

- What were you doing when things stopped working as they should?

- Did you hear any funny noises? (When hard drives start to go, they often sound like little birds chirping merrily away; you might, however, hear exorcist-quality screeches—not a good sign.)

- Did you recently make any changes in your System Software?

- How long were you working before the problem set in?

- What is your application and its version number?

- Which System Software version were you using?

- What, if any, System extensions and control panels were you using?

After you answer these questions, you can do several things to try to get your Macintosh back on the right track. First, try whatever you were doing again. You can't lose anything by trying again, so double-click the icon that won't open or reinsert the disk that your Macintosh tells you is unreadable. If trying again doesn't work, don't fret yet.

Fixing Startup Problems

If you are experiencing startup problems, try these solutions. If you're working from floppies, try a different startup disk. If your Macintosh starts up, you merely have a bad startup disk. If no startup disk starts your Macintosh, you most likely have a hardware problem and should see your dealer for service.

If you are working from a hard disk, your Macintosh does not start up, and you are using System 7, then hold down the Shift key as soon as the happy Mac icon appears. Holding down Shift keeps your extensions from loading. If your Macintosh starts up, you have a System extension conflict most likely; see the next section for suggestions. If you're using System 6, you can do the same by starting up from a floppy startup disk or another hard drive and removing all extensions and control panels from the suspect System Folder.

If your Macintosh never even reaches the happy Mac icon or you see a sad Mac icon with numbers below it (you also may hear musical notes), you need to see your dealer. You probably have a hardware problem that a professional must work on.

You can try starting up from the Disk Tools disk that came with your System Software set. If your Macintosh starts up, but your hard disk icon does not appear, try reinstalling the driver using the Apple HD SC 20 Setup program if you have an Apple disk drive. If your hard disk is from another company, you should have a utility that updates your hard disk driver and should use this one.

Another startup solution is to try running Disk First Aid on your hard disk. This utility also is on the Disk Tools disk and can fix some problems with hard disks. If neither your hard disk utility nor the Disk First Aid program can locate your hard drive, however, you may have a more serious problem that your dealer needs to attend to.

Several disk repair utilities are on the market. You should own one. Norton Utilities for the Mac by Symantec is the one I use. The package comes with an emergency startup disk that can repair many hard disk problems. The same is true of MacTools by Central Point Software. If you are concerned about potential hard disk crashes, you should purchase one of these utilities immediately and install it on your hard disk.

To help avoid disk problems, you should rebuild your Desktop regularly. Apple recommends once a month. I rebuild two to four times a month. To rebuild the Desktop easily, hold down the Command and Option key combination as your Macintosh starts up. You see a dialog asking if you want to rebuild; click the OK button. This process can take a while on large hard disks.

If you have a problem with a floppy disk, you can rebuild the Desktop file on the disk by holding down the Command and Option keys when you insert the disk.

Locating Software Conflicts

If your Macintosh starts up but crashes often, check control panels and extensions; they often can cause trouble. Consider the following:

Do you have any control panels or System extensions that perform similar functions?

Two System extensions or control panels that are intended to do similar functions often can conflict. Try removing one from your System Folder and restarting.

What System extension or control panel did you add last?

Many times, the last added is the one that "broke the camel's back." Remove that extension or control panel and try restarting.

What action did you perform when the crash occurred?

Not long ago, I had a crash that occurred every time I clicked a certain part of the menu bar. This coincidence made me suspect that a control panel or System extension that enhances menus was crashing. (It turned out to be true but was only the beginning; a menu enhancement extension was crashing, but another extension caused the menu enhancement extension to crash.)

Try the following steps to isolate problems:

1. Turn off half of your extensions and control panels; then restart.

   You can turn off extensions and control panels most easily with a utility such as Startup Manager by Now Software, but you also can remove the control panels and extensions from the System Folder (placing them on the Desktop is one suggestion).

2. If the problem occurs again, turn off the half of the control panels and extensions that you had left on; then restart.

   Repeat this halving until the problem goes away. Essentially, you are narrowing the number of extensions that are in your search for a cause of the problem. When the problem goes away, the likely suspect is one of the extensions or control panels in the last set you turned off.

3. Add back one of the extensions and control panels from the last set you turned off; then restart.

   If the problem reoccurs, the added item becomes your prime suspect. From here, you can go in a couple of directions. Call the manufacturer of your prime suspect and ask if there are any known conflicts between its extension or control panel with other software. The tech support department may be able to tell you right off what conflict is occurring or offer suggestions where you can look.

If you want to be more thorough on your own, you can continue the process by leaving your prime suspect on but turning off half of the other extensions and control panels and then restarting until the problem goes away. Generally, you find that you can narrow the problem down to two conflicting extensions or control panels.

To speed the process, keep in mind the most recent extensions and control panels you added. Even though you may have added your last a month ago, the problem could be a subtle one that takes time to appear. The extensions and control panels that have worked well for a long time are less likely to have developed a problem. Try combinations of your most recent extensions and control panel additions.

To avoid extension and control panel conflicts, don't add too many to your System Folder. Although a great number of extensions and control panels are available, you want only the one you are actually putting to use to reside in your System Folder. Too many of these items can cause conflicts or slow your Macintosh's performance.

If your problem occurs when all extensions are off and in a specific application, reinstall the application and try again. If the application now works, then the application file was most likely bad. If the application still does not work, you may have System problems. You should reinstall your System.

Keep in mind that sometimes applications store their settings in the program, and you lose any changes you made. Many of the major programs (Word, PageMaker, Excel) store their settings in the System file for that reason.

Recovering Lost Files

A good backup routine is the only way to reduce chances of losing data; but even if you are conscientious about backing up, you still may delete a file inadvertently. Deleting files from a disk does not erase them; it only makes them inaccessible through normal channels.

If you delete a file and have a backup, you need only load the backup, and you're ready to go again. If you don't have a backup, you need a file recovery tool such as Norton Utilities (from Symantec), MacTools (from Central Point Software), or Complctc Undelete from Microcom.

Before you can understand how file recovery tools work, you must understand what occurs when a file is deleted. First, deleting a file does not remove the contents of the file from the disk; deleting removes only the file's directory listing and address (also called a *path name*).

This directory, or table, is what the operating software uses to find a file that you retrieve. You erase this directory when you initialize, or reformat, a disk. You then have no hope of recovering the file, and any directory is gone for good. When you just place a file in the Trash can, you erase only a small part of the directory.

A file recovery program searches for deleted files and informs you whether they can be recovered. Many packages such as Norton Utilities enable you to install an extension that maintains information files which allow the package to recover a great number of files (as many as 500 is possible in Norton).

All users should have one of these packages to recover accidentally deleted files. But, as described in the following paragraphs, you should practice some preventive medicine as well.

Always back up applications as soon as you get them—even before you install them on your hard drive.

Keep a set of backup disks at a location other than where your computer is stored. If you don't, anything that destroys your hard disk (such as water or fire) also gets the backup disks. Make a total of three backup copies: one on your hard drive and two on floppy disks. You should have two backups on floppy disks just in case you lose a file on your hard drive and then find that your hard drive is erasing files—including the first backup disk. In such a scenario, you'll be glad you have a second backup disk.

If you didn't trash a file but instead find that your Macintosh is telling you that your disk is unreadable, try rebuilding the Desktop by holding down the Command and Option keys. This technique sometimes can work and gives you enough leeway to copy those important files to another disk that you know is good.

To avoid a situation in which you need Peter Norton to step in and save the day, use the following golden rules:

- Always make a backup.

- Before you trash a file, take your fingers off the keyboard and ask yourself whether you really want this file to disappear.

- Open a folder and examine its contents before you trash it. You never know what may be stored there.

- Always work from backups. Even the best Mac users have erased an application from the master disk.

- Use the write-protect notches on master disks.

- Always end a Macintosh session with the Shut Down command. This action places disk contents in order.

Locating Hardware Problems

Your computer still is not functioning properly, you cannot pin the problem to a particular software application, and the System seems to work. You could have a hardware problem.

At this point, you should begin a systematic testing of each peripheral attached to your Macintosh. First, disconnect all peripherals, including external disk drives, printers, plotters, scanners, and so on.

Then, for each peripheral, follow these steps:

1. Connect the peripheral.

2. Check the cable connections.

3. Try out the procedure again.

If the procedure works, the cables may not have been connected, or they may have been connected improperly. If the procedure doesn't work, try using another peripheral that is identical to yours. This idea may sound impractical with an item such as a printer; however, you may find a substitute easily if you have access to other Macs, and you may save yourself some money. If the substitute works, you know that your peripheral needs fine-tuning. If the substitute doesn't work, you still don't know whether the problem is the peripheral or your Macintosh.

Continue trying peripherals until you've systematically evaluated each one. If you have no success, you need to see your service department.

Fixing SCSI Problems

The biggest problem with hardware on the Macintosh today is the SCSI bus. SCSI problems crop up with maddening regularity when you add or remove a peripheral from a SCSI chain. If you have a SCSI peripheral (hard disk, CD-ROM, printer, etc.) that is behaving strangely or your Macintosh refuses to recognize that the peripheral exists, you may have a SCSI problem.

Consider the following points:

The shorter the SCSI cables are, the better.

Recently, a dealer sent me a six-foot SCSI cable for hooking up a hard disk (I had one already attached along with a CD-ROM player). I knew better but tried to use the cable. The hard disk never appeared on the Desktop. The dealer insisted the cable could not be the problem, but as soon as we swapped cables and I used a two-foot cable, everything was fine.

SCSI chains should be as short as possible. Apple recommends a length limit, but I can never recall it and the limit does not matter; I've encountered problems at a much shorter length. I checked the length limit then to verify it but promptly forgot it. The number is mostly useless in any case. Many people encounter problems with SCSI chains much shorter than Apple claims possible. The shorter-the-better rule is your best bet.

As a corollary to the preceding rule, forget about moving your SCSI peripheral to the other side of the room.

In fact, you may not even want to put your peripheral on the other side of the desk. Don't let anyone sell you a ten-foot SCSI cable; the Macintosh SCSI bus simply is too sensitive to be used at long distances.

Check your SCSI ID numbers. No peripheral should be set at 0 or 7. These numbers are reserved for the internal hard disk and the Macintosh itself, respectively.

Even the best Mac users manage to screw this one up. I nearly went insane trying to discover why a client's laser printer was acting strangely, only to find out that I had forgotten to check the SCSI ID number.

The number was set to 7, making the Macintosh think that the laser printer was a floppy disk from which it could boot. Bizarre events resulted.

Curious isn't it, that manufacturers even bother to put 0 and 7 as choices on Macintosh peripherals?

Some peripherals have SCSI ID switches that go beyond 7 into 8 and up to 15 (or after 9 go to A, B, C, D, E, and F). This numbering scheme enables you to switch the termination easily. Numbers 0 through 7 may be terminated, while 8 through 15 (or F) correspond to 0 through 7 without termination. Take two aspirin and check your manual.

If your internal hard disk is supplied by a company other than Apple, the ID used for the drive may be something other than 0. Although this numbering is not a good practice, some dealers set the internal drive to another number. To check your hard disk SCSI ID number, click the disk icon; then, from the File menu, choose Get Info. The Info window that appears tells you the SCSI ID number of the drive.

Check each device's termination. The rule is that the first and last device in a SCSI chain must be terminated.

Remember, if you have an internal drive, that drive is the first device in the SCSI chain and is terminated already. (The exception to this rule comes in Quadras. Check your Quadra manual carefully for more information on Quadra SCSI termination.)

You also can use SCSI Probe, a free utility available from most user groups and on-line services to tell you the SCSI ID numbers (and other information) about your disk drives. SCSI Probe also has the capability to force your hard disk to mount—which can be handy.

If all of these suggestions do not make the drive or other peripheral appear, you've entered the SCSI twilight zone where all bets are off and rules are meant to be bent and broken.

Try some of the following:

- Reorder the SCSI devices. The location of the device on the SCSI chain should make no difference. But sometimes it does. Try moving the problem device to the beginning or end of the SCSI chain rather than a middle position.

- Try different termination schemes. Be careful with these schemes, however. Don't do something too bizarre—like terminating every single device. Some users have found that removing the termination of the first device works. Try the reverse: terminate the problem device in addition to the usual terminations.

- Try reordering the SCSI ID numbers—another "shouldn't matter" that can sometimes.

If all else fails, call your dealer. You possibly may have a defective peripheral, or your Macintosh SCSI is failing. To narrow down this problem, connect only the problem device to the Macintosh and see if it works properly.

CAUTION

Whatever else you do, never touch the SCSI pins or plugs. Be careful when connecting devices. A tiny static discharge can damage your SCSI chip in your Macintosh and cost you an expensive repair.

Fixing Printer Problems

Although the thought is not pleasant, imagine your printer dying in the middle of an important job. You can't do much to repair your printer unless the problem is obvious, such as when a belt breaks or the print head on a dot-matrix printer needs to be replaced. Most printer repair jobs are best left for the pros.

The single-path repair method, however, is useful for fixing all hardware—including printers. This method works when only one thing goes wrong at a time, and it consists of the following six steps:

1. Trust your senses. By observing closely, you may be able to detect problems such as jammed paper, a ripped ribbon, or the smell of a wire with burned insulation.

2. Find the area that needs repair.

3. Remove the printer component that you think is faulty. Take out the old ribbon, for example.

4. Retest the system and see whether it works without the part you think is faulty. If the part is necessary for the system to work, you may have to get a replacement to complete this step.

5. Replace the defective part.

6. Test the system again.

NOTE

Before making any adjustments to your Mac hardware, check your warranty. Some do-it-yourself procedures void the warranty.

If you think that all cables are connected correctly and firmly, the next step is to be sure that you have installed the correct printer driver in the System folder and that you have selected the appropriate printer icon using the Chooser located on the Apple menu. One common problem with printers that don't print is that they are not selected in the Chooser. Make sure that you've selected the correct printer.

Sometimes the printer port can malfunction. Plug your printer cable into the modem port, select the modem port in the Chooser, and try to print. If the printer operates, shut down the Macintosh, reconnect to the printer port, and restart. In the Chooser, select Printer Port. Try printing again. Many times, this method resets the printer port. If the printer port is not reset, you have a damaged printer port.

If your printer is a SCSI printer, check the preceding section for more information.

Deciding Whether to Upgrade

Some problems can result because you are taxing your Macintosh beyond its limits. Crashes can occur, for example, because you are using almost all of the Macintosh's memory (called a *low memory condition* by Apple and an acknowledged Macintosh difficulty—rare but sometimes problematic).

You may be running software that is really intended for a more powerful machine. Software manufacturers—wanting as wide a market as possible—often list the lowest configuration that the program can run on, regardless of whether the program runs well on that configuration. You may want to consider memory expansion or acceleration.

One unfortunate example of a manufacturer that is a bit overly optimistic on the configurations that can run its software is Apple. System 7 (and the later 7.1 release) is recommended for machines as early as the Macintosh Plus. Yet machines with less power than the LC II or Classic II run very sluggishly with System 7. These earlier machines also tend to have too little memory to run the 2MB (and over) System 7 while also running other programs. The resulting low-memory conditions can cause crashes at worst, slow performance at best.

My personal recommendation is to use System 7 only on 68030 or later machines with at least 4MB of memory (preferably more).

At a point, upgrading becomes more costly than simply replacing your Macintosh with a newer model. The general rule of thumb is that the farther away your current system is from what you want, the more it will cost to upgrade and the more it's worth looking into a replacement.

Compare your ideal machine to the upgrades needed. Is it worth upgrading a IIsi to Centris power, for example? Boards that can make this upgrade do exist, but you need at least an accelerator card and probably a decent display card (see Chapter 26, "Expanding the Macintosh"). The cost for both cards runs from $2,200 to $2,500. A Centris 610 is not much more expensive than that—especially if you have a modular Macintosh (such as the IIsi) and can retain your monitor and keyboard, only purchasing the Centris 610 itself.

A memory upgrade often is one of the least expensive and most effective upgrades around. With SIMM prices down, memory upgrades can cost very little money. You can upgrade the LC, for example, from the base 2MB to 6MB for about $200 right now. An investment of $400 nets an LC user the maximum 10MB of memory. With more memory, your programs have more room and can run faster. You also can avoid low-memory conditions that can lead to crashes and other strange behavior.

The Big Mac Recommendation

The information in this chapter can help you prevent many serious breakdowns and help you keep your Macintosh running smoothly.

You should always observe these cardinal rules:

- Protect your Macintosh from dirt, dust, smoke, liquids, and food particles as much as possible.

- Keep your Macintosh cool, located in a cool room where direct sunlight does not fall on the machine.

- Back up your data regularly.

- Purchase and use a utility package such as Norton Utilities for the Macintosh to keep your machine healthy and to aid you in recovering from problems.

- Add System extensions and control panels sparingly. Although a great number of useful ones exist, avoid the temptation to add every one you see. If you find yourself not using one for a long time, remove it from your Macintosh.

- Rebuild your Desktop file regularly, at least once a month, if not more.

- Run a virus protection program on a regular basis.

Using System 6

I f you haven't upgraded to System 7, you might be feeling a bit left behind these days. And, in a way, the feeling is justified. System 7 is a major improvement in the System software and I, for one, haven't looked back since switching.

However, there are reasons for staying with System 6—and they can be good reasons. This chapter covers these reasons, so you can decide for yourself whether to make the switch.

In any case, the two versions of System software are similar enough that you can use most of the material in this book under either System without trouble. The biggest difference between the two Systems lies in the great number of advantages and options offered by System 7. In other words, the basics of the Macintosh System have not dramatically changed, but they have been greatly enhanced.

Considering a Switch to System 7

Before making the switch to System 7, consider a few points.

System 7 is memory intensive. In plain English, it's big. A hard drive is a necessity for running System 7—it will not even install without 1MB of available disk space. 4MB of memory is really a minimum to effectively use System 7.

System 7 operates slower than System 6 on older machines. Apple states that System 7 can be run on any machine from the Macintosh Plus up. I have found, however, that System 7 runs slowly on machines with 68000 CPUs (the Plus, the SE, the Portable, and the Classic), and does not run at all on machines that predate the Macintosh Plus. Basically, System 7 needs a 68020 CPU (the LC and the original Macintosh II, for example) or higher to run well. The System is most effective on 68030 and higher machines (the SE/30, the IIsi, the IIcx, and the Quadras, for example).

System 7 requires all software to be System 7 compatible. This should no longer be a problem. The System has been out long enough that software manufacturers have upgraded. If you upgrade your software on a regular basis, all your software is probably already System 7 compatible. If you do not upgrade your software regularly, check with the manufacturer to determine whether or not your software is compatible. When System 7 first appeared, upgrading every major item of software at once was a common complaint raised by Macintosh users—it can be expensive. But if you have upgraded your software punctually since System 7 appeared, you should not have a problem at all now.

System 7 is no longer new. In fact, it is now at Version 7.1. This should reassure those who fear new releases of software. (They do tend to be buggy—those of you who have been using a Mac for a while probably still remember the infamous System 3.0 fiasco.) System 7 even broke the old "never-buy-a-version-ending-in-a-zero" rule by being quite stable for a new release. In any case, two bug fixes and one feature enhancement have already passed. System 7 is now in use on millions of Macs—and is doing quite well.

System 7 is the first System software release that has cost Macintosh users money. Before System 7, we were used to going to the dealer or the user group with some disks and walking out with a free System copy. But the price of the software is not unreasonable considering the effort that went into the System software—and the fact that Apple now includes technical support for the System software. We can take comfort in the fact that IBM PC and clone users are now finding out their "less expensive" machines will end up costing them more than a comparable Macintosh if they want to use Windows. (Yes, I am chortling behind my hand. After all those years of being told that my computer of choice was "not a real computer," watching millions of PC users scramble to spend huge sums of money to make their "real" computers act like my "toy" is just *too* funny.)

In my recommendation, these are the only reasons that you shouldn't upgrade to System 7:

- You are using a Plus, Classic, or other 6800-based machine.

- You have less than 4MB of memory and cannot yet upgrade. The maximum memory limits for machines after the Classic are beyond 4MB, so there is no mechanical reason you cannot upgrade. Memory prices are quite low now, so the price should not hold you back unless you are on a very strict budget.

- Your software is not System 7 compatible.

- You do not have a hard drive.

If the first reason is why you have not made the switch, I concede the point. System 7 is just too slow on pre-Classic II machines. Don't switch until you upgrade the machine or buy a new one.

If one of the latter three points is holding you back, considering addressing the problem soon. Memory upgrades are an inexpensive way of gaining more power for your Macintosh with *any* System software. A hard drive is an upgrade you'll find immeasurably worth the expense. The expense of upgrading your software will be more than paid back by the gains in power and ease you'll find in the newer versions of the software and in the System 7 enhancements.

Considering Differences between Systems 6 and 7

Most of the commands and operations that you will need to do with System 7 are the same as those you do now with System 6. To copy a file from your hard disk to a floppy disk, for example, you drag the icon representing the file. The main difference between the Systems, as you have probably figured out by now, is not whether you can perform a task on one System or the other, or even *how* the basic Macintosh task is performed, but what tasks System 7 can do that System 6 cannot.

There are some other differences you will want to know about in order to use this book effectively.

Icons

Icons remain essentially the same. The biggest difference is that you change the name of an icon by clicking it, typing the new name, and then clicking on something else (such as the Desktop). You can now use the Return key to tell the Mac to accept the new name.

Menus

The application switching features located in System 6's Apple menu have been moved to this menu in System 7. The new menus are

- *Label.* Labeling is a System 7-specific feature. (System 6 included the "Color" menu, which had fewer capabilities than the Label menu has.)

- *Help.* Balloon Help is only available in System 7.

- *Application.* The application switching features located in this menu were handled by the Apple menu in System 6. The window-hiding features are unique to System 7.

If you used a color Macintosh under System 6, you might notice that System 7 has no Color menu. This menu allowed you to select an icon or icons and then choose a color. It operates much like the Label menu, but did not allow you to sort or find icons using their color—as you can using their label in System 7.

Some of the Finder menus have changed fundamentally and added new features. These changes include

- *Apple menu.* The Apple menu of System 6 is restricted to desk accessories—small, specific applications that must be installed using the utility Font/DA Mover. (Check your manual for more on this utility.)

  The Apple menu has changed significantly. System 6 does not have an Apple Menu Items folder. You must use the Font/DA Mover utility (which should be on your System disks) to install and remove items from the Apple menu. You are also limited to desk accessories. No other items can be installed into this menu in System 6.

The Apple menu of System 6 also handles the application switching functions of the Application menu (if you are running MultiFinder, which allows you to multitask). In System 7, this feature has been moved to the Application menu. System 7 also has the ability to hide application windows.

- *File menu.* The File menu of System 7 has additional commands. The Find, Find Again, Sharing, and Make Alias commands are available only in System 7. In System 6, the Eject Disk command is on this menu; in System 7, the Eject Disk command is on the Special menu.

- *View menu.* This menu functions the same in both Systems. The enhancement in System 7 is the ability to add more views to the menu.

- *Special menu.* The command in the Special menu that has changed most is the Clean Up command. The ability to sort icons by name, by size, and so on is not present in System 6. Holding down the Option key invokes a Clean Up command that organizes all icons, but you cannot control the order of the sort in System 6 the same way that you can do in System 7.

Windows

Windows have changed somewhat, but the basics of scrolling, resizing, and moving windows is the same. The zoom box works basically the same, but System 6 only allows zooming between a user-defined size and the full-screen size. System 7, on the other hand, zooms between a user-defined size and the smallest window that shows all items in the window.

Documents

The drag-and-drop method of opening documents is new in System 7. Double-clicking remains the same. The Open dialog is very similar, but the Drive button has been replaced by the Desktop button, which accesses the contents of the Desktop to be displayed in the dialog's list box—thus you can choose a disk drive to open. System 7 also enables you to access the Desktop by choosing it from the Folder menu of an Open dialog. System 6 only enables you to switch disk drives by clicking the Drive button.

Folders

Creating, deleting, opening, and closing a folder are the same. Using views is the same, but with System 7 you can customize the views in any way. System 7 enables you to click on the heading of a folder to change the view—a feature that is not available in System 6.

System 7 has a new Folder menu that can be popped up in folder windows. System 7 also has additional keyboard equivalents for folder operations. System 6 also has fewer keyboard equivalents for folder operations. Consult your manual for those that apply.

Control Panels

You access control panels in System 6 by choosing the Control Panels desk accessory from the Apple menu. A scrolling list of control panels appears in the desk accessory's window. Click the control panel you wish to use, and its controls appear in the Control Panel desk accessory's window. Control panels cannot be opened by double-clicking.

System 7 has a separate Memory control panel; the RAM cache is no longer part of the General control panel. System 6 does not have the 32-bit address mode or virtual memory features. These two features apply only to later Macintoshes running System 7, though upgrades may exist for your machine.

The Sound control panel is also different. You may be able to record sounds with System 6, but this may require a third-party recorder and software.

System 7 adds a View control panel that allows you to customize the views.

System 7 has a separate Control Panels folder. In System 6, all control panels reside in the System Folder. They are installed by dragging them into the System Folder and removed by dragging them out of the folder.

Extensions

Extensions do not have their own folders in System 6. They reside in the System Folder itself. You install and remove extensions by dragging them into and out of the folder, respectively.

Printers and Fonts

The main differences between System 6 and System 7 in the area of printers and fonts are

- System 6 printer drivers reside in the System Folder; there is no Extensions folder.

- TrueType is System 7 specific unless you have the System extension that allows you to use them in System 6. If you do not have this, your dealer or a user group may be able to help you locate it.

- Screen fonts and TrueType fonts are installed into the System file itself in System 6 by using the Font/DA Mover utility.

- Fonts can be previewed by double-clicking on them in System 7; this feature is not available in System 6.

Using MultiFinder

With System 7, Apple has integrated multitasking into the System software itself. Before this System version, Apple provided a separate Finder, called *MultiFinder*, that enabled you to run more than one application at a time.

MultiFinder is a system file like the System and Finder files. Like the original Finder, MultiFinder is a separate file located in the System Folder.

To switch between applications quickly in System 6, you must use MultiFinder.

The usefulness of MultiFinder is in how it switches between applications to complete more than one task (hence, the term "multitasking"). This switching takes place so fast that it appears the tasks are being completed simultaneously. This switching is not really multitasking in the sense that both sets of instructions are read at the same time. It is simultaneous in the sense that two tasks are being completed during the same time period, but not, strictly speaking, at the same moment in time. Keep in mind that the more applications you run under MultiFinder, the slower the Macintosh works.

Starting MultiFinder

Using MultiFinder is a simple and straightforward procedure. To set up MultiFinder, follow these steps:

1. From the Special menu, choose Set Startup.

   The Set Startup window for MultiFinder appears (see fig. A.1).

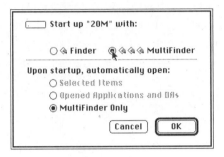

Fig. A.1
The Set Startup window.

2. Click the MultiFinder option button.

3. Click OK. MultiFinder will be installed the next time you start your Macintosh.

4. From the Special menu, choose Restart.

You also can double-click the MultiFinder icon (in the System Folder) to launch MultiFinder by pressing ⌘-Option when double-clicking the icon.

When your Macintosh starts up, MultiFinder is installed. A small Macintosh-like icon appears in the upper right corner of your screen to indicate that MultiFinder is active and ready to go (see fig. A.2).

Fig. A.2
The MultiFinder icon in the upper right corner.

MultiFinder icon ──

🍎 File Edit View Special

		20M		
Name	Size	Kind	Last Modified	
📁 Communications	--	folder	Fri, Aug 11, 1989	8:58 AM
📁 Excel	--	folder	Fri, Aug 11, 1989	9:38 AM
📁 Games	--	folder	Wed, Aug 2, 1989	8:39 AM
📁 Neil/Misc	--	folder	Fri, Aug 11, 1989	2:06 PM
📁 Paint	--	folder	Fri, Aug 4, 1989	2:50 PM
📁 Quark	--	folder	Sat, Aug 12, 1989	8:02 AM
📁 Quicken	--	folder	Sun, Aug 13, 1989	11:19 AM
📁 Res Meth Book	--	folder	Tue, Aug 8, 1989	10:16 AM
📁 Statistics	--	folder	Sat, Aug 12, 1989	7:30 AM
📁 System	--	folder	Thu, Aug 10, 1989	1:55 PM
📁 The Big Mac Book	--	folder	Fri, Aug 11, 1989	8:52 AM
📁 Utilities	--	folder	Sun, Aug 6, 1989	9:49 AM
📁 Wingz	--	folder	Sat, Aug 12, 1989	7:25 AM
📁 Word	--	folder	Sat, Aug 12, 1989	7:58 AM

Figure A.3 shows the Apple menu after both SuperPaint and Word have been opened under MultiFinder.

After you install MultiFinder, you can select applications in one of the following ways:

■ You can select the application from the Apple menu, which lists the running applications. For many people, this is the easiest and most logical way to access an application while another application is active.

■ You can resize the windows so that you have a separate window for each open application. If you have many applications open, however, your screen can become crowded.

■ You can go to the next active application by clicking the application icon located in the upper right corner of the MultiFinder screen. In figure A.3, for example, the current application is SuperPaint. If you are working in SuperPaint and want to switch to the next application, click the SuperPaint icon. Click the icon as often as necessary to switch to the desired application.

Fig. A.3

The Apple menu with SuperPaint and Word opened under MultiFinder.

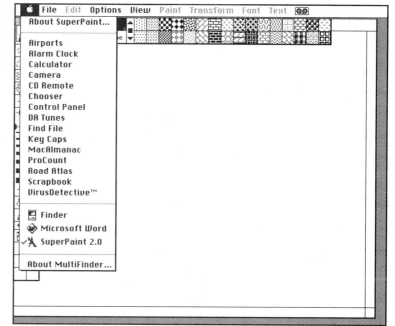

Adjusting Memory Use

MultiFinder features multitasking, easy switching between applications, and increased efficiency. Running more applications uses more memory, however.

If you try to run too many applications under MultiFinder, you receive an insufficient memory message. Many times you can get around this problem by adjusting the memory used by the applications you are running.

Suppose that you want to operate both Word and SuperPaint under MultiFinder, but when you try to open SuperPaint you receive the insufficient memory message. The first and most obvious remedy is to adjust the amount of memory used by the applications you are running.

To adjust memory allocation, follow these steps:

1. In the Finder, elect the icon for the application you want to use, and then choose Get Info from the File menu (or press ⌘-I).

2. The Info window shows you the amount of memory suggested to run this application and the amount of memory allocated (see fig. A.4). You can continue decreasing the amount of memory until the application launches. If you go below the required amount of memory, however, you eventually reach a point where the application no longer works at all. You will get unexpected results and system crashes.

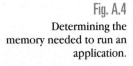

Fig. A.4

Determining the memory needed to run an application.

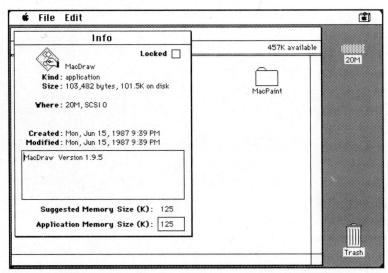

Some applications have two memory limits—a suggested and a minimum. If the available memory is less than what is suggested but more than the minimum required, you can reduce the memory size with reasonable safety.

Disabling MultiFinder

You can turn off, or *disable*, MultiFinder in two ways:

- From the Special menu, choose Set Startup. Click Finder instead of MultiFinder, and then restart your Macintosh.

  MultiFinder will be turned off until you later turn it on again.

- If you want to disable MultiFinder just for this specific session, hold down the Command key while starting your Mac.

  Although MultiFinder is still enabled on the Set Startup selections, MultiFinder will not start for this work session. The *next* time you start your machine, MultiFinder will be active.

Using Desk Accessories

When the first Macs came out, people found the mini-applications, called *desk accessories* (or DAs), to be useful tools. System 6 provides the Font/DA Mover, which enables you to move desk accessories and fonts in and out of the System file. Fonts and desk accessories are represented by the Suitcase icons you see in figure A.5.

Fig. A.5
The contents of the
Font/DA Mover folder.

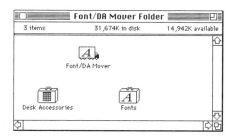

Font/DA Mover is represented by the truck icon.

Installing and Removing Desk Accessories

To use Font/DA Mover, follow these steps:

1. Double-click the Font/DA Mover icon.

   A list of all the fonts appears in the System file.

2. Click the Desk Accessory button to view the desk accessories now available, as shown in figure A.6.

Fig. A.6

The Font/DA Mover screen listing the current desk accessories.

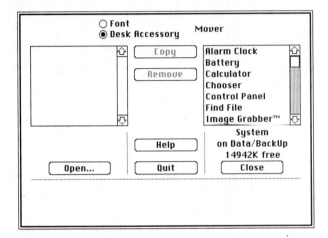

○ Font
● Desk Accessory   Mover

Copy
Remove

Alarm Clock
Battery
Calculator
Chooser
Control Panel
Find File
Image Grabber™

System
on Data/BackUp
14942K free

Help

Open...   Quit   Close

If you want to go directly to the listing of desk accessories, hold down the Option key while you double-click the Font/DA Mover icon.

3. Insert the floppy disk that contains the desk accessory you want to copy to your System.

4. In the left window, click the desk accessory you want to move.

   For example, click Calculator to highlight it. The two middle dimmed buttons, Copy and Remove, become active.

5. Click the Copy button.

Arrows in the Copy button point toward the System file where the desk accessory will be installed. You know the desk accessory is installed when you see the DA in the System file you copied it to.

If you want to remove a desk accessory or a font from a System file, click the desk accessory or font, and then click the Remove button (rather than the Copy button). You may want to remove a desk accessory from the System to free up space or to keep the number of desk accessories to 15, which is your limit.

CAUTION

Y ou must leave at least one desk accessory installed or the System will crash. Apple recommends leaving the Control Panel and the Chooser installed.

Accessing Desk Accessories

Desk accessories in System 6 are an imitation of the multitasking available with MultiFinder and System 7. Apple created the mini-applications so that you could enable any application at any time; you no longer have to quit Word, for example, to run a calculator.

Hence, the desk accessories in your System file are available at any time via the Apple menu. To run any desk accessory, choose its name from the Apple menu.

Installing and Removing Fonts

Fonts had to reside in the System file itself until System 7.1. While System 7.0 allowed you to drag fonts in and out of the System file, System 6 and previous versions required that you use Font/DA Mover.

The installation procedure for fonts is the same as for desk accessories with one difference. Skip step 2 in the desk accessory installation procedure. Font/DA Mover starts up and displays the fonts in your System file so that you do not need to click the Font option button (unless you have previously clicked the DA button, in which case you need to click the Font button to display fonts again).

Other than that, you use the same steps to install and remove fonts as you do to install and remove desk accessories.

System Specifications

This appendix gives the specifications for current and discontinued Macintosh models. You can use this information to make comparisons when you are deciding which new Mac to buy or when you are interested in purchasing a used Macintosh and want to make sure that the one you're considering meets your requirements.

T he Performa 200 has the same specifications as the Classic II.
The Performa 400 series (including the 400, 405, and 450), has the same specifications as the LC II. The Performa 600 has the same specifications as the IIvx.

	128K	Mac 512K	Mac 512KE	Mac Plus	Mac SE	Mac SE/30	Classic
System characteristics							
CPU	68000	68000	68000	68000	68000	68030	68000
CPU speed	8 MHz	8 MHz	8 MHz	8 MHz	8 MHz	16 MHz	8 MHz
Memory (standard)	128KB	512KB	512KB	1MB	1MB	1 or 4MB	1MB
Memory (maximum)	128KB	512KB	4MB	4MB	4MB	32MB	4MB
Min. RAM speed	150ns	150ns	150ns	150ns	150ns	120ns	120ns
PMMU	No	No	No	No	No	Yes	No
FPU	No	No	No	No	No	68882	No
Disk drives							
Int. floppy	400KB	400KB	800KB	800KB	(2) 800KB	1.44MB	1.44MB
Hard drive	No	No	No	No	Optional	Optional	Optional
SCSI	No	No	Yes	Yes	Yes	Yes	Yes
EtherNet	No	No	No	No	No	Optional	No
Dimensions	13.5x9 .7x10.9	13.5x9 .7x10.9	13.5x9 .7x10.9	13.5x9 .7x10.9	13.6x9 .6x10.9	13.6x9 .6x10.9	13.6x9 .6x10.9
Weight (lbs.)	16	16	16	16.5	17-21	21.5	21.5
Monitor Size	9" diag.	9" diag.	9" diag.	9" diag.	9" diag.	9" diag.	9" diag.
Color	No	No	No	No	No	No	No
Audio							
Out	Mono	Mono	Mono	Mono	Mono	Stereo	Mono
In	No	No	No	No	No	No	No
System Software							
System 6.0.5	No	No	No	Yes	Yes	Yes	No
System 6.0.7	No	No	No	Yes	Yes	Yes	Yes
System 6.0.8	No	No	No	Yes	Yes	Yes	Yes
System 7.0	No	No	No	Yes	Yes	Yes	Yes
System 7.0.1	No	No	No	Yes	Yes	Yes	Yes
System 7.1	No	No	No	No	Yes	Yes	Yes
A/UX 2.0.1	No	No	No	No	No	Yes	No
A/UX 3.0	No	No	No	No	No	Yes	No

	Classic II	Mac II	Mac IIx	Mac IIcx	Mac IIci
System characteristics					
CPU	68030	68020	68030	68030	68030
CPU speed	16 MHz	16 MHz	16 MHz	16 MHz	25 MHz
Memory (standard)	2 or 4MB	1 or 4M	4M	1 or 4M	5M
Memory (maximum)	10MB	20M	32M	32M	32M
Min. RAM speed	100ns	120ns	120ns	120ns	80ns
PMMU	Yes	Optional	Yes	Yes	Yes
FPU	No	68881	68882	68882	68882
Disk drives					
Int. floppy	1.44MB	1.44MB	1.44MB	1.44MB	1.44MB
Hard drive	Yes	Yes	Yes	Yes	Yes
SCSI	Yes	Yes	Yes	Yes	Yes
EtherNet	Optional	Optional	Optional	Optional	Optional
Dimension (in)	13.2x9 .7x11.2	5.5x18 .7x14.4	5.5x18 .7x14.4	5.5x18 .7x14.4	5.5x18 .7x14.4
Weight (lbs.)	16	24-26	24-26	24-26	24
Monitor Size	9" diag.	Varies	Varies	Varies	Varies
Color	No	With card	With card	With card	256
Audio					
Out	Mono	Mono	Mono	Mono	Stereo
In	Mono	No	No	No	No
System Software					
System 6.0.5	No	Yes	Yes	Yes	Yes
System 6.0.7	No	Yes	Yes	Yes	Yes
System 6.0.8	No	Yes	Yes	Yes	Yes
System 7.0	No	Yes	Yes	Yes	Yes
System 7.0.1	Yes	Yes	Yes	Yes	Yes
System 7.1	Yes	Yes	Yes	Yes	Yes
A/UX 2.0.1	No	With PMMU	Yes	Yes	Yes
A/UX 3.0	No	With PMMU	Yes	Yes	Yes

	Mac IIfx	Mac IIsi	PowerBook 100	PowerBook 140	PowerBook 170	Quadra 700	Quadra 900
System characteristics							
CPU	68030	68030	68000	68030	68030	68040	68040
CPU speed	40 MHz	20 MHz	16 MHz	16 MHz	25 MHz	25 MHz	25 MHz

continues

	Mac IIfx	Mac IIsi	PowerBook 100	PowerBook 140	PowerBook 170	Quadra 700	Quadra 900
Memory (standard)	4MB	3 or 5MB	2 or 4MB	2 or 4MB	4MB	4MB	8MB
Memory (maximum)	32MB	17MB	8MB	8MB	8MB	64MB	64MB
Min. RAM speed	80ns	100ns				80ns	80ns
PMMU	Yes	Yes	No	Yes	Yes	Yes	Yes
FPU	68882	Optional	No	No	68882	68882	68882
Disk drives							
Int. floppy	1.44MB	1.44MB	None	1.44MB	1.44MB	1.44MB	1.44MB
Hard drive SCSI	Yes	Yes	Yes	Yes	Yes	Yes	Yes
EtherNet	Optional	Optional	No	No	No	Yes	Yes
Dimensions (in)	5.5x18 .7x14.4	5.5x18 .7x14.4	8.5x11x 1.5	9.3x11 .25x2.25	9.3x11 .25x2.25	11.9x5. 5x14.4	18.6x8 .9x20.6
Weight (lbs.)	24	23	5.1	7	7	13	36
Monitor Size	Varies	Varies	9" passive	10" passive	10" active	Varies	Varies
Color	With card	256 colors	No	No	No	256 colors	256 colors
Audio							
Out	Stereo	Stereo	Mono	Mono	Mono	Stereo	Stereo
In	Mono	Mono	No	Mono	Mono	Mono	Mono
System Software							
System 6.0.5	Yes	No	No	No	No	No	No
System 6.0.7	Yes	Yes	No	No	No	No	No
System 6.0.8	Yes	Yes	No	No	No	No	No
System 7.0	Yes	Yes	No	No	No	No	No
System 7.0.1	Yes	Yes	Yes	Yes	Yes	Yes	Yes
System 7.1	Yes	Yes	Yes	Yes	Yes	Yes	Yes
A/UX 2.0.1	Yes	Yes	No	No	No	No	No
A/UX 3.0	Yes	Yes	No	No	No	Yes	Yes

	Mac IIvx	Centris 610	Centris 650	Quadra 800	Quadra 950
System characteristics					
CPU	68030	68LC040	68RC040	68040	68040
CPU speed	32 MHz	20 MHz	25 MHz	33 MHz	33 MHz
Memory (standard)	4 or 5MB	4MB	4MB	8MB	8MB
Memory (maximum)	20MB	68MB	132MB	136MB	64MB

	Mac IIvx	Centris 610	Centris 650	Quadra 800	Quadra 950
Min. RAM speed	80ns	80ns	80ns	80ns	80ns
PMMU	Yes	Yes	Yes	Yes	Yes
FPU	68882	No	Optional	Yes	Yes
Disk drives					
Int. floppy	1.44MB	1.44MB	1.44MB	1.44MB	1.44MB
Hard drive	Yes	Yes	Yes	Yes	Yes
SCSI	Yes	Yes	Yes	Yes	Yes
EtherNet	Optional	Optional	Optional	Yes	Yes
Dimensions (in)		3.4x 16.3x15.6	6x13x16.5	14.25x 8.9x16	18.6x8.9 x20.6
Weight (lbs.)		14	25	25.3	36
Monitor Size	Varies	Varies	Varies	Varies	Varies
Color	256 colors	256 colors	256/32,768	256/32,768	256 colors
Audio					
Out	Stereo	Stereo	Stereo	Stereo	Stereo
In	Mono	Mono	Mono	Mono	Mono
System software					
All new units use 7.1 or A/UX 3.0					

	Color Classic	LC II	LC III
System characteristics			
CPU	68030	68030	68030
CPU speed	16 MHz	16 MHz	25 MHz
Memory (standard)	4MB	4MB	4MB
Memory (maximum)	10MB	10MB	36MB
Min. RAM speed	100ns	100ns	80ns
PMMU	Yes	Yes	Yes
FPU	Optional	No	Optional
Disk drives			
Int. floppy	1.44MB	1.44MB	1.44MB
Hard drive	Yes	Yes	Yes
SCSI	Yes	Yes	Yes
EtherNet	No	No	No
Dimensions (in.)	14.5x9.9x12.6	3.2x12.2x15	3.2x12.2x15
Weight (lbs.)	23.2	8.8	8.8
Monitor Size	9" diag.	Varies	Varies
Color	256	256	32,768

continues

	Color Classic	LC II	LC III
Audio			
Out	Stereo	Stereo	Stereo
In	Mono	Mono	Mono

System software
All new units
use 7.1 or A/UX 3.0

	PowerBook 145	PowerBook 165c	Duo 210	Duo 230	PowerBook 160	PowerBook 180
System characteristics						
CPU	68030	68030	68030	68030	68030	68030
CPU speed	25 MHz	33 MHz	25 MHz	33 MHz	25 MHz	33 MHz
Memory (standard)	4MB	4MB	4MB	4MB	4MB	4MB
Memory (maximum)	8MB	14MB	24MB	24MB	14MB	14MB
Min. RAM speed						
PMMU	Yes	Yes	Yes	Yes	Yes	Yes
FPU	No	68882			No	Yes
Disk drives						
Int. floppy	1.44MB	1.44MB	1.44MB	1.44MB	1.44MB	1.44MB
Hard drive	Yes	Yes	Yes	Yes	Yes	Yes
SCSI	Yes	Yes	Yes	Yes	Yes	Yes
EtherNet	No	No	With dock	With dock	No	No
Dimensions (in)	9.3x11.25x (2.25)	9.3x11.25x (2.25)	9.3x11.25x (2.25)	9.3x11.25x (2.25)	9.3x11.25x (2.25)	9.3x11.25x (2.25)
Weight (lbs.)	7	7	6.8	6.8	6.8	6.8
Monitor Size	10" passive	9" passive	6" passive		6" passive	6" passive
Color	No	256	With dock	With dock	No	No
Audio						
Out	Stereo	Stereo	Stereo	Stereo	Stereo	Stereo
In	Mono	Mono	Mono	Mono	Mono	Mono

System software
All new units
use 7.1 or A/UX 3.0

System Error Codes

his appendix provides a quick reference to System error codes and Sad Mac codes.

Apple System Error Codes

The following Error Codes are generated by System 7. If you have a System error, the number you get may give you some insight into the problem.

General System

Code	Meaning
-1	A queue element not found during deletion
-2	Invalid queue element
-3	Core routine number out of range
-4	Unimplemented core routine
-5	Invalid queue element
-8	No debugger installed to handle debugger command

I/O System

Code	Meaning
-17	Driver cannot respond to Control call
-18	Driver cannot respond to Status call
-19	Driver cannot respond to Read call
-20	Driver cannot respond to Write call
-21	Driver reference number doesn't match unit table
-22	Driver reference number specifies NIL handle in unit table
-23	Requested read/write permission doesn't match driver's open permission, or attempt to open RAM SerD failed
-24	Close failed
-25	Tried to remove an open driver
-26	DrvrInstall couldn't find driver in resources
-27	I/O call aborted by KillIO
-27	I/O abort error (Printing Manager)
-28	Couldn't read/write/control/status because driver wasn't open

Code	Meaning
-29	Unit table has no more entries
-30	Dce extension error

File System

Code	Meaning
-33	Directory full
-34	Disk full
-35	No such volume
-36	I/O error
-37	There may be no bad names in the final System
-38	File not open
-39	End of file
-40	Tried to position to before start of file (read/write)
-41	Memory full (open), or file won't fit (load)
-42	Too many files open
-43	File not found
-44	Disk is write-protected
-45	File is locked
-46	Volume is locked
-47	File is busy (delete)
-48	Duplicate file name (rename)
-49	File already open with write permission
-50	Error in user parameter list
-51	Refnum error
-52	Get file position error
-53	Volume not on line error (was ejected)
-54	Permissions error on open file
-55	Drive volume already on-line at MountVol
-56	No such drive (tried to mount an incorrect drive number)

continues

Code	Meaning
-57	Not a Mac disk (sig bytes are wrong)
-58	Volume in question belongs to an external fs
-59	Internal file system error: during rename the old entry was deleted but could not be restored
-60	Bad master directory block
-61	Write permissions error

Disk

Code	Meaning
-64	Drive not installed
-65	Read/write requested for an off-line drive
-66	Couldn't find 5 nibbles in 200 tries
-67	Couldn't find valid address mark
-68	Read verify compare failed
-69	Address mark checksum didn't check
-70	Bad address mark bit slip nibbles
-71	Couldn't find a data mark header
-72	Bad data mark checksum
-73	Bad data mark bit slip nibbles
-74	Write underrun occurred
-75	Step handshake failed
-76	Track 0 detect doesn't change
-77	Unable to initialize IWM
-78	Tried to read second side on a one-sided drive
-79	Unable to correctly adjust disk speed
-80	Track number wrong on address mark
-81	Sector number never found on a track
-82	Cannot find sector 0 after track format
-83	Cannot get enough sync
-84	Track failed to verify

Memory Manager

Code	Meaning
-108	Not enough room in heap zone
-109	Handle was NIL in HandleZone or other
-110	Address was odd or out of range
-111	WhichZone failed (applied to free block)
-112	Trying to purge a locked or unpurgeable block
-113	Address in Zone Check failed
-114	Pointer Check failed
-115	Block Check failed
-116	Size Check failed
-117	Trying to move a locked block (Move HHi)

Resource Manager

Code	Meaning
-185	Extended resource has a bad format
-186	Cannot decompress a compressed resource because the resource is bent
-192	Resource not found
-193	Resource file not found
-194	AddResource failed
-195	AddReference failed
-196	RmveResource failed
-197	RmveReference failed
-198	Attribute inconsistent with operation
-199	Map inconsistent with operation

Sad Mac Codes

The Sad Mac Code is generated by the Mac during the startup process. It is usually indicative of a hardware or software problem that prevents the Mac from completing its startup.

128KB ROMs

The following codes are the different error codes that you can receive with the sad Mac if you are using a Macintosh Plus or earlier model of Mac.

Class Code	Reference	Class Code Meaning	Sub Code	Sub Code Meaning
01	ROM	ROM test failed	varying hexa-decimal number	Identifies the ROM chip that failed, usually meaningless
02	RAM	bus test failed	varying hexa-decimal number	Identifies the RAM chip that failed
03	RAM	write test failed	varying hexa-decimal number	Identifies the RAM chip that failed
04	RAM	pattern test failed	varying hexa-decimal number	Identifies the RAM chip that failed
05	RAM	address uniqueness test failed	varying hexa-decimal number	Identifies the RAM chip that failed

System Error Number	Sub Code	Error Meaning

0F Software Error (the column to the right are the numbers you will get as a sub code and indicate the type of software system error that occurred)

System Error Number	Sub Code	Error Meaning
01	0001	bus error
02	0002	address error
03	0003	illegal instruction
04	0004	zero divide
05	0005	check trap

System Error Number	Sub Code	Error Meaning
06	0006	overflow trap
07	0007	privilege violation
08	0008	trace trap
09	0009	trap dispatcher error
10	000A	line 1111 trap
11	000B	miscellaneous hardware trap
12	000C	unimplemented trap executed
13	000D	interrupt button pressed

Sad Mac Codes for Macs with 256KB and Larger ROMs

The Sad Mac code in a Macintosh SE or a Macintosh that was manufactured after the SE is two lines of eight characters. The characters in the first row are hexadecimal numbers that you need to decode to determine the problem. These numbers indicate the class code for the error. The following table lists the possible Sad Mac class codes you can receive. The numbers in the second row are decimal numbers that correspond to the System error codes from the System error table in the previous section.

Error Code	Description
0001	ROM checksum test failed. The ROMs are not responding correctly. Ignore the second line.
0002	The RAM in Bank B failed its first test. The second line indicates the address of the RAM bit that failed.
0003	The RAM in Bank B failed its second test. The second line indicates the address of the RAM bit that failed.
0004	The RAM in Bank A failed its test. The second line indicates the address of the RAM bit that failed.
0005	The RAM failed its external addressing test. The second line is the address that failed.
0006	Problem with the Versatile Interface Adapter (VIA) chip number 1. This chip controls the Mac's floppy disk drives, serial interface, and other I/O devices. Ignore the second code.

continues

Error Code	Description
0007	Problem with the Versatile Interface Adapter chip number 2. This chip controls the Mac's expansion slots and I/O devices not controlled by the VIA1. Ignore the second code.
0008	The Apple Desktop Bus failed its test. Keyboards, mice, and other input devices use the ADB. Ignore the second code.
0009	Problem with PMMU or the MMU chip. Ignore the second code.
000A	Problem with the NuBus controller or slots.
000B	Problem with the SCSI controller chip or bus. Ignore the second code.
000C	Problem with the chip that controls the floppy disk drives (SWIM or IWM chip). Ignore the second code.
000D	Problem with the chip that controls the serial ports (SCC chip). Ignore the second code.
000E	Problem with the data bus. The second code indicates the bad address.
000F	A software-related failure, such as a SCSI drive driver. The second line indicates the error code associated with the software failure (see the table in the System error code section).
FFXX	The CPU failed its power on test. XX indicates the number of a CPU exception. The number of the specific failure isn't very helpful. 33 possible numbers exist, ranging from a bus error to a PMMU Access Violation. Because these errors are directly related to the CPU, they indicate a CPU hardware failure.

Directory of Products

Product Listing by Category

Accounting

Aatrix modules (Aatrix)

Accountant, Inc. (Softsync)

ACCPACC Simply Accounting (Computer Associates)

APG Cash Drawer (APG)

atOnce! (Peachtree)

Back to Basics Accounting (Peachtree)

BPI General Accounting (Computer Associates)

Business Modules (Great Plains Software)

Business Plan Toolkit (Palo Alto Software)

Champion Accounting (Champion)

Computerized Classic Accounting (Absolute Solutions)

Cost Management System (Softouch Software)

DacEasy (DacEasy)

Dollars & Sense (BusinessSense)

Fiscal Knowledge (Mathesis, Inc.)

Flexware (Flexware)

Great Plains Accounting and Import Manager (Great Plains Software)

In-House Accountant (Migent)

Payroll, MultiLedger and Cash Ledger (CheckMark)

Plains & Simple (Great Plains Accounting)

POS/IM (Ensign System)

Quicken (Intuit)

Rags to Riches (Chang Labs)

SBT Accounting (SBT)

Service Industry Accounting (Brown-Wagh)

ShopKeeper (ShopKeeper Software)

Strictly Business (Future Design)

SuperMail Order (National Tele-Press)

SuperMOM (National Tele-Press)

Timeslips III (TimeSlips Corp.)

Up Your Cash Flow (Granville Publications Software)

Animation

Animation Works (Gold Disk)

DynaPerspective (Dyna)

Mac 3D (Challenger)

PictureBase (Symmetry)

StrataVision 3D (Strata)

Super 3D (Aldus)

Artificial Intelligence

ACPVision (Andyne Computing, Ltd.)

Adaflow (Iconix Software Engineering)

Blue/20 and /60 (Advanced Software Logic)

DEFT (Sybase)

MetaDesign (Meta Software Corporation)

ERVision (Andyne Computing, Ltd.)

Forms Programmer (OHM Software)

Foundation Vista (Menlo Business Systems)

Iconix PowerTools (Iconix Software Engineering)

MacDesigner, MetaDesigner, and MacAnalyst (Excel Software)

Macintosh Bubbles (Star Systems)

MacTech magazine

Silverrun (Peat Marwick)

Backup

911 (Microcom)

DiskFit Pro and DiskFit Direct (Dantz)

MacTools (Central Point)

MicroTest (Chariot)

Norton Utilities (Symantec)

Public Utilities (Fifth Generation)

Redux (Inline Design)

Retrospect and Retrospect Remote (Dantz)

Safe & Sound (Central Point)

CAD/CAM

Ashlar Vellum (Ashlar Inc.)

Aura CAD and Aura CAD/CAM (Aura CAD/CAM, Inc.)

AutoCAD (AutoDesk)

BluePrint (Graphsoft)

ClarisCAD (Claris Corporation)

Computer-Aided Design and Drafting (AutoDesk Retail Products)

Design Your Own Home Series (Abracadata)

DesignCAD, Inc. (DesignCAD, Inc.)

Generic CADD (AutoDesk Retail Products)

MacInteriors (Microspot)

MiniCad+ (Graphsoft)

RealCAD Level 1 (AutoDesk Retail Products)

Vellum 3D (Ashlar Inc.)

CD-ROM (Drives and Software)

AppleCD SC and CD Remote (Apple Computers, Inc.)

Beyond the Wall of Stars (CMC-Creative Multimedia Corp.)

CD-ROM drives (NEC)

CD-ROM drives (PLI)

CD-ROM drives (Relax Technology)

CD-ROM drives (Texel)

CD-ROM drives (Todd Enterprises)

CD-ROMs with shareware (Educorp)

Cell"abration" (Science for Kids)

ClipTime CD-ROM (Alpha Technologies)

Erasable Optical Drives (Storage Dimensions)

Family Doctor (CMC-Creative Multimedia Corp.)

Grolier's Electronic Encyclopedia (Grolier)

Living book series (Brøderbund)

Magneto-optical disk drives (Chimera Systems)

Multi-Ad Creator and Multi-Ad Search (Multi-Ad Services)

Optical Drives (NEC, PLI, and Toshiba)

Pro Art (Multi-Ad Services)

ProCDP Optical Drive (Optical Media)

Webster's Dictionary on CD (Highlighted Data)

Who Killed Sam Rupert? (CMC-Creative Multimedia Corp.)

Clip Art

American MediaCliptures (ATG, Inc.)

Artbeats (Artbeats)

ClickArt (T/Maker)

Clip Art (Educorp)

ClipTime CD-ROM (Alpha Technologies)

Cliptures (Dream Maker Software)

Images with Impact! (3G Graphics)

Marble and Granite (Artbeats)

ProArt Trilogy (ProArt)

QuickArt (Wayzata)

SmartArt (Emerald City)

TeXtures (Blue Sky Research)

Wallpaper (Thought I Could)

WetPaint (Dubl-Click Software)

Creativity Tools

IdeaFisher (Fisher Idea Systems)

Mindlink (MindLink)

Synchronicity (Visionary Software)

Data Analysis Programs

FASTAT (Systat)

Igor (WaveMetrics)

JMP (SAS Institute)

Mathematica (Wolfram Research)

MiniTab (MiniTab)

miniWriter (Maitreya)

MYSTAT (Systat)

Scientific Desk (C. Abaci, Inc.)

StatView II (Abacus Concepts)

SuperANOVA (Abacus Concepts)

SYSTAT (Systat)

Theorist (Prescience Corp.)

Databases

4th Dimension and 4D XREF (ACIUS)

Address Book Plus (Spinnaker)

C.A.T. (Chang Laboratories)

DAtabase (Baseline Publishing)

DaynaFile (Dayna Communications)

Double Helix and Helix Express (Helix Technologies)

Dynodex (Portfolio Systems)

EndNote Plus (Niles & Associates)

FileForce (Acius)

FileMaker (Claris)

Filevision IV (TSP)

FoxBASE+/Mac (Microsoft)

GrantManager (Niles & Associates)

Pro-Cite (Personal Bibliograhics Software)

Omnis Seven (Blyth Software)

QuickDEX (Casady & Greene)

Quickhelp (After Hours)

Retriever II (Exodus)

TouchBASE (After Hours)

Desktop Publishing

Cachet (Electronics for Imaging)

DTP Advisor (Brøderbund Software)

FrameMaker (Frame Technology)

Freedom of Press (Custom Applications)

Interleaf Publisher (Interleaf)

LetrTuck (EDCO)

Multi-Ad Creator (Multi-Ad Services)

PageMaker (Aldus)

Personal Press (Aldus)

PosterMaker Plus (Brøderbund Software)

Premiere (Adobe)

Publish It! Easy (Timeworks)

QuarkStyle (Quark)

QuarkXPress (Quark)

Ready,Set,Go! (Manhattan Graphics)

Disk Compression Programs

AutoDoubler (Salient)

DiskDoubler (Salient)

More Disk Space and Super Disk! (Alysis)

StuffIt Deluxe (Aladdin)

TimesTwo (Golden Triangle)

Draw/Paint Programs

Amazing Paint (CE Software)

Canvas (Deneba Software)

CorelDRAW! (Corel Systems)

Cricket Draw (Computer Associates)

CrystalPaint (Great Wave)

DeskPaint (Zedcor)

Easy 3D (Enabling Technologies)

ImageStudio (Fractal Design)

KidPix (Brøderbund)

MacDraw, MacDraw Pro (Claris)

MacPaint (Claris)

Modern Artist (Computer Friends)

Painter (Fractal Design)

PixelPaint (SuperMac)

Studio/8 (Electronic Arts)

Super 3D, SuperPaint (Aldus)

SuperPaint (Aldus)

Swivel 3D (Macromedia)

UltraPaint (Deneba)

Educational Programs

American Discovery and Daisy Quest (Great Wave)

A-Train (Maxis)

Carmen Sandiego series (Brøderbund)

Earthquest (Davidson & Associates)

Foreign language programs (Hyper-Glot)

Headline Harry (Davidson & Associates)

Heaven and Earth (Buena Vista Software)

HyperHebrew (Davka)

Individual Training systems (Individual Software)

Interactive Physics II (Knowledge Revolution)

Jungle Quest and Word Quest (Nordic Software)

KidsDesk (EdMark)

KidsMath and KidsTime (Great Wave Software)

KidsWorks (Davidson & Associates)

Living Books (Brøderbund)

Mavis Beacon Teaches Typing! (Software Toolworks)

Millie's Math House (EdMark)

Number Maze (Great Wave Software)

Reader Rabbit (The Learning Company)

ResumeMaker (Individual Software)

SimLife (Maxis)

Spelunx (Broderbund)

Swamp Gas (Inline Design)

Type! (Brøderbund Software)

Typing Instructor Encore (INDIVIDUAL Software)

Typing Tutor IV (Que Software)

Typist (Caere Corp.)

WillMaker (Nolo Press)

Fax Modem/Machines

BaxFax (Solutions International)

Home Office (Prometheus)

PowerPort series (Global Village Communications)

PowerPrint modems (Hayes)

PowerUser 24/96 (PowerUser)

RA2110M fax/modem (Relisys)

Shiva modems (Shiva)

Ultima Home Office (Prometheus)

File Management

At Ease (Apple Computers)

CanOpener (Abbott Systems)

DiskTop (CE Software)

FetchIt (Cra Z Software)

FileDuo (ASD Software)

FileForce (ACIUS)

FindAll (Abbott Systems)

FolderBolt (Kent Marsh, Ltd.)

HAM (Inline Design)

Hand-Off II (Connectix Corp.)

MacSafe II (Kent Marsh, Ltd.)

Nightwatch II (Kent Marsh, Ltd.)

On Cue (ICOM Simulations)

OnLocation (ON Technology)

Fonts

addDepth (Ray Dream, Inc.)

Adobe Type Manager (ATM) and Super ATM (Adobe)

Adobe Type Reunion (Adobe)

ASD Professional CAD Symbol Library (Advanced System Design)

Bitstream fonts (Bitstream)

FontMinder and FontMonger (Ares Software)

FONTographer (Altsys Co.)

Kadmos Greek font (Allotype)

KeyMaster (Altsys Co.)

Laser Fonts, Publishing Packs (Adobe Systems)

Licensed laser fonts (International Typeface Corporation)

MathWriter (Brooks/Cole Publishing)

Metamorphosis Pro (Altsys)

Multiple Master Typefaces (Adobe)

ParaFont (Design Science)

Suitcase II (Fifth Generation)

Tapestry (Pixar)

TrueForms (Adobe)

TypeAlign (Adobe)

World-Class Fonts (Dubl-Click Software)

Furniture

AnthroCart (Anthro Corp.)

MacTable and add-on cabinet modules (ScanCo Furniture)

MacTilt (Ergotron)

Mac Workstation and MacBuffer (Ergotron)

Games

3 in Three (Inline Design)

Beyond Dark Castle (Aldus)

CalendarMaker (CE Software)

Chuck Yeager's Advanced Flight Trainer (Electronic Arts)

Crystal Quest (Casady & Greene)

Dark Castle (Aldus)

Darwin's Dilemma (Inline Design)

Eight Ball (AMTEX)

Falcon (Spectrum Holobyte)

Ferrari Grand Prix (Bullseye Software)

Flight Simulator (Microsoft)

Fourth and Inches (Accolade)

Jack Nicklaus Golf series (Accolade)

KidsMath (Great Waves)

Klondike (Unison/Tymlabs Software)

Lemmings Mac (Psygnosis)

Mac Pro Football (Avalon Hill)

MacRacquetball (Practical Computer Applications)

MacSleuth (Dariana)

Mean 18 Ultimate Golf (Accolade)

Moriarty's Revenge (Bull City Software)

Orbiter (Spectrum Holobyte)

Pipe Dream (LucasFilm)

PT-109 (Spectrum Holobyte)

SimCity and SimCity Supreme (Maxis)

SpaceQuest and sequels (Sierra Online, Inc.)

Swamp Gas (Inline Design)

Synchronicity (Visionary Software)

Team Construction (Accolade)

Tessare (Inline Design)

Tetris (Spectrum Holobyte)

Tristan (AMTEX)

Ultimate Football (Accolade)

Welltris (Spectrum Holobyte)

Graphics/Screen Capture Programs

Adobe Illustrator (Adobe Systems)

Adobe PhotoShop (Adobe Systems)

Aldus FreeHand (Aldus)

Capture (Mainstay)

Clipper and SmartScrap (Portfolio Systems)

Color MacCheese (Delta Tao)

Cricket Graph (Computer Associates)

Exposure Pro (Baseline Publishing)

Image Analyst (Automatix)

ImageGrabber (Sebastian)

Morph (Gryphon Software)

PhotoEdge (Kodak)

QuickCapture (Data Translations)

Renaissance (Kodak)

SnapJot (Wildflower Software)

Home Finance

Calc+ (Abbott Systems)

CheckFree (CheckFree Corp.)

Dollars and Sense (Business Sense)

MacCalc (Bravo Technologies)

MacInTax (ChipSoft)

Managing Your Money (MECA)

M.Y.O.B. (Teleware)

Quicken (Intuit)

SuperMOM (National Tele-Press)

Up Your Cash Flow (Granville Publications Software)

Wealthbuilder (Reality Technologies)

HyperCard Programs

HyBase (Answer Software)

HyperAtlas (MicroMaps Software)

ScriptExpert (Hyperpress Publishing)

Supercard (Aldus)

Information/Time Management

Act! for Mac (Contact International)

Alarming Events (CE Software)

BizPlanBuilder (JIAN)

Business Sense (Business Sense)

Cathy Calendar (Amaze!)

DateBook (After Hours)

EndNote Plus (Niles Computing)

Far Side Calendar (Amaze!)

FastTrack Scheduler (AEC Management)

FlowMaster (Telmar)

Grant Manager (Niles Computing)

Hebrew Calendar Maker (Davka)

InTouch (Advanced Software)

MacPhonebook (Synex)

MacProject Pro (Claris)

Now Up-To-Date (Now Software)

Project Scheduler 4 (Scitar)

Thought Pattern (Bananafish Software, Inc.)

TimeWand Manager (Videx, Inc.)

TouchBASE (After Hours)

Integrated Software

ClarisWorks (Claris)

Microsoft Works (Microsoft)

WordPerfect Works (WordPerfect)

Keyboards

7' ADB Keyboard Cable (Kensington Microware)

12' and 25' keyboard cables (Your Affordable Software Company)

MAC-101 Keyboard (DataDesk International)

Mac-105 Keyboard (Cutting Edge)

MacPro Extended Keyboard (Keytronic Professional Series)
Mars-128 (Marstek)

Languages

ExperCommon Lisp (ExperTelligence)

HyperBASIC (Teknosys)

Mac C (Consulair)

MacForth Plus (Creative Solutions)

Mach II (Palo Alto Shipping)

Object Logo (Coral Software)

Pascal (TML Systems)

Prolog/m (Chalcedony Software)

Smalltalk (DigiTalk, Inc.)

THINK's Lightspeed C (Symantec)

TML (MacLanguage Series)

ZBasic (Zedcor)

Macros

QuicKeys (CE Software)

Tempo II Plus (Affinity Microsystems)

WorksPlus Command (Lundeen & Associates)

Math/Statistics Programs

Data Desk Professional (Odesta)

FASTAT (Systat)

Memory Upgrades/Accelerators

Accelerator II, Novy Mac20MX, File Server and Micro Channel
(Daystar)

AST TurboScan and NuBus card (AST Research)

Enhance (MicroFrontier)

Excelerator XL 20 and Excelerator XL 25 (Irwin Magnetics)

FastCache (Daystar Digital)

Knowledge Board (Products Diversified)

Macs-A-Million memory upgrades (Sophisticated Circuits)

MacSnap memory upgrades (Dove Computer)

MegaROM (Quantum Leap)

Memory Boards (Siclone)

Memory Upgrades (SuperMac Technologies)

NuSuper Coprocessor Board (YARC)

PowerCache accelerator card (Daystar Digital)

Prodigy 4 board for Mac Plus & 512K Mac, One Plus One (Levco)

Radius Accelerator 25, accelerator boards (Radius)

SIMMs (Micotech)

Spectrum FM Radio Board (Mosaic Development)

SpeedCard accelerator boards (SuperMac Technologies)

Standalone Expansion Systems (Second Wave, Inc.)

SuperRam 2 (SuperMac Technologies)

TokoMac accelerator cards (FusionData)

Transwarp accelerator cards (Applied Engineering)

Virtual and Maxima (Connectix)

Mice/Pointing Devices

A+ Mouse (Mouse Systems)

Abra 2000 and Abra Trak (Abra MacDabra)

Cordless Mouse (Practical Solutions)

CoStar Stingray trackball (CoStar Corp.)

Drawing pad graphics tablet (CalComp)

Expert Mouse (Kensington)

Gravis MouseStick (Advanced Gravis Computer Technology)

Kidz mouse (Logitech)

Kurta Tablets (Kurta)

Lynx Turbo Trackball (Lynx)

MousePenPro (Appoint)

MouseStick (Advanced Gravis)

SD-Series Digitizers (Wacom)

Thumbelina mouse (Appoint)

Trackball/ADB (Mouse Systems)

TrackMan (Logitech)

Turbo Mouse (Logitech)

Modems

2400XF Fax/Modem (Micro Electronic Technologies)

CONNECT V.32 Service (CONNECT)

Courier V.32 (US Robotics)

Digicom V.32 9624LE (Digicom)

FastComm FDX 9696 (FastComm)

Mac Modem with Red Ryder communications software (Prometheus Products)

Migent Pocket Modem (Migent)

Modems (NEC America)

Multi-Modem V32 (Multi-tech Systems)

NetModem (Shiva)

Nodem (Adaptec)

V-Series Smartmodem 9600 (Hayes)

Monitors

6' Mac II Monitor Cable extension kit (Kensington Microware)

Display Server SE (lapis)

DualPage Display System (Cornerstone Technology, Inc.)

EasyView Monitors (Nuvotech)

High resolution monochrome and color monitors (Taxan USA Corporation)

LaserView monitors (Sigma Designs)

MacLarger Monitors (Power R)

Macnifier (Premtech)

MagniView 480 (Dukane)

Monitors (E Machines)

Monitors (Radius)

Monitors (Seiko)

NoRad Shield (NoRad)

PrecisionColor and Pivot monitors (Radius)

Proxima Data Display (Computer Accessories)

RasterOps video boards (RasterOps)

RealTech monitors (Hardware That Fits)

View Frame Projection Panels (Nview)

Viking monitors (Moniterm)

Multimedia Tools

Action! (Macromedia)

American Media Cliptures (ATG, Inc.)

Animation Works (Gold Disk, Inc.)

CD Remote (Apple Computer, Inc.)

Fotoman (Logitech)

Macromind 3-D (Macromedia)

Macromind Director (Macromedia)

MacroModel (Macromedia)

MacRecorder (Macromedia)

MovieProducer bundle (Computer Friends/DIVA)

News Digest (Facts on File)

Photo CD Access (Kodak)

QuickTime (Apple Computers, Inc.)

Ray Dream Designer (Ray Dream, Inc.)

Swivel 3D Professional and Swivelman (Macromedia)

Variety's Video Directory (Bowker Electronic Publishing)

VideoSpigot (SuperMac Technologies)

VideoVision System (Radius)

Voice Navigator (Articulate Systems)

Music Programs

Beyond (Dr. T's Music Software)

Encore (Passport Designs)

HyperComposer (Addison-Wesley Publishing)

MIDI Conductor (Cambridge Automation)

Finale (Coda Music Software)

Master Tracks Pro (Passport Designs)

Music Mouse (Laurie Spiegal)

MusicProse (Coda)

Perceive (Coda)

Practica Musica (ARS Nova)

SoundMaster (Bruce Tomlin)

Toccata music notation program (Sun Valley Software)

Networking

480C PC Viewer (inFocus Systems)

AsanteHUB 1012 (Asante Technologies)

Asante MacCon+ Ethernet cards (Asante Technologies)

Cabletron Ethernet and NuBus cards (Cabletron Systems)

Central System Manager (Integrated Solutions)

ClassWorks (Computer Networking Specialists)

Common Link for Personal Computers (Pacific Microelectronics)

Corporate Communicator and Evolution (Interactive Solutions)

Ether2 TP (Compatible Systems)

EtherGate (Shiva)

EtherPeek (AG Group)

EtherPrint (Dayna Communications)

Evolution (Interactive Solutions)

Gridmaster (Numonics)

I-Server (Solana Electronics)

Lanview Network Analyzer (Cabletron)

LANWatch (FTP)

MacMainFrame (Avatar)

MacNOTIS (Sherrie Schmidt)

MacPROFF (Avatar)

MacTree Plus (Go Technologies)

Message Center (HyperMedia Publishing)

Microsoft Mail (Microsoft)

NetBridge (Shiva)

Novell (Novell)

Optix Network (Blueridge Technologies)

PhoneNet (Farallon Computing)

QuickMail (CE Software)

QuickShare (Compatible Systems)

Rapport and Drive 2.4 (Kennect Technology)

Software Bridge Macintosh (Systems Compatibility Corp.)

OCR Programs

Omni-page (Caere Corporation)

Read-It! (Olduvai)

ReadRight (OCR Systems)

Outliner

More (Symantec)

ThinkTank (Living Videotext)

Portable Macs

Cambridge 288 (Cambridge North America)

MacPort (DTC Technology)

PowerBooks (Apple Computer, Inc.)

Travel Mac (NexSys)

Presentation Programs

ADDmation (Motion Works, Inc.)

AudioMedia (Digidesign)

Cricket Presents (Cricket Software)

DeltaGraph (DeltaPoint)

Desktop Presentation System (HeyerTech)

Graph 3D (ACIUS)

MacMovies (Beck-Tech)

Persuasion (Aldus)

PowerPoint (Microsoft)

Presentation Pro (StradeWare)

Presenting Now (ISM)

Sound Manager Program (Ettore)

TableTools (Mansfield)

Video/FX (Digital FX, Inc.)

VideoShow Professional (General)

Visual Business #5 (Visual Business)

Printers

4693D Color Printer (Tektronix)

Accel-500 dot-matrix printer (Advanced Matrix Technology)

BLP laser printers (GCC Technologies)

Brother Desktop Laser Printers (Brother International)

Colorprint (I/O Design)

DeskJet and PaintJet printers (Hewlett-Packard)

Grappler LQ (Orange Micro)

ImageWriter and LaserWriter (Apple Computer)

JX Printers (Sharp)

LableWriter (CoStar)

Laser printer cartridge refills (Encore Ribbon)

MacBuffer (Ergotron)

MacPrint (Insight Development Corp.)

MacScanner (Infotek)

Printers (Computer Friends)

QMS Colorscript (QMS)

QMS-PS printers (QMS)

Qume printers (Qume)

Smart Label Printer (Seiko)

WriteMove, WriteImpact printers (GCC Technologies)

Programming

AppMaker (Bowers)

Design/OA (Meta)

Desktop Help (Help Software)

Dialoger (theResult Software)

ExperCommon LISP (ExperTelligence)

ExperLISP (ExperTelligence)

ExperLogo Plus (ExperTelligence)

HyperCard (Apple Computer, Inc.)

ithink (High Performance Systems)

Lasertalk (Emerald City Software)

MacFlow (Mainstay)

MacFORTRAN (Absoft)

MacTeX (FTL)

Microsoft QuickBasic 1.0 (Microsoft)

PDQ Pascal (Pecan Software Systems, Inc.)

Preditor (Evatec)

Think C (Symantec)

Think Pascal (Symantec)

Turbo Pascal Mac (Borland)

Visual Interactive Programming (Mainstay)

Resources

BMUG (Berkeley Macintosh User Group)

MacConnection

MacLand

MacTech Magazine

MacUser Magazine

Macwarehouse

MacWorld Magazine

Scanners/OCR Software

270A Hand Held Scanner (Accel Computer Corp.)

Agfa Focus scanners (AGFA)

Animas scanners (Animas)

Apple Scanner (Apple Computer)

AST TurboScan (AST Research)

BarneyScan XP (Barney Scan, Inc.)

Focus S800GS scanner (Agfa-Compugraphic)

JX Scanners (Sharp)

LaserPaint Color II (LaserWare)

Mac 286-10 (AST)

Microtek MSF-300C flatbed scanner (Microtek)

OmniDraft and OmniPage Professional (Caere)

PC Scan 1000 (Dest Corp.)

PixelScan (SuperMac Technologies)

Scan 300/S (Abaton Technology)

Scanners (Microtek, Xerox, Chinon)

TextPert (OCR) (CTA, Inc.)

ThunderScan and Lightning Scan (Thunderware)

TopScan (Calera Recognition Services)

TurboScan (AST)

WordScan Plus (Calera Recognition Systems)

Screen Savers

After Dark and More After Dark (Berkeley Systems)

Pyro (Fifth Generation)

Star Trek: The Screen Saver (Berkeley Systems)

Security Software

Advanced Security (Advanced Gravis)

FileGuard (ASD Software)

MacPassword and MacSnoop (Art Shumer)

MacSafe, FolderBOLT and other security software (Kent Marsh Limited)

MacTools (Central Point Software, Inc.)

TrashGuard (ASD Software)

Spelling Checkers

BigThesaurus and Spelling Coach (Deneba Software)

Correct Grammar (Lifetree)

Doug Clapp's Word Tools (Aegis Development)

GOfer (Microlytics)

Graham Speller (Graham Software)

Grammatik Mac (Reference)

Language Master (Franklin)

Liberty Spell Checker (DataPak Software)

MacProof (Automated Language Processing Systems)

Macspell+ (Creighton Development)

Sensible Grammar (Sensible Software)

Spelling Champion (Champion Software)

SpellsWell (Working Software)

Thunder 7 (Baseline Publishing)

WorksPlus Spell (Lundeen & Associates)

Spreadsheets

4D Calc (ACIUS)

BiPlane (Night Diamonds Software)

DataMerge (Seawell)

Excel (Microsoft)

Lotus 1-2-3 for the Mac (Lotus Development Corp.)

MacCalc (Bravo Technologies)

Theorist (Prescience Corp.)

Wingz (Informix)

Supplies

BakerForms (Baker Graphics)

Labels for printers and disks (Avery International)

Surge Protectors (Curtis Manufacturing)

Telecommunications

America Online (America Online)

CompuServe and CompuServe Navigator (CompuServe)

GEnie online service (General Electric)

MicroPhone II (Software Ventures)

Smartcom II (Hayes)

Prodigy online service (Prodigy)

White Knight (The Freesoft Company)

Utilities

Active Memory (ASD Software)

ALSoft Power Utilities (ALSoft)

AntiToxin (Mainstay)

Can Opener (Abbott Systems)

Capture (Mainstay)

ClickChange (Dubl-Click Software)

Complete Undelete (Microcom)

DiskDoubler (Salient)

DiskExpress II (ALSoft)

DiskInfo (Maitreya Design)

DiskTop (CE Software)

DiskTwin (Golden Triangle Computing)

DOS Mounter (Dayna Communications)

Drive 7 (Casa Blanca Works)

Findswell (Working Software)

Hand-Off II (Software Innovations)

Icon-It! (Olduvai)

In Control (Attain Corp.)

INIT Manager (Baseline Publishing)

INIThound (Cambridge Information Ware)

INITPicker (Inline Design)

LapLink Mac (Traveling Software)

Mac Rescue (Computer Care)

MacEKG (MicroMat Computer Systems)

MacInUse (Softview)

MacLinkPlus/PC and MacLinkPlus Translators (Dataviz)

MacTOPS (Sitka)

Master Juggler (ALSoft)

MenuFonts (Beyond)

MiniTab (MiniTab)

MultiFinder (Interleaf)

PrintBar (Bear Rock)

QuickTools (Advanced Software)

QuickDEX II (Casady & Greene)

RamSnap (Dove Computer)

Retriever II (Exodus Software)

Screen Eclipse (ALSoft)

Scuzzyview SCSI (Aura Systems)

SoftPC, SoftAT, Universal SoftPC (Insignia Solutions)

Sound Mover (Riccardo Ettore)

Stuffit (Aladdin)

Suitcase (Fifth Generation Systems)

SuperSpool (SuperMac Technologies)

Symantec Utilities for Macintosh (Symantec)

Talking Moose (Baseline Publishing)

Vaccine (CE Software)

Virex (Microcom)

Word Processing Programs

Authorware Professional (Authorware)

Expressionist (Prescience Corp.)

ExpressWrite (Exodus)

MacWrite Pro (Claris)

MORE (Symantec)

Nisus word processor (NISUS)

ResumExpert (A Lasting Impression)

Storyboarder and Scriptwriter (American Intelliware)

Taste (Deltapoint)

Word Mac (Microsoft)

WordPerfect (WordPerfect)

WriteNow (T/Maker)

Word Processing Add-Ons

DocuComp (Advanced Software)

KiwiEnvelopes (Kiwi)

MasterWord (Alki)

Pro-Cite (Personal Bibliographic Software)

Word Finder (Microlytics)

Word for Word Professional (Masterworks)

WorksPlus Command and WorksPlus Spell (Lundeen & Associates)

Writer's Dream Tools (Heizer Software)

Product Listing (Alphabetically Arranged)

12' and 25' keyboard cables (Your Affordable Software Company)

2400XF Fax/Modem (Micro Electronic Technologies)

270A Hand Held Scanner (Accel Computer Corp.)

3 in Three (Inline Design)

4693D Color Printer (Tektronix)

480C PC Viewer (inFocus Systems)

4D Calc (ACIUS)

4th Dimension and 4D XREF (ACIUS)

6' Mac II Monitor Cable extension kit (Kensington Microware)

7' ADB Keyboard Cable (Kensington Microware)

911 (Microcom)

A

A+ Mouse (Mouse Systems)

A-Train (Maxis)

Aatrix modules (Aatrix)

Abra 2000 and Abra Trak (Abra MacDabra)

Accel-500 dot-matrix printer (Advanced Matrix Technology)

Accelerator II, Novy Mac20MX, File Server and Micro Channel

Accountant, Inc. (Softsync)

ACCPACC Simply Accounting (Computer Associates)

ACPVision (Andyne Computing, Ltd.)

Act! for Mac (Contact International)

Action! (Macromedia)

Active Memory (ASD Software)

Adaflow (Iconix Software Engineering)

addDepth (Ray Dream, Inc.)

ADDmation (Motion Works, Inc.)

Address Book Plus (Spinnaker)

Adobe Illustrator (Adobe Systems)

Adobe PhotoShop (Adobe Systems)

Adobe Type Manager (ATM) and Super ATM (Adobe)

Adobe Type Reunion (Adobe)

Advanced Security (Advanced Gravis)

After Dark and More After Dark (Berkeley Systems)

Agfa Focus scanners (AGFA)

Alarming Events (CE Software)

Aldus FreeHand (Aldus)

ALSoft Power Utilities (ALSoft)

Amazing Paint (CE Software)

America Online (America Online)

American Discovery and Daisy Quest (Great Wave)

American Media Cliptures (ATG, Inc.)

Animas scanners (Animas)

Animation Works (Gold Disk, Inc.)

AnthroCart (Anthro Corp.)

AntiToxin (Mainstay)

APG Cash Drawer (APG)

Apple Scanner (Apple Computer)

AppleCD SC and CD Remote (Apple Computers, Inc.)

AppMaker (Bowers)

Artbeats (Artbeats)

Asante MacCon+ Ethernet cards (Asante Technologies)

AsanteHUB 1012 (Asante Technologies)

ASD Professional CAD Symbol Library (Advanced System Design)

Ashlar Vellum (Ashlar Inc.)

AST TurboScan (AST Research)

AST TurboScan and NuBus card (AST Research)

At Ease (Apple Computers)

atOnce! (Peachtree)

AudioMedia (Digidesign)

Aura CAD and Aura CAD/CAM (Aura CAD/CAM, Inc.)

Authorware Professional (Authorware)

AutoCAD (AutoDesk)

AutoDoubler (Salient)

B

Back to Basics Accounting (Peachtree)

BakerForms (Baker Graphics)

BarneyScan XP (Barney Scan, Inc.)

BaxFax (Solutions International)

Beyond (Dr. T's Music Software)

Beyond Dark Castle (Aldus)

Beyond the Wall of Stars (CMC-Creative Multimedia Corp.)

BigThesaurus and Spelling Coach (Deneba Software)

BiPlane (Night Diamonds Software)

Bitstream fonts (Bitstream)

BizPlanBuilder (JIAN)

BLP laser printers (GCC Technologies)

Blue/20 and /60 (Advanced Software Logic)

BluePrint (Graphsoft)

BMUG (Berkeley Macintosh User Group)

BPI General Accounting (Computer Associates)

Brother Desktop Laser Printers (Brother International)

Business Modules (Great Plains Software)

Business Plan Toolkit (Palo Alto Software)

Business Sense (Business Sense)

C

C.A.T. (Chang Laboratories)

Cabletron Ethernet and NuBus cards (Cabletron Systems)

Cachet (Electronics for Imaging)

Calc+ (Abbott Systems)

CalendarMaker (CE Software)

Cambridge 288 (Cambridge North America)

CanOpener (Abbott Systems)

Canvas (Deneba Software)

Capture (Mainstay)

Carmen Sandiego series (Brøderbund)

Cathy Calendar (Amaze!)

CD Remote (Apple Computer, Inc.)

CD-ROM (Drives and Software)

CD-ROM drives (NEC)

CD-ROM drives (PLI)

CD-ROM drives (Relax Technology)

CD-ROM drives (Texel)

CD-ROM drives (Todd Enterprises)

CD-ROMs with shareware (Educorp)

Cell"abration" (Science for Kids)

Central System Manager (Integrated Solutions)

Champion Accounting (Champion)

CheckFree (CheckFree Corp.)

Chuck Yeager's Advanced Flight Trainer (Electronic Arts)

ClarisCAD (Claris Corporation)

ClarisWorks (Claris)

ClassWorks (Computer Networking Specialists)

ClickArt (T/Maker)

ClickChange (Dubl-Click Software)

Clip Art (Educorp)

Clipper and SmartScrap (Portfolio Systems)

ClipTime CD-ROM (Alpha Technologies)

Cliptures (Dream Maker Software)

Color MacCheese (Delta Tao)

Colorprint (I/O Design)

Common Link for Personal Computers (Pacific Microelectronics)

Complete Undelete (Microcom)

CompuServe and CompuServe Navigator (CompuServe)

Computer-Aided Design and Drafting (AutoDesk Retail Products)

Computerized Classic Accounting (Absolute Solutions)

CONNECT V.32 Service (CONNECT)

Cordless Mouse (Practical Solutions)

CorelDRAW! (Corel Systems)

Corporate Communicator and Evolution (Interactive Solutions)

Correct Grammar (Lifetree)

Cost Management System (Softouch Software)

CoStar Stingray trackball (CoStar Corp.)

Courier V.32 (US Robotics)

Cricket Draw (Computer Associates)

Cricket Graph (Computer Associates)

Cricket Presents (Cricket Software)

Crystal Quest (Casady & Greene)

CrystalPaint (Great Wave)

D

DacEasy (DacEasy)

Dark Castle (Aldus)

Darwin's Dilemma (Inline Design)

Data Desk Professional (Odesta)

DAtabase (Baseline Publishing)

DataMerge (Seawell)

DateBook (After Hours)

DaynaFile (Dayna Communications)

DEFT (Sybase)

DeltaGraph (DeltaPoint)

Design Your Own Home Series (Abracadata)

Design/OA (Meta)

DesignCAD, Inc. (DesignCAD, Inc.)

DeskJet and PaintJet printers (Hewlett-Packard)

DeskPaint (Zedcor)

Desktop Help (Help Software)

Desktop Presentation System (HeyerTech)

Dialoger (theResult Software)

Digicom V.32 9624LE (Digicom)

DiskDoubler (Salient)

DiskExpress II (ALSoft)

DiskFit Pro and DiskFit Direct (Dantz)

DiskInfo (Maitreya Design)

DiskTop (CE Software)

DiskTwin (Golden Triangle Computing)

Display Server SE (lapis)

DocuComp (Advanced Software)

Dollars & Sense (BusinessSense)

DOS Mounter (Dayna Communications)

Double Helix and Helix Express (Helix Technologies)

Doug Clapp's Word Tools (Aegis Development)

Drawing pad graphics tablet (CalComp)

Drive 7 (Casa Blanca Works)

DTP Advisor (Brøderbund Software)

DualPage Display System (Cornerstone Technology, Inc.)

DynaPerspective (Dyna)

Dynodex (Portfolio Systems)

E

Earthquest (Davidson & Associates)

Easy 3D (Enabling Technologies)

EasyView Monitors (Nuvotech)

Eight Ball (AMTEX)

Encore (Passport Designs)

EndNote Plus (Niles & Associates)

Enhance (MicroFrontier)

Erasable Optical Drives (Storage Dimensions)

ERVision (Andyne Computing, Ltd.)

Ether2 TP (Compatible Systems)

EtherGate (Shiva)

EtherPeek (AG Group)

EtherPrint (Dayna Communications)

Evolution (Interactive Solutions)

Excel (Microsoft)

Excelerator XL 20 and Excelerator XL 25 (Irwin Magnetics)

ExperCommon Lisp (ExperTelligence)

ExperLISP (ExperTelligence)

ExperLogo Plus (ExperTelligence)

Expert Mouse (Kensington)

Exposure Pro (Baseline Publishing)

Expressionist (Prescience Corp.)

ExpressWrite (Exodus)

EZTax-Plan Business Edition (EZWare Corp.)

EZTax-Plan Personal Edition (EZWare Corp.)

EZTax-Prep 1040 (EZWare Corp.)

F

Falcon (Spectrum Holobyte)

Family Doctor (CMC-Creative Multimedia Corp.)

Far Side Calendar (Amaze!)

FASTAT (Systat)

FastCache (Daystar Digital)

FastComm FDX 9696 (FastComm)

FASTAT (Systat)

FastTrack Scheduler (AEC Management)

Fax Modem/Machines

Ferrari Grand Prix (Bullseye Software)

FetchIt (Cra Z Software)

FileDuo (ASD Software)

FileForce (ACIUS)

FileGuard (ASD Software)

FileMaker Pro (Claris)

Filevision IV (TSP)

Finale (Coda Music Software)

FindAll (Abbott Systems)

Findswell (Working Software)

Fiscal Knowledge (Mathesis, Inc.)

Flexware (Flexware)

Flight Simulator (Microsoft)

FlowMaster (Telmar)

Focus S800GS scanner (Agfa-Compugraphic)

FolderBolt (Kent Marsh, Ltd.)

FontMinder and FontMonger (Ares Software)

FONTographer (Altsys Co.)

Foreign language programs (Hyper-Glot)

Forms Programmer (OHM Software)

Fotoman (Logitech)

Foundation Vista (Menlo Business Systems)

Fourth and Inches (Accolade)

FoxBASE+/Mac (Microsoft)

FrameMaker (Frame Technology)

Freedom of Press (Custom Applications)

G

Generic CADD (AutoDesk Retail Products)

GEnie online service (General Electric)

GOfer (Microlytics)

Graham Speller (Graham Software)

Grammatik Mac (Reference)

Grant Manager (Niles Computing)

Graph 3D (ACIUS)

Grappler LQ (Orange Micro)

Gravis MouseStick (Advanced Gravis Computer Technology)

Great Plains Accounting and Import Manager (Great Plains Software)

Gridmaster (Numonics)

Grolier's Electronic Encyclopedia (Grolier)

H

HAM (Inline Design)

Hand-Off II (Connectix Corp.)

Headline Harry (Davidson & Associates)

Heaven and Earth (Buena Vista Software)

Hebrew Calendar Maker (Davka)

High resolution monochrome and color monitors (Taxan USA)

Home Office (Prometheus)

HyBase (Answer Software)

HyperAtlas (MicroMaps Software)

HyperBASIC (Teknosys)

HyperCard (Apple Computer, Inc.)

HyperComposer (Addison-Wesley Publishing)

HyperHebrew (Davka)

I

I-Server (Solana Electronics)

Icon-It! (Olduvai)

Iconix PowerTools (Iconix Software Engineering)

IdeaFisher (Fisher Idea Systems)

Igor (WaveMetrics)

Image Analyst (Automatix)

ImageGrabber (Sebastian)

Images with Impact! (3G Graphics)

ImageStudio (Fractal Design)

ImageWriter and LaserWriter (Apple Computer)

In Control (Attain Corp.)

Individual Training systems (Individual Software)

Information/Time Management

In-House Accountant (Migent)

INIT Manager (Baseline Publishing)

INIThound (Cambridge Information Ware)

INITPicker (Inline Design)

Integrated Software

Interactive Physics II (Knowledge Revolution)

Interleaf Publisher (Interleaf)

InTouch (Advanced Software)

ithink (High Performance Systems)

J

Jack Nicklaus Golf series (Accolade)

JMP (SAS Institute)

Jungle Quest and Word Quest (Nordic Software)

JX Printers (Sharp)

JX Scanners (Sharp)

K

Kadmos Greek font (Allotype)

KeyMaster (Altsys Co.)

KidPix (Brøderbund)

KidsDesk (EdMark)

KidsMath (Great Waves)

KidsWorks (Davidson & Associates)

Kidz mouse (Logitech)

KiwiEnvelopes (Kiwi)

Klondike (Unison/Tymlabs Software)

Knowledge Board (Products Diversified)

Kurta Tablets (Kurta)

L

Labels for printers and disks (Avery International)

LableWriter (CoStar)

Language Master (Franklin)

Lanview Network Analyzer (Cabletron)

LANWatch (FTP)

LapLink Mac (Traveling Software)

Laser Fonts, Publishing Packs (Adobe Systems)

Laser printer cartridge refills (Encore Ribbon)

LaserPaint Color II (LaserWare)

Lasertalk (Emerald City Software)

LaserView monitors (Sigma Designs)

Lemmings Mac (Psygnosis)

LetrTuck (EDCO)

Liberty Spell Checker (DataPak Software)

Licensed laser fonts (International Typeface Corporation)

Living book series (Brøderbund)

Lotus 1-2-3 for the Mac (Lotus Development Corp.)

Lynx Turbo Trackball (Lynx)

M

M.Y.O.B. (Teleware)

Mac 286-10 (AST)

Mac 3D (Challenger)

Mac C (Consulair)

Mac Modem with Red Ryder communications software

Mac Pro Football (Avalon Hill)

Mac Rescue (Computer Care)

Mac Workstation and MacBuffer (Ergotron)

MAC-101 Keyboard (DataDesk International)

Mac-105 Keyboard (Cutting Edge)

MacBuffer (Ergotron)

MacCalc (Bravo Technologies)

MacConnection

MacDesigner, MetaDesigner, and MacAnalyst (Excel Software)

MacDraw, MacDraw Pro (Claris)

MacEKG (MicroMat Computer Systems)

MacFlow (Mainstay)

MacForth Plus (Creative Solutions)

MacFORTRAN (Absoft)

Mach II (Palo Alto Shipping)

MacInTax (ChipSoft)

MacInteriors (Microspot)

Macintosh Bubbles (Star Systems)

Macintosh Pro Football (Avalon Hill)

MacInUse (Softview)

MacLand

MacLarger Monitors (Power R)

MacLinkPlus/PC and MacLinkPlus Translators (Dataviz)

MacMainFrame (Avatar)

MacMovies (Beck-Tech)

Macnifier (Premtech)

MacNOTIS (Sherrie Schmidt)

MacPaint (Claris)

MacPassword and MacSnoop (Art Shumer)

MacPhonebook (Synex)

MacPort (DTC Technology)

MacPrint (Insight Development Corp.)

MacPro Extended Keyboard (Keytronic Professional Series)
Mars-128 (Marstek)

MacPROFF (Avatar)

MacProject Pro (Claris)

MacProof (Automated Language Processing Systems)

MacRacquetball (Practical Computer Applications)

MacRecorder (Macromedia)

Macromind 3-D (Macromedia)

Macromind Director (Macromedia)

MacroModel (Macromedia)

Macs-A-Million memory upgrades (Sophisticated Circuits)

MacSafe II (Kent Marsh, Ltd.)

MacSafe, FolderBOLT and other security software (Kent Marsh Limited)

MacScanner (Infotek)

MacSleuth (Dariana)

MacSnap memory upgrades (Dove Computer)

Macspell+ (Creighton Development)

MacTable and add-on cabinet modules (ScanCo Furniture)

MacTech magazine

MacTeX (FTL)

MacTilt (Ergotron)

MacTools (Central Point Software, Inc.)

MacTOPS (Sitka)

MacTree Plus (Go Technologies)

MacUser Magazine

Macwarehouse

MacWorld Magazine

MacWrite Pro (Claris)

Magneto-optical disk drives (Chimera Systems)

MagniView 480 (Dukane)

Managing Your Money (MECA)

Marble and Granite (Artbeats)

Master Juggler (ALSoft)

Master Tracks Pro (Passport Designs)

MasterWord (Alki)

MathWriter (Brooks/Cole Publishing)

Mathematica (Wolfram Research)

Mavis Beacon Teaches Typing! (Software Toolworks)

Mean 18 Ultimate Golf (Accolade)

MegaROM (Quantum Leap)

Memory Boards (Siclone)

Memory Upgrades (SuperMac Technologies)

MenuFonts (Beyond)

Message Center (HyperMedia Publishing)

MetaDesign (Meta Software Corporation)

Metamorphosis Pro (Altsys)

MicroPhone II (Software Ventures)

Microsoft Mail (Microsoft)

Microsoft QuickBasic 1.0 (Microsoft)

Microsoft Works (Microsoft)

Microtek MSF-300C flatbed scanner (Microtek)

MicroTest (Chariot)

MIDI Conductor (Cambridge Automation)

Migent Pocket Modem (Migent)

Millie's Math House (EdMark)

MindLink (MindLink)

MiniCad+ (Graphsoft)

MiniTab (MiniTab)

miniWriter (Maitreya)

Modems (NEC America)

Modern Artist (Computer Friends)

Monitors (E Machines)

Monitors (Radius)

Monitors (Seiko)

MORE (Symantec)

More Disk Space and Super Disk! (Alysis)

Moriarty's Revenge (Bull City Software)

Morph (Gryphon Software)

MousePenPro (Appoint)

MouseStick (Advanced Gravis)

MovieProducer bundle (Computer Friends/DIVA)

Multi-Modem V32 (Multi-tech Systems)

Multi-Ad Creator and Multi-Ad Search (Multi-Ad Services)

MultiFinder (Interleaf)

Multiple Master Typefaces (Adobe)

Music Mouse (Laurie Spiegal)

MusicProse (Coda)

MYSTAT (Systat)

N

NetBridge (Shiva)

NetModem (Shiva)

News Digest (Facts on File)

Nightwatch II (Kent Marsh, Ltd.)

Nisus word processor (NISUS)

Nodem (Adaptec)

NoRad Shield (NoRad)

Norton Utilities (Symantec)

Novell Netware Mac (Novell)

Now Up-To-Date (Now Software)

Number Maze (Great Wave Software)

NuSuper Coprocessor Board (YARC)

O

Object Logo (Coral Software)

OmniDraft and OmniPage Professional (Caere)

Omnis Seven (Blyth Software)

On Cue (ICOM Simulations)

OnLocation (ON Technology)

Optical Drives (NEC, PLI, and Toshiba)

Optix Network (Blueridge Technologies)

Orbiter (Spectrum Holobyte)

P

PageMaker (Aldus)

Painter (Fractal Design)

ParaFont (Design Science)

Pascal (TML Systems)

Payroll, MultiLedger and Cash Ledger (CheckMark)

PC Scan 1000 (Dest Corp.)

PDQ Pascal (Pecan Software Systems, Inc.)

Perceive (Coda)

Personal Press (Aldus)

Persuasion (Aldus)

PhoneNet (Farallon Computing)

Photo CD Access (Kodak)

PhotoEdge (Kodak)

PictureBase (Symmetry)

Pipe Dream (LucasFilm)

PixelPaint (SuperMac)

PixelScan (SuperMac Technologies)

Plains & Simple (Great Plains Accounting)

POS/IM (Ensign System)

PosterMaker Plus (Brøderbund Software)

PowerCache accelerator card (Daystar Digital)

PowerPoint (Microsoft)

PowerPort series (Global Village Communications)

PowerPrint modems (Hayes)

PowerUser 24/96 (PowerUser)

Practica Musica (ARS Nova)

PrecisionColor and Pivot monitors (Radius)

Preditor (Evatec)

Premiere (Adobe)

Presentation Pro (StradeWare)

Presenting Now (ISM)

PrintBar (Bear Rock)

Printers (Computer Friends)

ProArt Trilogy (ProArt)

ProCDP Optical Drive (Optical Media)

Pro-Cite (Personal Bibliograhics Software)

Prodigy online service (Prodigy)

Project Scheduler (Scitar)

Proxima Data Display (Computer Accessories)

PT-109 (Spectrum Holobyte)

Public Utilities (Fifth Generation)

Publish It! Easy (Timeworks)

Pyro (Fifth Generation)

Q

QMS Colorscript (QMS)

QMS-PS printers (QMS)

QuarkStyle (Quark)

QuarkXPress (Quark)

QuickArt (Wayzata)

QuickCapture (Data Translations)

QuickDEX II (Casady & Greene)

Quicken (Intuit)

Quickeys (CE Software)

Quickhelp (After Hours)

QuickMail (CE Software)

QuickShare (Compatible Systems)

QuickTime (Apple Computers, Inc.)

QuickTools (Advanced Software)

Qume printers (Qume)

R

RA2110M fax/modem (Relisys)

Radius Accelerator 25, accelerator boards (Radius)

Rags to Riches (Chang Labs)

RamSnap (Dove Computer)

Rapport and Drive 2.4 (Kennect Technology)

RasterOps video boards (RasterOps)

Ray Dream Designer (Ray Dream, Inc.)

Read-It! (Olduvai)

Reader Rabbit (The Learning Company)

ReadRight (OCR Systems)

Ready,Set,Go! (Manhattan Graphics)

RealCAD Level 1 (AutoDesk Retail Products)

RealTech monitors (Hardware That Fits)

Redux (Inline Design)

Renaissance (Kodak)

ResumeMaker (Individual Software)

ResumExpert (A Lasting Impression)

Retriever II (Exodus Software)

Retrospect and Retrospect Remote (Dantz)

S

Safe & Sound (Central Point)

SBT Accounting (SBT)

Scan 300/S (Abaton Technology)

Scanners (Microtek, Xerox, Chinon)

Scientific Desk (C. Abaci, Inc.)

Screen Eclipse (ALSoft)

ScriptExpert (Hyperpress Publishing)

Scuzzyview SCSI (Aura Systems)

SD-Series Digitizers (Wacom)

Sensible Grammar (Sensible Software)

Service Industry Accounting (Brown-Wagh)

Shiva modems (Shiva)

ShopKeeper (ShopKeeper Software)

Silverrun (Peat Marwick)

SimCity and SimCity Supreme (Maxis)

SimLife (Maxis)

SIMMs (Micotech)

Smalltalk (DigiTalk, Inc.)

Smart Label Printer (Seiko)

SmartArt (Emerald City)

Smartcom II (Hayes)

Snap! (Forthought, Inc.)

SnapJot (Wildflower Software)

SoftPC, SoftAT, Universal SoftPC (Insignia Solutions)

Software Bridge Macintosh (Systems Compatibility Corp.)

Sound Manager Program (Riccardo Ettore)

Sound Mover (Riccardo Ettore)

SoundMaster (Bruce Tomlin)

SpaceQuest and sequels (Sierra Online, Inc.)

Spectrum FM Radio Board (Mosaic Development)

SpeedCard accelerator boards (SuperMac Technologies)

Spelling Champion (Champion Software)

SpellsWell (Working Software)

Spelunx (Brøderbund)

Standalone Expansion Systems (Second Wave, Inc.)

Star Trek: The Screen Saver (Berkeley Systems)

StatView II (Abacus Concepts)

Storyboarder and Scriptwriter (American Intelliware)

StrataVision 3D (Strata)

Strictly Business (Future Design)

Studio/8 (Electronic Arts)

Stuffit (Aladdin)

StuffIt Deluxe (Aladdin)

Suitcase (Fifth Generation Systems)

Super 3D, SuperPaint (Aldus)

SuperANOVA (Abacus Concepts)

Supercard (Aldus)

SuperMail Order (National Tele-Press)

SuperMOM (National Tele-Press)

SuperPaint (Aldus)

SuperRam 2 (SuperMac Technologies)

SuperSpool (SuperMac Technologies)

Surge Protectors (Curtis Manufacturing)

Swamp Gas (Inline Design)

Swivel 3D Professional and Swivelman (Macromedia)

Symantec Utilities for Macintosh (Symantec)

Synchronicity (Visionary Software)

SYSTAT (Systat)

T

TableTools (Mansfield)

Talking Moose (Baseline Publishing)

Tapestry (Pixar)

Taste (Deltapoint)

Team Construction (Accolade)

Tempo II Plus (Affinity Microsystems)

Tessare (Inline Design)

Tetris (Spectrum Holobyte)

TextPert OCR Software (CTA, Inc.)

TeXtures (Blue Sky Research)

Theorist (Prescience Corp.)

Think C (Symantec)

Think Pascal (Symantec)

THINK's Lightspeed C (Symantec)

ThinkTank (Living Videotext)

Thought Pattern (Bananafish Software, Inc.)

Thumbelina mouse (Appoint)

Thunder 7 (Baseline Publishing)

ThunderScan and Lightning Scan (Thunderware)

Timeslips III (TimeSlips Corp.)

TimesTwo (Golden Triangle)

TimeWand Manager (Videx, Inc.)

TML (MacLanguage Series)

TokoMac accelerator cards (FusionData)

TopScan (Calera Recognition Services)

TouchBASE (After Hours)

Trackball/ADB (Mouse Systems)

TrackMan (Logitech)

Transwarp accelerator cards (Applied Engineering)

TrashGuard (ASD Software)

Travel Mac (NexSys)

Tristan (AMTEX)

TrueForms (Adobe)

Turbo Mouse (Logitech)

Turbo Pascal Mac (Borland)

TurboScan (AST)

Type! (Brøderbund Software)

TypeAlign (Adobe)

Typing Instructor Encore (INDIVIDUAL Software)

Typing Tutor IV (Que Software)

Typist (Caere Corp.)

U

Ultima Home Office (Prometheus)

Ultimate Football (Accolade)

UltraPaint (Deneba)

Up Your Cash Flow (Granville Publications Software)

V

V-Series Smartmodem 9600 (Hayes)

Vaccine (CE Software)

Variety's Video Directory (Bowker Electronic Publishing)

Vellum 3D (Ashlar Inc.)

Video/FX (Digital FX, Inc.)

VideoShow Professional (General)

VideoSpigot (SuperMac Technologies)

VideoVision System (Radius)

View Frame Projection Panels (Nview)

Viking monitors (Moniterm)

Virex (Microcom)

Virtual and Maxima (Connectix)

Visual Business (Visual Business)

Visual Interactive Programming (Mainstay)

Voice Navigator (Articulate Systems)

W

Wallpaper (Thought I Could)

Wealthbuilder (Reality Technologies)

Webster's Dictionary on CD (Highlighted Data)

Welltris (Spectrum Holobyte)

WetPaint (Dubl-Click Software)

White Knight (The Freesoft Company)

Who Killed Sam Rupert? (CMC-Creative Multimedia Corp.)

WillMaker (Nolo Press)

Wingz (Informix)

Word Finder (Microlytics)

Word for Word Professional (Masterworks)

Word Mac (Microsoft)

WordPerfect (WordPerfect)

WordPerfect Works (WordPerfect)

WordScan Plus (Calera Recognition Systems)

WorksPlus Command (Lundeen & Associates)

WorksPlus Spell (Lundeen & Associates)

World-Class Fonts (Dubl-Click Software)

WriteMove, WriteImpact printers (GCC Technologies)

WriteNow (T/Maker)

Writer's Dream Tools (Heizer Software)

Z

ZBasic (Zedcor)

Vendor Guide

3G Graphics
114 Second Avenue South, Suite 104
Edmonds, WA 98020
Images with Impact!
(800) 456-0234
(206) 367-9321

A Lasting Impression
49 Thornberry Rd.
Winchester, MA 01890
RésumExpert
(617) 721-2037

Aatrix Software
523 N. Washington Avenue
Grand Forks, ND 58203
Aatrix accounting modules
(701) 746-6801

Abacus Concepts
1984 Bonita Ave.
Berkeley, CA 94704
StatView, SuperANOVA, and MacSpin
(510) 540-1949

Abbott Systems
62 Mountian Road
Pleasantville, NY 10570
Can Opener, FindAll, and Calc+
(800) 552-9157

Abracadata
P.O. Box 2440, Dept. MU
Eugene, OR 97402
Design Your Own Home Series for Macintosh,
Architecture
Interiors, and Landscape
(800) 451-4871
(503) 342-3030

Abra MacDabra Software
485 Pala Ave.
Sunnyvale, CA 94086
Abra 2000 and AbraTrak
(408) 737-9454

Absolute Solutions, Inc
P.O. Box 232400
Leucadia, CA 92023-2400
Computerized Classic Accounting
(800) 633-7666

Accel Computer Corp
188 Technology Drive, Suite B
Irvine, CA 92714
270A Hand held scanner
(714) 727-4311

Accolade
5300 Stevens Creek Blvd., Suite 500
San Jose, CA 95129
4th & Inches, Team Construction, Mean 18
Ultimate Golf, Jack Nicklaus Golf Series, and
Ultimate Football
(800) 245-7744
(408) 985-1700

ACIUS, Inc.
10351 Bubb Road
Cupertino, CA 95014
4th Dimension, FileForce, and 4D XREF
(408) 252-4444

Adobe Systems
1585 Charleston Road
Mountain View, CA 94039
TypeAlign, Illustrator, Photoshop, Premiere,
Adobe Type Manager (ATM), SuperATM,
Type Reunion, Type On Call CD-ROM,
TrueForms, and Multiple Master Typefaces
(415) 961-4400

Advanced Gravis Computer Technology, Ltd.
7400 MacPherson, Suite 111
Burnaby, BC
Canada V5J 4M6
Gravis MouseStick and Advanced Security
(604) 434-7274

Advanced Software
1095 E. Duane Avenue, Suite 103
Sunnyvale, CA 94086
InTouch, QuickTools, and DocuComp
(800) 346-5392
(408) 733-0745

Advanced System Design Inc.
1010 Stagecoach Blvd.
Evergreen, CO 80439
ASD Professional CAD Symbol Library
(303) 674-2222

Advent Computer Products
449 Santa Fe Dr., Suite 213
Encinitas, CA 92024
Colour Adaptor Module and TimeFrame
(619) 942-8456

AEC Software Inc.
22611 Markey Court, Bldg. 113
Sterling, VA 22166
FastTrack Schedule and Information Manager
(800) 346-9413

Affinity Microsystems
1050 Walnut St., Suite 425
Boulder, CO 80302
Tempo II Plus
(303) 442-4840

After Hours Software
5636 Van Nuys Blvd., Suite B
Van Nuys, CA 91401
TouchBASE, QuickHelp, and DateBook
(818) 780-2220

AG Group
2540 Camino Diablo, Suite 250
Walnut Creek, CA 94596
EtherPeek
(510) 937-2447

AGFA, Division of Miles
200 Ballardvale St.
Wilmington, MA 01887
Agfa Focus scanners and Arcus
(800) 685-4271

Aladdin Systems, Inc.
165 Westridge Drive
Watsonville, CA 95076
StuffIt Deluxe and StuffIt
(408) 761-6200

Albathion Software
P.O. Box 7926
San Francisco, CA 94120
Entrypaq
(415) 824-2737

Aldus Corporation
411 First Avenue South
Seattle, WA 98104
FreeHand, PageMaker, Super 3D, Beyond
Dark Castle, and Persuasion
(206) 622-5500

Aldus Corporation
Consumer Division
9770 Carroll Center Road, Suite J
San Diego, CA 92126
Personal Press, SuperPaint, SuperCard, and
Intellidraw
(206) 695-6958

Alki Software Corp.
219 First Avenue North, Suite 410
Seattle, WA 98109
Foreign language dictionaries and
MasterWord
(206) 286-2600

Allotype Typographics
1600 Packard Road, Suite 5
Ann Arbor, MI 48104
Kadmos Greek Font
(313) 663-1989

Alpha Technologies
6921 Cable Drive
Marriottsville, MD 21104
ClipTime Volumes
(410) 781-4200

Alphatronix
4022 Stirrup Drive, Suite 315
Durham, NC 27713
Inspire drives
(919) 544-0001

ALSoft Inc.
22557 Aldine Westfield Road, Suite 122
Spring, TX 77383
ALSoft Power Utilities, DiskExpress II, Screen
Eclipse, and Master Juggler
(713) 353-4090

Altra Technology
1200 Skyline Drive
Laramie, WY 82070
Felix
(800) 726-6153

Altsys Co.
269 W. Renner Road
Richardson, TX 75080
Fontographer, Virtuoso, and Metamorphosis
Professional
(214) 680-2060

Alysis Software Corp.
1231 31st Avenue
San Francisco, CA 94122
More Disk Space and SuperDISK!
(415) 566-2263

Amaze
11810 115th Avenue NE
Kirkland, WA 98034-6923
The Far Side Calendar and Cathy Calendar
(800) 345-1546
(206) 820-7007

America Online
8619 Westwood Center Drive
Vienna, VA 22182
Mac and IBM related online services
(800) 227-6364

Amtex Software
212 Albert Street
Belleville, Ontario, Canada K8N 3N7
Tristan and Eight Ball
(613) 967-7900

Andrew Corporation
19021 120th Avenue NE
Bothell, WA 98011
MacTwin
(800) 776-6174
(206) 485-8200

Andyne Computing Ltd.
552 Princess St.
Kingston, Ontario
Canada K7L1C7
ERVision and ACPVision
(800) 267-0665

Answer Software Corp.
20045 Stevens Creek Blvd.
Cupertino, CA 95014
HyBase
(408) 253-7515

Anthro Corp.
3221 N.W. Yeon St.
Portland, OR 97210
AnthroCart
(800) 325-3841
(503) 241-7113

APG (Cash Drawer Division of Upper
Midwest Industries)
1601 67th Avenue North
Brooklyn Center, MN 55430
APG Cash Drawer
(612) 560-1440

Apple Computer, Inc.
20525 Mariani Avenue
Cupertino, CA 95014
At Ease, System 7, Hypercard, CD Remote,
printers, monitors, CD-ROM drives, and
computer systems
(800) 776-2333
(408) 996-1010

Applied Engineering
3210 Beltline Road
Dallas, TX 75234
Transwarp accelerator cards
(800) 554-6227

Appoint
7026 Koll Center Pkwy., Suite 230
Pleasanton, CA 94566
MousePenPro and Thumbelina mouse
(800) 448-1184

Ares Software
561 Pilgrim Drive, Suite D
Foster City, CA 94404
FontMonger and FontMinder
(415) 578-9090

Ars Nova Software
P.O. Box 637
Kirkland, WA 98083
Practica Musica
(800) 445-4866

Artbeats
P.O. Box 1287
Myrtle Creek, OR 97457
Marble & Granite and Artbeats
(503) 863-4429

Articulate Systems
600 W. Cummings Park, Suite 4500
Woburn, MA 01801
Voice Navigator II
(800) 443-7077
(617) 935-5656

Asanté Technologies Inc.
821 Fox Lane
San Jose, CA 95131
Asanté MacCon+ Ethernet cards and
AsantéHUB 1012
(408) 435-8388

ASD Software
4650 Arrow Highway, Suite E-6
Montclair, CA 91763
FileGuard, WindowWatch, Active Memory,
FileDuo, TrashGuard, and Twins
(714) 624-2594

Ashlar Inc.
1290 Oakmead Pkwy., Suite 218
Sunnyvale, CA 94086
Ashlar Vellum and Vellum 3D
(408) 746-1800

AST Research, Inc.
16215 Alton Parkway
Irvine, CA 92715
AST TurboScan and NuBus card
(714) 727-4141

Attain Corp.
48 Grove Street
Somerville, MA 02144
In Control
(617) 776-1110

ATTO Technology
1567 Sweet Home Road
Amherst, NY 14228
SiliconExpress II
(716) 688-4259

Aura CAD/CAM, Inc.
2335 S. Alaska Ave.
El Segundo, CA 90245
AuraCAD and Aura CAD/CAM
(310) 643-5300

AutoDesk
2320 Marinship Way
Sausalito, CA 94965
AutoCAD
(415) 332-2344

AutoDesk Retail Products
11911 North Creek Pkwy. South
Bothell, WA 98011
Generic CADD
(206) 487-2233

Automatix
1000 Tech Park Drive
Billerica, MA 01821
Image Analyst
(508) 667-7900

Avatar Corporation
65 South St.
Hopkinton, MA 01748
MacMainFrame Series and MacPROFF
(508) 435-3000

Avenue Software
2162 W. Charest Blvd.
St. Foy, Quebec
Canada G1N 2G3
MacKeymeleon
(418) 682-3088

Avery/Dennison, Avery Division
20955 Pathfinder Drive
Diamond Bar, CA 91765
Labels for printers and disks
(909) 869-7711

Bananafish Software, Inc
730 Central Ave.
San Francisco, CA 94117
Thought Pattern
(415) 929-8135

Baseline Publishing
1770 Moriah Woods Blvd.
Memphis, TN 38117
Thunder 7, INIT Manager, DAtabase,
Exposure Pro, and Talking Moose
(901) 682-9676

Baudville
5380 52nd St. S.E.
Grand Rapids, MI 49508
AwardMaker Plus
(616) 698-0888

Bear Rock Technologies
4140 Mother Lode Drive, Suite 100
Shingle Springs, CA 95682
PrintBar
(800) BEAROCK

Beck-Tech
41 Tunnel Rd.
Alameda, CA 94705
MacMovies
(510) 748-1600

Berkeley Systems
1700 Shattuck Avenue
Berkeley, CA 94709
Stepping Out II, After Dark, More After Dark,
and Star Trek: The Screen Saver
(510) 540-5535

Berol Corp.
105 Westpark Dr.
P.O. Box 2248
Brentwood, TN 37024-2248
Products for the Macintosh
(615) 371-1199

Borland International
1800 Green Hill
Scotts Valley, CA 95066
Turbo Pascal Mac
(408) 438-8400

Boston Companies
15 Wake Robin Road
Sudbury, MA 01776
QuickShot
(508) 443-0075

Blueridge Technologies
P.O. Box 430
Flint Hill, VA 22627
Optix Network
(703) 675-3015

Blue Sky Research
534 S.W. Third Ave.
Portland, OR 97204
TeXtures
(503) 222-9571

Blyth Software
1065 E. Hillsdale Boulevard
Foster City, CA 94404
Omnis Seven and Teacher's Rollbook
(800) 346-6647
(415) 571-0222

BMUG (Berkeley Mac User's Group)
2055 Center Street
Berkeley, CA 94704
Macintosh user group
(415) 549-2684

Bowers Development
97 Lowell Road
Concord, MA 01742
AppMaker
(508) 369-8175

Bowker Electronic Publishing
Attn: Reed Reference Publishing
121 Chanlon Road
Providence, NJ 07974
Variety's Video Directory Plus and CD-ROM
products
(800) 323-3288

Bravo Technologies, Inc.
P.O. Box 10078
Berkeley, CA 94709
MacCalc and MacGraphX
(510) 841-8552

Brøderbund Software
500 Redwood Blvd.
Novato, CA 94948-6121
Carmen Sandiego Series, TypeStyler, DTP
Advisor, PosterMaker Plus, BannerMania,
Living Book series (*Arthur's Teacher Troubles*,
Just Grandma and Me, and *The Tortoise and the
Hare*)
(800) 521-6263
(415) 382-4400

Brooks/Cole Publishing
511 Forrest Lodge Rd.
Pacific Grove, CA 93950
MathWriter
(408) 373-0728

Brother International
200 Cottontail Lane
Somerset, NJ 08975
Brother laser printers and phase change
printers
(908) 356-8880

Brown-Wagh Publishers
130D Knowels
Los Gatos, CA 95030
Service Industry Accounting

Bruce Tomlin
15801 Chase Hill Blvd. #109
San Antonio, TX 78256
SoundMaster

Buena Vista Software
500 S. Buena Vista Street
Burbank, CA 91521-6385
Heaven and Earth
(818) 973-4303

Bullseye Software
P.O. Box 7900
Incline Village, NV 89450
Ferrari Grand Prix
(702) 831-2523

BusinessSense
448 E. 6400S, Suite 125
Salt Lake City, UT 84107
Dollars & Sense
(801) 261-7800

Byte by Byte
9442-A Capital of Texas Highway N., #650
Austin, TX 78759
Mac-related products
(512) 343-4357

C. Abaci, Inc
208 St. Mary's St.
Raleigh, NC 27605
Scientific Desk
(919) 832-4847

Cabletron Systems, Inc.
35 Industrial Way, P.O. Box 6257
Rochester, NH 03867
Cabletron Ethernet and NuBus cards
(603) 332-9400

Caere Corporation
100 Cooper Court
Los Gatos, CA 95030
Typist, OmniDraft, PageKeeper, and
OmniPage Professional
(800) 535-SCAN

CalComp
2411 West La Palma
Anaheim, CA 92801
Drawing pad graphics tablet and printers
(800) 445-6515

Calera Recognition Systems
475 Potrero Ave.
Sunnyvale, CA 94086
TopScan and WordScan Plus
(800) 544-7051

California Scientific Software
10024 New Town Road
Nevada City, CA 95959
BrainMaker Professional for the Macintosh
(916) 478-9040

Cambridge Information Ware
P.O. Box 1296
Cambridge, MA 02238
INIThound
(617) 484-8364

Cambridge Scientific Computing
875 Massachusetts, 6th Floor
Cambridge, MA 02139
Chem3D Plus
(617) 491-6862

Casa Blanca Works
148 Bon Air Center
Greenbrae, CA 94904
Drive 7
(415) 461-2227

Casady & Greene
22734 Portola Dr.
Salinas, CA 93908
Sky Shadow, Mission Starlight, QuickDEX II,
and Crystal Quest
(800) 359-4920
(408) 484-9228

CD Technology
766 San Aleso Avenue
Sunnyvale, CA 95086
Porta-Drive
(408) 752-8500

CE Software
1801 Industrial Circle
West Des Moines, IA 50265
DiskTop, QuicKeys, MacBillboard,
CalendarMaker, Vaccine, Amazing Paint,
PowerKey, Alarming Events, and QuickMail
(515) 224-1995

Central Point Software
15220 N.W. Greenbrier Parkway, #200
Beaverton, OR 97006
MacTools and Safe & Sound
(503) 690-8090

Champion Business System
6726 S. Revere Parkway
Englewood, CO 80112
Champion Accounting Software
(303) 792-3606

Chang Laboratories, Inc.
3350 Scott Blvd., Bldg. 25
Santa Clara, CA 95054
C.A.T. III and Rags to Riches
(408) 727-8096

CheckMark Software, Inc.
P.O. Box 860
Fort Collins, CO 80522
MultiLedger, CashLedger, and Payroll
(800) 444-9922

Chimera Systems
10540 Kinnard Ave.
Los Angeles, CA 90024
Magneto-Optical Disk Drives
(213) 249-2246

Chinon America, Inc.
615 Hawaii Avenue
Torrance, CA 90503
Scanners and CD-ROM drives
(800) 441-0222

ChipSoft
6330 Nancy Ridge Road
San Diego, CA 92121-2246
MacInTax
(619) 453-4446

Claris Corp.
5201 Patrick Henry Dr.
Santa Clara, CA 95052
Resolve, MacDraw Pro, FileMaker Pro,
MacProject Pro, and ClarisWorks
(408) 727-8227

Clear Access
200 W. Lowe
Fairfield, IA 52556
ClearAccess, External Macro Sets
(515) 472-7077

CMC ReSearch, Inc.
514 NW 11th Avenue, Suite 203
Portland, OR 97209
The Family Doctor CD-ROM, *Who Killed Sam Rupert?* CD-ROM, *Beyond the Walls of Stars* CD-ROM, and mulitmedia products
(800) 262-7668

CMS Enhancements, Inc.
2722 Michelson Dr.
Irvine, CA 92715
CMS Hard Drives
(714) 222-6000

Compatible Systems Corp.
P.O. Box 17220
Boulder, CO 80308
QuickShare and Ether2 TP
(800) 356-0283

CompuServe
5000 Arlington Centre Blvd.
Columbus, OH 43220
On-line service, The Navigator
(800) 848-8199
(614) 457-8600

Computer Accessories Corp.
6610 Nancy Ridge Drive
San Diego, CA 92121
Proxima Data Display VersaColor
(800) 582-2580

Computer Associates International
One Computer Associates Plaza
Islandia, NY 11788
ACCPACC Simply Accounting, BPI General Accounting, and CA-Cricket line of paint and draw programs
(800) 531-5236
(516) 342-5224

Computer Care
420 N. Fifth St., Suite 1180
Minneapolis, MN 55401
Mac Rescue
(800) 950-CARE

Computer Friends
14250 NW Science Park Drive
Portland, OR 97229
Modern Artist, ColorSnap 32+, and MovieProducer bundle
(800) 547-3303
(503) 626-2291

Connectix Corp.
2655 Campus Drive
San Mateo, CA 94403
Virtual, Maxima, CPU, and HAND-OFF II
(415) 571-5100

Contact Software International
1840 Hutton Drive, Suite 200
Carrollton, TX 75006
Contact! for the Mac
(214) 919-9500

Corel Systems
1600 Carling Ave.
Ottawa, ON,
Canada K1Z 8R7
CorelDRAW!
(416) 928-3110

CoStar Corp
22 Bridge St.
Greenwich, CT 06830
CoStar LabelWriter II and CoStar Stingray trackball
(203) 661-9700

Cra Z Software
P.O. Box 6379
Haverhill, MA 01831
FetchIt
(508) 521-5262

Creative Solutions
4701 Randolph Rd.
Rockville, MD 20852
MacForth Plus
(800) 367-8465
(301) 984-0262

Curtis Manufacturing Co., Inc.
30 Fitzgerald Drive
Jaffrey, NH 03452
Surge protectors, keyboard organizers,
and mice devices
(603) 532-4123

Custom Applications Inc.
900 Technology Park Drive, Building 8
Billerica, MA 01821
Freedom of Press
(508) 667-8585

Cutting Edge
97 S. Red Willow Rd.
Evanston, WY 82931
Mac-105 Keyboard and SCSI hard-disk drives
(800) 443-5199
(307) 789-3830

DacEasy, Inc.
17950 Preston Road, #800
Dallas, TX 75252
DacEasy Light Checkbook Accounting
(214) 248-0205

Dantz Development
1400 Shattuck Ave.
Berkeley, CA 94709
Retrospect, DiskFit, and DiskFit Pro
(415) 849-0293

Data Translation Inc.
100 Locke Drive
Marlboro, MA 01752
QuickCapture and VideoQuill
(508) 481-3700

Datability Inc.
1 Palmer Terrace
Carlstadt, NJ 07072
Mac Raf
(201) 438-2400

DataDesk International
9330 Eaton Ave.
Chatsworth, CA 91311
HyperDialer, MAC-101e and Switchboard
keyboards
(818) 998-4200

Dataproducts
6219 DeSoto Avenue
Woodland Hills, CA 91365
Phase change printers
(800) 334-3174

DataViz
55 Corporate Dr.
Trumbull, CT 06611
MacLinkPlus/PC and MacLinkPlus/
Translators
(203) 268-0030

Davidson and Associates
19840 Pioneer Avenue
Torrance, CA 90503
Headline Harry and the Great Paper Race,
KidWorks, and Earthquest
(310) 793-0600

Davka Corp.
7074 N. Western Ave.
Chicago, IL 60645
HyperHebrew, Otzar Plus, and Hebrew
Calendar Maker
(312) 465-4070

Dayna Communications
50 S. Main St., Fifth Floor
Salt Lake City, UT 84144
DaynaFile, DOS Mounter, and EtherPrint
(801) 531-0600

Daystar Digital, Inc.
5556 Atlanta Highway
Flowery Branch, GA 30542
FastCache and PowerCache accelerator cards
(800) 962-2077
(404) 967-2077

DCA
1000 Alderman Dr.
Alpharetta, GA 30202
MacIRMA Work Station
(404) 442-4000

Decathlon Corp.
4100 Executive Park Dr., #16
Cincinnati, OH 45241
LogoPower and Logo SuperPower
(800) 648-5646

Delta Tao Software, Inc.
760 Harvard Ave.
Sunnyvale, CA 94087
Color MacCheese, Zeus, Monet, Spaceward
Ho!, WonderPrint, and Strategic Conquest
(800) 827-9316
(408) 730-9336

Deltaic Systems
1701 Junction Ct., Suite 302B
San Jose, CA 95112
Optical drives and SCSI hard-disk drives
(408) 441-1240

DeltaPoint, Inc.
2 Harris Ct., Suite B1
Monterey, CA 93940
DeltaGraph, MindWrite, and TASTE
(800) 367-4334

Deneba Software
7400 SW 87th Avenue
Miami, FL 33122
Canvas, UltraPaint, and Spelling Coach
Professional
(800) 6-CANVAS
(305) 596-5644

Denon America
222 New Road
Parsippany, NJ 07054
(201) 575-7810

DesignCAD, Inc.
1 American Way
Pryor, OK 74361
DesignCAD
(918) 825-4848

Design Science
4028 Broadway
Long Beach, CA 90803
MathType and ParaFont
(310) 433-0685

Desktop Video Production
1000 Broadway, Suite 292
Oakland, CA 94607
Clip Animation Sampler
(415) 763-6243

DEST
1015 E. Brokaw Rd.
San Jose, CA 95131
PC Scan 3000
(408) 436-2700

Digidesign
1360 Willow Rd., Suite 101
Menlo Park, CA 94025
Audiomedia II and SampleCell
(415) 668-0600

Digital Technology International
500 W 1200 South
Orem, UT 84058
DTI SpeedView
(801) 226-2984

Dove Computer Corp.
1200 N. 23rd St.
Wilmington, NC 28405
RamSnap, MacSnap memory upgrades,
MaraThon Racer, and FastNet SE
(800) 788-3688

Dr. T's Music Software
100 Crescent Rd.
Needham, MA 02194
Beyond, Dr. T's Intro+, Music Mouse, and
UpBeat
(617) 455-1554

Dream Maker Software
925 W. Kenyon Avenue, Suite 16
Englewood, CO 80110
Cliptures and MacGallery
(800) 876-5665

Dubl-Click Software
9316 Deering St.
Chatsworth, CA 91311
ClickChange, World-Class Fonts, Big Caps,
and WetPaint
(818) 700-9525

Dynaware
950 Tower Lane, Suite 1150
Foster City, CA 94404
DynaPerspective
(415) 349-5700

E-Machines
9305 SW Gemini Drive
Beaverton, OR 97005
Monitors
(503) 646-6699

EDCO Services
12410 N. Dale Mabry Hwy.
Tampa, FL 33618
LetrTuck
(800) 523-8973
(813) 962-7800

EdMark
6727 185th Avenue, NE
P.O. Box 3218
Redmond, WA 98073-3218
Kids Desk and Millie's Math House
(800) 426-0856

Educorp Computer Services
7434 Trade St.
San Diego, CA 92121-2410
CD-ROM and shareware distributor
(800) 843-9497

Ehman Engineering
97 S. Red Willow Dr.
Evanston, WY 82931
Monitors and hard drives
(800) 257-1666
(307) 789-3830

Electronic Arts
1450 Fashion Island Blvd.
San Mateo, CA 94404
Chuck Yeager's Advanced Flight Trainer,
Seven Cities of Gold, DiskTools Plus,
Studio/32, and Studio/8
(800) 245-4525
(415) 571-7171

Electronics For Imaging
2855 Campus Drive
San Mateo, CA 94403
Cachet
(800) 285-4565
(415) 742-3400

Ensign Systems
26 N. Main
Layton, UT 84041
POS/IM
(801) 546-1616

Ergotron
3450 Yankee Dr., Suite 100
Eagan, MN 55121
MacTilt, Mac Workstation, and MacBuffer
(800) 888-8458
(612) 452-8135

Eric Snyder
4941 WoodCliff Hill Rd.
West Bloomfield, MI 48323
Baker's Dozen, Forty Thieves, and Montana
(313) 683-2918

Everex Systems, Inc.
48431 Milmount Drive
Fremont, CA 94538
Scan 300/S, ProPoint, and EMAC Metro drives
(800) 821-0806
(510) 498-1111

Exodus Software
800 Compton, Suite 9240
Cincinnati, OH 45231
Retriever II and ExpressWrite
(513) 522-0011

ExperTelligence
203 Chapala Street
Santa Barbara, CA 93101
ExperLISP, ExperCommon Lisp,
and ExperLogo Plus
(805) 962-2558

Facts on File
460 Park Avenue S.
New York, NY 10016
News Digest and CD-ROM products
(212) 683-2244

Farallon Computing
2000 Powell St., Suite 600
Emeryville, CA 94608
Timbuktu, PhoneNet, and MediaTracks
(510) 596-9303

FastComm Communications Corp
45472 Holiday Drive, Suite 3
Sterling, VA 20166
FastComm FDX 9696
(800) 521-2496

FGM Inc
131 Elden St., Suite 308
Herndon, VA 22070
Picture This
(703) 478-9881

Fifth Generation Systems
10049 North Reiger
Baton Rouge, LA 70809
Suitcase, Fastback Pro, The Local Connection,
Pyro!, Public Utilities, SafeLock, and DiskLock
(504) 291-7221

First Financial Technology
608 Silver Spur Road, Suite 230
Rolling Hills Estates, CA 90274
Arc Image
(213) 541-9446

Fisher Idea Systems
18881 Von Karman Ave., Ground Floor,
Irvine, CA 92715
IdeaFisher
(714) 474-8111

Flexware, Inc.
2255 Westlake Blvd.
Tahoe City, CA 96145
Flexware
(800) 527-6587
(916) 581-6999

Flight Engineering
615 Forrest Dr., #206
Miami Springs, FL 33166
Universal Calculator
(305) 884-1475

Forte Communications
1050 E. Duane Ave., Suite J
Sunnyvale, CA 94086
Remote Mouse
(408) 733-5100

Forthought, Inc
P.O. Box 32
Sunset, SC 29685
Snap!
(803) 878-7484

Fractal Design Corp.
385 Spreckles Drive, Suite F
Aptos, CA 95003
ImageStudio, Painter, Sketcher,
and ColorStudio
(408) 688-5300

Frame Technology
1010 Rincon Circle
San Jose, CA 95131
FrameMaker
(408) 433-3311

Franklin Software
122 Burrs Road
Mount Holly, NJ 08060
Language Master, Spelling Tutor,
and Elementary Spelling Ace
(609) 261-4800

FreeSoft Co., The
150 Hickory Drive
Beaver Falls, PA 15010
White Knight
(412) 846-2700

FWB, Inc.
2040 Polk St., Suite 215
San Francisco, CA 94109
Hard Disks and removable cartridge backup
system
(415) 474-8055

GCC Technologies
580 Winter St.
Cambridge, MA 02154
WriteMove, WriteImpact, and BLP printers
(617) 890-0880

GDT Softworks, Inc.
4664 Lougheed Highway, Suite 188
Burnaby, BC
Canada V5C 6B7
JetLink Express, GDT Softworks PowerPrint,
and PrintLink Collection
(800) 663-6222
(604) 291-9121

General Information Services
205 Bancroft Bldg., 3411 Silverside Rd.
Wilmington, DE 19810
Evaluation System
(302) 478-1000

General Parametrics Corp.
1250 Ninth St.
Berkeley, CA 94710
VideoShow Professional and thermal wax
color printers
(800) 223-0999

GEnie
Dept 02B
Rockville, MD 20850
On-line information service
(800) 638-9636
(301) 340-4494

Geocomp
66 Commonwealth Avenue
Concord, MA 01742
TechWords
(508) 369-8304

Global Village Communication
1204 O'Brien Drive
Menlo Park, CA 94025
PowerPort
(415) 329-0700

Gold Disk, Inc.
PO Box 789
Mississauga, Ontario
Canada L5M 2C2
Animation Works
(416) 602-4000

Golden Triangle Computing
4849 Ronson Court
San Diego, CA 92111
TimesTwo and DiskTwin
(619) 279-2100

GoldMind Publishing
4994 Tulsa Ave.
Riverside, CA 92505
MacGraphics
(714) 687-3815

Graphic Management Group Inc.
100-3 Summit Lake Drive
Valhalla, NY 10595
Aperture
(914) 769-7800

Graham Software
8609 Ingalls Circle
Arvada, CA 80003
Disk Ranger
(303) 422-0757

Graphsoft, Inc.
8370 Court Avenue, Suite 202
Ellicott City, MD 21043
MiniCAD+ and Blueprint
(301) 461-9488

Great Plains Software
1701 S.W. 38th Street
Fargo, ND 58103
Great Plains Accounting Series and
Plains & Simple
(800) 456-0025
(701) 281-0550

Great Wave Software
5353 Scotts Valley Drive, Suite E
Scotts Valley, CA 95066
ConcertWave, KidsMath, American Discovery,
Daisy Quest, Crystal Paint, and NumberMaze
(408) 438-1990

Grolier Electronic Publishing
Old Sherman Turnpike
Danbury, CT 06816
Grolier Electronic Encyclopedia and CD-ROM
products
(203) 797-3500

Gryphon Software
7220 Trade Street, Suite 120
San Diego, CA 92121
Morph
(619) 536-8815

Hardware That Fits
610 S. Frazier
Conroe, TX 77301
RealTech monitors
(800) 364-FITS

Harvard Associates
10 Holworthy St.
Cambridge, MA 02138
MacManager and DeskToppers
(617) 492-0660

Hayes Microcomputer Products, Inc.
P.O. Box 105203
Atlanta, GA 30348
V-Series Smartmodem 9600 and InterBridge
(404) 441-1617

Heizer Software
P.O. Box 232019
Pleasant Hill, CA 94523
CompileIt!, Writer's Dream Tools, and
Dialoger Professional
(510) 943-7667

Helix Technologies
4100 Commercial Avenue
Northbrook, IL 60062
Helix Express and Double Helix
(708) 205-1669

Hewlett-Packard
5301 Santa Clara Blvd.
Customer Information Center
MS #51-LSD
Santa Clara, CA 95022
LaserJet, DeskWrite, PaintWriter, and PaintJet
line of printers
(800) 752-0900

HeyerTech
726 Marion Ave.
Palo Alto, CA 94303
Desktop Presentation System
(415) 328-8269

Highlighted Data, Inc.
4350 N. Fairfax Dirve, Suite 450
Arlington, VA 22203
Webster's Dictionary on CD-ROM and other
CD-ROM products
(703) 519-9211

Hyper-Glot
PO Box 10746
Knoxville, TN 37939
Foreign language learning programs
(615) 558-8270

Hyperpress Publishing
P.O. Box 8243
Foster City, CA 94404
ScriptExpert and HyperBundle
(415) 345-4620

ICOM Simulations
648 S. Wheeling Rd
Wheeling, IL 60090
MacKern, TMON Professional, On Cue II,
and Formulator
(708) 520-4440

Ideaforms
P.O. Box 1540
Fairfield, IA 52556
DiskQuick and MacLabeler
(515) 472-7256

Image Club Graphics
1902 11th St. S.E., Suite 5
Calgary, Alberta
Canada, T2G 3G2
Fontpak, Digit-Art, and Artroom
(403) 262-8008

Individual Software, Inc.
5870 Stoneridge Drive, #1
Pleasanton, CA 94588
Typing Instructor Encore, ResumeMaker,
and Individual Training for Word
(510) 734-6767

Informix Software
P.O. Box 15902
Lenexa, KS 66219
Wingz
(913) 599-7100

Inline Design
308 Main Street
Lakeville, CT 06039
Darwin's Dilemma, HAM, INITPicker, Tessare,
3 in Three, and Swamp Gas
(800) 453-7671
(203) 435-4995

Innovative Data Design
2280 Bates Ave., Suite A
Concord, CA 94520
MacDraft and Dreams
(510) 680-6818

Insight Development Corp.
2200 Powell St., Suite 500
Emeryville, CA 94608
MacPrint
(415) 652-4115

Insignia Solutions
526 Clyde Ave.
Mountain View, CA 94043
SoftPC, SoftAT, Entry Level SoftPC, Universal
SoftPC, and AccessPC
(415) 694-7600

Inspiration Software
P.O. Box 1629
Portland, OR 97202
Inspiration
(503) 245-9011

Interactive Solutions
1730 S. Amphlett Blvd., Suite 220
San Mateo, CA 94402
MovieWorks and Evolution
(415) 578-1595

Interleaf Inc.
Prospect Place
9 Hillside Ave.
Waltham, MA 02154
Interleaf Publisher
(617) 290-0710

International Typeface Corporation
2 Hammarskjold Plaza
New York, NY 10017
licensed laser fonts
(212) 371-0699

Intuit
155 Linfield Avenue
Menlo Park, CA 94025
Quicken
(800) 624-8742
(415) 322-0573

Iomega Corp
1821 W 4000 South, Bldg. 4
Roy, UT 84067
removable cartridge drives
(801) 778-1000

Kensington Microware Ltd.
2855 Campus Drive
San Mateo, CA 94403
TurboMouse, PassProof, NoteBook keypad,
surge protectors, and Expert Mouse
(800) 535-4242
(415) 572-2700

Kent Marsh Ltd.
3260 Sul Ross
Houston, TX 77098
MacSafe II, NightWatch II, and FolderBolt
(800) 325-3587

Key Tronic Professional Series
P.O. Box 14687
Spokane, WA 99214
MacPro extended keyboard
(800) 262-6006

Kinetics, Inc.
1340 Treat Blvd., Suite 500
Walnut Creek, CA 94596
Fast Path and LAN Rover
(415) 947-0998

Kiwi Software
6546 Pardall Rd.
Santa Barbara, CA 93117
KiwiEnvelopes, Kiwi POWER WINDOWS,
and Kiwi Utilities
(805) 685-4031

Knowledge Revolution
15 Brush Place
San Francisco, CA 94103
Interactive Physics II and Fun Physics
(415) 553-8153

Kodak
Electronics Group
R-2 Riverwood
Rochester, NY 14650-5986
Photo CD Access, PhotoEdge, Renaissance,
and video display panels
(800) 242-2424

Kurta Corp.
3007 E. Chambers Street
Phoenix, AZ 85040
Kurta Tablets
(602) 276-5533

La Cie Ltd.
8700 SW Creekside Place
Beaverton, OR 97005
Tsunami Hard-disk drives
(800) 999-0143
(503) 520-9000

Language Systems Corp.
441 Carlisle Drive
Herndon, VA 22070
Wild Things
(800) 252-6479

Lapis Technologies
1100 Marina Village Pkwy., Suite 100
Alameda, CA 94501
Lapis PowerBase I display adapter
(800) 435-2747
(510) 748-1600

Learning Company, The
6493 Kaiser Drive
Freemont, CA 94555
Reader Rabbit and The Writing Center
(800) 852-2255
(510)713-0230

LetraSet USA, Inc.
40 Eisenhower Dr.
Paramus, NJ 07953
ImageStudio and LetraStudio
(201) 845-6100

Lightgate
6202 Christie Ave.
Emoryville, CA 94608
Felix
(415) 596-2350

LightSource
17 E. Sir Francis Drake Blvd., Suite 100
Larkspur, CA 94939
Ofoto OCR software
(800) 231-7226

Lionheart Press, Inc.
P.O. Box 379
Alburg, VT 05440
PERT Critical Path Techniques
(514) 933-4918

Logitech
6505 Kaiser Drive
Fremont, CA 94555
Kidz mouse, Turbo Mouse, MouseMan,
and TrackMan
(800) 231-7717

Lotus Development Corp.
55 Cambridge Pkwy.
Cambridge, MA 02142
Lotus 1-2-3 for the Mac
(617) 623-6572

LucasFilm Ltd., Games Division
P.O. Box 10307
San Rafael, CA 94912
Pipe Dream and other software
(800) 782-7927
(415) 721-3300

Lundeen & Associates
1000 Atlantic Avenue
Alameda, CA 94501
WorksPlus Command and WorksPlus Spell
(800) 233-6851
(510) 769-7701

Lynx Computer Products
P.O. Box 22727
Long Beach, CA 90802
Lynx Turbo Trackball
(800) 321-LYNX

MacConnection
14 Mill Street
Marlow, NH 03456
Mail order software and hardware
(800) 800-4444

MacLand
5006 S. Ash Ave.
Tempe, AZ 85282
Hard disk and optical drives
(800) 333-3353

Macromedia
600 Townsend St.
San Francisco, CA 94103
Action!, Macromind Director, Authorware,
Authorware Professional, MacRecorder Sound
System, Macromind 3D, and MacroModel
(415) 442-0200

MacShack Enterprises
191 Harrington Road
Cambridge, MA 02140
My Time Manager
(617) 876-6343

MacUser Magazine
Subscription Orders
P.O. Box 56986
Boulder, CO 80322-6986
Macintosh monthly magazine
(800) 627-2247
(303) 447-9330

MacWarehouse
1690 Oak Street
Lakewood, NJ 08701
Mail order software and hardware
(800) 255-6227

MacWorld Magazine
501 Second Street
San Francisco, CA 94107
Macintosh monthly magazine
(415) 243-0505

Mainstay
5311-B Derry Ave.
Agoura Hills, CA 91301
MacFlow, Visual Interactive Programming,
Capture, and AntiToxin
(818) 991-6540

Maitreya Design
PO Box 12085
Eugene, OR 97440
miniWriter
(503) 342-2834

Manhattan Graphics Corp.
250 E. Hartsdale Avenue, Suite 23
Hartsdale, NY 10530
Ready, Set, Go!
(914) 725-2048

Mastersoft, Inc.
6991 E. Camelback, Suite A-320
Scottsdale, AZ 85251
Word for Word Professional
(602) 277-0900

Mathesis Inc.
77 Mowat Avenue, Suite 201
Toronto ON M6K 3E3
Canada
Fiscal Knowledge
(416) 588-7592

MathSoft, Inc.
201 Broadway
Cambridge, MA 02139
Mathcad
(800) 628-4223
(617) 577-1017

MAXA Corp.
116 N. Maryland Avenue, Suite 100
Glendale, CA 91206
Snooper and Alert!
(818) 543-1300

Maxis Computing
2 Theatre Square, Suite 230
Orinda, CA 94563
SimCity, SimEarth, SimLife, and A-Train
(415) 376-6434

MECA Software
327 Riverside Avenue
Westport, CT 06880
Managing Your Money
(203) 226-2400

MECC
6160 Summit Drive N.
Minneapolis, MN 55430
Number Crunchers, Super Munchers,
and The Secret Island of Dr. Quandary
(800) 685-6322
(612) 569-1500

Meta Software
125 Cambridge Park Dr.
Cambridge, MA 02140
MetaDesign
(617) 576-6920

MetroImage Base
18623 Ventura Blvd., Suite 210
Tarzana, CA 91356
MetroImage Base Electronic Art
(800) 525-1552

Microcom Software Division
P.O. Box 51489
Durham, NC 27717
Carbon Copy Mac, 911 Utilities, Virex, Citadel
with Shredder, and Complete Undelete all in
Microcom Value Pak (MVP)
(919) 490-1277

Microlytics, Inc.
2 Tobey Village, Tobey Village Office Park
Pittsford, NY 14534
Word Finder Plus, Inside Information,
and GOfer
(716) 248-9150

MicroMaps Software
PO Box 757
Lambertville, NJ 08530
HyperAtlas
(800) 334-4291

MicroMat Computer Systems
7075 Redwood Blvd.
Novato, CA 94945
MacEKG
(415) 898-6227

MicroSeeds Publishing
5801 Benjamin Center Drive
Tampa, FL 33634
INITPicker, Redux, and Screen Gems
(813) 882-8635

Microsoft
1 Microsoft Way
Redmond, WA 98052
Microsoft Word, FoxBase+/Mac, Microsoft
Excel, Flight Simulator, Microsoft BASIC,
Microsoft Works, Microsoft Mail, Microsoft
Office on CD-ROM or disks, and PowerPoint
(206) 882-8088

MicroSpot
20421 Stevens Creek Blvd., Suite 240
Cupertino, CA 95014
MacInteriors and color printer ribbons
(408) 253-2000

MicroSpeed, Inc.
44000 Old Warm Springs Blvd.
Fremont, CA 94538
MacTRAC
(510) 490-1403

Microtek
680 Knox Street
Torrance, CA 90502
Microtek ScanMaker 600ZS
(800) 654-4160

Miles and Miles
704 N. Water, #1
Ellensburg, WA 98926
typefaces and fonts
(509) 925-5280

MindLink, Inc.
PO Box 247
North Pomfret, VT 05053
MindLink
(800) 253-1844

MiniTab, Inc.
3081 Enterprise Drive
State College, PA 16801
MiniTab
(800) 448-3555

Mirror Technologies
2644 Patton Rd.
Roseville, MN 55113
PowerVision
(800) 654-5294
(612) 633-4450

Motion Works, Inc.
1020 Mainland Street
Vancouver, BC
Canada V6B 2T4
ADDmotion
(604) 685-9975

Mouse Systems
47505 Seabridge Drive
Fremont, CA 94538
Trackball/ADB, The Little Mouse,
and A3 Mouse
(510) 656-1117

Multi-Ad Services
1720 W. Detweiller Drive
Peoria, IL 61615
Multi-Ad Creator
(309) 692-1530

National Instruments
6504 Bridge Point Pkwy.
Austin, TX 78730
LabVIEW
(512) 794-0100

National Semiconductor
P.O. Box 58090
Santa Clara, CA 95052
EtherNODE•16 NB-T
(800) 538-8510

National Tele-Press
Box 79
Mendecino, CA 95460
SuperMOM and SuperMailOrder
(800) 448-0988

Natural Intelligence
2067 Massachusetts Ave.
Cambridge, MA 02140
Inix, Shadow, and Easy4D
(617) 876-4876

NEC Technologies
1414 Massachusetts Avenue
Foxborough, MA 01719
Colormate PS Model 80 and Silentwriter
Model 90
(508) 264-8000

NetFrame Systems
894 Ross Drive, Suite 200
Sunnyvale, CA 94086
Network Server products
(408) 745-0633

Night Diamonds Software
P.O. Box 1608
Huntington Beach, CA 92647
BiPlane
(714) 842-2492

Niles & Associates
2000 Hearst St., Suite 200
Berkeley, CA 94709
MacInfo, EndNote Plus, and Grant Manager
(415) 655-6666

Nine to Five Software
PO Box 18899
Boulder, CO 80308
Reports
(800) 292-5925

Nisus
990 Highland Dr., Suite 102
Solano Beach, CA 92075
NISUS and QUED/M
(800) 922-2993
(619) 481-1477

Nolo Press
950 Parker St.
Berkeley, CA 94710
WillMaker and Personal RecordKeeper
(800) 992-6656
(510)549-1976

NoRad Corporation
1549 11th St.
Santa Monica, CA 90401
NoRad Shield
(213) 395-0800

Nordic Software
917 Carlos Drive
Lincoln, NE 68505
Word Quest, Jungle Quest, Turbo Math Facts,
and Preschool Pack
(402) 488-5056

Norstad, John
MacInit-macclub benelux
Wirtzfeld Valley 140
B-4761 Bullingen Belgium
Disinfectant
(*Editor's Note:* This program is freeware and
can be found on AppleLink, bulletin boards,
and through Mac user groups.)

Novell Inc.
122 East 1700 South
Provo, UT 84606
NetWare
(800) 453-1267

Now Software
319 SW Washington, 11th Floor
Portland, OR 97204
Now Utilities, Now Menus,
and Now-Up-to-Date
(503) 274-2800

Numonics Corp
101 Commerce Dr.
Montgomeryville, PA 18936
GraphicMaster
(215) 362-2766

Nuvotech
2015 Bridgeway, Suite 104
Sausalito, CA 94965
EasyView Monitors, NuvoLink II-T,
and TurboStar
(415) 331-7815

nView Corp
11836 Canon Blvd.
Newport News, VA 23606
View Frame Projection Panels
(804) 873-1354

OCR Systems
1800 Byberry Rd., Suite 1405
Huntingdon Valley, PA 19006
ReadRight for Macintosh
(215) 938-7460

Olduvai
7520 Red Rd., Suite A
South Miami, FL 33143
Icon-It!, Read-It! O.C.R. Pro, VideoPaint,
and MultiClip
(800) 822-0772
(305) 665-4665

ON Technology, Inc.
155 Second Street
Cambridge, MA 02141
On Location
(617) 876-0900

Opcode Systems
3641 Haven Dr., Suite A
Menlo Park, CA 94025
Cue and EZVision
(415) 369-8131

Optical Media International
180 Knowles Dr.
Los Gatos, CA 95030
Optical and CD-ROM drives
(800) 347-2664

Optima Technology
17526 Von Karman
Irvine, CA 92714
DisKovery and other hard disk drives
(714) 476-0515

Oracle
500 Oracle Parkway
Redwood Shores, CA 94065
Oracle SQL Database and Oracle for
Macintosh
(800) 345-3267

Orange Micro, Inc.
1400 N. Lakeview Ave.
Anaheim, CA 92807
Micro Grappler, TurboScan, and Micro
Grappler IIsp
(714) 779-2772

Palo Alto Software
260 Sheridan Avenue, Suite 219
Palo Alto, CA 94306
The Business Plan Toolkit and Sales/
Marketing Forecasting Toolkit
(415) 325-3190

PCPC
4710 Eisenhower Blvd., Bldg. A4
Tampa, FL 33634
MacBottom Hard Disk, DATStream, and HFS
Backup
(800) 622-2888
(813) 884-3092

Peachtree Software
1505 Pavillion Place
Norcross, GA 30093
Peachtree Accounting for the Mac and atOnce!
(800) 247-3224
(404) 564-5800

Peat Marwick
983 University Ave.
Los Gatos, CA 95030
Silverrun
(408) 395-1800

Personal Bibliographic Software Inc.
PO Box 4250
Ann Arbor, MI 48106
Pro-Cite
(313) 996-1580

Pinnacle Micro, Inc.
19 Technology
Irvine, CA 92718
Pinnacle optical drives
(800) 553-7070

Pixar
1001 W. Cutting Blvd.
Richmond, CA 94801
Tapestry
(510) 236-4000

PLI (Peripheral Land, Inc.)
47421 Bayside Pkwy.
Fremont, CA 94538
CD-ROM drives, external and internal hard
drives, and QuickSCSI
(800) 288-8754
(510) 657-2211

PMC TeleSystems, Inc.
P.O. Box 5127
Vancouver, BC
Canada V6B 4A9
Rendezvous
(604) 255-9949

Portfolio Systems
10062 Miller Avenue, Suite 201
Cupertino, CA 95014
Dynodex, SuperGlue, SmartScrap and
The Clipper II
(408) 252-0420

Postcraft International
27811 Hopkins, Suite 6
Valencia, CA 91355
Postility and LaserFX Effects Specialist
(805) 257-1797

Practical Solutions
1135 N. Jones Blvd.
Tucson, AZ 85716
The Cordless Mouse
(602) 322-6100

Prescience Corporation
939 Howard St.
San Francisco, CA 94103
Expressionist and Theorist
(415) 543-2252

Procom Technology
2181 Dupont Drive
Irvine, CA 92715
Hard disk and optical drives
(714) 549-9449

Prodigy
445 Hamilton Ave.
White Plains, NY 10601
Prodigy on-line service
(800) 822-6922, ext 205

Prometheus Products
9524 W. Tualatin Sherwood Road
Tualatin, OR 97062
The Home Office, Ultima Home Office,
and modem products
(503) 692-9600

Psygnosis
29 Saint Mary's Court
Brookline, MA 02146
Lemmings for the Mac
(617) 731-3553

QMS, Inc.
One Magnum Pass
Mobile, AL 36618
QMS printers
(205) 633-4300

Quantum Leap Technologies, Inc.
1399 SE Ninth Avenue, Suite 4
Hialeah, FL 33010
Aesopolis and other games
(305) 885-9985

Quark Inc.
300 S. Jackson, Suite 100
Denver, CO 80209
QuarkXPress and QuarkStyle
(800) 778-7835
(303) 934-2211

Que Software
11711 N. College Avenue
Carmel, IN 46032
Typing Tutor
(317) 573-2500

Queue
338 Commerce Drive
Fairfield, CT 06430
800 College Boards, other CD-ROM products,
and games
(800) 232-2224

Qume Corporation
260 S. Milpitas Blvd.
Milpitas, CA 95035
Qume printers
(408) 942-4000

Radius, Inc.
1710 Fortune Dr.
San Jose, CA 95131
PrecisionColor and Pivot monitors,
VideoVision System PowerView, and Rocket
accelerator boards
(800) 227-2795
(408) 434-1010

RasterOps
2500 Walsh Avenue
Santa Clara, CA 95051
Video Color Boards
(800) 729-2656
(408) 562-4200

Ray Dream, Inc.
1804 N. Shoreline Blvd.
Mountain View, CA 94043
Ray Dream Designer and addDepth
(415) 960-0765

Reality Technologies
2200 Renaissance Blvd.
King of Prussia, PA 19406
Wealthbuilder
(215) 277-7600

Relax Technology
3101 Whipple Road
Union City, CA 94587
CD-ROM and hard-disk drives
(800) 848-1313
(510) 471-6112

Relisys
320 S. Milpitas Blvd.
Milpitas, CA 95035
Tefax RA2110M Fax/Modem
(408) 945-9000

Riccardo Ettore
67 Rue de la Limite
1970 W-Oppem, Belgium
Sound Mover and Sound shareware

Salient Software
124 University Ave., #103
Palo Alto, CA 94301
DiskDoubler, Partner, and AutoDoubler
(415) 321-5375

SAS Institute, Inc.
SAS Campus Drive
Cary, NC 27513
JMP
(919) 677-8000

SBT
One Harbor Drive
Sausalito, CA 94965
SBT Accounting
(408) 331-9900

ScanCo Furniture
P.O. Box 3217
Redmond, WA 98073
MacTable and add-on cabinet modules
(800) 722-6263

Science for Kids
9950 Concord Church Road
Lewisville, NC 27023
"Cell"ebration
(800) KSCIENCE

Scitor
393 Vintage Park Dr., Suite 140
Foster City, CA 94404
Project Scheduler
(415) 570-7700

Sebastian Software
P.O. Box 70278
Bellevue, WA 98007
ImageGrabber
(206) 861-0602

Seiko Instruments USA, PC Products
Division
1130 Ringwood Court
San Jose, CA 95131
Color printers and monitors
(408) 922-5900

Shana Corporation
Avanced Technology Center
9650 20th Avenue, Suite 105
Edmonton, Alberta
Canada T6N 1G1
FastForms! Construction Kit, Informed Mini
Manager, and Informed Designer
(403) 463-3330

Sharp Electronics Corp.
Sharp Plaza, P.O. Box F1
Mahweh, NJ 07430
Color scanners, color printers, and video
display panels
(201) 529-8200
(800) 237-4277

Shiva Corp.
One Cambridge Center
Cambridge, MA 02142
EtherGate, Telebridge, and NetBridge
(617)252-6300

ShopKeeper Pub. International
3711 Shamrock W., Suite 110A
Tallahassee, FL 32308
ShopKeeper
(904) 222-8808

Siclone Sales and Engineering Corp.
1072 Saratoga-Sunnyvale Road, Bldg. A-107,
Suite 443
San Jose, CA 95129
Memory Boards and accelerators
(408) 534-1742

Sierra On-Line, Inc.
P.O. Box 485
Coarsegold, CA 93614
SpaceQuest! and Alphabet Blocks
(800) 326-6654
(206) 683-4468

Sitka
950 Marina Village Pkwy.
Alameda, CA 94501
MacTOPS
(510) 769-9669

Softstream International
10 Twin Ponds Drive
Dartmouth, MA 02748
HyperHIT Deluxe, Solitaire, Cribbage Tutor,
MacRummy, 22nd Street Whist Tutor,
MacMan, and Authenticate & Mutate
(800) 262-6610

Softsync, Inc.
800 S. W. 37th Ave., Suite 355
Coral Gables, FL 33134
Accountant, Inc
(800) 933-2537
(305) 444-0080

Software Toolworks
60 Leveroni Ct.
Novato, CA 94949
Mavis Beacon Teaches Typing
(800) 234-3088
(415) 883-3000

Software Ventures
2907 Claremont Avenue, Suite 220
Berkeley, CA 94705
MicroPhone II and Microphone Pro
(800) 336-6477
(800) 336-6478 (CA)
(510) 644-3232

Somak Software, Inc.
535 Encinitas Blvd., Suite 113
Encinitas, CA 92024
SharpenUp, Games Set, Casino Games,
and Card Games
(619) 942-2556

Sony Computer Peripherals Co.
655 River Oaks Pkwy.
San Jose, CA 95134
Sony monitors
(800) 352-7669
(408) 432-0190

Sophisticated Circuits
19017 120th Ave. N.E., Suite 106
Bothell, WA 98011
PowerPad and PowerKey
(206) 485-7979

Specular International
233 N. Pleasant St. P.O. Box 888
Amherst, MA 01004
Infini-D
(413) 549-7600

Spectrum HoloByte
2061 Challenger Drive
Alameda, CA 94501
Falcon, Welltris, PT-109, Orbiter, Tetris,
and WordTris
(510)522-3584

Spinnaker Software
201 Broadway
Cambridge, MA 02139
Address Book Plus
(617) 494-1200

Stac Electronics
5993 Avenida Encinas
Carlsbad, CA 92008
Stac for the Mac
(619) 431-7474

Storage Dimensions
1656 McCarthy Blvd.
Milpitas, CA 95035
Optical drives and SCSI cards
(408) 944-0710

Strata, Inc.
2 West St. George Blvd., Ancestor Square,
Suite 2100
St. George, UT 84770
StrataVISION 3d
(801) 628-5218

SuperMac Technology
485 Potrero Ave.
Sunnyvale, CA 94086
ThunderStorm, VideoSpigot, and PixelPaint
Professional
(800) 334-3005
(408) 245-2202

Survivor Software Ltd.
11222 La Cienega Blvd., Suite 450
Inglewood, CA 90304
MacMoney
(310) 410-9527

Sybase
557 Dixon Rd., Suite 111
Rexdale, Ontario
Canada M9W 1H7
Deft
(416) 249-2246

Symantec
10201 Torre Avenue
Cupertino, CA 95014
Norton Utilities for the Mac, MORE, SUM,
GreatWorks, Think C, Just Enough Pascal,
and SAM
(408) 253-9600

Synex
692 Tenth Street
Brooklyn, NY 11215
MacPhonebook
(800) 447-9639

Systat, Inc.
1800 Sherman Avenue
Evanston, IL 60201
SYSTAT, FASTAT, and MYSTAT
(708) 864-5670

Systems Compatibility Corp.
401 N. Wabash Ave, Suite 600
Chicago, IL 60611
Software Bridge for the Macintosh
(312) 329-0700

Tecmar
6225 Cochran Rd.
Solon, OH 44139
Backup tape drives
(216) 349-0600

Teknosys
3923 Coconut Palm Drive, Suite 111
Tampa, FL 33619
Help! and HyperBASIC
(800) 873-3494

Tektronix, Inc.
P.O. Box 1000
Wilsonville, OR 97077
ColorQuick and thermal wax color printers
(503) 627-7111

Teleware
300 Round Hill Drive
Rockaway, NJ 07866
M.Y.O.B.
(201) 586-2200

Telmar Information Services
902 Broadway
New York, NY 10010
FlowMaster
(212) 460-9000

Texas Instruments
5701 Airport Road
Temple, TX 76503
microlaser printers
(800) 527-3500
(214) 995-2011

TGS Systems
2745 Dutch Village Road., Suite 200
Halifax, NS,
Canada B3L 4G7
Prograph
(902) 455-4446

Third Wave Computing, Inc.
1826-B Kramer Lane
Austin, TX 78758
Third Wave drives and WindowTalk
Professional
(512) 832-8282

Thought I Could
107 University Place, #4D
New York, NY 10003
Wallpaper
(212) 673-9724

Thunderware
21 Orinda Way
Orinda, CA 94563
ThunderScan Plus, Thunderworks,
SnapGuide, and LightningScan products
(415) 254-6581

Timeslips Corp.
239 Western Ave.
Essex, MA 01929
Timeslips
(508) 768-6100

Timeworks
65 Academy Drive
Northbrook, IL 60062
Publish It! Easy, Color-It!, and Publish It!
(708) 559-1360

T/Maker Company
1390 Villa St.
Mountain View, CA 94041
ClickArt EPS Illustrations and ClickArt
(415) 962-0195

Toshiba Information Systems
9740 Irvine Blvd.
Irvine, CA 92713
Monitors, CD-ROM, and optical drives
(800) 456-3475

Traveling Software
18702 N. Creek Parkway
Bothell, WA 98011
Laplink Pro Mac
(800) 662-2652

Trend Micro Devices
2421 W. 205th Street, Suite D-100
Torrance, CA 90501
SafeLock
(310) 782-8190

Trendware
PO Box 2285
Huntington, CT 06484
XCAL
(203) 926-1116

Truevision
7340 Shadeland Station
Indianapolis, IN 46256
NuVista+ and Macintosh II Videographics
Card
(800) 344-8783
(317) 841-0332

TSP Software
4790 Irvine Blvd., Suite 105-294
Irvine, CA 92720
Filevision IV
(714) 731-1368

Unison/Tymlabs
675 Almanor Avenue, Suite 202
Sunnyvale, CA 94086
Klondike
(408) 245-3000

US Robotics, Inc.
8100 N. McCormick Blvd.
Skokie, IL 60076
Modems
(708) 982-5010

Varcon Systems Inc.
10509 San Diego Mission Rd., Suite K
San Diego, CA 91208
Manage That!
(619) 563-6700

Vertical Solutions
P.O. Box 1150
Beaverton, OR 9700
FastLabel
(800) 222-6032
(503) 524-7402

Virtus Corp.
117 Edinburgh S., Suite 204
Cary, NC 27511
Virtus WalkThrough
(919) 467-9700

Vision Software
3160 De La Cruz Blvd., Suite 104
Santa Clara, CA 95054
CameraMan
(408) 748-8411

Visionary Software
P.O. Box 69447
Portland, OR 97201
Synchronicity, LifeGuard, and First Things
First
(503) 246-6200

Visual Business Systems, Inc.
380 Interstate N. Pkwy., #190
Atlanta, GA 30339
GraphMaster
(404) 956-0325

Vividus Corporation
651 Kendall Avenue
Palo Alto, CA 94306
Cinemation
(415) 494-2111

Wacom Technology, Inc.
501 S.E. Columbia Shores Blvd.
Vancouver, WA 98661
Wacom SD-Series Digitizers and Wacom
tablets
(800) 922-6613

WaveMetrics
PO Box 2088
Lake Oswego, OR 97035
Igor
(503) 620-3001

Wayzata Technology, Inc.
P.O. Box 87
Prior Lake, MN 55372
Front Page News and other CD-ROM products
(612) 447-7321

Wildflower Software
21W171 Coronet Road
Lombard, IL 60148
SnapJot
(708) 916-9360

Wolfram Research
100 Trade Center Drive
Champaign, IL 61820
Mathematica
(217) 398-0700

WordPerfect Corp.
1555 N. Technology Way
Orem, UT 84057
WordPerfect, WordPerfect Works, Grammatik
Mac, and WordPerfect Office for Macintosh
(801) 225-5800

WordStar International
201 Alameda del Prado
Novato, CA 94968
Correct Grammar, Correct Quotes, WriteNow,
and American Heritage Dictionary
(415) 382-0606

Working Software, Inc.
P.O. Box 1844
Santa Cruz, CA 95061
Last Resort, Spellswell, and Findswell
(408) 423-5696

XTree Co.
4330 Santa Fe Road
San Luis Obispo, CA 93401
XTreeMac
(805) 541-0604

Zedcor
4500 E. Speedway, #22
Tucson, AZ 85712-5305
DeskPaint, DeskDraw, ZBasic, and Deskworks
(800) 482-4567
(602) 881-8101

Glossary

30 percent rule. Determines how points and Bézier control handles are positioned. According to Adobe Systems, Inc., the distance from a Bézier control handle to its point should be approximately 30 percent of the length of its segment. See also *Bézier curves*.

64KB ROM. Original ROM size used on the Mac 128 and 512. Followed by 128KB ROM. See also *read-only memory (ROM)*.

128KB ROM. Standard ROM on the Mac Plus, SE, and Mac 512KB enhanced. See also *read-only memory (ROM)*.

256KB ROM. Standard ROM on the Mac SE/30, II, IIx, and IIcx. See also *read-only memory (ROM)*.

Accelerator board. An option card that, when installed in the Macintosh, enables the computer to operate and manipulate data at a faster rate.

Acoustic modem. A modem with two cups that fit around a telephone's handset; converts a computer's signals into sound and back again. See also *modem*.

Active window. The top or front window on the Desktop. It has a highlighted title bar.

Alarm Clock. A desk accessory that displays the current date and time. The alarm can be set to alert you at a specified time.

Alert box. Contains a warning when you ask the Macintosh to do something that may cause loss of data or when other errors occur. See also *dialog box*.

Alias. An icon that represents an original file folder or disk.

Apple Desktop Bus (ADB). The connectors on the back of the Macintosh that allow connection of the keyboard, mouse, joysticks, graphics tablets, touch screens, track balls, and so on.

Apple HD SC Setup. A system utility file packaged with the Macintosh that initializes and sets up an Apple hard disk.

Apple key (⌘ or). When pressed in combination with other keys, performs an action or command. Also known as the Command key or "cloverleaf" key.

Apple menu. The far left menu at the top of the Macintosh screen.

Apple menu items. Items available on the Apple menu of the Desktop for immediate use. These applications, folders, and files are placed in the Apple Menu Items folder.

AppleShare. An operating system designed to enable a Macintosh to become a server to other Macs on the same network.

AppleTalk. A communications network used to connect Macs and share peripheral devices such as printers. AppleTalk is the communication protocol by which data is transferred. Also called LocalTalk.

Application. A program that enables the user to create, enter, and design information. Examples are word processors, spreadsheets, and paint programs.

Application template. A file developed to guide the creation of designs or documents. See also *template*.

Arrow keys. The four keys that move the insertion point left, right, up, and down in a word processor file and change the active cell in a spreadsheet.

ASCII (American Standard Code for Information Interchange). A standard computer text format in which each character is represented by seven bits. See also *text file*.

Assembler. A program that translates symbolic codes, or assembly language, to machine language. See also *compiler*.

Asynchronous communication. A means of transmitting data between computers. A special signal indicates when each character starts and stops.

Auto answer. The capability of a modem to answer an incoming call and establish communications without human assistance.

Autocall. The capability of a computer-controlled modem to place a telephone call.

Autotrace. A feature in drawing and page layout applications that enables the user to trace around shapes and lines of an image.

Background execution. A program that can continue operating without user commands and without interrupting a procedure operating in the foreground. See also *MultiFinder* and *multitasking*.

Balloon Help. Context-sensitive help available through System 7 and many System 7 applications.

Baseline. The horizontal line that defines the bottom of each character, excluding the descenders, in a font family.

BASIC (Beginner's All-Purpose Symbolic Instruction Code). A common programming language that is easy to learn but relatively inflexible.

Baud rate. A measure of speed equal to one signal per second. One baud represents one bit per second (bps). Common baud rates are 300, 1200, and 2400.

BBS. See *bulletin board system*.

Beta test. The first test of a new product outside the laboratory. This test is the final step before a full market release. Because many product bugs are found in the beta test release, producers do not consider the beta version to be a final version.

Bézier curves. Mathematically generated line that can display non-uniform curves; used to create PostScript fonts. See also *30 percent rule*.

Binary. A numbering system based on a series of ones (1s) and zeros (0s) used to encode text and numerical information.

Bit (binary digit). The smallest unit of computer information. A 1 or a 0 code electronically represents on or off, respectively.

Bit-mapped image. An image consisting of dots, in which one dot represents one or more bits of the image (depending on whether color or other attributes are used). A Mac Plus uses one bit per dot. See also *font*.

Bomb. An abnormal termination of a program. A bomb occurs when a program unexpectedly halts due to a bug or encounters data conditions it cannot handle. See also *bug*.

Boot. To start a computer by loading the operating system (System file and Finder) into memory. The operating system software tells the Macintosh how to load other programs.

Bridge. A device that enables you to connect networks so that members on one network can communicate with members on another network. See also *gateway*.

Buffer. A section of memory that temporarily holds information from I/O (input/output) communications, including data transfer through a modem or reading and writing to your disk. The buffer holds information when the computer is sending information faster than the device can receive it.

Bug. A problem in a software program. Initially named after a moth that caused the failure of an early computer (1945) at Harvard University. Today, a bug usually refers to an inappropriate or inaccurate line of programming code that causes the program to halt execution or respond incorrectly. See also *bomb*.

Bulletin board system (BBS). A telecommunications facility used to share information with others through the use of a modem and specialized communications software.

Bundled software. Software included with your Macintosh, such as the System Tools disk, Utilities disk, and HyperCard. Such a package deal includes hardware and software.

Bus. A path through which information is shared between one part of a computer and another.

Button. A location in a dialog box or HyperCard card where the user can click to initiate a command for the Macintosh to take some predefined action.

Byte. A measure of the amount of information equivalent to the memory needed to store a character of the alphabet. 1,024 bytes equal 1KB of memory. A byte consists of eight bits and has eight 1s and 0s.

Cache. A special section of RAM reserved for frequently used applications and utility information. See also *RAM cache*.

Calculator. A desk accessory that looks and acts like a four-function calculator.

Cancel button. A button in dialog boxes that the user may click to cancel a command. The Cancel command enables the user to stop a program or application that is running without saving any results or changes to that point.

Caps Lock key. A key located on the lower left corner of the Macintosh standard keyboard that, when pressed, causes alphabetic characters to be displayed in uppercase format but does not affect numeric keys or symbols.

Carrier detect. A modem function that detects whether another modem is sending a carrier signal. If the carrier signal is not detected, your modem generally disconnects itself and hangs up.

Cathode-ray tube (CRT). The screen used in computers in which light produced by a cathode strikes a phosphor coating on the screen.

Central processing unit (CPU). The computer's main information processing unit. In a Macintosh, the CPU is a single silicon chip called the microprocessor. See also *microprocessor*.

Character width. A term developed at Apple to refer to the number of bits (seven or eight) in a transmitted character. Also called number of data bits.

Chip. A tiny piece of silicon with an integrated electronic circuit photoengraved on its surface.

Chooser. A desk accessory that enables the user to choose the printer on which the document is to be printed. For the Chooser to function, the printer resource files must be installed in the current System file. In a networking environment, the Chooser can be used to connect and disconnect the Macintosh from the network and choose from among devices connected to the network.

Click. To place the mouse pointer (arrow) on an item on-screen and quickly press and release the mouse button.

Clip art. Artwork, bought on disk, that can consist of bit-mapped graphics, object graphics, or encapsulated PostScript files.

Clipboard. A temporary storage location that holds cut and copied information.

Clock speed. The actual operating speed of the computer's microprocessor.

Close. A command that closes a window or document.

Close box. A small box located at the top left of a document window. Clicking the Close box causes the program to prompt the user to save the last changes to the document and to close the current window.

CMYK. The four colors—cyan, magenta, yellow, and black—used in the color separation process that can be combined to form any other color.

Cold boot. Using the power switch to turn on your Macintosh.

Color separations. A process used in offset printing in which separate plates are used to print different colors of ink on a page producing multiple colors. As the name implies, each color has its own plate. When all color plates are placed atop each other, the final product is produced.

Command. A menu option that causes an action. A command tells the Macintosh what to do next.

Command key ⌘. See *Apple key*.

Commercial software. Software that is copyrighted and sold for profit. Commercial software cannot be copied and distributed to others without the approval of the software publisher.

Compiler. A program that translates source code to machine language. See also *assembler*.

Computer-aided design (CAD). Applications that take advantage of a computer's power to design architectural, mechanical, electrical, civil, schematic, IC, and various other types of drawings. Using the two- and three-dimensional capabilities of the application, the user can develop highly complex structures. Commonly referred to as computer-aided drafting and design (CADD).

Condensed type. A typeface in which the space between the characters is less than the normal spacing of the typeface. See also *font* and *kerning*.

Continuous tone image. An image that contains gradient tones from black to white. In a scanned image, the tones are converted from continuous to halftone images. See also *scanner* and *optical character recognition*.

Control (Ctrl) key. A key located on the left side of the standard keyboard, whose function varies depending upon the application being used.

Control panel. A desk accessory in System 6 that's used to personalize such features as the pattern on the Desktop, the speed of the mouse movement, and the volume of the warning beep.

Control Panels folder. A folder in System 7 that resides in the System Folder and contains control panels. Replaces the Control Panel desk accessory of System 6.

Coprocessor. A microchip that assists the main microprocessor with data-intensive tasks such as large spreadsheets, large databases, complex statistical analyses, or graphics activities.

Copy. A command used to make an exact replica of a letter, an entire document, a graphic, an application, or even a disk. The Copy command is located in the Edit menu. Using Copy does not modify or delete the original.

Copy protection. A method of preventing unauthorized duplication of software. See also *write-protect tab*.

Current startup disk. The startup disk whose System files the Macintosh is using.

Cursor. An icon indicating the current mouse location on-screen. The Macintosh has a variety of cursor shapes, including a vertical bar, I-beam, pointer, and wristwatch. See also *insertion point*.

Cut. A command that removes selected information from a document and temporarily places it in the Clipboard.

Cylinder. The total number of disk tracks that can be written or read for a specific disk-head position. On a double-sided floppy disk, a cylinder is two tracks; on a hard disk, it consists of four or more tracks. See also *track*.

DA. See *desk accessory*.

Data. The information processed with a computer application or program. Also called *information*.

Database. A collection of related information that is organized for storage and retrieval. A database may contain names, addresses, and phone numbers, for example.

Data fork. The portion of a Macintosh disk file containing the user's data.

Defragment. To increase the amount of usable space on a hard disk by rewriting files so that they are stored on contiguous sectors or parts of the hard disk.

Delete key. A key that you press to remove information from a document. Using this key is the same as using the Cut command except that the information is not placed on the Clipboard; it is deleted permanently. See also *cut*.

Delimiter. A special character used by applications and communications software to indicate the end of a line or to separate one field from another or one record from another.

Desk accessory (DA). A small application (located in the System file) that is accessible from the Apple menu. Examples are the Alarm Clock, Chooser, and Control Panel. Other more complex desk accessories are minispreadsheets, a thesaurus, and a bibliography maker.

Desktop. The work area of the Macintosh. The screen, disk icons, Trash can, and menu bar that you see when you start your Mac.

Desktop file. A file created on all Macintosh disks by the Finder. It is hidden from the user and contains information the Finder uses to locate files, folders, and icons.

Desktop publishing. An integrated package of certain applications that enables the user to design the layout of pages, determine the size and location of graphics, modify and locate text, and produce a document. Desktop publishing programs integrate page layout, text entry, graphics design, and printing into one overall application.

Dialog. A message from the Macintosh requesting further action or information from the user. In most instances, the user may respond by typing a response or clicking a button. When accompanied by a beep, the user is being warned that something may happen that the user has not anticipated. See also *alert box*.

Digitizer pad. A peripheral device that is similar to the mouse but enables the user to choose drawing tools, menu commands, and other functions, as well as to draw shapes without using the applications interface.

Dimmed command. A menu command that appears gray on-screen and cannot be used while dimmed. Usually another command must be completed or a selection made before the dimmed command can be accessed.

Dimmed icon. Represents a document, folder, or application on a disk that has been ejected. The image still resides on the Desktop, but the contents of the folder or disk cannot be opened.

Direct-connect modem. A modem that connects directly from the computer into the telephone line outlet and bypasses the telephone handset.

Directory window. The window that lists the contents of a disk. Using the View menu, the user can alter the appearance of the directory and have the contents displayed in small icons, large icons, and words.

Disk. A device that uses magnetic medium to store information. Disks can be floppy or hard. The Macintosh uses 3.5-inch, hard-case floppy disks. A typical floppy disk can be single-sided (400KB), double-sided (800KB), or high density (1.4MB). Hard disks can range from 10MB to 300+MB.

Disk drive. Holds the disk and retrieves information stored on the disk. The user must insert a floppy disk into the floppy disk drive. A hard disk drive has a built-in disk permanently installed.

Disk drive port. A port on the Macintosh designed to be connected to an external floppy disk drive. See also *port*.

Disk server. A disk drive, generally on a network, that is available to all users. A server divides the hard disk into several volumes and treats each volume as though it is a separate disk.

Document. A generic term describing whatever the user creates, using an application on the Macintosh. A document can be a letter, article, picture, table, or spreadsheet, among others. A document contains the information the user has entered and saved.

DOS (disk operating system). A shortened name for PC DOS and MS-DOS, which are the complete names of the operating system for IBM and IBM-compatible computers. DOS is a set of instructions. See also *operating system*.

Dot-matrix printer. A printer that forms characters and graphics from dots.

Dots per inch (dpi). A measure of screen and printer resolution by the number of dots per linear inch. The higher the number of dots, the better the resolution. The ImageWriter II operates at 144 dpi, and the LaserWriter operates at 300 dpi. See also *resolution*.

Double-click. An action used to open applications, documents, or folders. Double-clicking is performed by clicking the mouse button twice in rapid succession.

Download. A procedure in which a user transfers data from a remote computer's database to the user's computer and stores the data on a hard disk or floppy.

Downloadable font. A font that is downloaded (sent from your Macintosh to your printer).

Dpi. See *dots per inch*.

Drag. A technique used to move icons from one location to another. The user places the mouse pointer on the icon, presses and holds down the mouse button, moves the pointer to where the icon should be, and then releases the mouse button.

Driver. Software that tells the Macintosh how to operate an external device such as a printer. A driver is located in the System Folder.

Duplex. A communications protocol that allows for two-way communication. A half-duplex communication transmission can go only one direction at a time. In full-duplex communication, transmission occurs in both directions simultaneously.

Edit menu. A menu that contains the copying and cutting features and the Undo command.

Electronic mail. See *e-mail*.

e-mail. A messaging system that enables the user to send and receive messages to people in and outside the user's computer network. Outside messages are generally sent using telephone lines. A message can be as simple as a quick note or as complex as multiple documents and files.

Em dash. A dash the width of the capital letter *M*.

Em space. A space that is the width of the letter *M* of a specified typeface and type size. See also *en space*, *font*, *kerning*, and *leading*.

Emulation. A feature that enables one device to imitate another.

Encryption. To substitute characters to hide the original meaning of a document from those who do not have the enciphering program.

En dash. A dash the width of the capital letter *N*, usually half the width of an em space.

En space. A space that is the width of the letter *N* in a specified typeface and type size, usually half the width of an em space.

Enter key. A key that confirms an entry. Similar to the Return key.

EPS (encapsulated PostScript). A file format that uses PostScript language to store an image.

EtherNet. A standard for local area network hardware.

Expansion card. An internal card that enables additional features to be added to the computer's processing capability, telecommunications capability, and so on.

Expansion slot. A location inside the Macintosh that allows the installation of an option card to perform additional functions. See also *option card*.

Extension. A system program that extends the capabilities of System 7's features. See also *INIT*.

Field. A piece of data in a database record.

File. Information stored on disk. Also called a *document*.

File format. The set of instructions used to store information.

File server. A node on a network that has a disk drive, software, and processor that is available to all users. File-server software controls access to individual files, and multiuser software enables several users to access the same file simultaneously.

Fill. To paint an enclosed area with black, white, color, or shading.

Finder. A file and memory management utility that keeps the Desktop organized, thus enabling users to find and open files or folders. The Finder must always be in the System Folder for your Macintosh to operate properly (with the exception of HyperCard).

Fkey. A utility program similar to a desk accessory that runs when the user presses one of the number keys along the top of the keyboard in combination with the Command and Shift keys. An example is ⌘-Shift-1, which ejects a disk.

Floppy disk. A removable secondary storage medium that uses a magnetically-sensitive, flexible disk enclosed in a plastic envelope or case.

Folder. Holds related information in one location like the folders in an office file cabinet. A folder can contain files, other folders, graphics documents, or other information.

Font. A collection of letters, punctuation marks, numbers, and symbols that appear in the same typeface, style, and size. The Macintosh comes with a number of typefaces, such as Monaco, Chicago, and Geneva. See also *bit-mapped image*, *outline font*, and *PostScript*.

Font/DA. A System 6 utility that stores fonts and desk accessories, identified by a suitcase-shaped icon. To open a suitcase file and transfer its contents from one System file to another in System 6, you need the Font/DA Mover program packaged with your Macintosh software. System 7 eliminates the need for Font/DA Mover. See also *Font/DA Mover*.

Font/DA Mover. A Macintosh utility that moves fonts and DAs from one System to another or from a floppy disk to a System.

Font substitution. A Macintosh activity that substitutes one font for another when the font required by a particular application is not available.

Fragmentation. A situation in which various parts of a file are stored on more than one sector of a hard disk.

Freeware. Software shared without costs to the user, with the intention that the software be shared by others and distributed throughout a large network of users. See also *public domain software* and *shareware*.

Function key. A key that can be programmed to perform a particular function.

Gateway. In a computer network, the hardware and software used to connect two different types of computer networks. See also *bridge*.

Get Info. A command on the File menu that provides the following information on the file: locked or unlocked, creation date, modification dates, size, and user-entered notes.

Gigabyte (G). Around one billion bytes (1,073,741,824 bytes) or 1,024 megabytes.

Gray scale. A degree of screening ranging from white (0% screen) to black (100% screen) applied to images created with various graphics and drawing applications.

Grouping. A feature of drawing and page layout applications in which two or more objects are combined so that they are treated as one object.

GUI (graphical user interface). The way the Mac and the Mac user interact with each other. The GUI takes full advantage of graphics by using icons and the mouse.

Handshake. The protocol used to establish communication between the user and the computer, using a mouse and icons for giving commands; when two computers are able to connect and transmit information to each other; an electrical signal used by the receiving computer to stop transmission from the sending computer until the transmitted data can be received.

Hard disk drive. A disk drive contained inside or residing outside the Macintosh. The drive contains permanently installed disks that hold much more information than a floppy disk does and retrieves information faster.

Hardware. The physical parts of the Macintosh: the screen, keyboard, mouse, disk drives, casing, cables, and all the electronic mechanisms and boards inside the Macintosh. Hardware also includes other pieces of computer equipment, such as printers and modems.

Hanging indent. A word processing format in which the first line of a paragraph is flush with the left margin and all subsequent lines in the paragraph are indented.

Hayes-compatible modem. A modem that sets modes and features with the AT command set that was developed by Hayes Microcomputer Products.

Header. Text that is automatically printed at the top of each page. That portion of a Macintosh disk file containing the file's directory information such as name, type, and source. See also *data fork*.

Hierarchical database. A database that organizes information in tree-like structures.

Hierarchical File System (HFS). A system that enables the user to organize information with folders. The user can organize applications, documents, and other folders within folders to create levels in a hierarchy. See also *Macintosh File System*.

Highlight. Usually means to select something so that it appears different from the surrounding information. When a piece of information is highlighted, the user can initiate a command to modify that information—for example, you highlight a word when you are ready to make it bold.

High-profile SIMM. An in-line memory module that, when installed, is not flush with the motherboard.

HyperCard. An object-oriented application, developed by Bill Atkinson, that the user can modify. Using a scripting language called HyperTalk, you program HyperCard to create applications called stacks, which consist of cards that have buttons, icons, and fields that can perform other functions or can be linked to other stacks or cards. You can use HyperCard (which is ideal for sharing information in an approach that is visually appealing and understandable) to access many different types of information. See also *HyperTalk*.

HyperTalk. The programming language used to program HyperCard stacks and to create user-defined functions. HyperTalk is an "English-like" scripting language. HyperTalk uses scripts to reference information and build the command structure within the stack. See also *HyperCard*.

Hypertext. The retrieval of text and ideas throughout various documents and files without regard to order.

I-beam. The shape the mouse pointer takes when the user is entering information or editing text. The pointer resembles the uppercase letter *I*.

Icon. A graphic representation of a file, folder, disk, or command. A file is generally represented as a sheet of paper, for example, and a folder looks like a manila folder.

ImageWriter. The first dot-matrix printer designed specifically for use with the Macintosh.

ImageWriter font. A bit-mapped font designed to be printed using the ImageWriter.

Impact printer. A printer that forms characters by striking an inked ribbon against paper. See also *dot-matrix printer*.

Incremental backup. One of two types of backups in which only those files changed since the last backup are backed up.

Information service. A service accessed through telecommunications software that enables users to access financial, news, and entertainment databases. See also *bulletin board system* and *on-line services*.

INIT. A utility file (called *extension* in System 7) located in the System Folder. After you place an INIT file in the System Folder and restart the Macintosh, the INIT file becomes active. See also *extension*.

Initialize. To prepare a disk to be used by the Macintosh. Generally, when you initialize a disk, the Macintosh structures the disk into sectors and tracks. After a disk has been initialized, the Macintosh can use it to save information to and retrieve information from. Also called formatting a disk.

Inkjet printer. A printer that forms characters by spraying tiny streams of ink onto paper.

Input device. A device (such as a mouse, keyboard, trackball, or graphics tablet) that inputs information into your Macintosh.

Insertion point. The location in a document where the user may insert something. The insertion point is selected by placing the mouse pointer where you want the insertion to occur and clicking once. A blinking I-beam then appears at that point. See also *cursor*.

Installer. A separate application used to install software on your hard disk.

Integrated software. A software package containing spreadsheet, database, word processor, and telecommunications applications in which the component programs freely exchange data.

Interface. An electronic link between different computer devices, such as the computer and a mouse. The point where two elements meet. The connecting point between the Macintosh and the ImageWriter II, for example, is an interface. An interface may exist between two pieces of hardware, two pieces of software, or a piece of hardware and a piece of software.

Internal modem. A modem installed into a computer slot. A modem that is built directly into the computer. In the Macintosh, it can be installed only in the SE and II families.

Interpreter. A code built into PostScript-compatible printers that converts PostScript commands into a language the printer can process to create an image or character. See also *PostScript*.

Invisible file. A file that does not appear on the Desktop and that cannot be copied, erased, or moved.

Kerning. In word processors, page layout software, and advanced drawing applications, the process of adjusting the spacing between letters. Typically used to reduce the space between pairs of letters.

Kilobits per second (Kbps). A measure of data transfer speed, in thousands of bits per second.

Kilobyte (KB). 1,024 bytes. A common measure of file size. A typical double-spaced page is 1.5KB.

LAN. See *local area network*.

Landscape. A page orientation in which the printer prints the image horizontally. The page top is the longest side of the paper.

Laptop computer. A portable computer about the size of a small briefcase. Can be moved easily and accessed in any setting. Apple's line of laptops are the PowerBook series of Macs.

Laser font. An easily scaled font defined by mathematical formulas.

Laser printer. A printer that forms characters and graphics by moving a laser beam across a photoconductive drum. The printer then projects the image onto paper. Macintosh laser printers are called LaserWriters. See also *toner*.

Launch. The act of double-clicking an application to start it.

Leading. The amount of vertical spacing, in points, between baselines of type.

Lisa. The first computer to use the Mac interface, including the mouse and icons. The Lisa was unsuccessful due to its high cost.

Local area network (LAN). Computers linked with cables and software. The computers can share files and external devices such as printers and disk drives. Many offices are linked together with LANs to improve communication and efficiency.

LocalTalk. The hardware portion of Apple's LAN system used to connect Macs to LaserWriters and other Macs.

Logic board. The board inside the Macintosh responsible for organizing and executing instructions.

Lookup field. A database field that the database management system uses to find information contained in a table.

Low-profile SIMM. An in-line memory module flush with the motherboard when installed.

MacBinary. A format that enables Macintosh files to be stored on non-Mac machines without any loss of data.

Macintosh File System (MFS). A method of organizing files and folders where folders cannot be nested within folders. Followed by the Hierarchical File System (HFS). See also *Hierarchical File System*.

Macintosh User Group. An association of Macintosh enthusiasts of various levels of proficiency who meet to discuss issues relating to the Mac. User groups are located throughout the country. Many have a newsletter, which provides members with updated information and tips.

Macro. A small program of stored commands that, when retrieved, replays the commands to perform a task. It can be activated to do repetitive tasks simply by typing a letter or number that represents the macro program. Usually created with a macro application, although macro creation is available within some applications.

Mainframe. A large-capacity computer shared by many users. Its central processing unit (CPU) generally is housed in an air-conditioned room, and the terminals are located at various sites.

Marquee. The dotted line drawn around text or graphics by using the mouse pointer.

Megabyte (MB). A unit of measure representing 1,048,576 bytes (or 1,024KB) of storage capacity on a disk or in RAM. Hard disks are typically measured in terms of the amount of storage capacity. A 20MB hard disk indicates that the storage capacity of this disk drive is 20MB and will hold approximately 20,480KB of information.

Memory. The primary internal location within the computer where internal instructions are stored. The location in the Macintosh's central processing unit that holds information. Some of this memory is used by applications as necessary to do complex calculations or sort data (RAM). Other memory is permanently used by the Macintosh and is not accessible to the user (ROM). See also *random-access memory (RAM)* and *read-only memory (ROM)*.

Menu. A list of commands available to the user. You can open a menu by clicking the menu's name at the top of the screen. The user holds down the mouse button, moves the mouse pointer down the list of menu commands, and then releases the mouse button on the command needed.

Menu bar. The top line on-screen. It horizontally lists the menus available to the Macintosh user. See also *menu*.

MFS (Macintosh File System). The original filing system used by the Macintosh in which files and folders remain at the same organizational level. See also *Macintosh File System*.

Microcomputer. A small, relatively inexpensive computer developed primarily for use by one person. Also referred to as a personal computer or home computer. A Macintosh is a microcomputer.

Microfloppy disk. A 3.5-inch flexible disk contained within a semi-rigid plastic casing. See also *floppy disk*.

Microprocessor. A small silicon chip containing a large number of electronic components. The microprocessor chip can operate on large amounts of information when used with other computer components.

Minifloppy disk. A 5.25-inch flexible disk contained in a flexible plastic casing, used in many microcomputers. See also *microfloppy disk*.

Modem (modulator/demodulator). A peripheral device that enables computers to communicate by telephone lines.

Moiré. A screen saver that can be configured for a variety of geometric patterns.

Monitor. The screen associated with a computer. The light-blue Macintosh Plus and SE monitors are located directly above the disk drives, all contained in one cabinet. The Macintosh II has a separate monitor, which is not enclosed with the CPU or disk drives. Monitors can be color or monochrome.

Motherboard. The main board (also called the *logic board*) in the Macintosh that contains the central processing chips, RAM, and expansion slots.

Mouse. A hand-held device used to navigate on the Macintosh screen. The mouse can be used to access the menus and select information. When you move the mouse, the pointer moves on-screen in the corresponding direction.

Mouse button. The button located on the mouse. By pressing the mouse button (clicking), an action is initiated. By releasing the button, the action is acknowledged.

MultiFinder. A component of the Macintosh's System software that enables the user to load into memory multiple applications and switch among them. MultiFinder also allows for concurrent tasks to take place at seemingly the same time, which is known as *multitasking*.

Multimedia. Information presented in visual, auditory, and text formats.

Multitasking. A computer capability in which two or more programs are loaded into memory simultaneously. The CPU attends to all programs at once by switching back and forth between them—a process known as *time slicing*. See also *MultiFinder*.

Nanosecond. One billionth of a second.

Nesting. The placement of files within folders.

Network. A computer communication pathway using hardware and software that links multiple computers and peripheral devices so that each computer or device shares information. See *Node* and *Local area network*.

Node. A device on a network (such as a computer, a hard disk, or a printer) that can send and receive information. See also *network*.

NuBus. A high-speed information pathway for the Mac II family of computers.

Null modem. A cable connecting two computers. Used for communication purposes rather than a modem.

Object-oriented programming (OOP). A programming language in which program elements are conceptualized as objects that can pass messages to each other.

On-line help. A file contained within an application that can provide the user with help as the application continues.

On-line services. Various databases available to users who have a modem and telecommunications software. They offer access to business, education, travel, and entertainment databases (among others). Two popular on-line services are CompuServe and GEnie, which are offered to members who have paid a membership fee and a monthly access-time fee. In most instances, members can download information, files, and applications of interest. See also *bulletin board system*.

Open. The act of accessing a document for changing or viewing.

Open architecture. A computer design that enables third parties to design components and other improvements for use with the System.

Operating system. The System Software, which controls the functioning of the Macintosh and the direction of information flow among computer components. See also *System Software*.

Optical character recognition. A technology by which printed characters are optically scanned and translated into codes that the computer can process. The device that has this capability is known as an optical character reader (OCR) or scanner. See also *scanner*.

Optical disc. A disc on which music or data is recorded in the form of small pits. The data or music is retrieved with a laser beam.

Option card. Generally, a specialized piece of electronic circuits, installed by your Apple dealer, that enhances the performance of your Macintosh. An example is the installation of an accelerator card. See also *expansion slot*.

Option key. A Macintosh key used with other keys to perform particular operations.

Outline font. A PostScript font formed of outlines, which are then filled in. A printer font used to describe font characteristics for laser printers. Outline fonts generally have greater resolution than bit-mapped (screen) fonts. See also *bit-mapped image*, *font*, and *PostScript*.

Pack/unpack. To compress data for the purpose of storage or transmission. Unpacking is decompressing a file and returning it to its normal state.

Page description language (PDL). A language used to describe printer output.

Page preview. A feature of many Macintosh applications that gives the user a view of the printed page before actually printing the document.

Pantone Matching System. A standard system for choosing colors based upon ink mixes. A color wheel generally provides the necessary information for choosing colors for color applications and monitors.

Parallel port. A connection to a computer through which eight or more bits are transmitted simultaneously in one direction. See also *disk drive port*.

Parameter RAM. Memory devoted to certain System settings such as the time, date, and the alarm clock.

Parity bit. An extra bit appended to a character whose value is used to check for errors in the transmission of data. If the total number of 1s in a byte is even, the parity bit is set to 1; if the number is odd, the bit is set to 0. If sending and receiving devices arrive at the same number after independently checking parity, the character is correct.

Partition. A physically separate section on a hard disk that can be used with the same or a different operating system.

Paste. A command that retrieves from the Clipboard a copied or cut piece of data and places the data at the insertion point in a document.

Path. The hierarchical path to a folder, application, or document file that reflects the organization of a particular group of information. A hard disk, for example, contains a folder called Folder 1, which contains a second folder called Folder 2. Within Folder 2 are three letters (Let1, Let2, Let3). To identify the path of Let3, you identify the name of the disk and progress toward document Let3 in this manner: Hard disk→Folder 1→Folder 2→Let3.

Peripheral device. A unit of computer hardware such as a printer, modem, or external hard disk drive. Peripheral devices usually are connected to the Macintosh with cables.

Personal computer (PC). A generic term used to describe a computer designed for use at home or in a small-business setting. In general, a Macintosh is not referred to as a PC. The term has come to mean any IBM computer or IBM-compatible computer.

Phosphor. A chemical material used to coat the inside of cathode ray tubes (CRTs) on which electrons are targeted to produce images.

Pica. A unit of measure equal to 12 points, or approximately one-sixth of an inch.

PICT. An object-oriented graphic format used to store MacDraw documents.

Pixel (picture element). A single dot or picture element on the Macintosh display. A pixel is the visual representation of a bit in which a pixel is white if the bit is equal to 0 and black if the bit is equal to 1.

Platter. The glass or metal circular component of a hard disk that spins and on which data is written and from which data is read.

Point. A unit of measure used to indicate size of line or type. An inch consists of 72 points.

Pointer. An icon, usually arrow-shaped, that reflects the movement of the mouse.

Port. A connection socket on the back of the Macintosh that enables the user to connect a printer cable, hard disk drive, modem, keyboard, or mouse to the Macintosh.

Portrait mode. A page orientation in which the top of the printed image is along the short side of the paper.

PostScript. A page description programming language written by Adobe, Inc. to prepare an image for printing on a laser printer. PostScript fonts are used with PostScript-compatible printers. These fonts are widely recognized as the standard in near-typeset quality printing. Also called encapsulated PostScript (EPS) format.

PostScript interpreter. A code built into PostScript-compatible printers that converts PostScript commands into a language the printer can process to create an image or character. See also *PostScript*.

Printer buffer. Additional memory storage that enables the computer to send data for printing at a faster rate than the printer can accept.

Printer driver. The software containing the instructions that enable the computer to communicate with the printer.

Printer font. A font designed for printing and not just for display.

Printer port. A serial port designed for the connection of a printer or modem to the computer. See also *serial port*.

Printer server. On a network, a printer available to all network users.

Printer spooling. The process by which documents to be printed are stored in a memory outside the computer's RAM, enabling computer processing to continue while the printer is working.

Program. A set of instructions, usually in the form of a programming language, that tells a computer what to do.

Programmer's switch. A switch on the side of many Macintosh computers that enables you to reboot the computer and access the Macintosh's debugging utility.

Programming language. A language used to write programs for the Macintosh. Many languages are available, including Object Pascal, C++, BASIC, FORTRAN, and SmallTalk/V. The code, words, and symbols used to send commands and instructions to the computer.

Proportional spacing. In typesetting or printing, the characteristic in which wider letters take up more space than narrower letters.

Protocol. In computer telecommunications, the set of commands, rules, and procedures determining how information travels between computers. See also *handshake*.

Public domain software. Software that can be copied without copyright infringement. See also *shareware* and *freeware*.

Pull-down menu. A menu that appears only when accessed by the user. At all other times, only the menu titles are visible.

QuickDraw. A computer code that resides in the Macintosh's ROM and facilitates the generation of images for the screen and printer. Primarily used with dot-matrix printer output.

Radio button. A round button, found in dialog boxes, that you click to choose a particular option.

RAM. See also *random-access memory*.

RAM cache. A portion of the RAM memory that can be designated to hold data that is used repeatedly by an application.

RAM disk. A program that sets aside part of the Macintosh's memory and programs the computer to recognize this memory as a disk drive.

Random-access memory (RAM). The part of the Macintosh's memory that allows temporary storage of data. Because RAM is only temporary, any information left in RAM is lost when the computer is turned off.

Raw data-transfer rate. The fastest speed in which data is transferred to and from a disk drive to a computer.

Readme file. A file often included on applications that updates the user as to any changes made in the accompanying documentation.

Read-only memory (ROM). The part of the Macintosh's memory that permanently stores System information and contains the information needed to start up. Also called *firmware*.

Reboot. The act of restarting the computer.

Record. A set of related fields in a database. A record contains information unique to an individual or object.

Relational database. A database in which any field or record of one file can be tied to any other field or record by using a common key field.

Removable media. Typically a cartridge containing magnetic media such as a disk or tape that can be removed from the computer's storage device.

ResEdit. A utility application capable of editing the resources of other applications. ResEdit enables you to customize such applications as the Finder, to change menu commands, or to modify the appearance of icons.

Resolution. The number of dots per inch (dpi) displayed on a screen or a printed document. The Macintosh Plus and SE screens have a resolution of 72 dpi. The LaserWriter has a resolution of 300 dpi. See also *dots per inch*.

Restart. To reset a computer to its startup state without turning off the power. The Macintosh has two procedures for restart: a menu command and the programmer's switch. Also referred to as a *warm boot*.

Return key. The key, located to the right side of the main keyboard, that instructs the Macintosh to move the cursor to the next line. Similar to the Enter key.

ROM. See also *read-only memory*.

Root directory. The first level of organization of the top level created when the disk is formatted.

Run. The act of executing a program or an application.

Save. A command instructing the Macintosh to store information on disk.

Save As. A command instructing the Macintosh to save the current document using a different name or file format or on a different disk drive.

Scanner. A device used to capture graphics and text for use in Mac applications. See also *optical character recognition*.

Scrapbook. A desk accessory used to store pictures and text. The Scrapbook, located in the System Folder, can be accessed in the Apple menu. In contrast to the Clipboard, the Scrapbook permanently stores information.

Screen dump. A picture of the screen sent to a file or to a printer for printing.

Screen font. A font used for display and for printing on dot-matrix printers.

Screen saver. A utility, usually in the form of a desk accessory, FKey, extension, or control panel, that prevents image "burn in" by automatically filling the screen with a form of animation during a period of user inactivity.

Script. A series of commands written in the HyperTalk programming language for HyperCard.

Scroll. A method of moving within a document. Using the scroll bars located on the right and bottom of the screen, the user can move forward, backward, left, and right to see other portions of the document. Scroll arrows, located in the scroll bars, move the document one line or column at a time in the direction desired. The user can scroll continuously through a document by clicking the arrow and holding the mouse button.

SCSI port. A port located on the back of the Macintosh that enables the user to connect a SCSI cable from a peripheral device to the Macintosh.

Sector. On a disk, the smallest continuous physical space for saving data. Multiple sectors define a track. See also *track* and *cylinder*.

Security system. A password-protection software utility that enables the user to protect files or disks from unwanted intruders. Most security utilities enable the user to set a password and to encrypt files.

Select. An operation used to indicate where the next action should take place. To select an object, the user double-clicks the icon or word or drags the mouse across the object.

Serial interface. A form of data transmission in which the bits of each character are transmitted sequentially one by one over a single channel or wire. The most common serial interface is the RS-232 cable and connector.

Serial port. A connector on the back of the Macintosh that enables the user to connect serial devices using a serial interface. See also *printer port*.

Serif. A kind of typeface that has small cross strokes across the ends of the main strokes of each character. Typefaces without the cross strokes are referred to as *sans serif*.

Server. On a network, any device or computer that all users can share.

Shareware. Copyrighted computer programs that users can try on a trial basis. If you like the software, you are expected to pay a fee to the program's author. See also *public domain software* and *freeware*.

Shutdown. The process of saving all work, closing all folders and files, ejecting all disks, and turning off the power of the computer.

Signal-to-noise ratio (S/N). The ratio of the level of a received electric signal to the level of the interfering noise.

SIMM. An in-line memory module that plugs into the motherboard or the logic board.

Size box. A box located in the lower right corner of the active window that contains two overlapping smaller boxes. Clicking and dragging in the smaller of the two boxes enables the user to decrease the size of the active window. Clicking and dragging in the larger box increases the size of the active window.

Slot. A location on an internal board where additional cards can fit.

Small Computer System Interface (SCSI). A standard interface that enables the user to connect a peripheral device to the Macintosh.

Software. A generic term for computer programs. Software tells the computer hardware how to perform its work. Software can be categorized into many areas, including systems software, utility software, and applications software.

Spooler. A printer software utility that enables the user to send multiple documents to the printer and continue working while the printer receives each spooled document for printing.

Spooling. The act of storing data in a buffer until it is needed.

Spreadsheet. A program using a rectangular grid of rows and columns. The intersection of a row and a column is a cell. The spreadsheet can manipulate values, and the user can specify interrelationships among the values. The program can calculate results using formulas and macros. Advanced spreadsheets integrate graphics, charts, buttons, macros, and functions.

Stack. A HyperCard document or application. A group of related cards. Each card is a record and each record (card) has a number of fields.

Star network. A network with the central processor at the center of the network and a series of nodes surrounding it in a star pattern.

Startup disk. A disk that contains the System files the Macintosh needs to get started. A startup disk must contain the System file and Finder and generally contains printer resources and desk accessories. The start-up disk is the first disk inserted into a floppy disk system. In a hard disk system, the startup disk is contained on the hard disk and automatically boots when the power switch is turned on. See also *boot*.

Startup screen. The opening screen containing words and graphics that appears when booting the Macintosh. Many utilities enable the user to customize the startup screen.

String. A specified sequence of characters (a word, phrase, or number).

Style. A variation of a font that can be displayed in boldface, italic, shadow, outline, underline, and strikethrough styles, to name a few.

Style sheet. A set of predefined format and text commands that can easily and quickly be incorporated into a new document.

Suitcase. The icon that represents a set of fonts or desk accessories.

Switcher. A Macintosh System utility that enables up to four different applications to be loaded into RAM at once. MultiFinder has generally replaced the Switcher.

SYLK (Symbolic Link). A file format developed by Microsoft for spreadsheets and databases. Used for transferring data between incompatible applications.

System 7. Apple's latest version of the Macintosh operating system.

System file. A file that contains information the Macintosh uses to operate and start up. System files cannot be opened in the usual manner but can be modified. The Macintosh cannot operate without a System file.

System Folder. The folder that contains the important System and Finder files necessary to boot up and run the Macintosh.

System heap. The area of memory set aside for storing system information about files and resources.

System software. The files, extensions, control panels, utilities, desk accessories, fonts, and resources located in the System Folder as provided by Apple. This software is all the Macintosh needs to run properly. See also *operating system*.

System Tools disk. Software disks packaged with the Macintosh that provide the user with various tools to facilitate using the Macintosh.

Tab-delimited file. A data file in which tabs separate individual records or data elements. See also *delimiter*.

Tear-off menu. A feature of some Macintosh applications that enables the user to pull down a menu and to keep the menu visible while working. The menu also can be moved to a more convenient location within the active window.

Telecommunications. Sharing information over phone lines through the use of a modem and telecommunications.

Template. A document created for repeated use. By using the Save As command, the user can save each use of the template with a unique name and still maintain the original template for future use.

Terminal emulation. To make a computer act like a terminal for use with a modem and host computer such as a mainframe. Terminal emulation software enables the user to customize the Macintosh to recognize and use the control codes required to access the host's data.

Text file. A computer file that contains sequences of bits that represent characters. Also known as an ASCII file. See also *ASCII*.

Thermal-transfer printer. A dot-matrix printer that uses heated pins to melt dots of pigment on paper.

TIFF (Tagged Image File Format). A scanned image-saving format. See also *optical character recognition*.

Title bar. The multilined bar at the top of the active window that displays the title of the document or window.

Token-ring network. A network in which information is passed from one node through another in a ring-like shape.

Toner. A black powder used in laser printers and photocopiers that serves as ink in the printing of characters and images. See also *Laser printer*.

Tool Box. A collection of drawing and painting tools found in many applications such as HyperCard, MacDraw, and MacPaint.

Touch pad. A pointing device that is used by moving a finger over a receptive flat surface.

Touch screen. A computer screen that enables the user to touch the screen to activate computer actions and commands.

Track. A location on magnetic media that stores data. Tracks are concentric circles on the surface of a disk made up of sectors. One or more tracks make up a cylinder of disk space. See also *cylinder* and *sector*.

Trackball. A pointing device that essentially is an inverted mouse, in which the ball is located on top of the device. The user moves the ball rather than the device, which remains stationary. A pointed arrow on-screen reflects the ball's movement just as though a mouse is being used. See also *mouse*.

Tractor-feed printer. A printer that advances paper through the use of pins that fit into preformed holes on the edges of the computer paper.

Trash can. A storage location on the Desktop used to discard documents, folders, and applications. The Trash can is not emptied until the user selects Empty Trash from the Special menu or until other disk operations are performed. If the Trash can has not been emptied, documents that have been trashed can be reclaimed by double-clicking the Trash can and retrieving the document. The retrieved document then must be placed back into the folder from which it originally came.

Type effect. Typeface changes that include heavy, shadow, and outline effects. See also *font*, *typeface*, and *typestyle*.

Typeface. The basic font family design, such as Times or Monaco. See also *font*.

Type size. The height in points of the characters in a font. See also *font*.

Typestyle. Versions of a typeface that have become known as separate fonts. Examples include italic and boldface. See also *font*.

UNIX. An operating system developed by Bell Laboratories for minicomputers. UNIX, regarded as a powerful, general-purpose operating system, enables several programs to run simultaneously. It can easily be transferred from one computer type to another.

Upload. A procedure in which a user transfers information from his or her computer to a remote computer.

User group. A group of people who have an interest in a particular computer or a particular type of application such as desktop publishing.

User level. The setting on a HyperCard stack that indicates what actions a user may access. User levels can be set at browsing, typing, painting, authoring, and scripting. Each level allows greater flexibility in the tools available and the actions the user may take.

Utilities disk. A disk packaged with the Macintosh that contains utilities used to maintain your computer system. Examples of utility programs contained on this disk are the Font/DA Mover and the Installer.

Video card. A circuit board containing the video controller and related components that connects into a computer to control the video display. See also *video controller circuit*.

Video controller circuit. A circuit that modifies digital information to create the signal necessary for display on a computer screen. See also *cathode ray tube (CRT)*.

Video RAM. A section of RAM devoted to screen information. In the Macintosh, the video RAM stores a bit-mapped image of the screen display. See also *random-access memory (RAM)*.

Virtual memory. The use of the available space on a hard disk to increase the RAM available for application use.

Virus. A series of computer program lines designed to alter the normal functioning of a computer by destroying data, corrupting system files, locking users out of the computer, or flashing messages on-screen at predetermined times. In many cases, the user may be unaware that a virus exists in the system until it is too late to protect the existing data. A virus is generally passed from disk to disk and from computer to computer through disk sharing or telecommunication file transfers.

Virus-protection software. A utility software program designed to check existing files and applications for the presence of a virus. Some protection software identifies the strain of virus and tries to eradicate it. Other software just informs the user that a virus exists.

Visual interface. The system of representing files, folders, and commands in symbols, such as icons, that easily can be recognized.

Volatile memory. Memory that loses its contents when the power is removed.

Warm boot. The act of selecting the Restart command on the Special menu so that the computer boots without turning the power off and on.

Window. The area on the Desktop that displays information. To view a document, the user uses a window. Windows can be opened or closed, moved around on the Desktop, resized, and scrolled through.

Word processor. An application that enables the user to enter characters to create documents, including letters, newsletters, and graphics. Examples include MacWrite II, Microsoft Word, and WordPerfect. Word processors are becoming more advanced with features such as macro support, page layout capabilities, file import/export, mail-merge features, footnoting, and spell-checking features.

Word wrap. In word processing, a text-entry feature in which typed text automatically advances to the next line at the end of a line.

Wristwatch cursor. Appears on-screen when the Macintosh is busy performing some activity. During the time that the wristwatch is on the screen, the user cannot access additional commands. The wristwatch's hands turn, indicating that the Macintosh is working.

Write-protect tab. A small tab or box built into a 3.5-inch disk casing to prevent accidental erasure or overwriting of disk contents. See also *copy protection*.

Zone. An AppleTalk network in a series of interconnected networks joined by bridges.

Zoom box. A box located on the right side of the title bar that the user clicks to expand the active window to its maximum size. By clicking the zoom box again, the user can return the window to its previous size.

Index

Symbols

#AND# operator, 397
#NOT# operator, 397
#OR# operator, 397
2-D drop shadows, 543
3-D shadowing, 543
32-bit address modes, 223
68020 /68030CPU Macintoshes,
 virtual memory, 221
680x0 series microprocessors,
 850-851

A

About This Macintosh command
 (Apple menu), 128-129
accelerator cards, 765-766
 DayStar Digital, 766
 Rocket series (Radius), 766
 TokaMac series (Fusion), 766
 Transwarp series (Applied
 Engineering), 766
access time, 161-162
accessing
 DAs, 911
 shared items (File Sharing),
 802-803
accessories
 anti-glare filters, 772-773
 carrying cases, 771-772
 disk files, 773-774
 diskettes, 773-774
 furniture, 775-776
 power line protectors,
 770-771
 security devices, 772
 stands and bases, 774-775
AccessPC 2.0 (Insignia Solutions),
 810
accounting programs, 471-474
 Aatrix modules, 481
 Accounting (Champion), 477
ACCPAC Bedford (Computer
 Associates), 477
AtOnce! (Layered), 477
Back to Basics Accounting,
 481
BPI General Accounting, 481
Cost Management System
 (Softouch Software), 480
Credit Card DA (E.E.S.
 Companies), 480
Fiscal Knowledge (Mathesis,
 Inc.), 478
Great Plains Software,
 475-476
Insight Expert (Layered), 476
Plains & Simple (Great Plains
 Software), 477
Print Bar (BearRock), 480
Quicken (Intuit), 471
Rags to Riches, 481
SBT Database Accounting
 Library (Mac/Series, Six
 Plus), 471-474
Service Industry Accounting
 (Brown-Wagh Publishing),
 479
ShopKeeper (ShopKeeper
 Software), 479
Simply Accounting, 481
Strictly Business, 481
Super Mail Order Manager
 (National Tele-Press),
 478-479
TimeSlips III (NorthEdge),
 480
Up Your Cash Flow (Granville
 Publications Software), 479
accounts, 460-461
 transactions, 462-463
 payable, 472
 receivable, 472
add-ons, 420
 to word processors, 375
WorksPlus Command
 (Lundeen & Associates),
 455
WorksPlus Spell (Lundeen &
 Associates), 455
addDepth (Ray Dream, Inc.), 314
Addison-Wesley
 Human Interface Guidelines,
 859
 Inside Macintosh, 856-861
 Macintosh X-Ref, 856
address modes, 32-bit, 223
address-and-name databases, 431
addresses, 386
Adobe Systems
 Illustrator, 293, 546-547,
 553-554
 Premiere 2.0, 623
 Publishing Packs, 523-524
 SmartArt, 519-521
 SuperATM package, 317-319
 TrueForms, 420
 Type On Call CD-ROM, 317
 TypeAlign, 314, 521
 Type Manager (ATM),
 302-303, 314-315, 739-741
 Type Reunion, 317
advertisements, 502, 524
AFE (Apple File Exchange),
 809-810
After Dark (Berkley Systems), 735
AIFF files, 615
airbrushes, 553
Aladdin Systems
 StuffIt, 435
 Stuffit Deluxe, 170, 583
 Stuffit Deluxe 3, 639-640
 Stuffit SpaceSaver, 170
Alarm Clock, 132-133
Aldus
 Designs for Business
 Communications, 524
 Designs for Manuals, 524

Designs for Newsletters, 524
FreeHand, 293, 546-547,
    553-554
PageMaker, 174, 502, 523,
    525-526
Personal Press, 174, 529
SuperPaint 3.0, 548-550
alerts, 85-86
    boxes, ResEdit, 874
Alert Sounds list box, 249-250
aliases
    adding/removing items to
        Apple menu, 251
    files, 191-195
    icons, 120-121
    pointers to icons, 120-121
aligning
    cell contents, 390-391
    objects, 543
allocating memory, 859
ALSoft
    DiskExpress II, 169
    MasterJuggler, 315, 321, 643
    Power Utilities Bundle
        MultiDisk, 167
        Screen Eclipse, 735
America Online information
    service, 578, 580, 602-603,
    689, 877
    programs, 596, 597
analog-to-digital converter chips,
    614
anti-glare filters, purchasing
    guidelines, 772-773
APDA (Apple Programmers
    Developers Association), 876
    APDALog, 876
    New Inside Macintosh, 876
APL (Programming Language),
    864
APL 68000 for the Apple
    Macintosh (Spencer Organiza-
    tion), 864

APL*Plus System for the
    Macintosh (STSC, Inc.), 864
Apple At Ease program, Desktop,
    53
Apple Computers, Inc.
    8•24 video card, 731
    Apple File Exchange, 809-810
    CD-ROM drives, 174
    Color OneScanner, 719
    Desktop Bus Mouse II, 717
    keyboards
        Apple Extended, 716
        Apple Extended II, 86, 89
        Apple Keyboard, 86
        ergonomic, 717
    Macintosh Development Tools
        and Languages Guidebook,
        877
    Macintosh PC Exchange, 810
    monitors, 728-731
    printers
        Color inkjet printer, 739,
            742
        dot-matrix, 739-742
        laser, 742-745
        LaserWriter printers, 305
    QuickTime, 616-618
    scanners, 573
    TrueImage, 302
Apple File Exchange, 809-810
Apple HD SC Setup program,
    165-168
Apple HD SC 20 Setup program,
    889
Apple II cards, 767
Apple menu, 132, 250-251
    Alarm Clock, 132-133
    Calculator, 134
    Chooser, printers, 279-285
    commands, About This
        Macintosh, 128-129
    items, 108
        adding and removing, 251

    choosing, 131-132
    sorting, 251-255
    Key Caps, 135-136
    Puzzle, 137
    Scrapbook, 137-139
Apple Programmers Developers
    Association, 876
Apple Programmers Develop-
    ment Association, MacsBug,
    849
AppleCD 300 CD-ROM drive,
    173-175
AppleColor High Resolution RGB
    Monitor, 728
AppleLink, 639, 876
AppleTalk
    communications module,
        ClarisWorks, 449
    LaserWriter, 281
    printers, 51-52, 281
        bridges, 786-787
    protocol, 781-782
    software, 781
    zones, 786
Application Heap, 859
application icons, 182
application layer, ISO model, 581
Application menu
    commands, 127
    Finder, 54, 71
applications
    copying between, 126
    hiding windows, 126-127
    quitting, 127
    starting, 122-124
    switching, 124-125
    see also DAs; programs;
        software; utilities
appointment manager databases,
    see information/time manage-
    ment programs
archiving files, 170
area charts, 566

arrow keys, 90
  moving insertion point, 94
arrows, 543
  scroll, 21, 75, 186
artificial intelligence (AI),
  868-869
Artrix modules, 481
ascenders, 298
ASCII format
  exporting to other programs,
    376-377
  files, 579
assembly language, 852-853
asset accounts, 460
association/prediction statistics,
  492
asynchronous communication,
  584
AT&T
  3210 DSP (digital sound
    processor), 713
  public E-mail, 597
ATM, see Adobe Systems, Type
  Manager
audio feedback, setting on/off,
  247
audio/video interface cards,
  VideoVision System (Radius),
  626
AutoCAD, 563
autodimensioning, 562
AutoDoubler (Salient), 170, 640
automatic OCR programs, 571
automatic startups, 255-256

B

backbone topology, 784
background
  copying, 130
  images, clip art, 554
  printing, 284-286

backing up
  disks, 205-208
  files, 345
backup programs, 630
  DiskFit Direct (Dantz
    Development), 630-631
  DiskFit Pro (Dantz Develop-
    ment), 630-631
  Retrospect (Dantz Develop-
    ment), 630-632
  Retrospect Remote (Dantz
    Development), 630-632
backups
  files, 884, 892-893
  tapes, 144
Balloon Help, 140-141
banners, 680
bar charts, 566
bars
  menu, 19
  scroll, 21, 75, 186
  title, 21, 73
Baseline
  Exposure Pro, 532-533
  INIT Manager, 642
  Thunder 7, 369
baseline of type, 298
bases for computers, purchasing
  guidelines, 774-775
BASIC (Beginner's All-purpose
  Symbolic Instruction Code),
  860-862
baud rates, 579, 582-583
BBSs (Bulletin Board Systems),
  578-579, 599-600
  AppleLink, 876
Berkeley Macintosh User's Group
  (BMG), 877
Berkeley Systems, After Dark, 735
Bernoulli standard, removable
  hard disks, 163
best mode, 739

Bézier curves, 543, 552
bibliographical databases
  EndNote Plus (Niles Associ-
    ates), 430
  Grant Manager (Niles
    Associates), 430
  Pro-Cite (Personal Biblio-
    graphic), 430
bill-paying service (electronic),
  CheckFree, 465-467
bit-mapped
  fonts, 302
  images, 543
bits, 579
  start and stop, 584
blinking rates
  insertion point, 211
  menus, 212
blocks of text, moving, 347
BMUG (Berkeley Macintosh
  User's Group), CD clip art, 555
borders, clip art, 554-555
Borland International
  Roundtable (GEnie), 877
  Turbo Pascal for the
    Macintosh, 862
Boston Computer Society (BCS)
  Macintosh User's Group, 877
  CD clip art, 555
boxes
  alert, ResEdit, 874
  check, 83
  close, 21
  list, 84, 186
  scroll, 21, 75
  size, 21
  text, 83-84
  zoom, 21
bridges, 786-787
  gateways, 787
  The I-Server (Solana
    Electronics), 787

InterBridge (Hayes), 787
NetBridge (Shiva), 787
Brightness control panel, 227
brochures, 502
Brøderbund, 658
    Arthur's Teacher Troubles
        CD-ROM, 657
    Carmen San Diego series, 661
    DTP Advisor, 534
    KidPix, 541, 647
    PinBall, 675
    PosterMaker Plus, 680-681
    TypeStyler, 313, 521
buffers, screen, 856
Bulletin Board Systems, see BBSs
bulletins, 502
burning images, 734
business
    clip art, 554-555
    letter models, 375
    programs, 327
business/finance information
    services, Dow Jones News/
    Retrieval, 604
buttons
    command, 82-83
    desktop, 186
    radio, 83
bytes, 579

C

C, 860-863
C++, 860-863
cables, 780
    printer, troubleshooting, 897
caching disks, 221
CAD (computer-aided design),
    542
    programs, 561
        AutoCAD, 563
        Blueprint (Graphsoft), 564
        ClarisCAD, 562-563

Design Home-Interiors
    (Abracadata), 564
Design Your Own Home
    (Abracadata), 563
Design Your Own Home
    Architecture
    (Abracadata), 563
MacInteriors (MicroSpot),
    564
MiniCad Plus (Graftsoft),
    564
Real CAD Level 1 (Ge-
    neric), 561-562
CAD/CAM (computer-aided
    design/ computer-aided
    manufacturing), 275
Calculator, 134
calendars, 524
CAM (computer-aided manufac-
    turing) programs, 561
cameras, still image
    Canon, 626
    FotoMan (Logitech), 626
Canon
    H850 Insertable Graphic Clips
        (Canon), 721
    Hi8 Stereo 8 mm (Canon),
        721
    RC-250, 721
    RC-570, 721
    still image cameras, 626
    UC1 8 mm, 720
cap height, 298
capacity, hard disks, 757-758
Caps Lock key, 87-89
capturing screens, 532-534
card game programs
    22nd Street Whist Tutor
        (SoftStream), 675-676
    Cribbage Tutor (SoftStream),
        675
    MacRummy (SoftStream), 675

Solitaire (SoftStream), 675
see also game programs
cards
    accelerator, 765-766
    Apple II, 767
    controller, 160
    expansion, purchasing
        guidelines, 762-767
    greeting, 680
    MAC286.10 (AST Research),
        811
    NuBus, 764
    PDS (Processor Direct Slot),
        764-765
    SIMMs (Single In-Line
        Memory Modules), 763-764
care and maintenance
    disks
        hard, 171
        floppy, 157-158
    printers, 748-750
        dot-matrix, 750-752
        laser, 752-753
Carmen San Diego series
    (Brøderbund), 661
carpal tunnel syndrome, 33,
    887-888
carrying cases
    MacLuggage, 771
    purchasing guidelines,
        771-772
cartoon clip art, 554
CASE, 869
cash accounts, 460
catalogs, 502
CD Remote (audio CDs), 175-176
CD Technology, CD-ROM drives,
    174
CD-ROM (Compact Disc-Read
    Only Memory)
    clip art, 555

clip media
   American Media Clip Time
      series (ATG Inc.), 624
   "Business and Technol-
      ogy," ClipMedia 1
      (MacroMedia), 624
   drives, 145, 172-176
      AppleCD 300, 173
      purchasing guidelines,
         759-760
   Phil and Dave's Excellent CD
      (Apple), 876
   photos, 624-625
   programs
      Berlitz language series,
         663
      HyperGlot language series,
         663
      QuickTime, 617
      VocabuLearn series, 663
CDEV (Control panel DEVice),
   see control panels
CE Software
   Alarming Events, 433
   CalendarMaker, 682-683
   DiskTop, 532
   DiskTop 4.0, 643
   MacBillboard, 680-681
   PowerKey, 771
   QuicKeys 2, 646-647
   QuickMail, 597
cells, 382, 386
   aligning contents, 390-391
centered text, 354, 514
Central Point Software
   MacTools, 634-636, 649
      Optimizer, 169
   Safe & Sound, 634-636
Centris 610 model, Macintosh,
   41, 698-699
Centris 650 model, Macintosh,
   41, 698-699

chamfers, 562
characters, 298
   special, 99-101
      viewing with Key Caps,
         135-136
charts, 400, 502, 565
   adding text, 402
   area, 566
   bar, 566
   creating, 402
   formatting, 402-403
   high-low-close, 566
   line, 566
   pie, 566
   text, 566
check boxes, 83
checking
   grammar, 371-373
   spelling, 341, 360, 369-370
checks, printing, 461, 465-467
chemistry dictionaries, 370
chips
   analog-to-digital converter,
      614
   RISC (Reduced Instruction Set
      Computer) chip, 850
Chooser
   printer drivers, Background
      Printing option, 284-285
   printers, 279-282
CISC microprocessor, 850
Claris
   ClarisCAD, 543-545, 562-563
   ClarisWorks, 413, 438,
      450-451, 486
   FileMaker Pro, 416, 419,
      422-428
   MacDraw Pro, 543-546
   MacPaint 2.0, 540
   MacProject II, 847
ClarisWorks, 413, 438, 450-451,
   486

modules, 440
   communications, 440, 449
   database, 440-442, 449
   graphics, 440, 447
   integrating, 443-446
   spreadsheet, 440, 444-448
   transferring information
      between, 440-443
   word processing, 439,
      444-447
programs, transferring
   information between,
   449-450
Classic model, Macintosh, 36-38,
   704
Classic II model, Macintosh,
   36-38, 695
Clean Up by Label command
   (Special menu), 191
Clean Up command (Special
   menu), 239-240
cleaning mouse, 882
Clear command (Edit menu), 95
click art, *see* clip art, 506
clicking, 18, 56-57
client/employee manager
   databases
   ABRA 2000 (Abra MacDabra),
      434
   AbraTrak, 434
   CLIENTmac (Software
      Complement), 435
clip art, 506
   CD-ROM, 555
   creating, 555
clip art libraries, 554-555
clip art tracking programs,
   556-558
clip media
   American Media Clip Time
      series (ATG Inc.), 624
   "Business and Technology,"
      ClipMedia 1
      (MacroMedia), 624

Clipboard, 26, 96-97, 108
    text, moving, 347-352
close box, 21
Close View control panel,
    242-243
closing windows, 22, 76
CMYK method, 273
COBOL, 864
codes
    creator, 180-181
    object, 853
    type, 180-181
collections, *see* files
college boards tests, CDs, 175
collisions, 781
color, 551-552
    documents, printing, 553-554
    inkjet printers, 273
    mixing, on-screen, 553
    options, monitors, 224-225
    output, 508
    paint programs, 552-553
    printers, 739-748
        continuous-tone, 275
        inkjet, 273
        phase-change, 274
        thermal-wax transfer,
            273-274
    scanners, 574
        Barneyscan system
            (Barneyscan), 574
        files, importing, 553
    slides, generating with
        PowerPoint, 553
    utilities, Colorizer (Palomar),
        554
Color Classic model, Macintosh,
    36, 695-696
Color control panel, 234-237
color-separation programs,
    553-554
    FreeHand (Aldus), 553-554

Illustrator (Adobe Systems),
    553-554
    QuarkXPress, 554
colors
    editing, 553
    labels, 259
    setting
        color wheel, 236-237
        text highlight, 234-235
        window frames, 235
    smoothing, 553
columns, 382, 386
    list views, 241-242
Command (⌘) key, 87-89
command buttons, 82-83
Command key, shortcut keys, 70
command line interface (CLI),
    855
commands
    Apple menu, About This
        Macintosh, 128-129
    Application menu
        Hide, 127
        Hide Others, 127
        Show All, 127
    Desktop, 91-92
    Edit menu
        Clear, 95
        Copy, 26, 97, 126, 347
        Cut, 26, 97, 347
        Paste, 27, 97-98, 126, 347
        Undo, 98, 346
    ellipses (...), 64
    Excel
        Data Extract, 410
        Data Find, 407
        Data Set Database, 405
        Data Sort, 405
        Edit Copy Down, 396
    File menu
        Duplicate, 113
        Find, 195-196
        Find Again, 196

Get Info, 117-118, 128,
    160, 193, 200, 908
Make Alias, 120, 192
New, 344, 389
New Folder, 189
Open, 116, 185, 343
Page Setup, 280
Print, 27, 281
Put Away, 115, 148
Save, 340
Save As, 344
grayed out, 62
Help menu
    Finder Shortcuts, 141
    Hide Balloons, 140
    Show Balloons, 139-140
Lotus 1-2-3, Range Format,
    391-393
menu, ResEdit, 874
PostScript, 288, 292
selecting, 21, 61-64
Special menu
    Clean Up, 239-240
    Clean Up by Label, 191
    Eject, 154
    Empty Trash, 114, 231
    Erase Disk, 152
    Restart, 105, 149, 906
    Set Startup, 906
toggling, 65
View menu, Label, 191
Comment option, viewing
    folders, 202
commercial sources, software,
    329
COmmon Business-Oriented
    Language, *see* COBOL
communications
    asynchronous, 584
    digital, 585
    protocols, 580-582
        MacBinary, 585

remote, LANs (local area
networks), 792-793
synchronous, 584
see also telecommunications
modules
ClarisWorks, 440, 449
Microsoft Works, 453
programs, 328, 576-577,
590-591
MicroPhone II (Software
Ventures), 591-595
MicroPhone Pro (Software
Ventures), 595
Smartcom II for the Mac
(Hayes), 596
White Knight (FreeSoft),
595-596
Compact Disc-Read Only
Memory, *see* CD-ROM
compact model Macintoshes, 16,
36-38
Classic II, 695
Color Classic, 695-696
Performa 200, 695
video display, 732
compatibility
software, evaluating, 331-333
spreadsheet programs,
411-413
compilers, 853-854
components, integrated software
packages, 438
compressing hard disks, 170
CompuServe Information
Service, 578-580, 592-597,
601-602, 689
forums, Apple and Symantec,
877
programs
CompuServe Information
Manager, 596-597
Navigator, 596-597
virus definitions, 636

computer furniture
Anthro, 775
ScanCo, 776
computer science dictionaries,
370
computer-aided design, *see* CAD
computer-aided design/com-
puter-aided manufacturing,
see CAD/CAM
computer-aided manufacturing,
see CAM
computer-aided software
engineering, *see* CASE
computers
carrying cases, 771-772
compilers, 853-854
dust covers, 772
furniture, 775-776
hosts, 579
interpreters, 853-854
keyboard position, 33-34
languages
assembly, 852-853
machine, 851-852
object-oriented program-
ming, 854-855
microprocessors, 850-851
monitors, 32-33
office furniture, 34-35
power line protectors,
770-771
security devices, 772
stands and bases, 774-775
concurrent programming, 864
configuration of networks, *see*
topologies
configuring, File Sharing (System
7), 793-798
connecting
hard disks, 164-165
Macintoshes, 47-48
modems, 578
connectors, 781

consistence design basic, 509
contact manager databases, *see*
name-and-address databases
content free presentations, 612
contents, tables, 365-366
continuous-tone printers, 275
Control key, 87-89
shortcut keys, 70
control panels, 109, 260
Brightness, 227
Close View, 242-243
Color, 234-237
Date & Time, international
options, 213-218
Easy Access, 243-247
folder, 210
General Controls, 210-213
installing, 260
Keyboard, 219-220
Memory, 220-223
Monitor, 223-226
Mouse, 226-227
removing, 261
Sound, 228-230, 248-250
Startup Disk, 230-231
Startup Manager, 891
System 6 versus System 7, 904
troubleshooting, 890-892
Views, 237-242
controller cards, 160
converting files, word processing
to other formats, 368
copiers, 609
coprocessors, math, 766-767
Copy (⌘-C) shortcut key, 97
Copy (F3) shortcut key, 97
Copy command (Edit menu), 26,
97, 126, 347
copying
between applications, 126
floppy disks to hard disks,
155-156

graphics, 97
  into Puzzle, 137
icons, 112-113
  in background, 130
into Scrapbook, graphics,
    text, or sounds, 138-139
text, 97
coupons, 524
cover letter templates, 375
CPUs (central processing units),
    330
  68020 or 68030, virtual
      memory, 221
creating
  accounts, 461
  charts, 402, 565-569
  clip art, 555
  databases, 404-405, 422
  files, word processing,
      339-343
  folders, 189
  fonts, 311
  graphs, 565-569
  reports, personal finance
      programs, 464-465
  tables, 354
  worksheets, 389
creator codes, 180-181
Cut (⌘-X) shortcut key, 97
Cut (F2) shortcut key, 97
Cut command (Edit menu), 26,
    97, 347
cylinders, see tracks

D

daisy chain topology, 783-784
DAs, see desk accessories
DAT (Digital Audio Tape), 762
data
  communications telephones,
      577
    dedicated lines, 590
  databases, entering, 425

transfer rate, 161-162
ClarisWorks
  transferring between
      modules, 440-443
  transferring between
      programs, 449-450
forks, 869
link layer, ISO model, 581
recovery programs, see
    utilities
worksheets, entering, 389-390
database
  forms, 416
  information services, 601
    BRS (Bibliographic
        Retrieval Services), 603
    Dialog, 603
  modules, ClarisWorks,
      440-442, 449
databases, 403-404, 416-418
  appointment managers,
      431-433
  bibliographical, 430
  client/employee manager,
      434-435
  creating, 404-405, 422
  designing, 422-424
  desk accessories
    DAtabase (Preferred
        Publishers), 428
    QuickDEX (Greene, Inc.),
        428
    Retriever II (Exodus), 429
  evaluating programs, 421-422
  files, 424-425
  finding data, 407-410
  flat-file, comparison to
      relational-file, 418-421
  grade managers, 433-434
  graphical, 430
  layouts, 427
  merging data with word
      processing documents, 361

name-and-address, 431-432
on-line, 578
programs, 326-327
records
  finding, 425-427
  importing/exporting,
      427-428
  sorting, 405-407
DataViz
  MacLink Plus, 806-807, 812
  MacLink Plus/PC, 808-810
Date & Time control panel,
    213-217
Date option, viewing folders, 202
dates
  international options, 213-216
  setting, 212-213
dBASE, SBT Database Accounting
    Library, 472
dealers, software sources, 329
debugging programs, 849
  MacsBug (Apple Programmers
      Development Association,
      849
  TMON (Icon Simulations),
      849
DEC (Digital Equipment
    Corporation), interfaces with
    Macintoshes, 813
dedicated data lines, 590
default pages, 523
defragmenting, see optimizing
Del key, 90
deleting
  folders, 189
  fonts, 309-310
  from Scrapbook, graphics,
      text, or sounds, 139
  graphics, 95-96
  icons, 114-116
  items from Apple menu, 251
  text, 95-96, 346
demodulation, 576

descenders, 298
descriptive statistics, 489-490
design in desktop publishing
    basics, 507-509
    techniques, 509-515
designing databases, 422-424
desk accessories, 104, 132
    accessing, 911
    Alarm Clock, 132-133
    Calculator, 134
    Canvas (Deneba), 542
    database
        DAtabase (Preferred
            Publishers), 428
        QuickDEX, 428
        Retriever II (Exodus), 429
    DeskPaint (Zedcor), 532, 542
    ExpressWrite (Exodus), 376
    Key Caps, 135-136
    miniWRITER (Maitreya), 376
    Puzzle, 137
    Scrapbook, 137-139
    Scriptor (Screenplay Systems),
        376
    Vantage (Preferred Publish-
        ers), 376
    word processing, 376
    Font/DA Mover, 909
        installing/removing, 910
Desktop, 210
    blinking rate
        insertion point, 211
        menus, 212
    commands, 91-92
    files, 55, 153, 181
        printing, 28
    Finder, 54-55
    KidDesk (EdMark Corp.),
        652-653
    pattern, 210-211
    programs, Apple At Ease, 53
    recommendations, 890

    settings, dates and times,
        212-213
    viewing, 52-54
desktop button, 186
desktop publishing, 502-504
    compared to traditional
        publishing, 505-507
    design
        basics, 507-509
        techniques, 509-515
    learning, 534
    PageMaker, 502, 523
    programs, 327, 525
        Interleaf Publisher,
            527-528
        Multi-Ad Creator (Multi-Ad
            Services), 528
        PageMaker (Aldus),
            525-526
        Personal Press (Aldus),
            529
        Publish It! Easy
            (Timeworks), 528-529
        purchasing guidelines,
            530-531
        QuarkXPress (Quark),
            522-523, 527
        Ready, Set, Go! (LetraSet),
            526-527
        UltraSpec (Publication
            Technologies), 530
        Writing Center (Learning
            Company), 529
    service bureaus, 504-505
    special effects, 515-518
    style sheets, 522-524
    templates, 522-524
    type-enhancing programs,
        519-522
    utilities, 532-533
destination document, 126
detecting viruses, 635-637

development environments, 849
diagnostic programs, 637
    Help! (Teknosys), 637-638
    MacEKG II (MicroMat), 638
    MacSleuth (Dariana, Inc.),
        638
dialog boxes
    Open File, 185
    Print, 27
    Save, 340
Dialog database information
    service, 603
dialogs
    boxes
        check, 83
        list, 84
        text, 83-84
    buttons
        command, 82-83
        radio, 83
    controlling from keyboard,
        84-85
    controls, 81-82
dictionaries, 370
    specialized, 369
digital communications, 585
Digital Darkroom (FotoMan), 626
Digital Darkroom (Silicon
    Beach), 573-574
Digital Equipment Corporation
    (DEC), interfaces with
    Macintoshes, 813
digital sound processors, AT&T
    3210 DSP, 713
digital tape drives (DAT), 762
dimensioning tools, 562
dimmed options, 20
DIP (Dual In-line Package)
    switches, 758
dirt-free systems, 881
disabling MultiFinder, 909
Disk Doubler (Salient), 170, 640

disk drives
  floppy, 144-158
  floptical, 145, 177
  hard, 144, 158-162, 757
    capacity, 757-758
    care and maintenance, 171
    compressing, 170
    connecting, 164-165
    copying floppy disks to, 155-156
    external, 163
    history, 159-160
    initializing, 165-166
    internal, 163
    optimizing, 168-169
    partitioning, 166-168
    purchasing guidelines, 757-759
    removable, 163
    SCSI devices, 758
    SCSI interface, 160-161
    security, 170
    seek time, 758
  SuperDrive (FDHD), 145
  see also drives
Disk First Aid, 890
Disk Tools disk icon, 165
diskette purchasing guidelines, 773-774
disks
  backing up
    floppy, 205
    hard, 206-207
  caching, 221
  compression programs, 639
    AutoDoubler (Salient), 640
    DiskDoubler (Salient), 640
    More Disk Space (Alysis Software), 640
    Stuffit Deluxe 3 (Aladdin), 639-640
    SuperDisk! (Alysis Software), 640

    TimesTwo (Golden Triangle), 641
  copy utilities, 155
  Disk First Aid, 890
  DOS Mounter System extension, 807
  emergency, 634
  error codes, 922
  files
    creator and type codes, 180-181
    storing, 180
  floptical, 145
  formatting, 809-810
  fragmented, 180
  icons, 148, 165, 181-182
  indicators, 186
  information, 241
  locking and unlocking, 156-157
  mounting DOS, 810
  MS-DOS-formatted, 145
  optimizing, 180
  reading DOS, 809-810
  servers, 782
  source, 154
  target, 154
  writing to, 809-810
  see also floppy disks; hard disks
DiskTop (CE Software), 532
DiskTop 4.0 (CE Software), 643
displays
  Apple Macintosh Portrait Display, 728
  AppleColor High Resolution RGB Monitor, 728
  full-page, 725
  landscape, 725
  Lapis PowerBase 1, 732
  Macintosh 12" Monochrome Display, 728
  Macintosh 12" RGB, 728

  Macintosh 16" Color Display, 729
  Macintosh 21" Color Display, 729
  Macintosh Color Display, 728
  monochrome, 725
  NEC, 730
  portrait, 725
  PowerBooks, 732
  PowerView (Radius), 732
  PowerVision (Mirror Technologies), 732
  protecting, 734-735
  purchasing guidelines, 727-728
  radiation from, 886-887
  Radius, 730
  RealTech series monitors (Hardware That Fits), 730-731
  RGB, 725-726
  Scuzzy View (Aura Systems), 732
  Seiko, 730
  Sony, 730
  video cards, 731
    Apple 8•24, 731
    Macintosh Display Card 8•24GC, 731
    PrecisionColor series (Radius), 731
    SuperMac, 731
    Video+ PB140/170 (LifeTime Memory Products), 732
distributed file servers, 783
distribution-free statistics, *see* nonparametrics
dithering, 273, 553
documents
  destination, 126
  predesigned, 375
  printing in color, 553-554
  source, 126

System 6 versus System 7, 903
see also files
DOS Mounter (Dyna), 807, 810
dot-matrix printers, 269
  Apple ImageWriter II, 739,
    741-742
  care and maintenance,
    750-752
  color, 553
dots per inch, *see* dpi
double-clicking, 18, 57-58
  icons, 116
  opening files, 183-184
  speed, 227
Dow Jones News/Retrieval
  business/finance information
  service, 592, 604
downloading
  files, 579-580
  fonts, 305, 311-312
dpi (dots per inch), 738
draft mode (printers), 739
drag-and-drop (icons), 101, 116
dragging, 58-61, 185
draw programs, 542
  Claris CAD, 543-545
  FreeHand (Aldus), 546-547
  Illustrator (Adobe Systems),
    546-547
  MacDraw Pro (Claris),
    543-546
drawing tools
  CAD programs, 562
  intuitive, 543
  PostScript, 546-547
drivers (printer), 277
  background printing, 284-286
  Chooser, 279-285
  GDT Softworks, 745
  installing, 278-279
  Orange Micro, 746

drives
  CD-ROM, 145, 172-176
  magneto-optical, 144, 176-177
    DisKovery 128MO (Optima
      Technology), 761
    MEOD 128 (Procom
      Technology), 761
  purchasing guidelines
    CD-ROM, 759-760
    magneto-optical, 761
    optical, 759
    tape, 762
    WORM, 760-761
  tape
    digital, 762
    PowerUser Pr 160MB, 762
  WORM (Write Once Read
    Many), 144
drives, *see also* disk drives
drop caps (type), 518
DTP, *see* desktop publishing
dumb terminals, 579
Duo series, Macintoshes, 45-46
Duplicate command (File menu),
  113
dust-free systems, 881
Dvorak keyboards, 101, 220, 263,
  664, 888

E

E-mail (electronic mail), 597-599
Easy Access control panel,
  243-244
  audio feedback, 247
  Mouse Keys, 244-245
  Slow Keys, 246
  Sticky Keys, 246-247
echoplex protocol, 582
Edit menu commands
  Clear, 95
  Copy, 26, 97, 126, 347
  Cut, 97, 347

  Paste, 27, 97-98, 126, 347
  Undo, 98, 346
editing
  colors, 553
  files
    Macintosh, 869-872
    word processing, 341-343,
      346-352
  fonts, 311
  icon names, 111-112
  pictures, 626
  text, 101
education clip art, 554
educational programs, 328,
  652-653
  A-Train (Maxis), 661
  Adventure Learning Series
    (Great Wave Software), 654
  American Discovery (Great
    Wave Software), 659-660
  Arthur's Teacher Troubles
    CD-ROM (Brøderbund),
    657
  ASKit (True Basic), 659
  Carmen SanDiego series
    (Brøderbund), 661
  DaisyQuest (Great Wave
    Software), 653-654, 657
  Headline Harry (Davidson
    and Associates), 661
  Interactive Physics (Knowl-
    edge Revolution), 658
  JungleQuest (HyperCard),
    654-655
  Kid Pix (Brøderbund), 657
  Kids Works 2 (Davidson), 656
  Millie's Math House
    (EdMark), 654-655
  Muppets On Stage (Sesame
    Street), 654-656
  Spelunx (HyperCard), 657
  Swamp Gas Visits Europe, 660

Swamp Gas Visits the USA, 661
Time Treks (EarthQuest), 661
EduCorp, 174, 555
Eject command (Special menu), 154
ejecting floppy disks, 148-150
electronic bill-paying service (CheckFree), 465-467
electronic mail networks, 578, 592
electronic mail, *see* E-mail
elementary skills educational programs, 652-658
ellipses (...) in commands, 64
emergency disks, 634
EMI protection, 770
emphasis/contast design basic, 508
Empty Trash command (Special menu), 114, 231
Encapsulated PostScript (EPS) files, 294, 551
enclosures, 502
End key, 90
environments
    object-oriented programming, 860, 865-868
    procedural programming, 860
EPS (Encapsulated PostScript) files, 294, 551
Erase Disk command (Special menu), 152
ergonomics, 886-888
    carpal tunnel syndrome, 887-888
    eye strain, 886
    glare, 886
    keyboards (Apple), 717
    mouse, 717
    muscle strain, 887-888
    radiation, 886-887

error checking, *see* parity checking
Error Codes
    disk, 922
    file system, 921-922
    general, 920
    I/O, 920-921
    Memory Manager, 923
    Resource Manager, 923
Esc (escape) key, 89
etching on screens, 734
EtherNet, 791
    FastNet (Dove Computer), 791
    Fastpath (Kinetics), 791
    LAN Ranger (Kinetics), 791
evaluating software, 329-330
    compatibility, 331-333
    Macintosh considerations, 330-331
    memory, 330
    return policies, 333-334
    technical support, 334-335
    versions, 331-333
    warranties, 333-334
Excel, 382-393, 397-403, 407, 410-413, 486-487
Excel commands
    Data menu
        Extract, 410
        Find, 407
        Set Database, 405
        Sort, 405
    Edit menu, Copy Down, 396
Excel Software
    MacAnalyst, 869
    MacDesigner, 869
    MetaDesigner, 869
expansion cards
    accelerator, 765-766
    Apple II, 767
    math coprocessors, 766-767

NuBus, 764
PDS (Processor Direct Slot), 764-765
purchasing guidelines, 762-767
SIMMs (Single In-Line Memory Modules), 763-764
expert systems, 868
exporting database records, 427-428
express mail services, 589
extensions, 108
    System, 261
        installing, 262
        preventing startup, 262-263
        removing, 262
    System 6 versus System 7, 904
external hard disks, 163, 757
external modems, 580
extruding objects, 559
eye strain, 886

F

facsimile, *see* fax
fax
    forms, 524
    modems, 586
        programs, 608-609
        Relisys RA2110M, 609
    protocols, 586, 589
FDHD (Floppy Drive High Density), *see* SuperDrive
fields, 404, 416-419
Fifth Generation Systems
    The Local Connection, 792-793
    SafeLock, 646
    Suitcase 2.0, 642-643
file formats
    draw programs, 543
    EPS (Encapsulated PostScript), 551

Graphic Image File (GIF), 551
PICT, 550
PNT, 550
PNTG, 550
TIFF, 551
file icons, 181-182
File menu commands
    Duplicate, 113
    Find, 195-196
    Find Again, 196
    Get Info, 117-118, 128, 160,
        193, 200
    Make Alias, 120, 192
    New, 344, 389
    New Folder, 187-189
    Open, 116, 185, 343
    Page Setup, 280
    Print, 27, 281
    Put Away, 115, 148
    Save, 340
    Save As, 344
    Get Info, 908
file servers, 783
    allShare (Everyware), 783
    distributed, 783
    EasyShare (ShirtPocket
        Software), 783
    TOPS (Transcendental
        Operating System), Sun
        Microsystems, 783
File Sharing (System 7), 793
    accessing shared items,
        802-803
    configuring, 793-798
    controlling, 800-802
    disks, 798-800
    folders, 798-800
    options, 800
file system error codes, 921-922
file translation programs
    AccessPC 2.0 (Insignia
        Solutions), 810

Apple File Exchange (Apple),
    809, 810
DOS Mounter (Dyna), 810
LapLink (Traveling Software),
    808-809, 812
MacLink Plus, 806-807, 812
MacLink Plus/PC (DataViz),
    808-810
Macintosh PC Exchange
    (Apple), 810
Software Bridge/Mac (Argosy
    Software Inc.), 809
FileMaker Pro (Claris), 422-428
files, 180, 416-418
    aliasing, 191-195
    archiving, 170
    ASCII, 579
    backing up
        floppy disk, 205
        hard disk, 206-207
        Microsoft Word, 345
        Nisus, 345
        tape backup, 207-208
        WordPerfect, 345
    backups, 884, 892-893
    converting word processing
        to other formats, 368
    creating word processing,
        339-343
    creator and type codes,
        180-181
    database, 424-425
    Desktop, 55, 153, 181
    DiskDoubler, 639
    downloading, 579-580
    editing
        Macintosh, 869-872
        word processing, 341-343,
            346-352
    Encapsulated PostScript
        (EPS), 294

finding
    Find command, 195-196
    Find dialog options,
        196-199
    original of aliases, 192-193
folders, System 6 versus
    System 7, 904
formatting word processing
    files, 352-359
fragmented, 168
IBM PC ZIP, 639
importing, color scanner, 553
labeling, 190
metrics, 320
MultiFinder, 905
    disabling, 909
    installing, 905-907
    memory allocation,
        908-909
opening, 183-186
organizing hard disks,
    186-190
printing, 27-28
recovering, 892-893
removing labels, 191
saving
    as stationery pads, 200
    graphics, 550-551
    word processing, 344-346
sharing, 294-296
sorting by labels, 191
sound
    AIFF, 615
    SoundEdit, 615
    System 7, 615
storing, 180
System, 109
translating to/from Apple
    systems, 806-810
uploading, 580
viewing in folders, 201
viruses, 883-884

fillets, 562
filters, anti-glare, 772-773
finance programs, 327, 460
    accounts, 460-463
    Dollars & Sense (Business
      Sense), 468-469
    Managing Your Money (Meca)
      5.0, 466-468
    Quicken, 465-466
    reports, 464-465
    Wealth Builder (Reality
      Technologies), 471
financial planning strategies, 471
Find Again command (File
    menu), 196
Find command (File menu),
    195-196
Finder, 54-55, 109
    applications
      hiding windows, 126-127
      starting, 122-124
      switching, 124-125
    background copying, 130
    File menu commands, 187
    memory usage, 128-130
    menus, 70-71
    shortcuts, 141
Finder enhancement programs,
    643
    CanOpener 2.0 (Abbot
      Systems), 643
    DiskTop 4.0 (CE Software),
      643
    HAM (Hierarchical Apple
      Menu) (InLine Design), 645
    Hand-Off II (Connectix
      Corporation), 643
    Now Menus, Now Utilities,
      644-645
    On Cue II (ICOM Simula-
      tions), 643
    SuperBoomerang, Now
      Utilities, 643-644

Finder Shortcuts command (Help
    menu), 141
finding
    files, 195
      Find command, 195-196
      Find dialog options,
        196-199
      original of aliases, 192-193
    records in databases,
      407- 410, 425-427
    text, 350-352
flat scanners, 569
flat-file databases, 418
    disk-based, 419
    memory-resident, 419
fliers, 502, 524
Flight Simulator (Microsoft), 669
Floating Point Units (FPUs), 766
floating-point decimals in CAD
    programs, 562
floating-point unit (FPU), 330
floppy disks, 144-145
    3.5 inch, 145
    backing up, 205
    care and maintenance,
      157-158
    copying to hard disks,
      155-156
    ejecting, 148-150
    initializing, 150-153
    inserting, 148-149
    locking, 154
    structure, 146
    types, 146-148
floptical disks, 145, 177
flow charts, 847
flying/driving game programs
    Falcon (Spectrum Holobyte),
      670
    Flight Simulator (Microsoft),
      669
    Grand Prix (Bullseye
      Software), 668

    Mustang Flight Simulator
      (Donald Hill Jr.), 669
    Orbiter (Spectrum Holobyte),
      670
    The Duel-Test Drive II,
      668-669
    see also game programs
FolderBolt (Kent Marsh), 645-646
folders, 201
    Control Panels, 210
    creating, 189
    deleting, 189
    icons, 181-182
    menus, 186
    naming, 189
    navigating, 203-205
    nesting, 182-183, 189-190
    Preferences, 109
    sizes, 240-241
    Startup Item, 255-256
    System, 187
    System 6 versus System 7, 904
    viewing
      by Name option, 201-202
      by outline views, 202-203
      by Small icons, 201
      files from, 201
Font Creator, 320
font utilities, 312
    addDepth (Ray Dream, Inc.),
      314
    Adobe Type Manager (ATM),
      315
    Adobe Type Reunion, 317
    Adobe TypeAlign, 314
    conversion, 315
    Incubator Pro 2.0 (Type
      Solutions), 315
    managers, 315
    Master Juggler (ALSoft), 315,
      321-322
    Metamorphosis Professional,
      315

Suitcase (Fifth Generation), 315, 321-322
SuperATM package (Adobe Systems), 317-319
Tapestry (Pixar), 314
type enhancement, 313-314
TypeStyler (Brøderbund), 313
Font/DA Mover, 909
  icon, 909
  installing/removing, 910
fonts, 298-302, 356-358, 543
  creating, 311
  deleting, 309-310
  downloading, 305, 311-312
  editing, 311
  installing, 308-309
  installing/removing, 911
  monospaced, 307
  PostScript, 739-743
  previewing, 312
  printers
    PostScript, 304-306
    QuickDraw, 303-304
  raster image processing (RIP), 302-303
  ResEdit, 874-875
  screen, 307
  sizes, 356-358
  special characters, 135-136
  System 6 versus System 7, 905
  TrueType, 288, 302, 739, 742-743
  view, 238-239
  worksheets, 393-394
forecasting/planning programs, 481
  Business Plan Toolkit (Palo Alto Software), 482
  Forecaster (Palo Alto Software), 481
  HyperCard Stack, 482-483
  Sales Marketing Forecasting Toolkit, 483

foreign keyboards, 263
forks, data and resource, 869
formats (documents)
  ASCII, 376-377
  converting word processing files to other, 368
  file, draw programs, 543
  graphics, 550-551
  international options
    dates, 213-216
    numbers, 217-218
    times, 213-217
  sound, 615
formatting
  charts, 402-403
  disks
    DOS, 809-810
    floppy, 150-153
    hard, 165-166
  files, 352-359
  numbers, 391-393
  text
    fonts, 356-358
    justification, 354-356
    line spacing, 358
    margins, 352-353
    pages, 358-359
    sizes, 356-358
    styles, 356-358
    tables, 354
    tabs, 353-354
formulas
  entering, 394-397
  functions, 398-400
  operators, 397-398
FORTRAN (FORmula TRANslator), 864
FORTRAN Converter (True BASIC), 864
FoxBase+, 420
FoxBase+/Mac (Microsoft), 416
FPU (floating-point unit), 330, 766

fractal lines, 552
fragmented
  disks, 180
  files, 168
FreeHand (Aldus), 546-547, 553-554
freeware, 329
full duplex protocol,579-581
full-page displays, 725
function keys, 89
functions, 398-400
furniture (office), 34-52, 775-776
future model Macintoshes, 712-713
FWB, DAT tape drives, 762

G

game programs
  22nd Street Whist Tutor (SoftStream), 675-676
  4th and Inches (Accolade), 667
  Battle Stations (TimeLine), 671
  Beyond Dark Castle (Silicon Beach), 671
  Bomber (Deadly Games), 670
  Cribbage Tutor (SoftStream), 675
  Crystal Quest (Cassady and Greene), 674
  Falcon (Spectrum Holobyte), 670
  Flight Simulator (Microsoft), 669
  Fool's Errand (Miles Computing), 671-672
  GATO (Spectrum Holobyte), 670
  Glider (Cassady and Greene), 674-675

Go-Man-Ku (Toyogo), 673-674
Grand Prix (Bullseye Software), 668
Hard Ball (Accolade), 665
Leader Board (Access), 667
Lemmings (Psygnosis), 677
Mac Pro Football (Avalon Hill), 667
MacRacquetball (Practical Computer Applications), 667
MacRummy (SoftStream), 675
Mean 18 Ultimate Golf (Accolade), 665-667
Moriarity's Revenge (Bull City Software), 671
Mustang Flight Simulator (Donald Hill Jr.), 669
Orbiter (Spectrum Holobyte), 670
PinBall (Brøderbund), 675
purchasing guidelines, 664-665
Puzzle Gallery (Miles Computing), 671
Solitaire (SoftStream), 675
Tetris (Spectrum HoloByte), 672-673
The Duel-Test Drive II, 668-669
Welltris (Spectrum HoloByte), 673-674
gateways, 787
GCC series of laser printers, 746
General Controls control panel, 210
  blinking rate, 211-212
  Desktop pattern, 210-211
  settings, 212-213
general information services
  America Online, 602-603
  CompuServe, 601-602
  CONNECT, 605
  GEnie, 602
  NewsNet, 604
  Prodigy, 604
  purchase guidelines, 605-606
  Well (Whole Earth Lectronic Link), 605
general ledger programs, 472, 478
GEnie on-line service, 578, 592, 602, 877
Get Info command (File menu), 117-118, 128, 160, 193, 200, 908
GIF (Graphic Image File) file format, 551
glare, 886
glossaries, 363
glossary terms, 455
grade manager databases, 433-434
grammar checkers, 371-373
graph/chart programs, 565-566
  Cheshire (Abbot), 568-569
  CricketGraph (Cricket Software), 566-567
  DeltaGraph (DeltaPoint), 568
  KaleidaGraph (Ablebeck), 566-568
graphical statistical programs
  FASTAT (Systat), 493
  Igor (WaveMetrics), 493-495
  JMP (SAS), 494
  Mathematica, 493
  SuperAnova (Abacas), 494
  Theorist (Prescience Corporation), 493
graphical user interface, see GUI
graphics
  clip art, 554
  copying, 97, 138-139
  deleting, 95-96, 139
  desktop publishing, 533
  formats, 550-551
  module
    ClarisWorks, 440, 447
    Microsoft Works, 452
  moving, 97-98
  programs, 538-539
  puzzles, 137
  replacing, 96
  tablets
    DrawingPad Graphics Tablet (Calcomp), 719
    purchasing guidelines, 719
    UnMouse, 719
    Wacom series, 719
  word processing, 366-368
  wraparounds, 511-513
graphics programs, 327, 558-561
  Animation Works (Gold Disk), 561
  DynaPerspective, 560
  Mac3D (Challenger), 558
  StratsVISION 3D (Strata), 560
  Super 3D (Silicon Beach), 558
  Zing (Enabling Technologies), 560
graphs, see charts
gray scaling, 543
gray-scale scanning, OCR (Optical Character Recognition), 573
grayed commands in menus, 62
grayscale monitors, 725
greeting cards, 680
grids, 239-240, 382, 386
group difference statistics, 490-491
Group III fax protocol, 586, 589
grouping objects, 543
GUI (graphical user interface), 537, 855-856

H

half duplex protocol, 579-581
HAM (Hierarchical Apple Menu)
    (InLine Design), 645
hand-held scanners, 570
handshaking, 582
hard disks, 144, 158-162, 757
    backing up, 206-207
    capacity, 757-758
    compressing, 170
    connecting, 164-165
    copying floppy disks to,
        155-156
    external, 163
    file organization, 186-190
    history, 159-160
    initializing, 165-166
    internal, 163
    maintenance programs, 171,
        632
        911 Utilities (Microcom),
            635
        MacTools (Central Point
            Software), 634
        Norton Utilities 2.0
            (Symantec/Peter
            Norton), 632-634
        Public Utilities (Fifth
            Generation Systems,
            Inc.), 634-635
        Safe & Sound (Central
            Point Software),
            634-635
    optimizing, 168-169
    partitioning, 166-168
    purchasing guidelines,
        757-759
    removable, 163
    SCSI interface, 160-161, 758
    security, 170
    seek time, 758

hard partitions, 167
hardware
    multimedia, purchasing
        guidelines, 626
    OCR (Optical Character
        Recognition), purchasing,
        572-573
    purchasing guidelines,
        690-691
    return policies, 690-691
    running IBM programs on
        Macintoshes, 811
    sources, 688-689
    troubleshooting, 893-896
    warranties, 690-691
Hayes
    InterBridge, 787
    Smartcom II for the Mac, 596
    Ultra 144 modems, 588
    Ultra 24 modems, 588
    Ultra 96 modems, 588
Hayes-compatible modems, 587
headings, 386
Help, 140
    Balloon Help, 140-141
    Help key, 90
    Help menu commands
        Finder Shortcuts, 141
        Hide Balloons, 140
        Show Balloons, 139-140
    programs, 142
Hewlett-Packard
    DeskWriter C, 747
    ScanJet series, 720
HFS (Hierarchical File System),
    182-183
HFS tree, 188
Hide Balloons command (Help
    menu), 140
Hide command (Application
    menu), 127

Hide Others command (Applica-
    tion menu), 127
hiding application windows,
    126-127
Hierarchical File System, see HFS
hierarchical menus, 66-67
High charts, 566
Home key, 90
horizontal scan rate, 724
hosts, 579
HyperCard, 429
    JungleQuest, 654-655
    Spelunx, 657
HyperCard Stack, 482-483
HyperGlot language series, 663
HyperTalk, 860
hyphenation, 514-515

I

I-beam pointer, 94
I/O system error codes, 920-921
IBM-type PCs
    emulator programs
        Entry Level SoftPC 2.5
            (Insignia Solutions),
            812
        SoftNode 1.0 (Insignia
            Solutions), 812
        Universal SoftPC 2.5
            (Insignia Solutions),
            811
    mounting disks, 810
    translating files to/from Apple
        systems, 806-812
icons, 104, 110
    aliases, 120-121
    application, 182
    copying, 113, 130
    customizing appearance,
        256-257
    deleting, 114-116
    disk, 148, 181-182

Disk Tools disk, 165
double-clicking, 183-184
editing names, 111-112
file, 181-182
folder, 181-182
Font/DA Mover, 909
Get Info command, 117-118
grids, 239-240
labeling, 190-191
labels
    applying, 258
    customizing, 258-259
Lock, 156
locking and unlocking, 119
moving, 19, 112-113
opening, 116-117
printer driver, 279-282
ResEdit, 872-873
selecting, 19, 110-111
sizes, 240
System 6 versus System 7, 902
Trash, 114-116, 148, 231
idea processor programs, 483
    IdeaFisher (Mel Fisher),
      483-484
    MindLink (MindLink), 484
    Synchronicity (Visionary), 485
identifying, 225-226
Illustrator (Adobe Systems),
    546-547, 553-554
ImageWriter print head scanners,
    570
ImageWriter II, 269, 553, 739-742
ImageWriter LQ, 282-283
importing
    database records, 427-428
    files, 553
income tax preparation, *see* tax
    preparation
indexes, 365-366
inference engine, 868
Info window icons, 117-118

information services, 578-579,
    600
    billing problems, 606-608
    business/finance, Dow Jones
      News/Retrieval, 592, 604
    database, 601
      BRS (Bibliographic
        Retrieval Services), 603
      Dialog, 603
    general, 600
      America Online, 578,
        592-597, 602-603, 689
      CompuServe, 578,
        601-602, 689
      CONNECT, 605
      Delphi, 578
      GEnie, 578, 592, 602
      NewsNet, 595, 604
      Prodigy, 604
      Well (Whole Earth
        Lectronic Link), 605
    Macintosh, 600
    on-line addiction, 606-608
    purchase guidelines, 605-606
    software sources, 329
    technical/scientific, 603-604
    Telenet, 578
inkjet printers, 270
    Apple, 739, 742
    color, 553, 747
inserting
    floppy disks, 148-149
    text, 346-347
insertion point, 92
    blinking rate, 211
    moving, 93-94
Inside Macintosh, 856-857,
    860-861
Insignia Solutions
    AccessPC 2.0, 810
    Entry Level SoftPC 2.5, 812
    SoftAT 2.5, 812

    SoftNode 1.0, 812
    Universal SoftPC 2.5, 811
install base, 697
installing
    control panels, 260
    Font/DA Mover, 910
    fonts, 308-309, 911
    keyboard layouts, 263
    MultiFinder, 905-907
    printer drivers, 278-279
    System 7, 105-107
    System extensions, 262
integrated software packages,
    438-439
    ClarisWorks, 439-451
    Microsoft Works, 451-456
interfaces, 32, 849
    AppMaker (Bowers Develop-
      ment), 857
    command line (CLI), 855
    GUI (graphical user interface),
      855-856
    The Human Interface
      Guidelines, 859
    Musical Instrument Digital
      Interface (MIDI), 679
    SCSI (Small Computer System
      Interface), 50-51, 160-161,
      756-757
Interleaf Publisher, 527-528
interleave ratio, 161-162
internal hard disks, 163, 757
internal modems, 580
Internal Revenue Service forms,
    469
international options
    dates, 213-216
    numbers, 217-218
    times, 213-217
International Standards Organiza-
    tion (ISO) model, 581-582
interpreters, 853-854

interprocess messaging, 713
intuitive drawing tools, 543
Investigator, 677
invitations, 502, 524
ISO, *see* International Standards
Organization

J-K

justifying text, 354-356, 514-515

Kermit protocol, 580
kerning, 355, 509-510
Key Caps, 135-136
key fields, 419
Keyboard control panel, 219-220
keyboards, 86-87
Apple Extended Keyboard, 716
Apple Extended Keyboard II, 86, 89
controlling dialogs, 84-85
Desktop commands, 91-92
Dvorak, 101, 263, 664, 888
ergonomic (Apple), 717
foreign, 263
keys
arrow, 90
Del, 90
End, 90
Esc (escape), 89
function, 89
Help, 90
Home, 90
modifier, 87-89
numeric, 90
Page Down, 90
Page Up, 90
Power on, 90
layouts, 219-220
choosing, 264
installing, 263
removing, 263-264

MAC-101e Keyboard
(DataDesk International), 717
MacPro (KeyTronic), 717
NoteBook KeyPad
(Kensington), 717
Plusware Numeric Keypad, 717
positions, 33-34
PowerPad (Sophisticated
Circuits), 717
purchasing guidelines, 716-717
QWERTY, 101
Switchboard (DataDesk
International), 717
KeyFinder, Norton Utilities, 648
keys
arrow, 90, 94
combinations pressed
separately, 246-248
Del, 90
delaying acceptance of
presses, 246
Desktop commands, 91-92
End, 90
Esc (escape), 89
function, 89
Help, 90
Home, 90
modifier, 87-89
numeric, 90
Page Down, 90
Page Up, 90
Power on, 90
repeat rate, 219
special characters, 99-101
see also shortcut keys
Kind option, viewing folders, 202
Kodak
DataShow, 733

overhead projection tools, 734
Photo CD Access Software, 624-625

L

Label command (View menu), 191
Label menu (Finder), 71
Label option, viewing folders, 202
labeling files, 190
labels
colors, 259
files, 191
icons, 258-259
landscape
displays, 725
orientation, 359
language instruction programs
Berlitz language series, 663
Elementary Spelling Ace
(Franklin Electronics), 663
HyperGlot language series, 663
Picture it! (Penton Overseas), 663
Spelling Tutor (Franklin
Electronics), 663
VocabuLearn series, 663
languages
macro, 410-411
page-description (PDLs), 287-288
PostScript, 519-521
programming, 846
APL (Programming
Language), 864
artificial intelligence (AI), 868-869
assembly, 852-853
BASIC, 861-862

books, 861
C, 862-863
C++, 862-863
COBOL, 864
compilers, 853-854
Forth, 864
FORTRAN, 864
interpreters, 853-854
LISP, 863
LOGO, 863
machine, 851-852
Modula-2, 864
object-oriented, 854-855,
    860, 865-868
Pascal, 862
procedural, 860
VIP (Visual Interactive
    Programming) (Main-
    stay), 865
scripting, 595
see also printer languages
LANs (local area networks)
communicating remotely,
    792-793
constructing, 788-790
EtherNet, 791
peripherals, 792
PhoneNET (Farallon),
    790-791
planning setup, 787-788
see also networks
LapLink (Traveling Software),
    808-809, 812
laptop model Macintoshes,
    42-47, 699-700
PowerBook 145, 700
PowerBook 160, 700
PowerBook 165c, 700-701
PowerBook 180, 701
PowerBook Duo 210/230,
    701-702
starting, 16

laser printers, 271-273, 742-746
care and maintenance,
    752-753
color, 553
laser-printer languages, 286-293
LaserWriter Font Utility, 311-312
LaserWriter Pro 600/630, 744-745
LaserWriter Select 300/310, 742
layers, ISO model, 581-582
layouts
databases, 427
keyboards, 219-220, 263-264
LC series Macintoshes, 39, 767
LCD (liquid crystal display), 733
leading, 299, 511
leased lines, 590
left-justified text, 354
liability accounts, 460
libraries
clip art, 554-555
shared, 713
symbol, 562
light shading, 559
line charts, 566
line length of text, 515
lines, 543
3-D graphics, 559
fractal, 552
spacing, 358
Linotronic typesetters, 276
Lisa computer, 867
LISP, 863
list views
columns, 241
icon size, 240
local area networks, *see* LANs
LocalTalk networks, 51, 781-782
Lock icon, 156
locking
disks, 154-157
icons, 119
object arrangements, 543

logical operators, 397
Lotus 1-2-3, 382-384, 388-391,
    396, 400, 403, 410-412, 486
Low charts, 566
low memory condition, 897

M

MAC-101e Keyboard (DataDesk
    International), 717
Mac-to-mainframe programs,
    MacMainframe (Avatar), 813
MacBinary protocol, 585
MacDraw Pro (Claris), 543-546
MacFORTRAN (Absoft Corp.),
    864
machine language, 851-852
Macintosh Development Tools
    and Languages
    Guidebook(Apple), 877
Macintosh Display Card 8•24GC
    video card, 731
Macintosh PC Exchange (Apple),
    810
Macintosh RoundTable, 602
Macintosh X-Ref, 856
Macintoshes
America Online roundtables,
    877
associations, 876
connecting, 47-48
Duo series, 45-46
ergonomics, 32-35
future models, 712-713
GUI (graphical user interface),
    855
hardware
    12" Monochrome Display,
        728
    12" RGB, 728
    16" Color Display, 729
    21" Color Display, 729
    512K/512Ke, 709

II, 39, 710
IIci, 40, 705-706
IIcx, 40, 705
IIfx, 39, 706
IIsi, 40, 704-705
IIvx, 41, 175, 698
IIx, 39, 710
Centris 610, 41
Centris 650, 41
Classic, 36-38
Classic II, 36-38
Color Classic, 36
keyboards, 86-92
LC III, 39, 696-697
LC/LC II, 39, 706-707
Motorola microprocessors, 850-851
Performa 200, 36, 38
Performa 400, 39
Performa 600, 41
Performa 600 CD, 41
Plus, 36-37, 709
PowerBook series, 45
Quandra 800, 702
Quandra 950, 703
SE, 36-37
SE/30, 36-37, 705
information services, 600
laptop models, 699-700
modular, 696-699
obsolete models, 708-710
older models, 703-708
overhead displays, 733-734
Portable, 42-44
printer setup, 48-52
publications, 876-877
purchasing guidelines, 710-712
quitting, 28
running IBM PC programs, 810-812
software evaluation, 330
starting, 16-17

MacLink Plus (DataViz), 806-807, 812
MacLink Plus/PC (DataViz), 808-810
MacPaint 2.0 (Claris), 540
MacProject (Claris), 496-499, 847
MacRacquetball (Practical Computer Applications), 667
macro utilities, 646
    QuicKeys 2 (CE Software), 646-647
    Tempo II Plus (Affinity), 646
macros, 364, 846
MacTech magazine, 876
MacTech Quarterly (TechAlliance), 876
MacTools (Central Point Software), 169, 634-636, 649, 883, 890
MacUser magazine, 158, 587, 689-690, 710
MacWeek, 689
MacWorld magazine, 158, 587, 689-690, 710
MacWrite Pro
    graphics, 366-367
    text
        converting to other formats, 368
        finding/replacing, 352
        fonts, 357
        merging, 361
        spell checkers, 360
        tables, 354
magazines, 502, 525
    hardware information, 689-690
    Macintosh information, 710
    MacUser, 158, 587
    MacWorld, 158, 587
magnetic storage devices, 756
magneto-optical drives, 144, 176-177

DisKovery 128MO (Optima Technology), 761
MEOD 128 (Procom Technology), 761
purchasing guidelines, 761
mail merging, 361
mail services (electronic)
    compared to telecommunications, 589
mainframes, connecting Macintoshes, 812-813
Make Alias command (File menu), 120, 192
managing memory, 858-859
manipulating
    objects in three dimensions, 559
    text, 519-522
margins, 352-353
masking objects, 552
master pages, 523
MasterJuggler (ALSoft), 315, 321, 643
math coprocessors, 766-767
MCI Mail on-line service, 592
memory
    32-bit address mode, 223
    allocating in MultiFinder, 908-909
    disk caching, 221
    low memory condition, 897
    memory control panel, 220
    ROM (read-only memory), 104
    SIMMs (Single In-Line Memory Modules), 763-764
    upgrade considerations, 898
    usage, 128-130
    virtual, 221-223
memory-resident databases, 419
memos, 524

menus, 61
  adding and removing items, 251
  bars, 19
  choosing items, 131-132
  commands, 20
  items, 108, 132-139
  blinking rate, 212
  folder, 186
  hierarchical, 66-67
  options, 64-66
  pop-up, 68-69
  scrolling, 67-70
  selecting commands, 61-64
  System 6 versus System 7, 902-903
    Apple menu, 902-903
    File menu, 903
    Special menu, 903
    View menu, 903
merging text, 360-362
messaging interprocess, 713
metrics files, 320
micro-to-mainframe programs
  DynaComm Asynchronous (Future Soft Engineering), 813
  MacIRMA Workstation (Digital Communications), 813
Microcom
  911 Utilities, 635
  Carbon-Copy Mac, 792
  Citadel with Shredder, 646
  Complete Undelete, 635
  Virex, 636
MicroPhone II (Software Ventures), 591-595
MicroPhone Pro (Software Ventures), 595
microphones, recording sounds, 248-250
microprocessors, 850-851

Microsoft
  BASIC, 862
  Flight Simulator, 669
  FoxBase+/Mac, 416
  PowerPoint, 553
  TrueImage, 302
  Windows, 856
  Word
    dictionaries, 370
    files, 345
    glossaries, 363
    graphics, 367
    indexes, 365
    PostScript commands, 291
    table of contents, 365-366
  Works, 419, 438-439, 451-456
MicroSpeed (MacTrac 2.0), 718
MicroSpot (MacInteriors), 564
MIDI (Musical Instrument Digital Interface), 679
mini-applications, *see* desk accessories
mnemonics, 852
MNP-5 error correction, 585-589
modems, 576, 579, 587-589
  baud rates, 582-583
  communications module (ClarisWorks), 449
  communications programs, 576-577
  connections, 578
  external, 580
  fax, 586
    programs, 608
    Relisys RA2110M, 609
  The Home Office (Prometheus), 578
  internal, 580
  parity checking, 583-585
  programs, 586-588
  protocols, 580-582

  purchasing guidelines, 586-588
  surge protectors, 880
  Telax System (Relisys), 609
  telephones, 577-578
modes
  32-bit address, 223
  best, 739
  draft, 739
modified clicking and dragging, 61
modifier keys, 87-89
modular Macintoshes, 39-42
  Centris 610, 698-699
  Centris 650, 698-699
  Macintosh LC III, 696-697
  Macintosh IIvx, 698
  Performa 400 series, 697
  Performa 600 series, 697
  starting, 16
modulation, 576
modules
  ClarisWorks
    communications, 440, 449
    database, 440-442, 449
    graphics, 440, 447
    integrating, 443-446
    spreadsheet, 440, 444-448
    transferring data between, 440-443
    word processing, 439, 444-447
  integrated software packages, 438
  Microsoft Works
    communications, 453
    graphics, 452
    spreadsheet, 453-454
    word processing, 452-454
  SBT Database Accounting Library (Mac/Series Six Plus), 473-474

Monitor control panel, 223-224
    color options, 224-225
    identifying and arranging
        monitors, 225-226
monitors, 724-725
    anti-glare filters, 772-773
    Apple Macintosh Portrait
        Display, 728
    AppleColor High Resolution
        RGB Monitor, 728
    color, 552
    displays, 725
    eye strain, 886
    glare, 886
    grayscale, 725
    height and distance, 32-33
    Lapis PowerBase 1, 732
    Macintosh Color Display,
        728-729
    Macintosh Monochrome
        Display, 728
    NEC, 730
    PowerBooks, 732
    PowerView (Radius), 732
    PowerVision (Mirror
        Technologies), 732
    protecting, 734-735
    purchasing guidelines,
        727-728
    Radius, 730
    RealTech series monitors
        (Hardware That Fits),
        730-731
    screens, preventing glare, 33
    Scuzzy View (Aura Systems),
        732
    Seiko, 730
    Sony, 730
    video cards, 731
        Apple 8•24, 731
        Macintosh Display Card
            8•24GC, 731

    PrecisionColor series
        (Radius), 731
    SuperMac, 731
    Video+ PB140/170 (LifeTime
        Memory Products), 732
monochrome displays, 725
monospaced fonts, 307
Motorola microprocessors,
    850-851
mounting disks (IBM PC), 810
mouse, 55-56
    A3 Mouse (Mouse Systems),
        718
    cleaning, 882
    clicking, 18, 56-58, 61
    dragging, 18, 58-61
    ergonomic, 717
    Kidz Mouse, 718
    Little Mouse (Mouse Systems),
        718
    MouseMan, 718
    MousePenPro (Appoint), 718
    moving pointer, 244-245
    pads, 17
    pen-like, 718
    purchasing guidelines,
        718-719
    selecting icons, 19
    UnMouse, 719
Mouse control panel, 226-227
movies
    QuickTime, 618
    video/multimedia, 616
moving
    graphics, 97-98
    icons, 19, 112-113
    insertion point, 93-94
    text, 97-98, 347-349
    windows, 22-23, 73
MS QuickBASIC, 862
MS-DOS-formatted disks, 145

MultiFinder, 122, 905
    disabling, 909
    installing, 905-907
    memory allocation, 908-909
multimedia, 612-613
    hardware purchasing
        guidelines, 626
    programs, 328
        Action! for the Mac
            (MacroMedia), 619-622
        Kodak Photo CD Access
            Software, 624-625
        MacroMind Director
            (MacroMedia), 618-619
        Magic (MacroMedia), 623
        Movie Producer Bundle
            (Computer Friends/
            DiVA), 623
        Premiere 2.0 (Adobe
            Systems), 623
        QuickTime (Apple
            Computers), 616-618
    sound, 613-615
    utilities, 623
        American Media Clip Time
            series (ATG Inc.), 624
        AudioShop, 624
        "Business and Technol-
            ogy," ClipMedia 1, 624
        CameraMan (Vision
            Software), 624
        Cinemation (Vividus
            Corporation), 624
        "Industry at Work,"
            ClipMedia 2, 624
        MacroMind Three-D
            (MacroMedia), 623
        MacroModel
            (MacroMedia), 623
        Swivel 3D Professional
            (MacroMedia), 624

SwivelMan (MacroMedia), 623
video, 615-616
multiple windows, 76-79
multitasking, 104, 122-130, 712
multithreading, 712
Muppets On Stage (Sesame Street), 654-656
muscle strain, 887-888
music programs
  ConcertWare+ (Great Wave Software), 678
  Encore (Passport), 679
  Miracle Piano Teaching System Bundle (Software Too, 680
  Musical Instrument Digital Interface (MIDI), 679
  Practica Musica (ARS Nova), 678-679
Musical Instrument Digital Interface (MIDI), 679

N

Name option (viewing folders), 201-202
name-and-address databases
  Address Book Plus (Power Up), 431-432
  MacPhonebook (Synex), 431
  TouchBase 2.0 (After Hours Software), 431
names of icons, editing, 111-112
naming folders, 189
Nautilus CD-ROM monthly "magazines", 173
navigating folders, 203-205
nesting folders, 182-183, 189-190
network layer, ISO model, 581
networks, 780
  AppleTalk zones, 786
  bridges, 786-787
  electronic mail, 578, 592
  LocalTalk, 781-782
  servers, 782-783
  topologies, 783
    backbone, 784
    daisy chain, 783-784
    star, 785
    token ring, 786
    see also LANs
New (⌘-N) shortcut key, 344
New command (File menu), 344, 389
New Folder command (File menu), 189
New Folder command (Finder's File menu), 187
New Inside Macintosh (APDA), 876
New Wave (Hewlett-Packard) GUI (graphical user interface), 856
news articles CD, 175
NewsFlash, 604
newsletters, 502, 522-524
NewsNet information service, 595, 604
newspapers, 525
Nisus (NISUS)
  Clipboard, 348
  files, backing up, 345
  graphics, 366
  indexes, 365
  macros, 364
  QUED/M, 375-376
  table of contents, 365
  text
    converting to other formats, 368
    deleting, 346
    finding/replacing, 351
    inserting, 347
    moving, 348
  spell checkers, 360
  tables, 354
  tabs, 353
  thesauruses, 370
nodes, 579-780
nonparametrics, 492-493
nontrainable OCR software, 571
Norton Utilities, 632-634, 890
  Backup, 648
  Disk Doctor, 632-633
  Encrypt, 648
  FileSaver, 169
  for the Macintosh, 155, 648
  Partition, 167, 648
  Speed Disk, 169
  UnErase, 632-633
Note Pad, 109
Now Utilities, 252, 431, 532, 641-648
NTSC video standard, 616
NuBus cards, 764
null modems, 579
numbers
  formatting, 391-393
  international options, 217-218
numeric keypad, 90
  moving mouse pointer, 244-245

O

object code, 853
Object Pascal, 860
object-oriented programming, 854-855, 860, 865-868
objects
  aligning, 543
  assigning to multiple layers, 562
  extruding, 559
  filling with text, 522
  grouping/ungrouping, 543

locking/unlocking arrangements, 543
manipulating in three dimensions, 559
masking, 552
order, 543
reshaping, 559-560
rotating, 559-560
snapping to, 562
wireframe views, 559
zooming, 559, 562-563
OCR (Optical Character Recognition), 720
hardware, 572-573
programs, 571-573
office furniture, computers, 34-35
on-line, 579
on-line addiction, 606-608
on-line databases, 578
on-line services, *see* information services
on-screen color mixing, 553
OOP, *see* object-oriented programming
Open (⌘-O) shortcut key, 343
Open command (File menu), 116, 185, 343
Open File dialog box, 185
opening
files, 183
by double-clicking, 183-184
by dragging and dropping, 185
within application programs, 185-186
word processing, 343-344
icons, 116-117
windows, 20-21, 25-26
operators, 397-398
Optical Character Recognition, *see* OCR

optical drives, 759
optical storage devices, 756
optimizing
disks, 180
hard disks, 168-169
Option key, 87-89
shortcut keys, 70
special characters, 99-101
option-drag method of copying icons, 112-113
options
file sharing, 800
menus, 64-66
Page Setup, 282-283
Print, 283-284
toggling, 65
order of sorting
Apple menu items, 252-255
objects, 543
organizing files on hard disk, 186-190
orientation of pages, 359
OS/2 (IBM) GUI (graphical user interface), 856
outline views, folders, 202-203
overhead display, 733
Kodak DataShow, 733
purchasing guidelines, 733-734

P

Page Description Language (PDL), 739
Page Down key, 90
Page Setup command (File menu), 280
Page Setup options, 282-283
Page Up key, 90
page-description languages (PDLs)
PostScript, 287
TrueImage, 288

Paged Memory Management Unit (PMMU), 221, 331
PageMaker, *see* Aldus PageMaker
pages, 358-359
default, 523
master, 523
pages per minute (ppm), 738
paint programs, 539-540
Canvas (Deneba), 542
color, 552-553
Modern Artist (Computer Friends), 552
PixelPaint (SuperMac), 552
Studio/8 (Electronic Arts), 552
UltraPaint (Deneba), 552
Color MacCheese (Delta Tao), 540-541
Crystal Paint (Great Wave), 541
DeskPaint (Zedcor), 542
KidPix (Brøderbund), 541
MacCalligraphy (Enzan-Hoshigumi), 541
MacPaint 2.0 (Claris), 540
paint/draw programs, 548
Canvas (Deneba), 548
SuperPaint 3.0 (Aldus), 548-550
parallel devices, connecting, 792
parallel printers, 745-746
parity checking, 583-585
partitioning hard disks, 166-168
Pascal, 860-862
Paste (⌘-V) shortcut key, 97-98
Paste (F4) shortcut key, 97-98
Paste command (Edit menu), 27, 97-98, 126, 347
pause key, 89
payroll records, 472
PDL (Page Description Language), 739

pen-like mouse, 718
Performa series, Macintosh 36-41, 54, 175, 695, 697
personal finance programs, 460
　accounts, 460-463
　Dollars & Sense (Business Sense), 468-469
　Managing Your Money 5.0 (Meca), 466-468
　Quicken, 465-466
　reports, 464-465
　Wealth Builder (Reality Technologies), 471
Personal LaserWriters, 272, 280-281, 287, 743
phase-change printers, 274
PhoneNET (Farallon), 790-791
photo Cds, 624-625
PhotoCD, 174
physical layer, ISO model, 581
physics dictionaries, 370
picas, 299
PICT file format, 550
pictures, editing, 626
pie charts, 566
PixelPaint (SuperMac), 552
pixels, 724
planning/forecasting programs, 481
　Business Plan Toolkit (Palo Alto Software), 482
　Forecaster (Palo Alto Software), 481
　HyperCard Stack, 482-483
　Sales Marketing Forecasting Toolkit, 483
platforms, universal
　Institutional File System (IFS) project (University of Michigan), 813
PLI
　DAT tape drives, 762
　Infinity Optical 3.5", 176

plotters, 275
Plus model, 36-37
Plusware Numeric Keypad, 717
PMMU (Paged Memory Management Unit), 221, 331
PMO-650 drive, 176
PMT function, 398
PNT file format, 550
PNTG file format, 550
point-of-sale systems, 479-480
points, 299, 356
pop-up menus, 68-69
portability, 861
Portable model, Macintosh, 42-44
Portfolio Systems
　SmartScrap II, 556-557
　SuperGlue II, 557-558
portrait displays, 725
portrait orientation, 359
ports, printers, 897
poster programs
　MacBillboard (CE Software), 680-681
　PosterMaker Plus (Brøderbund), 680-681
posters, 502
PostScript
　drawing tools, 546-547
　files, sharing, 294-296
　fonts, 302, 311, 739, 741, 743
　laser printers, 272
　page-description language (PDL), 287, 519, 521
　printer language, 272-273, 287-288
　printers, 289, 304-306
　programming, 290
　programs, 293-294
　utilities, 290-293
power line protectors, 770-771
Power on key, 90
PowerBook series, 45, 700-702, 708, 732

PowerPoint (Microsoft), 553
ppm (pages per minute), 738
predesigned documents, 375
prediction/association statistics, 492
preemptive multitasking, 712
Preferences folder, 109
presentation layer, ISO model, 581
presentation programs
　PowerPoint (Microsoft), 553
presentations, content free, 612
preventive maintenance, 880-886
　dirt, 881
　dust, 881
　insurance, 886
　mouse cleaning, 882
　static, 882-883
　surge protectors, 880
　temperature, 880-881
　theft, 885
　transporting systems, 884-885
　viruses, 883-884
previewing fonts, 312
Print command (File menu), 27, 281
Print dialog box, 27
print head scanners, 570
Print Monitor, 109
Print options, 283-284
Print Preview option, 359
print screen key, 89
printer drivers, 277
　background printing, 284-286
　Chooser, 279-285
　GDT Softworks, 745
　installing, 278-279
　Orange Micro, 746
printers, 268-269
　Apple LaserWriter, 305
　AppleTalk, 51-52, 281
　CAD programs, 562

care and maintenance,
748-750
color, 273, 747
   Apple Color inkjet, 739,
742
   Brother, 748
   CHC-S445 (Mitsubishi),
748
   CHC-S446i ColorStream/
DS (Mitsubishi), 748
   ColorPoint PS (Seiko), 747
   ColorPoint PSX Model 14
(Seiko), 747
   continuous-tone, 275
   CorrectPrint 300
(RasterOps), 748
   Dataproducts, 748
   Hewlett-Packard
DeskWriter C, 747
   ImageWriter II, 739-742
   inkjet, 273
   phase-change, 274
   Spectra Star 430 (General
Parametrics), 747
   Tektronix ColorQuick, 747
   Tektronix Phaser 200, 747
   Tektronix Phaser III PXi,
748
   thermal-wax-transfer,
273-274
dot-matrix, 269
   Apple, 739-742
   care and maintenance,
750-752
   color, 553
fonts, downloading, 311-312
inkjet, 270
   Apple, 739-742
   color, 553
languages, 272-273
laser, 271-273, 286-293, 746
   Apple, 742-745

care and maintenance,
752-753
   color, 553
options
   Page Setup, 282-283
   Print, 283-284
parallel, 745-746
Personal LaserWriter NTR,
287
plotters (alternative), 275
PostScript, 289, 304-306
PowerPoint, 745-746
purchasing guidelines, 738
QuickDraw, 303-304
SCSI, 50-51, 281
serial, 49, 280
setting up, 48-49
System 6 versus System 7, 905
Telax System (Relisys), 609
troubleshooting, 896-897
typesetters (alternative),
276-277
printing
   background, 284-286
   checks, 461, 465-467
   documents, color, 553-554
   files, 27-28
PrintMonitor program, 285-286
private E-mail, 597-599
procedural programming
language, 860
Prodigy information service, 604
programmers, 846
programming, 846-847
   CASE, 869
   concurrent, 864
   Toolbox, 856-858
   with PostScript, 290
programming languages, 846
   APL (Programming Language),
864
   artificial intelligence (AI),
868-869

   assembly, 852-853
   BASIC, 861-862
   books, 861
   C, 862-863
   C++, 862-863
   COBOL, 864
   compilers, 853-854
   Forth, 864
   FORTRAN (FORmula
TRANslator), 864
   interpreters, 853-854
   LISP, 863
   LOGO, 863
   machine, 851-852
   microprocessors, 850-851
   Modula-2, 864
   object-oriented, 854-855, 860,
865-868
   Pascal, 862
   procedural, 860
   VIP (Visual Interactive
Programming) (Mainstay),
865
programs, 326, 846
   accounting, 471-481
   add-ons, 420
   Apple At Ease, Desktop, 53
   Apple HD SC Setup, 165-168
   Apple HD SC 20 Setup
program, 889
   backup, 630-632
   CAD (computer-aided
design), 561-564
   calendar, 682-683
   CAM (computer-aided
manufacturing), 561
   characteristics, 848-849
   ClarisWorks, 439-451
   clip art tracking, 556-558
   color-separation, 553-554
   communications, 328,
576-577, 590-591, 596

Complete Undelete program, 892

data compression, 639-641

data recovery, 632-635

databases, 326-327, 416-418
    creating, 422-428
    evaluating, 421-422
    flat-file, 418-421
    relational-file, 418-421
    specialized, 430-435

debugging, 849

desktop publishing, 327, 509, 525
    Interleaf Publisher, 527-528
    Multi-Ad Creator (Multi-Ad Services), 528
    PageMaker (Aldus), 502, 523, 525-526
    Personal Press (Aldus), 529
    Publish It! Easy (Timeworks), 528-529
    QuarkXPress (Quark), 522-523, 527
    Ready, Set, Go! (LetraSet), 526-527
    UltraSpec (Publication Technologies), 530
    Writing Center (Learning Company), 529

diagnostic, 637-638

dictionaries, 370

Disinfectant (virus protection program), 883

draw, 542-547

E-mail, 597-598

educational, 652-661

educational and recreational, 328

file transfer, 806-809, 812

file translation, 809-810

financial/business, 327

Finder enhancement, 643-645

fine-tuning scanned images, 573-574

Font Creator, 320

Fontographer (Altsys), 311

forecasting/planning, 481-483

games, 667-675

grammar checkers, 371-373

graph/chart, 565-568

graphics, 327, 538-539

hard disk maintenance, 632-635

Help, 142

IBM PC
    emulators, 811-812
    running on Macintoshes, 810-812

idea processor, 483-485

integrated, see integrated software packages

language instruction, 663

Mac-to-mainframe, MacMainframe (Avatar), 813

macro, 646-647

MacTools, 883, 890

micro-to-mainframe, 813

Microsoft Works, 451-456

modems, 587
    purchasing guidelines, 586-588

multimedia, 328
    Action! for the Mac (MacroMedia), 619-622
    Kodak Photo CD Access Software, 624-625
    MacroMind Director (MacroMedia), 618-619
    Magic (MacroMedia), 623
    Movie Producer Bundle (Computer Friends/ DiVA), 623

Premiere 2.0 (Adobe Systems), 623

QuickTime (Apple Computers), 616-618

music, 678-680

Norton Utilities, 890

OCR (Optical Character Recognition), 571-572
    gray-scale scanning, 573
    purchasing, 572-573

opening files, 185-186

paint, 539-540
    Canvas (Deneba), 542
    color, 552-553
    Color MacCheese (Delta Tao), 540-541
    Crystal Paint (Great Wave), 541
    DeskPaint (Zedcor), 542
    KidPix (Brøderbund), 541
    MacCalligraphy (Enzan-Hoshigumi), 541
    MacPaint 2.0 (Claris), 540

paint/draw, 548
    Canvas (Deneba), 548
    SuperPaint 3.0 (Aldus), 548-550

personal finance, 460-471

poster, 680-681

PostScript, 293-294

PrintMonitor, 285-286

project management, 495-496
    FastTrack Scheduler (AEC), 499
    MacFlow (Mainstay), 847
    MacInUse (Softview), 499
    MacProject, 496-499
    MacProject II (Claris), 847
    Manage That! (Varcon Systems), 847
    TopDown (Kaetron), 499-500

resource manager, 642-643
running IBM PC on
    Macintoshes, 811-812
security, 645-646
simulation games, 661-662
software training, 662
spell checkers, 369
spreadsheet, 326, 381-382,
    413-414
    benefits, 384-385
    BiPlane, 414
    charts, 400-403
    ClarisWorks, 413
    compatibility, 411-413
    components, 382
    databases, 403-410
    financial tools, 486-488
    formulas, 394-400
    macros, 410-411
    uses, 383-384
    worksheets, 385-390
Startup Manager, 641-642,
    891
statistical analysis, 487-494
Symantec Anti-Virus, 883
tax preparation, 469-470
TeachText, 92, 184
TechWords (specialized
    dictionaries), 370
telecommunications
    CompuServe Information
        Manager, 596-597
    Navigator, 596-597
    Pro-Search (Personal
        Bibliographic Software),
        601
text editors, 375-376
thesaurus, 370
three-dimensional graphics,
    558-561
type-enhancing, 519-521
typing, 663-664

UNIX emulator, MACIDRIS
    (Whitesmiths), 812
utility packages, 328
    MacTools (Central Point
        Software), 649
    Norton Utilities for the
        Macintosh 2.0 (Sym....),
        648
    Now Utilities 3.0 (Now
        Software), 647
Virex, 883
virus protection/detection,
    635-637, 580
word processing, 326
    Expressionist (Prescience),
        375
    MathType (Design
        Science), 374
    purchasing guidelines, 377
WordPerfect Works, 456-457
writing assistants
    Correct Quotes (WordStar
        International), 373-374
    EndNote Plus, 373-374
    Writer's Dream Tools
        (Heizer Software), 373
see also applications; DAs;
    macros; software; utilities
Prograph (TGS Systems), 866-867
project management programs,
    495-496
    FastTrack Scheduler (AEC),
        499
    MacFlow (Mainstay), 847
    MacInUse (Softview), 499
    MacProject, 496-499
    MacProject II (Claris), 847
    Manage That! (Varcon
        Systems), 847
    TopDown (Kaetron), 499-500
Project Modula (MacLogimo
    Plus), 864

projection tools, 733-734
Prometheus (The Home Office),
    587
Prometheus Ultima Home Office
    modems, 589
proportion design basic, 507
protecting
    power lines, 770-771
    screens, 734-735
    viruses, 635-637
protocols, 577, 580-582
    AppleTalk, 781-782, 786
    fax, 586, 589
    full duplex, 579
    half duplex, 579
    MacBinary, 585
Psygnosis (Lemmings), 677
Pterodactyl Software
    (PCMacBASIC), 862
public E-mail, 597
    programs, 598
    services, 597-598
Public Utilities (Fifth Generation
    Systems, Inc.), 634-635
Publication Technologies
    (UltraSpec), 530
publications (Macintoshes),
    876-877
Publish It! Easy (Timeworks),
    524, 528-529
Publishing Packs (Adobe
    Systems), 523-524
publishing, see desktop
    publishing
purchasing guidelines
    anti-glare filters, 772-773
    carrying cases, 771-772
    disk files, 773-774
    diskettes, 773-774
    drives
        CD-ROM, 759-760
        magneto-optical, 761
        optical, 759

tape, 762
   WORM (Write Once Read
      Many), 760-761
expansion cards, 762-767
furniture, 775-776
game programs, 664-665
graphics tablets, 719
hard drives, 757-759
hardware, 690-691
   modems, 586-588
   multimedia, 626
   OCR (Optical Character
      Recognition), 572-573
information services, 605-606
keyboards, 264, 716-717
Macintoshes, 710-712
monitors/displays, 727-731
mouse, 718-719
overhead displays/projection
   tools, 733-734
power line protectors,
   770-771
printers, 738
programs
   desktop publishing,
      530-531
   modems, 586-588
   OCR (Optical Character
      Recognition), 572-573
   word processing, 377
scanners, 719-720
security devices, 772
software, return policies,
   333-334
stands and bases, 774-775
trackballs, 718-719
video cameras, 720-721
Put Away command (File menu),
   115, 148
Puzzle, 137
Puzzle Gallery (Miles Computing), 671

Q

Quadra series, Macintoshes, 42,
   161, 702-703, 707-708
Quantum Leap Technologies,
   658
Quark
   QuarkStyle, 524
   QuarkXPress, 294, 522-523,
      527, 554
QuickDraw, 739-742
   printer language, 272, 273
   printers, 303-304
Quicken (Intuit Software),
   465-466, 471
QuicKeys 2 (CE Software),
   646-647
QuickTime, 615-618
quitting
   applications, 127
   Macintoshes, 28
QWERTY keyboards, 101,
   219-220

R

radiation from displays, 886-887
radio buttons, 83
Radius
   monitors, 730
   PowerView, 732
   PrecisionColor series video
      cards, 731
   Rocket series accelerator
      cards, 766
   VideoVision System, 626
ragged-left text, 514
ragged-right text, 514
range of cells, 388
raster image processing (RIP),
   302-303
RasterOps (CorrectPrint 300),
   748

rates
   data transfer, 161-162
   horizontal scan, 724
   refresh, 724
RCMD commands, scripting
   language, 595
read-only memory (ROM), 104
reading disks (DOS), 809-810
recording sounds, 229, 248-250,
   626
records, 404, 416-418
   databases
      finding, 425-427
      importing/exporting,
         427-428
   payroll, 472
recovering files, 892-893
recreational programs, 328
Reduced Instruction Set
   Computer (RISC) chip, 850
refresh rate, 724
regression statistics, 492
relational-file databases, 418-421,
   472
remote communciations, 792-793
removable hard disk drives, 163
removing
   control panels, 261
   file labels, 191
   Font/DA Mover, 910-911
   fonts, 911
   keyboard layouts, 263-264
   sounds, 250
   System extensions, 262
repeat rate of keys, 219
repetitive strain injuries (RSI), 33
replacing
   graphics, 96
   text, 96, 350-352
reports, 502
   corporate annual (Annual
      Reports, Inc., 524

creating (personal finance programs), 464-465

ResEdit, 869-875
  alert boxes, 874
  fonts, 874-875
  icons, 872-873
  menu commands, 874

resizing windows, 22-24

reshaping, *see* shaping

resolution, 724, 738

resource editors (ResEdit), 869-872

resource forks, 869

Resource Manager error codes, 923

resource manager programs, 642-643

resource templates, ResEdit, 871

resources, 109

Restart command (Special menu), 105, 149, 906

resume templates, 375

return policies (hardware), 690-691

reverse type, 515, 516

RFI protection, 770

RGB display, 725-726

right-justified text, 354

RIP (raster image processing), 302-303

RISC (Reduced Instruction Set Computer) chip, 850

ROM (read-only memory), 104

rotating objects, 559-560

roundtables
  America Online, 877
  Delphi, 877
  GEnie, 877

rows, 382, 386

RSI (repetitive strain injuries), 33

rulers, 543

runarounds, 511-513

S

Sad Mac Code, 924-926
  128K ROM, 924-926
  256K ROM and up, 925-926

Salient
  AutoDoubler, 170, 640
  Disk Doubler, 170
  DiskDoubler, 640
  Partner, 533

sampling rate, sounds, 614

sans serif typefaces, 299

Save (⌘-S) shortcut key, 340

Save As command (File menu), 344

Save command (File menu), 340

Save dialog box, 340

saving files
  as stationery pads, 200
  graphics, 550-551
  word processing, 344-346

scaling, gray, 543

scan rate, horizontal, 724

ScanJet series (Hewlett-Packard), 720

ScanMaker IIXE, 720

scanned images, 573-574

scanners, 569-570
  Animas True-Color Scanner, 720
  Apple Computer, Inc., 573
  color, 574
    Barneyscan system (Barneyscan), 574
    importing files, 553
  Color OneScanner (Apple), 719
  LightningScan 400 (Thunderware), 720
  LightningScan Compact (Thunderware), 720
  LightningScan Pro 256 (Thunderware), 720

Microtek MSF300Q scanner, 573
  purchasing guidelines, 719-720
  ScanJet series (Hewlett-Packard), 720
  ScanMaker IIXE, 720
  Telax System (Relisys), 609
  ThunderScan (ThunderWare), 570-571
  Typist Plus Graphics, 720

scanning gray-scale, 573

scientific/technical information services (Orbit), 603

Scrapbook, 137-139

Scrapbook File, 109

Scrapbook, Now Utilities, 532

screen fonts, 302, 307

screen savers, 734-735

screens
  brightness, 227
  buffers, 856
  capturing, 532-534
  clutter, 76, 126
  graphics, 518
  magnifying images, 242-243
  preventing glare, 33
  protecting, 734-735
  worksheet, 386-389

scripting languages (RCMD commands), 595

scroll arrows, 21, 75, 186

scroll bars, 21, 75, 186

scroll boxes, 21, 75

scroll lock key, 89

scrolling windows, 24-25, 75-76

scrolling menus, 67-68

SCSI (Small Computer System Interface), 160-161
  bus
    cable length, 894
    device termination, 895-896

ID numbers, 894-895
    troubleshooting, 894-896
chain, 160
devices, 164-165
    drives, CD-ROM, 173
    hard disks, 758
ID number, 160
interface, 756-757
printers, 50-51, 281
SE model, Macintosh, 36-37
SE30 model, Macintosh, 36-37
searching, *see* finding
secondary skills, educational
    programs, 658-662
sectors, 153, 180
security
    hard disks, 170
    devices, purchasing guide-
        lines, 772
    utilities, 645
        Citadel with Shredder
            (Microcom), 646
        FolderBolt (Kent Marsh),
            645-646
        MacSafe II (Kent Marsh),
            645
        NightWatch II (Kent
            Marsh), 645-646
        SafeLock (Fifth Generation
            Systems), 646
seek time, 161-162, 758
selecting
    commands, 20, 61-64
    icons, 19, 110-111
    items
        clicking, 56-57
        double-clicking, 57-58
send-and-receive fax modems,
    586
send-only fax modems, 586
separating colors, 553
sequence/direction design basic,
    507

serial devices, connecting, 792
serial ports, 449
serial printers, 49, 280
serif typefaces, 299
servers, 782-783
service bureaus, desktop
    publishing, 504-505
servicing printers, 749-750
session layer, ISO model, 581
Set Startup command (Special
    menu), 906
setting colors
    color wheel, 236-237
    text highlight, 234-235
    window frames, 235
setting up Macintoshes, 32
    ergonomics, 32-35
    printers, 48-52
shading, 559
shadowed pop-up menus, 68
shadows, 543
shaping objects, 559-560
shareware, 329
sharing
    disks, 798-800
    files
        accessing shared items,
            802-803
        controlling, 800-802
        File Sharing (System 7),
            793-798
        options, 800
        PostScript, 294-296
    folders, 798-800
Shift key, 70, 87-89
shortcut keys, 69-70
    Copy (⌘-C), 97
    Copy (F3), 97
    Cut (⌘-X), 97
    Cut (F2), 97
    New (⌘-N), 344
    Open (⌘-O), 343
    Paste (⌘-V), 97-98

Paste (F1), 98
Paste (F4), 97-98
Save (⌘-S), 340
Undo (⌘-Z), 98
Show All command (Application
    menu), 127
Show Balloons command (Help
    menu), 139-140
Silicon Beach
    Beyond Dark Castle, 671
    Digital Darkroom, 573-574
    Super 3D, 558
silicon storage devices, 756
SIMMs (Single In-Line Memory
    Modules) cards, 763-764
simulation games programs,
    661-662
sink design concept, 508
size
    design basic, 507
    fonts, 543
    type, 299-301
    windows, 73-74
size box, 21
Size option, viewing folders, 202
Slow Keys, 246
Small Computer System
    Interface, *see* SCSI
Small icons, viewing folders, 201
soft partitions, 168
software, 326
    AppleTalk, 781
    communications, 328
    conflicts, 890-892
    database, 326-327
    desktop publishing, 327
    educational and recreational,
        328
    evaluating, 329-330
        compatibility, 331-333
        Macintosh considerations,
            330-331

memory, 330
return policies, 333-334
technical support, 334-335
versions, 331-333
versions, System, 331
warranties, 333-334
financial/business, 327
graphics, 327
GrayShare, 740-743
integrated packages, 327,
438-439
ClarisWorks, 439-451
Microsoft Works, 451-456
multimedia, 328
sources, 328-329
spreadsheet, 326
System, 104
installing, 105-107
versions, 104-105
utilities, 328
word processing, 326
WordPerfect Works, 456-457
see also programs
software training programs, 662
Software Ventures
MicroPhone II, 591-595
MicroPhone Pro, 595
Solarian II, 677
Sony monitors, 730
sorting
Apple menu items, 251-255
databases, 405-407
files by labels, 191
text, 362
Sound control panel, 228
alerts, 228-229
sounds
adding, 248-250
removing, 250
volume, 229-230
SoundEdit files, 615
sounds, 613-615, 626

copying into Scrapbook,
138-139
deleting from Scrapbook, 139
recording, 248-250, 626
removing, 250
source disks, 154
source document, 126
spacing lines, 358
special characters, 99-101
viewing with Key Caps,
135-136
Special menu commands
Clean Up, 239-240
Clean Up by Label, 191
Eject, 154
Empty Trash, 114, 231
Erase Disk, 152
Finder, 71
Restart, 105, 149, 906
Set Startup, 906
Specifications, system, 913-918
Speed Disk, Norton Utilities, 169,
648
speeds
hard disks, 161-162
mouse, 226-227
spelling checkers, 341, 360,
369-370
splitting transactions, 463
sports clip art, 554-555
sports statistics CD, 175
spreadsheet module
ClarisWorks, 440, 444-448
Microsoft Works, 453-454
spreadsheet programs, 326,
381-382, 413-414
as financial tools, 486-488
benefits, 384-385
BiPlane, 414
charts, 400-403
ClarisWorks, 413
compatibility, 411-413

components, 382
databases, 403-410
formulas, 394--400
macros, 410-411
uses, 383-384
worksheets, 385-390
standards, removable hard disks,
163
stands for computers (purchasing
guidelines), 774-775
star topology, 785
start and stop bits, 584
starting
applications, 122-124
Macintoshes, 16-17
Startup Disk control panel,
230-231
Startup Items folder (automatic
startups), 255-256
startup manager programs,
641-642
startups
problems, 889-890
System extensions
preventing, 262-263
static (effects on systems),
882-883
stationery pads (saving files as),
200
statistical analysis programs,
487-488
FASTAT (Systat), 489, 492-493
Igor (WaveMetrics), 493-495
JMP (SAS), 494
Mathematica, 493
MiniTab (MiniTab), 489-491
MYSTAT (Systat), 489
StatView, 492
SuperAnova (Abacas), 491,
494
SYSTAT (Systat), 489

Theorist (Prescience Corporation), 493
statistics
    association/prediction, 492
    descriptive, 489-490
    group difference, 490-491
    regression, 492
Stick Keys, 246-247
still image cameras
    Canon, 626
    FotoMan (Logitech), 626
storage devices, 756
    list, 144-145
storing files, 180
Stuffit (Aladdin Systems), 170, 435, 583, 639-640
Stuffit SpaceSaver (Aladdin Systems), 170
style sheets, 522
    predesigned, 523-524
    Publishing Packs (Adobe Systems), 523
styles
    fonts, 356-358, 543
    type, 301
StyleWriter, 270, 280, 739-741
Suitcase (Fifth Generation), 315, 321, 642-643
suitcases of fonts, 308
SuperATM package (Adobe Systems), 317-319
SuperDrive, 145, 806, 809
SuperMac
    PixelPaint, 552
    Video Spigot, 626
SuperMac video cards, 731
SuperPaint 3.0 (Aldus), 548-550
surge protectors, 880
Switchboard (DataDesk International), 717
switching applications, 124-125

Swivel 3D Professional (MacroMedia), 624
SwivelMan (MacroMedia), 623
Symantec
    Anti-Virus program, 883
    Just Enough Pascal, 862
    Norton Utilities 2.0
        FileSaver, 169
        Norton Partition, 167
        Speed Disk, 169
    SAM, 580
    Think C, 860, 862
Symantec Anti-Virus for the Macintosh (SAM), 636-637
Symantec Utilities for the Macintosh, hard drive partitioning, 782
Symantec/Peter Norton
    Norton Utilities 2.0, 632-634
    Norton Utilities for the Macintosh 2.0, 648
symbol libraries, 562
synchronous communication, 584
SyQuest standard (removable hard disks), 163
System, 109
    Clipboard, 96-97
    Error Codes, 920-923
        disk, 922
        file system, 921-922
        general, 920
        I/O, 920-921
        Memory Manger, 923
        Resource Manager, 923
    information, 139-140
    maintenance rules, 898
    Sad Mac Code, 924-926
        128K ROM, 924-925
        256K ROM and up, 925-926

software, 104
    installing, 105-107
    versions, 104-105
    upgrading considerations, 897-898
system specifications, 913-918
System 6, 900
    desk accessories, 376
    software evaluation, 331
    startup problems, 889
    versus System 7, 901-905
        control panels, 904
        documents, 903
        extensions, 904
        folders, 904
        icons, 902
        menus, 902-903
        printers and fonts, 905
        windows, 903
System 7
    File Sharing, 793
        accessing shared items, 802-803
        configuring, 793-798
        controlling, 800-802
        disks, 798-800
        folders, 798-800
        options, 800
    files, aliasing, 191-195
    installing, 105-107
    installing/deleting fonts, 308-310
    keyboards, 91
    software evaluation, 331
    sound files, 615
    startup problems, 889
    switching to from System 6, 900-901
    upgrading considerations, 897
    versus System 6, 901-905
        control panels, 904

documents, 903
extensions, 904
folders, 904
icons, 902
menus, 902-903
printers and fonts, 905
windows, 903
System 7.1, 213-218
System extensions, 234, 261
installing, 262
preventing startup, 262-263
removing, 262
System files (MultiFinder), 905
disabling, 909
installing, 905-907
memory allocation, 908-909
System Folder, 107-110, 187-189
Control Panels folder, 210
Brightness, 227
Date & Time, 213-218
General Controls, 210-213
Keyboard, 219-220
Memory, 220-223
Monitor, 223-226
Mouse, 226-227
Sound, 228-230
Startup Disk, 230-231
installing fonts, 309
Startup Items, 255
System Heap, 859

T

Tab key, 87
table of contents, 365-366
tables, creating, 354
tabs, 353-354
tag image file format, *see* TIFF
tape backups, 144, 207-208
tape drives, 762
target disks, 154
tax preparation programs,
469-470

TeachText program, 92, 184
TechAlliance (*MacTech* Quarterly), 876
technical support (software),
334-335
technical/scientific information
services (Orbit), 603-604
telecommunications, 576
communications programs,
576-577
compared to mail services,
589
costs, 589-590
International Standards
Organization (ISO) model,
581-582
modems, 576, 578, 580-586
programs
CompuServe Information
Manager, 596-597
Navigator, 596-597
Pro-Search (Personal
Bibliographic Software),
601
see also communications
telephones, 577-578
terminology, 578-580
Telenet, 578, 603, 606
telephones, 576-578
temperature effects on system,
880-881
templates, 522
Annual Reports, Inc., 524
cover letter, 375
Designs for Business
Communications, 524
Designs for Manuals, 524
Designs for Newsletters, 524
predesigned, 523
Publish It! Easy, 524
QuarkStyle, 524
resource, ResEdit, 871

resumes, 375
wills, 375
see also stationery pads
Tempo II Plus (Affinity), 646
terminals
dumb, 579
emulating, 580
TTY, 579
terminology in telecommunications, 578-580
Texas Instruments
Micro Explorer NuBus boards,
863
microLaser Plus, 746
microLaser Turbo, 746
text
3-D graphics, 559
charts, 402
copying, 97, 138-139
deleting, 95-96, 139, 346
drop caps, 518
editing, 101
filling objects, 522
finding, 350-352
formatting
fonts, 356-358
justification, 354-356
line spacing, 358
margins, 352-353
pages, 358-359
size, 356-358
styles, 356-358
tables, 354
tabs, 353-354
highlight color, 234-235
hyphenation, 514-515
inserting, 346-347
justification, 354-356, 514-515
kerning, 509-510
leading, 511
line length, 515
manipulating, 519-522

merging, 360-362
moving, 97-98, 347-349
multiple-clicking, 58
replacing, 96, 350-352
reverse type, 515-516
runarounds, 511-513
screens, 518
sorting, 362
spell checkers, 360
thesauruses, 360
tracking, 510
typing, 92-93
wraparounds, 511-513
text boxes, 83-84
text charts, 566
text editors, 375-376
thermal-wax-transfer printers, 273-274, 747
thesauruses, 341, 360, 370
Think C
    Apple Programmers Developers Association, 863
    CompuServe forums, 877
    Symantec Corp., 860, 862
Think Pascal, CompuServe forums, 877
thought processors, see idea processor programs
three-dimensional graphics programs
    Animation Works (Gold Disk), 561
    DynaPerspective, 560
    Mac3D (Challenger), 558
    StratsVISION 3D (Strata), 560
    Super 3D (Silicon Beach), 558
    Zing (Enabling Technologies), 560
Thunderware
    LightningScan 400, 720
    LightningScan Compact, 720
    LightningScan Pro 256, 720
    ThunderScan, 570-574

TIFF file format, 551
tiling windows, 78
Timbuktu (Farallon), 792
time/information management programs, see information/time management programs
times
    international options, 213-214, 216-217
    setting, 212
title bars, 21, 73
toggling of options, 65
token ring topology, 786
toner, 742
Toolbox, 104
    managers
        Event, 858
        Memory, 858-859
    programming, 856-858
tools
    dimensioning, 562
    drawing
        CAD programs, 562
        PostScript, 546-547
topologies, 783
    backbone, 784
    daisy chain, 783-784
    star, 785
    token ring, 786
Toshiba CD-ROM drives, 174
trackballs, 718
    MacTrac 2.0 (MicroSpeed), 718
    purchasing guidelines, 718-719
    Stingray (CoStar), 718
    Thumbelina Mac, 719
    TurboMouse 4.0 (Kensington), 718
tracking, 356, 510
tracking speeds (mouse), 226-227

tracks, 153, 180
trainable OCR programs, 571
transactions (accounts), 462-463
transferring
    data between modules (ClarisWorks), 440-443
    data between programs (ClarisWorks), 449-450
    icons, 112
translating
    files
        from DOS, 809-810
        to/from Apple systems, 806-809
        to IBM compatible PCs from Apple systems, 806-812
            file transfer programs, 806
            SuperDrive, 806-812
transport layer, ISO model, 581
transporting systems, 884-885
Trash icon, 114-116, 148
Trash options, 231
Traveling Software (LapLink), 808-809, 812
trees (HFS), 188
troubleshooting, 888-897
    determining problem, 888-889
    Disk First Aid, 890
    hardware problems, 893-894
    MacTools, 890
    Norton Utilities, 890
    printer problems, 896-897
    recovering files, 892-893
    SCSI buses, 894-896
        cable length, 894
        device termination, 895-896
        ID numbers, 894-895
    software conflicts, 890-892
    startup problems, 889-890
TrueType fonts, 288, 302, 311, 739, 742-743

Turbo Pascal Borland Roundtable
(GEnie), 877
Turbo Pascal for the Macintosh
(Borland International), 862
type
characters, 298
drop caps, 518
hyphenation, 514-515
justification, 514-515
kerning, 509-510
leading, 511
line length, 515
reverse, 515-516
runarounds, 511-513
size, 299-301
style, 301
tracking, 510
weight, 301
wraparounds, 511-513
type codes, 180-181
type-enhancing programs,
519-521
typefaces, 298
types of fonts, 302
typesetters, 276-277
typing
special characters, 99-101
text, 92-93
typing programs, 663-664

UL (Underwriters Laboratory)
certification, 770
Undo (⌘-Z) shortcut key, 98
Undo (F1) shortcut key, 98
Undo command (Edit menu), 98,
346
undoing mistakes, 98, 101
ungrouping objects, 543
unit measurements (CAD
programs), 562
unity design basic, 508

universal platforms
Institutional File System (IFS)
project (University of
Michigan), 813
UNIX emulator programs
MACIDRIS (Whitesmiths), 812
unlocking
disks, 156-157
icons, 119
object arrangements, 543
upgrading
considerations, 897-898
memory, 898
System 7, 897
uploading files, 580
user groups
Berkeley Macintosh User's
Group), 877
Boston Computer Society
(BCS), 877
software sources, 329
users (shared files), 795-796
utilities, 328
color, Colorizer (Palomar),
554
data recovery programs,
632-635
desktop publishing programs,
532
Capture! (Mainstay),
532-533
Clipper (Solutions), 532
DeskPaint (Zedcor), 532
DiskTop (CE Software),
532
Exposure Pro (Baseline),
532-533
ImageGrabber (Sebastian),
532-533
MathType (Design
Science), 532

OnLocation (Go Technol-
ogy), 532
Scrapbook, Now Utilities,
532
SmartScrap (Solutions),
532
disk copy, 155
font, 312
addDepth (Ray Dream,
Inc.), 314
Adobe Type Manager
(ATM), 315
Adobe Type Reunion, 317
Adobe TypeAlign, 314
conversion, 315
Incubator Pro 2.0 (Type
Solutions), 315
managers, 315
Master Juggler (ALSoft),
315, 321-322
Metamorphosis Profes-
sional, 315
Suitcase (Fifth Genera-
tion), 315, 321-322
SuperATM package (Adobe
Systems), 317-319
Tapestry (Pixar), 314
type enhancement,
313-314
TypeStyler (Brøderbund),
313
LaserWriter Font Utility,
311-312
multimedia, 623
American Media Clip Time
series (ATG Inc.), 624
AudioShop, 624
"Business and Technol-
ogy," ClipMedia 1, 624
CameraMan (Vision
Software), 624

Cinemation (Vividus
Corporation), 624
"Industry at Work,"
ClipMedia 2, 624
MacroMind Three-D
(MacroMedia), 623
MacroModel
(MacroMedia), 623
Swivel 3D Professional
(MacroMedia), 624
SwivelMan (MacroMedia),
623
PostScript, 290-293
Stuffit Deluxe (Aladdin
Systems), 583
utility packages
MacTools (Central Point
Software), 649
Norton Utilities for the
Macintosh 2.0 (Symantec),
648
Now Utilities 3.0 (Now
Software), 647

V

V.42bis error correction, 585, 589
Varityper typesetters, 276
VAX computers (interfaces with
Macintoshes), 813
Version (viewing folders), 202
versions
software, 331-333
System software, 104-105
video, 615-616, 626
cameras
H850 Insertable Graphic
Clips (Canon), 721
Hi8 Stereo 8 mm
(Canon), 721
purchasing guidelines,
720-721
RC-250 (Canon), 721

RC-570 (Canon), 721
UC1 8 mm (Canon), 720
cards, 731
Apple 8•24, 731
Macintosh Display Card
8•24GC, 731
PrecisionColor series
(Radius), 731
SuperMac, 731
PowerBooks
Lapis PowerBase 1, 732
PowerView (Radius), 732
PowerVision (Mirror
Technologies), 732
Scuzzy View (Aura
Systems), 732
Video+ PB140/170
(LifeTime Memory
Products), 732
memory, VRAM, 726-727
View menu commands (Label),
191
View menu (Finder), 71
viewing
Desktop, 52-54
files in folders, 201
folders
by Name option, 201-202
by outline views, 202-203
by Small icons, 201
fonts, special characters,
135-136
views, CAD programs, 562
Views control panel, 237-238
disk information, 241
folder sizes, 240-241
fonts, 238-239
icon grids, 239-240
list views
columns, 241-242
icon sizes, 240
Virex (Microcom), 636, 883

virtual memory, 221-223
virus detection programs, 580
virus protection/detection
programs, 635
Disinfectant (John Norstad),
636
MacTools (Central Point
Software), 636
Safe & Sound (Central Point
Software), 636
Symantec Anti-Virus for the
Macintosh (SAM), 636-637
Virex (Microcom), 636
viruses, 883-884
VisiCalc, 384
voice telephones, 577
volumes, 782
VRAM (video memory), 726-727

W

war game programs
Battle Stations (TimeLine),
671
Bomber (Deadly Games), 670
GATO (Spectrum Holobyte),
670
see also game programs
warranties
hardware, 690-691
software, 333-334
weights of type, 301
Well (Whole Earth Lectronic
Link) information network,
605
what-if analysis, 385
White Knight (FreeSoft), 595-596
wills, templates, 375
windows, 72-73
closing, 22, 76
color, 235
Info icons, 117-118
moving, 22, 73

multiple, 76-79
opening, 20-21, 25-26
resizing, 22-24
scrolling, 24-25, 75-76
sizing, 73-74
System 6 versus System 7, 903
tiling, 78
types, 79-80
zooming, 75
Wipe Info, Norton Utilities, 648
wireframe views of objects, 559
word processing
ASCII format, 376-377
desk accessories, 376
dictionaries, 370
files
converting to other
formats, 368
creating, 339-343
editing, 341-343, 346-352
formatting, 352-359
opening, 343-344
saving, 344-346
glossaries, 363
graphics, 366-368
indexes, 365-366
macros, 364
modules
ClarisWorks, 439, 444-447
Microsoft Works, 452-454
predesigned documents, 375
programs, 326
equation generators,
374-375
Nisus, 339
purchasing guidelines, 377
specialized, 376
spell checkers, 360, 369-370
table of contents, 365-366
text, 360-362
thesauruses, 360, 370
writing assistants, 373

Word, see Microsoft Word
word wrap, 93, 543
Word Wrapper, 377
WordPerfect
Clipboard, 348
files, backing up, 345
graphics, 366
indexes, 365
macros, 364
table of contents, 365
text
converting to other
formats, 368
finding/replacing, 350-352
fonts, 357
inserting, 347
moving, 348
sorting, 362
tables, 354
WordPerfect Corp.
Grammatik Mac, 371
PostScript commands, 292
Works, 456-457
WordScrambler, 677
WordStar International
American Heritage Electronic
Dictionary, 370
Correct Grammar, 371-373
Correct Letters, 375
Correct Quotes, 373-374
Working Software (Spellswell 7),
369
worksheets, 385-390
cells, aligning contents,
390-391
creating, 389
data, entering, 389-390
Excel, 486-487
fonts, 393-394
numbers, formatting, 391-393
screen, 386-390
workstation Macintoshes, 702

world flags clip art, 555
WORM (Write Once Read Many)
drives, 144, 677, 760-761
wraparounds, 511-513
WriteNow
files, saving, 346
text, font sizes, 357
writing to disks, DOS, 809-810
writing assistants, 373
WYSIWYG Menus, Now Utilities
3.0, 647

X-Z

x-height, 298
X-Windows, GUI (graphical user
interface), 856
Xerox STAR, 867
XMODEM protocol, 580-581
XTND technology, 341, 368
XTND translation system, 551,
808

YMODEM protocol, 580

zones AppleTalk, 786-787
zoom box, 21
Zoom series modems, 589
zooming
objects, 559, 562-563
windows, 75